BUILDING
PASCAL PROGRAMS

BUILDING
PASCAL PROGRAMS

An Introduction to Computer Science

STUART REGES
Stanford University

LITTLE, BROWN AND COMPANY
Boston   Toronto

Library of Congress Cataloging-in-Publication Data

Reges, Stuart
    Building Pascal programs.
    (Little, Brown computer science series)
    Includes index.
    1. PASCAL (Computer program language)   I. Title.
II. Series.
QA76.73.P2R44   1987   005.13'3   86-34422
ISBN 0-316-73854-9

Library of Congress Catalog Card No. 86-34422

ISBN 0-316-73854-9

9 8 7 6 5 4 3 2 1

MV

Published simultaneously in Canada by Little, Brown & Company (Canada) Limited

Printed in the United States of America

PREFACE FOR INSTRUCTORS

A trip to the computer section of your local bookstore will show you that introductory Pascal books are proliferating almost as quickly as diet books. Until I convinced myself that I could do something original, I was hesitant to add to this avalanche. As you look at the books, you will find that they fall into two main categories, which I call old style and new style. Authors of old-style books concentrate on rigorous computer science and the properties of the Pascal programming language. These are written almost like some mathematics texts, terse, formal, and difficult to read. Books of the new style start chronologically with the first edition of *Oh! Pascal!* More conversational in tone, these authors concentrate on the process of programming, describing it in terms of problem solving and distinguishing between general problem-solving strategies and their application to specific programming tasks. You get the feeling in these books that the authors are wise old programmers who are passing on their secrets to new, inexperienced programmers. These books are quite successful in teaching people how to program.

We are, I believe, about to experience a kind of book that incorporates recent advances in computer science. For example, the problem-solving paradigm explains only part of what a programmer does. A good programmer will try to create a program whose parts are independent enough that they can be used again to solve other programming tasks. In this way, the programmer is like an engineer. Thus, the new generation of books will be written using the software-engineering paradigm instead of the problem-solving paradigm.

As another example, consider the coverage of data abstraction versus procedural abstraction. Authors of current books carefully explain the principles of procedural abstraction, usually introducing procedures early and using them to motivate discussion of specific topics. Almost all those principles have parallel data abstraction principles, yet you hardly ever find mention of them. In the new generation of books, authors will carefully explain these principles, introducing abstract data types early and using them to motivate discussion of specific topics.

Building Pascal Programs is the first in this new generation of introductory programming texts. Mindful of the needs described above, I have consistently stressed the software-engineering paradigm over the problem-solving paradigm. Likewise, I have used the concept of the abstract data type throughout the book to underpin the discussion of specific topics. I have introduced, too, some fundamental concepts on program logic from the new field of program verification.

To carry through these ideas, I have had to reshape and rethink the traditional approach to the organization and coverage of topics. Although this book is intended for a quarter or semester course equivalent to CS1, as outlined by the ACM, it is somewhat larger than it needs to be because the boundary between CS1 and CS2 is not universally agreed upon. For one thing, I believe that simple data abstraction needs to be emphasized in CS1 so that bad habits do not have to be unlearned in CS2, and so that recursion can be postponed until CS2. Many instructors believe just the opposite. For this reason, I include enough material for you to be able to choose the subset of topics that you want to include in your course.

The book is divided into two major parts: Foundations and Extensions. The first ten chapters (foundations) represent the fundamental concepts upon which students build to understand more advanced topics. In the next seven chapters (extensions) we explore different advanced topics. To understand the other structural aspects of the book, you have to understand the compromises that I made to achieve the competing goals of writing a book that is:

- pedagogically sound

- easy to read

- full of helpful examples

- flexible

Imagine a tree representing the body of knowledge in CS1. You will find that it is both broad (loops, selection, simple types, structured types, logic, information hiding, and so on) and deep (three kinds of loops, two kinds of selection, four simple types). An important decision was to use a breadth-first rather than depth-first traversal of this tree. Students do not learn to manipulate characters until Chapter 6. But look at what they learn in the meantime: in Chapter 1 they learn to decompose programs into procedures; in Chapter 2 they learn about abstract data types, looping, and information hiding; in Chapter 3 they learn to use value parameters to generalize tasks; in Chapter 4 they learn about functions, selection, and interactive programs; and in Chapter 5 they learn about VAR parameters and the design of good programs. This approach I find to be the most pedagogically sound. In the breadth-first approach difficult concepts are explained gradually, so that students gain a first-order approximation, then a finer second-order approximation, and so on. Delaying the details of a topic also helps the student to see the whole picture more clearly. At the end of Chapter 3 students know about procedural decomposition, data types, variables, constants, looping, and parameters. They do not understand all the details, but they know that these are most of the important topics of the course.

A drawback to the breadth-first approach is the difficulty in deviating from the book's order of topics covered. And here I have compromised: the first eight chapters are breadth-first. It is not possible to significantly alter the order of topics in these chapters. But the remaining chapters are written with flexibility in mind, as described below.

Other decisions relate to the level of difficulty and the target audience. I have class tested this textbook at Stanford in both a service course for engineering and science students and in our first course for CS majors. This audience is fairly sophisticated, but I have targeted their lowest level. The students who have difficulty in understanding the concepts need the book most. Thus, I include many examples, often saying the same thing several times, and usually explaining topics in almost tedious detail. As a result, I believe this book is appropriate to use at any school either in a course for CS majors or in a service course for science and engineering students.

One final decision is a factor making the book longer than it might have been: the case studies. Many of the most interesting properties of large programs do not surface in a cursory review. If you think of the decomposition tree of the program, the most interesting nodes are the internal ones, yet most textbook authors concentrate on the root node and the leaves. They do so because it is difficult to discuss the internal nodes without going into great detail about how the program is designed and developed. But to truly appreciate the issues that arise in creating large programs, some close attention needs to be given to at least a few large programs. Several such case studies appear in this book and can serve that purpose. In the interest of flexibility, however, I have made it possible for the case studies to be skipped: you can either ignore them or use them as a model for creating different case studies.

The textbook lays a firm foundation in the first eight chapters and then allows branching into different topics. This diagram illustrates most of the dependencies in the book:

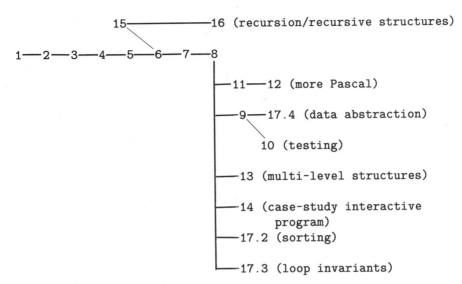

Pascal topics illustrating specific points are woven into the text in the first eight chapters in such a way that it would be difficult to change the order of presentation. Teaching WHILE loops before FOR loops using this text would be hard.

Other Pascal topics are really independent of the text. For flexibility, I have separated these topics into Chapter 11 (more on data) and Chapter 12 (more on control). The material can, however, be assigned to students early in the course. It is possible to introduce REPEAT loops in parallel with WHILE loops, though these topics are grouped into chapters. The sections of the chapters are fairly independent: you can study section 5 of Chapter 12 without reading anything else in Chapters 11 and 12.

This books is by no means the last Pascal book you will see at the bookstore, but it does include some of the best ideas floating around computer-science circles. I hope you and your students find that it has something new to teach you.

Acknowledgments

My first thanks go to the publishing staff. Tom Casson, my editor, made everything possible; Daniel Smail, his assistant, managed to make even bad news sound cheerful; and Jane Muse and Victoria Keirnan, the production staff, turned my wrinkled pages into a real book and managed not to get too angry when the pages showed up late.

Every book needs reviewers, and I managed to get some of the best. My thanks go to each of the people who reviewed the manuscript in one form or another: Stephen J. Allan, Utah State University; Sara Baase, University of

California at Berkeley; Marsha J. Berger, New York University; Tim Corica, the Peddie School; Henry A. Etlinger, Rochester Institute of Technology; David Gelernter, Yale University; Terry A. Gill, Carnegie-Mellon University; Harry R. Lewis, Harvard University; Rich Pattis, University of Washington; Jean B. Rogers, University of Texas at Austin; Henry D. Shapiro, University of New Mexico; Robert S. Streett, Mills College; Caroline E. Wardle, Boston University; Stephen Weiss, University of North Carolina, Chapel Hill; and Marvin V. Zelkowitz, University of Maryland.

I have had tremendous support at Stanford and would like to thank Gene Golub, who hired me and gave support to my initial projects; Nils Nilsson, who continues to find new ways to harness my keen interest in undergraduate computer-science education; the students of CS105A, CS106A, and CS106X, who suffered through drafts of this textbook ("We need an index!"); the student instructors, TAs, and section leaders, who constantly gave me advice about improving the book; and Mike Padilla, who reviewed some of my early work and helped me to improve my grammar and English usage.

Finally, I would like to acknowledge four colleagues whose intelligence and stubbornness (sometimes even arrogance) make them experts on what should be in a first course in computer science. Many of the best ideas in this book come from arguments with Mike Clancy, University of California at Berkeley; Phil Miller, Carnegie-Mellon University; Fred Schneider, Cornell University; and Rich Pattis, University of Washington. Rich has the special distinction of thinking up all my best ideas just before I do.

Stuart Reges

Lecturer and Assistant Chairman for
Education, Department of Computer
Science, Stanford University

Chief Reader, Advanced Placement
Examination in Computer Science

PREFACE FOR STUDENTS

Engineers build things, sometimes for ordinary people to use, like television sets. They also build tools, such as oscilloscopes. In this book we examine the building not of tangible tools but of programs, which are built by software engineers, building things that are made of bits and bytes instead of resistors and capacitors or nuts and bolts. When working on a program, a software engineer considers not just the problem at hand, but general-purpose tools that will be useful in later programs.

You make use of programming languages like Pascal to build programs. The emphasis in this book, however, is on the process of building, not on a specific language such as Pascal. Thus, most of the concepts and techniques that you learn will be applicable to any language in which you decide to program.

This book will also expose you to some of the basic concepts of computer science. Contrary to popular belief, computer programming is not the same as computer science. Programming is to the study of computer science what writing is to the study of literature. Programs are often used to express computer-science ideas, and computer science often examines the process of programming, but programmers are not necessarily computer scientists, and vice versa.

CONTENTS

PART TWO
EXTENSIONS

PART ONE

FOUNDATIONS

1

INTRODUCTION

1.1 Introduction

This chapter introduces some basic terminology and discusses Pascal's status as a programming language. You will learn the basics of how a computer works and how a person gives instructions to a computer. The chapter closes with a brief look at Pascal, examining how to write simple but structured programs that produce output.

1.2 Languages in General

People use language to communicate, to transfer information. Linguists call languages such as English, French, and German *natural languages*, because people use them to communicate with one another. The languages people use to communicate with computers are called *programming languages*.

You may wonder why English or some other natural language isn't used to communicate with computers. Unfortunately, not enough is known about such languages to do it. Natural language is rich in expression and freedom, and contrary to what you may believe, computers are quite simple-minded. Consequently, computer scientists have had limited success getting computers to understand natural languages. Computer scientists are still struggling to get a computer to demonstrate the same comprehension of English that you expect of a 5-year-old.

3

In the meantime, you have to settle for programming languages. You make your wishes known to the computer by talking to it in a programming language such as Pascal. Pascal is only one such language, one that is particularly well-suited to teaching good programming practices. It was designed in 1968 by Niklaus Wirth to be simple yet powerful. He wanted a single language that embodied all the major constructs of existing languages, yet one that was simple enough to be taught easily to nonprogrammers. Wirth named his language after Blaise Pascal, a seventeenth-century mathematician whom he admired.

Languages used by professional programmers are called *applications languages*. Wirth never intended to develop an applications language. Nevertheless, Pascal has become a popular applications language for microcomputers. Furthermore, the core of the new Department of Defense language, Ada, is similar to Pascal. Many programming languages are used today, and some of them are very old. The following all predate Pascal:

- FORTRAN (FORmula TRANslation) is the most commonly used applications language for science and engineering. It has changed a great deal over the years and now has constructs that parallel Pascal.

- COBOL (COmmon Business Oriented Language) is widely used for business applications.

- LISP (LISt Processing) is the chief language for artificial intelligence applications (trying to develop computer programs that reason the way people do).

- BASIC (Beginner's All-purpose Symbolic Information Code), according to its designers, is simple to learn and facilitates later learning of more complex languages such as FORTRAN. Because BASIC is simpler than these others, it runs more easily on microcomputers, which traditionally have had severe restrictions on the size of computer memory. This has made it the most commonly used language for microcomputers, a situation that is, however, rapidly changing as the cost of computer memory goes down.

Other widely used applications languages include ALGOL, APL, C, FORTH, PL1, and PROLOG. A language that might become important is Modula II. It is Niklaus Wirth's "next" language after Pascal. Wirth believes he has overcome many of the shortcomings of Pascal while still providing a language that is easy for novices to learn and which can be run on almost any computer.

1.2.1 Computer Languages

You tell the computer what to do by writing a program.

PROGRAM

A set of instructions that are to be carried out by a computer.

The word code describes program fragments ("these four lines of code") or the act of programming ("Let's code this into Pascal"). Once a program has been written, you can execute it.

PROGRAM EXECUTION

The act of carrying out the instructions contained in a program.

The process of execution is often called *running*. It can be used as a verb, "When my program runs it does something strange...," or as a noun, "The last run of my program produced these results...."

All computers have primitive operations, or primitives. A *primitive operation* is one you can ask for without further explanation, something the computer understands automatically. The set of primitive operations of a computer is called the *machine language* of that computer. Different computers have different machine languages, just as different makes of automobiles have different parts. Machine languages are usually very simple, with a relatively small set of available operations. In fact, such languages are so primitive that their programs are expressed as a series of numbers.

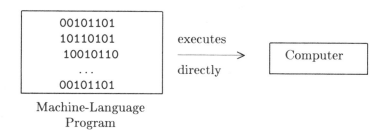

Because people do not think well in numbers, most machines have a higher-level language called an *assembly language*. Assembly languages use short abbreviations rather than numbers and are closely tied to their corresponding machine languages. Each assembly language instruction will expand into just a few machine primitives when translated into machine language. Programs that translate assembly language into machine language are called *assemblers*.

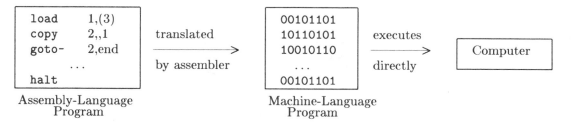

Because an assembly language is so close to its machine language, and because machine languages vary from computer to computer, assembly languages also vary from computer to computer. Even assembly language, however, is not a convenient language to work with. Its operations are so low level that you have to write very long programs to express simple ideas, and because different machines use different assembly languages, it is impossible to move programs from one machine to another. For these reasons, very high level programming languages have been designed. All the programming languages mentioned, i.e., Pascal, FORTRAN, COBOL, LISP, and even BASIC, are high-level languages.

Programs written in high-level languages are, like assembly-language programs, first translated into the computer's machine language. The machine-language translation is then executed. The big difference between assembly language and higher-level languages is the translation gap. Assembly language translates almost directly into machine language, each instruction translating into a few machine primitives at most. High-level languages are usually so much higher than machine language that a single instruction can translate into dozens and dozens of machine primitives.

Therefore, a program written in a language such as Pascal can be run on many different machines as long as each machine has a method for translating Pascal into the machine language of the computer. Programs that perform this translation are called *compilers*. The process of translation is called *compilation*. This, then, is a third way to execute programs. You can write a program in a high-level language and use a compiler to translate it into machine language.

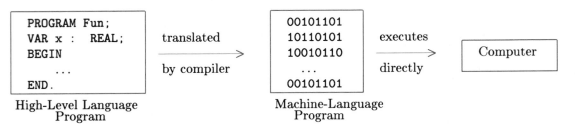

Pascal is a simple enough language that virtually every computer on the market today has the ability to compile Pascal programs.

1.2.2 Language Interpreters

There is a fourth way to execute programs without using a compiler. It is possible to program in a high-level language using a language *interpreter*. The distinction between a compiler and an interpreter is similar to the distinction between a foreign translator and an interpreter. If you have a manuscript written in German that you wish to have translated into English, you send off the entire manuscript to a translator. You receive back a translated version of the manuscript in English. You are then free of the translator. If, however, you have a German dignitary visiting, you pair the dignitary up with a German translator who translates on the spot.

Compilers work like translators. The programmer writes a complete program and passes it on to the compiler to translate. The compiler generates a machine-language version of the program that can then be executed directly. Executing a program using a compiler is a two-step process—first, the compiler translates the program into machine language, and then, the machine-language version is executed.

Language interpreters are more dynamic. The interpreter executes the program piece by piece, translating the code as it goes along. Executing using an interpreter is a one-step process—you start the interpreter executing and it translates as it goes along.

Interpreters are generally better than compilers for educational environments. Students working on programming problems usually execute many versions of a program until they find a correct solution. Thus they are interested in the fast start-up time provided by a one-step interpreter. Once you have a program that seems to work, however, it is wise to compile it into machine language so it won't have to be translated anymore and will run more quickly.

1.3 Hardware Terms

A computer system is composed of *hardware*, a computer and other physical devices attached to it, and *software*, a set of programs that can be executed on the computer. Inside a computer are two basic units: a memory unit and a processing unit. The *memory unit* stores information—both programs and data. Additional memory is attached to the outside of the computer. The internal memory is called *main memory* and the external memory is called *secondary memory* in order to distinguish them. The *central processing unit* (*CPU*) is the master control of the computer. It decides what operation to carry out next. The CPU and main memory unit are the core of the computer. You can usually attach several things to this core, however. Such attachments are called *peripheral devices*, or *peripherals*.

Computer

| CPU (processing unit) | | Peripheral |
| Main memory | $\longleftrightarrow$ | devices |

The size of the main memory unit puts limitations on the size of programs that can be executed. Program size will be very high if the program is very complex or if it has a lot of data to process. For example, the Ada language is sufficiently complex that an Ada compiler takes up more space than most modern microcomputers have in their main memory.

Part of the main memory is called *Read Only Memory* (*ROM*). ROM does not change; it stores permanent information. The other part of main memory is called *Random Access Memory* (*RAM*). Peripherals fall into four main categories:

Category	Examples
Input	Keyboard, card reader, joystick, mouse
Output	Terminal screen, printer, sound synthesizer
Storage	Disk drive, tape drive
Communications	Modem, network connection

Input devices allow information to flow into the computer. *Output devices* allow the computer to send information outside. *Storage devices* are in some sense both input and output, because information flows in both directions. Storage devices extend the normal capabilities of the internal memory. *Communications devices* allow connections between computers or connections through unusual channels (e.g., over telephone lines). Let's look at each of these categories in more depth.

1.3.1   Input Devices

You will probably enter information into your computer using a typewriter-like keyboard. This is your way of communicating with the computer. Older computer systems used punched paper cards to enter data. Users first typed information onto the paper cards and then fed a "stack" of cards into a device called a *card reader*. Fortunately, card readers have almost disappeared from college campuses and are starting to disappear from older computer-oriented businesses. Most home computers provide a *joystick* that can be rotated to various angles for use in video games. The joystick supplies input such as "shoot in this direction" or "move King Kong this way." Many newer computers have a device called a *mouse* that lets users point at objects on different parts of the screen. By moving the mouse around on a flat surface, you can select a different part of the screen. By pressing a button on the mouse, you can tell the computer to do something with whatever appears on that part of the screen. (See Fig 1.1.)

1.3.2   Output Devices

A typical terminal has both a keyboard for input and a television-type monitor for output. The computer displays text and, on more advanced monitors, pictures. You will want to obtain paper versions of information, in which case you

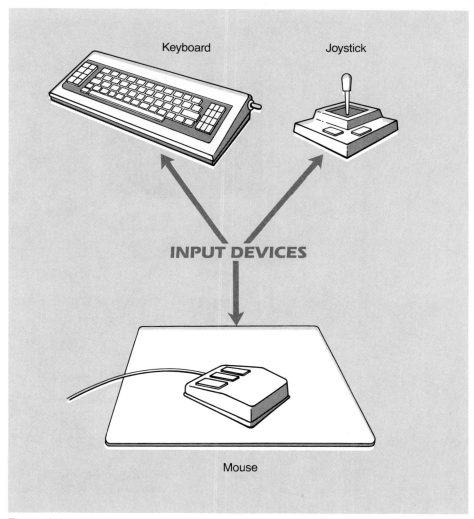

Figure 1.1

will direct output to a printer. Many computers also have output devices that generate sound—that beep, play music, or speak. (See Fig. 1.2.)

1.3.3 Storage Devices

Because the main memory of a machine is often limited, you will usually have only one program and its data in main memory at a time. Programs not being used are generally stored, along with their data, in a secondary storage unit. The most typical external storage unit is a disk drive. Disk drives allow fast access to information. Just as a record player has a needle that can be positioned to

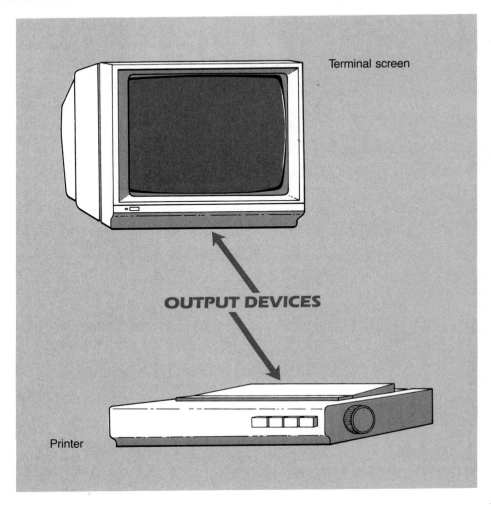

Terminal screen

OUTPUT DEVICES

Printer

Figure 1.2

any song, a disk drive has a head that can be positioned to any data. This way of accessing information is called *random access*, because you can access the information in any order, not just in the order it was recorded.

Another kind of storage device is a tape drive, which stores information on a magnetic tape. As with a tape recorder, to get information near the end of the tape, the tape drive must pass through all the entries that come before. This kind of access is called *sequential access*, because you can only access information in the order it was recorded. Sequential access is slower than random access.

Because of their fast access time, disk drives are used to store the most frequently used information. Information that is used only occasionally is generally stored on magnetic tape and is transferred onto the disk drive when needed. The formats used for storing information on magnetic tapes are more standard than the formats used for storing information on disk drives. Thus magnetic tapes are often used for transferring information from one computer system to another. (See Fig. 1.3.)

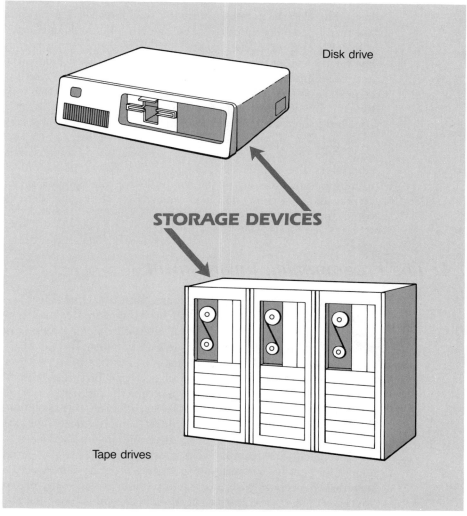

Figure 1.3

1.3.4 Communications Devices

Communications peripherals link computer peripherals together or link computers together. Terminals and computers usually pass information back and forth by creating electric impulses on a wire that joins them. If you want to connect to a computer that is very far away (in some cases thousands of miles), it is not practical to run a wire directly from your terminal to the computer. A _modem_ frees you from this restriction by allowing you to communicate over a phone line. The electric impulses normally sent between the terminal and computer are translated into sounds by the modem. These sounds can be sent through a telephone to anyplace on earth. Such communication requires two modems, one for the computer and one for the terminal. Each modem does the encoding and decoding necessary to send and receive tones over the phone line. When a message is sent, the first modem translates the electric impulses into tones for transmission on the phone line; the second modem hears these tones and translates them back into the original electric impulses. (See Fig. 1.4.)

A _network_ allows communication among a cluster of computers and peripherals. You might, for example, use a network to allow data sharing among five computers, one printer, and one large disk drive. In such an environment it is usually possible for any of the computers on the network to share the common printer and disk drive, and it is usually easy to transfer data from computer to computer.

1.4 The Programming Environment

You must become familiar with your computer setup before you start programming. First, you have to figure out how the computer and its peripherals work. Each computer provides a different environment for program development, but there are common elements that deserve comment.

The basic unit of storage on most computers is a _file_. You will create files whose contents are Pascal programs. Some programs you run will generate output files. You might write a program that makes a calendar, for example. Your programs will specify exactly what information to include in these files and in what order. Some programs will read information from external files. Such files are usually stored on the disk drive and are created either by your instructor or by yourself. For example, your instructor might make an input file of students' names and grades and ask you to write a program that processes this input file, generating a report with grade-point averages and a list of students with high averages. When you start writing such programs, your instructor will tell you what set of instructions to use on your specific computer to access the file.

Some programs you write will be _interactive_—they will interact with a user at the terminal. In this case, the output of your program is directed to a user's

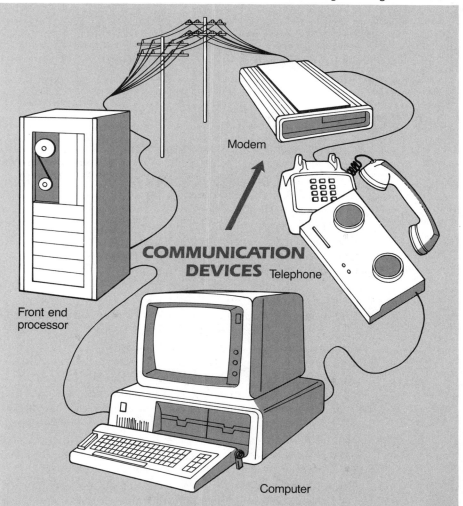

Modem

COMMUNICATION
DEVICES Telephone

Front end
processor

Computer

Figure 1.4

terminal screen and the input comes from the characters typed by the user on the keyboard.

Your computer has a built-in operating system that controls the functioning of the computer and its peripherals. The *operating system* of a computer provides a set of programs for manipulating these resources. There will be some kind of editor for creating program files. Editors are sometimes called *word processors* if they are used mainly for creating documents. There will also be commands available to execute programs created by the editor. Other programs might allow you to print your program and output files on the printer. Sometimes many of these elements are combined into one uniform environment, as in

UCSD Pascal, MacPascal for the Apple Macintosh, and Waterloo Pascal for the IBM PC. There is no single description for all, or even most, systems. Again, your instructor will describe the relevant features of your particular operating system.

1.5 Program Errors

When professional programmers write large, complex programs, they test extensively before releasing the program to users. Even so, any seasoned programmer will admit the impossibility of anticipating all cases. Even programs that sell for hundreds of thousands of dollars have little mistakes buried in them. Very few programs are perfect.

Little errors are called *bugs*. Computer programmers use such words as *bug-ridden* and *buggy* to describe poorly written programs. The term dates back to an old story about a group of programmers who couldn't figure out what was wrong with their programs, until they opened up the computer and found a moth trapped inside. The process of finding and eliminating bugs from programs is called *debugging*.

The terms *syntax* and *semantics* are used throughout this book to differentiate errors. Syntax is the linguist's word for grammar. It is the set of rules that specify a language's legal constructs. Syntax describes how to put the pieces of a language together and what a language looks like on the surface. The semantics of a language are the set of interpretations of the various constructs, the meaning of the language. For example, "Will develop the mind—programming" contains a syntactic mistake because the subject of a sentence should appear at the beginning: "Programming will develop the mind." "The abstract sheep wore beauteous arguments" contains a semantic error. The sentence meets all the syntactic rules of English, but it doesn't make sense.

In translating your program from a high-level language into machine language, the computer will run into difficulties if the program is not legal (i.e., if it is syntactically or semantically flawed). All syntactic errors are caught at compile time, because if you misspell words or punctuate your program incorrectly, the compiler will be unable to translate it. Only some of the semantic errors will be caught at compile time, however. For example, your program might tell the computer to divide a number by zero. Division by zero is not allowed, so such a program is semantically flawed. It is usually possible to translate such a program into machine language, however, so it does not generate any errors during translation. An error detected during compilation is called a *compilation error*.

When the compiler encounters a mistake, it generates a message describing the problem. Unfortunately, once the compiler becomes a little confused, it often quickly becomes very confused. One error in a program can generate many different error messages. Often the first message is the only significant one.

A program that generates compilation errors cannot be executed. If you submit your program to the compiler and have errors reported, you must fix the errors and resubmit the program to the compiler. You will not be able to proceed until your program is free of compilation errors.

Once your program compiles properly, it generates a machine-language translation than can be executed. This does not mean it is free of errors. Even a program that is syntactically perfect can instruct the computer to do something illegal. Such an error is called an *execution error* because it is encountered during execution. An execution error is a message from the computer that says, "You've done something illegal here, and as a result, I can't continue."

An *intent error* is saying one thing when you really mean something else. An intent error occurs when you fail to consider all possibilities or when your reasoning is faulty. Unless you are dealing with an extremely simple program, you will probably never type in a perfect, error-free program the first time. Thus you need to learn to find and correct errors systematically.

If you use an interpreter rather than a compiler, you will find that many compilation errors reduce to execution errors. An interpreter usually makes a quick pass through a program, making sure that it looks okay on the surface. It might miss spelling errors or other syntactic mistakes. As it executes individual parts of the program, however, it will discover these mistakes and report them during execution. Another property of interpreters is that they generally provide better error messages than compilers do.

1.6 Some Problem-Solving Terminology

People have only a modest capacity for detail and generally can't solve complex problems with one flash of insight. Instead, they structure their problem solving by dividing the problem into manageable pieces and conquering each piece individually. The same strategy works in programming a computer. To solve a complex problem using Pascal, you should decompose the overall task into logical subtasks and then solve each subtask individually. If a subtask proves too complex to solve easily, you break it down into subtasks as well. You continue breaking down the problem until you reach a task you can implement easily. This process is called *structured decomposition* or *stepwise refinement*— decomposition in that you are decomposing the task into smaller pieces, refinement in the sense that the list of subtasks is more detailed than the name of the overall task.

DECOMPOSITION

A separation into discernible parts, each of which is simpler than the whole.

Consider the problem of baking a cake. You can divide this problem into the following subproblems.

- Make the batter.
- Bake the cake.
- Make the frosting.
- Frost the cake.

Each of these four tasks has details associated with it. To make the batter, for example, you:

- Mix the dry ingredients.
- Cream the butter and the sugar.
- Beat in the eggs.
- Stir in the dry ingredients.

Thus you divide the overall task into subtasks and further divide these subtasks into smaller subtasks. Eventually, you reach descriptions that are so simple they require no further explanation (i.e., primitives).

A diagram of this partial solution would look like this:

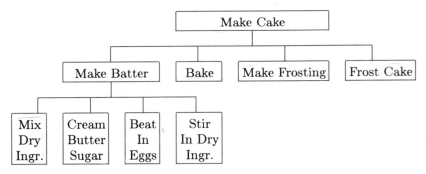

"Make Cake" is the highest-level operation of all. It is defined in terms of four lower-level operations called "Make Batter," "Bake," "Make Frosting," and "Frost Cake." The "Make Batter" operation is defined in terms of even lower-level operations. Diagrams such as this appear throughout the book. They are called *structure diagrams*, and are intended to show how a problem is broken down into subproblems. In this diagram, you can also tell in what order operations are performed by reading left to right. This will not be true of most structure diagrams. To determine the actual order that subprograms are performed in, you will usually have to refer to the program itself.

A related set of terms is *bottom-up* and *top-down*. To make a cake, you might start at the top and reason, "I can make a cake by first making batter, then baking it, then making frosting, and finally putting the frosting on the cake. I could make the batter by first...." This is a top-down solution; it starts at the highest level and proceeds downward. A bottom-up solution involves reasoning such as, "What can I do now? I could put together dry ingredients. If I then creamed the butter and sugar, and then beat in eggs, and then mixed in dry ingredients, I'd have some batter. If I then baked that batter, I'd have an unfrosted cake. If I then...." This is a bottom-up solution because it starts with low-level operations and puts them together to form higher-level operations.

1.7 And Now—Pascal

Here is a short but complete program that shows the basic structure common to all Pascal programs.

```
PROGRAM Fun (OUTPUT);
BEGIN
    WRITELN ('This is a very simple Pascal Program');
    WRITELN ('That produces two lines of output.')
END.
```

The first line is called the *program header*. It tells you that the program is called Fun and that it produces output. The subsequent lines are called the *body of the program*. The body specifies the series of actions to be performed. This program has two commands in it, each of which causes the computer to write a line of output.

This program has four *elements*. Each element has special rules associated with it.

1. *Identifiers*: Words that the programmer introduces into a program. In this program, the word Fun, the name of the program, is an identifier.
2. *Keywords*: The predefined, built-in vocabulary of Pascal. In this example, the keywords are PROGRAM, OUTPUT, BEGIN, WRITELN, and END. The keywords in all program examples in this book are capitalized.
3. *String constants*: Text that can be sent to the output file. This program has two string constants, one inside the parentheses of each WRITELN statement.
4. *Punctuation*: The special characters used to separate items and to indicate special operations. This program uses semicolons, parentheses, quotation marks, and a period.

1.7.1 Identifiers and Keywords

The words used in a Pascal program are called *identifiers*. Identifiers must start with a letter and then can be followed by any number of letters and digits. The following are legal identifiers.

```
first          HiThere        NumStudents    TwoBy4
```

The following are illegal identifiers.

```
two+two        Hi There        Hi-There        2by4
```

Because `hi there` written with a space is considered two identifiers in Pascal, you should write it instead as `hithere`. In distinguishing identifiers, Pascal ignores the case of letters: `hithere` is the same as `HITHERE`, `HIthere`, and `hiTHERE`. Your programs will be easier to read if you choose a consistent scheme. Whenever I concatenate words (put them together), I capitalize the first letter of each word and leave the rest in lowercase, as in `HiThere`.

Don't hesitate to use long identifiers. The more descriptive your names, the easier it will be for people (including yourself) to read your programs. Long identifiers are worth the time they take to type.

Pascal has a set of predefined identifiers called *keywords*. As you read this book, you will learn these keywords and what they are used for. Some, but not all, of Pascal's keywords are reserved. You can only use reserved keywords for their intended purpose. You must be careful to avoid using these words for definitions that you make. For example, if you name your program `Repeat`, your program header will look like this:

```
PROGRAM Repeat (OUTPUT);
```

This will cause a problem, however, because `REPEAT` is a reserved keyword. Here is the complete list of reserved keywords.

AND	END	MOD	REPEAT
ARRAY	FILE	NIL	SET
BEGIN	FOR	NOT	THEN
CASE	FORWARD	OF	TO
CONST	FUNCTION	OR	TYPE
DIV	GOTO	PACKED	UNTIL
DO	IF	PROCEDURE	VAR
DOWNTO	IN	PROGRAM	WHILE
ELSE	LABEL	RECORD	WITH

1.7.2 String Constants

When you want to send literal text to the output file, you enclose it inside single quotation marks. This is called a *string constant* because you string together a series of characters to form something that always stays the same. The following is a string constant.

```
'This is a bunch of text surrounded by quotation marks.'
```

You use single quotation marks, not double quotation marks. The following is not a string constant.

```
"Bad stuff here."
```

But the following is a string constant.

```
'This is a quote even with "these" quotes inside.'
```

String constants must not span more than one line of a program. The following is not a string constant.

```
'This is really
bad stuff
right here.'
```

If you want to include a single quotation mark within a string,

```
'Is what I've typed a string constant?'
```

you must use two apostrophes to represent the apostrophe in the word *I've*:

```
'Is what I''ve typed a string constant?'
```

The two apostrophes together are called an *apostrophe image* and represent one real apostrophe. If you output this string constant, it produces one apostrophe.

1.7.3 The WRITELN Statement

As you have seen, the body of a program contains a series of commands for the computer to carry out. Each command is called a *statement*. The first statement you will study is the WRITELN statement (pronounced "write line" or "write lin"). It is the principal way of producing output in Pascal. Programs wouldn't be terribly interesting if they didn't produce results. The computer "speaks" by generating this output, which can be directed to a user's terminal screen, a printer, or a file. Every program should produce output.

The simplest form of the WRITELN statement is the word itself. The following statement commands the computer to produce a blank line of output.

```
WRITELN
```

WRITELN statements often command the computer to produce lines with text. To output text on a line, you convert the text into a string constant, parenthesize it, and put it after the word WRITELN.

```
WRITELN ('This is a write line statement.')
```

This statement commands the computer to produce the following line of output.

```
This is a write line statement.
```

Each WRITELN statement produces a different line of output. These three statements

```
WRITELN ('This is the first line of output.');
WRITELN;
WRITELN ('And this is the third, below a blank line.');
```

will produce these three lines of output:

```
This is the first line of output.

And this is the third, below a blank line.
```

As noted, if you include an apostrophe image in a WRITELN statement, you will see one apostrophe on output.

1.7.4 Punctuation and Simple Program Structure

Consider this program:

```
PROGRAM NewFun (OUTPUT);
BEGIN
    WRITELN ('This is a program');
    WRITELN ('with four statements.');
    WRITELN ('Notice it has only');
    WRITELN ('three semicolons.')
END.
```

The program header indicates that the name of the program is NewFun and that it produces output. A semicolon separates the header from the body. The words BEGIN and END denote the execution part of the body—the series of statements the computer will carry out. The computer executes the statements sequentially. Control flows from one statement to the next in a forward direction, from the first statement after the BEGIN to the last statement before the END. The program body has a period after the END to indicate the end of the program file.

The three semicolons separate the four statements in the program. A fourth semicolon is not needed, because you use semicolons to separate statements rather than to terminate them. The reasoning is simple if you think of the BEGIN as a left parenthesis and the END as a right parenthesis. Consider the list (Joe, Jane, Jim, Janis). You only need three commas to separate the four names. You don't need a comma to separate Janis from the right parenthesis. Similarly, you don't need a semicolon to separate the last statement of a program from the END. The END acts as a punctuation mark in itself.

Semicolons are a required part of the syntax. If any are left out, the program will have a compilation error. Adding an extra semicolon before the END, however, will not cause an execution error, even though it is not needed. Most professional programmers choose to put it in, claiming it reduces syntax errors. If you always put in the extra semicolon, you don't have to worry about adding or deleting semicolons when you add or delete code later on. You merely put a semicolon at the end of every statement and forget about it.

Here is a more complicated program example. Notice that it uses two empty WRITELN statements to produce blank lines.

```
PROGRAM DrawFigures1 (OUTPUT);
BEGIN
    WRITELN ('   /\');
    WRITELN ('  /  \');
    WRITELN (' /    \');
    WRITELN (' \    /');
    WRITELN ('  \  /');
    WRITELN ('   \/');
    WRITELN;
    WRITELN (' \      /');
    WRITELN ('  \    /');
    WRITELN ('   \/');
    WRITELN ('   /\');
    WRITELN ('  /  \');
    WRITELN (' /    \');
    WRITELN;
    WRITELN ('   /\');
    WRITELN ('  /  \');
    WRITELN (' /    \');
    WRITELN ('+------+');
    WRITELN ('|      |');
    WRITELN ('|      |');
    WRITELN ('+------+');
    WRITELN ('|United|');
    WRITELN ('|States|');
    WRITELN ('+------+');
    WRITELN ('|      |');
    WRITELN ('|      |');
    WRITELN ('+------+');
    WRITELN ('   /\');
    WRITELN ('  /  \');
    WRITELN (' /    \')
END.
```

Here is the output it generates:

```
       /\
      /  \
     /    \
     \    /
      \  /
       \/


     \   /
      \ /
       \/
       /\
      /  \
     /    \


       /\
      /  \
     /    \
   +------+
   |      |
   |      |
   +------+
   |United|
   |States|
   +------+
   |      |
   |      |
   +------+
     /\
    /  \
   /    \
```

1.8 Procedures

The procedure construct in Pascal allows you to build new commands. While you may be dismayed that Pascal does not provide a primitive command for drawing a box, you can get around it by writing your own procedure for doing so. *Procedures* define new actions, new verbs. Once you define a new action, you can use it freely throughout the program. If you define a procedure called **DrawBox**, for example, you can cause its actions to be executed by "calling" the procedure using its name.

Procedures are the tools you use to break down programming tasks into subtasks, to perform decomposition. A procedure is a miniprogram. Like a

program, it has a header and a body. The header names the procedure, and
the body specifies the actions it is to perform. You place procedure definitions
between the program header and the program body. You use semicolons to
separate procedure declarations from each other and from the body of the main
program (i.e., you put a semicolon after the END of each procedure, but put a
period after the END of the program). Consider this sample program:

```
PROGRAM DrawFigures2 (OUTPUT);

PROCEDURE DrawBox;
BEGIN
    WRITELN ('+------+');
    WRITELN ('|      |');
    WRITELN ('|      |');
    WRITELN ('+------+')
END;

PROCEDURE DrawCone;
BEGIN
    WRITELN ('   /\');
    WRITELN ('  /  \');
    WRITELN (' /    \')
END;

PROCEDURE DrawV;
BEGIN
    WRITELN (' \    /');
    WRITELN ('  \  /');
    WRITELN ('   \/')
END;

PROCEDURE DrawDiamond;
BEGIN
    DrawCone;
    DrawV;
    WRITELN
END;

PROCEDURE DrawX;
BEGIN
    DrawV;
    DrawCone;
    WRITELN
END;
```

```
PROCEDURE DrawRocket;
BEGIN
    DrawCone;
    DrawBox;
    WRITELN ('|United|');
    WRITELN ('|States|');
    DrawBox;
    DrawCone;
    WRITELN
END;

BEGIN
    DrawDiamond;
    DrawX;
    DrawRocket
END.
```

This is a structured version of the **DrawFigures1** program you saw earlier. The output generated is identical. The program is named **DrawFigures2** and has six procedures defined within it. The first three procedures contain only simple WRITELN statements. Each of the next three procedures calls the earlier procedures and has an empty WRITELN at the end to produce a blank line to separate it from the other figures. The main program calls these last three procedures in order.

The program is easier to read backwards, starting with the final BEGIN/END in the body of the main program. Here is a structure diagram that shows which procedures the main program (**DrawFigures2**) calls and which procedures are called by each of them:

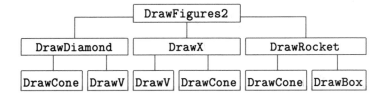

As you can see, this program has three levels of structure and two levels of decomposition. The overall task is split into three subtasks, and each of those subtasks has two subtasks.

A program with procedures has a more complex flow of control than one without them. The rules are still fairly simple, however. When a procedure is called, the computer executes the statements in the body of that procedure; then control proceeds to the statement after the procedure call. Program **DrawFigures2** first executes the body of procedure DrawDiamond, which executes procedures DrawCone and DrawV (in that order). When DrawDiamond finishes executing, control shifts to the next statement in the body of the main program, the call on procedure DrawX.

```
BEGIN
    DrawDiamond;
```

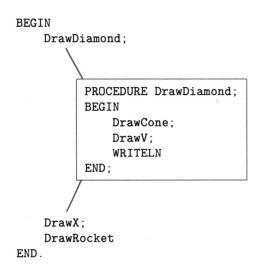

```
    PROCEDURE DrawDiamond;
    BEGIN
        DrawCone;
        DrawV;
        WRITELN
    END;
```

```
    DrawX;
    DrawRocket
END.
```

A complete breakdown of the flow of control from procedure to procedure in DrawFigures2 follows.

1st	DrawDiamond
2nd	DrawCone
3rd	DrawV
4th	DrawX
5th	DrawV
6th	DrawCone
7th	DrawRocket
8th	DrawCone
9th	DrawBox
10th	DrawBox
11th	DrawCone

The order in which you define procedures does not have to parallel the order in which they are executed. The order of execution is determined by the body of the main program and by the bodies of procedures called from the main program. A procedure declaration is like a dictionary entry—it defines a word, but it does not specify how the word will be used. The body of this main program says to first execute DrawDiamond, then DrawX, then DrawRocket. This is the order of execution, regardless of the order they were defined in.

The order of procedure declaration is not totally arbitrary, however. One of Pascal's rules is that you must define words before you can use them. For example, procedure `DrawDiamond` calls procedures `DrawCone` and `DrawV`. This means that you must define `DrawCone` and `DrawV` before `DrawDiamond`. The `DrawX` and `DrawRocket` procedures have similar dependencies. The procedures could have been defined as follows without violating this rule: `DrawV`, `DrawCone`, `DrawX`, `DrawDiamond`, `DrawBox`, `DrawRocket`.

Procedure structure adds to program readability. A well-structured solution is easier to comprehend, and the procedures themselves become a means of explaining a program. Also, programs with procedures are more flexible, more easily adapted to a similar but different task. For example, you can take the six procedures defined in `DrawFigures2` and write the following new program to produce a larger and more complex output file. Building procedures to create new commands increases your flexibility without adding unnecessary complication.

```
BEGIN
    DrawCone;
    DrawCone;
    DrawRocket;
    DrawX;
    DrawRocket;
    DrawDiamond;
    DrawBox;
    DrawDiamond;
    DrawX;
    DrawRocket
END.
```

1.9 Comments and Readability

While procedures address some of the need for explaining how a program works, they are not enough. The layout of a program can also enhance its readability. Pascal is a free-format language. This means you can put in as many or as few spaces and blank lines as you like, as long as you put at least one space or other punctuation mark between words. The following program is legal, but hard to read.

```
PROGRAM Bad (OUTPUT); BEGIN WRITELN ('How short I am!'); WRITELN END.
```

Here are some simple rules to follow that will make your programs more readable.

- Put procedure/program headers on lines by themselves.

- Put no more than one statement on each line.

- Indent statements inside a `BEGIN`/`END` by a consistent number of spaces.

- Use blank lines to separate parts of the program (e.g., procedures).

Using these rules to rewrite the program above yields the following:

```
PROGRAM Bad (OUTPUT);
BEGIN
    WRITELN ('How short I am!');
    WRITELN
END.
```

Well-written Pascal programs are often quite readable, but there will still be times when you will want to include some explanations that are not part of the program itself. You can annotate programs by putting comments in them. Comments are enclosed in curly braces

```
{like this}
```

or by a left parenthesis immediately followed by an asterisk and an asterisk immediately followed by a right parenthesis

```
(* just like this *)
```

You must not put spaces between the asterisks and the parentheses.

```
( * this is bad * )
```

You can put almost any text you like, including carriage returns inside the comment characters, for example,

```
(* Thadeous Martin
   Assignment #1
   Instructor:  Professor Wallingford
   Grader:      Hillary Wilson        *)
```

or

```
(* This is a long comment here, with some open braces {{{{{
   a second line with some other comment openings (*(*(*(*(*
   and a final line with just some text on it and one comment end *)
```

The only thing you aren't allowed to put inside a comment is the comment end character(s). The following is not legal.

```
(* This comment has an asterisk (*) in it
   which prematurely closes the comment   *)
```

The two sets of comment characters are interchangeable. The following are both legal comments.

```
(* This is legal }
{  As is this    *)
```

You must be very careful to close all of your comments. Consider the following.

```
(* This is a bad program.

PROGRAM Bad (OUTPUT);
BEGIN
    WRITELN ('Hi there.')
END.   (* main program *)
```

This is not a program; it is one long comment. Because the comment on the first line is not closed, the entire program is swallowed up. To avoid such mistakes and to make comments stand out, I suggest making one-line comments only. If you have a block of text to comment, put a series of one-line comments in a block.

Don't confuse comments with the text of the WRITELN statements. The text of your comments will not be displayed as output when the program executes. The comments are to help examine and understand the program.

The following are all good places to add comments.

- Include a description of the program at the beginning. Always include your name and the date you last modified the program. You may want to include other information such as class name, grader, and assignment number.

- Include a brief description of what that procedure does at the beginning of each procedure.

- Add a comment at the END of each procedure, so that you can easily pick out the extent of a procedure (from procedure header to commented END).

- Add a comment at the BEGIN and END of the main program, so they are easily found.

1.10 Key Concepts

- Pascal is one of a family of high-level programming languages, one that is highly suited to the teaching of programming.

- Programs written in a high-level language are either translated directly into machine language by a program called a compiler or are dynamically executed by a program called an interpreter.

- A computer system is composed of a Central Processing Unit (CPU), a main memory, and a collection of peripheral devices that provide input, output, storage, and communications.

- The programs that you write will probably contain errors. Compilation errors are mistakes in syntax discovered at compilation time. Execution errors result from programs instructing the computer to perform illegal actions at execution time. Errors of intent result from faulty reasoning.

- Complex problems are solved by decomposing the overall task into subtasks, each of which is simpler than the whole, and further decomposing those subtasks until you reach tasks that are simple enough to write without further decomposition. Procedures are used in Pascal to accomplish this stepwise refinement.

- All words used in a Pascal program are either identifiers introduced by the programmer or keywords that are part of the Pascal language.

- Some of Pascal's keywords are reserved and cannot be used as programmer-defined identifiers.

- Comments and program layout add to the readability of a program.

1.11 Self-Check Exercises

1. If you were going to use a computer to help you write a novel, would you be more likely to want a great deal of main memory or a great deal of secondary memory?

2. What kind of peripheral device is a robot arm?

3. Which of the following can be introduced into a Pascal program as identifiers?

    ```
    writeln         first-name      AnnualSalary    label
    22Skidoo        loop            sum_of_terms    Warp8Scotty
    ```

4. What series of WRITELN statements would produce the following output?

    ```
    This is a test of your
    knowledge of "quotes" used
    in 'string constants.'

    You're bound to get it right
    if you read the section on
    ''quotes.''
    ```

5. Draw a structure diagram for the following program. Could its procedures be defined in a different order?

    ```
    PROGRAM Strange (OUTPUT);

    PROCEDURE First;
    BEGIN
        WRITELN ('Inside first procedure.')
    END;
    ```

```
PROCEDURE Second;
BEGIN
    WRITELN ('Inside second procedure.');
    first
END;

PROCEDURE Third;
BEGIN
    WRITELN ('Inside third procedure.');
    first;
    second
END;

BEGIN    (* main program *)
    first;
    third;
    second;
    third
END.     (* main program *)
```

6. What is the output of the program in Exercise 5?

7. The following program is legal under the free format rules of Pascal, but it is difficult to read. Reformat it following the rules described in Section 1.9.

```
PROGRAM GiveAdvice(OUTPUT);BEGIN WRITELN(
'Programs can be easy or difficult');WRITELN
('to read, depending upon their format.'
);WRITELN
;WRITELN('Everyone, including yourself, will be');WRITELN
(
'happier if you choose to format your');WRITELN('programs.'
)END
```

1.12 Programming Problems

1. Write a program to spell out MISSISSIPPI using block letters like the following:

```
MMM          MMM
 MMM        MMM
 MMMM      MMMM
 MM MM    MM MM
 MM   MMMM   MM
 MM    MM    MM
 MM          MM
 MM          MM
MMM          MMM
```

2. Write a program that produces several letters. You should create low-level procedures that write out individual paragraphs and then write high-level procedures that produce letters by combining paragraphs.

3. Write a program that produces as output a song. Use procedures for each verse and the refrain.

4. Write a program that produces as output the words of "The Twelve Days of Christmas." (Hint: Procedures simplify this task.)

2

BASIC PROBLEM-SOLVING TECHNIQUES

2.1 Introduction

Now that you know something about the basic structure of Pascal programs, you are ready to start solving complex problems. You will still be restricted to programs that produce output. As you progress through the chapter, you will examine some basic problem-solving techniques used by software engineers and some software engineering goals other than programs that work.

The first half of the chapter fills in three important areas. First, it examines expressions, that is, how values are expressed in Pascal, and in particular, how the values of integers are described. Second, it discusses program objects called variables that can change in value as the program executes. Third, it details the workings of the Pascal statements WRITELN and WRITE, which produce output.

The second half of the chapter introduces your first control structure: the FOR loop. You use this structure to repeat actions in a program. This is useful whenever you find a pattern in a complex figure, because you can use a FOR loop to repeat an action that creates a pattern. The challenge is finding each pattern and figuring out what repeated action will reproduce it.

2.2 Data Objects

Think of a computer as a manipulator of objects. The objects that a program manipulates are individual pieces of information. For example, the computer might have one object for storing a taxpayer's gross income and another object for storing the taxpayer's total deductions. A third object might be a place for storing the adjusted gross income. The program might ask a user at the terminal to give a value to the first two objects and would give a value to the third by a manipulation on the first two that we call subtraction. The program might have further objects used to calculate the tax owed, by performing operations such as multiplication and addition.

All Pascal programs specify what objects are to be used in the program and how the objects are to be manipulated. These objects fall into different categories. For example, the following are three simple categories of objects and the names that Pascal gives to them:

Category	Description	Examples
INTEGER	Whole numbers	$-2, -1, 0, 1, 2$
REAL	All numbers	$2.3, 19.8, -94.332$
CHAR	Characters	X, Y, Z, a, b, c, !, ?

These categories are called *types* and are described by abstract data types.

ABSTRACT DATA TYPE ————————

A description of the domain of a type and the *set of operations* that can be performed on objects of that type.

The *domain of values* describes what values are considered part of the type. For example, a character type would probably have a domain that includes letters, punctuation marks, and digits. The *set of operations* is the set of manipulations that can be performed on elements of the type. For example, for a character type, you might have operations such as capitalizing a character.

2.2.1 Expressions

When you specify the series of actions that a program is to perform, you will often refer to specific values. For example, you probably wouldn't say, "Draw stars"; you would say, "Draw 10 stars," or "Draw 100 stars." In Pascal, you refer to values by using an expression.

EXPRESSION

A description of how to obtain a value.

Consider the problem of describing the net pay of an employee after taxes have been taken out. You can refer to the value directly:

$20,395

A direct reference to a value is the simplest possible expression. While this doesn't quite fit the definition of "how to obtain" because there is nothing to be done to obtain it, Pascal is simpler to define and understand when you consider constants such as these to be expressions rather than something else.

A second way to refer to a value involves referring to an object. Each object manipulated in a program has a name and a value. For example, you can define an object called `NetPay` that has the value described above. Thus another way to describe how to obtain this value is by referring to the object:

    NetPay

In this case, the way you obtain the value is to look up the value that this object has. Neither of these references is very specific about where the value comes from.

A third way to refer to the value is by describing more specifically how it is obtained. For example, if you have objects called `GrossPay` and `Taxes`, you can refer to this value by saying:

    GrossPay - Taxes

In this expression, you are describing not just a value, but rather a rule to follow for obtaining it. Like this more typical example, most expressions involve some kind of calculation. With the rule, you can calculate the net pay of many employees if you know their gross pay and taxes, making this expression more useful in solving different tasks.

Expressions can be very complex. To group various parts of an expression, you can use parentheses:

    (3 + 29) - (4 + 5)

The parentheses here cause the expression to be calculated as follows:

    (3 + 29) - (4 + 5)
    (32) - (9)

23

2.2.2   Terminology of Expressions

The simplest expression is a direct reference to a value. Such a value is called a *constant* because it does not change in value. Later in this chapter, Section 2.5.6 explains how to create program objects, also called constants, that are guaranteed not to change in value.

> **CONSTANT**
>
> A specific value; also, an object in a program that is guaranteed not to change in value.

Consider the expression:

```
GrossPay - Taxes
```

The minus sign is called an *operator*, and GrossPay and Taxes are called *operands*. An operator is a special symbol (such as + or -) used to indicate an operation to be performed on one or more values. An operand is a value used by an operator. Here is a complex expression with its operators and operands indicated:

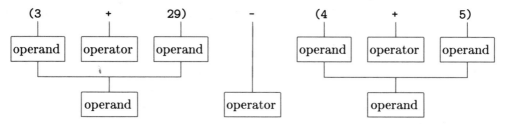

Operands need not be simple. The first plus operator has simple operands of 3 and 29, and the second plus operator has simple operands of 4 and 5, but the minus operator has operands that are each parenthesized expressions with operators of their own. Thus you can see that expressions are built from smaller expressions. At the lowest level, you have constants and names of objects that describe values. These are used as operands to make more complex expressions, which in turn can be used as operands in even more complex expressions.

You will see many different operators as you progress through this book, all of which can be used to form expressions. Expressions can be arbitrarily complex, with as many operators as you like. For this reason, when I tell you, "An expression can be used here," I will often point out that I mean "arbitrary expressions" to emphasize that you can use complex expressions as well as simple values and names of objects.

The computer determines the value of an expression by evaluating it.

> **EVALUATION**
>
> The process of obtaining the value of an expression.

The value obtained when an expression is evaluated is called the *result*. Using objects called `first`, `second`, and `third`, with the values 5, 10, and 20, respectively, here is a table of some expressions and their results:

Expression	Result
23	23
2 + 2	4
first	5
second	10
third	20
second − first	5
first + third − second	15

2.2.3 Precedence

Pascal expressions are like complex noun phrases in English. The net pay expression could be worded as "the difference between gross pay and taxes." Such phrases are subject to ambiguity, as in "the man on the hill by the river with the telescope." Is the river by the hill or by the man? Is the man holding the telescope, or is the telescope on the hill, or is the telescope in the river? You don't know how the various parts are grouped together.

You can get the same kind of ambiguity if parentheses aren't used to group the parts of a Pascal expression. For example, the expression (`first + third - second`) has two operators. Which is performed first? You could interpret the expression two ways:

```
(first + third) - second
first + (third - second)
```

While either grouping here yields the same answer, this is not always true. To deal with the ambiguity, Pascal has rules of precedence that determine how the various parts are grouped together.

> **PRECEDENCE**
>
> The relative importance of one operator over another.

Rules of precedence are applied when the grouping of operators in an expression is ambiguous. An operator with low precedence is evaluated after operators of higher precedence.

2.2.4   Type INTEGER

In order to explore expressions, you first need to learn about one of Pascal's types. The simplest one to examine first is type INTEGER.

The domain of type INTEGER is the set of whole numbers 0, 1, 2, 3, ... and the negative counting numbers -1, -2, -3, ... Theoretically, this domain is unbounded, but for practical reasons, there are limits. There are many manipulations that can be performed on objects of type INTEGER. Most common are the arithmetic operations and the built-in procedures that allow you to input and output integer values.

Type INTEGER is language-independent, because it describes only the domain and the operations. It doesn't specify how to refer to values of the domain or how to refer to the operations. Those are implementation details. For example, in the programming language LISP, you calculate "two plus two" by saying

```
(PLUS 2 2)
```

This is very different from the way it is done in Pascal:

```
2 + 2
```

Both, however, represent the same abstract calculation. This distinction between abstract specification and detailed implementation is an important one for a software engineer to understand.

Let's examine the details of Pascal's implementation of type INTEGER. Constants of the domain are expressed as a series of digits. You can put a plus or minus sign in front of the digits. Here are some legal INTEGER constants:

```
18              2781359         -456            +208
```

The following are not legal INTEGER constants:

```
18.0            2,781,359       -456.           +208.5
```

Integers are whole numbers: no decimal point is needed (or allowed). Also, commas are not used to break up groups of three digits in large integers.

There are some integer values that are too large in magnitude to be manipulated, because computers have limited storage space. Different computers have different limits. A small microcomputer, for example, will not be able to distinguish as many different values as a large time-sharing system. Thus type INTEGER will in general be more limited on smaller computers.

To recognize this variety, Pascal puts no absolute limitations on what the domain should be. But it does require that there be a way to find out the limits. Every Pascal system is required to have a predefined object called MAXINT that describes the largest value of type INTEGER. The domain of INTEGER is defined to be $-$MAXINT to $+$MAXINT. Every Pascal system will set MAXINT to the appropriate value. MAXINT is a *predefined object*, which means that you can refer to it without defining it yourself.

The basic arithmetic operators for type INTEGER are:

Operator	Meaning	Example	Value
+	Addition	2 + 2	4
−	Subtraction	53 − 18	35
*	Multiplication	3 * 8	24
DIV	Truncated division	19 DIV 5	3
MOD	Remainder	19 MOD 5	4

The addition and subtraction operators should be familiar to you. The asterisk as a multiplication operator might be a surprise for nonprogrammers. You don't use an X because you don't want to confuse multiplication operations with the identifier X, and the dot that is sometimes used to denote multiplication does not exist on most keyboards.

The last two operators, DIV and MOD, are the most confusing. Division presents a problem in the domain of integers. When you divide 119 by 5, for example, you do not get an integer. Therefore, integer division is expressed as two different integers—a quotient and a remainder:

$\frac{119}{5} = 23$ (quotient) with 4 (remainder)

In terms of INTEGER operators,

```
119 DIV 5 = 23
119 MOD 5 =  4
```

If you remember long division, you remember doing calculations such as this:

```
         31
    34 )1079
        102
        ──
         59
         34
         ──
         25
```

Here, dividing 1079 by 34 yields 31 with a remainder of 25. Using INTEGER operators, the problem would be described like this:

```
1079 DIV 34 = 31
1079 MOD 34 = 25
```

DIV and MOD do not have this behavior for negative numbers. Appendix A contains all these details.

2.2.5 Precedence for Type INTEGER

Consider the expression:

    24 + 2 * 2

There are two ways to evaluate it:

    (24 + 2) * 2 = 26 * 2 = 52
    24 + (2 * 2) = 24 + 4 = 28

Such ambiguities are cleared up by rules of precedence for type INTEGER. The additive operators (+ and -) form one level of precedence, and the multiplicative operators (*, DIV, and MOD) form another. The additive operators have a lower level of precedence than the multiplicative operators.

The right answer to the problem above is 28, because you would multiply first. If you want to, you can use parentheses to override precedence:

    (24 + 2) * 2

Some cases are not answered by levels of precedence alone:

    13 DIV 2 * 3

With two operators of the same precedence level, you do not know which is the correct order of evaluation:

    13 DIV 2 * 3 = 13 DIV (2 * 3) = 13 DIV (6) = 2
    13 DIV 2 * 3 = (13 DIV 2) * 3 = (6) * 3 = 18

You need another precedence rule. When operators of the same precedence appear in an expression or subexpression that is not grouped by parentheses, the operators are evaluated left to right.

According to this rule, the expression above evaluates to 18. If you want the multiplication to take place first, you can force the order of evaluation by using parentheses. When in doubt, it is wise to use parentheses.

2.3 Variables

An object that can change in value as the program executes is called a *variable*. The computer's main memory is divided into individual memory cells where values can be stored. A program has many different memory cells available to it and can access them by using variables.

VARIABLE

A memory cell with a name and a type that stores a value.

As with all Pascal words, variables are named by legal identifiers. Pascal is particular about the type of each object, so you must tell the computer the type of every variable you plan to use. Every variable has a memory cell set aside where it stores its value. Values can change, but only one value can be stored at a time. When the variable changes, the old value goes away.

Every variable initially has an undefined value. Usually this means that the variable has some random value. A good way to think of this is to imagine a memory cell containing a big question mark. Some Pascal systems initialize the variables to zero or some other value that seems appropriate, but there is no universal rule. Even if you are using a Pascal system that does initialize, it is best to be safe and assume you are starting with a question mark.

The names that you give to variables must be defined, just as all identifiers that you introduce in a program must be defined. You do so with the **VAR** declaration. A declaration comprises, in order, the word **VAR**, a series of identifiers separated by commas, a colon, a type, and a semicolon. The following declaration defines three variables of type **INTEGER**:

```
VAR first, second, sum :  INTEGER;
```

The preceding declaration has a list of three identifiers that are all given the same type. You may also give types to the identifiers individually:

```
VAR first  : INTEGER;
    second : INTEGER;
    sum    : INTEGER;
```

A colon separates each variable name from its type. Each declaration is terminated with a semicolon. The word **VAR** appears once at the beginning. Some programmers prefer individual declarations such as this because they can be read more easily, especially if the colons are lined up so that the variable names can easily be distinguished from the types.

Here is a general description of the **VAR** declaration's syntax:

```
VAR  <identifier list>  :  <type>;
     <identifier list>  :  <type>;

        .  .  .

     <identifier list>  :  <type>;
```

Anything inside <*braces*> should be interpreted as "put this here." This is called a *syntax template* because it shows the general form (i.e., syntax) of a language construct. Such templates appear throughout the book.

The syntax of an identifier list can also be described by a syntax template:

<*identifier*>,   <*identifier*>, <*identifier*>, . . . , <*identifier*>

This template shows that an identifier list is composed of as many identifiers as you like, separated by commas.

2.3.1   Program and Procedure Blocks

Now that you know the syntax of variable declarations, you have to learn how to include them in a program or procedure. Programs and procedures have both declaration parts and execution parts. The combination is called a *block*.

The declarations you know about so far are for variables and procedures. You will also see other declarations that define new words. Declarations must appear in a particular order. Variables, for example, must be defined before procedures, and all declarations must precede the execution part of the block. The syntax of a program block as you understand it so far can be described as

> *<variable declarations>*
> *<procedure declarations>*
> *<execution part>*

Because a procedure is considered a miniprogram, this syntax describes not only program blocks, but also procedure blocks. Just about anything a program can do, a procedure can do. Thus a procedure is allowed to define its own variables and procedures.

2.3.2   Assignment Statement

The simplest way to give a value to a variable is to use an assignment statement:

```
first := 47;
```

This statement stores the value 47 in the memory cell for the variable `first`. The general syntax of the statement is

> *<variable>* := *<expression>*

The special symbol made from a colon and an equals sign (`:=`) separates the two sides of this statement. When the statement executes, the computer first evaluates the expression on the right side; then it stores the result in the memory cell for the given variable. The type of the variable and expression must match (no mixing of apples and oranges).

This assignment statement is more complicated:

```
second := 37 - 18 + 3;
```

Here, arithmetic operations form an `INTEGER` expression. The expression evaluates to 22, giving the value 22 to the variable `second`.

Expressions need not contain only constants:

```
sum := first + second;
```

To calculate the value of this expression, the computer adds together the current values of the variables `first` and `second` and comes up with the answer 69. This value is stored in the variable `sum`. Pascal uses the symbol `:=` to emphasize that this is not a statement of equality, but a command to perform some action. This is not a legal assignment statement:

```
47 := first;
```

This does not fit the template. The left side must have a variable and the right side must have an expression, not vice versa. Some programming languages allow you to do multiple assignments with one statement:

```
first := second := 0;
```

This is not legal in Pascal. Each variable must be initialized separately:

```
first  := 0;
second := 0;
```

The assignment statement does not represent an algebraic relationship. This statement of equality

$$x = y + 2$$

is very different from a statement like

```
second := first + 2
```

When you say that x is equal to y plus 2, you are stating a fact for now and forever. If x changes, y will change accordingly. The assignment statement, on the other hand, is a command to perform an action at some moment in time. It does not represent a lasting relationship between variables. Consider this short program:

```
PROGRAM Sample (OUTPUT);
VAR first  : INTEGER;
    second : INTEGER;
BEGIN
    first := 13;
    second := first + 2;
    first := 50;
    WRITELN (first, second)
END.
```

Initially, **first** and **second** have random values:

```
first  ?              second  ?
```

The first assignment statement gives an initial value to **first**:

```
first  13             second  ?
```

And the second gives an initial value to the variable `second`:

first | 13 | second | 15 |

While there now exists an algebraic relationship between `first` and `second` similar to $x = y + 2$, this relationship is temporary, because the third assignment statement reassigns the value of `first`:

first | 50 | second | 15 |

`second` is no longer 2 more than `first`. The last assignment statement wipes out the old value of `first` and leaves `second` unchanged. This temporary quality of the assignment statement is sometimes difficult for beginners to grasp. Remember that in algebra one reasons about permanent relationships, whereas in programming one reasons about sequences of actions. The best habit to get into is to read the `:=` as "gets" or "becomes."

One very common assignment statement that points out the difference between algebraic relationships and program statements is

```
first := first + 1;
```

This statement says "`first` gets the value of `first` plus one." This may seem a rather odd statement, but you should be able to decipher it given the rules outlined above. Suppose that the current value of `first` is 19. To execute the statement, you first evaluate the expression to obtain the result 20. The computer stores this value in the variable named on the left, in variable `first`. Thus this statement increments the value of `first` by one.

2.4   Output Revisited

You saw in Chapter 1 that you can output string constants using the `WRITELN` statement. You can also output `INTEGER` expressions using `WRITELN`:

```
WRITELN (12 + 3 - 1);
```

This statement causes the computer to first evaluate the expression, which yields the value 14, and then to write 14 to the output file. In addition, the `WRITELN` statement can output more than one value on a line. If you want to output several items, you list them inside parentheses and separate them by commas. The items can be any combination of string constants and `INTEGER` expressions. Thus the general syntax is

```
WRITELN ( <item>, <item>, <item>, ... , <item>);
```

Here is a WRITELN statement with four items:

```
WRITELN ('First answer =', 6 * 2, '   Second answer =', 12 + 3);
```

This is easier to see in the following illustration:

```
WRITELN ('First answer ='  ,  6 * 2  ,  '   Second answer ='  ,  12 + 3);
```

| string | expression | string | expression |

This statement produces this line of output:

```
First answer =          12, Second answer =          15
```

There are several leading spaces printed out before each of these integers because my computer uses twelve columns to display each integer unless I specify otherwise. In the next section you will see how to get rid of such leading spaces.

Consider the following example of a program with complex WRITELN statements:

```
PROGRAM ReportDomain (OUTPUT);
BEGIN
    WRITELN ('An integer on this system can take on any value between');
    WRITELN ('plus ', MAXINT, ' and minus ', MAXINT, '.')
END.
```

This program reports the limits on the domain of type INTEGER. It will produce different outputs on different machines. On my machine, it produces this output:

```
An integer on this system can take on any value between
plus   34359738367 and minus   34359738367.
```

As you can see, my computer has a large domain for type INTEGER. You should run this program on your own system to find out its domain for type INTEGER.

2.4.1 Field-Width Specifications

The number of columns used for an output item is called the *field-width* of that item. My computer uses a field width of 12 for integers. You can change the field width of any item in a WRITELN statement by putting a colon after the item and a different field width:

```
WRITELN ('First answer =', (6 * 2):3, ', Second answer =', (12 + 3):3);
```

This WRITELN still has four items being output. The second and fourth items are integer expressions with field widths of 3. Notice that the field-width specification appears after the expression. There are parentheses around the expressions for readability, but they are not required. This statement produces the following output:

```
First answer = 12, Second answer = 15
```

If the field width specified for an INTEGER expression is not large enough, the computer will expand it to whatever is necessary. Thus a statement such as

```
WRITELN ('number = ', number:1);
```

will write out the variable **number** in as much space as is required. A field width of 1 is often used for this purpose.

You can use field widths for string constants as well. As with integers, the text is right-justified within the field, so setting field widths can be useful for centering lines and other tasks that involve creating leading blanks:

```
WRITELN ('How to Use Format Specifications':55);
WRITELN ('by Mona Tyler':46);
```

These lines produce this output:

```
          How to Use Format Specifications
                  by Mona Tyler
```

If the field width for a string is not large enough, the string is truncated to that number of characters. For example,

```
WRITELN ('A long string here':7, 'and some more':8);
```

produces this output:

```
A long and some
```

2.4.2 WRITE versus WRITELN

The computer has a pointer or output cursor to keep track of where to send the next output. Initially this pointer is at the beginning of the first line. As you execute various statements, it is advanced across lines and down the page.

Pascal has a second statement that produces output known as the WRITE statement. It has the same form as the WRITELN statement, but it has a different effect on the output cursor. The WRITELN statement does two things: it produces output on the current line, and it positions the output cursor to the beginning of a new line. The WRITE statement does only the first of these. It produces output on the current line, but the output cursor remains on the same line. A series of WRITE statements, therefore, will generate output all on the same line. Only a WRITELN statement will cause the current line to be completed and a new line to be started.

Consider these six statements:

```
WRITE ('Hi Ho, ');
WRITE ('my man.');
WRITE ('Where are you bound?  ');
```

```
WRITELN ('My way, I hope.');
WRITE ('This is');
WRITELN (' for the whole family!')
```

These statements produce two lines of output. Remember every WRITELN statement produces exactly one line of output. Because there are two WRITELN statements here, there are two lines of output.

After the first statement executes, the current line looks like this:

```
Hi ho,
       ↑
```

The arrow below the output line indicates the position of the output cursor. It is at the end of this line. Notice that it is preceded by a space. That is because the string constant ends with a space. Pascal will not insert a space to separate items on a line.

After the next WRITE, the line looks like this:

```
Hi ho, my man.
              ↑
```

The output cursor doesn't have a space before it now because the string constant written out ends in a period, not a space.

After the next WRITE, the line looks like this:

```
Hi ho, my man.Where are you bound?
                                  ↑
```

There is no space between the period and the word Where because there was no space before the output cursor. Because the string constant in the third statement has spaces at the end, the output cursor is positioned two spaces after the question mark.

After the next statement executes, the output looks like this:

```
Hi ho, my man.Where are you bound?  My way, I hope.

↑
```

Because this fourth statement is a WRITELN statement, it finishes the output line and positions the cursor at the beginning of the second line.

The next statement is another WRITE that produces this:

```
Hi ho, my man.Where are you bound?
This is
       ↑
```

The final WRITELN completes the second line and positions the output cursor at the beginning of a new line:

```
Hi ho, my man.Where are you bound?
This is for the whole family!
```

↑

These six statements are equivalent to these two single statements:

```
WRITELN ('Hi ho, my man.Where are you bound?  My way, I hope.');
WRITELN ('This is for the whole family!')
```

It seems a bit silly to have both the WRITE and the WRITELN statement for producing lines such as this, but you will see that there are more interesting applications of WRITE.

It is possible to have empty WRITELN statements:

```
WRITELN;
```

Because there is nothing inside of parentheses to be written to the output line, this positions the output cursor to the beginning of the next line. If there are WRITE statements before this empty WRITELN, it finishes out the line made by those WRITE statements. If there are no previous WRITE statements, it produces a blank line. An empty WRITE statement is meaningless and is illegal.

2.5 The FOR Loop

Programming often involves specifying redundant tasks. The FOR loop helps to avoid such redundancy. Suppose you want to write out the squares of the first 5 integers. You can say

```
PROGRAM WriteSquares (OUTPUT);
BEGIN
    WRITELN (1:1, ' squared = ', (1 * 1):2);
    WRITELN (2:1, ' squared = ', (2 * 2):2);
    WRITELN (3:1, ' squared = ', (3 * 3):2);
    WRITELN (4:1, ' squared = ', (4 * 4):2);
    WRITELN (5:1, ' squared = ', (5 * 5):2)
END.
```

This produces the following output:

```
1 squared =  1
2 squared =  4
3 squared =  9
4 squared = 16
5 squared = 25
```

This is a tedious solution to the problem. The program has five statements that are very similar. They are all of the form

```
WRITELN (number:1, ' squared = ', (number * number):2);
```

where Number is either 1, 2, 3, 4, or 5.

The FOR loop allows you to avoid such redundancy. It has the following syntax:

FOR *<variable>* := *<starting expression>* TO *<ending expression>* DO
   <controlled statement>

This template has four pieces to be filled in: a variable, two expressions, and a statement. The variable is used to carry out the looping. It is given all of the values between the starting expression and the ending expression inclusive. For each value the variable takes on, the controlled statement is executed once. The FOR loop is the first example of a *control structure*, a syntactic structure that controls another statement.

Here is an equivalent program using a FOR loop:

```
PROGRAM WriteSquares (OUTPUT);
VAR number : INTEGER;
BEGIN
    FOR number := 1 TO 5 DO
        WRITELN (number:1, ' squared = ', (number * number):2)
END.
```

The starting value is 1, the ending value is 5, and the statement controlled by the loop is the WRITELN. This WRITELN, then, will be executed a total of 5 times, first with **number** equal to 1, then with **number** equal to 2, and so on until **number** equals 5.

The variable that controls a FOR loop is called a *control variable*. Each execution of the controlled statement of a loop is called an *iteration*, as in "The loop halted after four iterations." Iteration also refers to looping in general, as in "I solved the problem using iteration."

Consider another FOR loop:

```
FOR number := -100 TO +100 DO
    WRITELN (number:4, ' squared = ', (number * number):5)
```

This loop executes a total of 201 times, producing the squares of all the integers between −100 and +100 inclusive. The starting and ending values, then, can be any integers. They can, in fact, be arbitrary integer expressions:

```
FOR number := (2 + 2) TO (17 * 3) DO
    WRITELN (number:2, ' squared = ', (number * number):4)
```

This loop will generate the squares between 4 and 51 inclusive. The parentheses are not necessary, but they improve readability.

Consider the following loop:

```
FOR number := 1 TO 30 DO
    WRITELN ('+--------+')
```

This loop generates 30 lines of output, all exactly the same. This loop is slightly different from the previous one because the statement controlled by the FOR loop makes no reference to the control variable. Thus

```
FOR number := -30 TO -1 DO
    WRITELN ('+--------+')
```

generates exactly the same output. The behavior of such a loop is determined solely by the number of iterations it performs.

The number of iterations is given by

$$(\text{Ending value}) - (\text{starting value}) + 1$$

You should adopt the convention of starting with the value 1 in such cases, so that the ending value indicates how many times the loop will execute. It is much simpler to see that the first of these loops iterates 30 times. Thus

```
FOR number := 1 TO 1 DO
    WRITELN ('+--------+')
```

iterates once because there is exactly one value between 1 and 1 inclusive. What about

```
FOR number := 1 TO 0 DO
    WRITELN ('+--------+')
```

This loop performs no iterations at all. It will not cause an execution error; it will merely not execute the controlled statement. Whenever the final value is less than the starting value, the loop performs no iterations.

2.5.1 Controlling Multiple Statements

What if you want to write a FOR loop that executes two statements? What if, for example, you want to produce 20 pairs of lines, the first of which has the word Hi on it and the second of which has the word Ho? You might try the following:

```
FOR number := 1 TO 20 DO
    WRITELN ('Hi!');
    WRITELN ('Ho!');
```

The indentation here indicates that you want both WRITELN statements to be controlled by the FOR. However, this indentation means nothing to the computer. The FOR loop controls whatever single statement follows the DO, no matter how you indent the program.

You could define a procedure called `TwoLines` that performs these two
`WRITELN`s:

```
FOR number := 1 TO 20 DO
    TwoLines;
```

However, there is another way to do this. You can turn a series of statements
into a single statement by using a compound statement. A *compound statement*
is a series of statements separated by semicolons and surrounded by `BEGIN` and
`END`. You have already used compound statements to define the execution parts
of procedures and programs.

The following syntax template illustrates the syntax of a compound statement:

```
BEGIN
    <statement> ;
    <statement> ;
      . . .
    <statement>
END
```

The compound statement groups statements so that they behave syntactically
like a single statement. Thus to make your `FOR` loop execute both `WRITELN`
statements, you could use the following:

```
FOR number := 1 TO 20 DO
BEGIN
    WRITELN ('Hi!');
    WRITELN ('Ho!')
END;
```

The correct syntactic interpretation of this fragment is that the `FOR` loop controls
a single statement, a compound statement. However, the compound statement
has within it two `WRITELN` statements, so the loop is, in effect, controlling two
statements.

You can put as many statements as you like inside the `BEGIN/END`:

```
FOR number := 1 TO 20 DO
BEGIN
    WRITELN ('Hi!');
    WRITELN ('Ho!');
    WRITELN ('My');
    WRITELN ('Man!')
END;
```

As always, you must be careful to separate the statements by semicolons. No
semicolon is required before the `END`. When I use a compound statement in a
control structure such as a `FOR` loop, I indent my `BEGIN/END` blocks as follows:

```
FOR number := 1 TO 20 DO
BEGIN
    WRITELN ('Hi!');
    WRITELN ('Ho!')
END;
```

I always put the BEGIN and END at the same level of indentation as the control structure itself. Inside the BEGIN/END, I indent the controlled statements. You should choose some indentation scheme for yourself and use it consistently. A few other schemes follow. The second of these seems to be most popular among professional Pascal programmers.

```
FOR number := 1 TO 20 DO
    BEGIN
    WRITELN ('Hi!');
    WRITELN ('Ho!')
    END;

FOR number := 1 TO 20 DO BEGIN
    WRITELN ('Hi!');
    WRITELN ('Ho!')
END;

FOR number := 1 TO 20 DO
    BEGIN
        WRITELN ('Hi!');
        WRITELN ('Ho!')
    END;
```

2.5.2 FOR Loops within FOR Loops

The FOR loop controls a statement, and the FOR loop is itself a statement. This makes the following legal:

```
FOR number1 := 1 TO 10 DO
    FOR number2 := 1 TO 5 DO
        WRITELN ('Hi there.');
```

This is probably easier to read from the inside out. The WRITELN statement produces a single line of output. The number2 loop executes this statement 5 times, producing 5 lines of output. The outer loop executes the inner loop 10 times, producing 10 sets of 5 lines, or 50 lines of output. The code above, then, is equivalent to:

```
FOR number := 1 TO 50 DO
    WRITELN ('Hi there.');
```

This example shows that a FOR loop can be controlled by another FOR loop. Such a loop is called a *nested loop*.

Let's look at another nested loop. Consider how to generate a single line of output with 30 asterisks on it. You could do the following:

```
WRITELN ('******************************');
```

This solution is not very adaptable or readable. It isn't immediately obvious how many asterisks are being written out, nor is it simple to change that number.

There is a better way. You can use a loop to write the 30 asterisks:

```
FOR column := 1 TO 30 DO
    WRITE ('*');
WRITELN;
```

You use WRITE instead of WRITELN to output the asterisks on one line. You follow this with an empty WRITELN to finish the line of output. This solution is more readable and is more easily changed to produce a line of different length. This code produces a single line. If you want to produce 50 lines, you can nest these statements inside another loop. The following fragment produces 50 lines of output, each with 30 asterisks on it.

```
FOR row := 1 TO 50 DO
BEGIN
    FOR column := 1 TO 30 DO
        WRITE ('*');
    WRITELN
END;
```

2.5.3　Levels of Control

Compound statements and control structures introduce different statement levels, the relative levels of control of statements within a block. Statements controlled at the outer level are assigned level 1; statements controlled by level 1 statements are assigned level 2; statements controlled by level 2 statements are assigned level 3; and so on.

In my indentation scheme, each level of indentation corresponds to one of these levels of structure. This allows me to visually scan the structure of a piece of code. Sometimes it is useful to actually annotate the program and list the level of each statement. For example, here is a listing of the loops examined in the last section. The level has been included as an extra column to the left of the code. Since BEGIN and END are not statements, I don't assign them a level.

Instead, I list them as parentheses to indicate their grouping function. This fragment has three levels of structure:

```
1      FOR row := 1 TO 50 DO
(      BEGIN
2          FOR column := 1 TO 30 DO
3              WRITE ('*');
2          WRITELN
)      END;
```

Here is a more complicated program fragment with four levels of structure:

```
1      FOR row := 1 TO 5 DO
(      BEGIN
2          FOR column := 1 TO 15 DO
(          BEGIN
3              WRITE ('|');
3              FOR dashes := 1 TO 3 DO
4                  WRITE ('-')
)          END;
2          WRITELN ('|')
)      END;
```

This fragment produces 5 rows each with 15 columns composed of a vertical bar and 3 dashes. Thus the output of this code is

```
|---|---|---|---|---|---|---|---|---|---|---|---|---|---|---|
|---|---|---|---|---|---|---|---|---|---|---|---|---|---|---|
|---|---|---|---|---|---|---|---|---|---|---|---|---|---|---|
|---|---|---|---|---|---|---|---|---|---|---|---|---|---|---|
|---|---|---|---|---|---|---|---|---|---|---|---|---|---|---|
```

There is no limit to the number of times you can nest one loop inside another, so your statement levels can be arbitrarily high.

I should admit a bias of mine before I finish this topic. Compound statements are a source of great controversy when instructors discuss structure, indentation, and control. Reconsider this simple loop:

```
FOR number := 1 TO 20 DO
BEGIN
    WRITELN ('Hi!');
    WRITELN ('Ho!')
END;
```

I describe this as "Here is a FOR loop controlling two statements wrapped up in a compound statement." Others would say "Here is a FOR loop controlling a compound statement, and the compound statement controlling two inner statements." The subtle difference is the implication of control on the part of the compound statement.

If you view the compound statement as controlling its two inner statements, then your definition of statement level requires that you analyze the fragment differently:

```
1       FOR number := 1 TO 20 DO
2       BEGIN
3           WRITELN ('Hi!');
3           WRITELN ('Ho!')
2       END;
```

This leads to both a different indentation scheme and a different assignment of statement level. A **FOR** loop at level 1 controls a compound statement at level 2 that controls two **WRITELN** statements at level 3. This is in some sense the correct interpretation given the underlying philosophy of Pascal. But like many instructors, I don't like this way of doing things. I stretch the language a bit and interpret the **BEGIN** and **END** as syntactic tools used for grouping, but not as a means of control. This leads to the indentation scheme and definition of statement level used in this book.

2.5.4 Programming with Pseudocode

The programs that you write describe a particular algorithm for solving a problem.

> **ALGORITHM**
> A precise, step-by-step description of how to solve a problem.

As you develop more and more complex algorithms, you will want to make use of the technique of writing pseudocode.

> **PSEUDOCODE**
> English-like descriptions of algorithms. Programming with pseudocode involves successively refining an informal description until it is easily translated into Pascal.

For example, you can describe the problem of drawing a box as

draw a box with 50 lines and 30 columns of asterisks.

While this describes the figure, it is not specific about how to draw it, i.e., what algorithm to use. Do you draw the figure line-by-line or column-by-column? In Pascal, figures such as these must be generated line-by-line because once a

WRITELN has been performed on a line of output, that line cannot be changed. There is no command for going back to a previous line in an output file. Therefore, the first line must be output in its entirety first, then the second line in its entirety, and so on. This means your decompositions for these figures will be line-oriented at the top level. Thus a closer approximation is

```
for (each of 50 lines) do
        draw a line of 30 asterisks.
```

Even this can be made more specific by introducing the idea of writing a single character on the output line versus moving to a new line of output:

```
for (each of 50 lines) do
begin
        for (each of 30 columns) do
                write one asterisk on the output line.
        go to a new output line.
end
```

Using pseudocode, you can gradually convert an English description into something easily translated into a Pascal program. The simple examples you have seen so far are hardly worth the application of pseudocode, so you will now examine the problem of generating a more complex figure:

```
********
 *******
  *****
   ***
    *
```

This figure must also be generated line-by-line:

```
for (each of 5 lines) do
        draw one line of the triangle.
```

Unfortunately, each line is different. Therefore, you must come up with a general rule that fits all lines. The first line of this figure has a series of asterisks on it with no leading spaces. The subsequent lines have a series of spaces followed by a series of asterisks. Using your imagination a bit, you can say that the first line has zero spaces on it followed by a series of asterisks. This allows you to write a general rule for making this figure:

```
for (each of 5 lines) do
begin
        write some spaces (possibly 0) on the output line.
        write some asterisks on the output line.
        go to a new output line.
end
```

In order to proceed, you must determine a rule for the number of spaces and a rule for the number of asterisks. Assuming that the lines are numbered 1 through 5 and looking at the figure, you can fill in the following chart:

Line	Spaces	Asterisks
1	0	9
2	1	7
3	2	5
4	3	3
5	4	1

You want to find a relationship between line number and the other two columns. This is simple algebra, because these columns are related in a linear way. The second column is easy to get from `line`; it equals (`line - 1`). The third column is a little tougher. Because it goes down by 2 every time and the first column goes up by 1 every time, you need a multiplier of -2. Then you need an appropriate constant. The number 11 seems to do the trick, so that the third column equals (`11 - 2 * line`). You can improve your pseudocode, then, as follows:

```
for line going 1 to 5 do
begin
    write (line − 1) spaces on the output line.
    write (11 − 2 * line) asterisks on the output line.
    go to a new output line.
end
```

This is simple to turn into a program:

```
PROGRAM DrawV (OUTPUT);
VAR line   : INTEGER;
    column : INTEGER;
BEGIN
    FOR line := 1 TO 5 DO
    BEGIN
        FOR column := 1 TO (line - 1) DO
            WRITE (' ');
        FOR column := 1 TO (11 - 2 * line) DO
            WRITE ('*');
        WRITELN
    END
END.
```

2.5.5   DOWNTO Loops

How would you produce this figure?

```
    *
   ***
  *****
 *******
*********
```

You could follow the same process you did above and find new expressions that produce the appropriate number of spaces and asterisks. However, there is an easier way. This figure is the same as the previous one, except the lines appear in reverse order. Pascal provides a mechanism for doing a FOR loop in reverse order. In place of the word "TO" between the starting and ending values, you can use the word "DOWNTO." When you do so, the control variable decreases in value rather than increasing in value.

Thus the loop

```
FOR number := 10 DOWNTO 1 DO
    WRITELN (number, ' squared = ', number * number);
```

will produce the squares of the first 10 integers, but in reverse order. The simple way to produce the upward-pointing triangle, then, is as follows:

```
PROGRAM DrawCone (OUTPUT);
VAR line   : INTEGER;
    column : INTEGER;
BEGIN
    FOR line := 5 DOWNTO 1 DO
    BEGIN
        FOR column := 1 TO (line - 1) DO
            WRITE (' ');
        FOR column := 1 TO (11 - 2 * line) DO
            WRITE ('*');
        WRITELN
    END
END.
```

2.5.6   Magic Numbers

The DrawCone program in the last section draws a cone with 5 lines. How would you modify it to produce a cone with 3 lines? One simple strategy is to change all the 5s to 3s, which will produce the output on page 58.

```
*****
*******
*********
```

This is obviously wrong. If you work through the geometry of the figure, you will discover that the problem is with the number 11 in one of the expressions. The number 11 comes from this formula:

2 * (number of lines) + 1

Thus for 5 lines the appropriate value is 11. But for 3 lines the appropriate value is 7. Programmers call numbers such as these *magic numbers*. They are magic in the sense that they seem to make the program work, but their definition is not always obvious. Glancing at the program, one is apt to ask, "Why 5? Why 11? Why 3? Why 7? Why me?"

To make programs more readable and more adaptable, you should try to avoid magic numbers whenever possible. You do so by creating objects that store the magic values. The first advantage of such an object is that you can name it. This allows you to choose a descriptive name that explains what the value represents. You can then use that name instead of referring to the specific value to make your programs more readable and adaptable. For example, in the `DrawCone` program you might want to introduce an object called `NumberOfLines` that will replace the magic number 5. Also, you can use the object as part of an expression to calculate a value. This allows you to replace the magic number 11 with a formula such as (2 * `NumberOfLines` + 1).

What objects should you use to store magic numbers? You could use variables, but that is misleading, given that you are trying to represent constant values. Pascal offers an alternative. You can create objects that are guaranteed to have constant values. Not surprisingly, they are called *constants*, and they are declared with the `CONST` declaration:

```
CONST   <identifier> = <constant> ;
        <identifier> = <constant> ;
            . . .
        <identifier> = <constant> ;
```

As in

```
CONST height = 10;
      width  = 20;
```

As with the `VAR` declaration, the keyword `CONST` appears only once, even though several constants might be declared. The equals sign is used because this represents true equality. This declaration creates objects called `height` and `width` that will always have the values 10 and 20. These objects are like rocks with their values carved into them; their values never change.

How would you rewrite the `DrawCone` program with a constant to eliminate the magic numbers? You would introduce a constant for the number of lines:

59

2.5 The FOR Loop

```
CONST NumberOfLines = 5;
```

Next, you would replace the 5 in the outer loop with this constant. Then, you would replace the 11 in the second inner loop with the expression (2 * NumberOfLines + 1). Simplifying the expressions a bit, you obtain this program:

```
PROGRAM DrawCone (OUTPUT);
CONST NumberOfLines = 5;
VAR   row            : INTEGER;
      column         : INTEGER;
BEGIN
    FOR row := NumberOfLines DOWNTO 1 DO
    BEGIN
        FOR column := 1 TO (row - 1) DO
            WRITE (' ');
        FOR column := 1 TO (2 * (NumberOfLines - row) + 1) DO
            WRITE ('*');
        WRITELN
    END
END.
```

The advantage of this program is that it is more readable and more adaptable. You can make a simple change in the constant NumberOfLines to make it produce a different-sized figure.

You are not restricted to numerical constants. You can also give names to string constants, as in

```
CONST MyName   = 'Dr. Joseph Martin ';
      MyNumber = '(708) 555-2189 ';
      MyOffice = '394-H ';
```

Once you define constants such as these, you can use them in WRITE and WRITELN statements the same way you use the original string constants. In other words, if you say

```
WRITELN ('Dr. Joseph Martin ', '(708) 555-2189 ', '394-H');
```

with the definition of the three string constants above, you can instead say

```
WRITELN (MyName, MyNumber, MyOffice);
```

2.5.7 Back to Procedures

You can now combine FOR loops, variables, and constants with what you know about procedures. Suppose you want to turn the DrawCone program into a DrawCone procedure. Since a procedure is a miniprogram, you should be able to simply change the word "PROGRAM" to the word "PROCEDURE," eliminate the word "OUTPUT" in the header, and end it with a semicolon instead of a period:

```
PROCEDURE DrawCone;
VAR line   : INTEGER;
    column : INTEGER;
BEGIN
    FOR line := 5 DOWNTO 1 DO
    BEGIN
        FOR column := 1 TO (line - 1) DO
            WRITE (' ');
        FOR column := 1 TO (11 - 2 * line) DO
            WRITE ('*');
        WRITELN
    END
END;
```

This procedure works. It has something new: two variables called **line** and **column** defined inside of the procedure. This is allowed, because procedures and programs have the same block structure. These variables are called *local variables*. Local variables belong to the procedure that declares them and cannot be used by any other. If you want to turn the **DrawV** program into a procedure as well, you make the same changes:

```
PROCEDURE DrawV;
VAR line   : INTEGER;
    column : INTEGER;
BEGIN
    FOR line := 1 TO 5 DO
    BEGIN
        FOR column := 1 TO (line - 1) DO
            WRITE (' ');
        FOR column := 1 TO (11 - 2 * line) DO
            WRITE ('*');
        WRITELN
    END
END;
```

Notice that this procedure also uses the variables **line** and **column**. This is not a conflict, because these particular **line** and **column** variables are local to this procedure, just as the other variables are local to their procedure.

By declaring a variable locally, its existence is known only within the procedure. No other procedure of the program nor the program itself will be able to see the local variables, because they are hidden from sight.

This principle is similar to the use of refrigerators in dormitories. Every dorm room can have its own refrigerator for use in that room. If you are outside of a room, you don't even know that it has a refrigerator in it. The contents of the room are hidden from you.

Localizing variables leads to some duplication, but guarantees more security. Procedures use variables to store values, just as students use refrigerators to store beer, ice cream, and other valuables. The last time I was in a dorm I noticed that most of the individual rooms had refrigerators in them. This seems terribly redundant, but the reason is obvious. If you want to guarantee the security of something, you put it where nobody else can get it. You will use local variables in much the same way. Each individual procedure will have its own local variables to use, which means you don't have to consider possible interference from other procedures. Also, if you make your procedures independent of each other, they will be more easily transported from one program to another to be used again.

As for constants, just as procedures can define their own local variables, procedures can also define their own local constants. As with local variables, they are invisible to the rest of the program. They are only accessible inside the procedure.

2.5.8 A Complex Figure

Now consider an example that is even more complex. To solve it, you will use procedures to decompose the task into subtasks. Consider the following figure:

In order to generate this figure, you have to first break it down into subfigures. In doing so, you should look for lines that are similar in one way or another. The first and last lines are exactly the same, the three lines after the first line all fit one pattern, and the three lines after that fit another. Thus you can break the problem down as

> draw a solid line.
> draw the top half of the hourglass.
> draw the bottom half of the hourglass.
> draw a solid line.

You should solve each independently. Before you do so, however, you should think a moment about possible magic numbers this figure might generate. It has a specific height and width that might introduce magic numbers. Because of the regularity of the figure, though, the height is determined by the width, and vice versa. For example, if you change the height of the two hourglass halves from 3 to 4, you have to increase the overall width from 8 to 10 to make the diagonals line up properly. Therefore, you should define only one constant.

Suppose you choose the height of the hourglass halves:

```
CONST SubFigureHeight = 3;
```

Given this constant, you can calculate the other magic numbers that are related to size. For example, the overall width of the figure is

```
(2 * SubFigureHeight + 2)
```

And the number of dashes in a solid line is

```
(2 * SubFigureHeight)
```

Thus you can use these expressions to avoid magic numbers. The solid-line task can be further specified as

write a plus on the output line.
write (2 * SubFigureHeight) dashes on the output line.
write a plus on the output line.
go to a new output line.

This translates easily into a procedure:

```
PROCEDURE DrawLine;
VAR column : INTEGER;
BEGIN
    WRITE ('+');
    FOR column := 1 TO (2 * SubFigureHeight) DO
        WRITE ('-');
    WRITELN ('+')
END;    (* DrawLine *)
```

The top half of the hourglass is more complex. Here is a typical line:

```
| \ / |
```

This has four printing characters and some spaces that separate them:

	\	/	
bar	spaces backslash spaces	slash spaces	bar

Thus a first approximation in pseudocode is

for (each of SubFigureHeight lines) do
begin
    write a bar on the output line.
    write some spaces on the output line.
    write a backslash on the output line.
    write some spaces on the output line.

> write a slash on the output line.
> write some spaces on the output line.
> write a bar on the output line.
> go to a new line of output.
>
> end

Again, you can make a table to figure out the desired expressions. Writing the single characters will be easy enough to translate into Pascal, but you need to be more specific about the spaces. This line really has three sets of spaces. Here is a table that shows how many to use in each case:

Line	Spaces	Spaces	Spaces
1	0	4	0
2	1	2	1
3	2	0	2

The first and third sets of spaces fit the rule (`line` - 1), and the second number of spaces is (6 - 2 * `line`). But how do you account for possible magic numbers? There are many ways to do so. You could find the expressions for different heights and see how they differ. Or you could analyze the geometry of the figure and try to deduce the expressions. Or you could guess and hope that you are right. Any of these solutions would inevitably lead to the conclusion that the only magic number in the expressions above is 6, which comes from (2 * `SubFigureHeight`). Thus the correct expressions are (`line` - 1) and 2 * (`SubFigureHeight` - `line`). Therefore, the pseudocode should read:

> for line going 1 to SubFigureHeight do
> begin
> > write a bar on the output line.
> > write (line − 1) spaces on the output line.
> > write a backslash on the output line.
> > write 2 * (SubFigureHeight − line) spaces on the output line.
> > write a slash on the output line.
> > write (line − 1) spaces on the output line.
> > write a bar on the output line.
> > go to a new line of output.
>
> end

This is easily translated into a procedure. A similar solution exists for the bottom half of the hourglass. Put together, the program looks like this:

```
PROGRAM DrawFigure (OUTPUT);
CONST SubFigureHeight = 3;
```

```
PROCEDURE DrawLine;
(* Produces a solid line *)
VAR column : INTEGER;
BEGIN
    WRITE ('+');
    FOR column := 1 TO (2 * SubFigureHeight) DO
        WRITE ('-');
    WRITELN ('+')
END;   (* DrawLine *)

PROCEDURE DrawTop;
(* This produces the top half of the hourglass figure *)
VAR line   : INTEGER;
    column : INTEGER;
BEGIN
    FOR line := 1 TO SubFigureHeight DO
    BEGIN
        WRITE ('|');
        FOR column := 1 TO (line - 1) DO
            WRITE (' ');
        WRITE ('\');
        FOR column := 1 TO 2 * (SubFigureHeight - line) DO
            WRITE (' ');
        WRITE ('/');
        FOR column := 1 TO (line - 1) DO
            WRITE (' ');
        WRITELN ('|')
    END
END;   (* DrawTop *)

PROCEDURE DrawBottom;
(* This produces the bottom half of the hourglass figure *)
VAR line   : INTEGER;
    column : INTEGER;
BEGIN
    FOR line := 1 TO SubFigureHeight DO
    BEGIN
        WRITE ('|');
        FOR column := 1 TO (SubFigureHeight - line) DO
            WRITE (' ');
        WRITE ('/');
        FOR column := 1 TO 2 * (line - 1) DO
            WRITE (' ');
        WRITE ('\');
```

```
            FOR column := 1 TO (SubFigureHeight - line) DO
                WRITE (' ');
            WRITELN ('|')
        END
    END;    (* DrawBottom *)

    BEGIN   (* main program *)
        DrawLine;
        DrawTop;
        DrawBottom;
        DrawLine
    END.    (* main program *)
```

This solution may seem cumbersome, but it is easier to adapt to a new task. It would be simple, for example, to modify this program to produce the figure below. All you have to do is reverse the order of the calls on procedures `DrawTop` and `DrawBottom` in the main program.

```
+------+
|  /\  |
| /  \ |
|/    \|
|\    /|
| \  / |
|  \/  |
+------+
```

2.5.9 Global versus Local Constants

The program written in the last section raises an important issue. It declares a constant known as `SubFigureHeight` that is used throughout the program. But the constant is not declared locally in the individual procedures. Such a constant is called a *global constant*. Remember that for variables, local variables should be used whenever possible. The same, however, is not true for constants. In this case, the object should be used in a global manner.

One of the arguments against global variables is interference from other procedures. This argument doesn't hold for constants, since they are guarantied not to change. The other argument for using local variables is that they make procedures more independent. This argument has some merit, but not enough. It is true that global constants introduce procedural dependencies, but often this is really what you want. For example, the three procedures of the hourglass program should not be independent of each other when it comes to the size of figures. Each subfigure has to use the same size constant. Imagine the potential disaster if each procedure had its own `SubFigureHeight`, each with a different value. None of the pieces would fit together.

The following analogy gives some perspective on this point. Imagine having a passbook account at a bank. You need a personal passbook because you don't want anyone to interfere with your account (i.e., you want control) and because you care about privacy. Thus a passbook is like a local variable, accessible only to you. But interest rates are different. You don't need a personal list of rates. The rates are bound to change, which means such a list will eventually be incorrect. A more reliable system is to call the bank for the current rates whenever you need them. This is like using a global constant. The information is stored in one central place, which means that everybody gets the same information. It also means that changing requires only a change at the central location. Global constants provide this flexibility. Since all procedures look to one place in the program for a particular value, they are guaranteed to use the same value, and you can change their behavior simply by making a change in one place.

2.5.10 Some Caveats about FOR Loops

There are several special rules that you should keep in mind when using `FOR` loops. Not all Pascal systems enforce these rules, but they are good guidelines to follow.

■   The control variable of a `FOR` loop must be a local variable.

In other words, my recommendation to avoid using global variables is more than just a recommendation. Not only will I encourage you to use local variables, Pascal will as well.

■   The value of a `FOR` loop control variable will be undefined after the loop terminates.

This means that the control variable is uninitialized after the loop is done executing. Trying to manipulate its value after the loop terminates will lead to unpredictable results, perhaps even an execution error.

■   The expressions that determine the starting and ending values of a `FOR` loop are evaluated once, just before the loop starts executing.

This is a very subtle point about loops. To understand it better, consider the following:

```
number := 20;
FOR count := 1 TO number DO
BEGIN
    WRITELN ('Hi there!');
    number := number - 1
END;
```

The odd thing about this loop is that it is supposed to iterate from 1 to **number**, but **number** changes as the loop executes. For example, after 10 iterations of the loop, **number** will have the value 10. Does the loop stop at that point? The answer is no. According to the rule above, before the loop executes, the computer evaluates the starting and stopping expressions:

```
Starting Value = 1
Stopping Value = 20
```

These limits are not evaluated again, even if the expressions that define them change in value. Thus it doesn't matter that **number** changes from 20 to something else. The loop will iterate from 1 to 20 no matter what.

■ The value of a **FOR** loop control variable is not to be threatened within the loop.

To understand what this means, you have to remember that Pascal gives an initial value to the control variable and increments it each time through the loop. In other words, the computer automatically manipulates the variable because it is controlling a **FOR** loop. The rule says that other parts of your program cannot manipulate the value of the control variable as well. You are not allowed to increment the variable yourself, nor are you allowed to assign it a different value. Such actions are considered a threat to the value of the control variable. You can't, for example, do this:

```
FOR count := 1 TO 10 DO
BEGIN
    WRITELN ('great fun!');
    count := 5
END;
```

In this case, the computer is supposed to manipulate the variable **count** so that it starts at 1 and takes on all the integer values up to 10. You would expect, as a result, that 10 lines of output would be produced. But the assignment statement inside the loop threatens the computer's manipulaton of the variable by resetting it to 5 each time through the loop. This statement is a violation of the rule above and is therefore illegal.

A more common example of threatening is

```
FOR number := 1 TO 10 DO
    FOR number := 1 TO 5 DO
        WRITELN ('Hi.');
```

This loop uses the same control variable, **number**, for both the inner and outer loops. That is a violation of the rule because execution of the inner loop threatens the value of the control variable of the outer loop. You could fix this problem by introducing a second variable to control the inner loop. Notice, however, that loops that follow one right after the other do not threaten control variables. The following is perfectly legal and safe. The first loop executes in its entirety before the second loop even starts; therefore, the same variable can be used to control both.

```
FOR number := 1 TO 10 DO
    WRITELN ('Hi.');
FOR number := 1 TO 20 DO
    WRITELN ('How are you?');
```

2.6 Key Concepts

- The objects manipulated by a program are individual pieces of information. Such objects fall into natural categories called data types.

- A data type is described by an abstract data type: a specification of the domain of the type and the set of operations that can be performed on objects of that type.

- Pascal programs can manipulate data objects that never vary in value (program constants) and data objects that can change in value as the program executes (program variables).

- An expression is a description of how to obtain a value. Such a description can contain references to variables and constants and to operations to be performed on those objects, often described using operators such as "+".

- An expression is evaluated during program execution to determine its value. If more than one operator appears in an expression, rules of precedence determine which operator to apply first. Multiplicative operators have higher precedence than additive operators, and within a level of precedence, operators are evaluated left to right. Use parentheses to override precedence.

- A FOR loop controls an inner statement. If several statements are to be controlled by the loop, use BEGIN and END to group them. Because FOR loops can appear within FOR loops, it is possible to have many levels of control within a program.

- An algorithm can be easier to develop if you start with a very English-like description and successively turn the pseudocode into something that approximates Pascal.

- Magic numbers should be turned into global constants.

- Use local variables in procedures whenever possible to make them more self-contained.

2.7 Self-Check Exercises

1. Which of the following are not legal INTEGER constants?

    MAXINT   1.   304   2.5   2,349   -0   429   2.0   -MAXINT

2. The following is a trace of the evaluation of $(7 * 12 - 3 * 4)$:

Expression	Operator	Operands	Result
7 * 12 − 3 * 4	*	7, 12	84
84 − 3 * 4	*	3, 4	12
84 − 12	−	84, 12	72
72			

    Trace the evaluation of the following:

    ```
    2 + 3 * 4 - 6
    (12 + 3) DIV 4 * 2
    (238 MOD 10 + 3) MOD 7
    (18 - 7) * (43 MOD 10)
    ```

3. What are the four different VAR declarations that can be used to define two INTEGER variables called Num1 and Num2?

4. Suppose that you have an INTEGER variable called **number**. What Pascal expression describes the last digit of the number (the 1s digit)? What Pascal expression describes the second to last digit (the 10s digit)?

5. Suppose that you have INTEGER variables **first** and **second** with values 8 and 19, respectively. What are their values after executing the following code?

    ```
    first := first + second;
    second := first - second;
    first := first - second;
    ```

    How would you characterize the net effect of these three statements?

6. What is the output of the following code fragment?

```
WRITELN ('1':10, '2':10, '3':10);
WRITELN ('12345678901234567689901234567890');
WRITELN ('This is long':4, (45 + 3):2, 'wow':8, 13:9, ' ':4, 245:-1);
```

7. Rewrite the following code as a series of equivalent WRITELN statements (i.e., without any WRITE statements):

    ```
    WRITE('Twas');
    WRITE('brillig and the');
    WRITELN(' ');
    WRITE('slithy toves did');
    WRITE(' ');
    WRITELN    ('gyre and');
    WRITELN    (' gimble');
    ```

```
WRITELN    ;
WRITELN (   'in the wabe.'  );
```

8. Use nested **FOR** loops to produce this output:

```
    |          |          |          |          |          |
123456789012345678901234567890123456789012345678901234567890
------------------------------------------------------------
```

9. Use nested **FOR** loops to produce the following output. Indicate the level of each statement in your code.

```
000111222333444555666777888999
000111222333444555666777888999
000111222333444555666777888999
```

Modify the code so that it now produces this output:

```
999998888877777666665555544444333332222211111100000
999998888877777666665555544444333332222211111100000
999998888877777666665555544444333332222211111100000
999998888877777666665555544444333332222211111100000
999998888877777666665555544444333332222211111100000
```

10. Suppose that you are trying to write a program that produces this output:

```
1, 3, 5, 7, 9, 11, 13, 15, 17, 19, 21
1, 3, 5, 7, 9, 11
```

The following program is an attempt at a solution, but it contains four major errors. Identify each.

```
PROGRAM BadNews (OUTPUT);
CONST MaxOdd = 21;
VAR   count  : INTEGER;

PROCEDURE WriteOdds;
BEGIN
    FOR count := 1 TO (MaxOdd - 2) DO
    BEGIN
        WRITE (count:1, ', ');
        count := count + 2
    END;
    WRITELN ((count + 2):1)
END;

BEGIN
    WriteOdds;
    MaxOdd := 11;
    WriteOdds
END.
```

11.   What is the output of the following loop:

```
PROCEDURE OddStuff;
VAR count  : INTEGER;
    number : INTEGER;
BEGIN
    number := 4;
    FOR count := 1 TO number DO
    BEGIN
        WRITELN (number);
        number := number DIV 2
    END
END;    (* OddStuff *)
```

2.8 Programming Problems

1.   Write a program that produces the following output:

```
****** //////////// ******
*****  /////////\\   *****
****   ////////\\\\   ****
***    //////\\\\\\    ***
**     ////\\\\\\\\     **
*      //\\\\\\\\\\      *
       \\\\\\\\\\\\
```

2.   Write a program that produces the following output:

```
+---------+
|    *    |
|   /*\   |
|  //*\\  |
| ///*\\\ |
| \\\*/// |
|  \\*//  |
|   \*/   |
|    *    |
+---------+
| \\\*/// |
|  \\*//  |
|   \*/   |
|    *    |
|    *    |
|   /*\   |
|  //*\\  |
| ///*\\\ |
+---------+
```

3. Write a program that displays Pascal's triangle:

```
                        1
                      1   1
                    1   2   1
                  1   3   3   1
                1   4   6   4   1
              1   5   10  10   5   1
            1   6   15  20  15   6   1
          1   7   21  35  35  21   7   1
        1   8   28  56  70  56  28   8   1
      1   9   36  84 126 126  84  36   9   1
    1  10   45 120 210 252 210 120  45  10   1
```

4. Write a program that produces the following output. Use a program constant to make it possible to change the number of stairs in the figure.

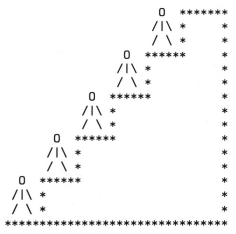

```
                        0  *******
                       /|\ *      *
                       / \ *      *
                    0  *****      *
                   /|\ *          *
                   / \ *          *
                0  ******         *
               /|\ *              *
               / \ *              *
            0  ******             *
           /|\ *                  *
           / \ *                  *
        0  ******                 *
       /|\ *                      *
       / \ *                      *
    0  ******                     *
   /|\ *                          *
   / \ *                          *
   ******************************
```

3

INTRODUCTION TO PROGRAMMING METHODOLOGY

3.1 Introduction

Chapter 2 discussed techniques for solving complex problems and global constants that can add to the flexibility of a program solution. This chapter explores a more powerful technique for obtaining such flexibility. You will learn how to use value parameters to create procedures that solve not just single tasks, but whole families of tasks. Creating such procedures requires an insight into problems called *generalization*. It requires looking beyond a specific task to find a more general task for which this is just one instance. The ability to generalize is one of the most important qualities of a software engineer, and the generalization technique you will study in this chapter is one of the most powerful features of Pascal.

After exploring value parameters, this chapter examines the process of producing programs. More specifically, it examines the steps involved in producing a program and the order in which those steps should be performed. The chapter ends with a case study of a table-producing program.

3.2 Lifetime of Objects

Pascal is a dynamic language in which objects exist sometimes for only a short part of program execution and then go away. Every object occupies a certain amount of space in the computer's memory. The computer can allocate that space when necessary and then deallocate it when it is no longer needed. This provides an efficient use of the computer's memory, because space is only allocated as it is needed. The *lifetime of an object* is the period of program execution in which the object exists (i.e., when space is allocated for it).

When a procedure or program is executed, its block is activated. Activation causes the computer to first allocate any objects defined in the declaration part and then to start executing the statements in the execution part. When the computer has executed the last of the statements in the execution part, it deallocates the block's objects.

Consider variables defined in the main program. They are allocated when the program block is activated and are not deallocated until the program terminates. Thus these objects exist throughout program execution, so their lifetime is the same as that of the program. Local variables are different. Because they are defined by the declaration part of a procedure, they are allocated only when the procedure is activated and are deallocated when the procedure terminates. Thus their lifetime is the period of time during which the procedure executes. Because a procedure can be executed more than once, these objects can have several lifetimes, being "reincarnated" each time the procedure is activated. However, the computer does not reincarnate them to what they were in their former lives. Local variables always start out uninitialized, even if they are on their second or subsequent lifetimes.

3.3 The Black Box Model

Anything you build, programs included, should be as self-contained as possible, a black box that does something useful. Users shouldn't have to look inside the black box to be able to use it. When an electrical engineer puts a chassis around a television, he is trying to create a black box. The engineer places the innards of a television, a maze of wires and circuits, inside a chassis (the black box), so that users won't have to deal with them. If all goes well, the television should do just what the users want without them having to see the insides of the machine.

You must try as much as possible to put the innards of your procedures inside black boxes. Since you build your programs from information and not from electronic parts, this principle, when applied to software engineering, is called *information hiding.* You want to hide from the user as much of the information of a procedure as possible, so that it is simple to use. Local variables are the first example you have seen of information hiding, because they are visible only to the procedure that declares them.

It is not always possible or desirable to build totally self-contained black boxes. For example, a radio that always uses the same volume and station setting is not very useful. Thus you will often build black boxes that have information flowing in or out. The values that come in or out are the parameters of the task. A radio with volume and station adjustments is an excellent example of a *parameterized task*. The settings are the parameters that determine how the radio behaves. Given a specific volume and station setting, the radio performs a specific task. You change the parameter settings to make the radio perform a different task.

PARAMETER (PARAMETERIZE)

Any of a set of characteristics that distinguish different members of a family of tasks. To parameterize a task is to identify a set of its parameters.

Thus many radio-playing tasks can be characterized by the volume and station settings, two parameters of radio-playing tasks. These two characteristics distinguish the different members of the family of tasks. This relationship is indicated by the following information flow diagram:

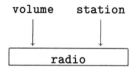

3.3.1   Value Parameters

The `DrawFigure` program in Chapter 2 performs its task adequately, but there are several things wrong with it. For example, there are six different places where a `FOR` loop writes out spaces. This is redundant and should be consolidated into a single procedure that performs all space-writing tasks.

Each space-writing task requires a different number of spaces, so you can't build a totally self-contained procedure. If you did, it would always produce the same number of spaces. You need something more flexible.

Just as you can parameterize a radio, you can also parameterize procedures. For example, you can design a `WriteSpaces` procedure that produces any number of spaces. The parameter is the number of spaces to write. This number characterizes the different space-writing tasks in your family. This number comes from outside the procedure, so a black box diagram of its information flow is

This diagram indicates that `WriteSpaces` must be fed a number before it can perform its task. Once it is fed a number, it will perform the task. It is possible to write such a procedure in Pascal using a value parameter:

```
PROCEDURE WriteSpaces (number: INTEGER);
VAR count : INTEGER;
BEGIN
    FOR count := 1 TO number DO
        WRITE (' ')
END;
```

The value parameter appears in the procedure header after the name and before the semicolon. This procedure uses a parameter called **number** of type `INTEGER`. The parameter declaration is in many ways the opposite of a local variable declaration. By declaring **count** as a local variable, the procedure says, "This object belongs to me. Its lifetime will be the same as mine. I will take responsibility for it." Declaring **number** as a value parameter says, "This object comes from the outside. Somebody else has responsibility for it. If I am provided with one, though, I will manipulate it."

How do you give a value to the parameter? How do you feed something into this black box? You can no longer call the parameterized procedure by using its name

```
WriteSpaces;
```

You must now say something like

```
WriteSpaces (20);
WriteSpaces (4);
WriteSpaces (2 * 3 + 4);
```

Every call on procedure `WriteSpaces` must specify what number of spaces to write. As the third call above indicates, you can use any integer expression.

Computer scientists use the word "parameter" liberally to mean both what appears in the procedure declaration (the formal parameter) and what appears in the procedure call (the actual parameter).

> **FORMAL PARAMETER**
>
> The generalized parameter that appears in the header of a procedure declaration and which is used to generalize the procedure's task.

> **ACTUAL PARAMETER**
>
> The specific parameter that appears in a procedure call and which is used to perform a specific task from the family of tasks.

The term *formal parameter* is not very descriptive of its purpose. A better name would be *generic parameter*. In the procedure above, **number** is the generic parameter that appears in the procedure declaration. It is a placeholder for some unspecified value. The values appearing in the procedure calls are the actual parameters, because each call indicates a specific task to perform. In other words, each call provides an actual value to fill the placeholder.

Using procedure **WriteSpaces**, you can rewrite the **DrawTop** procedure as follows:

```
PROCEDURE DrawTop;
VAR line : INTEGER;
BEGIN
    FOR line := 1 TO SubFigureHeight DO
    BEGIN
        WRITE ('|');
        WriteSpaces (line - 1);
        WRITE ('\');
        WriteSpaces (2 * (SubFigureHeight - line));
        WRITE ('/');
        WriteSpaces (line - 1);
        WRITELN ('|')
    END
END;    (* DrawTop *)
```

Notice that you call **WriteSpaces** three different times, specifying how many spaces you want in each case. Similarly, you can also modify the **DrawBottom** procedure to simplify it.

3.3.2 The Mechanics of Value Parameters

When the computer activates a procedure, it initializes all value parameters. For each value parameter, it first evaluates the expression passed as the actual parameter and then uses the result to initialize a local variable whose name is given by the formal parameter.

This is best explained by example.

```
PROGRAM Fun (OUTPUT);
VAR first  : INTEGER;
    second : INTEGER;
```

```
PROCEDURE WriteSpaces (number: INTEGER);
VAR count : INTEGER;
BEGIN
    FOR count := 1 TO number DO
        WRITE (' ')
END;

BEGIN
    first := 8;
    second := 10;
    WRITE ('*');
    WriteSpaces (first);
    WRITELN ('*');
    WRITE ('!');
    WriteSpaces (second);
    WRITELN ('!');
    WRITE ('"');
    WriteSpaces (30);
    WRITELN ('"');
    WRITE ('<');
    WriteSpaces (first * second - 30);
    WRITELN ('>')
END.
```

When the computer activates the program's block, it allocates space for the variables the block defines:

first | ? | second | ? |

Next, it starts the execution part of the program block. The first two statements initialize these variables:

first | 8 | second | 10 |

The next three lines of code:

```
WRITE ('*');
WriteSpaces (first);
WRITELN ('*');
```

produce an output line with 8 spaces bounded by asterisks on either side. You can see where the asterisks come from, but look at the procedure call that produces the spaces. When the computer activates the block for procedure **WriteSpaces**, it must set up two local objects: the value parameter and the local variable. To set up the value parameter, it first evaluates the expression being passed as the actual parameter. The expression is simply the variable `first`, which has the value 8. Therefore, the expression evaluates to 8. The computer uses this result to initialize a local variable whose name is that of the formal parameter, `number`. Thus you get:

first | 8 | second | 10 | number | 8 |

The net effect of this process is that you have a local copy of the variable `first`. To set up the local variable `count`, the computer allocates an uninitialized memory cell, as it always does with local variables:

first | 8 | second | 10 | number | 8 | count | ? |

Since `number` has the value 8, the `FOR` loop in the procedure iterates 8 times and produces 8 spaces on the line. On exiting the procedure, the computer deallocates both the value parameter and the local variable:

first | 8 | second | 10 |

You finish this line with the `WRITELN` that appears after the procedure call. The next line starts by writing an exclamation mark at the left margin, and then `WriteSpaces` is called again, this time with the variable `second` as its actual parameter. The computer evaluates this expression, obtaining the result 10. This value is used to initialize `number`. Thus this time it creates a copy of variable `second`:

first | 8 | second | 10 | number | 10 | count | ? |

Because `number` has a different value this time (10 instead of 8), the procedure produces a different number of spaces. After this execution, the computer again deallocates the local objects:

first | 8 | second | 10 |

The output line is finished with the `WRITELN` after the procedure call, and the computer starts the third line of output. It writes a quotation mark at the left margin and then activates procedure `WriteSpaces` again. This time it uses the constant 30 as the expression, which means it makes the value parameter `number` into a copy of it:

first 8   second 10   number 10   count ?

Again, the procedure will behave differently because of the different value of **number**. Finally, for the fourth call to procedure **WriteSpaces**, the computer must evaluate a complex expression with arithmetic operators:

first * second - 30 = (8 * 10) - 30 = 80 - 30 = 50

The computer uses this result to initialize **number**:

first 8   second 10   number 50   count ?

Thus **number** is now a copy of the value described by this complex expression. Therefore, the total output of this program is

```
*         *
!              !
"                           "
<                                   >
```

3.3.3   Value Parameters and Defensive Programming

You will see that the value parameter allows the flow of information into a procedure but prevents the flow of information back out. There are distinct advantages to this one-way data flow. I'll give you an example from my own experience.

When I was an undergraduate, I kept orderly notes which I loaned to fellow students who skipped class. The loaned notes would provide my classmates with information they required and would be returned for my use. However, what I got back was not what I gave. The notes were returned with frayed edges, pages hopelessly out of order, missing pages, coffee stains, "happy faces," and so on. I didn't want my notes to be altered, so I made copies of the notes and gave the copies to my fellow students. That way they could do whatever they wanted to their copies while my notes remained untouched.

The value parameter uses the same principle. When the value parameter is set up, a local variable is created and is initialized to the value being passed as the actual parameter. The net effect is that the local variable is a copy of the value coming from the outside. Since it is a local object, it can't influence any objects on the outside.

Consider this procedure:

```
PROCEDURE DoubleNumber (number : INTEGER);
BEGIN
    WRITELN ('Initial value of number = ', number:1);
    number := number * 2;
    WRITELN ('Final value of number = ', number:1)
END;
```

Suppose you have the same program variables and starting values as you did in the previous section:

first ⬚8⬚   second ⬚10⬚

What happens if the computer executes this statement?

```
DoubleNumber (first);
```

It evaluates the expression being passed and obtains the result 8. Thus it creates a local variable called **number** with the initial value 8:

first ⬚8⬚   second ⬚10⬚   number ⬚8⬚

The computer starts by writing out the current value of this local variable:

```
Initial value of number = 8
```

This value is then doubled to 16. Since it is a local variable, this process does not affect the program variables:

first ⬚8⬚   second ⬚10⬚   number ⬚16⬚

The third statement of the procedure reports this new value:

```
Final value of number = 16
```

When the procedure is done executing, the computer deallocates **number** to again obtain:

first ⬚8⬚   second ⬚10⬚

Thus the local manipulations of the value parameter do not change these variables on the outside. The following illustrates the data flow for the `DoubleNumber` procedure:

number

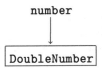

The use of copies guarantees protection against unwanted changes and is an important property of value parameters. A variable passed as the actual parameter to a value parameter is guaranteed not to change as a result of manipulations to the value parameter. In other words, the value parameter allows information to flow into a procedure, but it won't let anything flow back out.

You should exploit this protection mechanism whenever possible. Doing so is part of what is called *defensive programming*, a programming philosophy that says "better safe than sorry." People who program defensively do not always avoid mistakes, but they often manage to sort them out more quickly. This protection mechanism gives programmers confidence.

There is one other benefit of the value parameter's copying mechanism. There are some programming tasks that are more easily written if you can temporarily modify a variable. Value parameters facilitate such temporary changes. For example, a procedure that manipulates a variable that stores a word might want to make all the letters into capitals so that it does the same thing for 'hello,' 'HeLlO,' and 'HELLO'. If the word is passed as a value parameter, then the change will influence only the local copy of the word and will leave the variable outside intact.

3.3.4 More Value Parameter Details

So far, the discussion of value parameter syntax has been informal. Before discussing procedures with more than one value parameter, here is a precise description of the rules of value parameters.

The general syntax for a procedure header is

PROCEDURE *<name>* (*<formal parameter group>*;
                    <formal parameter group>;
                    . . .
                    <formal parameter group>) ;

This template indicates that after the procedure name, there is a set of parentheses that contains a series of parameter groups separated by semicolons. After the parentheses is a semicolon that separates the procedure header and the procedure block. Each parameter group has this syntax:

<identifier list> : *<type>*

You saw this template before when you examined `VAR` declarations. It shows that a parameter group is described by a list of identifiers followed by a colon and a type. Individual identifiers in the identifier list, as in the `VAR` declaration, are separated by commas.

Procedures `WriteSpaces` and `DoubleNumber` each had a single parameter group with a single parameter. To understand their syntax, imagine starting with the identifier list:

```
number
```

This list has only one element in it, but it is a list nonetheless. It becomes a parameter group when you specify its type:

```
number : INTEGER
```

You can now place this parameter group inside parentheses and into the procedure header:

```
PROCEDURE WriteSpaces  (number : INTEGER);
PROCEDURE DoubleNumber (number : INTEGER);
```

Now consider a procedure with more than one parameter. For example, suppose you are going to make a table with rows and columns. You will probably want to have a value parameter to specify the number of rows and another value parameter to specify the number of columns. Suppose you are going to call the parameters `NumRows` and `NumColumns` and are going to call the procedure `MakeTable`. Here is one way of composing a procedure header. Start with an identifier list:

```
NumRows, NumColumns
```

This list has two parameters separated by a comma. Turn this list into a parameter group by specifying its type:

```
NumRows, NumColumns : INTEGER
```

Place the parameter group inside parentheses in a header:

```
PROCEDURE WriteTable (NumRows, NumColumns : INTEGER);
```

There is another way to compose a procedure header. Start with two identifier lists:

```
NumRows
NumColumns
```

Turn them into parameter groups by specifying their types:

```
NumRows    : INTEGER
NumColumns : INTEGER
```

Separate the two groups with a semicolon:

```
NumRows    : INTEGER;
NumColumns : INTEGER
```

And put them inside of parentheses in a procedure header:

```
PROCEDURE WriteTable (NumRows    : INTEGER;
                      NumColumns : INTEGER);
```

There is no rule that parameter groups must appear on separate lines, but it is a convention that makes programs easier to read. This is an alternative procedure header that also declares two value parameters of type **INTEGER**. These two declarations of the procedure are functionally equivalent. It doesn't matter whether you declare one parameter group with two parameters or two groups each with one.

Consider the syntax of the procedure call:

<procedure name> (*<actual parameter list>*) ;

This template says that procedures are activated by specifying the name of the procedure and the actual parameters to be used for this execution. The format of the actual parameter list is

<actual parameter>, *<actual parameter>*, . . . , *<actual parameter>*

For value parameters, these actual parameters can be arbitrary expressions. Therefore, examples of legal calls on this procedure are

```
WriteTable (10, 10);
WriteTable (2 + 2, 5 * 5);
```

How are these actual parameters tied to the formal parameters? Order determines the correspondence. For example, if you call your table procedure with these values

```
WriteTable (6, 8);
```

these two actual parameters would correspond to the formal parameters of the procedure declaration in the order they appear here:

```
PROCEDURE WriteTable    (NumRows,   NumColumns   :   INTEGER);
                           |            |
WriteTable              (   6,         8                    ):
```

This procedure call will create a table with 6 rows and 8 columns. If you want to instead create a table with 8 rows and 6 columns, you reverse the order in the call:

```
WriteTable (8, 6);
```

This correspondence would result:

```
PROCEDURE WriteTable   (NumRows,   NumColumns   :   INTEGER);
                           |           |
WriteTable             (   8,         6                     ):
```

The number of parameters passed in the actual parameter list must be the same as the number of parameters in the formal parameter list or this correspondence will not be possible.

To summarize, the number of parameters in the actual parameter list of a procedure call must match exactly the number of parameters in the formal parameter list of the procedure declaration. Formal parameters are bound to actual parameters according to order, the first actual parameter being bound to the first formal parameter, the second actual parameter being bound to the second formal parameter, and so on.

3.3.5 Value Parameters versus Global Constants

How does this new technique relate to what you already know? The most important technique you learned in Chapter 2 for creating program flexibility is the use of global constants. By using such constants, you make it easy to modify a program. The value parameter provides much of the same flexibility, and more. Consider the WriteSpaces procedure. Suppose you wrote it using a global constant:

```
CONST NumberOfSpaces = <something>;
```

This gives you the flexibility to produce a different number of spaces, but it has one major limitation. The constant can change only from execution to execution. It cannot change within a single execution. In other words, you can execute the program once with one value and then execute it again with a different value, but you can't use different values in a single execution of the program using a global constant.

Value parameters are more flexible. Because you specify the value to be used each time you call the procedure, you can use several different values in a single program execution. As you have seen, you can call a procedure with a value parameter many different times within a single program execution and have it behave differently every time. At the same time, however, the value parameter is more work for the programmer than the global constant. It makes your procedure headers and procedure calls more tedious, not to mention making the execution (and thus the debugging) more complex.

Therefore, you will probably find occasion to use each technique. The basic rule is to use a global constant when you only want to change the value from execution to execution. If you want to use different values within a single execution, use the value parameter. Parameterizing a procedure will pay off if and only if you actually use the procedure to execute different specific tasks within a single program execution.

3.4 The Software Life Cycle

There are several discernible phases that a software engineer goes through in dealing with a software product. This book concentrates on three: design, coding, and testing.

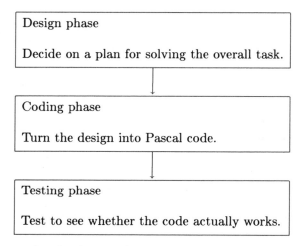

In the design phase, you need to consider how a piece of software can be implemented. The questions to consider include: how to decompose the overall task into procedures, how the program will store its information, and in what order to develop the various procedures. In the coding phase, you follow the plan worked out in the design phase to produce a program. In the testing phase, you attempt to verify that the program works properly and to fix any bugs that you find. These phases don't always happen in succession. Software engineers find that they are often redoing work they did in one phase because of insights they have gained working in another.

When left to their own devices, beginners often concentrate almost exclusively on the coding phase of program development. This text has a fairly balanced discussion of all three phases because all three are essential to the writing of complex programs.

The software life cycle has other phases, but these are traditionally covered in more advanced software engineering courses, because they become critical only as programs become very large.

3.4.1 Adaptable Code and the Software Library

Software engineers try to develop *software tools*, procedures that perform commonly encountered tasks and are easily fit into new programs. They collect their tools into a *software library*.

When you build powerful tools, you can use them over and over to perform new tasks. For example, the `WriteSpaces` procedure that simplified the drawing of the hourglass figure is also useful in other programs. As you start writing large programs later in this book, you will notice that you constantly make use of previously defined tools.

It is possible to easily transport a procedure such as `WriteSpaces` from one program to another, because all its data objects are either localized or parameterized. The local variables guaranty that any unimportant details are contained within the procedure, i.e., hidden within the black box. The parameters guaranty that the procedure can be easily adapted to a variety of tasks. These are the kind of procedures you want to write, because they become tools that will make your job easier later on.

Software engineers collect useful tools. When they build a powerful tool, they make it part of their collection, part of their library. Developing and using a software library is really a problem-solving skill, because good use of the library makes it easier to solve future problems. Before you write a program, you should consider any tools available in your software library to simplify the task. You may find that some tools are almost, but not quite, suitable. If so, you should improve the tools so that you can use them to solve the old problems and the new one. Next, return to the problem at hand. Copy the useful tools from the library into your program, then build any extra tools you need for the task. When you are done, examine the new tools you built to see if you should add them to the library.

Software engineers with large libraries of tools find they rarely write code. They merely adapt existing tools to new uses. The process of software engineering, then, often reduces to managing a large collection of pieces of old programs.

You should add WriteSpaces to your software library as a start. It is general enough that you will certainly find a use for it later. As you examine other useful tools in this book, you should add them to your software library also.

3.5   A Case Study with Tables and Fence Posts

A lesson you should learn early is that while computers are very good at producing detail, people are often overwhelmed by it. For example, to produce a report about how many hours a group of employees has worked and how much they are getting paid, young programmers often have the computer produce verbose output such as

```
Mona Kane worked 32.8 hours at $6.50 per hour and made $ 213.20.
```

Unfortunately, when you get many such lines of output, you end up with a mess:

```
Jesse Hubbard worked 40.0 hours at $8.00 per hour and made $ 320.00.
Jeremy Hunter worked 39.8 hours at $8.00 per hour and made $ 318.40.
Mona Kane worked 32.8 hours at $6.50 per hour and made $ 213.20.
```

```
Greg Nelson worked 19.4 hours at $7.50 per hour and made $ 145.50.
Clifford Warner worked 23.5 hours at $8.50 per hour and made $ 199.75.
```

When you present a series of related data values, try to structure them so that people can read the results easily. A simple way to do this is to produce a table.

```
-------------------------------------------------------------------
| Employee              Hours          Hourly         Total    |
|                       Worked         Wage ($)        Pay ($)  |
-------------------------------------------------------------------
| Jesse Hubbard    |    40.0     |     8.00     |     320.00 |
| Jeremy Hunter    |    39.8     |     8.00     |     318.40 |
| Mona Kane        |    32.8     |     6.50     |     213.20 |
| Greg Nelson      |    19.4     |     7.50     |     145.50 |
| Clifford Warner  |    23.5     |     8.50     |     199.75 |
-------------------------------------------------------------------
```

Tables are easier to comprehend than a mass of sentences. Producing them, however, often leads to what computer scientists call *fence-post problems*. An examination of the general solution to the fence-post problem follows.

The problem is this: You want to put up a fence with both posts and wire that alternates like this:

post, wire, post, wire, . . . , post, wire, post

Because you want posts on both the far left and the far right, you can't use the following simple loop because it doesn't plant the final post.

```
for (the length of the fence) do
begin
      plant a post.
      attach some wire.
end
```

Switching the order of the two operations doesn't help, because you miss the first post. The problem with this loop is that the number of posts always equals the number of sections of wire, whereas the fence you want to build has one more post than section of wire. The solution is to plant one of the posts either before or after the loop. The usual solution is to do it before.

```
plant a post.
for (the length of the fence) do
begin
      attach some wire.
      plant a post.
end
```

In addition to helping you produce tables, this general solution will help with many other programming problems.

3.5.1 Designing a Table-Making Program

When you were young, you probably worked with tables for addition, subtraction, and multiplication. How would you write a program that creates the following multiplication table?

```
---------------------------------------------------
! 1 !  2 !  3 !  4 !  5 !  6 !  7 !  8 !  9 ! 10 !
---------------------------------------------------
! 2 !  4 !  6 !  8 ! 10 ! 12 ! 14 ! 16 ! 18 ! 20 !
---------------------------------------------------
! 3 !  6 !  9 ! 12 ! 15 ! 18 ! 21 ! 24 ! 27 ! 30 !
---------------------------------------------------
! 4 !  8 ! 12 ! 16 ! 20 ! 24 ! 28 ! 32 ! 36 ! 40 !
---------------------------------------------------
! 5 ! 10 ! 15 ! 20 ! 25 ! 30 ! 35 ! 40 ! 45 ! 50 !
---------------------------------------------------
```

To write the pseudocode for the main program, you will, because of the limitations of Pascal, again produce the figure line-by-line. One simple observation you can make is that the table has two kinds of lines: rows of the table and solid lines. To write the main program, you have to specify in what order these two kinds of lines should appear. Here is your first fence-post problem. The solid lines and table rows alternate this way:

solid line, row, solid line, row, . . . , solid line, row, solid line

Because you want solid lines at both the top and bottom, you use the standard fence-post solution of writing the first solid line before the loop:

```
write a solid line.
for (each of 5 rows) do
begin
    write the next row of the table.
    write a solid line.
end
```

You can easily turn this pseudocode into a main program that produces the table once you develop procedures for each kind of line.

Next, you should consider in what order to develop the procedures. There is no reason to create both at once. In fact, there are good reasons not to. One of the principal advantages of program decomposition is that you can develop the pieces of a program separately. You do so by producing a first version of the program with only one procedure and then a second version with both. By developing the program incrementally, you can develop and debug each procedure separately. Therefore, you should first create a program that produces the rows of the table; then create a procedure for producing the solid lines.

What about variables in this program? You need a variable to control the loop that produces the different rows, so you will need at least a variable for current row number. Nothing else in the pseudocode indicates the need for a variable.

Are there any important conventions to be decided on in this program? You need to decide what field width to use for values in the table. If you limit yourself to row and column numbers less than or equal to 30, the largest possible integer in the table is $30 * 30 = 900$, and you can use a field width of 3.

Next, consider whether you want to introduce global constants. There are three magic numbers that might easily appear in your code: field width, number of rows, and number of columns. Which should be made into global constants? To answer, think about the general task you are solving. You are writing code to generate multiplication tables. Is it likely that you will want to produce more than one table of different dimensions with a single program execution? Yes, you might want to create a series of different tables with different sizes. Global constants are not sufficiently flexible to allow this. You will need to use value parameters instead.

What about the field width? It isn't likely that you will want to create different tables with different field widths from a single program execution. Tables are usually written out in a standard format where each column takes up the same amount of space. Also, the field widths you are likely to use do not vary greatly. Most people would consider a table uninteresting if it listed only one-digit or two-digit numbers, so the field width will usually be at least 3. On the other hand, it is unlikely that you would ever want a field width greater than 4. Consider, for example, numbers up to $99 * 99$. Such a multiplication table would fit in a field width of 4 and when printed would probably cover a large table. You probably won't have a field width other than 3 or 4, and consequently, you should declare it as a global constant.

Now that you have planned your program construction, you can begin the implementation phase of program development.

3.5.2   Writing Code for WriteRowOfTable

Following your design, you first write a procedure for writing a row of the table. Think about a single row of the table. Here is row 3:

```
!   3 !   6 !   9 ! 12 ! 15 ! 18 ! 21 ! 24 ! 27 ! 30 !
```

This line has a series of columns with table values and exclamation marks. Here is your second fence-post pattern:

exclamation, value, exclamation, . . . , exclamation, value, exclamation

Because you want exclamations at both the left and right, you again use the standard fence-post solution. Thus your pseudocode begins:

write an exclamation mark.
for (each column) do
begin
    write a table value.
    write an exclamation mark.
end
go to new output line.

To refine the pseudocode further, you need to explain what you mean by "each column" and "a table value." You can refine both by changing the loop to one that iterates from 1 to the number of columns. You can use the control variable for the loop to calculate the table value, (`row * column`). You can also make the table easier to read by inserting a space between the table value and the exclamation mark:

write an exclamation mark.
for column going 1 to (number of columns) do
begin
    write (row * column) in given field width.
    write a space.
    write an exclamation mark.
end
go to new output line.

You can translate this easily into Pascal. You only have to consider where various values come from. According to the pseudocode, this procedure needs to know the field width, the number of columns, and the current value of `row`. In the design phase, you decided that the field width would be a global constant, so the procedure can refer to it without declaring it locally. For the number of columns, you chose to use a value parameter. For the current row number, since you decided that `row` would be a variable in the main program, you also have to use a value parameter.

```
PROGRAM TableMaker1 (OUTPUT);
CONST FieldWidth = 3;
VAR   row       : INTEGER;

PROCEDURE WriteRowOfTable (row, NumColumns : INTEGER);
VAR column : INTEGER;
BEGIN
    WRITE ('!');
    FOR column := 1 TO NumColumns DO
        WRITE ((row * column):FieldWidth, ' !');
    WRITELN
END;   (* WriteRowOfTable *)
```

```
BEGIN    (* main program *)
    FOR row := 1 TO 5 DO
        WriteRowOfTable (row, 10)
END.    (* main program *)
```

Here is the output for this program:

```
!  1 !  2 !  3 !  4 !  5 !  6 !  7 !  8 !  9 ! 10 !
!  2 !  4 !  6 !  8 ! 10 ! 12 ! 14 ! 16 ! 18 ! 20 !
!  3 !  6 !  9 ! 12 ! 15 ! 18 ! 21 ! 24 ! 27 ! 30 !
!  4 !  8 ! 12 ! 16 ! 20 ! 24 ! 28 ! 32 ! 36 ! 40 !
!  5 ! 10 ! 15 ! 20 ! 25 ! 30 ! 35 ! 40 ! 45 ! 50 !
```

3.5.3   Writing Code for WriteSolidLine

Following your design plan, you now write the procedure for producing a solid line.

```
----------------------------------------------------
```

You can use a FOR loop to write out this series of dashes. The challenge is figuring out how many dashes to write. The line above has 51. How do you express that without using a magic number? The easiest way is to realize that the line produced by procedure **WriteRowOfTable** has the same length as this solid line. Thus you can analyze **WriteRowOfTable** to find out the appropriate width.

Most of the characters written out by **WriteRowOfTable** are output by the FOR loop. During each iteration of the loop, the procedure writes out an integer and two other characters: a space and an exclamation. The field width used for the integer is given by **FieldWidth**, which means that the number of characters output on each iteration is

```
(FieldWidth + 2)
```

The number of iterations performed by the loop equals **NumColumns**, so the total number of characters output by the loop is

```
NumColumns * (FieldWidth + 2)
```

The procedure outputs only one other character, an exclamation written just before the loop. This means that the total number of characters output by the procedure is

```
NumColumns * (FieldWidth + 2) + 1
```

This expression describes how many dashes to write. A quick verification for **FieldWidth** of 3 and **NumColumns** of 10 yields

NumColumns * (FieldWidth + 2) + 1 = 10 * (3 + 2) + 1 = 51

You can now finish the procedure. Because its action depends on the value of FieldWidth and NumColumns, you need to decide how it obtains these values. Because FieldWidth is a global constant, you don't need to pass it as a parameter, as you do with NumColumns. Thus your program becomes

```
PROGRAM TableMaker2 (OUTPUT);
CONST FieldWidth = 3;
VAR    row        : INTEGER;

PROCEDURE WriteSolidLine (NumColumns : INTEGER);
VAR count : INTEGER;
BEGIN
    FOR count := 1 TO (NumColumns * (FieldWidth + 2) + 1) DO
        WRITE ('-');
    WRITELN
END;    (* WriteSolidLine *)

PROCEDURE WriteRowOfTable (row, NumColumns : INTEGER);
VAR column : INTEGER;
BEGIN
    WRITE ('!');
    FOR column := 1 TO NumColumns DO
        WRITE ((row * column):FieldWidth, ' !');
    WRITELN
END;    (* WriteRowOfTable *)

BEGIN   (* main program *)
    WriteSolidLine (10);
    FOR row := 1 TO 5 DO
    BEGIN
        WriteRowOfTable (row, 10);
        WriteSolidLine (10)
    END
END.    (* main program *)
```

The output appears on page 94.

```
------------------------------------------------------
!  1 !  2 !  3 !  4 !  5 !  6 !  7 !  8 !  9 ! 10 !
------------------------------------------------------
!  2 !  4 !  6 !  8 ! 10 ! 12 ! 14 ! 16 ! 18 ! 20 !
------------------------------------------------------
!  3 !  6 !  9 ! 12 ! 15 ! 18 ! 21 ! 24 ! 27 ! 30 !
------------------------------------------------------
!  4 !  8 ! 12 ! 16 ! 20 ! 24 ! 28 ! 32 ! 36 ! 40 !
------------------------------------------------------
!  5 ! 10 ! 15 ! 20 ! 25 ! 30 ! 35 ! 40 ! 45 ! 50 !
------------------------------------------------------
```

3.5.4   Coding One More Level of Structure

You now have a program that works, but it is not quite done. One of the goals of your design was to produce a program that is easily adapted to produce multiple tables of differing dimensions. To produce a table with different dimensions, you would have to make major modifications to the main program, and this is not acceptable.

You can fix this problem by creating another level of structure. Your current decomposition looks like this:

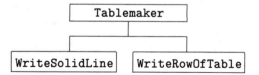

You have procedurized the line tasks, but you haven't procedurized the overall table task. The main program specifies in what order to produce the different lines. You can move these details into a new procedure that creates a single table, leaving you with the following decomposition

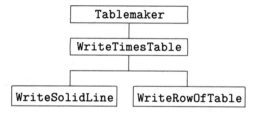

Your main program now will be able to call up this new procedure several times to produce several tables. The number of rows and columns for a table

should be parameterized, so this new procedure will have those as value parameters. Below is a program with this new procedure and a main program that calls it twice to create two different tables. Notice that the variable for current row number has become local to the new procedure.

```
PROGRAM TableMaker3 (OUTPUT);
CONST FieldWidth = 3;

PROCEDURE WriteSolidLine (NumColumns : INTEGER);
VAR count : INTEGER;
BEGIN
    FOR count := 1 TO (NumColumns * (FieldWidth + 2) + 1) DO
        WRITE ('-');
    WRITELN
END;   (* WriteSolidLine *)

PROCEDURE WriteRowOfTable (row, NumColumns : INTEGER);
VAR column : INTEGER;
BEGIN
    WRITE ('!');
    FOR column := 1 TO NumColumns DO
        WRITE ((row * column):FieldWidth, ' !');
    WRITELN
END;   (* WriteRowOfTable *)

PROCEDURE WriteTimesTable (NumRows, NumColumns : INTEGER);
VAR row : INTEGER;
BEGIN
    WriteSolidLine (NumColumns);
    FOR row := 1 TO NumRows DO
    BEGIN
        WriteRowOfTable (row, NumColumns);
        WriteSolidLine (NumColumns)
    END
END;   (* WriteTimesTable *)

BEGIN   (* main program *)
    WriteTimesTable (5, 10);
    WRITELN;
    WriteTimesTable (4, 12)
END.    (* main program *)
```

The output appears on page 96.

```
-------------------------------------------------------
! 1 ! 2 ! 3 ! 4 ! 5 ! 6 ! 7 ! 8 ! 9 ! 10 !
-------------------------------------------------------
! 2 ! 4 ! 6 ! 8 ! 10 ! 12 ! 14 ! 16 ! 18 ! 20 !
-------------------------------------------------------
! 3 ! 6 ! 9 ! 12 ! 15 ! 18 ! 21 ! 24 ! 27 ! 30 !
-------------------------------------------------------
! 4 ! 8 ! 12 ! 16 ! 20 ! 24 ! 28 ! 32 ! 36 ! 40 !
-------------------------------------------------------
! 5 ! 10 ! 15 ! 20 ! 25 ! 30 ! 35 ! 40 ! 45 ! 50 !
-------------------------------------------------------


-----------------------------------------------------------------
! 1 ! 2 ! 3 ! 4 ! 5 ! 6 ! 7 ! 8 ! 9 ! 10 ! 11 ! 12 !
-----------------------------------------------------------------
! 2 ! 4 ! 6 ! 8 ! 10 ! 12 ! 14 ! 16 ! 18 ! 20 ! 22 ! 24 !
-----------------------------------------------------------------
! 3 ! 6 ! 9 ! 12 ! 15 ! 18 ! 21 ! 24 ! 27 ! 30 ! 33 ! 36 !
-----------------------------------------------------------------
! 4 ! 8 ! 12 ! 16 ! 20 ! 24 ! 28 ! 32 ! 36 ! 40 ! 44 ! 48 !
-----------------------------------------------------------------
```

The important point to make about this final version of the program is that you make the flexibility of producing different tables in a single execution of the program possible by creating another procedure with value parameters to generalize that new procedure. If you use global constants, you have to either make major modifications to the program or execute the program once for each different table.

3.6 Key Concepts

- Data objects in Pascal are dynamically allocated only when they are needed. Local variables, for example, are allocated when a procedure is activated and deallocated when it terminates.

- Procedures should be as self-contained as possible—black boxes whose details are hidden. To make more flexible procedures that perform a family of tasks, however, you identify parameters of the task, using a set of formal parameters to define a procedure in a general way. You cause the procedure to perform a specific task by supplying a set of actual parameters.

- Value parameters allow values to flow into a procedure. A value parameter causes a local copy of a value to be created. Because it is a copy, it cannot change anything outside the procedure.

- Value parameters and global constants both provide adaptability in a program. Global constants should be used when you are unlikely to use more than one value in one execution of a program. Value parameters should be used if you expect to call the procedure several times with different actual parameters.

- Creating a piece of software involves several phases. In this book we concentrate on the design phase in which a plan is created; the coding phase, in which Pascal code is written; and the testing phase, in which the code is tested.

- As you write more and more programs you will find that some of the procedures you develop are useful enough that they should be incorporated into a software library that will be helpful in the writing of other programs.

3.7 Self-Check Exercises

1. Under what circumstances would there be more than one object of the same name active at the same time?

2. Suppose that a program has a variable X in the main program, a variable Y in a procedure called **Task1**, and a variable Z in a procedure called **Task2**. If **Task1** is called three times by the main program and is not called anywhere else, and **Task2** is called four times by **Task1** and nowhere else, how many times are each of X, Y, and Z allocated and deallocated?

3. In what way is a value parameter outside the black box defined by a procedure? In what way is it inside?

4. What is the output of the following program?

```
PROGRAM Weird (OUTPUT);
VAR number : INTEGER;

PROCEDURE HalfTheFun (number : INTEGER);
VAR count : INTEGER;
BEGIN
    number := number DIV 2;
    FOR count := 1 TO number DO
        WRITE (count:2);
    WRITELN
END;
```

```
BEGIN
    number := 8;
    HalfTheFun (11);
    HalfTheFun (2 - 3 + 2 * 8);
    HalfTheFun (number);
    WRITELN ('number = ', number:1)
END.
```

5. Suppose that you are going to write a program that produces a table of prime numbers. For each question listed below, indicate at what phase of program development the question should be considered (design, coding, or testing).

    When should a `WRITELN` be executed to go to a new line?

    How do you calculate the next prime?

    Are the numbers produced by the program really prime?

    Should the field width for the table be a global constant or parameter?

    What will be the principal procedures of the program?

6. Consider the problem of writing out positive integers in sequence, as in

    1, 2, 3, 4, 5, 6, 7, 8, 9, 10, 11, 12, 13, 14, 15

    Write a procedure that performs this task. It should have a parameter that specifies the largest integer to write out (15 here).

7. Program `TableMaker3` at the end of this chapter has four objects: `FieldWidth`, defined in the main program; `count`, defined in procedure `WriteSolidLine`; `column`, defined in `WriteRowOfTable`; and `row`, defined in `WriteTimesTable`. How many times is each allocated and deallocated?

8. What modifications would have to be made to program `TableMaker3` that appears at the end of this chapter in order to make it calculate sums rather than products?

9. In the table-maker program you wrote a procedure called `WriteSolidLine` that uses the global constant `FieldWidth` and the value parameter `NumColumns` to produce a line of dashes like the two lines that border this table entry:

    ```
    ---------------------------------------------------
    ! 1 ! 2 ! 3 ! 4 ! 5 ! 6 ! 7 ! 8 ! 9 ! 10 !
    ---------------------------------------------------
    ```

    Write a new version of the procedure that uses not only dashes, but also plus signs to mark the columns, as in

    ```
    +----+----+----+----+----+----+----+----+----+----+
    ! 1 ! 2 ! 3 ! 4 ! 5 ! 6 ! 7 ! 8 ! 9 ! 10 !
    +----+----+----+----+----+----+----+----+----+----+
    ```

10. For program `TableMaker3` that produces a times table (showing `row * column`), it was appropriate to make `FieldWidth` a global constant rather than a parameter. Would the same be true if the program produced a table of powers instead (showing `row`^{`column`})? Briefly explain.

3.8 Programming Problems

1. Write a program that produces Christmas trees as output. It should have a procedure with two parameters: one for the number of segments in the tree and one for the height of each segment. For example, the tree on the left below has 3 segments of height 4, and the one on the right has 2 segments of height 5.

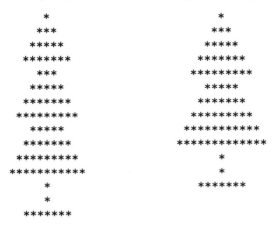

2. Write a program that produces several calendars. It should have a procedure that produces a single month's calendar like the one below given parameters that specify how many days are in the month and what the date of the first Sunday is (31 and 6, respectively, here).

```
Sun  Mon  Tue  Wed  Thu  Fri  Sat
+----+----+----+----+----+----+----+
|    |    |    |  1 |  2 |  3 |  4 |  5 |
|  6 |  7 |  8 |  9 | 10 | 11 | 12 |
| 13 | 14 | 15 | 16 | 17 | 18 | 19 |
| 20 | 21 | 22 | 23 | 24 | 25 | 26 |
| 27 | 28 | 29 | 30 | 31 |    |    |
+----+----+----+----+----+----+----+
```

3. A certain bank offers 12.7 percent interest on loans compounded annually. Create a table that shows how much money a person will accumulate over a period of 25 years assuming an initial investment of $1000 and assuming that $100 is deposited each year after the first. Your table should indicate for each year the current balance, the interest, the new deposit, and the new balance.

4. Write a program that produces a table showing all the factors of the integers between 1 and 50. For example, the factors of 30 are 1, 2, 3, 5, 6, 10, 15, and 30.

5. Write a program that shows the total number of presents received on each day according to the song "The Twelve Days of Christmas," as indicated on page 100.

Day	Presents Received	Total Presents
1	1	1
2	2	3
3	3	6

4

INTERACTIVE PROGRAMS

4.1 Introduction

The last three chapters examined programs that produce output. This chapter examines the more interesting side of communication: programs that interact with a user. Because humans and computers don't communicate very well, these programs are the most challenging to write.

The chapter begins with an examination of how values are obtained from the user and the basic structure of an interactive program. Next, it introduces a new type used to store all real numbers, not just integers, that you will need whenever you want to talk to the user about numbers that aren't always integers (e.g., money). The chapter then examines a Pascal construct called a function that extends your ability to form expressions. This will be important in performing complex calculations for the user.

After covering this basic background, you will learn an important new control structure: the IF/THEN/ELSE. Called a conditional or selection construct, it allows you to select from among alternatives depending on certain conditions. This new structure, like the FOR loop, is so powerful that you will wonder how you managed to write programs without it.

Finally, the chapter examines writing subprograms that are very like procedures except that they return values. These subprograms allow you to replace certain tedious sequences of statements with elegant expressions that make your programs more readable and less monotonous.

4.2 The READLN Statement

The **READLN** statement obtains input. It is appropriate for terminal input on most Pascal systems. Its general syntax has a series of variable names separated by commas inside parentheses:

READLN (*<variable>*, *<variable>*, ..., *<variable>*)

Here is an example:

READLN (first, second, third);

This **READLN** statement reads in values for three variables. **READLN** is a second way of assigning values to variables, values entered by a user. When your program executes a **READLN** statement in an interactive program, it pauses and waits for a user at the terminal to type a line of input.

If you ask the program to read in values for three numbers, as in the example above, it stores the first number typed by the user in the memory cell for **first**, the second number from the user in **second**, and the third number in **third**. This makes perfect sense, but don't be fooled into thinking the computer understands your variable names. If you execute the following statement:

READLN (third, first, second);

the first number typed by the user will go into **third**, the second into **first**, and the third into **second**. Values typed by the user are assigned to variables in the order you specify in the **READLN**.

When executing a **READLN**, the computer will wait until it has been given the correct amount of data. If a user types in only two numbers when the computer needs values for three variables, it will pause and wait for the user to type a second line. If after reading this second line, it doesn't have enough values, the computer will wait for the user to type a third line, and so on.

The **READLN** statement obtains the data it requires. If a user types in four numbers, the first three are read into the three variables and the fourth number is thrown away. This is true of any other data on the input line that appears after the desired three values.

If a user types something that isn't a number, such as **XYZZY**, the program will probably reach an execution error.

4.2.1 Elements of an Interactive Program

Now that you know how to read information from the user, you can write your first interactive program. Here is a simple program that reads in two integers and does some calculations.

```
(* This program prompts the user for two integers and reports various *)
(* arithmetic calculations using those numbers.                       *)
```

```
PROGRAM Math (INPUT, OUTPUT);
VAR first  : INTEGER;    (* first number typed by user  *)
    second : INTEGER;    (* second number typed by user *)
BEGIN  (* main program *)
    WRITELN ('Hi there!');
    WRITELN ('This program does some simple math on two integers.');
    WRITELN ('If you give me two numbers to work with, I''ll do');
    WRITELN ('some calculations for you.  Here we go . . .');
    WRITELN;
    WRITE ('Give me two numbers  ---> ');
    READLN (first, second);
    WRITELN;
    WRITELN (first:1, ' + ', second:1, ' = ', (first + second):1);
    WRITELN (first:1, ' - ', second:1, ' = ', (first - second):1);
    WRITELN (second:1, ' - ', first:1, ' = ', (second - first):1);
    WRITELN (first:1, ' * ', second:1, ' = ', (first * second):1);
    WRITELN (first:1, ' div ', second:1, ' = ', (first DIV second):1);
    WRITELN (first:1, ' mod ', second:1, ' = ', (first MOD second):1);
    WRITELN (second:1, ' div ', first:1, ' = ', (second DIV first):1);
    WRITELN (second:1, ' mod ', first:1, ' = ', (second MOD first):1)
END.   (* main program *)
```

Because you want both for this program, INPUT and OUTPUT are inside parentheses in the program header. After the program header, a VAR declaration defines first and second as variables of type INTEGER.

The program starts by explaining what is going to happen. This is essential for interactive programs. If READLN statements appear first, users would be expected to type input without knowing what to type. The fifth statement generates a blank line of output to separate the introductory text from what will follow.

The sixth statement is a prompt, a request for information from the user. I use a WRITE statement instead of a WRITELN so that the user will type the values on the same line as the prompt (i.e., to the right of the prompt).

After prompting for values, the program reads in two numbers and writes out the results. I use formatted output in this WRITELN statement, giving each integer expression a field width of 1 so that it will be written out in exactly as much space as it takes. The execution of this program would go something like this:

```
Hi there!
This program does some simple math on two integers.
If you give me two numbers to work with, I'll do
some calculations for you.  Here we go . . .
```

```
Give me two numbers  ---> 29   536

29 + 536 = 565
29 - 536 = -507
536 - 29 = 507
29 * 536 = 15544
29 div 536 = 0
29 mod 536 = 29
536 div 29 = 18
536 mod 29 = 14
```

4.3 REAL Expressions and Variables

It's time to learn a new type: the type **REAL**. The domain of type **REAL** is the set of all numbers. Type **REAL** contains not only the **INTEGER**s, but also the decimal numbers, such as 3.45.

Simple **REAL** constants have a decimal point with an integer on either side. They can also have a sign in front of them. For example,

17.0	0.23	-19.4	+76.3

There must be digits on either side of the decimal. The following are not real constants.

17.	.23	-19	+76.

It is also possible to express **REAL** constants in scientific notation, as powers of 10. Each constant is expressed as a mantissa, followed by 'e' and an exponent. The mantissa can be either a simple **REAL** or **INTEGER** constant, and the exponent must be an **INTEGER**, as in

3.2e10	4e-6	7.3e+19	+234.4e-17

These should be interpreted as

$$3.2 * 10^{10} \qquad 4 * 10^{-6} \qquad 7.3 * 10^{19} \qquad 234.4 * 10^{-17}$$

The operations defined on type **REAL** are the standard arithmetic operations:

Operator	Meaning	Example	Value
+	Addition	2.3 + 2.2	5.5
-	Subtraction	36.4 - 18.3	18.1
*	Multiplication	3.4 * 4.8	16.32
/	Division	398.43/45.35	8.786

These are the same as for integers except you now use the usual division operator (/). The same precedence rules apply: the multiplicative operators (*, /) over the additive operators (+, -).

You can use the VAR declaration to define variables of type REAL, just as you defined variables of type INTEGER:

```
VAR first, second, third : REAL;
```

or individually:

```
VAR first  : REAL;
    second : REAL;
    third  : REAL;
```

If you want to have two INTEGER variables as well, you make the declaration longer:

```
VAR first  : REAL;
    second : REAL;
    third  : REAL;
    num1   : INTEGER;
    num2   : INTEGER;
```

Some statements that use variables of type INTEGER work for REALs and some do not. You can use the assignment statement for REALs, and it works the same way. You can also use WRITE and WRITELN, but they work slightly differently. You cannot, however, use the FOR loop with REALs.

```
FOR count := 34.5 TO 47.8 DO
    WRITELN (count);
```

You use a starting value to execute a FOR loop once, use the next value to execute it again, then use the next, and so on, until you reach the ending value. This won't work for REALs, however, because there is no "next" real number after 34.5.

This points out an important difference between type REAL and type INTEGER. Reals are continuous because between any two values there is another. Type INTEGER is discrete, or ordinal, because you can order the elements so that there is a first element, a next element, and so on. This is similar to the difference between the words "much" and "many." We use "much" for continuous quantities, as in "How much do you weigh?" because weight can vary by indefinitely small amounts (175 pounds, 175.1 pounds, 175.01 pounds, etc.). We use "many" for ordinal quantities, as in "How many brothers do you have?" because brothers vary by discrete amounts (two brothers, three brothers, four brothers, etc.).

4.3.1 Mixing Types

The assignment statement works for REAL variables as well as INTEGERs, but you must be careful. The assignment statement has the form:

<variable> := *<expression>*

Not all combinations of variables and expressions are legal. The type of the expression must be compatible with the type of the variable. Suppose you have the following VAR declaration:

```
VAR RealVar    : REAL;
    IntegerVar : INTEGER;
```

Given this declaration, the following are legal assignment statements, because you can always assign a variable to a constant of that type:

```
RealVar := 34.5;
IntegerVar := 12;
```

But is it legal to mix the types? That is,

```
RealVar := 12;
IntegerVar := 34.5;
```

The first assignment statement has a REAL variable and an INTEGER constant. This is allowed, even though the types do not match. The INTEGER on the right is converted into a REAL. This is possible because all integers are also reals. The computer usually performs an actual conversion because integer values are generally stored in a different format than real values at the machine level.

The second assignment statement has an INTEGER variable and a REAL constant. This is not legal. There is no automatic conversion from REAL to INTEGER, however, as you will see, there are ways of converting if you're willing to specify how to deal with the fractional part of the number. Pascal is strict about this rule, even when the REAL expression happens to coincide with an INTEGER:

```
IntegerVar := 12.0;
IntegerVar := 4.8/2.4;
```

Both these statements are illegal. An INTEGER variable cannot be assigned a REAL expression, even if the expression happens to have an integer value.

The rule for determining whether an expression is of type REAL or type INTEGER is not complex. The presence of any REAL variable, constant, or division operator will make the overall expression a REAL. The table on page 107 lists some examples.

Expression	Type	Explanation
2 + 2	INTEGER	No REALs
34 - 8 DIV 5	INTEGER	No REALs
4 DIV 2	INTEGER	No REALs
4/2	REAL	REAL division operator (/)
2 + 3 - 4 * 1.8	REAL	REAL constant (1.8)
RealVar + 4 - 9 * 2	REAL	REAL variable (RealVar)

The operators DIV and MOD are (not) defined for REALs. They require INTEGER operands. Thus, the following expression is illegal.

```
22.8 DIV 2.0
```

4.3.2 Formatted REALs

You can use the WRITE and WRITELN statements to write out REAL values as well as INTEGER values:

```
WRITELN (34.8, 109.45);
```

This statement produces the following output:

```
3.480000E+01    1.094500E+02
```

Pascal displays REALs in scientific notation. The output above should be interpreted as

```
3.48 * 10¹  = 3.48 * 10 = 34.8
1.0945 * 10²  = 1.0945 * 100 = 109.45
```

This is not a convenient form of output for most people. However, just as with INTEGERs, you can specify output formats to change the way the computer displays REAL values. For example, if your computer, by default, displays REAL values in a field width of 16, you can change that field width the same way you did with INTEGERs and string constants:

```
WRITELN (34.8:8, 109.45:9);
```

This statement produces the following output:

```
3.5E+01 1.09E+02
```

You still have scientific notation, but the width is smaller. Notice that when the computer displays 34.8 with only two significant digits, it rounds to the value 35. The final displayed digit of a REAL is always rounded.

To get around the scientific notation, you must specify a second format that tells the computer where to put the decimal point:

```
WRITELN (34.8:8:2, 109.45:9:3);
```

Notice the second colon and second integer. This second integer specifies how many digits should appear after the decimal point. Here is the output of this statement:

```
34.80   109.450
```

The first number has two digits after the decimal point, and the second has three, as specified in the format. In this case, the computer displays zeros because the format has more digits than are significant.

Positive REAL numbers are always written out with a leading blank (presumably to make them line up with negative numbers that have a leading minus sign). Thus, to write the number 34.80, the minimum field width you need is 6 for the two digits on either side of the decimal point, the leading blank, and the decimal point. If you use a field width less than 6, it will be expanded (as with INTEGERs) to accommodate the number.

You will generally use one of two specifications. You might use a format such as :1:2 to call for as much space as is necessary with two digits after the decimal point. This specification will not work well if you are trying to line up a column of numbers, however. The expansion of the field can force decimal points out of line and create the following unsightly accounting statement.

```
  3.45
 29.84
109.34
 72.45
-18.94
-------
196.14
```

The minimum field width necessary to make these numbers line up is seven columns for the numbers 109.34 and 196.14 (five digits, one decimal point, and one leading space for the sign). The numbers will line up as long as no expansion occurs. This means you should choose a large field width, using a format specification such as :7:2, as in the following example. To be prudent, you might want to use a format specification such as :9:2 or :10:2 in case some numbers are larger.

```
   3.45
  29.84
 109.34
  72.45
 -18.94
 -------
 196.14
```

4.4 Cumulative Sum

A common programming task is finding the sum of a series of numbers. An earlier program added two numbers together using variables `first`, `second`, and `sum`. It would not be convenient, however, to define 100 variables to add together 100 numbers.

The trick is to keep a running tally and to process one number at a time. If you have a variable called `sum`, for example, you would add in the next number by saying

```
sum := sum + next;
```

This statement says to take the old value of `sum`, add the value of a variable called `next`, and store this as the new value of `sum`. This operation is performed for each number to be summed. There is a slight problem when executing this statement for the first number, because there is no old value of `sum` the first time around. To get around this, you initialize `sum` to a value that will not affect the answer—zero.

Rather than obtaining all the numbers first and then doing all the processing, you alternate obtaining a number and processing it. This allows you to use a single variable `next` rather than many variables. Here is a pseudocode description of the cumulative-sum algorithm:

```
sum := 0.
for (all numbers to sum) do
begin
    obtain next.
    sum := sum + next.
end
```

To implement this algorithm, you must decide how many times to go through the loop and how to obtain a next value. Here is an interactive program using both REALs and INTEGERs that prompts the user for how many numbers to sum together and for the numbers themselves.

```
(* This program adds together a series of numbers for the user at *)
(* the terminal.  It first asks the user how many numbers to sum, *)
(* then asks for the series of numbers  and reports the sum.      *)

PROGRAM FindSum (INPUT, OUTPUT);
VAR count   : INTEGER;    (* loop counter                 *)
    HowMany : INTEGER;    (* number of numbers to sum     *)
    sum,    : REAL;       (* running tally                *)
    next    : REAL;       (* next number to sum           *)
```

```
BEGIN    (* main program *)
    WRITELN ('This program will add together a series of');
    WRITELN ('real numbers for you.');
    WRITELN;
    WRITE ('How many numbers do you want to add together? ');
    READLN (HowMany);
    sum := 0;
    FOR count := 1 TO HowMany DO
    BEGIN
        WRITE ('    next ---> ');
        READLN (next);
        sum := sum + next
    END;
    WRITELN ('Sum =', sum:1:2)
END.    (* main program *)
```

Notice that INPUT and OUTPUT appear in the header. Also notice that in the VAR declaration, to enhance readability, there is one variable per line, each with comments regarding its use. The program will execute something like this:

```
This program will add together a series of
real numbers for you.


How many numbers do you want to add together?  5
    next --->  13.5
    next --->  12.85
    next --->  -109.8
    next --->  102.45
    next --->  213.8
Sum = 232.80
```

The cumulative-sum algorithm and variations on it will be useful in many of the programming tasks you solve. How would you do a cumulative product, for example? Here is the pseudocode:

```
product := 1;
for (all numbers) do
begin
    obtain next.
    product := product * next.
end
```

4.5 Built-in Functions

Pascal has many built-in mathematical functions. For example, if you want the square root of a number, the built-in function **SQRT** performs this operation:

```
number := SQRT (45.8 - 3.4);
```

This assignment statement calculates the square root of 42.4 and puts the answer in the variable **number**, presumably of type **REAL**. The value you want **SQRT** to use (i.e., the parameter you want **SQRT** to use) appears inside parentheses. Parameters of functions are called *arguments of the function*. The answer is called the *result*. Each function will return values of a particular type, called the *result type of the function*. **SQRT** has the result type **REAL**.

As you see, you can use complex expressions as arguments. In evaluating such an expression, Pascal first evaluates the expression inside the parentheses, and then passes this as the argument to the function. The overall expression evaluates to whatever is returned by the function.

You can, however, have expressions that use more than one function call:

```
number := SQRT (SQRT (4) + 7) - SQRT (25);
```

The overall expression uses the subtraction operation. Before you can subtract, however, you first must evaluate the two values to be used. Suppose that the left side is evaluated first and then the right. As with all parenthesized expressions, you evaluate the innermost expressions first. Once you calculate the left value, you calculate the value to the right of the minus and then subtract. Here is a trace of the evaluation:

```
SQRT (SQRT (4) + 7) - SQRT (25) =
SQRT (     2.0 + 7) - SQRT (25) =
SQRT (     9.0    ) - SQRT (25) =
         3.0          - SQRT (25) =
         3.0          -    5.0   =
               -2.0
```

Before going further, consider the power the function gives you. Why do you need functions when you have procedures? Why can't Pascal provide a procedure **FindSquareRootOf** rather than providing a **SQRT** function? If it were a procedure, you would expect to use it like this:

```
FindSquareRootOf ((45.8 - 3.4), number);
```

In this procedure, you would provide two parameters: the first indicating what value to find the square root of and the second indicating where to store the result. Thus the procedure call above would be equivalent to

```
number := SQRT (45.8 - 3.4);
```

In this case, a single procedure call could replace the single function call.

But consider a more complicated function use:

```
number := SQRT (25) - SQRT (16);
```

To use a procedure here instead of the function, you must have three different commands. You have to call up the procedure twice to find the roots and then you have to perform the subtraction. You also have to introduce variables to store the roots:

```
FindSquareRootOf (25, FirstRoot);
FindSquareRootOf (16, SecondRoot);
number := FirstRoot - SecondRoot;
```

This is more tedious than the manipulations on the function. The function allows you to condense your commands by giving a single command that expresses more. Functions, then, extend your ability to form complex yet meaningful expressions, simplifying programs by shortening the number of commands and the number of variables you must use.

The syntax of the function call is like the syntax of the procedure call:

<function name> (*<specific parameters>*)

You can use the function call in an expression in place of an object of the result type. For example, you can form **REAL** expressions like the following:

```
3.0 * 4.0
```

Thus you can use calls on a **REAL**-valued function instead of either or both of these **REAL** constants:

```
SQRT (9) * SQRT (16)
```

You must realize, however, that function calls act syntactically like nouns, not like imperative sentences. The following is not a command:

```
2.3 + 2.7;
```

Similarly, the following is not a command:

```
SQRT (25);
```

Both these are **REAL** expressions; they represent values (nouns). To make them into imperative sentences, you must say something like

```
number := 2.3 + 2.7;
number := SQRT (25);
```

Many of the statements you have seen (assignment, **FOR**, **WRITE**, **WRITELN**) are defined in terms of expressions. This means that you can use function calls in those statements to form expressions:

```
WRITELN ('Hypotenuse = ', SQRT (x * x + y * y));
```

The following table shows the built-in numerical functions:

Function	Meaning	Argument Type	Result Type
ABS	Absolute value	REAL/INTEGER	REAL/INTEGER
ARCTAN	Arctangent	REAL/INTEGER	REAL
COS	Cosine	REAL/INTEGER	REAL
EXP	Power of e	REAL/INTEGER	REAL
LN	Natural logarithm	REAL/INTEGER	REAL
SIN	Sine	REAL/INTEGER	REAL
SQR	Square	REAL/INTEGER	REAL/INTEGER
SQRT	Square root	REAL/INTEGER	REAL

Notice that the **ABS** and **SQR** functions return the same type as their argument. ABS (-34.5) and SQR (46.85) are of type **REAL**. ABS (-97) and SQR (17) are of type **INTEGER**. Appendix A discusses the details of the numerical functions.

Pascal also provides two functions for converting values of type **REAL** into **INTEGER**s:

Function	Meaning	Example	Value
TRUNC (x)	Truncation	TRUNC (34.9)	34
ROUND (x)	Rounding	ROUND (34.9)	35

Both take arguments of type **REAL** and return an **INTEGER**. To find the largest **INTEGER** less than the square root of 300, you would say

```
answer := TRUNC (SQRT (300));
```

If you want the closest **INTEGER** to this square root, you would say

```
answer := ROUND (SQRT (300));
```

The **TRUNC** operation ignores all digits after the decimal:

```
TRUNC (-12.0)  = -12          TRUNC (12.0)  = 12
TRUNC (-12.5)  = -12          TRUNC (12.5)  = 12
TRUNC (-12.99) = -12          TRUNC (12.99) = 12
```

ROUND rounds to the nearest **INTEGER**:

```
ROUND (-12.0)  = -12          ROUND (12.0)  = 12
ROUND (-12.5)  = -13          ROUND (12.5)  = 13
ROUND (-12.99) = -13          ROUND (12.99) = 13
```

For those of you who like mathematics, here is a more precise description of the relationship between **TRUNC** and **ROUND**.

$$\text{ROUND (x)} = \begin{cases} \text{TRUNC (x - 0.5), for x <= 0} \\ \text{TRUNC (x + 0.5), for x > 0} \end{cases}$$

4.6 IF/THEN/ELSE Statements

The programs you write will often make decisions between different possible actions. The simplest way to introduce a decision branch into a program is using an IF/THEN statement.

```
IF <test> THEN
    <statement>
```

An IF/THEN statement allows you to put a condition on the execution of a statement. The statement will be executed only if the test is true.

```
IF number > 0 THEN
    answer := SQRT (number);
```

This test is useful because you wouldn't want to ask for the square root of a negative number. Notice that there is no semicolon after the THEN. This is because the IF/THEN, like the FOR loop, is a control structure. The assignment statement is controlled by the IF/THEN and, therefore, is indented to indicate the structure.

The most common form of the IF statement includes an ELSE clause:

```
IF <test> THEN
    <statement>
ELSE
    <statement>
```

as in

```
IF number > 0 THEN
    answer := SQRT (number)
ELSE
    answer := 0;
```

There is no semicolon before the ELSE because this is all one statement. The statement in the THEN part is executed if the test returns TRUE, but if the test returns FALSE, the statement in the ELSE part is executed. Thus the IF/THEN/ELSE controls two different statements, one to be executed when the test returns TRUE and the other to be executed when the test returns FALSE.

Some people prefer this format:

```
IF number > 0
    THEN answer := SQRT (number)
    ELSE answer := 0;
```

This style has some advantages because it makes it obvious that this is one statement controlled by a test. People who program this way are less likely to make the mistake of putting a semicolon before the ELSE. The style also indicates that the two branches are equally weighted. This style is not as convenient, however, when the controlled statements are BEGIN/END blocks.

The IF/THEN/ELSE is controlled by a test. Simple tests compare two expressions to see if they are related in some way. Such a test is itself an expression that returns either TRUE or FALSE and is of the form

<expression> <relational operator> <expression>

To evaluate such a test, you first evaluate the two expressions and then see if the given relation holds between the value on the left and the value on the right. If the relation does hold, the test evaluates to TRUE. If not, the test evaluates to FALSE.

The relational operators are

Operator	Meaning	Example	Value
=	Equality	2 + 2 = 4	TRUE
<>	Nonequality	3.2 <> 4.1	TRUE
<	Less than	4 < 3	FALSE
>	Greater than	4 > 3	TRUE
<=	Less than or equal	2 <= 0	FALSE
>=	Greater than or equal	2.4 >= 1.6	TRUE

Because you use the relational operators as a new way of forming expressions, you must reconsider precedence. The following expression is made up of the constants 3, 4, 9, and the operations plus and equals.

```
3 + 4 = 9
```

Which of the operations is performed first? Because the relational operators have a lower level of precedence than the arithmetic operators, the answer is plus. You now have three levels of precedence:

```
* / DIV MOD          Multiplicative operators
+ -                  Additive operators
= < > <= >= <>       Relational operators
```

This precedence scheme frees you from parenthesizing the left and right sides of a test using a relational operator. Using these precedence rules, the following expression is evaluated like this:

```
3 + 2 * 2 = 9
3 + 4 = 9
7 = 9
FALSE
```

You can put arbitrary expressions on either side of the relational operator as long as they are of a compatible type. REALs and INTEGERs can always be compared, but when you examine characters and other types, you must be more careful. Here is a test with complex expressions on either side:

```
(2 - 3 * 8) DIV (435 MOD (7 * 2)) <= 3.8 - 4.5/(2.2 * 3.8)
```

To write an IF statement that executes more than one statement, you again use a BEGIN/END block:

```
IF number > 0 THEN
BEGIN
    answer := SQRT (number);
    number := number * 2
END
```

If you have an ELSE part for this statement, it would look like this:

```
IF number > 0 THEN
BEGIN
    answer := SQRT (number);
    number := number * 2
END
ELSE
BEGIN
    answer := 0;
    number := -number
END;
```

Be very careful with semicolons. There is no semicolon before the ELSE because this is one statement. It is a single IF/THEN/ELSE statement with two branches, each specified by a BEGIN/END block with two statements inside.

Some programmers who prefer shorter programs use indentation like the following. This style can minimize common semicolon mistakes.

```
IF number > 0 THEN BEGIN
    answer := SQRT (number);
    number := number * 2
END ELSE BEGIN
    answer := 0;
    number := -number
END;
```

4.6.1 Nested IF/THEN/ELSE

Many beginners write code that looks like this:

```
IF <test1> THEN
    <statement1>;
IF <test2> THEN
    <statement2>;
```

```
IF <test3> THEN
    <statement3>;
```

This sequential structure is appropriate if you want to execute any combination of the three statements. You might write this code in a program for a questionnaire with three optional parts, any combination of which might be applicable for a given person. Often, however, you only want to execute one of a series of statements. In such cases, it is better to nest the IFs:

```
IF <test1> THEN
    <statement1>
ELSE
    IF <test2> THEN
        <statement2>
    ELSE
        IF <test3> THEN
            <statement3>;
```

nested

one semicolon only

With this construct, you can be sure that one statement at most is executed. The first test to return TRUE has its corresponding statement executed. If no tests return TRUE, no statement is executed. If this is your objective, this construct is more appropriate than the sequential IF/THEN structure because it reduces the likelihood of errors and simplifies the testing process.

Another structure that is useful is the following:

```
IF <test1> THEN
    <statement1>
ELSE
    IF <test2> THEN
        <statement2>
    ELSE
        <statement3>;
```

In this construct, the final statement is controlled by an ELSE instead of a test. This branch will always be taken when the earlier tests fail, and thus the construct will always execute exactly one of the three statements.

For example, suppose you want to write out whether a number is positive, negative, or zero.

```
IF number > 0 THEN
    WRITELN ('Number is positive.');
IF number = 0 THEN
    WRITELN ('Number is zero.');
IF number < 0 THEN
    WRITELN ('Number is negative.');
```

To determine how many of the WRITELNs are potentially executed, you have to stop and think about the tests being performed. You shouldn't have to put that much effort into understanding this code. It would be more efficient and more clear to say instead:

```
IF number > 0 THEN
    WRITELN ('Number is positive.')
ELSE
    IF number = 0 THEN
        WRITELN ('Number is zero.')
    ELSE
        IF number < 0 THEN
            WRITELN ('Number is negative.');
```

This construct executes at most one of the statements. Notice that this nested IF/THEN/ELSE has no semicolons: it is one statement with several levels of structure.

This solution, however, is not the best. You know that you want to execute one and only one WRITELN statement. This nested structure does not preclude the possibility of no statement being executed. If all three tests fail, no statement would be executed. With these particular tests, this will never happen. If a number is neither positive nor zero, it must be negative. Thus the final test here is unnecessary and misleading. You must think about the tests in order to know whether or not it is possible for all three of these branches to be skipped.

The best solution is the nested IF/THEN/ELSE with a final branch that is always taken if the first two tests fail:

```
IF number > 0 THEN
    WRITELN ('Number is positive.')
ELSE
    IF number = 0 THEN
        WRITELN ('Number is zero.')
    ELSE
        WRITELN ('Number is negative.');
```

You can glance at this construct and see that exactly one WRITELN will be executed. You don't have to look at the tests being performed in order to realize this; it is a property of this kind of nested IF/THEN/ELSE.

When you have alternatives such as this, you should decide how many of the branches you want to be taken. If any combination can be taken, use sequential IF/THEN statements. If you want one or none of the branches to be taken, use the nested IF/THEN/ELSE with a test for each statement. If you want exactly one branch to be taken, use the nested IF/THEN/ELSE with a final branch controlled by an ELSE rather than by a test.

4.6.2   The Dangling ELSE

Nested **IF/THEN/ELSE** statements present a special problem known as the dangling **ELSE**. Suppose you are writing some code to calculate grades for students in a class and you have three variables that have been given values in this program:

`Total`	raw score not counting bonus projects
`Project1`	score received on one extra project (0 if not done)
`Project2`	score received on another extra project (0 if not done)

Also suppose you decide to add 5 points to the total if a student did one or the other project, but not to add more than 5 if he did both. Writing this in pseudocode you get

    if (either project was done) then
        add 5 points to total.

Unfortunately, you don't yet know how to express the intent of "either project was done." You have to figure out how to say this using simple tests. One first attempt might be

    if (first project was done) then
        add 5 points to total.
    if (second project was done) then
        add 5 points to total.

This is not what you want, though, because it adds 10 points to the total if both projects are done. You need a nested **IF/THEN/ELSE** construct to make sure that you add 5 points at most:

    if (first project was not done) then
        if (second project was done) then
            add 5 points to total.
    else
        add 5 points to total.

The outer **IF/THEN/ELSE** distinguishes whether or not the first project was done. If it wasn't (the **THEN** part), the student gets the extra points only if the second project was done. If it was (the **ELSE** part), the student gets the extra points no matter what.

Here is some Pascal code that tries to implement this pseudocode:

```
IF project1 = 0 THEN
    IF project2 > 0 THEN
        total := total + 5
ELSE
    total := total + 5;
```

Unfortunately, this code doesn't work. If you test it, you will find that it gives a student 5 extra credit points for doing neither project and fails to give 5 points for doing the first project.

The problem with this code is that you have two nested IF/THEN statements and only one ELSE clause. Which IF/THEN is this dangling ELSE matched up with? The answer is the closest one. In this case, the ELSE is matched up with the inner IF/THEN, which means the indentation is not correct in the code above. It should be

```
IF project1 = 0 THEN
    IF project2 > 0 THEN
        total := total + 5
    ELSE
        total := total + 5;
```

This is obviously not what you intended. Beginning students tend to suggest fixing this by introducing semicolons in the middle of the code. This will not work, however, because you cannot have a semicolon before an ELSE.

One good solution would be to introduce a BEGIN/END. The BEGIN/END pair effectively puts parentheses around the inner IF/THEN so that the ELSE will not be matched up with it:

```
IF project1 = 0 THEN
BEGIN
    IF project2 > 0 THEN
        total := total + 5
END
ELSE
    total := total + 5;
```

A second solution is to reverse the meaning of the outer test, allowing you to exchange the THEN and ELSE parts. This solves the dangling else by putting the second IF after the ELSE:

```
IF project1 > 0 THEN
    total := total + 5
ELSE
    IF project2 > 0 THEN
        total := total + 5
```

4.6.3 Factoring IF/THEN/ELSE Statements

Suppose you are writing a program that plays a betting game with a user at a terminal and you want to give the user different warnings about his cash holdings depending on how he is doing. The following nested IF/THEN/ELSE distinguishes three different cases: money less than $500, which is considered low; money between $500 and $1000, which is considered okay; and money over $1000, which is considered good. Notice that the user is given different advice in each branch:

```
IF money < 500 THEN
BEGIN
    WRITELN ('You have, $' money:1:2, ' left.');
    WRITE ('Your cash is dangerously low.  Bet carefully.');
    WRITE ('How much do you want to bet? ');
    READLN (bet)
END
ELSE
    IF money < 1000 THEN
    BEGIN
        WRITELN ('You have, $' money:1:2, ' left.');
        WRITE ('Your cash is somewhat low.  Bet moderately.');
        WRITE ('How much do you want to bet? ');
        READLN (bet)
    END
    ELSE
    BEGIN
        WRITELN ('You have, $' money:1:2, ' left.');
        WRITE ('Your cash is in good shape.  Bet liberally.');
        WRITE ('How much do you want to bet? ');
        READLN (bet)
    END;
```

This construct is repetitious and can be reduced using a technique called *factoring*. With it, you factor out common pieces of code from the different branches of the IF/THEN/ELSE. The technique is simple. The preceding construct creates three different branches depending on the value of **money**. You start by writing down the series of actions being performed in each branch and comparing them:

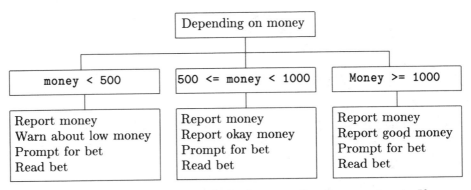

You can factor at both the top and the bottom of such a construct. If you notice that the top statement in each branch is the same, you factor it out of the branching part and put it before the branch. Similarly, if the bottom statement in each branch is the same, you factor it out of the branching part and put it after the loop. You can factor the top statement in each of these branches and the bottom two statements.

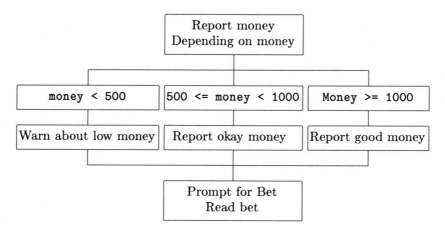

Thus the preceding code can be reduced to the following, which is more succinct:

```
WRITELN ('You have, $' money:1:2, ' left.');
IF money < 500 THEN
    WRITE ('Your cash is dangerously low.  Bet carefully.')
ELSE
    IF money < 1000 THEN
        WRITE ('Your cash is somewhat low.  Bet moderately.')
    ELSE
        WRITE ('Your cash is in good shape.  Bet liberally.');
WRITE ('How much do you want to bet? ');
READLN (bet)
```

4.7 User-Defined Functions

Pascal allows you to define your own functions, just as it allows you to define your own procedures. As an example, let's define a simple conversion function. Consider a function that converts feet to miles:

```
miles (0)        should equal  0.0
miles (2640)     should equal  0.5
miles (3960)     should equal  0.75
miles (5280)     should equal  1.0
    . . .
```

Assume that the feet are expressed as an INTEGER. The result is a REAL. Thus you want a function that will take an INTEGER object or expression as an argument and will return a REAL object. Examine the following function definition:

```
FUNCTION Miles (feet : INTEGER) : REAL;
BEGIN
    miles := feet/5280
END;
```

You will notice many similarities to a procedure definition. The word "PROCEDURE" is replaced with the word "FUNCTION" in the header, but the header line still has a name and a parameter list. The parameter list for this function defines one value parameter called feet. After the parameter list, you will notice something that is different from a procedure definition. There is a colon and the word "REAL" between the parameter list and the semicolon that separates the header from the body of the function. This specifies the result type of the function. This header, then, says that you are defining a function called miles that will return a REAL result when passed an INTEGER value as its parameter.

Notice that the function has a BEGIN/END block just as a procedure does. This block has only a single assignment statement in it. However, this assignment statement is not of the form

<variable> := *<expression>*

This assignment statement is of the form

<function name> := *<expression>*

This assignment statement is where you specify what value the function is to return. Let's look at a complete program that uses this function:

```
(* This program prompts the user at the terminal for the dimensions of  *)
(* a field in feet and tells him what the area is in square miles.       *)

PROGRAM CalculateArea (INPUT, OUTPUT);
VAR length : INTEGER;     (* length of field in feet       *)
    width  : INTEGER;     (* width of field in feet        *)
    area   : REAL;        (* area of field in square miles *)

FUNCTION Miles (feet : INTEGER) : REAL;
BEGIN
    miles := feet/5280
END;    (* miles *)

BEGIN    (* main program *)
    WRITELN ('This program will calculate the square mileage of a field');
```

```
      WRITELN ('given its dimensions.');
      WRITELN;
      WRITE ('How many feet wide is the field? ');
      READLN (width);
      WRITE ('How many feet long is the field? ');
      READLN (length);
      area := miles (width) * miles (length);
      WRITELN;
      WRITELN ('The square mileage is', area:1:3)
END.    (* main program *)
```

Here is a sample of its execution:

```
This program will calculate the square mileage of a field
given its dimensions.

How many feet wide is the field? 4000
How many feet long is the field? 8000

The square mileage is 1.148
```

4.7.1 Syntax of Functions

In Chapter 2 you learned that constant declarations appear before variable declarations and that variable declarations appear before procedure declarations. Function declarations can be mixed in anywhere with procedure declarations. Thus the proper order of declaration is

```
CONST <declarations>
VAR    <declarations>
PROCEDURE and FUNCTION <declarations>
```

Now that you've seen the definition of a simple function, look at its general syntax:

```
FUNCTION <function name> ( <parameter list> ) : <result type>;
<declarations>
BEGIN
    <statements>
END;
```

As you saw in the last section, this syntax is similar to that of the procedure. It has a header; it has a declaration part where local constants, types, and variables can be defined; and it has a BEGIN/END block with a series of statements. All these are exactly the same as the procedure. The only difference indicated is the result type after the parameter list in the header.

Within the set of statements for the function, there should be at least one statement of the form

<function name> := *<value>*;

This is the statement that determines what value is returned. You can have more than one such statement, and you can even have the function execute more than one. It will return the last value it was assigned during the function's execution.

Let's look at a more complex example that has more than one such assignment statement—the **min** function that calculates the minimum of two numbers:

```
FUNCTION Min (first, second : REAL) : REAL;
BEGIN
    IF first < second THEN
        min := first
    ELSE
        min := second
END;
```

This function has two statements that assign a value to the function. Depending on the parameters passed, one or the other statement will be executed.

It is an error for a function to terminate without executing at least one such statement (i.e., functions must always return a value). You will have to be careful to write functions that always do. The computer cannot check this for you at compile time. To do so, the compiler would have to be able to make logical deductions about the execution of your function. Only with very simple function definitions can the compiler make such a judgment. Such errors, then, become execution errors. If you execute a program and such an error occurs, your Pascal system should warn you that a function has terminated without assigning a value to be returned. Unfortunately, however, this is one of the most difficult errors to catch, and many Pascal systems will not inform you of the error. The system usually uses some random value and continues executing. This means that such errors can be difficult to find in programs, so you want to do your best to avoid them.

Don't be led astray by the fact that an assignment statement appears inside the function body assigning a value to the function name. This does not mean that the function name has the power of a local variable. For example, suppose you want to define a factorial function. The factorial is defined by

n! (which is read as "*n* factorial") $= 1 * 2 * 3 * \cdots * n$

You can calculate it with a cumulative product:

```
product := 1;
FOR count := 2 TO n DO
    product := product * count;
```

You might guess, then, that you can do the following:

```
FUNCTION Factorial (n: INTEGER): INTEGER;
VAR count : INTEGER;
BEGIN
    factorial := 1;
    FOR count := 2 TO n DO
        factorial := factorial * count
END;
```

not allowed

You aren't allowed to do this, however. The first assignment statement is okay; it merely says to give the function the value 1, and the presence of the FOR loop doesn't cause a problem. However, the assignment statement controlled by the FOR loop is a problem. The word `factorial` appears on the right side of the assignment statement. The assignment statement says, "Take the old value of `factorial` and multiply by `count` to get the new value of `factorial`." This is not allowed. You can't ask for the old value of `factorial`. You are only allowed to do this kind of manipulation on variables.

To fix the procedure, you would introduce a local variable that you can manipulate in this way and then assign the function the value that this local variable ends up with:

```
FUNCTION Factorial (n: INTEGER): INTEGER;
VAR fact  : INTEGER;
    count : INTEGER;
BEGIN
    fact := 1;
    FOR count := 2 TO n DO
        fact := fact * n;
    factorial := fact
END;
```

A simple rule to follow for function names inside of functions is that they should be used only on the left side of an assignment statement. Such a statement assigns a value to the function and is the only way that the function name can be employed inside the function. You will see one exception to this rule when you consider recursive functions that call themselves, but this simple rule will be valid for the nonrecursive programs you will be writing in the next few chapters.

4.8 Key Concepts

- Some programs interact with a user. Such programs must prompt for input before reading.

- Even though integers are a subset of real numbers, type INTEGER is different from type REAL. Mixed expressions can be formed, but they are always of type

REAL. You cannot use the INTEGER operators DIV and MOD on expressions of type REAL and you cannot assign a REAL value to an INTEGER variable.

- Nested IF/THEN/ELSE constructs provide different kinds of flow of control. In a nested construct, each ELSE clause is paired with the nearest IF/THEN. In a nested IF/THEN/ELSE construct with different branches, any statement that appears at either the beginning or the end of each branch can be factored out of the branches.

- Pascal provides many useful built-in functions and you can define your own functions. The declaration of a FUNCTION is much like that of a PROCEDURE, the main difference being that a FUNCTION has an extra statement, usually at the end, in which the return value of the FUNCTION is specified.

4.9 Self-Check Exercises

1. The last chapter discussed a procedure called WriteTimesTable with the following header:

   ```
   PROCEDURE WriteTimesTable (NumRows, NumColumns : INTEGER);
   ```

   Assume that this procedure is already defined. Write an interactive program that allows a user to display a times table of any size.

2. Which of the following are not REAL constants in Pascal?

   ```
   34.5     18.     19.73    123     .75     2.3     -43.2    +19.8
   ```

3. Some of the expressions below are legal and some are not. What are the values of the legal expressions?

   ```
   2.5 MOD 1.2              10.0 DIV 3
   2.0 * 3.2 + 6.4          12 + 15/3
   2.5 - 3.5 * 2.0/0.7      8 MOD 3 + 4.5
   (3.5 * 2) MOD 5          17 MOD 6 * 2/5
   -2.0 * 3.1               -3.1 * -2.0
   ```

4. Why would the following statement be inappropriate for producing checks?

   ```
   WRITELN ('$', amount:12:2);
   ```

5. Suppose that you have a program that produces a column of numbers using the format :8:3. If the column is skewed (i.e., the decimal points don't line up), what is the likely problem?

6. You have just arrived at the automated teller as you make preparations for a fun weekend. Suppose that you need money for purchasing a drink called a Blue Moon at your favorite bar. If the variable NumMoons stores the number of Blue Moons you plan to consume, and if each Blue Moon costs $4.50, and if you can withdraw only $20 bills from your teller, what Pascal expression will tell you how many $20 bills to withdraw in order to finance your debauchery?

7. Suppose that you are going to store an amount of money in two ways, as a single **REAL** variable called **money** or as two **INTEGER** variables called **dollars** and **cents**. What statement will give a value to **money** if an amount is stored in **dollars** and **cents**? What statements will give values to **dollars** and **cents** if an amount is stored in **money**? What **WRITELN** statement will output **dollars** and **cents** in the standard format of dollar sign, dollars, and cents (e.g., $4.75 and $123.00)?

8. You are going to translate some English descriptions into simple tests that can be used to control **IF/THEN/ELSE** statements. For each description below, give a Pascal test that captures the same idea. Assume that three **INTEGER** variables called **x**, **y**, and **z** have been defined.

   z is odd

   z is not greater than y's square root

   y is positive

   one of x and y is even and one is odd

   y is a multiple of z

   z is not zero

   y is greater in magnitude than z

   x and z are of opposite sign

   y is a one-digit number

   z is nonnegative

   x is even

   x is closer in value to y than z is

9. You are to write a function with the following header that returns the minimum of three integers. Write one version of the function that makes use of function **min** defined earlier and write another version that doesn't require **min**.

   ```
   FUNCTION Min3 (first, second, third : INTEGER) : INTEGER;
   ```

10. The following code is poorly structured:

    ```
    WRITE ('Is your money multiplied 1, 2, or 3 times? ');
    READLN (times);
    IF (times = 1) THEN
    BEGIN
        WRITE ('And how much are you contributing? ');
        READLN (donation);
        sum := sum + donation;
        count1 := count1 + 1;
        TotalPrivate := TotalPrivate + donation
    END;
    ```

```
IF (times = 2) THEN
BEGIN
    WRITE ('And how much are you contributing? ');
    READLN (donation);
    sum := sum + 2 * donation;
    count2 := count2 + 1;
    TotalPrivate := TotalPrivate + donation
END;
IF (times = 3) THEN
BEGIN
    WRITE ('And how much are you contributing? ');
    READLN (donation);
    sum := sum + 3 * donation;
    count3 := count3 + 1;
    TotalPrivate := TotalPrivate + donation
END;
```

Rewrite it so that it has a better structure and avoids redundancy. In order to simplify things, you can assume that the user enters either a 1, 2, or 3 when asked how many times the money is multiplied.

4.10   Programming Problems

1. Write a program that prompts for two numbers and reports their greatest common divisor (i.e., the largest integer that goes evenly into each).

2. Write a program that prompts for the lengths of the sides of a triangle and reports the three angles.

3. Write a program that prompts for a number and displays it in Roman numerals.

4. Write a program that prompts for a date (month, day, year) and reports the day of the week for that date. It might be helpful to know that January 1, 1601, was a Monday.

5. A new tax law has just been passed by the government: the first $3,000 of income is free of tax, the next $5,000 is taxed at 10 percent, the next $20,000 is taxed at 20 percent, and the rest is taxed at 30 percent. Write an interactive program that prompts for a user's income and reports the corresponding tax.

6. A useful technique for catching typing errors is to use a check-digit. For example, suppose that a school assigns a six-digit number to each student. A seventh digit can be determined from the other digits, as in

    (1 * (1st digit) + 2 * (2nd digit) + ... + 6 * (6th digit)) MOD 10

    When someone types in a student number, he types all seven digits. If the number is typed incorrectly, the check-digit will fail to match in 90 percent of the cases. Write an interactive program that prompts for a six-digit student number and reports the check digit for that number using the scheme described above.

5

INTRODUCTION TO PROGRAM DESIGN

5.1 Introduction

This chapter examines the issues of program and procedure design. To build well-designed procedures, you must learn a second kind of parameter: the **VAR** parameter. This parameter complements the value parameter by allowing you to send values out of procedures. Because you will be writing more sophisticated procedures, you need this new parameter if you want to continue to write self-contained procedures. After an introduction, a discussion of how the **VAR** parameter differs from the value parameter and some hints to help you decide when to use which parameter follow.

The chapter then presents some tools for obtaining unpredictable values within a program. While the tools will be useful throughout the book, their immediate application is for interactive programs that require an element of uncertainty. For example, many game-playing programs need an element of chance to keep the games exciting.

Next, the chapter focuses directly on design issues. You will study a poorly designed interactive program that uses global variables. You will rewrite the program so that it has better internal structure and adapt it to a new task. You will see that better internal design makes adaptation easier. Then you will examine the biggest design issue you will face in the next few programs you write: the problem of decomposing a large program into procedures. After some

130

basic terminology, a discussion of some general decomposition guidelines follows. The chapter closes with a substantial sample program.

5.2 VAR Parameters

The **VAR**, or variable, parameter is a new way of generalizing. It works by playing games with the names of objects. Here is an example to help you understand the basic idea. If you were interviewing John and Jane, applicants for a job, you might describe the process using this pseudocode:

```
Read John's application.
If (John looks bad) then
     Reject John.
else
begin
     Interview John.
     Call John's references.
     If (John looks bad now) then
          Reject John.
     else
          Hire John.
end
Read Jane's application.
If (Jane looks bad) then
     Reject Jane.
else
begin
     Interview Jane.
     Call Jane's references.
     If (Jane looks bad now) then
          Reject Jane.
     else
          Hire Jane.
end
```

This is redundant code. It would be even worse if there were more than two people. To avoid this redundancy, you should choose a generic term to describe the task more generally. You can describe, for example, how to consider "the applicant":

```
How to Consider "the applicant":
begin
     Read the applicant's application.
     If (the applicant looks bad) then
          Reject the applicant.
     else
     begin
          Interview the applicant.
```

>   Call the applicant's references.
>   If (the applicant looks bad now) then
>   Reject the applicant.
>   else
>   Hire the applicant.
>   end
>   end

Once you have a general description such as this, you can say

>   Consider John.
>   Consider Jane.

The whole idea is that you use two names for the same thing. In the general procedure, you use a generic name such as "the applicant" to describe the task. To carry out the task, you provide a specific person, which provides a specific name. For example, you decide to carry out the task on John. "John" and "the applicant" are both names for John. So if you hire "the applicant," you have, in effect, hired John. Anything that happens to "the applicant" also happens to "John," because the two names are synonymous while you carry out this task. Later on, you can perform the task using a different person, such as Jane. During the second execution, all references to "the applicant" are references to "Jane."

If you understand this kind of generalization, you understand the basic idea of the VAR parameter. Here is a simple example. Suppose you have three different INTEGER variables that you want to triple. You might write a program such as the following:

```
PROGRAM Triples (OUTPUT);
VAR first  : INTEGER;
    second : INTEGER;
    third  : INTEGER;

PROCEDURE TripleFirst;
BEGIN
    first := 3 * first
END;

PROCEDURE TripleSecond;
BEGIN
    second := 3 * second
END;

PROCEDURE TripleThird;
BEGIN
    third := 3 * third
END;
```

```
BEGIN
    first := 3;
    second := 6;
    third := 17;
    WRITELN ('Values before tripling are:', first, second, third);
    TripleFirst;
    TripleSecond;
    TripleThird;
    WRITELN ('Values after tripling are: ', first, second, third)
END.
```

There are two problems with this program. First, its procedures make non-local references. This is bad style, but there is a no way around it in this case (you will see why in a minute). Second, the three procedures are redundant. Each of them manipulates an object identically (i.e., it triples it). The only difference between the procedures is that they manipulate different objects.

To improve the situation, you must create a single procedure that has a generic name for the object to be manipulated. Then you execute the procedure three times, using different objects each time. Here is such a program:

```
PROGRAM Triples2 (OUTPUT);
VAR first  : INTEGER;
    second : INTEGER;
    third  : INTEGER;

PROCEDURE Triple (VAR number: INTEGER);
BEGIN
    number := 3 * number
END;

BEGIN
    first := 3;
    second := 6;
    third := 17;
    WRITELN ('Values before tripling are:', first, second, third);
    triple (first);
    triple (second);
    triple (third);
    WRITELN ('Values after tripling are: ', first, second, third)
END.
```

Look closely at the definition of procedure **triple**. It has a single parameter called **number**. The parameter name is preceded by the word "**VAR**." The **VAR** indicates that this is a **VAR** parameter and not a value parameter. The procedure is defined in terms of this generic parameter **number**. When the procedure is called, you name a variable to use as the specific parameter. This procedure call does not cause the creation of a new object. Instead, it binds the name **number** to the object being passed as a parameter.

Consider what happens when the program executes. You have three global variables that are allocated before execution begins:

first   `?`   second   `?`   third   `?`

The first three statements initialize these variables:

first   `3`   second   `6`   third   `17`

Next, you call the **triple** procedure using the variable **first** as the specific parameter. To set up the generic parameter **number**, you don't create a new object. Instead, you bind the name to an existing object, the variable **first**, so that **number** and **first** refer to the same variable:

number = first   `3`   second   `6`   third   `17`

Any changes to **number** change **first**. When the procedure triples **number**, you get

number = first   `9`   second   `6`   third   `17`

When the procedure is done executing, the local definition of **number** goes away:

first   `9`   second   `6`   third   `17`

On the second procedure call, you use the variable **second** as the specific parameter, thus **number** and **second** are synonymous:

first   `9`   number = second   `6`   third   `17`

When **number** is tripled, **second** is tripled. When the procedure is done executing, you have

first   `9`   second   `18`   third   `17`

In the final procedure call, **number** becomes synonymous with **third**, which is also tripled:

first   9   **second**   18   **third**   51

If you are naturally skeptical, which I hope most of you are, you should be asking "So what?" just about now. Obviously, the **VAR** parameter allows you to generalize tasks, but so did the value parameter. However, while the value parameter did allow you to generalize many tasks, it would prove inadequate to generalize this task.

Consider procedure **triple** above. A value goes into **triple**—the original value of the variable—and a value comes out of **triple**—the final value of the variable. The procedure is modifying an object. This is a case where you want the object to go in and out:

number

This is a very different use of an object than with the value parameter. Here, you have an object going into the procedure and coming out with a changed value. Remember, the value parameter, designed specifically to prevent this kind of two-way flow, manipulates local copies and has no effect on anything outside the procedure. The **VAR** parameter, then, gives you some power that you wouldn't have otherwise. It allows two-way flow.

5.2.1 The Other VAR Parameter Use

What if you want information to flow out of, but not into, a procedure, as is the case when you are initializing a variable? For example, to write a procedure that asks a user for an angle, you want this information flow:

angle

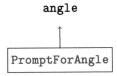

This procedure initializes a variable that stores an angle. The procedure does not use the initial value of the variable, so the value doesn't flow into the procedure. The only flow of information is the angle that comes back from the procedure.

You use the **VAR** parameter for this kind of information flow. Here is a simple program that demonstrates the use of such a procedure.

```
PROGRAM Angles (INPUT, OUTPUT);
VAR angle1 : REAL;
    angle2 : REAL;

PROCEDURE PromptForAngle (VAR angle: REAL);
BEGIN
    WRITE ('    Give me an angle in degrees ---> ');
    READLN (angle)
END;

BEGIN
    WRITELN ('This program will tell you the third angle of a');
    WRITELN ('triangle given the other two.');
    WRITELN;
    WRITELN ('Please input the first angle:');
    PromptForAngle (angle1);
    WRITELN ('Please input the second angle:');
    PromptForAngle (angle2);
    WRITELN;
    WRITELN ('The third angle is ', (180 - angle1 - angle2):1:2)
END.
```

The program would execute like this:

```
This program will tell you the third angle of a
triangle given the other two.

Please input the first angle:
    Give me an angle in degrees ---> 32.5
Please input the second angle:
    Give me an angle in degrees ---> 48.9

The third angle is  98.60
```

Let's trace this program's execution to make sure you understand it. The computer allocates space for two global variables before executing the program:

angle1 ?   angle2 ?

The first three **WRITELN** statements tell the user what is going on. The fourth asks the user to input the first angle. The next statement calls procedure **PromptForAngle** using **angle1** as the specific parameter. That means the computer sets up **angle** as follows:

angle = angle1   `?`   angle2   `?`

No value flows into the procedure because **angle1** is uninitialized. This will not cause an error, however, unless you try to manipulate this object before you initialize it. You obviously aren't going to do that because you immediately prompt the user for an angle and read the result into **angle**. If the user enters 32.5, this gives you

angle = angle1   `32.5`   angle2   `?`

Because they are synonymous as a result of the **VAR** parameter mechanism, when the computer changes **angle**, it also changes **angle1**. When this statement is done executing, you exit the procedure and eliminate the definition of **angle**:

angle1   `32.5`   angle2   `?`

The next statements tell the user that you want him to enter the second angle and call the **PromptForAngle** procedure again using **angle2** as the actual parameter:

angle1   `32.5`   angle = angle2   `?`

Again, no value flows into the procedure because the variable is uninitialized. You prompt the user for an angle and read the value into **angle2**:

angle1   `32.5`   angle = angle2   `48.9`

The procedure exits and the definition of **angle** goes away:

angle1   `32.5`   angle2   `48.9`

Finally, you report the answer to the user.

5.2.2   VAR versus Value

Now that you know two different parameters, you must distinguish between them when you write procedures. The distinction is easy to make if you consider the flow of information in your program. You can reduce manipulations on variables and values to one of four categories.

Information Flow	Task	Object to Use
None	Use a variable internally	Local variable
In	Use an external value	Value parameter
Out	Initialize an external variable	VAR parameter
In/Out	Modify an external variable	VAR parameter

The VAR parameter is in some sense more powerful than the value parameter because it can change variables outside the procedure. If you were to choose only one parameter, you would probably choose the VAR. FORTRAN, for example, has only VAR parameters.

The value parameter is useful, however. First, it allows you to pass expressions rather than variables as specific parameters. While it makes sense to say

```
DrawBox (10, 20);
DrawBox (2 + 2, 94 * 36);
```

it doesn't make sense to say

```
triple (15.95);
```

As noted earlier, the value parameter also protects the value of any objects passed to it. Finally, making the distinction between value and VAR parameters adds to the readability of the procedure. A person reading the header can more easily understand the intended flow of information.

There are two statements that you have learned that may elucidate this distinction. The WRITELN statement uses values passed to it, as is the case with the value parameter. It makes sense to say both

```
WRITELN (number);
WRITELN (2 + 2);
```

The READLN statement initializes variables and is therefore like the VAR parameter. The first example makes sense and the second does not:

```
READLN (number);
READLN (2 + 2);
```

Here is a summary of the differences between the two parameter types:

VAR Parameter	Value Parameter
VAR in declaration	No VAR in declaration
Must be passed a variable	Can be passed an expression
Local synonym for variable	Local copy of object
Used for output (initialize)	Used for input (utilize)
Used for input/output (modify)	
Like READLN	Like WRITELN

5.2.3 More on Parameter Syntax

Now that you know a second kind of parameter, let's see how it fits with your understanding of parameter syntax. Remember, the syntax of procedure and function headers is

```
PROCEDURE <name> (<formal parameters>);
FUNCTIOON <name> (<formal parameters>) : <type>;
```

This syntax is unchanged. The syntax of the formal parameters for each is

<formal parameter group>;
<formal parameter group>;
. . .
<formal parameter group>

This syntax is also unchanged.

At the next level, however, there is a difference. You indicate that a parameter group is a **VAR** parameter group by adding the word "**VAR**" at the beginning of the group and excluding it if it is a value parameter group. Here is that syntax:

[**VAR**] *<formal parameter list>* : *<type>*

The brackets around the word "**VAR**" indicate that it can either be there or not. The syntax of the parameter list is also unchanged:

<formal parameter>, *<formal parameter>*, ..., *<formal parameter>*

Each parameter group is of exactly one type (**INTEGER**, **REAL**, etc.) and of exactly one kind (**VAR** or value). You have to introduce a different parameter group for each different combination. For example, if you have four value parameters to define, two of type **REAL** and two of type **INTEGER**, you will need at least two parameter groups to define them since there are two types involved. Here is a sample procedure header:

```
PROCEDURE Fun (a, b : REAL;
               c, d : INTEGER);
```

If you want the parameters to have the types specified above, but you want the first parameter to be a **VAR** parameter and the rest to be value parameters, you will need at least three parameter groups:

Kind	Type	Parameter Group		
VAR	REAL	VAR	a	: REAL
Value	REAL		b	: REAL
Value	INTEGER		c, d	: INTEGER;

If you put this all together, you get

```
PROCEDURE Fun (VAR a    : REAL;
                   b    : REAL;
                   c, d : INTEGER);
```

If you want the INTEGER parameters to be VAR parameters, you add the word "VAR" at the beginning of the parameter group:

```
PROCEDURE Fun (VAR a    : REAL;
                   b    : REAL;
               VAR c, d : INTEGER);
```

This use of VAR is quite different from variable declarations, where you use the word "VAR" once no matter how many groups of variables are to be defined. In this case, the word "VAR" only applies to a single parameter group. Every parameter group that you want to be a VAR parameter group must be preceded by the word "VAR."

Any confusion lessens if you put only one parameter per group:

```
PROCEDURE Fun (VAR a : REAL;
                   b : REAL;
               VAR c : INTEGER;
               VAR d : INTEGER);
```

Putting one parameter per line and lining up the colons and the variable names make it easy to see the kinds and types of each parameter.

5.3 When to Use Functions

So far you have seen several functions. Consider the corresponding headers if you were to define them as procedures:

```
PROCEDURE ConvertFeet  (VAR miles   : REAL;
                            feet     : REAL);

PROCEDURE GetMinimum   (VAR minimum : REAL;
                            first    : REAL;
                            second   : REAL);

PROCEDURE GetFactorial (VAR factorial : INTEGER;
                            number     : INTEGER);
```

Notice the commonalities of these procedures. Each has a single VAR parameter. More specifically, each procedure has a single parameter whose information flow is out. In each case, the value parameters uniquely determine the VAR parameter. Using the black box paradigm, these procedures are boxes that have one or more values coming in and exactly one value coming out. For a given set of inputs, there is exactly one output:

inputs   output

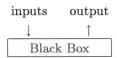

You can convert boxes that fit this criterion into functions. They are calculating boxes that calculate single results based on inputs and should be written as functions.

This matches the usual mathematical definition of a function. Mathematicians say that "y is a function of several variables" if there is a single y value for each set of values of the other variables.

Most of the functions you write, then, will have parameter lists that contain just value parameters.

5.4 Pseudorandom Number Tools

This section introduces tools that let you generate a sequence of pseudorandom numbers. The numbers are not entirely random because they are calculated using a well-defined algorithm and the sequence repeats itself. Anyone who examines the code or observes the sequence long enough can deduce the next number. However, in practice, as long as the algorithm is not known to the person using the program, the numbers will seem random.

The inner details of these tools are not simple to understand, but there is a brief description of them in Appendix A for those who are interested. One detail you do need to understand is that the tools for generating the random sequence depend on the use of an INTEGER variable known as a seed. You use a seed to determine the next number in the sequence. It is modified so that the next time a value is requested, a different number from the sequence will be returned. You have to give an initial value to this variable, usually by prompting the user for it; then you must pass it to the random number generator each time you request a new number. You must remember when you use these tools that you have to declare a seed variable and be sure to initialize it and pass it properly.

Here is the first tool, a procedure for obtaining a value for the seed.

```
PROCEDURE GetSeed (VAR seed: INTEGER);
(* This procedure prompts the user for a value to initialize seed. *)
BEGIN
    WRITELN ('I need an integer to seed the random number generator.');
    WRITE ('Give me a seed ---> ');
    READLN (seed);
    WRITELN
END;   (* GetSeed *)
```

You must call this tool before the others. Two other tools obtain pseudorandom values in a given range. One is for REAL numbers and one for INTEGERs:

```
FUNCTION Random (      low  : REAL;
                       high : REAL;
                  VAR seed : INTEGER) : REAL;
(* This function uses the provided seed to return a pseudorandom  *)
(* real such that low <= Random < high. Seed is modified so that  *)
(* the next call will provide a different result.                 *)
BEGIN
    seed := (29 * seed + 1) MOD 1024;
    random := (seed/1024) * (high - low) + low
END;   (* Random *)
```

```
FUNCTION RandomInt (     low  : INTEGER;
                         high : INTEGER;
                    VAR seed : INTEGER) : INTEGER;
(* This function uses the provided seed to return a pseudorandom *)
(* integer such that low <= Random <= high.  Seed is modified so *)
(* that the next call will provide a different result.           *)
BEGIN
    seed := (29 * seed + 1) MOD 1024;
    RandomInt := TRUNC ((seed/1024) * (high - low + 1)) + low
END;   (* RandomInt *)
```

Notice that random and RandomInt are functions. You intuitively think of them as values, and thus it is natural to think of a "random-value expression" rather than a "getting a random value action." For example, it makes sense to calculate a random sum of three numbers by saying

```
sum := random (seed) + random (seed) + random (seed);
```

instead of saying:

```
GetRandom (seed, num1);
GetRandom (seed, num2);
GetRandom (seed, num3);
sum := num1 + num2 + num3;
```

Nevertheless, random and RandomInt are unorthodox functions in that they have a VAR parameter. While the usual situation is for a function to have all value parameters, these functions have a VAR parameter because the value of seed must be updated each time. This is an example of a function with a side effect. The side effect is that seed is set to the next value in the sequence. You should, in general, try to avoid such side effects, but in this case, the side effect is not as important as the intuition about `random` and `RandomInt` as values and not actions.

5.5   The Engineering of Good Procedures

My sister once bought an all-in-one stereo set that had a radio, tape player, record player, and speakers in one box. It was easy to use, but not very adaptable. She could use it for only one thing at a time. She wasn't able to loan me the tape player without giving me everything else. Pulling out the tape player would have meant ripping apart a huge mass of wires and other electronic parts. When I did rip out the tape player, after my sister had abandoned the system for something better, all the other parts of the stereo were permanently disabled.

The better system my sister bought was a component stereo. It was more complicated to use, but more adaptable. Setting it up took time, because we had to figure out how to make the various components fit together. We found that we could fit them together in different ways, however, to produce different results. This is typical of a well-engineered set of components. They are more adaptable, but their interconnections are more complex.

The all-in-one stereo is like a program that is not well-engineered. It might perform its overall task, but it isn't easily separated into distinct components that can be used in different ways. A component stereo system is like a well-engineered program, where each procedure is a powerful component.

Some of the properties of a well-designed stereo component correspond to those of a well-designed procedure. A good stereo component is a black box that doesn't need to be opened up to be used. It needs only to be connected properly and switched on. Well-designed procedures are similar. To use one, you simply connect it properly with parameters and let it execute. Your goal for a procedure is to design a box that you can easily pull out of one program and fit into another.

A stereo component should not have stray wires sticking out of it that connect to other parts of the system. Some interconnection is necessary, but most wires should be housed inside a chassis so that the user doesn't have to fiddle with its innards. Nonlocal references used by procedures are like stray wires. To pull out a procedure that uses global variables, for example, you must bring along the global variables it uses. Localizing variables is like putting things inside a chassis. The user doesn't even have to know that there are local variables, because they are invisible from the outside. Therefore, you should put as many of the details as possible inside the box by using local variables.

Even so, most boxes are not totally self-contained. A loudspeaker, for example, requires a signal as input to perform its task. On a well-designed loudspeaker there is a place to plug in a cable for input. The plug should not be buried inside the box, it should be on the outside. Parameters provide this functionality for procedures. They are outside the box; they appear in the procedure header, not within it. When a procedure requires something that comes from the outside, or when it produces a result that needs to go out of the box for use elsewhere, you should use parameters. These parameters provide the interface between the procedure and other parts of the program.

If you keep this analogy in mind, you should easily be able to decide when to use a parameter and when to use a local variable. A parameter, like a plug, indicates that the object is not inside the box, that it comes from elsewhere. Local variables are the opposite; they indicate that the object is inside the box. Local variables are like the innards of stereo components. When a procedure declares a local variable, it makes a statement of ownership. It says, "This object belongs to me. I am responsible for all manipulations on it, and I will initialize it and utilize it. This object's lifetime is the same as mine: it will serve its complete purpose during my execution." A parameter declaration is a statement of manipulation, not ownership. It says, "I don't own this object. It is controlled by some other part of the program. However, if I am provided one, I will manipulate it in a certain way."

Plugs make stereo components more difficult to fit together, because the user has to figure out what goes where. Parameters make procedures more difficult to call, because the user has to figure out what to include in the procedure call. Every plug in a well-engineered stereo system has a reason for being there and adds to the versatility of the system. Every parameter in a well-engineered procedure also has a reason for being there and should add to the versatility of the procedure.

5.5.1 Examples of Good and Bad Engineering

The following program performs a simple task. It is a banking program that lets a customer perform a series of deposit and withdrawal transactions. It is not a well-engineered program. You will note many of the problems discussed previously. An examination of how to fix these problems follows.

```
(* This is a simple banking program that prompts the user for a series *)
(* of deposit/withdrawal transactions and keeps track of the balance.  *)

PROGRAM Banking (INPUT, OUTPUT);
VAR balance     : REAL;     (* customer's current balance         *)
    amount      : REAL;     (* amount of next transaction         *)
    transaction : INTEGER;  (* which transaction (1 or 2)         *)
    HowMany     : INTEGER;  (* number of transactions to perform  *)
    count       : INTEGER;  (* loop counter                       *)
```

```
PROCEDURE GiveIntroduction;
(* Explains the program to the user. *)
BEGIN
    WRITELN ('This is a simple banking program that will perform a');
    WRITELN ('series of transactions for you.  Transactions are either');
    WRITELN ('deposits or withdrawals.  I will keep track of the current');
    WRITELN ('balance as you perform these various operations.  I will');
    WRITELN ('ask you to enter a 1 for a deposit and a 2 for a withdrawal.');
    WRITELN
END;   (* GiveIntroduction *)


PROCEDURE InitializeVariables;
(* Initializes the number of transactions and starting balance. *)
BEGIN
    WRITE ('How many transactions would you like to perform? ');
    READLN (HowMany);
    WRITE ('What is the starting balance? ');
    READLN (balance);
    WRITELN
END;   (* InitializeVariables *)


PROCEDURE Deposit;
(* Prompts for an amount to deposit and adds that amount to balance. *)
BEGIN
    WRITE ('    amount ---> ');
    READLN (amount);
    balance := balance + amount
END;   (* Deposit *)

PROCEDURE Withdraw;
(* Prompts for an amount to withdraw and deducts that amount from *)
(* balance.  If insufficient funds, an error is reported instead. *)
BEGIN
    WRITE ('    amount ---> ');
    READLN (amount);
    IF amount <= balance THEN
        balance := balance - amount
    ELSE
        WRITELN ('    insufficient funds, unable to withdraw that much.')
END;   (* Withdraw *)
```

```
PROCEDURE PerformTransaction;
(* Prompts for which transaction the customer wishes to perform and *)
(* carries out that transaction.                                    *)
BEGIN
    WRITE ('   transaction (1 = deposit, 2 = withdrawal) ---> ');
    READLN (transaction);
    IF transaction = 1 THEN
        deposit
    ELSE
        withdraw;
    WRITELN
END;    (* PerformTransaction *)


PROCEDURE SayGoodBye;
(* Reports final balance. *)
BEGIN
    WRITELN ('Nice doing business with you.');
    WRITELN ('Final balance = $', balance:1:2, '.')
END;    (* SayGoodBye *)


BEGIN    (* main program *)
    GiveIntroduction;
    InitializeVariables;
    FOR count := 1 TO HowMany DO
        PerformTransaction;
    SayGoodbye
END.    (* main program *)
```

To understand the program better, here is a sample of its execution:

```
This is a simple banking program that will perform a
series of transactions for you.  Transactions are either
deposits or withdrawals.  I will keep track of the current
balance as you perform these various operations.  I will
ask you to enter a 1 for a deposit and a 2 for a withdrawal.

How many transactions would you like to perform? 4
What is the starting balance? 234.98

    transaction (1 = deposit, 2 = withdrawal) ---> 1
    amount ---> 29.34

    transaction (1 = deposit, 2 = withdrawal) ---> 2
    amount ---> 185.42
```

```
transaction (1 = deposit, 2 = withdrawal) ---> 2
amount ---> 304.85
insufficient funds, unable to withdraw that much.

transaction (1 = deposit, 2 = withdrawal) ---> 1
amount ---> 607.42
```

```
Nice doing business with you.
Final balance = $ 686.32.
```

The problem with this program is that it uses three global variables: `balance`, `amount`, and `transaction`. You should either localize them (put them inside a box) or parameterize them (make a plug for them).

You can easily fix `transaction`. Because you use it only in procedure `PerformTransaction`, you can make it local to that procedure.

You use both `amount` and `balance` in more than one procedure. You can localize one and not the other. To understand why, consider the following analogy. Suppose you want to have 20 people sign a birthday card. To do so, each person needs a pen. You could have 1 pen for everyone to use (this is the case of no localizing, everyone sharing the same object), or you could have 20 pens (each individual having his own "local" pen to sign the card). However, you cannot have 20 cards. The card cannot be localized, because it must be signed (manipulated) by 20 people.

The variable `amount` is like the pen. If you look at the `deposit` and `withdraw` procedures, you will notice that the variable `amount` in each procedure is initialized and used completely within the procedure. Its initial value doesn't come from the outside, and there is no reason why its ending value needs to be kept. Therefore, you can localize it within each procedure.

The variable `balance` is like the card. It cannot be localized because the value manipulated by `deposit` must be shared with the value manipulated by `withdraw`. The banking program will not be representative of the real world if deposits and withdrawals aren't remembered. `Balance` is the sum of all the individual transactions, so each transaction has to act on a single balance variable.

Because you cannot localize `balance`, you should ask, "Who owns it? Who should take responsibility for it?" Looking at the main program, you will see that it initializes `balance` and manipulates it through successive calls on `Perform-Transaction`. Thus the main program must take responsibility for `balance`. `Balance` will have to be a global variable. But that doesn't mean you have to use it in a sloppy manner. You don't have to bury references to `balance` inside procedures; you can parameterize them instead, building plugs for them.

Because the `deposit` and `withdraw` procedures modify the balance, it needs to flow in and out. This is a perfect application for a `VAR` parameter:

```
PROCEDURE Deposit (VAR balance: REAL);
VAR amount : REAL;
BEGIN
    WRITE ('    amount ---> ');
    READLN (amount);
    balance := balance + amount
END;
```

This differs from the first version because it has a local variable, **amount**, and a **VAR** parameter, **balance**. Because **balance** is defined as a parameter in the procedure header, the reference to it in the procedure body is a local reference to the parameter, not a nonlocal reference to the global variable. Using the analogy, there is no longer a stray wire connecting the inside of this box to the global variable. This internal wire is connected to a plug (the parameter), and the global variable is attached to the procedure through the plug. The changes to procedure **withdraw** are almost identical.

Notice that procedures **InitializeVariables** and **SayGoodbye** also use **balance**. The first gives an initial value to the variable; the second reports its final value. Thus the first is a natural **VAR** parameter application; the second is a natural value parameter application. In fact, the different manipulations of **balance** show all the typical parameter-passing situations.

Procedure	Task	Information Flow	Parameter
InitializeVariables	Initialize	Out	VAR
Deposit	Modify	In/out	VAR
Withdraw	Modify	In/out	VAR
SayGoodBye	Use	In	Value

You still aren't done. The structure diagram of the program should make this clear:

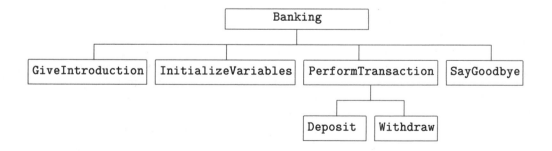

The `deposit` and `withdraw` procedures manipulate `balance`, but `balance` is controlled by the main program. You have parameterized both these low-level procedures, but procedure `PerformTransaction` is in the middle. This is a very common information-flow situation. The answer is to parameterize `PerformTransaction`, building a plug into it so that the global variable can be connected to it. `PerformTransaction` can then plug this parameter into the two low-level procedures. Thus the global variable gets passed two levels down. `Balance` is a `VAR` parameter to this procedure, for the same reason that it is a `VAR` parameter to `deposit` and `withdraw`. The value needs to flow in and out of `PerformTransaction` so the effect of a transaction is remembered.

Here, then, is the fully parameterized and localized version of the `banking` program, the well-engineered solution:

```
(* This is a simple banking program that prompts the user for a series *)
(* of deposit/withdrawal transactions and keeps track of the balance.  *)

PROGRAM Banking2 (INPUT, OUTPUT);
VAR balance     : REAL;      (* customer's current balance           *)
    HowMany     : INTEGER;   (* number of transactions to perform *)
    count       : INTEGER;   (* loop counter                         *)

PROCEDURE GiveIntroduction;
(* Explains the program to the user. *)
BEGIN
    WRITELN ('This is a simple banking program that will perform a');
    WRITELN ('series of transactions for you.  Transactions are either');
    WRITELN ('deposits or withdrawals.  I will keep track of the current');
    WRITELN ('balance as you perform these various operations.  I will');
    WRITELN ('ask you to enter a 1 for a deposit and a 2 for a withdrawal.');
    WRITELN
END;    (* GiveIntroduction *)

PROCEDURE InitializeVariables (VAR HowMany : INTEGER;
                               VAR balance : REAL);
(* Initializes the number of transactions and starting balance. *)
BEGIN
    WRITE ('How many transactions would you like to perform? ');
    READLN (HowMany);
    WRITE ('What is the starting balance? ');
    READLN (balance);
    WRITELN
END;    (* InitializeVariables *)
```

```
PROCEDURE Deposit (VAR balance : REAL);
(* Prompts for an amount to deposit and adds that amount to balance. *)
VAR amount : REAL;    (* amount of next transaction *)
BEGIN
    WRITE ('    amount ---> ');
    READLN (amount);
    balance := balance + amount
END;    (* Deposit *)


PROCEDURE Withdraw (VAR balance: REAL);
(* Prompts for an amount to withdraw and deducts that amount from *)
(* balance.  If insufficient funds, an error is reported instead. *)
VAR amount : REAL;    (* amount of next transaction *)
BEGIN
    WRITE ('    amount ---> ');
    READLN (amount);
    IF amount <= balance THEN
        balance := balance - amount
    ELSE
        WRITELN ('    insufficient funds, unable to withdraw that much.')
END;    (* Withdraw *)


PROCEDURE PerformTransaction (VAR balance: REAL);
(* Prompts for which transaction the customer wishes to perform and *)
(* carries out that transaction.                                     *)
VAR transaction : INTEGER;    (* which transaction (1 or 2) *)
BEGIN
    WRITE ('    transaction (1 = deposit, 2 = withdrawal) ---> ');
    READLN (transaction);
    IF transaction = 1 THEN
        deposit (balance)
    ELSE
        withdraw (balance);
    WRITELN
END;    (* PerformTransaction *)


PROCEDURE SayGoodBye (balance : REAL);
(* Reports final balance. *)
BEGIN
    WRITELN ('Nice doing business with you.');
    WRITELN ('Final balance = $', balance:1:2, '.')
END;    (* SayGoodBye *)
```

```
BEGIN   (* main program *)
    GiveIntroduction;
    InitializeVariables (HowMany, balance);
    FOR count := 1 TO HowMany DO
        PerformTransaction (balance);
    SayGoodbye (balance)
END.    (* main program *)
```

Notice that the procedure `InitializeVariables` has two parameters of differing types, so it has two parameter groups. The word "VAR" must appear at the beginning of each to make the parameter a `VAR` parameter.

5.5.2 Power of Good Design

In the last section you went to great lengths to engineer a good solution to the banking program. You might wonder what that gains you. The answer is power.

What if you want to modify the banking task to deal with more than one customer? This will involve keeping track of more than one balance. The first version of the banking program that made numerous nonlocal references to `balance` would be difficult to modify for more than one balance because of all the stray connections to the single global variable.

Fortunately, the parameters make modifications simple. The parameter **balance** in your procedures acts as a plug for any balance variable. More specifically, any variable of type `REAL` can be passed as the specific parameter. You can write a new program with two variables: `balance1` and `balance2`. Using the parameter, you can plug in whichever variable you want to. If you have done a good job of engineering, you won't have to modify the black boxes which perform the transactions. The procedures here are, in fact, designed well enough to do this. The only procedures that you need to change are `GiveIntroduction`, `InitializeVariables`, and `SayGoodBye`.

Here is a solution to the banking program with two customers:

```
(* This is a simple banking program that prompts two users for a series  *)
(* of deposit/withdrawal transactions and keeps track of their balances.  *)

PROGRAM Banking3 (INPUT, OUTPUT);
VAR balance1 : REAL;        (* customer #1's current balance        *)
    balance2 : REAL;        (* customer #2's current balance        *)
    HowMany  : INTEGER;     (* number of transactions to perform    *)
    count    : INTEGER;     (* loop counter                         *)
```

```
PROCEDURE GiveIntroduction;
(* Explains the program to the user. *)
BEGIN
    WRITELN ('This is a simple banking program that will perform a');
    WRITELN ('series of transactions for two customers.  Transactions');
    WRITELN ('are either deposits or withdrawals.  I will keep track of');
    WRITELN ('the current balances as you perform these various');
    WRITELN ('operations.  I will ask you to enter the customer number');
    WRITELN ('(either 1 or 2) and a 1 for deposit, 2 for withdrawal.');
    WRITELN
END;   (* GiveIntroduction *)

PROCEDURE InitializeVariables (VAR HowMany  : INTEGER;
                               VAR balance1 : REAL;
                               VAR balance2 : REAL);
(* Initializes the number of transactions and starting balances. *)
BEGIN
    WRITE ('How many transactions would you like to perform? ');
    READLN (HowMany);
    WRITE ('What is the starting balance for customer #1? ');
    READLN (balance1);
    WRITE ('What is the starting balance for customer #2? ');
    READLN (balance2);
    WRITELN
END;   (* InitializeVariables *)

PROCEDURE Deposit (VAR balance : REAL);
(* Prompts for an amount to deposit and adds that amount to balance. *)
VAR amount : REAL;   (* amount of next transaction *)
BEGIN
    WRITE ('    amount ---> ');
    READLN (amount);
    balance := balance + amount
END;   (* Deposit *)

PROCEDURE Withdraw (VAR balance: REAL);
(* Prompts for an amount to withdraw and deducts that amount from *)
(* balance.  If insufficient funds, an error is reported instead. *)
VAR amount : REAL;   (* amount of next transaction *)
BEGIN
    WRITE ('    amount ---> ');
    READLN (amount);
    balance := balance - amount
END;   (* Withdraw *)
```

```
PROCEDURE PerformTransaction (VAR balance: REAL);
(* Prompts for which transaction the customer wishes to perform and *)
(* carries out that transaction.                                    *)
VAR transaction : INTEGER;    (* which transaction (1 or 2) *)
BEGIN
    WRITE ('   transaction (1 = deposit, 2 = withdrawal) ---> ');
    READLN (transaction);
    IF transaction = 1 THEN
        deposit (balance)
    ELSE
        withdraw (balance);
    WRITELN
END;    (* PerformTransaction *)


PROCEDURE HelpOneCustomer (VAR balance1 : REAL;
                           VAR balance2 : REAL);
(* prompts for customer number and performs a transaction. *)
VAR customer : INTEGER;    (* Which customer for this transaction *)
BEGIN
    WRITE ('   which customer? ');
    READLN (customer);
    IF customer = 1 THEN
        PerformTransaction (balance1)
    ELSE
        PerformTransaction (balance2)
END;    (* HelpOneCustomer *)


PROCEDURE SayGoodBye (balance1 : REAL;
                      balance2 : REAL);
(* Reports final balances. *)
BEGIN
    WRITELN ('Nice doing business with you.');
    WRITELN ('Customer #1, final balance = $', balance1:1:2, '.');
    WRITELN ('Customer #2, final balance = $', balance2:1:2, '.')
END;    (* SayGoodBye *)


BEGIN    (* main program *)
    GiveIntroduction;
    InitializeVariables (HowMany, balance1, balance2);
    FOR count := 1 TO HowMany DO
        HelpOneCustomer (balance1, balance2);
    SayGoodbye (balance1, balance2)
END.    (* main program *)
```

Notice that `PerformTransaction`, `Deposit`, and `Withdraw` are unchanged because of the parameters and local variables.

To make sure you understand this version of the program, examine this sample execution.

```
This is a simple banking program that will perform a
series of transactions for two customers.  Transactions
are either deposits or withdrawals.  I will keep track of
the current balances as you perform these various
operations.  I will ask you to enter the customer number
(either 1 or 2) and a 1 for deposit, 2 for withdrawal.

How many transactions would you like to perform? 5
What is the starting balance for customer #1? 12.45
What is the starting balance for customer #2? 3092.34

    which customer? 1
    transaction (1 = deposit, 2 = withdrawal) ---> 2
    amount ---> 11.29

    which customer? 2
    transaction (1 = deposit, 2 = withdrawal) ---> 2
    amount ---> 1098.45

    which customer? 2
    transaction (1 = deposit, 2 = withdrawal) ---> 2
    amount ---> 1845.23

    which customer? 1
    transaction (1 = deposit, 2 = withdrawal) ---> 1
    amount ---> 245.98

    which customer? 2
    transaction (1 = deposit, 2 = withdrawal) ---> 1
    amount ---> 204.32

Nice doing business with you.
Customer #1, final balance = $ 247.14.
Customer #2, final balance = $ 352.98.
```

5.6 *Terminology of Decomposition*

Before you begin reading the discussion of decomposition strategies, you must understand some decomposition terminology.

Communication between subtasks is the sharing of information from one subtask to another. This sharing is usually accomplished using parameters, although it can also be accomplished using global variables or global constants. A good example of this is evident in the following structure diagram. The `WriteWord` task is supposed to write out the word read in by the `ReadWord` task. To do this, there must be communication between the procedures. It isn't possible for each procedure to declare its own local word variable. Therefore, each procedure manipulates the word variable as a parameter, and the word variable itself is controlled by some other procedure.

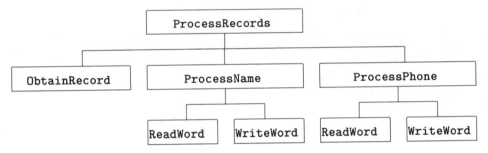

The *owner of an object* is the task or subtask that causes an object to be allocated. The owner of a global variable is the main program. The owner of a local variable is the procedure that declares it. When procedures such as `ReadWord` and `WriteWord` must share a variable, the variable is owned by some higher-level task. For example, `ProcessName` can declare a word variable and can pass it as a parameter to the `ReadWord` and `WriteWord` procedures. Thus `ProcessName` can own the word variable and can establish the communication between `ReadWord` and `WriteWord`. Similarly, `ProcessPhone` can own a different word variable that is passed as a parameter to `ReadWord` and `WriteWord`. Another alternative is to have the main program own a word variable that is passed as a parameter to both `ProcessName` and `ProcessPhone`. These two procedures can then pass on the word variable to the low-level procedures. This way there would only be one word variable owned by the main program. However, as you will see, this isn't a very good idea.

This points out an important relationship between ownership and communication. In general, the need for communication limits the possibility of ownership. In the case of `ReadWord` and `WriteWord`, for example, because the word variable has to be communicated from one to the other, it can't be owned by either (i.e., it can't be declared as a local variable in either).

5.6.1 What Is a Good Decomposition?

To examine what constitutes a good decomposition is difficult. The concept is often vague and the techniques often elusive. Talking about a good decomposition is like talking about a good marriage. It isn't easy to define what one is or how a person gets one. It is usually easier to talk about what it isn't rather than what it is. Nevertheless, some guidance in this area is presented here.

You will understand decomposition better if you recognize that it is not something specific to computer science or computer programs. Decomposition is something that many people do. A corporate manager makes decisions about how to divide the corporation into divisions and how those divisions are to interact. A curriculum expert looks at "that which is knowable" and divides it up into discrete subject areas, courses, and curricula. A grocery store owner plans the layout of merchandise so that different items are grouped together into sections and aisles that have an element of unity. Each of these people is applying decomposition techniques, and many of the properties each looks for are the same. An explanation of some of these properties and how they relate to programming follows.

Compare the program decomposition discussed earlier with this organizational chart of a business:

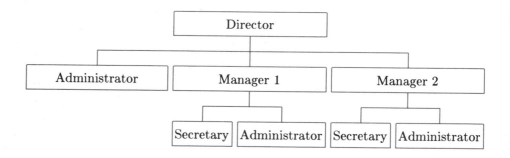

Just as the earlier task is divided into three subtasks, this organization is divided into three departments. Two of the departments are overseen by a manager and are further divided into a secretary and administrator.

As you study the various rules of a good decomposition, remember that they are not independent of each other. If a program is missing one of these properties, it will tend to miss the others as well. By discussing the properties separately, you can see the general goals to strive for.

RULE ONE OF A GOOD DECOMPOSITION

The responsibilities of different subtasks should be clearly delineated.

In the business analogy, each department must have a clear idea of what its part of the whole is. Disasters occur when two or more departments claim responsibility for a job or when no department claims responsibility for a job.

In programming, a clear delineation implies that there is no confusion about which subtask is responsible for which part of the overall task. For example, if you are creating subtasks to process a complex input, you should know exactly which subtask will process each part of the input. Ideally, there will be no crossover of responsibilities between subtasks and no responsibilities that are left uncovered.

RULE TWO OF A GOOD DECOMPOSITION
Communication between subtasks should be minimal.

In the business analogy, this means that staff members should not have to rely on other staff members to get their work done. As much as possible, each staff member should operate independently, and dependencies should exist only when they are absolutely necessary. This minimizes possible conflicts and makes each piece of the whole run more smoothly.

In programming, subtasks communicate through parameters. Consider a main program decomposed two different ways, each time into three procedures. Suppose that no global variables or global constants are used in either program, but that the first decomposition passes no variables as parameters and the second passes 10 parameters for each procedure. You can conclude that the second has more communication than the first. This means the procedures in the second program are more dependent on each other because they must pass many variables back and forth. It also means that the main program must control all the variables and establish the communication between procedures. Dealing with excessive communication requires much concentration on the programmer's part. This diminishes the concentration given other aspects of decomposition. It also leads to programs that are more difficult to modify and subtasks that are not easily adapted to new tasks. Excessive communication is symptomatic of subtasks that have not been clearly delineated.

RULE THREE OF A GOOD DECOMPOSITION
Objects should be owned at the lowest possible level.

Using the business analogy, this means that decisions should be made at the lowest possible level in the organizational chart. This is a simple rule. It implies that individuals should be allowed to make their own decisions whenever possible and shouldn't have to consult with a higher authority. Some decisions, however, can't be made individually. If the secretary and administrator who work for manager 1 have a dispute, neither should make the final decision. The decision should belong to a higher authority, the manager. The decision should not be bumped higher unless it is absolutely necessary. In other words, you don't bother the boss unless you have to—you deal with the lowest-level person you can.

Consider the application of this principle to programs. Its immediate implication is that you should use local variables whenever possible. If a procedure is manipulating a variable, it can't possibly be owned any lower than in the procedure itself. Declaring it locally satisfies the criterion that it be declared as low as possible. This is like allowing staff members to make their own decisions whenever possible.

However, it is not always possible to declare variables locally. You saw an example of this earlier in the discussion of what task or subtask should own the word variable used to process the name and phone of a record. You saw that `ReadWord` and `WriteWord` couldn't own the word variable because they need to communicate the value between themselves. One possibility was to have `ProcessName` and `ProcessPhone` each own a word variable that is passed as a parameter to `ReadWord`/`WriteWord`:

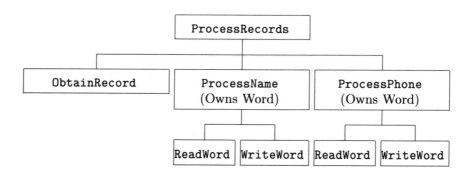

This solution is the best you can do by the preceding criterion, given that `ReadWord` and `WriteWord` can't own the variables. This is like having managers settle the disputes between their own staff members.

Another possibility is to have the main program own the word variable and have it pass it to `ProcessName` and `ProcessPhone`, which in turn pass it to `ReadWord` and `WriteWord`:

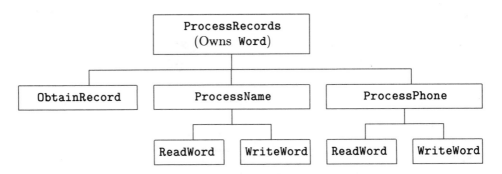

Given the simple rule that objects should be owned at the lowest possible level, this is a bad idea. It's like having the director settle disputes that the managers can handle. It increases the parameter passing between the main program and `ProcessName/ProcessPhone`, which will make the main program more difficult to manage. It makes `ProcessName` and `ProcessPhone` less independent, which means they will be more difficult to adapt to new tasks. In addition, it introduces a possibility of interference between `ProcessName` and `ProcessPhone` when there was no such possibility before. In short, it complicates the program tremendously and gains nothing for you.

RULE FOUR OF A GOOD DECOMPOSITION

The distance in the structure diagram between the owner of each object and the manipulator(s) of that object should be minimal.

Using the business analogy, this means the distance in the organizational chart between someone making a decision and someone significantly influencing a decision should be minimal. Each decision has a natural level at which it should be made. Corporate executives decide whether or not to launch a new product line or approve a merger without consulting many low-level staff members. They only consult with the next level or two in order to make such a decision. Without this freedom, the corporate executive would be unable to make important decisions.

Distance in the structure diagram means the number of levels of subtasks. This is a great distance:

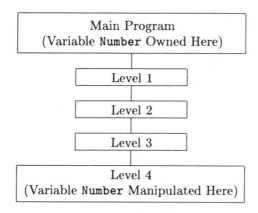

The distance between the ownership of **number** in the main program and the manipulation of **number** at level 4 is great. In a program, each variable has a natural level at which it should be owned and manipulated. A situation such as the one above causes many problems. First, the variable **number** would have to be passed as a parameter through all four levels, or it would have to be declared as a global variable. You want neither. Second, this leads to an extremely low-level procedure manipulating a high-level variable. This is usually inappropriate. It is like a corporation letting a filing clerk decide whether or not to release a new product line. This decomposition defect is usually symptomatic of one of two problems. Either the low-level procedure is not really low-level, or the high-level object **number** is not high-level.

5.7 A Complex Interactive Program

Let's examine a complex interactive program that uses most of the language features and tools covered in the last two chapters. Consider a program that plays roulette with the user. To get an idea of how it works, examine the following log of execution.

```
I am going to let you play some roulette.  The game works this
way.  The roulette wheel has numbers on it ranging from 0 to
36.  I will spin the wheel as many times as you tell me to and
will let you bet each time on what number will come up.
Before I spin, I will ask you to make a bet.  You will tell me
how much to bet and what to bet on.  There are three kinds of
bets.  You can bet on whether the number is odd or even;
whether the number is high or low (low means between 1 and 18
and high means between 19 and 36); or that a specific number will
come up.  If you win odd/even or high/low, you get even money
($1 for every $1 you bet).  If you win on a specific number,
```

you win 36 times your bet ($36 for every $1 you bet). If a 0
comes up on the wheel, you automatically lose. You start out
with $1000. Good luck.

How many spins do you want today? 6

I need an integer to seed the random number generator.
Give me a seed ---> 942

How much of your $1000 do you want to bet? 100
Category (1 = odd/even, 2 = high/low, 3 = a specific number)? 1
And which do you want (1 = odd, 2 = even)? 2
Around and around and around it goes. And it lands on . . . number 25
Sorry, you lose.

How much of your $900 do you want to bet? 200
Category (1 = odd/even, 2 = high/low, 3 = a specific number)? 2
And which do you want (1 = high, 2 = low)? 1
Around and around and around it goes. And it lands on . . . number 25
Congratulations, you win!

How much of your $1100 do you want to bet? 200
Category (1 = odd/even, 2 = high/low, 3 = a specific number)? 1
And which do you want (1 = odd, 2 = even)? 1
Around and around and around it goes. And it lands on . . . number 30
Sorry, you lose.

How much of your $900 do you want to bet? 400
Category (1 = odd/even, 2 = high/low, 3 = a specific number)? 1
And which do you want (1 = odd, 2 = even)? 1
Around and around and around it goes. And it lands on . . . number 34
Sorry, you lose.

How much of your $500 do you want to bet? 300
Category (1 = odd/even, 2 = high/low, 3 = a specific number)? 2
And which do you want (1 = high, 2 = low)? 1
Around and around and around it goes. And it lands on . . . number 0
Sorry, you lose.

How much of your $200 do you want to bet? 200
Category (1 = odd/even, 2 = high/low, 3 = a specific number)? 1
And which do you want (1 = odd, 2 = even)? 2
Around and around and around it goes. And it lands on . . . number 19
Sorry, you lose.

```
You ended up with $0.
I guess you're just too cool for this game, dude.
```

There is not enough space to develop the program in detail, but a discussion of some of its critical points follows. Most of the pieces of this program are either very simple or already developed. To simulate the spinning of a roulette wheel, for example, you use the `RandomInt` function to return a random value between 0 and 36. This means you need to call up `GetSeed` at some point to initialize the seed variable.

The most difficult part of this program is the code that takes a bet and evaluates the result. One way to represent a bet is to store it as two different integers: one to describe the category of bet (`category`) and one to describe the specific bet being made (`value`). The following table explains the conventions:

Kind of Bet	Category	Value
Odd/even	1	1 for odd, 2 for even
High/low	2	1 for high, 2 for low
Specific number	3	Whatever number is being bet on

To prompt the user for a bet, you have to obtain a value for both `category` and `value`. Because you want to obtain the category first, you ask a simple question and read a simple answer:

```
WRITE ('Category (1 = odd/even, 2 = high/low, 3 = a specific number)? ');
READLN (category);
```

The prompt to the user explains the encoding scheme. Then you prompt for `value`. The prompt is different for each category, but the reading is always the same. Thus you can bottom factor out the reading. This leads to the pseudocode

Give one of three prompts, depending upon value of category.
Read value.

This is easily translated into Pascal:

```
IF category = 1 THEN
    WRITE ('And which do you want (1 = odd, 2 = even)? ')

ELSE
    IF category = 2 THEN
        WRITE ('And which do you want (1 = high, 2 = low)? ')
    ELSE
        WRITE ('And what number do you want? ');
READLN (value)
```

Putting these two together, you have the basic routine for prompting the user for a bet. Next is the problem of figuring whether the user wins or loses. A nested IF/THEN/ELSE is very useful here. You start by distinguishing four cases: the case where everyone loses because the spin is 0 and the three different cases that depend on what category the user bet on:

```
IF (spin = 0) THEN
    <user loses>
ELSE
    IF (category = 1) THEN
        <evaluate category 1>
    ELSE
        IF (category = 2) THEN
            <evaluate category 2>
        ELSE
            <evaluate category 3>
```

Each of the three category evaluations requires an IF/THEN/ELSE that distinguishes between winning and losing. Because there are many ways to win and many ways to lose, you should create some procedures that take care of each. Call them YouWin and YouLose. You should also create a third procedure, YouWinBig, to take care of a win in the third category, where the user is paid 36 times the bet.

Once you write these simple procedures, you can set about evaluating each category. The expression (spin MOD 2 + 1) is handy for deciding wins and losses for category 1. Remember that MOD gives the remainder of integer division. Therefore, this expression will be 1 for even numbers (when the remainder of division by 2 is 0) and will be 2 for odd numbers (when the remainder is 1). The variable value is 1 when the user is betting on odds and 2 when betting on evens, so the user wins when the bet is not equal to this expression and loses when it is equal:

```
IF (value = spin MOD 2 + 1) THEN
    <user loses>
ELSE
    <user wins>
```

You can form a similar IF/THEN/ELSE using the expression (spin DIV 19 + 1) for category 2. Since DIV performs truncated division, this expression will return 1 when spin is between 1 and 18 (i.e., when it is low) and will return 2 when it is between 19 and 37 (i.e., when it is high). The user is betting 1 for high and 2 for low, so again the user wins when the variable value is not equal to this expression:

```
IF (value = spin DIV 19 + 1) THEN
    <user loses>
ELSE
    <user wins>
```

For category 3 the test is easier because the user is betting on a specific number. The user wins if **value** equals **spin** and loses otherwise:

```
IF (value = spin) THEN
ELSE
```

These three tests complete the procedure for evaluating the result of one spin. The rest of the program is straightforward:

```
(* This program plays the game of roulette with a user.  See procedure *)
(* GiveIntro for more details.                                         *)

PROGRAM Roulette (INPUT, OUTPUT);
CONST high        = 36;        (* high number on roulette wheel   *)
      mid         = 19;        (* should equal (high DIV 2) + 1.  *)
      StartingMoney = 1000;    (* how much money user starts with *)
VAR   seed        : INTEGER;   (* used for pseudorandom numbers   *)
      count       : INTEGER;   (* loop counter for spins          *)
      money       : INTEGER;   (* how much money user has now     *)
      NumSpins    : INTEGER;   (* number of spins user wants      *)

PROCEDURE GiveIntro;
(* This procedure introduces the program to the user. *)
BEGIN
    WRITELN ('I am going to let you play some roulette.  The game works this');
    WRITELN ('way.  The roulette wheel has numbers on it ranging from 0 to');
    WRITELN (high:1, '.  I will spin the wheel as many times as you tell me',
             ' to and');
    WRITELN ('will let you bet each time on what number will come up.');
    WRITELN ('Before I spin, I will ask you to make a bet.  You will tell me');
    WRITELN ('how much to bet and what to bet on.  There are three kinds of');
    WRITELN ('bets.  You can bet on whether the number is odd or even;');
    WRITELN ('whether the number is high or low (low means between 1 and ',
             (mid - 1):1);
    WRITELN ('and high means between ', mid:1, ' and ', high:1, '); or that a',
             ' specific number will');
    WRITELN ('come up.  If you win odd/even or high/low, you get even money');
    WRITELN ('($1 for every $1 you bet).  If you win on a specific number,');
    WRITELN ('you win ', high:1, ' times your bet ($', high:1, ' for every $1',
             ' you bet).  If a 0');
    WRITELN ('comes up on the wheel, you automatically lose.  You start out');
    WRITELN ('with $', StartingMoney:1, '.  Good luck.');
    WRITELN
END;    (* GiveIntro *)
```

```
PROCEDURE YouLose (VAR money : INTEGER;
                       bet    : INTEGER);
(* Reports that the user has lost and adjusts money accordingly. *)
BEGIN
    WRITELN ('Sorry, you lose.');
    money := money - bet
END;    (* YouLose *)

PROCEDURE YouWin (VAR money : INTEGER;
                      bet    : INTEGER);
(* Reports that the user has won and adjusts money accordingly. *)
BEGIN
    WRITELN ('Congratulations, you win!');
    money := money + bet
END;    (* YouWin *)

PROCEDURE YouWinBig (VAR money : INTEGER;
                         bet    : INTEGER);
(* Reports that the user has won at the high stakes and adjusts *)
(* money accordingly.                                           *)
BEGIN
    WRITELN ('Congratulations, you really win this time!');
    money := money + bet * high
END;    (* YouWinBig *)

PROCEDURE SayGoodbye (money : INTEGER);
(* This procedure gives a goodbye salutation to the user. *)
BEGIN
    WRITELN ('You ended up with $', money:1, '.');
    IF money <= StartingMoney THEN
        WRITELN ('I guess you''re just too cool for this game, dude.')
    ELSE
        WRITELN ('Say, dude, you cleaned up!')
END;    (* SayGoodbye *)

PROCEDURE GetSeed (VAR seed: INTEGER);
(* This procedure prompts the user for a value to initialize seed. *)
BEGIN
    WRITELN ('I need an integer to seed the random number generator.');
    WRITE ('Give me a seed ---> ');
    READLN (seed);
    WRITELN
END;    (* GetSeed *)
```

```
FUNCTION RandomInt (     low  : INTEGER;
                        high : INTEGER;
                   VAR seed : INTEGER) : INTEGER;
(* This function uses the provided seed to return a pseudorandom *)
(* integer such that low <= Random <= high.  Seed is modified so *)
(* that the next call will provide a different result.           *)
BEGIN
    seed := (29 * seed + 1) MOD 1024;
    RandomInt := TRUNC ((seed/1024) * (high - low + 1)) + low
END;   (* RandomInt *)


PROCEDURE DoSpin (VAR spin : INTEGER;
                  VAR seed : INTEGER);
(* This procedure uses the pseudorandom number generator to simulate *)
(* the spinning of a roulette wheel.                                 *)
BEGIN
    spin := RandomInt (0, high, seed);
    WRITELN ('Around and around and around it goes.  And it lands on . . .',
             ' number ', spin:1)
END;   (* DoSpin *)


PROCEDURE SetUp (VAR seed     : INTEGER;
                 VAR NumSpins : INTEGER;
                 VAR money    : INTEGER);
(* This procedure gives an introduction and initializes program variables. *)
BEGIN
    GiveIntro;
    WRITE ('How many spins do you want today? ');
    READLN (NumSpins);
    WRITELN;
    GetSeed (seed);
    money := StartingMoney
END;   (* SetUp *)


PROCEDURE GetBet (VAR bet      : INTEGER;
                  VAR category : INTEGER;
                  VAR value    : INTEGER);
(* This procedure prompts the user for a bet. *)
BEGIN
    WRITE ('How much of your $', money:1, ' do you want to bet? ');
    READLN (bet);
    WRITE ('Category (1 = odd/even, 2 = high/low, 3 = a specific number)? ');
    READLN (category);
```

```
    IF category = 1 THEN
        WRITE ('And which do you want (1 = odd, 2 = even)? ')
    ELSE
        IF category = 2 THEN
            WRITE ('And which do you want (1 = high, 2 = low)? ')
        ELSE
            WRITE ('And what number do you want? ');
    READLN (value)
END;    (* GetBet *)


PROCEDURE AdjustMoney (VAR money    : INTEGER;
                           spin     : INTEGER;
                           bet      : INTEGER;
                           category : INTEGER;
                           value    : INTEGER);
(* Adjusts the user's money according to the bet made and *)
(* the number that appears on the wheel.                  *)
BEGIN
    IF spin = 0 THEN
        YouLose (money, bet)
    ELSE
        IF category = 1 THEN
            IF (value = spin MOD 2 + 1) THEN
                YouLose (money, bet)
            ELSE
                YouWin (money, bet)
        ELSE
            IF category = 2 THEN
                IF (value = spin DIV mid + 1) THEN
                    YouLose (money, bet)
                ELSE
                    YouWin (money, bet)
            ELSE
                IF spin = value THEN
                    YouWinBig (money, bet)
                ELSE
                    YouLose (money, bet);
    WRITELN
END;    (* AdjustMoney *)


PROCEDURE SpinOnce (VAR seed  : INTEGER;
                    VAR money : INTEGER);
(* This procedure performs one spin, adjusting money and seed as a result. *)
```

```
VAR spin          : INTEGER;
    bet           : INTEGER;
    category      : INTEGER;
    value         : INTEGER;
BEGIN
    GetBet (bet, category, value);
    DoSpin (spin, seed);
    AdjustMoney (money, spin, bet, category, value)
END;   (* SpinOnce *)

BEGIN   (* main program *)
    SetUp (seed, NumSpins, money);
    FOR count := 1 TO NumSpins DO
        SpinOnce (seed, money);
    SayGoodbye (money)
END.    (* main program *)
```

5.8 Key Concepts

- VAR parameters allow information to flow both in and out of a subprogram (PROCEDURE or FUNCTION). With VAR parameters, the formal parameter becomes a synonym for the variable passed as the actual parameter. Thus, any changes made to the formal parameter also cause a change in the variable passed as the actual parameter.

- Tasks and their corresponding information flow can be characterized by four categories. Using an internal variable involves no information flow and calls for a local variable. Using an external value involves information flow into a subprogram and calls for a value parameter. Initializing an external variable involves information flow out of a subprogram and calls for a VAR parameter. Modifying an external variable involves information flow both into and out of a subprogram and also calls for a VAR parameter.

- A subprogram should generally be defined as a FUNCTION whenever it has a single value flowing out given one or more values flowing in.

- A well-designed subprogram uses local variables for any pieces of information that don't add to its adaptability and uses parameters for those pieces of information which are likely to vary from one execution of the procedure to another. A well-engineered program will be easier to modify.

- Different decompositions of a problem will lead to different kinds of flow of information and different dependencies between the subprograms. A good decomposition leads to easily distinguished subtasks that are fairly independent of one another.

5.9 Self-Check Exercises

1. The following code is redundant:

```
WRITE ('Longitude (degrees, minutes, seconds) ---> ');
READLN (degrees, minutes, seconds);
longitude := degrees + minutes/60 + seconds/3600;
WRITE ('Latitude (degrees, minutes, seconds) ---> ');
READLN (degrees, minutes, seconds);
latitude := degrees + minutes/60 + seconds/3600;
```

Suppose we want to rewrite it as

```
WRITE ('Longitude');
GetAngle (longitude);
WRITE ('Latitude');
GetAngle (latitude);
```

Write procedure **GetAngle** (assuming **degrees**, **minutes**, and **seconds** are of type **INTEGER** and **latitude** and **longitude** are of type **REAL**).

2. Which do you suppose uses less space in memory when a procedure is activated, a **VAR** parameter or a value parameter?

3. Suppose that procedure **WriteSpaces** from the last chapter were written with a **VAR** parameter, so that its header became

```
PROCEDURE WriteSpaces (VAR number : INTEGER);
```

Why would this version be less useful than the original?

4. Consider:

```
PROCEDURE IncrementTwo (VAR first  : INTEGER;
                        VAR second : INTEGER);

BEGIN
    first := first + 1;
    second := second + 1
END;
```

If we have an **INTEGER** variable called **number** with initial value 9, what is the effect of the following call?

```
IncrementTwo (number, number);
```

5. Given this procedure header:

```
PROCEDURE DoCalculation (VAR result1, result2 : INTEGER;
                         value1               : REAL;
                         value2               : INTEGER);
```

and given **INTEGER** variables **int1**, **int2**, and **int3** and **REAL** variable **real1**, which of the following are legal calls?

```
DoCalculation (int1, int2, real1, int3);
DoCalculation (int1, int2, 32.9, 27);
DoCalculation (int1, int2, 35/4, 2 * 3);
DoCalculation (10, 20, 30.5, 40);
DoCalculation (int1, int1, real1, int3);
DoCalculation (int1, int2, 10, 20);
DoCalculation (int2, int1, 10.5, 20.5);
```

6. What is the output of the following program?

```
PROGRAM Mystery (OUTPUT);
VAR a, b, c, d : INTEGER;

PROCEDURE Strange (VAR a, b : INTEGER;
                        c    : INTEGER);
VAR d : INTEGER;
BEGIN
    d := 10;
    c := c * 2;
    a := b + c + d;
    b := a + d - c
END;

BEGIN
    a := 1;
    b := 2;
    c := 3;
    d := 4;
    strange (a, b, c);
    WRITELN (a, b, c, d);
    strange (b, a, d);
    WRITELN (a, b, c, d);
    strange (c, d, c);
    WRITELN (a, b, c, d)
END.
```

7. Consider two schemes for expressing a position on a two-dimensional map. One scheme uses two numbers to express the horizontal and vertical positions. Another scheme uses two numbers to express the distance and direction from a specified origin. If you want to write a single subprogram to convert from the first scheme to the second, would you use a procedure or function?

8. Assuming you have an initialized **seed** variable, use the pseudorandom-number tools to form an expression that simulates the sum obtained when two dice are rolled once (assuming each die has faces numbered 1 through 6).

9. Draw a decomposition tree for program **roulette**.

10. What variable(s) is(are) manipulated the farthest distance from their ownership in program **roulette**?

5.10 Programming Problems

1. Write a program that simulates a slot machine, asking a user how many times to play the game and then showing the results of each spin of the machine. The program should report appropriate winnings/losses.

2. The game of craps can be implemented on a computer by simulating the rolling of two dice. Write a program that allows two users to play craps, making bets on the outcome of a series of rolls.

3. Simple computer-aided instruction takes the form of drill and practice. Write a program that makes up a series of arithmetic problems for a user. The program should report the problem, prompt for an answer, and report whether or not the user is correct.

4. Write a program that tests the extrasensory perception (ESP) of a person. It should randomly pick a series of numbers between 1 and 10 and ask the user to guess each number. It should report at the end what percentage of the numbers the user guessed correctly.

5. Write an interactive program that allows a user to keep track of gas mileage assuming that the tank is filled every time. The program should prompt for an initial odometer reading and should ask for the total number of times the tank has been filled up. Then, for each reading, the program should prompt for the new odometer reading and the number of gallons added. It should report for each reading how many miles per gallon were achieved since the last reading. It should also report at the end the overall miles per gallon that have been achieved.

6

CHARACTER AND
FILE PROCESSING

6.1 Introduction

This chapter introduces a Pascal primitive type that stores textual information. It is called type CHAR, short for character. The chapter begins with an examination of the basic manipulations on type CHAR and the basic structure of files of characters.

Before you can understand complex manipulations on such files, you must know more about the reading operations, READ and READLN, and about a new kind of loop, the WHILE loop. Unlike the FOR loop, this loop allows you to iterate an indefinite number of times. This is an important property for processing text files which vary in the numbers of lines and the lengths of those lines.

After covering these Pascal details, the chapter examines typical file processing algorithms and concludes by examining how to read both numbers and characters from a file. A complex program is presented at the end.

6.2 Type CHAR

So far you have only manipulated numbers. Type CHAR manipulates textual information. Its domain is the set of all individual characters, including letters of the alphabet, digits, punctuation marks, and certain nonprinting characters called *control characters*.

To distinguish character constants from other parts of the program, you enclose them in single quotation marks. Here are some legal character constants:

```
'A'    'Z'    'a'    'z'    '5'    '!'    '?'    '"'    ''''
```

There are a few things you should note. First, Pascal distinguishes between uppercase and lowercase letters. Second, when you enclose a digit inside quotation marks, the program treats it as a character constant rather than an integer constant. Finally, to describe the apostrophe character, you must use an apostrophe image (i.e., four apostrophes describe the single apostrophe character).

Many beginners forget the quotation marks and run into trouble. Given these variables:

```
VAR a : CHAR;
    b : CHAR;
```

suppose you wrote the following code:

```
a := 'X';
b := 'a';
```

These two statements direct the computer to store the `'X'` character in the memory cell for variable a and to store the `'a'` character in the memory cell for variable b. This differs from

```
a := 'X';
b := a;
```

Without the quotation marks, the second statement directs the computer to copy the value of variable a into the memory cell for variable b, giving it the value `'X'`. You will not have problems like this if you remember to use quotation marks and avoid using one-letter variable names.

Many languages provide a primitive type, usually called a *string*, that lets you make assignments such as the following:

```
name := 'Hillary';
```

There is no such simple type in Pascal. The domain of type CHAR includes only single characters. If you want a type such as this (and you will), you must define it yourself.

Remember, a type is defined not only by its domain, but also by the operations that can be performed on objects of that type. With a variable of type CHAR, you can use READ and READLN to input characters. This is described later in this chapter. You can also use WRITE and WRITELN to display the value of a character. Character constants are not written out with the single quotation marks, they are written as the individual characters they represent. Consider the following procedure.

```
PROCEDURE Example;
VAR OneChar: CHAR;
BEGIN
    OneChar := 'C';
    WRITE (OneChar);
    OneChar := '3';
    WRITE (OneChar);
    OneChar := 'P';
    WRITE (OneChar);
    OneChar := 'O';
    WRITELN (OneChar)
END;
```

This procedure is equivalent to the statement:

```
WRITELN ('C3PO');
```

Most of the other character operations are derived from the fact that type **CHAR** is ordinal. Ordinal types were discussed in Chapter 4, where it was pointed out that type **REAL** differs from type **INTEGER** in that real numbers are continuous (between any two, there is a third), whereas integers are ordinal because they can be ordered so that there is a first element, a next element, a next after that, and so on). Type **CHAR**, like type **INTEGER**, is ordered.

Constants of type **CHAR** are given a particular order in the *collating sequence of the character set*. One character is designated as the lowest-order character, another is designated as the second, another as the third, and so on. The collating sequence makes type **CHAR** ordinal.

Because encoding schemes vary from machine to machine, the Pascal standard does not specify a particular collating sequence. Different Pascal systems can have different collating sequences. This way people who write the Pascal compiler on a particular machine can use whatever collating sequence matches their own machine level encoding of characters.

One of the most common collating sequences is called ASCII (American Standard Code for Information Interchange). Most computer manufacturers have abandoned their own codes and have adopted this standard specified by the American National Standards Institute. Many IBM computers, however, still use an encoding scheme called EBCDIC (Extended Binary Coded Decimal Interchange Code). If you program properly, it shouldn't matter which collating sequence your Pascal system uses. Because ASCII is the standard, it is used in this book as an example.

ASCII has 128 characters, of which 33 are nonprinting control characters (the first 32 and the 128th). Here are the 95 printing characters in their proper order:

```
!"#$%&'()*+,-./0123456789:;<=>?@ABCDEFGHIJKLMNOPQRSTUVWXYZ
[\]^_`abcdefghijklmnopqrstuvwxyz{|}~
```

The first printing character is a space (this may not be obvious from the list above).

Because type CHAR is an ordinal type, it can be compared using the relational operators. The collating sequence determines the order of the characters. Thus you can say such things as

```
IF 'A' < 'a' THEN
    WRITELN ('Capital A less than small a')
ELSE
    WRITELN ('Capital A greater than small a');
```

If ASCII is your collating sequence, this IF/THEN/ELSE will execute the THEN clause, because a capital 'A' does in fact precede small 'a' in the sequence.

Besides relational comparisons, there are four built-in functions that manipulate characters:

Name	Meaning	Argument Type	Result Type	Example	Value
SUCC	Successor	CHAR	CHAR	SUCC ('A')	'B'
PRED	Predecessor	CHAR	CHAR	PRED ('D')	'C'
ORD	Ordinal value	CHAR	INTEGER	ORD ('A')	65
CHR	Character value	INTEGER	CHAR	CHR (97)	'a'

The successor function (SUCC), when passed a character, returns the next character from the collating sequence. The predecessor function (PRED) does the opposite, returning the previous character in the collating sequence. It is an error to ask for the predecessor of the first element or the successor of the final element.

The ordinal and character value functions (ORD and CHR) are transfer functions. When passed a character, the ORD function returns an integer corresponding to that character's position in the collating sequence. The first character in the collating sequence is given ordinal value 0, the second is given ordinal value 1, and so on. There are 32 nonprinting characters before the space in ASCII, which means the space has ordinal value 32. As indicated in the table, the capital 'A' has ordinal value 65 in ASCII. The CHR function is the inverse. Given an integer, it returns the character that has that ordinal value. Thus the CHR of 32 is a space and the CHR of 97 is a small 'a'.

CHR is a special-purpose function for the type CHAR. The SUCC, PRED, and ORD functions, however, are not specific to type CHAR. You can use them for any ordinal type. Addition and subtraction have provided an alternative to the SUCC and PRED functions for type INTEGER:

```
number := number + 1;
number := number - 1;
```

You can also write these statements as

```
number := SUCC (number);
number := PRED (number);
```

You use the ORD function to convert an ordinal type into an INTEGER. There is no need to convert an INTEGER into an INTEGER, so the ORD function is not useful when applied to INTEGERs (it merely returns the same value it is passed as an argument). However, all three functions are important for the other ordinal types.

Because the successor function gives you a next value, you can use character variables to control FOR loops:

```
PROCEDURE WriteAlphabet;
VAR letter: CHAR;
BEGIN
    FOR letter := 'A' TO 'Z' DO
        WRITE (letter)
END;
```

This loop will execute 26 times, with the control variable taking on all the values between 'A' and 'Z'. Each time through the loop, the control variable is set to the successor of its previous value. This procedure prints the alphabet using uppercase letters.

Similarly, because of the predecessor function, you can obtain the alphabet in reverse order by using a DOWNTO loop instead of a TO loop:

```
PROCEDURE WriteBackwardsAlphabet;
VAR letter: CHAR;
BEGIN
    FOR letter := 'Z' DOWNTO 'A' DO
        WRITE (letter)
END;
```

Consider the following expression:

```
SUCC (SUCC (SUCC (SUCC (SUCC ('a')))))
```

This is the fifth character after a small 'a'. In ASCII, this is the character 'f'. This is a tedious way to express the idea. The ORD and CHR functions allow you to write this expression more simply, by converting to type INTEGER and then using addition:

```
CHR (ORD ('a') + 5)
```

This converts the character to its integer ordinal value, adds 5 to the integer, and then converts back to a character. This can prove useful. For example, consider the relationship between lowercase and uppercase letters in ASCII:

ORD ('A') = 65	ORD ('a') = 97	difference = 32
ORD ('B') = 66	ORD ('b') = 98	difference = 32

```
ORD ('C') = 67        ORD ('c') = 99        difference = 32
ORD ('D') = 68        ORD ('d') = 100       difference = 32
                       . . .
```

If you have a lowercase letter, you can obtain the ordinal value of its uppercase equivalent by subtracting 32 from its ordinal value. Thus, if you have a variable called `letter` in lowercase, you can uppercase it with the following statement:

```
letter := CHR (ORD (letter) - 32);
```

Thirty-two is the right number to use for ASCII. But you should figure out where it comes from and write that instead:

```
letter := CHR (ORD (letter) + ORD ('A') - ORD ('a'));
```

This makes your statement independent of the particular ordinal values in the ASCII character set. This statement will work provided the ordinal values of the lowercase letters follow the same pattern as the ordinal values of the uppercase letters. This is true in all the major character codes, including IBM's EBCDIC.

Another useful application of the `CHR` function would be to produce a table of the collating sequence:

```
FOR count := 0 TO 127 DO
    WRITE ('Character #', count:3, ' = "', CHR (count), '"');
```

On an ASCII machine, this produces a table of the 128 ASCII characters and their ordinal values.

6.3 Set Constants

A *set* contains a collection of values. In Chapter 11 you will see how to define set variables that can change in value as the program executes. In other words, you will be able to add or delete elements from such sets. For convenience at this point, however, you will examine set constants and learn one operation that can be performed on a set. *Set constants* provide you with a convenient way of describing a collection of values. They are useful in writing file-processing programs because you are often interested in special groups of values (e.g., the alphabet).

You specify set constants by listing the values, separated by commas, inside brackets:

```
[ <value>, <value>, . . ., <value> ]
```

The following set has four different integer values in it:

```
[1, 6, 19, 24]
```

The following set has three characters in it.

```
['a', 'z', 'X']
```

The following set is illegal because you aren't allowed to mix types. A set can contain elements of only one base type. In addition, the base type must be ordinal. Thus you can have sets of INTEGER or CHAR, but not sets of REAL.

```
[1, 'a', 6, 'z', 19, 'X', 24]
```

There is a shorthand notation that lets you specify a range of values using a low value, two dots, and a high value. This means that the syntax really is

```
[ <value or list>, <value or list>, . . ., <value or list> ]
```

where a list is defined as

```
<low value> .. <high value>
```

You cannot put a space between the two dots separating the two values. The first of these sets contains all the integers between 1 and 100 inclusive. The second set contains the lowercase letters:

```
[1..100] or ['a'..'z']
```

You can have more than one range:

```
[1..100, 200..300] or ['a'..'z', 'A'..'Z']
```

and, as the syntax above implies, you can mix individual elements with ranges:

```
[1..100, 150, 200..300, 350] or ['a'..'z', '!', 'A'..'Z', '$']
```

The one set operation that you will study now is the IN operator. It tests for set inclusion and its syntax is

```
<value> IN  <set>
```

This expression is a test. It returns either TRUE or FALSE depending on whether the given value is in the set. You can use an expression such as this to control an IF/THEN/ELSE statement. For example, here is a procedure that turns its parameter to uppercase if it is lowercase:

```
PROCEDURE TurnToUppercase (VAR character : CHAR);
BEGIN
    IF (character IN ['a'..'z']) THEN
        character := CHR (ORD (character) - ORD ('a') + ORD ('A'))
END;
```

This procedure is useful enough that you should add it to your software library. The parentheses here are not required, but add to readability.

The type of the <value> and the <set> must match. You can't test to see whether an INTEGER is in a set of characters. However, you can use arbitrary expressions for the <value> being tested, as long as the result of the expression matches in type the base type of the set. For example,

```
(2 + 2 - 3 * 4 + 15) IN [1..10]
```

This expression returns **TRUE** because the expression inside the parentheses evaluates to 7, and 7 is between 1 and 10.

Sets are implemented differently in different versions of Pascal. Some Pascal versions (such as UCSD Pascal) have a very general implementation of sets that allow you to have a great number of elements. Other Pascal versions, however, limit the size of sets severely. It is usually possible, however, to at least use sets of **CHAR**.

The **IN** operator has the same precedence as the relational operators and is unlikely to cause you any trouble in formulating expressions. The following expression is fine. Because the **IN** operator has a lower precedence level than the plus, the computer adds first and then tests for set inclusion. However, it is more readable to use parentheses.

```
3 + 4 IN [1..10]
```

6.4 External Files

You have already examined programs that obtain numerical input from the terminal. In this section you will study external files rather than terminal **INPUT**. An *external file* is a collection of characters and numbers that appear on one or more lines. They are external because they are not contained within the program and are not obtained from the user during execution. They are outside the scope of the program and its execution. You create external input files before the execution of a program. For example, you might create a file of student names and grades:

```
Jane Dobrin   :  A B A C-
Jesse Hubbard :  C D A B A+
Robin MoCall  :  B A A+ A-
```

and then you might write a program that processes this external input file and produces some kind of report. Such a program should be general enough that it could process any external input file that matches a specified format.

You can usually use the same editor to create both your program files and your external input files. Once an external file is created, you can use **READ** and **READLN** statements to process it.

Just as programs can **READ** from external input files, they can also **WRITE** to external output files. By directing output to a file rather than to a terminal, the program creates a more permanent record of its results.

On most Pascal systems, terminal interaction is the default. To use external files, you often have to include some special statements in the program. Consider the following file.

```
This file contains
two separate lines
```

This file has 18 characters on both lines. The following program echoes the first three characters of each input line to the output file. While it may seem useless to echo the input to the output, you will see that many programming tasks involve a variation of echoing.

```
PROGRAM EchoThree (INPUT, OUTPUT);
VAR first   : CHAR;
    second  : CHAR;
    third   : CHAR;
    row     : INTEGER;
BEGIN
    FOR row := 1 TO 2 DO
    BEGIN
        READLN (first, second, third);
        WRITELN (first, second, third)
    END
END.
```

Given this input file, the program would produce the following output:

```
Thi
two
```

This program reads an entire input line first, and then creates an entire output line. The pseudocode would be

```
for (each of two lines) do
begin
    process an entire input line.
    produce a complete output line.
end
```

The more usual case would be to process the line character-by-character, reading and writing as you go along:

```
for (each of two lines) do
begin
    for (each character on the line) do
    begin
        read a character.
        write the character.
    end
    go to a new input line.
    go to a new output line.
end
```

This pseudocode produces the output line as it is reading the input line. This is like the cumulative-sum algorithm that calculates its sum as it reads numbers. You would use the following program to process all 18 characters of the two lines:

```
PROGRAM EchoEighteen (INPUT, OUTPUT);
VAR next    : CHAR;
    row     : INTEGER;
    column  : INTEGER;
BEGIN
    FOR row := 1 TO 2 DO
    BEGIN
        For column := 1 TO 18 DO
        BEGIN
            READ (next);
            WRITE (next)
        END;
        READLN;
        WRITELN
    END
END.
```

Rarely do you have input lines with exactly 18 characters. However, before you can deal with input lines of differing lengths, you must learn a new loop construct, the WHILE loop.

6.5 WHILE Loops

The FOR loop is a *definite loop* because it iterates a specified number of times. *Indefinite loops* are not fixed in the number of iterations they will perform. They continue iterating as long as their continuation condition is satisfied. The WHILE loop is the first indefinite loop you will study. It has the following syntax:

```
WHILE <test> DO
    <statement>
```

The test is a continuation condition. The WHILE loop performs its test and, if the test returns true, executes the controlled statement. It continually tests again and executes again if the test returns TRUE. When the test returns FALSE, the loop terminates.

Here is an example of a WHILE loop:

```
number := 1;
WHILE (number <= 200) DO
    number := number * 2;
```

The parentheses are not necessary, but they add to readability. On the surface, this statement looks like

```
number := 1;
IF (number <= 200) THEN
    number := number * 2;
```

while and if

The difference between the two is that the WHILE executes multiple times; it loops until the test returns FALSE. The IF statement executes the inner assignment statement once, leaving **number** equal to 2. The WHILE loop executes the statement indefinitely until the test returns FALSE. This WHILE loop executes the assignment statement eight times, setting **number** to the value 256 (the first power of 2 that is greater than 200).

The WHILE loop tests its condition before executing the statement it controls. It performs its test at the top of the loop, as indicated in this pseudocode:

```
loop
        perform test.
        exit if test returns false.
        execute controlled statement.
end of loop
```

A WHILE loop will not execute its controlled statement if its test returns FALSE the first time. In some loops it is not necessarily meaningful to test on the first iteration. If the test makes reference to variables that are given values inside of the loop, the variables might be undefined on the first iteration. You have to watch for such possibilities. You can get around them by *priming*, ensuring that the loop works properly on the first iteration. Later you will study an indefinite loop that doesn't require priming because it performs its test at the bottom of the loop.

Here is a WHILE with two statements in the loop:

```
number := 1;
WHILE (number <= max) DO
BEGIN
    WRITELN ('Hi there');
    number := number + 1
END;
```

As with the FOR loop and IF/THEN/ELSE, you use a BEGIN/END block when you want to control more than one statement. This loop executes a WRITELN statement repeatedly and increments **number** until it is greater than **max**. This WHILE loop is more or less equivalent to the following FOR loop:

```
FOR number := 1 TO max DO
    WRITELN ('Hi there');
```

You can write all FOR loops as WHILE loops. The reverse, however, is not true. Suppose you want to find the smallest divisor of a number other than 1. Here are some examples of what you are looking for:

Number	Factors	Smallest Divisor
10	2 * 5	2
15	3 * 5	3
25	5 * 5	5
31	31	31
77	7 * 11	7

Here is a pseudocode description of how you might do this:

start divisor at 2.
while (the current value of divisor does not work) do
    increase divisor.

You don't start divisor at 1 because you are looking for the first divisor greater than 1. To modify this code, you must be more explicit about what makes a divisor work. A divisor of a number has no remainder when the number is divided by it. You can rewrite this as

start divisor at 2.
while (the remainder of $\frac{number}{divisor}$ is not 0) do
    increase divisor.

Here is a use for the MOD operator which gives the remainder for integer division. The following WHILE loop performs this task:

```
divisor := 2;
WHILE (number MOD divisor <> 0) DO
    divisor := divisor + 1;
```

One problem you will undoubtedly encounter in writing your WHILE loops is the infamous *infinite loop*. Consider the following code:

```
number := 1;
WHILE (number > 0) DO
    number := number + 1;
```

Because **number** begins as a positive value and the loop makes it larger, this loop will continue indefinitely. It will terminate on an execution error when **number** becomes larger than **MAXINT**. You must be careful in formulating your WHILE loops to avoid situations where a piece of code will never finish executing. Every time you write a WHILE loop, you should consider when and how it will finish executing.

6.5.1 Sentinel Loops

Reconsider the problem of echoing a line of input to the output file. Suppose you have these input lines:

```
This line of input ends in a period.
As does this line.
And this one.
```

If you want to write a procedure that echos one line of input, you would write the task in pseudocode.

echo each character of input to output until you reach a period.

You can express this more precisely using the concepts of reading, writing, and looping:

```
for (each character up to a period) do
begin
      read a character.
      write the character.
end
```

You can't express this as a **FOR** loop, however, because you don't know how many characters are on a line. You need to use the new concept of indefinite looping:

```
while (you haven't seen a period) do
begin
      read a character.
      write the character.
end
```

This loop requires some priming. The test is worded in terms of a character, so you have to assign a value to the character variable outside the loop before it executes. Any value other than period will do. You can't assign the character a period because it would look like the loop had read a period and it would therefore never iterate. This example uses a space:

```
set the character to a space.
while (the character is not a period) do
begin
      read a character.
      write the character.
end
```

You can convert this pseudocode into Pascal code by adding a variable of type **CHAR**:

```
PROCEDURE Echo;
VAR next   : CHAR;
```

```
BEGIN
    next := ' ';
    WHILE (next <> '.') DO
    BEGIN
        READ (next);
        WRITE (next)
    END
END;
```

This loop is a *sentinel loop*. The period acts as a sentinel, or marker, for the end of input. In this case, you echo the sentinel as well as the rest of the input line. Typical sentinel loops echo up to, but not including, the sentinel. This is a fence-post problem. For the nonsentinel characters, you want to

read, write, read, write, ..., read, write

The final character is to be read but not written. The final **READ** is the classic extra post:

read, write, read, write, ..., read, write, read

You solve this by putting an extra **READ** before the loop:

read a character.
while (the character is not a period) do
begin
    write the character.
    read a character.
end

The initial **READ** primes the **WHILE** loop, so you don't need an extra assignment statement. Here is the Pascal version:

```
PROCEDURE Echo;
VAR next : CHAR;
BEGIN
    READ (next);
    WHILE (next <> '.') DO
    BEGIN
        WRITE (next);
        READ (next)
    END
END;
```

The basic problem with sentinel loops, however, is that they depend on the presence of the sentinel. If it is missing, the loop becomes infinite and executes indefinitely. If this **WHILE** loop were executed on a file that contained no periods, the program would read characters until it reached the end of the file and cause an execution error when it attempted to **READ** beyond it. It is difficult to control errors in the input file with such loops. To write better loops, you first have to examine the structure of files.

6.6 The Structure of TEXT Files

Files are a new kind of object that programs can manipulate. Because external files are a new kind of object, Pascal has a type that describes them. They are different from the objects you have examined before in that they are structured and not simple.

STRUCTURED TYPE

A type of object that has individual components.

The *components* of a file are the characters and numbers stored within it. Simple external files are of type TEXT. The domain of type TEXT is the set of all possible files (i.e., all possible combinations of characters and numbers appearing on one or more lines). Later, you will see some of the operations that can be performed on objects of type TEXT.

Let's examine the structure of TEXT files in more detail. Consider this three-line input file:

```
I have
some text
here.
```

Each line is terminated by a special character called an EOLN (end of line).

```
I have<eoln>
some text     <eoln>
here.<eoln>
```

Notice that the <*eoln*> character can follow immediately after the last printing character of a line (as in the first and third) or after some trailing blanks at the end of the line (as in the second). Blanks at the ends of lines can appear for many reasons. If the file is created by a person using an editing system, the person can type some spaces at the end of a line before going to a new line. Some editing systems strip these trailing spaces, but many do not.

In addition to the <*eoln*> character, there is a special character called <*eof*> (end of file) that appears after the last line of the file:

```
I have<eoln>
some text     <eoln>
here.<eoln>
<eof>
```

There is only one $<eof>$ in a file and it always is preceded by an $<eoln>$. Pascal guarantees that you won't have to deal with a file like the following:

```
I have<eoln>
some text     <eoln>
here.<eof>
```

However, there can be a blank line preceding the <eof>:

```
I have<eoln>
some text     <eoln>
here.<eoln>
<eoln>
<eof>
```

It is natural to think of a file as a two-dimensional object with both rows and columns. That will lead you astray, however, because Pascal thinks of a file as a one-dimensional, or linear, object. For example, you can collapse the two-dimensional file above to a one-dimensional sequence:

```
I have<eoln>some text     <eoln>here.<eoln><eoln><eof>
```

Because of the $<eoln>$ characters, you do not lose any information by putting the characters in one row. You can still see where the line breaks are and could write out the file row by row. This one-dimensional representation is equivalent to the two-dimensional one.

One-dimensional objects are simpler to manipulate than two-dimensional objects, so Klaus Wirth chose the one-dimensional representation of a file. While this does simplify the language, it makes it conceptually more difficult for many beginners.

Here's an analogy to help you understand Pascal's file objects. A Pascal file is like a deck of cards. Each single character from an input file is on an individual card. Remember, $<eoln>$ and $<eof>$ are single characters, so some cards will have $<eoln>$ on them and one will have $<eof>$ on it. The deck is in the exact same order as the input file. Using the input file above as an example, the top card would be 'I' and the bottom card $<eof>$.

A deck of cards has many of the properties of the file. First, it is one-dimensional in the sense that it is a single sequence of cards. There is a first card, second, third, and so on. It doesn't matter what row and column a given character comes from. In Pascal, the important thing is where a character appears in the linear sequence. Pascal files are processed in sequential order. This is the same as saying that you can only take cards off the top of the deck. You cannot grab something out of the middle; you must take the cards in sequence. This is a limitation of a file object.

Pascal keeps track of the top card of the deck by keeping an internal pointer into the file. This pointer is the *input cursor*. The input cursor is like the output cursor discussed earlier, only it keeps track of the next character to read rather than the next position where a character will be written.

Initially, the input cursor is positioned at the first character of a file:

```
I have<eoln>some text     <eoln>here.<eoln><eoln><eof>
↑
```

As the computer reads characters, the cursor moves from left to right, just as taking cards off the top of a deck will position you at the next card.

Let's trace some reading operations on characters to see how this works. Suppose you define these variables:

```
VAR one   : CHAR;
    two   : CHAR;
    three : CHAR;
```

To begin, consider this simple statement:

```
READ (one);
```

The position of the input cursor determines what value is given to the variable. Whatever character it is pointing at is the value you use. The input cursor then moves one to the right so that it points to the next character. It is like taking the top card off the deck, using that value for the variable, and discarding it so that the next character from the deck is on top.

This statement is a bit more complex:

```
READ (one, two, three);
```

Instead of using a single character, you use three. Instead of taking one card off the deck, you take three. For example, if this statement executes once on this input file:

```
I have<eoln>some text     <eoln>here.<eoln><eoln><eof>
↑
```

you would obtain the following:

```
one  │'I'│      two  │' '│      three  │'h'│
```

The input cursor then moves to the fourth character in the file. A space is read as a character, as in the case of variable **two**. In the deck, spaces appear on cards just like all the other characters:

```
I have<eoln>some text     <eoln>here.<eoln><eoln><eof>
  ↑
```

After a second execution, you would get:

one   `'a'`   two   `'v'`   three   `'e'`

The input cursor then moves to the seventh character:

`I have`*<eoln>*`some text     `*<eoln>*`here.`*<eoln>**<eoln>**<eof>*
      ↑

The seventh character (the top card of the deck) is the *<eoln>* character at the end of the first line. You can read this *<eoln>* character. Because the *<eoln>* is a special character, when the computer reads it, it turns it into a space. Thus it assigns a space to the variable in the **READ**. The *<eoln>* is a character just like any other, however, in the sense that once it is read, the cursor moves to the next character. If you take an *<eoln>* card off the deck, you interpret it as a space. The third execution of the statement would yield:

one   `' '`   two   `'s'`   three   `'o'`

The input cursor then moves to the tenth character in the file:

`I have`*<eoln>*`some text     `*<eoln>*`here.`*<eoln>**<eoln>**<eof>*
       ↑

As you continue to read characters, the input cursor will slowly move to the right. When the input cursor reaches the *<eof>*, your program is not allowed to **READ** any more (you cannot take a card from an empty deck). Your program will generally cause an execution error if it attempts to do this.

6.6.1   READ versus READLN

The relationship between **READ** and **READLN** is similar to the relationship between **WRITE** and **WRITELN**. The **READ** statement obtains values for variables and moves the input cursor forward. The **READLN** statement does the same thing and then skips to the beginning of the next input line. For example, consider this input file:

`I have`*<eoln>*`some text     `*<eoln>*`here.`*<eoln>**<eoln>**<eof>*
↑

What would happen if you used this statement?

`READLN (one, two, three);`

First the computer reads values for the variables as before:

one $\boxed{\texttt{'I'}}$ two $\boxed{\texttt{' '}}$ three $\boxed{\texttt{'h'}}$

The **READLN**, however, instead of leaving the input cursor at the fourth character, scans over the input until it finds an *<eoln>* and positions the cursor after it, at the first character of the second line:

```
I have<eoln>some text     <eoln>here.<eoln><eoln><eof>
        ↑
```

In terms of the deck, the **READLN** does the **READ** operation first, and then discards cards until it discards an *<eoln>* card.

A second execution of this **READLN** statement yields these values:

one $\boxed{\texttt{'s'}}$ two $\boxed{\texttt{'o'}}$ three $\boxed{\texttt{'m'}}$

The input cursor then moves to the beginning of the third line.

```
I have<eoln>some text     <eoln>here.<eoln><eoln><eof>
                                 ↑
```

The **READLN** is not as simple as it seems, however. Because the *<eoln>* character looks like a space when reading characters, you might end up processing more than one line with a single **READLN**. Consider this input file:

```
I
am
happy!
```

Assuming it has no spaces at the ends of lines and no blank lines, it would be interpreted by Pascal as the following linear sequence:

```
I<eoln>am<eoln>happy!<eoln><eof>
↑
```

The first character of this file is the '**I**'. The second character is the *<eoln>* at the end of the first line. The third character is the '**a**' of the second line. If you execute

```
READLN (one, two, three);
```

you would obtain these values:

one $\boxed{\texttt{'I'}}$ two $\boxed{\texttt{' '}}$ three $\boxed{\texttt{'a'}}$

The input cursor then moves beyond the next *<eoln>*:

I<*eoln*>am<*eoln*>happy!<*eoln*><*eof*>
    ↑

Thus the single **READLN** statement processed two lines of input because the first <*eoln*> was read as a character. The deck made from this input file would have 'I' written on the first card, <*eoln*> on the second, and 'a' on the third. To perform the **READLN** on three variables, you first do the **READ** part of the statement by taking off the top three cards and assigning values to the variables. This skips past the first <*eoln*>. Because it was a **READLN**, however, you then have to start discarding cards until you have discarded an <*eoln*> (you don't count the one that you already discarded by accident). The 'm' card that appears fourth in the deck and the <*eoln*> card that follows it are discarded, leaving the 'h' card on the top of the deck.

This example should serve as a warning that the **READLN** statement has the potential to do something you don't intend. This is generally considered a "bad" thing for a program to do. You should process each line of data separately. Programs such as the one above can accidentally try to read characters when the input cursor is positioned at the <*eof*>, and you should, therefore, avoid them.

6.6.2   More File Processing Loops

The most common way to process a line of input is to use a line-oriented or **EOLN** loop. A built-in function called **EOLN** performs a test on the input file and returns **TRUE** if the input cursor is positioned at an <*eoln*> and **FALSE** otherwise. It does not move the input cursor. In the card-deck analogy, **EOLN** allows you to peek at the top card without removing it. If it is an <*eoln*>, then **EOLN** is **TRUE**; otherwise, it is **FALSE**.

Using this function, you can write a line processing loop:

```
while (the top card is not an end-of-line) do
begin
    read a character.
    write the character.
end
```

This loop will echo every character from the input line to the output line. Its logic is simple. You take cards off the top of the deck until you see the <*eoln*> card. Then you stop. If you try to echo an empty input line, you will see the <*eoln*> card right away and won't do anything. Notice that this loop leaves an <*eoln*> card on the top of the deck so you must be careful to discard that <*eoln*> card before trying to process the next line.

Here is the Pascal version of this code written as a procedure:

```
PROCEDURE EchoLine;
VAR next : CHAR;
BEGIN
    WHILE NOT EOLN DO
    BEGIN
        READ (next);
        WRITE (next)
    END
END;
```

Notice that the EOLN function call is preceded by the word "NOT." The NOT operator is a way of expressing the negation of a test. In this case you are saying that if EOLN is FALSE (i.e., NOT EOLN is TRUE), then you want to continue. Chapter 8 discusses the NOT operator in more detail.

In addition to the EOLN function, Pascal has another function called EOF that tells if the input cursor is positioned at the <*eof*> character. It peeks at the top card like EOLN. You use this function to write file-oriented or EOF loops:

```
PROCEDURE EchoFile;
BEGIN
    WHILE NOT EOF DO
    BEGIN
        EchoLine;
        READLN;
        WRITELN
    END
END;
```

Again, notice the use of the NOT operator to express the negation of a condition. Remember, the EchoLine procedure echoes the text of the line but leaves the input cursor positioned at the <*eoln*> (i.e., it processes all the cards up to the <*eoln*> card, but leaves the <*eoln*> card on the top of the deck). To proceed to the next input line (i.e., to discard the <*eoln*> card), you need a READLN following it. And if you want your output file to match your input file, you need to go to a new line of output at the same time using a WRITELN.

6.6.3 Program Example—Uppercasing a File

The task of uppercasing a file is a simple modification of the echoing process. Here is the general echoing pseudocode:

```
while (not at end of file) do
begin
     while (not at end of line) do
     begin
          read a character.
          write the character.
     end
     go to new input line.
     go to new output line.
end
```

The only modification you need to make is to uppercase any lowercase letters. You can insert a line for doing so between the reading and the writing:

```
while (not at end of file) do
begin
     while (not at end of line) do
     begin
          read a character.
          turn the character to uppercase.
          write the character.
     end
     go to new input line.            readln;
     go to new output line.           writeln
end
```

Earlier in this chapter you saw a procedure for turning a character to uppercase. Therefore, you have all the pieces you need to implement the pseudocode. Here is the complete program:

```
(* This program takes a text file as input and produces an uppercase   *)
(* version of it as output.                                             *)

PROGRAM Uppercase (INPUT, OUTPUT);
VAR next : CHAR;        (* next character to be processed *)

PROCEDURE TurnToUppercase (VAR character : CHAR);
(* Turns character to uppercase if it is lowercase. *)
BEGIN
    IF (character IN ['a'..'z']) THEN
        character := CHR (ORD (character) - ORD ('a') + ORD ('A'))
END;    (* TurnToUppercase *)
```

```
BEGIN    (* main program *)
    WHILE NOT EOF DO
    BEGIN
        WHILE NOT EOLN DO
        BEGIN
            READ (next);
            TurnToUppercase (next);
            WRITE (next)
        END;
        READLN;
        WRITELN
    END
END.     (* main program *)
```

Given this input file:

```
This file starts out
with both uppercase
and lowercase letters.
How do you suppose it ends up?
```

program **uppercase** will produce the following output:

```
THIS FILE STARTS OUT
WITH BOTH UPPERCASE
AND LOWERCASE LETTERS.
HOW DO YOU SUPPOSE IT ENDS UP?
```

6.6.4 Reading Both Characters and Numbers

In earlier chapters you examined programs that read numbers. In this chapter you have seen programs that read characters. A discussion of programs that do both follows. Consider this file:

```
12+18
94-407
938+2
```

The file has two numbers per line, separated by a plus or a minus character. Using a deck of cards as an analogy to understand files, how would you represent this file? Using *<eoln>*s and an *<eof>*, you need to represent it in a one-dimensional way:

12+18*<eoln>*94-407*<eoln>*938+2*<eoln><eof>*

To represent this as a deck of cards, imagine one character or one number on each card. Your deck would look like this:

```
12
'+'
18
<eoln>
94
'-'
407
<eoln>
938
'+'
2
<eoln>
<eof>
```

Here is a short program that would process this input file, adding or subtracting the numbers depending on the character in between:

```
PROGRAM AddOrSubtract (INPUT, OUTPUT);
VAR first    : INTEGER;
    second   : INTEGER;
    result   : INTEGER;
    operator : CHAR;
BEGIN
    WHILE NOT EOF DO
    BEGIN
        READLN (first, operator, second);
        IF operator = '+' THEN
            result := first + second
        ELSE
            result := first - second;
        WRITELN (first:1, operator, second:1, ' = ', result:1)
    END
END.
```

Given the input file above, this program produces the following output:

```
12+18 = 30
94-407 = -313
938+2 = 940
```

As you will see in later chapters, it is not really correct to write one number per card in your deck of cards. Pascal allows you to read the individual characters that make up a number if you want to. For the time being, however, consider numbers in input files to be indivisible.

6.7 A Large Program Example

Suppose you have an input file of employee names followed by the hours worked by each employee:

```
Tad Martin: 3  4.5  2  1.75
Phoebe Wallingford: 2  3.25  8.5  9.25  4.5  1.5
Greg Nelson:  1.5  2
Adam Chandler: 3.8 5.9 6.7 8.5
```

This is a fairly complex input file because the name length and the list of hours vary from line to line. Also, you don't know how many lines the input file will have. Suppose you want to produce a table showing how many hours each employee worked. The overall task is solved by an EOF loop:

while (not at end of file) do
      process one line.

To expand this pseudocode, you must figure out how to process a line. Each line is composed of two parts, the name and the list of hours. Because the name appears first on the line, you must process it first:

while (not at end of file) do
begin
      process name.
      process hours.
end

Processing the name is a simple combination of several tools you have examined. You start with a simple sentinel loop:

read a character.
while (the character is not the sentinel) do
begin
      write the character.
      read a character.
end

To line things up in proper columns for a table, you need to keep track of how many characters you echo. For example, if the width of the name column is 35 and you echo a 15-character name, you will have to know to echo 20 spaces afterwards to fill up the column. You can keep track of the length by applying the cumulative-sum technique to this loop:

read a character.
start length at 0.
while (the character is not the sentinel) do
begin
      write the character.
      read a character.

```
        increment length.
end
```

Finally, you can use the **WriteSpaces** tool to write out the appropriate number of spaces to fill up the column. The following pseudocode translates easily to Pascal:

```
read a character.
start length at 0.
while (the character is not the sentinel) do
begin
        write the character.
        read a character.
        increment length.
end
write ((width of name column) − (actual name length)) spaces.
```

Processing the list of hours involves finding their sum and then writing it to the output file. For the loop to work correctly, you also need to go to a new input line at the end of the loop so that you will be ready to process the next line:

```
while (not at end of file) do
begin
        echo name.
        find sum of list of hours.
        report sum.
        go to new input line.
end
```

Because the list of hours is terminated by an $<eoln>$, you can use an EOLN loop for reading them and a cumulative sum to add them up.

Let's add one more element to the program: have the program figure out the maximum and minimum number of hours worked. The simplest algorithm to use for calculating the minimum of a sequence of numbers is

```
set minimum to the first value.
for (each remaining value) do
        if value < minimum then
                set minimum to value.
```

There is a corresponding pseudocode for maximums:

```
set maximum to the first value.
for (each remaining value) do
        if value > maximum then
                set maximum to value.
```

To fit this algorithm into your pseudocode, you have to change the WHILE loop so that it processes the first line before the loop. Because this first line of input provides the initial value for maximum and minimum, it is worthwhile to say that the following operations from the pseudocode will become a procedure for processing the line:

echo name.
find sum of list of hours.
report sum.
go to new input line.

You can combine these different pseudocode descriptions into one piece of code:

process next line.
set minimum to sum.
set maximum to sum.
while (not at end of file) do
begin
    process next line.
    if sum > maximum then
        set maximum to sum.
    if sum < minimum then
        set minimum to sum.
end

Here is the program that expands this pseudocode:

```
(* This program processes input files of the form:                *)
(*                                                                *)
(*      <name>   :  <list of hours>                               *)
(*      <name>   :  <list of hours>                               *)
(*                   . . .                                        *)
(*      <name>   :  <list of hours>                               *)
(*                                                                *)
(* as in:                                                         *)
(*                                                                *)
(*      Tad Martin: 3  4.5  2  1.75                               *)
(*      Phoebe Wallingford: 2  3.25  8.5  9.25  4.5  1.5          *)
(*      Greg Nelson:  1.5  2                                      *)
(*                                                                *)
(* Notice that names need not be the same length, but that the colon *)
(* must be present to separate the name from the list of hours.  The *)
(* program produces a table that lists the number of hours worked by *)
(* each employee and the maximum and minimum hours worked overall.   *)

PROGRAM TotalUpHours (INPUT, OUTPUT);
CONST width     = 6;     (* field width for REAL values              *)
      digits    = 2;     (* # of digits after decimal for REAL values *)
      separator = ':';   (* character separating name from hours     *)
      NameLength = 25;   (* field width to use for names             *)
```

```
VAR   total       : REAL; (* total hours for next employee     *)
      max         : REAL; (* maximum hours for any employee     *)
      min         : REAL; (* minimum hours for any employee     *)

PROCEDURE WriteSpaces (number : INTEGER);
(* This procedure writes out the specified number of spaces. *)
VAR count : INTEGER;
BEGIN
    FOR count := 1 TO number DO
        WRITE (' ');
END;

PROCEDURE EchoName;
(* This procedure uses a sentinel loop to echo the name. *)
VAR next    : CHAR;     (* next name character *)
    count   : INTEGER; (* loop counter          *)
BEGIN
    READ (next);
    count := 0;
    WHILE (next <> separator) DO
    BEGIN
        WRITE (next);
        READ (next);
        count := count + 1
    END;
    WriteSpaces (NameLength - count)
END;    (* EchoName *)

PROCEDURE ReadHours (VAR sum : REAL);
(* This procedure uses an EOLN loop and cumulative sum to find the  *)
(* total hours worked.                                              *)
VAR next : REAL; (* next number of hours *)
BEGIN
    sum := 0;
    WHILE NOT EOLN DO
    BEGIN
        READ (next);
        sum := sum + next
    END
END;
```

(handwritten annotations: "'Please enter your name');" after BEGIN in EchoName; "number in Procedure WriteSpaces" pointing to count := count + 1)

```
PROCEDURE ProcessLine (VAR total : REAL);
(* This procedure processes one line and returns the total hours worked.  *)
BEGIN
    EchoName;
    ReadHours (total);
    WRITELN ('      ', total:width:digits);
    READLN
END;  (* ProcessLine *)

BEGIN  (* main program *)
    WRITELN ('Employee                             Hours');
    WRITELN ('---------------------------------------------');
    ProcessLine (total);
    min := total;
    max := total;
    WHILE NOT EOF DO
    BEGIN
        ProcessLine (total);
        IF total > max THEN
            max := total;
        IF total < min THEN
            min := total
    END;
    WRITELN;
    WRITELN ('Maximum hours worked =', max:width:digits);
    WRITELN ('Minimum hours worked =', min:width:digits)
END.    (* main program *)
```

The program produces the following output given the input file above.

```
Employee                     Hours
-------------------------------
Tad Martin                   11.25
Phoebe Wallingford           29.00
Greg Nelson                   3.50
Adam Chandler                24.90

Maximum hours worked = 29.00
Minimum hours worked =  3.50
```

6.8 Key Concepts

- Textual information is manipulated in Pascal programs character by character using type **CHAR**. Type **CHAR** includes alphabetic characters, punctuation marks, digits, and other special characters. A collating sequence defines a first element of type **CHAR**, a second, third, and so on.

■ Programs can read from external input files and can create external output files. External files are stored in the secondary memory of the computer.

■ Actions that are to be performed an indefinite number of times should be expressed using a **WHILE** loop rather than a **FOR** loop. A **WHILE** loop will often have to be primed so that the first evaluation of the test is meaningful.

■ A structured type is one that has individual components.

■ Normal external files are of the structured type **TEXT**. Such files are composed of a series of characters with special end-of-line characters and a special end-of-file character.

■ An input cursor keeps track of the next character to be read from a file. If a character is read while the input cursor is positioned at an end-of-line, a space will be read in and the input cursor will position to the first character of the next line. It is illegal to perform a reading operation when the input cursor is positioned at the end-of-file character.

6.9 Self-Check Exercises

1. What is the output of the following program?

```
PROGRAM Strange (OUTPUT);
VAR w, x, y, z : CHAR;
BEGIN
     w := 'w';
     x := 'y';
     y := '!';
     z := x;
     WRITELN (w, x, y, z);
     x := y;
     w := z;
     WRITELN (w, x, y, z)
END.
```

2. Assume that in the collating sequence of type **CHAR** the digit characters appear in order from '0' to '9'. A single digit can be expressed either as an **INTEGER** value or as the corresponding character of type **CHAR**. You are to write two functions that convert between the representations using the headers below.

```
FUNCTION IntDigit (CharDigit : CHAR) : INTEGER;
(* returns the integer corresponding to CharDigit *)

FUNCTION CharDigit (IntDigit : INTEGER) : CHAR;
(* returns the character corresponding to IntDigit *)
```

3. Rewrite the following expression so that it uses `CHR` and `ORD` rather than `PRED`:

    ```
    PRED (PRED (PRED (PRED (TheChar))))
    ```

4. You are to write a function with the following header that encodes letters of the alphabet:

    ```
    FUNCTION EncodedChar (OriginalChar : CHAR) : CHAR;
    ```

    The function should return the original character if it is not a letter of the alphabet. If, however, it is alphabetic, the function should return the letter that appears 10 positions later in the alphabet. For example, `'A'` (position 1) is turned into `'K'` (position 11); `'B'` (position 2) is turned `'L'` (position 12); and so on. Notice that `'P'` (position 16) is turned into `'Z'` (position 26). After `'P'`, you should follow the pattern that `'Q'` (position 17) is turned into `'A'` (position 1); `'R'` (position 18) is turned into `'B'` (position 2); up to `'Z'` (position 26) turned into `'J'` (position 10). The function should make the appropriate conversion both for lowercase and uppercase letters. You can assume that `'a'` through `'z'` appear in sequential order and that `'A'` through `'Z'` also appear in sequential order.

5. Which of the following would you expect to find stored in an external file?

    numbers   dates   names   addresses   programs

6. What will the following loop do (note the semicolon after the `DO`)?

    ```
    number := 1000;
    WHILE (number <> 0) DO;
    BEGIN
        WRITELN (number);
        number := number DIV 2
    END;
    ```

7. What output will the following code generate?

    ```
    number := 1;
    WHILE (number < 100) DO
        WRITELN (number);
        number := number * 3;
    ```

8. Is the end-of-line character in the domain of type `CHAR`?

9. Given variables `first`, `second`, `third`, and `fourth` of type `CHAR`, consider the statements:

    ```
    READLN (first, second);
    READLN (third);
    READLN (fourth);
    ```

    What values are given to the variables if these statements are executed with the input cursor positioned at the beginning of the following file?

```
1: Line #1.
2: Line #2.
3: Line #3.
```

What values are given if the following file is used instead (note that each line has only one character on it)?

```
1
2
3
4
5
6
```

10. Files often have sequences of spaces in them that create lines such as:

    ```
    many    spaces        on    this        line!
    ```

    Write a procedure that reads a line of input and echoes it to output with all sequences of spaces reduced to single spaces. The procedure should reposition both the input and output cursors to the beginning of the next line before terminating.

6.10 Programming Problems

1. Write an interactive program that prompts for an integer and displays the same number in binary. How would you modify the program to make it display in base 3 rather than base 2?

2. Write a program that takes as input a single-spaced text file and produces as output a double-spaced text file.

3. Suppose that you are given a file with all its letters in uppercase. A program cannot distinguish all cases where a word should be capitalized, but it can distinguish some of them. Write a program that capitalizes the first word of every sentence and lowercases the rest, assuming that sentences are terminated by either a period, question mark, or exclamation mark.

4. Students are often told that their term papers should have a certain number of words in them. Counting words in a long paper is a tedious task, but the computer can help. Write a program that counts the number of words in a paper, assuming that consecutive words are separated either by spaces or end-of-line characters.

5. Write a program that takes as input a series of student names and their grades and produces as output a list of the grade-point averages of the students.

6. Write a program that takes as input lines of text such as

   ```
   This is some
   text here.
   ```

and produces as output the same text inside a box, as in

```
+--------------+
| This is some |
| text here.   |
+--------------+
```

Your program will have to assume some maximum line length (e.g., 12 above).

7

SIMPLE ARRAYS

7.1 Introduction

The sequential nature of the file severely limits the number of interesting things you can easily do with it. The algorithms you have examined so far have all been sequential algorithms: algorithms that can be performed by examining each data item once in a sequence. There is an entirely different class of algorithms that can be performed when you have random access of the data, and when you can access the data items as many times as you like and in whatever order you like.

This chapter examines a new object that provides this random access—the array. The discussion of array applications begins with some sequential algorithms that are enhanced by arrays.

Before the introduction of arrays and an example of a typical array application, the chapter introduces a new kind of type—subrange types. These are important because you cannot define arrays without them. A discussion of giving names to array structures, an important engineering technique that allows you to more clearly express yourself and adds to the adaptability of the procedures you write, follows. Next, this chapter examines some more array applications using arrays with varying structure and concludes by pointing out some of the limitations of arrays and giving some guidelines on documentation.

7.2 Subrange Types

In Pascal, you can make a new type by using a subrange of an existing ordinal type (the ordinals include `INTEGER` and `CHAR`). The type `INTEGER`, for example, includes all values between $-$`MAXINT` and $+$`MAXINT`. You can introduce a new type by using a low and high value to define the subrange:

```
VAR score: 0..100;
```

The general form of the subrange type follows. You cannot insert a space between the two dots in a subrange type, but there can be spaces before or after the dots.

<*constant*> .. <*constant*>

The domain of the subrange type is the set of all values between the first and second constant inclusive. The operations allowed on the type are the same as the operations allowed on the type from which it is derived. Thus, with a variable that is a subrange of type `INTEGER`, you can still perform addition, subtraction, and the other `INTEGER` operations. Because subrange types come from ordinal types, they are themselves ordinal.

Subrange types let you describe more precisely how you intend to use a particular variable. For example, if you were writing a program to read in test scores you might use the declaration

```
VAR score : 0..100;
```

to indicate that all the scores will be between the values of 0 and 100 inclusive. If the variable takes on a value outside of this range, most Pascal systems will generate a message indicating that an error has occurred. This allows many mistakes to be caught early rather than letting a program continue to execute.

You can also define subranges of type `CHAR`. The following declaration restricts the variable `letter` to the range of characters between capital 'A' and capital 'Z':

```
VAR letter: 'A'..'Z';
```

Subranges are most useful, however, when used in conjunction with a new data structure called an array.

7.3 Arrays

Arrays, like files, are structured objects that have individual components. The array structure, however, allows random access. You can access any component at any time, no matter what you have accessed already.

An *array* is a collection of data objects that have the same type. These different components are indexed by some sequence of ordinal values. The indexes differentiate the different components. This is similar to the way post office boxes are set up. Each post office has a series of boxes that all store the same thing—mail. The boxes are indexed with numbers so that you can refer to an individual box by using a description such as "post office box 884."

In a banking program, for example, you might have a collection of variables that represent the balances of different customers. If you have a banking program that keeps track of three balances in three different variables, that is,

```
VAR bal1 : REAL;
    bal2 : REAL;
    bal3 : REAL;
```

you can simplify this scheme by using an array:

```
VAR bal : ARRAY [1..3] OF REAL;
```

This description says that variable `bal` is indexed by numbers 1 through 3 and has components for each of the values of the index type (i.e., for every value between 1 and 3, there is a corresponding component). It also says that each component of `bal` is of type `REAL`. Thus you might picture `bal` like this (there are three components, one for each of the values in the range of the index type):

```
            bal

[1]    ┌──────────┐
       │   12.34  │
[2]    ├──────────┤
       │    9.28  │
[3]    ├──────────┤
       │  1243.19 │
       └──────────┘
```

In describing an array, you must describe the range of its index and the type of each individual component. Here is the syntax of an array declaration:

```
ARRAY [<index type>] OF <element type>
```

The index range is specified by an ordinal type. Normally, this will be a subrange type, although you can use the name of any ordinal type. It is not difficult to see why Pascal requires that the index be ordinal. Consider an array indexed over `REAL`s. If the array went from 2.5 to 3.5, you would need a component for each value in that range. Because there are infinitely many values in that range, you could not store them all. Ordinal types, however, always have a finite number of values between any two.

The *<type>* that follows can be any type in Pascal, including (as you will see later) other arrays. There is no restriction on what can be stored in an array. The only restrictions are on how the array is indexed.

To keep track of 100 bank customers, you would use this description:

```
VAR bal : ARRAY [1..100] OF REAL;
```

If you put some values into the components of `bal`, it might look like this:

bal

[1]	12.34
[2]	9.28
[3]	1243.19
[4]	12.32
[...]	...
[100]	983.23

You refer to a single component of the array by using its index inside the square bracket characters. For example,

```
bal [3]
```

is a reference to the object corresponding to the index 3. This object has the value 1243.19. You are not restricted to constant values inside of these brackets. You can use any expression that matches the type of the index type. This lets you use variables to process large parts of the array. For example, the following is quite tedious:

```
bal [1]  := 0;
bal [2]  := 0;
bal [3]  := 0;
bal [4]  := 0;

       . . .
bal [100]  := 0;
```

Assuming you have an INTEGER variable called `index`, you can use it to index over the entire range of values. This single FOR loop will set all the components of the array to 0:

```
FOR index := 1 TO 100 DO
    bal [index] := 0;
```

If you want to write out all the values of an array, you could do something like the following:

```
FOR index := 1 TO 100 DO
    WRITELN ('Value for element #', index:3, ' is ', bal [index]:7:2);
```

If you use an index value that is outside the legal range, e.g.,

```
WRITELN (bal [101]);
```

your program will reach an execution error. The usual error message is "subscript out of bounds" or "array index out of bounds."

7.3.1 Program Example—Tally

Consider a program that uses an array. Suppose you have an input file of INTE-GERs between 1 and 10:

```
2 8 7 4 12 2 1 8 7 1 7 4 4 6 79 5 8 5 1 2 7 4 3 2 4
2 7 4 5 4 10 2 275 93 1 5 4 5 6 8 1 2 6 -999 9 5 7
64 3 4 2 3 10 2 4 9 5 3 -36 9 1 6 2 2 1 6 6 1 3 8 6
```

To add how many times each number appears in the input file, you would

tally occurrences.
report results.

Tallying the occurrences involves reading in all the numbers, so you will want some file processing loops:

```
while (not at end of file) do
begin
     while (not at end of line) do
     begin
          read a number.
          process the number.
     end
     go to a new line of input.
end
report results.
```

Now all you have to do is figure out how to tally a number and how to report the results. To do so, you must first recognize that you are doing 10 separate tallies. You are tallying the occurrences of the number 1, the number 2, the number 3, and so on up to and including the number 10. You will more easily solve the overall task if you first solve the task of performing one tally. To tally the occurrences of the number 1, you would want a simple INTEGER variable. You can perform the tally by a straightforward cumulative sum, initializing your tally variable to 0 outside the loop and incrementing it every time you see an occurrence of 1:

set total to 0.
while (not at end of file) do

```
begin
    while (not at end of line) do
    begin
        read a number.
        if the number is 1 then
            increment total.
    end
    go to a new line of input.
end
report the value of total.
```

To solve the task of tallying all 10 numbers, you can use an array with one component for tallying each value. The index is from 1 to 10, one for each value to be tallied. Because your single tally used a simple INTEGER variable, you will want your array to have INTEGER components. This way you will have a different INTEGER variable for each of the 10 tallying tasks. Here is the declaration you would use for the array:

```
VAR total : ARRAY [1..10] OF INTEGER;
```

Here is what **total** looks like initially:

```
        total

[1]     ?

[2]     ?

[...]   ...

[10]    ?
```

You can solve this problem by processing the file once looking for 1s, then on a second pass looking for 2s, then a third pass looking for 3s, and so on. This is highly inefficient, however. It is more efficient to do all the tallying operations in parallel. Thus your pseudocode becomes

```
set each component of total to 0.
while (not at end of file) do
begin
    while (not at end of line) do
    begin
        read a number.
        increment the total for the component corresponding to number.
    end
    go to a new line of input.
end
report the value of each component of total.
```

In the last section you learned how to set every component of an array to 0 and how to report the value of each component. The only thing left to figure out is how to increment the appropriate component of total depending on the number read in. This is quite simple. You use the variable `number` to index the component you are interested in. Thus, instead of saying

increment the total for the component corresponding to number.

you can approach Pascal more by saying

increment total [number].

One last point you should consider is what happens if a number is out of range. What if the file contains a number that is less than 1 or greater than 10? You would obtain an array index out of bounds. There are many ways to account for this problem. One simple solution is to keep track of how many illegal values appear. Thus the line above is replaced by

if (number is in range) then
    increment total [number].
else
    increment number of illegal values.

This requires introducing a new variable that tallies the number of illegal values. You would initialize the variable to 0 before the loop.

You can easily translate this pseudocode. Notice that the particular subrange used by this program is a nice application for named constants and that variable `index` is of a subrange type while the variable `next` is of type INTEGER.

```
(* This program takes an input file of values between "low and "high" *)
(* and reports the frequency of occurrence of each value.              *)

PROGRAM Tally1 (INPUT, OUTPUT);
CONST low   = 1;                                (* lowest value in file     *)
      high  = 10;                               (* highest value in file    *)
VAR   total : ARRAY [low..high] OF INTEGER;     (* occurrences of each value *)
      next  : INTEGER;                          (* next input value         *)
      index : low..high;                        (* loop counter             *)
      NumBad : INTEGER;                         (* number of illegal values *)

BEGIN   (* main program *)
    FOR index := low TO high DO
        total [index] := 0;
    NumBad := 0;
    WHILE NOT EOF DO
    BEGIN
        WHILE NOT EOLN DO
```

good example

```
    BEGIN
        READ (next);
        IF (next IN [low..high]) THEN
            total [next] := total [next] + 1
        ELSE
            NumBad := NumBad + 1
    END;
    READLN
END;
WRITELN ('Value    Occurrences');
FOR index := low TO high DO
    WRITELN (index:3, total [index]:12);
WRITELN ('Other', NumBad:10)
END.    (* main program *)
```

If this program were executed using the earlier input file, it would produce the following output:

Value	Occurrences
1	8
2	11
3	5
4	10
5	7
6	7
7	6
8	5
9	3
10	2
Other	7

This program uses a sequential algorithm that has been improved by the array. You could have written the program without an array using many simple tally variables.

7.3.2 Giving Names to Types

Before there were televisions, there was no word "television" in our vocabulary. The first television built was probably described as "a cathode-ray tube sitting in a box that picks up electrical transmissions and displays them on a phosphorus screen." Rather than use that complicated description, someone created a single word to describe the object: "television."

When programmers describe the types of variables in Pascal, they often create complicated descriptions. Consider the declaration of the array in **tally1**:

```
VAR    total : ARRAY [low..high] OF INTEGER;
```

You could describe the type of variable `total` as "a collection of INTEGER variables indexed from `low` to `high`." No single word names the type. Such types are called *anonymous types*.

Pascal puts severe limitations on variables of anonymous type. They cannot be passed as **VAR** parameters, for example. The following is prohibited:

```
PROCEDURE BadStuff (VAR list: ARRAY [1..10] OF INTEGER);
```

The types used in parameter declarations must be named types. You cannot use complicated descriptions such as the one above. This restriction exists for several reasons. First, it is easier for the compiler writer if he has an easy way to verify that a variable is of the same type as a parameter. If he has a single name describing the type, he can compare the names. If he has a complicated description, however, he has to compare the structures. Another reason Pascal has this restriction is that when you introduce a new type, it is best to indicate in some straightforward way what objects of the program are of that type. The easiest way to do this is by having a single name that describes the type.

Because you will certainly want to pass parameters and to clearly indicate the type of all the objects used in your programs, you need to learn how to give names to types. To do so, you use a TYPE declaration which has the following syntax:

```
TYPE   <identifier>  =  <type>;
       <identifier>  =  <type>;
             . . .
       <identifier>  =  <type>;
```

For example, you could give a name to the `tally` program types by saying:

```
TYPE range = low..high;
     list  = ARRAY [range] OF INTEGER;
```

This declaration defines the words **range** and **list** as new types. Notice that you can use the name of the subrange inside the brackets of the array declaration. That is so because **range** is an ordinal type, so you can use it to index the array. You could then define variables to be of these types.

Pascal requires that declarations be in a particular order (no jumbling is allowed). Because many TYPE declarations depend on constants (in subranges, for example), and because variable declarations depend on the type declarations (you have to describe the classes of objects before you can describe the objects), it is not difficult to realize what order makes sense. The proper order of declaration is as follows:

CONST declarations
TYPE declarations
VAR declarations

Here is another version of the `tally` program that gives names to all the constants, types, and variables and that introduces some procedures. Notice that just as you use program constants in a global way, you also use TYPE declarations in a global way.

```
(* This program takes an input file of values between "low and "high" *)
(* and reports the frequency of occurrence of each value.             *)

PROGRAM Tally2 (INPUT, OUTPUT);
CONST low   = 1;                         (* lowest value in file      *)
      high  = 10;                        (* highest value in file     *)
TYPE  range = low..high;                 (* range of values           *)
      list  = ARRAY [range] OF INTEGER;  (* a list of totals          *)
VAR   total : list;                      (* occurrences of each value *)
      NumBad : INTEGER;                   (* number of illegal values  *)

PROCEDURE Initialize (VAR total  : list;
                      VAR NumBad : INTEGER);
(* Sets NumBad and all the components of Total to 0. *)
VAR index : range;    (* loop indexer *)
BEGIN
    FOR index := low TO high DO
        total [index] := 0;
    NumBad := 0
END;   (* Initialize *)


PROCEDURE Tally (VAR total  : list;
                 VAR NumBad : INTEGER);
(* Processes the input file, tallying the occurrences of each value. *)
VAR next : INTEGER;    (* next value in input file *)
BEGIN
    WHILE NOT EOF DO
    BEGIN
        WHILE NOT EOLN DO
        BEGIN
            READ (next);
            IF (next IN [low..high]) THEN
                total [next] := total [next] + 1
            ELSE
                NumBad := NumBad + 1
        END;
        READLN
    END
END;   (* Tally *)
```

```
PROCEDURE Report (total  : list;
                  NumBad : INTEGER);
(* Reports the occurrences of each value. *)
VAR index : range;    (* loop counter *)
BEGIN
    WRITELN ('Value    Occurrences');
    FOR index := low TO high DO
        WRITELN (index:4, total [index]:10);
    WRITELN ('Other', NumBad:9)
END;   (* Report *)

BEGIN    (* main program *)
    Initialize (total, NumBad);
    Tally (total, NumBad);
    Report (total, NumBad)
END.     (* main program *)
```

A type declaration is very different from a variable declaration. A type declaration is like a blueprint for a building. It describes the structure but is not itself a building. Thus, even though list is defined as a type in the preceding program, you can't make a reference to

```
list [1]
```

This is like asking who lives in apartment 1 of a blueprint. Once you have a blueprint, you can make specific instances of it. In other words, once you have your blueprint, you can actually build some objects that follow the blueprint. For example, the **tally** program defines a variable **total** of type list. It makes perfect sense to refer to

```
total [1]
```

because total is an object (a variable), whereas list is simply a description of an object.

7.3.3 Noninteger Indexing of Arrays

Just as subranges can be defined over both INTEGER and CHAR values, arrays can be indexed over both INTEGER and CHAR values. Here is an array indexed over a subrange of type CHAR:

```
VAR list: ARRAY ['A'..'F'] OF INTEGER;
```

This variable has the following structure:

```
          List

['A']    |  2  |

['B']    | 12  |

['C']    |  4  |

['D']    |  5  |

['E']    | 16  |

['F']    |  3  |
```

If ASCII is the collating sequence, this array will have six elements (one for each letter between 'A' and 'F'). You might use a structure such as this to tally up the number of occurrences of the letters 'A' through 'F' in an input file. You can, in fact, make the following minor modification to the `tally` program to make it tally these letters instead of the numbers 1 through 10:

```
CONST low  = 'A';   (* lowest value in input file  *)
      high = 'Z';   (* highest value in input file *)

VAR   next : CHAR;  (* next input value *)
```

Changing the values of two constants and the type of one variable changes everything in the program that needs to be changed, because the types were defined in terms of the constants and the variables and parameters were defined in terms of the types. The `tally` program is remarkably adaptable because of its use of named constants and types. You should aim for this kind of adaptability, even though it is usually more difficult to achieve.

7.3.4 Variable Length Data

So far we have discussed an array that is in some sense full: all its elements were in use. This is not the usual case. Usually you build an array with a maximum in mind, but only fill it up partially.

If you want to use an array to process some lines of characters from an input file, you use a single array to store the characters of one input line. Because the lines differ in length, you don't know how big to make the array. Therefore, the best you can do is to set some arbitrary maximum for the length of a line and make the array that large. There is no way to change the size of an array while the program is executing. Some programming languages do allow you to define such things (they are called *dynamic arrays*), but not Pascal. You have to make a decision when you write your program as to how big the array should be.

In defining the types for such an array, you might write declarations such as the following:

```
CONST LineMin    = 1;         (* starting length    *)
      LineLength = 70;        (* maximum line length *)
TYPE  LineRange  = LineMin..LineLength;  (* range of line length *)
      LineList   = ARRAY [LineRange] OF CHAR;  (* stores one data line *)
```

These are not, however, the typical declarations. There is no need to declare the LineMin, because in such applications you almost always use 1 as the lower index. There is also no good use for the LineRange type. You might at first think that the length variable can be defined to be of this type. This is not so because sometimes the array will be empty. If there are no active components in the array, then you set length to 0. This presents a problem, though, because the LineRange starts at 1, not 0. If you change your index range to start at 0, you introduce an extra element in the array. You could define two different subrange types, one for the index and one for the length. This is rather tedious, however. The simplest alternative is to give up on subrange types and go back to the broader type INTEGER. Many people argue that Pascal has failed to provide the kind of subrange definitions that a programmer wants.

The more typical definitions of such a structure, then, would be

```
CONST LineLength = 70;
TYPE  LineList   = ARRAY [1..LineLength] OF CHAR;
VAR   line       : LineList;
      length     : INTEGER;
```

You define not only an array to hold the contents of the line, but also an INTEGER variable called length to keep track of how many elements of the array are currently being used. If you were to read the following input line:

Wowy!

you would expect the variables line and length to look like this:

The word "Wowy!" appears in the first five memory cells of this array. Because five memory cells of the array are in use, you store the value 5 in the memory cell for length. The elements 6 through 70 are uninitialized, as indicated by the question marks above. If you keep track of the length, however, you can be sure to use only elements of the array that are currently active, which means that you will avoid using an uninitialized value.

Let's examine a program that uses this data structure. Consider the problem of reversing all the lines of a file. Given this input file:

```
How would you get this line of text here
into reverse order?
<------*** radar ***------>
And what about this one?
```

The output file should look like this:

```
ereh txet fo enil siht teg uoy dluow woH
?redro esrever otni
>------*** radar ***------<
?eno siht tuoba tahw dnA
```

Why does this problem require an extra structure? With a file you can read the characters of a line in sequential order. You can't, however, read them backwards. An array has no such limitations. To reverse the line, you read it into an array and then manipulate the array. You should think of this as a transfer of information. The characters from the input line are transferred from the file structure to the array structure. Once transferred, you can manipulate the characters using the array and not worry about the file until it is time to process another line. Thus your pseudocode description would be

```
while (not at end of file) do
begin
     transfer line from file to array.
     write array contents in reverse order.
end
```

The transfer operation involves an EOLN loop.

```
while (not end of line) do
     read a character into the next array component.
```

To improve this pseudocode you need to specify what you mean by the next array component. Because you want to store the first character in component [1], the next in component [2], and so on, you need an integer variable to keep track of this. You also need to keep track of the length. Fortunately, you can easily combine these two tasks:

```
set length to 0.
while (not end of line) do
begin
     increment length.
     read a character into line [length].
end
```

Some novices write the following pseudocode:

```
set length to 1.
while (not end of line) do
```

```
begin
     read a character into line [length].
     increment length.
end
```

The problem here is that **length** ends up being one more than it should be, because you chose the wrong starting value for the length. Before the loop executes, no characters have been read, so the length is 0.

Writing the contents of the array in reverse order is a simple operation. You merely use a DOWNTO loop to index the array backwards. Here is the complete program:

```
(* This program takes a text file as input and produces an output file  *)
(* with all the lines reversed.                                          *)

PROGRAM ReverseLines (INPUT, OUTPUT);
CONST LineLength = 70;                      (* maximum line length    *)
TYPE  LineList   = ARRAY [1..LineLength] OF CHAR;  (* stores one data line *)
VAR   line       : LineList;                (* current input line     *)
      length     : INTEGER;                 (* current line length    *)

PROCEDURE TransferLineTo (VAR line    : LineList;
                          VAR length  : INTEGER);
(* This procedure transfers the characters of the next line from the *)
(* file  structure into the array structure.                         *)
BEGIN
    length := 0;
    WHILE NOT EOLN DO
    BEGIN
        length := length + 1;
        READ (line [length])
    END;
    READLN
END;   (* TransferLineTo *)


PROCEDURE WriteReverse (line    : LineList;
                        length  : INTEGER);
(* This procedure writes the contents of the line in reverse order. *)
VAR count : INTEGER;   (* loop counter *)
BEGIN
    FOR count := length DOWNTO 1 DO
        WRITE (line [count]);
    WRITELN
END;   (* WriteReverse *)
```

```
BEGIN   (* main program *)
    WHILE NOT EOF DO
    BEGIN
        TransferLineTo (line, length);
        WriteReverse (line, length)
    END
END.    (* main program *)
```

7.3.5 Another Application of LineList

The ReverseLines program may not seem terribly useful, but it provides a framework for a whole class of line-oriented programs. For example, let's take an input file of text and center the lines in a field `LineLength` wide. Here is the input file:

```
We are all in the gutter, but some of us are looking at the stars.
--Oscar Wilde

You are not consistent, you cannot be programmed, you are inferior.
--Ruk, Star Trek

Many men stumble upon truth, but most manage to pick themselves up
and continue unscathed.
--Winston Churchill

It is only shallow people who do not judge by appearances.
--Oscar Wilde
```

You want to produce the following output.

```
 We are all in the gutter, but some of us are looking at the stars.
                            --Oscar Wilde

You are not consistent, you cannot be programmed, you are inferior.
                        --Ruk, Star Trek

 Many men stumble upon truth, but most manage to pick themselves up
                      and continue unscathed.
                        --Winston Churchill

     It is only shallow people who do not judge by appearances.
                        --Oscar Wilde
```

This program is simple to write if you use the work you have already done. The basic task is to put enough spaces at the beginning of each line to center it. The number of leading spaces you write depends on the line length. You must calculate how many spaces are not taken up by the line itself. If a line is 40 characters long, there are 30 leftover spaces in a line 70 characters long. You put half of these to the left and half to the right to center the line. Therefore, you use 15 leading spaces. If the line is 30 characters long, there are 40 leftover spaces, and you put half, 20, to the left. You can express the number of leading spaces you require as follows:

```
(70 - length)/2
```

You can improve this expression by realizing that 70 is a magic number that you have called `LineLength` and by realizing that the `DIV` operator would be more appropriate because you want to produce an integral number of leading spaces. Thus a better expression for leading spaces is

```
(LineLength - length) DIV 2
```

The file has many lines in it, and you must center each. To center an individual line, you write the appropriate number of leading spaces and then echo the line. Therefore, your starting pseudocode is

```
while (not at end of file) do
begin
        write (LineLength — length) DIV 2 leading spaces.
        echo line.
end
```

The problem here is that in order to write out the appropriate number of leading spaces, you need to know the length of the line before you start echoing it. This means you can't echo the line character-by-character. You must use the strategy employed in the last section. First, transfer the contents of the line from the file to an array. Then, knowing the length, you can write out the appropriate number of leading spaces and write out the contents of the array. Here is the modified pseudocode:

```
while (not at end of file) do
begin
        transfer line from file to array.
        write (LineLength — length) DIV 2 leading spaces.
        write contents of array.
end
```

Most of this pseudocode has already been implemented. You have a tool for transferring a line from the file to the array and a procedure for writing out an arbitrary number of spaces. All you have to do is write out the contents of the array. This can be done with a simple `FOR` loop. Here is a complete program that implements this strategy:

```
(* This program takes a text file as input and produces an output file  *)
(* with all the lines centered in a field LineLength wide.                *)

PROGRAM CenterLines (INPUT, OUTPUT);
CONST LineLength = 70;                              (* maximum line length  *)
TYPE  LineList   = ARRAY [1..LineLength] OF CHAR;   (* stores one data line *)
VAR   line       : LineList;                        (* current input line   *)
      length     : INTEGER;                         (* current line length  *)

PROCEDURE WriteSpaces (number: INTEGER);
(* This procedure writes "number" spaces on the output line *)
VAR count : INTEGER;    (* loop counter *)
BEGIN
    FOR count := 1 TO number DO
        WRITE (' ')
END;    (* WriteSpaces *)

PROCEDURE TransferLineTo (VAR line   : LineList;
                          VAR length : INTEGER);
(* This procedure transfers the characters of the next line from the *)
(* file structure into the array structure.                          *)
BEGIN
    length := 0;
    WHILE NOT EOLN DO
    BEGIN
        length := length + 1;
        READ (line [length])
    END;
    READLN
END;    (* TransferLineTo *)

PROCEDURE WriteCentered (line   : LineList;
                         length : INTEGER);
(* This procedure writes the line centered. *)
VAR count : INTEGER;    (* loop counter *)
BEGIN
    WriteSpaces ((LineLength - length) DIV 2);
    FOR count := 1 TO length DO
        WRITE (line [count]);
    WRITELN
END;    (* WriteCentered *)
```

```
BEGIN   (* main program *)
     WHILE NOT EOF DO
     BEGIN
         TransferLineTo (line, length);
         WriteCentered (line, length)
     END
END.    (* main program *)
```

7.3.6 Limitations of Array Types

You should be aware of some general limitations of the array type. For example, using the `LineList` type, suppose you have the following variables defined:

```
VAR FirstLine    : LineList;
    SecondLine   : LineList;
    FirstLength  : INTEGER;
    SecondLength : INTEGER;
```

You should not assume that you can perform the operations that you are used to performing on simple types on these variables. For example, you cannot use the relational operators on structured objects. The following are not legal statements:

array

```
IF FirstLine < SecondLine THEN
    WRITELN ('I got this to work.');
IF FirstLine = SecondLine THEN
    WRITELN ('I got this to work as well.');
```

You also cannot use such objects in **READ/READLN** or **WRITE/WRITELN** statements.

You can, however, use them in an assignment statement, as long as it is between two variables of the same type. For example, you can say

```
FirstLine := SecondLine;
```

This statement will copy each individual component of `FirstLine` to the corresponding component of `SecondLine`.

Just because you can't do things the normal way doesn't mean that you can't do them. You can't say

```
WRITELN (FirstLine);
```

But you can build a procedure for writing out one of these objects:

```
PROCEDURE WriteLineList (line   : LineList;
                         length : INTEGER);
VAR index : INTEGER;
BEGIN
    FOR index := 1 TO length DO
        WRITE (line [index]);
    WRITELN
END;   (* WriteLineList *)
```

This procedure uses the WRITE statement to write out the individual components of variable line. Because these components are all of type CHAR, you can do this by taking advantage of the fact that CHAR objects can be written. You are building a writing procedure on top of the facility for writing simple characters. All you have to do is tell the computer which of the components to write and in what order.

Similarly, you can build tools to compare such structures for equality. You can't do this directly on the structured variables, but you can do it on the components of the variables. Thus, if you build a procedure where you specify the components to compare and in what order, you can build a tool for comparing the structured objects.

7.4 Documentation Revisited

Now that you are starting to develop some useful tools, let's review how to make sure these tools are well documented. Some of the basic ideas of documentation and some specific techniques that you can use follow.

First, you should use the language as much as possible to write readable code. If you can name a procedure TransferLineTo rather than x, do it. Push the language as far as it will go, trying to make the code itself the documentation. This requires you to find the name most appropriate for each object. Pondering such mysteries takes time, but the results are well worth it.

There are limitations to the amount of documentation the program itself can provide, however. Some code will take you hours to get right. This code is usually so dense that it can't serve as its own documentation. For these parts of a program, you should provide supplemental documentation in the form of comments. These comments should be inserted right along with the code:

```
(* We convert the angle from radians to degrees by using the *)
(* fact that 180 degrees = pi radians.  We do so because the *)
(* Pascal angle operations are defined only for radians.     *)
angle := AngleInDegrees * pi/180;
```

The amount of documentation you provide should be proportional to the difficulty of the code. There is no need to document lines of code that are obvious. Documenting the obvious detracts from the readability of your program.

You should provide some kind of documentation for each structural unit of your program. For example, each new procedure should be commented. A good way to do this is to attach a block of comments to each procedure. Here are the things you should describe:

- Parameters   The names of the parameters and whether each is in (value being used), in/out (variable being modified), or out (variable being initialized).
- Task   What task is performed by this procedure (usually described in terms of its parameters).
- Requirements   Lists any dependencies (procedures, variables, types, and constants declared outside the scope of this procedure).
- Structure   What kind of data structure is used.
- Algorithm   What kind of algorithm is used. If the algorithm has a name (e.g., sentinel loop), the name is used. Otherwise, if the algorithm is complicated enough, a brief description of the algorithm is included.

The first three of these describe the procedure's linkage to the outside world, i.e., how to use this tool. The other two describe the internal details of the procedure, i.e., how it does what it does. The first three are the specification, the last two the implementation. From here on, this book will include such comments in all procedures.

The program itself is a structural unit that should have documentation attached to it. You can use a block similar to the procedure comments to describe the program. The only difference is that the parameters for the program are the input and output files. The documentation for your program is also a convenient place to list information about yourself: your name, the date you last worked on the program, what assignment number it is, and so on.

Finally, you should document all objects and types that you define. Every variable, constant, and type should have a brief comment attached to it to describe what it is to be used for.

Here is an example of complete documentation, using the line-centering program:

```
(* parameters : INPUT-in, OUTPUT-out.                              *)
(* task       : Every line of the INPUT file is echoed to the OUTPUT *)
(*             : file in a centered field "LineLength" long.         *)
(* structure  : One-dimensional array of characters to store each line. *)
(* algorithm  : EOF loop; each line is transferred from the file to the *)
(*             : array, then written out with leading spaces to center  *)
(*             : the line.                                            *)
```

```
PROGRAM CenterLines (INPUT, OUTPUT);
CONST LineLength = 70;                           (* maximum line length  *)
TYPE  LineList   = ARRAY [1..LineLength] OF CHAR; (* stores one data line *)
VAR   line       : LineList;                      (* current input line   *)
      length     : INTEGER;                       (* current line length  *)

PROCEDURE WriteSpaces (number: INTEGER);
(* parameters : Number-in.                                              *)
(* task       : The specified number of spaces is written to output. *)
VAR count      : INTEGER;   (* loop counter                          *)
BEGIN
    FOR count := 1 TO number DO
        WRITE (' ')
END;   (* WriteSpaces *)


PROCEDURE TransferLineTo (VAR line    : LineList;
                          VAR length  : INTEGER);
(* parameters : Line-out, Length-out.                                  *)
(* task       : Contents of current input line stored in Line; Length *)
(*            : set to number of characters transferred; input cursor *)
(*            : at beginning of next line.                             *)
(* requires   : type LineList.                                        *)
(* algorithm  : EOLN loop.                                            *)
BEGIN
    length := 0;
    WHILE NOT EOLN DO
    BEGIN
        length := length + 1;
        READ (line [length])
    END;
    READLN
END;   (* TransferLineTo *)


PROCEDURE WriteCentered (line    : LineList;
                         length  : INTEGER);
(* parameters : Line-in, Length-in.                                    *)
(* task       : Given Line with given Length is written to output file *)
(*            : centered in a field LineLength wide.                   *)
(* requires   : constant LineLength; type LineList.                    *)
VAR count      : INTEGER;   (* loop counter                          *)
BEGIN
    (* We calculate the number of unused spaces on the line, divide by *)
    (* two, and write that number of leading spaces, so that half will *)
```

```
    (* appear to the left of the line.
    WriteSpaces ((LineLength - length) DIV 2);
    FOR count := 1 TO length DO
        WRITE (line [count]);
    WRITELN
END;   (* WriteCentered *)

BEGIN   (* main program *)
    WHILE NOT EOF DO
    BEGIN
        TransferLineTo (line, length);
        WriteCentered (line, length)
    END
END.   (* main program *)
```

7.5 Key Concepts

- Any ordinal type can lead to a subrange type whose domain is a subset of the overall domain. You can perform the same operations on objects of the subrange type as you can on objects of the overall type.

- An array is a structured type that allows random access to an individual element by referring to its index value. Such references to the index value can be made using arbitrary expressions, so that you can write simple code that manipulates many elements of an array structure.

- Use the TYPE declaration to name any new type that you introduce into a program if you intend to declare variables of that type. Variables that are of an unnamed type cannot be passed as parameters.

- Arrays can be indexed by any ordinal type and can store elements of any type.

- You will often store a length variable along with an array if you don't intend to fill the array completely.

7.6 Self-Check Exercises

1. Given these constants:

```
CONST low  = 1;
      high = 10;
```

   which of the following are legal subrange types?

```
0..5                    '0'..9
-10..+10                1..2+2
low..high               'a'..'z'
10..10                  high..low
-high..-low             low..50
```

2. What type does not have subrange types?

3. Given these types:

```
TYPE RangeType = 1..20;
     Alphabet  = 'A'..'Z';
```

which of the following are legal array types? For the legal types, indicate how many elements each has.

```
ARRAY [INTEGER] OF CHAR;
ARRAY [1..20] OF RangeType;
ARRAY [1..100] OF CHAR;
ARRAY [0..10] OF alphabet;
ARRAY [alphabet] OF alphabet;
ARRAY ['A'..20] OF alphabet;
```

4. How many elements are there in the following array?

```
VAR strange : ARRAY [-100..100] OF REAL;
```

5. Given the following declarations:

```
TYPE ListType = ARRAY [1..10] OF CHAR;
VAR  first    : ListType;
     second   : ARRAY [1..10] OF CHAR;
     third    : ARRAY [1..10] OF CHAR;
```

Are **first** and **second** of the same type? **first** and **third**? **second** and **third**?

Questions 6 to 9 refer to the following:

A sequence of numbers is stored in an array with the following declarations:

```
CONST MaxLength = 100;
TYPE  ListType  = ARRAY [1..MaxLength] OF INTEGER;
VAR   list      : ListType;
      length    : INTEGER;
```

6. Write some code that stores the even numbers between 1 and 35 in **list**, giving an appropriate value to **length**.

7. Write a function with the following header that returns the sum of the numbers stored in **list**:

```
FUNCTION Sum (list   : ListType;
              length : INTEGER) : INTEGER;
```

8. Write a procedure with the following header that eliminates any zeros stored in `list`, resetting `length` appropriately. The nonzero elements should remain in the same order. For example, if `list` stores the numbers (1, 7, 0, 3, 8), it should be changed to (1, 7, 3, 8) and `length` should be reset to 4.

```
PROCEDURE EliminateZeros (VAR list   : ListType;
                          VAR length : INTEGER);
```

9. Write a procedure with the following header that reverses the order of elements in `list`:

```
PROCEDURE Reverse (VAR list   : ListType;
                       length : INTEGER);
```

7.7 Programming Problems

1. Every Pascal implementation places a limit on the largest integer that can be manipulated. This limit can be circumvented by representing an integer as an array of digits. Write an interactive program that adds two integers of up to 50 digits each.

2. Personal mailing labels can prove quite useful. Write a program that reads a five-line address from an input file and produces an output file with the address repeated 50 times in three columns.

3. Write a program that reads an input file of numbers and reports the average of the numbers as well as how far each number is from the average.

4. Write a program that plays a variation of the game of Mastermind with a user. For example, the program can use pseudorandom numbers to generate a four-digit number. The user should be allowed to make guesses until he gets the number correct. Clues should be given to the user indicating how many digits of the guess are correct and in the correct place and how many are correct but in the wrong place.

5. Write a program that reads an input file and reports the longest word appearing in the file.

6. Write a program that prompts the user for two words and compares them alphabetically to see which is less. Identify which procedures are likely to be useful later as software tools.

7. Write a program that decodes a file. Assume that the first line of the file contains 26 letters which specify how the file was encoded. The first letter describes how to decode 'A', the second describes how to decode 'B', and so on.

8

PROGRAM LOGIC

8.1 Introduction

This chapter explores how you can apply logic to computer programs. After reviewing some basic concepts of propositional logic and learning a new type that stores true/false information, you will see how operations on this type let you write more complex loops than you have been able to write before and how precedence of expressions works given these new operations.

With the background given, you can then explore some more significant applications of logic to programming: how you can reason logically about a program and how you can prove various properties of programs. In this light, verification takes on new meaning. You will see that programs can not only be tested, but actually proved to be correct. You will also see, however, that most such proofs are currently too difficult to construct. Reasoning about programs this way not only allows you to see how a computer scientist analyzes a program, but also gives you a basis for working out the logic of complex programs. While good programmers instinctively program this way, people who don't have programming in their blood will find this helpful.

Next, the chapter examines ways to describe the logical connections between different pieces of a program. These methods give you a more sophisticated vocabulary for discussing whether or not a piece of code works. Last, the chapter discusses how logic relates to documentation, problem solving, and debugging.

8.2   Assertions and Propositions

Before examining how to apply logic to the writing of programs, you need to review some of the basics of propositional logic. Those of you who have had a course in propositional logic should move ahead to Section 8.3.

Logicians concern themselves with *assertions*.

ASSERTION

A declarative sentence.

The following are all assertions:

$2 + 2 = 4$

The sun is larger than the earth.

$x > 45$

It was raining.

The rain in Spain falls mainly on the plain.

Edsgar Dijkstra thinks BASIC is better than Pascal.

The following are not assertions (the first is a question and the second is a command):

How much do you weigh?

Please take me home.

Some assertions are either true or false. They are called *propositions*.

PROPOSITION

An assertion that is either true or false.

The following assertions are not propositions because they can be true or false depending on context:

$x > 45$	This depends on x.
It was raining.	This depends on when and where.

You can make such assertions propositions by providing a context:

When $x = 13$, $x > 45$.

On July 4, 1776 in Philadelphia, it was raining.

In algebra, you use variables as placeholders for numbers. You can then use the arithmetic operators (+, −, *, /) to form complex expressions of numbers and variables. In logic, you use variables as placeholders for propositions. The variables P, Q, and R could represent the following propositions:

p: $2 + 2 = 4$.
q: The sun is larger than the earth.
r: Edsgar Dijkstra thinks BASIC is better than Pascal.

8.2.1 Negation and Logical Connectives

You represent the logical negation of a proposition by putting the word "not" in front of it. You read the negation operator "It is not the case that . . . ."

not $(2 + 2 = 4)$

not (The sun is larger than the earth.)

not (Edsgar Dijkstra thinks BASIC is better than Pascal.)

or

not p

not q

not r

The negation operator reverses the truth value of the proposition. If a proposition is true, its negation is false, and vice versa. You can express this using a truth table. The following truth table has two columns, one for a variable and one for its negation. The table shows for each value of the variable, the corresponding value of the negation.

p	not p
true	false
false	true

In addition to the negation operator, there are two logical connectives you will use, "and" and "or." You use these connectives to tie two propositions together, thus creating a new proposition. The "and" operator is also called the *conjunction*. For example,

$(2 + 2 = 4)$ and (The sun is larger than the earth.)

or using propositional variables,

p and q

The truth table shows that the conjunction is true only when both of its individual statements are true:

p	q	p and q
true	true	true
true	false	false
false	true	false
false	false	false

You could form the following conjunctions:

$(2 + 2 = 4)$ and (The sun is larger than the earth.)

$(2 + 2 = 4)$ and (Edsgar Dijkstra thinks BASIC is better than Pascal.)

The first is true, because both its individual propositions are true. The second is false, because the second proposition is false.

The second connective, "or," is also called the *disjunction*. For example,

$(2 + 2 = 4)$ or (The sun is larger than the earth.)

or written with propositional variables,

p or *q*

The truth table shows that the disjunction is true except when both statements are false.

p	q	p or q
true	true	true
true	false	true
false	true	true
false	false	false

The following statement is true because the first proposition is true:

$(2 + 2 = 4)$ or (Edsgar Dijkstra thinks BASIC is better than Pascal.)

The following overall proposition is false because both the propositions that make it up are false:

$(2 > 4)$ or (Edsgar Dijkstra thinks BASIC is better than Pascal.)

The disjunction has a slightly different meaning from the English "or." In English you say, "I'll study tonight or I'll go to a movie." One proposition or the other will be true, but not both. The logical "or" behaves differently. If both propositions are true, the overall proposition is true.

When you work with complex logical expressions, it is useful to apply rules that simplify expressions. For example, negating a proposition twice yields the original logic value of the proposition. Therefore, if you ever find yourself with

not not p

you replace it with

p

You use the symbol " $<\longrightarrow$ " to express such replacement rules. This symbol indicates that one logical formula is equivalent to another. You would, therefore, express the double negation rule as

not not p $<\longrightarrow$ p

Here is a list of replacement rules that may prove useful in writing your programs and the names usually given to them:

Replacement Rule	Name
not not p $<\longrightarrow$ p	Double negation
not (p and q) $<\longrightarrow$ not p or not q	De Morgan's law
not (p or q) $<\longrightarrow$ not p and not q	De Morgan's law
p and q $<\longrightarrow$ q and p	Commutative property
p or q $<\longrightarrow$ q or p	Commutative property
(p and q) and r $<\longrightarrow$ p and (q and r)	Associative property
(p or q) or r $<\longrightarrow$ p or (q or r)	Associative property
p and (q or r) $<\longrightarrow$ (p and q) or (p and r)	Distributive property
p or (q and r) $<\longrightarrow$ (p or q) and (p or r)	Distributive property

8.3 Type BOOLEAN

George Boole was such a good logician that a type has been named for him. You use the Pascal type BOOLEAN to describe logical true/false relationships (propositions).

Without realizing it, you have already used BOOLEANs. IF/THEN/ELSE statements and WHILE loops are controlled by expressions that specify tests. The expression

```
number MOD 2 = 0
```

is a test for divisibility by 2. It is also a BOOLEAN expression. This at first looks like an assertion but not a proposition. However, it is neither true nor false because it depends on the value of the variable number. You provide this assertion with a context by performing the test at a specific point in program execution. At this specific point, the assertion is either true or false, so you can think of it as a proposition.

BOOLEAN expressions are meant to capture the concepts of truth and falsity, so it is not surprising that the domain of type BOOLEAN has only two values— TRUE and FALSE. The words TRUE and FALSE are keywords in Pascal. They are the constant values of type BOOLEAN. All BOOLEAN expressions, when evaluated, will return one or the other of these constants.

To understand this better, remember what these terms mean for INTEGERs. The domain of the INTEGERs is the set of whole numbers. This means an INTEGER variable can take on many different values. The constants of type INTEGER include 0, 1, 2, and so on. Because these are constants of type INTEGER, you can do things such as the following (assuming variables called number1 and number2 of type INTEGER):

```
number1 := 1;
number2 := 0;
```

Consider what you can do with variables of type BOOLEAN. Suppose you define variables called test1 and test2 of type BOOLEAN. These variables can only take on two possible values—TRUE and FALSE. You can say

```
test1 := TRUE;
test2 := FALSE;
```

You can also write a statement that copies the value of one BOOLEAN variable to another, as with variables of any other type:

```
test1 := test2;
```

You also know that the assignment statement can use expressions:

```
number1 := 2 + 2;
```

and that the simple tests you have been using are BOOLEAN expressions:

```
test1 := (2 + 2 = 4);
test2 := (3 * 100 < 250);
```

These assignment statements say "set this BOOLEAN variable according to the truth value of the following proposition." The first statement sets the variable test1 to TRUE, because the proposition is true. The second sets the variable test2 to FALSE, because the second proposition is false. The parentheses are not needed, but they make the statement more readable.

Many beginners don't understand these assignment statements and write such code as the following:

```
IF (first < second) THEN
    less := TRUE
ELSE
    less := FALSE;
```

This is a redundant statement. First, it evaluates the truth value of the test (`first < second`). If the result is `TRUE`, it executes the `THEN` part and assigns `less` the value `TRUE`. If the result is `FALSE`, is executes the `ELSE` part and assigns `less` the value `FALSE`. Since you are assigning `less` the truth value of the `IF/THEN/ELSE`'s test, you should do it directly:

```
less := (first < second);
```

Obviously, then, the assignment statement is one of the operations you can perform on variables of type `BOOLEAN`. In addition, you can use the `WRITE` and `WRITELN` statements to output a `BOOLEAN` expression. The computer writes `BOOLEAN` expressions as the word "true" or the word "false." Therefore, this program:

```
PROGRAM foo (OUTPUT);
VAR test1 : BOOLEAN;
    test2 : BOOLEAN;
BEGIN
    test1 := (3 = 1 + 2);
    test2 := (97 < 5);
    WRITELN (test1, test2)
END.
```

produces this output:

```
true false
```

Note that type `BOOLEAN` is an ordinal type. Unfortunately, this does not turn out to be very useful. Because type `BOOLEAN` is an ordinal type, you can do comparisons on `BOOLEAN`s (`FALSE` is less than `TRUE`). You can also use the `PRED`, `SUCC`, and `ORD` functions and have `FOR` loops controlled by `BOOLEAN` variables.

You form complicated `BOOLEAN` expressions using the following operators:

Operator	Meaning	Example	Value
AND	Logical conjunction	(2 = 2) AND (3 < 4)	TRUE
OR	Logical disjunction	(1 < 2) OR (2 = 3)	TRUE
NOT	Logical negation	NOT (2 = 2)	FALSE

How does this relate to the propositional variables you manipulated earlier? Consider the following expression:

```
((2 = 3) AND (NOT (3 < 4))) OR (0 < 1)
```

Using propositional variables, that is,

```
P:      (2 = 3)
Q:      (3 < 4)
R:      (0 < 1)
```

makes the expression easier to read:

```
(P AND (NOT Q)) OR Q
```

In this example, P is **FALSE** and Q and R are **TRUE**. Thus you have

```
(FALSE AND (NOT TRUE)) OR TRUE
```

You can reduce this using the truth tables for these operators:

```
(FALSE AND (NOT TRUE)) OR TRUE
(FALSE AND ( FALSE  )) OR TRUE
(       FALSE        ) OR TRUE
                TRUE
```

Thus the overall expression evaluates to **TRUE**.

People use the words "and" and "or" all the time. Pascal only allows you to use them in the strict logical sense, however. So be careful not to write code such as the following:

```
IF (X = 1 OR 2 OR 3) THEN        not
    something;
```

You can use the **AND** and **OR** operators only to join propositions together. Otherwise, the computer will not understand what you mean. To express this using the **BOOLEAN OR**, you have to string three different propositions together:

```
IF (X = 1) OR (X = 2) OR (X = 3) THEN
    something;                        yes
```

8.3.1 Use of Logical Operators

You have already seen an application for the **NOT** operator to negate **EOLN** and **EOF**. The **NOT** is useful whenever you have a test you need to express the opposite way.

You generally use the other logical operators when what you have to say does not reduce to one test. For example, consider the problem of reading a series of scores from an input line. If you have a fixed number of scores per line:

```
98 100 95
85 84 100
75 80 83
98 93 95
```

you can use a **FOR** loop to find the sum:

```
sum := 0;
FOR count := 1 to 3 DO
BEGIN
    READ (number);
    sum := sum + number
END;
```

If you aren't sure how many numbers there are, you use a WHILE loop:

```
sum := 0;
WHILE NOT EOLN DO
BEGIN
    READ (number);
    sum := sum + number
END;
```

If you want something that is in between the two, such as reading numbers from the input line but limiting the number of iterations (e.g., reading a series of not more than 10 scores), you want a combination of the above. Because you want the loop to exit if you run out of data (if you reach EOLN) or if you have read 10 scores, you want a WHILE loop with two exit conditions. You would say

exit if (end-of-line) or (you have read 10 scores).

This test is worded in terms of an exit condition. The WHILE loop's test, however, is worded in terms of a continuation condition, not an exit condition. Thus you have to negate the expression. Putting parentheses around the whole expression and putting NOT in front is one way to negate it.

continue if NOT ((end-of-line) or (you have read 10 scores)).

By applying one of De Morgan's Laws (Section 8.2.1), however, you can reduce this to:

continue if (NOT end-of-line) and (you have not read 10 scores).

You can write this as a WHILE loop using the AND and NOT operators:

```
sum := 0;
count := 0;
WHILE NOT EOLN AND (count < 10) DO
BEGIN
    READ (number);
    sum := sum + number;
    count := count + 1
END;
```

Another application of this can ensure you don't overfill an array. A program that reads single lines of input using the following pseudocode does not account for the fact that the array has a fixed size:

set length to 0.
while (not end-of-line) do
begin
    increment length.
    read a character into line [length].
end

You want to exit from the loop if length ever becomes equal to `LineLength`, because that would indicate that the array can hold no more. Thus you want the exit condition to be

exit if (end-of-line) or (you have read LineLength characters).

You negate this to form a continuation condition and apply De Morgan's law:

continue if (not end-of-line) and (you have not read LineLength characters).

You fine-tune this using the `length` variable:

continue if (not end-of-line) and (length < LineLength).

Thus your pseudocode becomes

set length to 0.
while (not end-of-line) and (length < LineLength) do
begin
    increment length.
    read a character into line [length].
end

Here is the modified procedure:

```
PROCEDURE TransferLineTo (VAR line   : LineList;
                          VAR length : INTEGER);
(* This procedure transfers the characters of the next line from the *)
(* file structure into the array structure.                          *)
BEGIN
    length := 0;
    WHILE NOT EOLN AND (length < LineLength) DO
    BEGIN
        length := length + 1;
        READ (line [length])
    END;
    READLN
END;   (* TransferLineTo *)
```

8.3.2 Precedence Revisited

Now that you have seen the operators AND, OR, and NOT, you must again consider the precedence of operators. Here are the four levels from highest to lowest:

Level	Name	Operators
1	Negation	NOT
2	Multiplicative	* / DIV MOD AND
3	Additive	+ − OR
4	Relational	= <> < > <= >= IN

Notice the inclusion of the set operator IN. These levels of precedence answer questions that arise when evaluating such expressions as

```
IF NOT test1 AND test2 OR test3 THEN
    something;
```

Here, the computer evaluates the NOT first, the AND second, and then the OR. Something unusual happens when it tries to evaluate the following expression:

```
3 < 4 AND 12 = 6 + 6
```

The operator with the highest level of precedence is the AND, but if the computer tries to first evaluate

```
4 AND 12
```

it doesn't make sense and would generate a compiler error. The AND operator requires two BOOLEAN arguments. To evaluate the AND last, you need parentheses:

```
(3 < 4) AND (12 = 6 + 6)
```

Remember, NOT, AND, and OR usually need to have their operands parenthesized.

8.4 Flags and Other BOOLEAN Variables

IF/THEN/ELSE statements are controlled by a BOOLEAN test. The test can be a BOOLEAN variable as well as a BOOLEAN expression. The following code:

```
IF (number > 0) THEN
    WRITELN ('positive')
ELSE
    WRITELN ('negative')
```

could be rewritten as

```
positive := (number > 0);
IF positive THEN
    WRITELN ('positive')
ELSE
    WRITELN ('negative')
```

This code is legal assuming you have a BOOLEAN variable called `positive`. BOOLEAN variables add to the readability of programs because they allow you to give names to tests. Consider the kind of code you would generate for an address book program. You might have some INTEGER variables that describe certain attributes of a person: `looks`, to store a rough estimate of physical beauty (on a scale of 1 to 10); IQ, to store intelligence quotient; `income`, to store gross annual income; and `snothers`, to track intimate friends ("snother" is short for significant other). Given these variables to specify the attributes of a person, you can develop various tests of suitability. BOOLEAN variables are useful here to give names to those tests and add greatly to the readability of the code:

```
cute := (looks >= 9);
smart := (IQ > 125);
rich := (income > 50000);
available := (snothers = 0);
awesome := cute AND smart AND rich AND available;
```

You will use a BOOLEAN variable, called a *flag*, often. You will typically use flags within loops to record error conditions or to signal completion. Different flags test different conditions. Suppose you have a football game and you hire 10 flagmen to watch for certain illegal actions. One flagman might look for offsides, another for excessive holding, another for out-of-bounds, and so on. The flagmen all start with their flags down. When the teams execute a play, each man watches and raises his flag if the condition he is looking for occurs. Once a flag is up, it stays up. It doesn't matter, for example, if a player runs back in bounds after running out of bounds. The flag stays up. After a play, the referees check the raised flags and impose penalties accordingly. The flags then go down and the game proceeds.

To see how to use a flag, let's look at a pseudocode description of the flagman watching for offsides. You can describe players stepping over the line of scrimmage in terms of the steps they take.

```
for (each step taken by a team member) do
begin
    if (this step puts the player over the scrimmage line) then
        set offsides to true.
    else
        set offsides to false.
end
if offsides then
    impose penalty.
```

This does not perform the way you want it to because offsides can be reset to false after having been set to true (i.e., the flag can be lowered after it has been raised). This was not your intention. A team is not forgiven by stepping back to their side of the scrimmage line. You need something like this:

```
for (each step taken by a team member) do
      if (the step puts the player over the scrimmage line) then
            set offsides to true.
if offsides then
      impose penalty.
```

You want to raise the flag and not allow it to go down. There is one problem with this pseudocode. What happens if nobody goes offsides? How does the flag get a value? You need to initialize it. The simple fix is to start the flag out as false outside the loop (i.e., start with the flag down), assuming innocence until guilt is proven. Here is the pseudocode. It shows you the basic way to use flags in programs.

```
set offsides to false.
for (each step taken by a team member) do
      if (the step puts the player over the scrimmage line) then
            set offsides to true.
if offsides then
      impose penalty.
```

8.4.1   A Sample Program with Flags and Fence Posts

Many banks impose minimum-balance restrictions and charge a fee if you don't maintain a minimum balance. If you write a program that balances your checkbook for a given month, assuming that you can give the credits and debits in the order they appeared at the bank, it should be possible to figure out whether the minimum balance is maintained. You use a BOOLEAN variable to flag the balance if it ever dips below the minimum. You start with a minor variation of the usual pseudocode for flags:

```
set WeDipped to false.
for (each transaction) do
begin
      perform transaction.
      if (the new balance is below the minimum) then
            set WeDipped to true.
end
if WeDipped then
      impose the service charge.
```

This is not quite right, however. The checkbook program presents a fence-post problem. The program involves transactions and checking a balance, but there is one more balance to check than there are transactions to perform. If you perform five transactions, for example, each produces a different balance (five new balances). But there is also an initial balance that you carry over from the previous month that needs to be checked:

check, transact, check, transact, ..., check, transact, check

This pattern is the same as the fence post and the same solution solves it. You have to do one extra balance check before the loop. Because the flag needs to be initialized anyway, you might as well perform a check to give it its starting value. Here is the complete pseudocode:

set WeDipped to the truth value of (starting balance is below minimum).
for (each transaction) do
begin
    perform transaction.
    if (the new balance is below minimum) then
        set WeDipped to true.
end
if WeDipped then
    impose the service charge.

Here is a program that follows this pseudocode:

```
(* This is a simple checkbook program that prompts the user for   *)
(* one month's transaction amounts and reports the final balance. *)
(* If the balance ever dips below $2,000, a $5 fee is charged.    *)

PROGRAM Checkbook (INPUT, OUTPUT);
VAR balance    : REAL;      (* customer's current balance          *)
    amount     : REAL;      (* amount of next transaction          *)
    HowMany    : INTEGER;   (* number of transactions to perform *)
    count      : INTEGER;   (* loop counter                        *)
    dip        : BOOLEAN;   (* flag for balance dipping too low  *)
BEGIN
    WRITELN ('Time to balance the checkbook again. Describe transactions to');
    WRITELN ('me as positive numbers (credit) or negative numbers (debit).');
    WRITELN ('Please enter the transactions in order, so that the minimum');
    WRITELN ('balance can be checked.');
    WRITELN;
    WRITE ('What was last month''s ending balance? ');
    READLN (balance);
    WRITE ('How many transactions would you like to perform? ');
    READLN (HowMany);
    dip := (balance < 2000);
```

```
    FOR count := 1 TO HowMany DO
    BEGIN
        WRITE ('Next transaction amount ---> ');
        READLN (amount);
        balance := balance + amount;
        IF balance < 2000 THEN
            dip := TRUE
    END;
    WRITELN;
    IF dip THEN
    BEGIN
        WRITELN ('I''m afraid you dipped below the minimum this month.');
        balance := balance - 5
    END
    ELSE
        WRITELN ('Financial planning is good, no service charge this month.');
    WRITELN ('Ending balance = $', balance:1:2);
    WRITELN ('See you again next month!')
END.
```

Here are two executions to show how the program works:

```
Time to balance the checkbook again.  Describe transactions to
me as positive numbers (credit) or negative numbers (debit).
Please enter the transactions in order, so that the minimum
balance can be checked.

What was last month's ending balance? 2009.14
How many transactions would you like to perform? 4
Next transaction amount ---> 100
Next transaction amount ---> -125
Next transaction amount ---> 750
Next transaction amount ---> -39.50

I'm afraid you dipped below the minimum this month.
Ending balance = $ 2689.64
See you again next month!


Time to balance the checkbook again.  Describe transactions to
me as positive numbers (credit) or negative numbers (debit).
Please enter the transactions in order, so that the minimum
balance can be checked.

What was last month's ending balance? 2689.64
```

```
How many transactions would you like to perform? 5
Next transaction amount ---> -213.94
Next transaction amount ---> 2000
Next transaction amount ---> -2119.24
Next transaction amount ---> -120
Next transaction amount ---> -19.55


Financial planning is good, no service charge this month.
Ending balance = $ 2216.91
See you again next month!
```

8.5   Full Evaluation and Its Consequences

Because of the properties of the logical operators, it is not always necessary to evaluate both the operands. Consider the BOOLEAN expression controlling the WHILE loop of the rewritten TransferLineTo procedure:

```
NOT EOLN AND (length < LineLength)
```

If you reach the end-of-line character, EOLN is FALSE. This is sufficient information to know that the overall BOOLEAN expression is FALSE. There is no need to test whether length is less than LineLength. Even so, most Pascal systems will perform the test. Such systems perform full evaluation of the expression. The Pascal standard leaves it up to the implementor to decide whether or not to perform full evaluation. Most systems do.

There are cases where full evaluation is a problem. Suppose you have the following declarations:

```
CONST LineLength = 70;
TYPE  LineList   = ARRAY [1..LineLength] OF CHAR;
VAR   list       : LineList;
      length     : INTEGER;
```

If you want to find the second unique value appearing in list, you want to skip over all the occurrences of the first value until you find something that is different. If the variables have these values:

	[1]	[2]	[3]	[4]	[5]	[6]	[7]	[...]	[70]		
list	'a'	'a'	'a'	'a'	'b'	?	?	...	?	length	5

you skip over the first four elements to find the second unique value in element [5]. If you have a variable called index that is to store the index of the second unique value, your problem reduces to giving index an appropriate value. Here is a simple attempt to do so:

```
index := 1;
WHILE (list [1] = list [index]) DO
    index := index + 1;
```

This code starts `index` at the second element of the array (`list [1]`) and increments `index` until it finds an element (`list [index]`) that differs from the first element (`list [1]`). If there is no difference, if the first value appears in every element of the array, this `WHILE` loop will eventually try to examine an element of the array that is uninitialized. And if the array is full (i.e., `length` = `LineLength`), then it will try to examine an element of the array that doesn't exist (i.e., `list [71]`).

You must take this special case into account. Start by fixing your specification. Adopt the convention that if all the elements 1 ⋯ `length` have the same value, you will set `index` to the value (`length + 1`). Now fix the implementation. The `WHILE` loop has two reasons for exiting:

exit if (no more elements to examine) or (difference encountered).

Using De Morgan's law to convert to a continuation condition, you get:

continue if (more elements to examine) and (elements are same).

You can translate this easily into Pascal:

```
index := 1;
WHILE (index <= length) AND (list [1] = list [index]) DO
    index := index + 1;
```

Consider what this code does, however, when all elements of the array have the same value. After the computer compares `list [1]` and `list [length]`, it increments `index` to (`length + 1`). When it then performs the test of the `WHILE` loop, it sees that the first of the two parts returns `FALSE`:

```
(index <= length)
```

This part of the expression is `FALSE`, so the overall expression must be `FALSE`. But unfortunately, if full evaluation is performed, then it also evaluates the test

```
(list [1] = list [index])
```

Since `index` equals (`length + 1`), the computer reaches an execution error when it examines an uninitialized array element or, in the case when `length` equals `LineLength`, when it tries to examine an array element that is out of bounds. Thus the simple strategy won't work because even though you have a new test that will stop the loop from executing, the time when that test becomes useful is a time when the other test causes an error.

Your first inclination is probably to have the loop iterate one less time by changing the less than or equal to a less than:

```
index := 1;
```

```
WHILE (index < length) AND (list [1] = list [index]) DO
    index := index + 1;
```

By changing the relational operator this way, the loop will never allow `index` to become larger than `length`. As soon as `index` takes on the value `length`, the first test causes the computer to exit the loop. While this fixes the earlier problem, it introduces a bug. It gives the wrong answer when all elements of the array are the same. `index` should be set to (`length + 1`) in this case. If this loop never sets `index` higher than `length`, then it must not be complete.

You can fix it by adding an extra test after the loop:

```
index := 1;
WHILE (index < length) AND (list [1] = list [index]) DO
    index := index + 1;
IF (list [1] = list [index]) THEN
    index := index + 1;
```

This `IF/THEN` performs what used to be the last iteration of the loop after the loop is done executing. This solution works, but it is not very elegant. The elegant solution is provided by a flag.

By introducing a `BOOLEAN` flag, called `MoreToDo`, and allowing it to control the loop, the basic pseudocode becomes

```
set MoreToDo to true.
while MoreToDo do
    look at next element.
```

You can refine this pseudocode by introducing `index`:

```
set index to 0.
set MoreToDo to true.
while MoreToDo do
begin
    increment index.
    see if more to do.
end
```

All that remains is to refine what is meant by "see if more to do." The problem encountered with

```
continue if (test1) and (test2)
```

is that the computer evaluates the second test when it doesn't need to. The fix is to use an `IF/THEN/ELSE` to say that the second test will be performed only if the first succeeds:

```
if (test1) then
    continue if (test2).
else
    don't continue.
```

Here, you explicitly state that the second test is to be performed only if the first returns **TRUE**. If the first is not true, you stop immediately. This introduces an explicit hierarchy, specifying the order the tests are to be performed in and solves the problem:

```
if (index <= length) then
    set MoreToDo to the truth value of (list [1] = list [index]).
else
    set MoreToDo to false
```

You refer to `list [index]` only if you know that `index` is within the correct range. Otherwise, you are done. Now, you can easily translate this pseudocode into Pascal:

```
index := 0;
MoreToDo := TRUE;
WHILE MoreToDo DO
BEGIN
    index := index + 1;
    IF (index <= length) THEN
        MoreToDo := (list [1] = list [index])
    ELSE
        MoreToDo := FALSE
END;
```

Here, you use a flag to control a complex loop. Flags offer a nice solution to the problems presented by full evaluation of **BOOLEAN** expressions.

8.6 Reasoning about Programs

To write programs correctly and efficiently, you must learn to make assertions about your programs and to understand the contexts in which those assertions will be true. For example, if you are trying to obtain a nonnegative number from the user, you want the assertion "**number** is nonnegative" to be true. What happens if you use a simple prompt and **READLN**?

```
WRITE ('Please input a nonnegative number ---> ');
READLN (number);
(* Is number nonnegative here? *)
```

The user can ignore your request and input a negative number anyway. In fact, users often input values that you don't expect, most often because they are confused. Given the uncertainty of user input, this particular assertion is sometimes true and sometimes false. It might be important to be certain that this assertion is true for something that appears later in the program. For example, if you are going to take the square root of that number, you must be sure it is nonnegative. Otherwise, you might end up with an execution error. Here is a way of making sure:

```
WRITE ('Please input a nonnegative number ---> ');
READLN (number);
WHILE (number < 0) DO
BEGIN
    WRITE ('That number is negative!  Give me a nonnegative one ---> ');
    READLN (number)
END;
(* number is definitely nonnegative now. *)
```

You know that **number** will be nonnegative after the WHILE loop; otherwise, the WHILE loop would not have terminated. As long as a user gives negative values, he stays in the WHILE loop and can't break out of it until the continuation condition of the WHILE loop fails (i.e., when **number** ≥ 0).

This doesn't mean that the number "should be nonnegative" after the loop. It means the number "will be nonnegative." By working through the logic of the program, you can see that this is a certainty. It is an assertion of which you are sure. You could even prove it if need be. Such an assertion is called a *provable assertion*.

Provable assertions help to identify unnecessary bits of code. Consider these statements:

```
x := 0;
IF x = 0 THEN
    WRITELN ('This is what I expect.')
ELSE
    WRITELN ('how can that be?')
```

The IF/THEN/ELSE is not necessary. It tests something you know is a fact because you know how assignment statements work and you notice the assignment statement before the IF/THEN/ELSE setting the variable x to zero. Testing whether or not it's zero is like saying, "Before I proceed, I'm going to check that $2 + 2$ equals 4." Because the THEN part of this IF/THEN/ELSE is always executed, you can prove that these lines of code always do the same thing as

```
x := 0;
WRITELN ('This is what I expect.')
```

These lines of code are simpler and, therefore, better. Programs are complex enough without adding unnecessary code.

Let's consider a case that requires more thought—the EchoLine procedure:

```
PROCEDURE EchoLine;
VAR next : CHAR;
BEGIN
    WHILE NOT EOLN DO
    BEGIN
        READ (next);
        WRITE (next)
    END
END;
```

What can you deduce as true after the procedure is done executing?

```
EchoLine;
(* What is true now? *)
```

The procedure has only one statement in it—a WHILE loop. It can exit that loop only when its test returns FALSE. Thus you can conclude that

```
EchoLine;
(* Condition of EchoLine's WHILE loop is now FALSE *)
```

Looking at the WHILE loop, you will realize that this means

```
EchoLine;
(* EOLN is now TRUE *)
```

EOLN is a provable assertion at this point in program execution. Otherwise, you would not have exited the WHILE loop. It would be silly to say something like

```
EchoLine;
IF EOLN THEN
    READLN;
```

You must remember, however, that things change as a program executes. While you can prove that EOLN must be true immediately after EchoLine executes, it doesn't mean EOLN will always be true:

```
EchoLine;
(* EOLN is now TRUE *)
READLN;
(* EOLN might be TRUE or FALSE now *)
```

Another example of this kind of reasoning is provided by this code fragment:

```
index := 1;
WHILE (index < length) AND (list [1] = list [index]) DO
    index := index + 1;
(* what do we know is true here? *)
```

This is a more complex WHILE loop because it has two possible reasons for exiting. The answer is

```
either   (index >= length)
or       (list [1] <> list [index])
or       both of the above
```

Assuming that `length` is greater than 2, you know that `index` starts at a value less than `length` and is incremented toward it. Therefore, you can be more precise and rule out the possibility that `index` is greater than `length`. Thus one of the following is true:

```
either (index = length)
or     (list [1] <> list [index])
or     both of the above
```

Recalling your task, these two tests can be written in English.

```
either   (you have reached the end of the array)
or       (you have encountered a difference)
or       both of the above
```

The loop was intended to find a difference between `list [1]` and `list [index]`. If it doesn't, there is still work to do. Thus the first of these cases is the one that causes worry, the one where you exit the loop because you ran out of array elements but still haven't encountered a difference. Because of this case, it is necessary to add an extra IF/THEN after the loop and to possibly increment `index`:

```
IF (index = length) AND (list [1] = list [index]) THEN
    index := index + 1;
```

But what can you reason about this IF/THEN?

```
IF (index = length) AND (list [1] = list [index]) THEN
    (* what is true here? *)
    index := index + 1;
```

You know that if the overall test of the IF/THEN returns TRUE, both its parts must be true:

```
index = length
list [1] = list [index]
```

If both these conditions are TRUE, you can reason that the following are also TRUE:

```
index = length
list [1] = list [length]
```

This follows from the fact that (`index = length`). Because you know it is true, you can apply it as a substitution in your second fact. Likewise, if you know that these two statements are true, you can substitute back to the original statements, reasoning that they are TRUE. The first pair of statements imply that the second pair are true, and the second pair imply that the first are TRUE. Therefore, they are logically equivalent.

Another equivalent way of wording your IF/THEN is as follows:

```
IF (index = length) AND (list [1] = list [length]) THEN
    index := index + 1;
```

To carry this further, you can use the substitution in the assignment statement:

```
IF (index = length) AND (list [1] = list [length]) THEN
    index := length + 1;
```

These are three different ways of saying the same thing. There is no good argument for one over the other. You should use the one that suits you best.

8.6.1   Preconditions and Postconditions

You can formally describe the workings of a procedure using assertions. For example, you can give a series of assertions that describe what will be true when a procedure is done executing. Such assertions are called *postconditions* of a procedure. For example, to describe the job of a person on an auto assembly line, you might use a postcondition such as, "The bolts that secure the left front tire are on the car and tight."

Postconditions are not the whole story. Employees on an assembly line depend on each other. A line worker can't add bolts and tighten them if the left tire isn't there or if there are no bolts. You specify such conditions as these by using *preconditions*, assertions that must be true before a task is performed. The assembly line worker might have preconditions such as, "The left tire is mounted properly on the car; there are at least eight bolts in the supply box; and a working wrench is available." You describe the task fully, then, by saying that the worker can make the postconditions true if the preconditions are true before starting.

Procedures, like workers on an assembly line, need to work together, each solving its portion of the task, in order to solve the overall task. The preconditions and postconditions describe the dependencies between procedures. To understand this better, consider this nonprogramming example with the following procedures and their conditions.

MakeBatter

        pre : bowl is clean.

        post: bowl has batter in it; bowl is dirty.

BakeCake

        pre : bowl has batter in it; pan is clean.

        post: cake is baked; pan is dirty.

WashDishes
> pre : none.
> post: bowl and pan are clean.

When you call these procedures, you must fit them together so the preconditions are always satisfied before a procedure executes. For example, if you suppose that the bowl and pan are initially clean, you can make a cake by

MakeBatter.
BakeCake.

Here is a trace of its execution.

————> bowl and pan are clean.
MakeBatter.
————> bowl has batter in it; bowl is dirty; pan is clean.
BakeCake.
————> cake is baked; bowl and pan are dirty.

The preconditions are satisfied before each procedure is executed. However, if you want a loop to make cakes, you can't do it:

while (more cakes to make) do
begin
     MakeBatter.
     BakeCake.
end

The first cake is made properly, but not the second. The error occurs because the preconditions for MakeBatter are not satisfied on the second execution of the loop. You need a clean bowl and pan to execute MakeBatter.

————> bowl and pan are clean.
MakeBatter.
————> bowl has batter in it; bowl is dirty; pan is clean.
BakeCake.
————> cake is baked; bowl and pan are dirty.
MakeBatter.

You need to change your solution:

while (more cakes to make) do
begin
     MakeBatter.
     BakeCake.
     WashDishes.
end

The execution of WashDishes leaves you with a clean bowl and pan and guarantees that you satisfy the preconditions of MakeBatter on the next iteration.

Consider an example closer to Pascal programming tasks with the following procedures and conditions:

procedure ReadLine
        pre : input cursor at beginning of line.
        post: input cursor at EOLN; line read in.
procedure ProcessLine
        pre : line read in.
        post: information from line is processed.
procedure NewLine
        pre : none.
        post: input cursor at beginning of next line.

Initially, the input cursor is at the beginning of the first line of the input file and you can process it with

ReadLine.
ProcessLine.

If you want to set up a loop, however, you can't say

while (not at end-of-file) do
begin
    ReadLine.
    ProcessLine.
end

The loop fails on its second pass because the preconditions for ReadLine are not satisfied, the cursor is not positioned at the beginning of the second line. You need to fix the loop:

while not at (end-of-file) do
begin
    ReadLine.
    ProcessLine.
    NewLine.
end.

The NewLine action is usually accomplished by a simple READLN. The missing READLN is a common mistake of novice programmers. You will make these mistakes less often if you remember to write procedures with preconditions and postconditions and use them to figure out how to fit the procedures together into a sequence of calls that makes sense.

8.6.2 Proving Programs Correct

Thinking logically about your programs is essential. You should always be asking "What do I know is true now? What needs to be true next? How will I make that true so that I can proceed?" Only through this kind of thinking will you be able to verify that a program works. Using logic to prove the correctness of programs is the subject of a relatively new field of computer science called *program verification*, or *program proving*. While a formal program-verification model is beyond the scope of this book, many of the principles can be applied to improve the process of program development.

Ideally, a programmer would be able to prove all kinds of assertions about a program: to confidently say that it reaches no execution errors by saying that it never divides by zero, never takes the square root of a negative number, never asks for an array index that is out of bounds, and so on. A programmer would also be able to say that it always finishes executing, which means that it has no infinite loops, and, finally, that it performs the specified task. The combination of all these assertions is a basic assertion: "It works."

A bug indicates that there is at least one context where one of these assertions is false. Bugs arise most often because of flaws in logic. Programmers don't have the time to construct elaborate proofs of large chunks of code, so they write something that they are pretty sure will work rather than something they are sure will work.

How can you be sure of a piece of code? Consider a procedure that is supposed to exchange two values. Its header might look like this:

```
PROCEDURE Swap (VAR first  : INTEGER;
                VAR second : INTEGER);
```

You can describe its preconditions and postconditions as

```
pre  : first and second have values.
post : values of first and second are exchanged.
```

These conditions are fairly informal for a program prover, so you should make them a little more rigorous. To do so, you need a way of describing the initial values of the variables. The usual notation for doing so is `first'` and `second'` (read as "first prime" and "second prime"). Using this notation you can be more specific:

```
pre  : first = first', second = second'.
post : first = second', second = first'.
```

As a program prover, you start with preconditions and assume they are true. This gives you a set of assertions to work with. Then you see how each statement of the procedure changes that set of assertions. For example, when an assignment statement is executed, three things happen:

1. You use all the current assertions to evaluate the expression on the right.

2. You eliminate any assertions concerning the value of the variable being assigned to.

3. You add a new assertion that the variable has the value calculated from the expression.

Try to evaluate whether this version of the procedure works:

```
PROCEDURE Swap (VAR first  : INTEGER;
                VAR second : INTEGER);
BEGIN
    first := second;
    second := first
END;
```

You start with the preconditions:

```
first = first', second = second'.
```

Next, you execute statements. To execute the first assignment statement, you go through the three steps:

1. Evaluate the expression and obtain `second'`.
2. Eliminate the assertion that `first = first'`.
3. Add new assertion that `first = second'`.

Then you obtain:

```
first = second', second = second'.
```

Following the same steps on the next statement, you get

```
first = second', second = second'.
```

The second assignment statement has no effect. The assertions do not match the desired postconditions, so this procedure does not work. Look at another version:

```
PROCEDURE Swap (VAR first  : INTEGER;
                VAR second : INTEGER);
VAR temp : INTEGER;
BEGIN
    temp := first;
    first := second;
    second := temp
END;
```

Again, start with the preconditions:

```
first = first', second = second'.
```

In executing the first assignment statement, you gain an assertion about the local variable `temp`:

```
first = first', second = second', temp = first'.
```

The second assignment statement creates a new assertion about variable `first`:

```
first = second', second = second', temp = first'.
```

Finally, the last statement creates a new assertion about variable **second**:

```
first = second', second = first', temp = first'.
```

This shows that the postconditions hold after this procedure executes, so you have proven that it works.

You were probably able to realize that the first version of **swap** wouldn't work and that the second version would without having to apply these techniques, but consider another version and use your program-proving technique to see if it works:

```
PROCEDURE Swap (VAR first  : INTEGER;
                VAR second : INTEGER);
BEGIN
    first := first + second;
    second := first - second;
    first := first - second
END;
```

You start with

```
first = first', second = second'.
```

Go through the three steps for the first statement:

1. The value of the expression is (**first'** + **second'**).
2. Eliminate the current assertion about **first**.
3. Add a new assertion that **first** equals the expression value.

This leads to

```
first = (first' + second'), second = second'.
```

Go through the three steps for the second statement:

1. The value of the expression is ((**first'** + **second'**) - **second'**) = **first'**.
2. Eliminate the current assertion about **second**.
3. Add a new assertion that **second** equals the expression value.

This leads to

```
first = (first' + second'), second = first'.
```

Go through the three steps a last time for the third statement:

1. The value of the expression is ((**first'** + **second'**) - **first'**) = **second'**.
2. Eliminate the current assertion about **first**.
3. Add a new assertion that **first** equals the expression value.

This leads to

```
first = second', second = first'.
```

This matches the postconditions, so you have proven that this version works.

Proving the correctness of a piece of code is often quite straightforward, but it is not always easy. Computer scientists are just beginning to understand how to use these techniques to prove the correctness of complex pieces of code.

8.7 Logic and Documentation

Now that you have a new way of describing procedures, add these three new keywords to your comment blocks:

pre	What must be true before executing this procedure?
post	What will be true after executing this procedure?
errors	What errors are checked for?

Notice that in and in/out parameters introduce some preconditions of their own, namely, that the parameters are initialized. Don't bother to list these as separate preconditions. The **pre/post** comments replace the old **task** comments. Use the errors clause to describe any error recovery the procedure performs when one of the preconditions does not hold.

8.7.1 Logic and Problem Solving

You have seen many properties of a good decomposition. Preconditions and postconditions provide a new vocabulary for describing a property that wasn't included earlier. If you try to measure the amount of work being done by a procedure, you would express it roughly as

(postconditions - preconditions)

In other words, you can measure the amount of work done by a procedure by seeing how much more is true after it is done executing than was true before. If there are few preconditions (little done in advance) and many postconditions (much accomplished by the end), the procedure is responsible for a lot of work. If, however, there are few new postconditions (little accomplished by the end), the procedure is responsible for little work.

It isn't enough to simply have the problem decomposed into parts. In a good decomposition, the higher subtasks should be doing a lot of work and the lower subtasks should be doing very little work. Often, beginning students try writing low-level procedures that do lots of work, a strategy that will fail. When you confront a problem too complex to solve in one step, you must break it up into pieces that are less complex. If the pieces are each as complex as the overall task, the breakdown is of no benefit.

For example, if you are writing a program to read in a dictionary of words, you want a low-level procedure to read a single word. A typical set of conditions for such a procedure are

> pre : input cursor is positioned at an alphabetic character.
> post: characters are read until the first nonalphabetic character is encountered; the word read in is returned via a VAR parameter.

Saying that the input cursor is positioned at an alphabetic character is a strong statement. It means that some other part of the program, some higher-level procedure, must deal with the complexity of positioning the cursor properly, including dealing with other garbage that might appear in the file. This strong assumption, however, makes this procedure easy to write. This should be true of all your low-level procedures. They should be easy to write, because they should all have very strong assumptions about what the higher-level procedures will do before calling them. You don't want too strong a postcondition:

> post : characters are read until the first nonalphabetic character is encountered; the word read in is placed in the dictionary.

A low-level procedure should not even know that there is a dictionary. This procedure should know about something simple, such as a word. If it deals with the more complex problem, it will become complex to write. Bringing the complexity of the overall problem into a low-level procedure will ruin you.

8.7.2   Logic and Debugging

Program logic contributes much to better debugging. The most significant contribution comes from the preconditions and postconditions. If you develop this logical framework for a program as you write it, you will have a solid framework for pinpointing errors as you go along.

The most difficult bugs to trace are the ones in which one part of the program appears to be flawed, but in fact another part of the program has the error. These bugs are especially prevalent among less seasoned programmers who don't know how to guard against them.

A bad diagnosis is often made because students can't see inside the computer to know what their program is really doing. A student knows a program starts executing and that it reaches an execution error. A student rarely knows what happens in between. In the absence of better knowledge, the novice usually uses the execution error as a clue to what went wrong, and this is often not the right thing to do.

The procedures of a program are like the workers of an assembly line who each take their turn trying to make something happen. At some point, one of them makes a mistake. Does the assembly line stop? Not right away. Usually things keep going until the error compounds into something that causes an execution error (like an array index out of bounds or a divide by zero).

The execution error that finally stops the whole system from running is rarely the problem. It is an indication that something went wrong, but usually that something happened earlier. Unfortunately, many students seem to think that the computer knows where the problem is and that the execution-error message describes it. The computer has no idea of what should be going on in your program, and it has even less of an idea of what went wrong. Your program will usually go quite a bit past the original error because even though your program is doing the wrong things, it isn't doing anything illegal. A computer only catches illegal actions; it has no idea of what should be going on.

How can you avoid such problems? The easiest way is to build your own early warning system into the program. If an error occurs in your assembly line, you want to find out about it as soon as possible. Because the computer can't detect errors early enough, your program must.

I have suggested that you include precondition and postcondition comments in your procedures. You can in many cases make them part of the code. For example, if you are writing a procedure called `ReportResults` whose precondition is

```
pre  :  1 <= length <= LineLength.
```

you can insert some actual code at the beginning of the procedure that checks the precondition. You would write something like this:

```
PROCEDURE ReportResults (length : INTEGER);
BEGIN
    IF (length < 1) OR (length > LineLength) THEN
        WRITELN ('argh! precondition of ReportResults is not true!!');
    . . .
END;
```

With this statement at the beginning of the procedure, you will receive a warning if the procedure is called with an illegal value. You can do an analogous test at the end of the procedure to make sure that the postcondition is true just before you exit the procedure.

You should try to turn many of your preconditions and postconditions into tests such as these. Some, however, are not easy to write as Pascal tests. There are some alternatives. Suppose you are writing a procedure to uppercase a word and your header looks like this:

```
PROCEDURE UpperCase (VAR word   : WordType;
                         length : INTEGER);
```

The conditions of the procedure are

```
pre  :  1 <= length <= LineLength.
        characters stored in elements 1..length are all letters.
```

> post : characters stored in elements 1..length are turned into
>   corresponding uppercase letters.

These conditions say that given a word whose length is in the legal range and whose characters are all letters, this procedure will uppercase all the letters. The constraint on the value of length is easily translated into a BOOLEAN test. The others, however, are probably more trouble than they are worth, and this is where the alternative comes in. If this is part of a program that manipulates words, there is probably a procedure for writing out a single word. Suppose there is and that it is called WriteWord. You can keep your eye on all these conditions by doing the following:

```
PROCEDURE UpperCase (VAR word   : WordType;
                         length : INTEGER);
BEGIN
    IF (length < 1) OR (length > LineLength) THEN
        WRITELN ('argh! precondition of UpperCase is not true!!');
    WRITE ('Entering UpperCase, this should be all letters --> "');
    WriteWord (word, length);
    WRITELN ('"');
    . . .
    WRITE ('Exiting UpperCase, this should be all uppercase --> "');
    WriteWord (word, length);
    WRITELN ('"')
END;
```

With these extra WRITE statements you will see messages such as

```
Entering UpperCase, this should be all letters --> "cola"
Exiting UpperCase, this should be all uppercase --> "COLA"
Entering UpperCase, this should be all letters --> "oscar"
Exiting UpperCase, this should be all uppercase --> "OSCAR"
```

Messages such as these are quickly read and verified. If you put this kind of code into each of your procedures, you will probably generate many such messages and, therefore, will be able to see what is going on inside the computer. You can tell what procedures are being called and with what values. The whole process becomes visible.

Most messages that the program generates will say the right thing and will roll past on the screen. But you might get a message such as

```
Entering UpperCase, this should be all letters --> "freeble&*!"
Exiting UpperCase, this should be all uppercase --> "FREEBLE+{["
```

Here you have encountered something wrong and should investigate.

There is one problem with such messages. You don't want the final version of your program to produce them. Users of your program don't want all this detailed information, and there is an elegant way to avoid this. The solution is to introduce a global BOOLEAN flag called **debugging** that controls whether or not the debugging code is executed. When you want to see debugging information, you set the flag to TRUE. When you don't, you set it to FALSE. Thus the main program starts

```
PROGRAM Complex (INPUT, OUTPUT);
CONST Debugging = TRUE;   (* whether or not you are debugging *)
```

and you can rewrite the procedure:

```
PROCEDURE UpperCase (VAR word   : WordType;
                         length : INTEGER);
BEGIN
    IF debugging THEN
    BEGIN
        IF (length < 1) OR (length > LineLength) THEN
            WRITELN ('argh! precondition of UpperCase is not true!!');
        WRITE ('Entering UpperCase, this should be all letters --> "');
        WriteWord (word, length);
        WRITELN ('"')
    END;

    .  .  .

    IF debugging THEN
    BEGIN
        WRITE ('Exiting UpperCase, this should be all UpperCase -->"');
        WriteWord (word, length);
        WRITELN ('"')
    END
END;
```

With the global constant, you can change the value of **debugging** to FALSE when you are ready to generate the final version and the extra lines of output will no longer appear.

Writing debugging code is time-consuming, but the potential savings are enormous: the time you spend on writing the debugging code will probably be made up by shorter debugging sessions; writing code may be tedious, but fighting against bugs is frustrating; if you ever come back to the code to modify it later, you will already have your debugging facility built-in; if you build such code into tools of your software library, you get the debugging for free every time you reuse the tool; and finally, instructors and graders love this kind of code, so you will probably get a higher grade for doing it this way.

If you decide not to write debugging code for all your procedures, you should at least include it in your key procedures: the ones that are called the most often, that perform the most complex tasks, or that are most likely to be used again in another program.

8.8 Key Concepts

- An assertion is a declarative sentence. A proposition is an assertion that has a proper context to make it either true or false.

- Just as INTEGER variables are used to store the numeric value of some expressions, BOOLEAN variables are used to store the truth value of some propositions. The operators AND, OR, and NOT are used to form complex BOOLEAN expressions.

- BOOLEAN variables add to the readability of programs because they give names to tests.

- One common application of a BOOLEAN variable is to use it as a flag. A flag variable is used to keep track of whether a condition is true or was true.

- BOOLEAN expressions are potentially evaluated fully, even when there is no need to do so. It is therefore difficult to express some continuation conditions of WHILE loops. You can use a flag to fix such loops.

- It is important to reason about the logic of a program as you write it, keeping track of the assertions you know are true at each step in program execution. Some assertions can be proven to hold at specific points in a program, allowing you to construct a proof that a program or program fragment is correct.

- The task of a subprogram can be precisely described using a precondition that describes what is true before the subprogram is executed and a postcondition describing what should be true after the subprogram is executed.

8.9 Self-Check Exercises

1. Which of the following are assertions? Which are propositions?

   $x < y$.

   Write a program that adds together two numbers.

   The moon is made of green cheese.

   $z = 2 + 2$.

   What is your name?

   All FOR loops can be rewritten as WHILE loops.

2. Given the following logical variables:

   p: $x > 0$
   q: $y > 0$
   r: $z < 0$

Express the following ideas using P, Q, and R and the logical connectives AND, OR, and NOT.

One or both of X and Y is (are) positive.
X is positive and Z is negative.
One of X and Y is positive and the other is not.
X and Y are positive whenever Z is negative.

3. Assume that you have variables X and Y with values 10 and 12, respectively. The following is a trace of the evaluation of (x > 2) AND NOT (y = 6):

Expression	Operator	Operands	Result
(x > 2) AND NOT (y = 6)	>	X, 2	TRUE
(TRUE) AND NOT (y = 6)	=	Y, 6	FALSE
(TRUE) AND NOT (FALSE)	NOT	FALSE	TRUE
(TRUE) AND TRUE	AND	TRUE, TRUE	TRUE
TRUE			

You should assume, as in the preceding exercise, that parenthesized expressions are evaluated left to right. Trace the evaluation of the following:

```
(x > y) OR (x > 0) AND (y > 0)
NOT (x + 2 = y) OR (x < y)
```

4. Is the following code legal? If so, what does it do?

```
VAR test : BOOLEAN;
BEGIN
    FOR test := TRUE DOWNTO FALSE DO
        WRITELN (test);
```

5. Rewrite the nested IF/THEN/ELSE construct below as a single assignment statement:

```
IF (x < 0) THEN
    test := TRUE
ELSE
    IF (y > z) THEN
        test := FALSE
    ELSE
        test := TRUE;
```

6. Here is a loop that reads numbers from an input line and calculates their product:

```
product := 1;
WHILE NOT EOLN DO
BEGIN
    READ (number);
    product := product * number
END;
```

This code terminates when `EOLN` is reached. How would you modify it so that it also terminates if the product becomes zero?

7. Suppose that you have an array called `list` that stores integers and a variable called `length` that tells how many elements of `list` are currently in use. Write some code that gives a value to a variable called `position` such that `list [position]` is the first element of `list` that is greater than 10. If no value is greater than 10, set `position` to (`length + 1`), but be careful never to examine the value of `list [length + 1]`.

8. Given the following loop:

```
length := 0;
READ (number);
WHILE NOT EOLN AND (length < MaxLength) AND (number <> -1) DO
BEGIN
    length := length + 1;
    list [length] := number;
    READ (number)
END;
```

which of the following can't be `TRUE` immediately after the loop terminates?

```
EOLN AND (length = 0)
(list [length] = -1)
NOT EOLN AND (number = -1)
NOT EOLN AND (length < MaxLength) AND (number <> -1)
EOLN AND (length = MaxLength) AND (number <> -1)
EOLN AND (length = MaxLength + 1) AND (number = -1)
```

9. What are the preconditions and postconditions of Pascal's square root function (`SQRT`)?

10. Suppose that you have `INTEGER` variables `x`, `y`, and `z` and that you want to write code that changes the values of the variables so as to satisfy these conditions:

```
pre  : x = x', y = y', z = z'.
post : x = z', y = x', z = y'.
```

Use program-proving techniques to prove or disprove that the following code satisfies the conditions:

```
z := x + y + z;
x := z - (x + y);
y := z - (x + y);
z := z - (x + y);
```

8.10 Programming Problems

1. Suppose that a text file has some comments added to it that appear inside of [square brackets]. Write a program that strips the comments from the file. (*Hint:* Use a flag to keep track of whether or not you are echoing.)

2. Write a program that plays a number-guessing game with two players. The program should alternate prompting for guesses from the players and should indicate in some way how close the guess is. For example, if a player is not right, the program could write out a certain number of stars, writing out more stars when the player is closer. The program should stop when one of the players guesses the number correctly. You should also allow the players to quit by typing 0 as a guess.

3. Write an interactive program that screens prospective credit card holders. The program should ask the user various questions about income, dependents, and credit history in order to determine whether or not the user gets a credit card. A card should be granted only if the user passes all the tests.

4. Write a program that plots a two-dimensional figure. The program should draw X and Y axes and should use a special character such as an asterisk to indicate points that are included in the figure. The program should use a BOOLEAN function with the following header to determine whether or not a given row and column position is considered part of the figure:

   ```
   FUNCTION Included (row, column : INTEGER) : BOOLEAN;
   ```

   The program should be general enough that changing function Included will cause the program to plot a different figure.

5. Write an interactive program that simulates the landing of a spaceship on the moon. Start the user 1000 meters above the ground and ask him to specify how much fuel to burn every 10 seconds. Stop the simulation when the user either successfully lands the ship or when the ship crashes into the surface.

9

BUILDING
LINEAR DATA TYPES

9.1 Introduction

Complex computer programs use many structures for storing data. A linear structure has a first element, a second element, and so on to a final element. This book has examined two linear structures in Pascal—files and arrays—describing their structures and telling you what you can do with them. While learning Pascal, you do need some of this kind of education. However, you shouldn't habitually look to the language to provide you with data structures. If you do, you will find your programs limited by the language. This chapter explores a different way of looking at data structures, building your own using your imagination and intelligence.

In the early design phase of program development, you shouldn't think at all about specific structures such as files or arrays. You should think more abstractly about the kinds of data you want to store and the kinds of manipulations you want to perform on those data. First, you examine the domain of the type; then you look at the operations that can be performed on objects of that domain.

After you have a good idea of what you want, then you should start thinking about possible implementations. If your specification matches a built-in type such as a file or array, that's great. If it doesn't, you must do some extra work. This usually involves choosing a built-in structure similar to, but not the same as, what you envision. In this case, you simply enhance the built-in type to give it the extra features it needs.

267

In this chapter you will explore two such structures that are extensions of the simple array. To use these new structures you must understand a new Pascal structure: the record. After covering some language details associated with records you will study thoroughly how to create a data type and build two of them, developing a program for each.

9.2 Records

Arrays are structured objects whose components are all of the same type. Because it is sometimes useful to form structured objects whose components are of different types, Pascal provides the record structure to build such objects.

For example, suppose you are doing a confidential study of introductory computer science students and are investigating the possible relationship between performance in a computer science course and factors such as gender, family income, age, and so on. Because of confidentiality, you store no names, but you do store such information as the following:

Attribute	Type	Description
Age	INTEGER	How many years old the person is
Experience	INTEGER	Prior experience with computers, rating 1 to 10
Gender	CHAR	Either M for male or F for female
Income	INTEGER	Total family income (in thousands of dollars)
Minority	BOOLEAN	Whether or not a member of a targeted minority
Private	BOOLEAN	Whether the person went to private school
Score	INTEGER	Measure of success in computer science course, rating 0 to 100

An array is not flexible enough to store all these components in one structured object because the components of an array must all be of the same type. However, you can use the record structure to store such a hodgepodge. Here is a declaration for a record type called **PersonInfo** that stores the combination of attributes above:

```
TYPE PersonInfo    = RECORD
          Age        : INTEGER;
          Experience : INTEGER;
          Gender     : CHAR;
          Income     : INTEGER;
          Minority   : BOOLEAN;
          Private    : BOOLEAN;
          Score      : INTEGER
      END;
```

The general syntax of the record type is:

```
RECORD
    <identifier list>  :  <type>;
    <identifier list>  :  <type>;
             . . .
    <identifier list>  :  <type>;
END
```

You enclose the contents of a record in the keywords `RECORD` and `END`. Notice that there is no corresponding `BEGIN` for this `END`. There is no semicolon before the `END` in this template, but you can put it in if you want to.

As with the `VAR` declaration, the identifier list can have any number of identifiers separated by commas. Each identifier introduces a new component of the record. Each of these components is a field of the record.

An object of type `PersonInfo` has seven different components or fields. The names and types of the components are listed in the type declaration. Therefore, if you were to define a variable of this type:

```
VAR OnePerson : PersonInfo;
```

You expect that `OnePerson` has a structure like this:

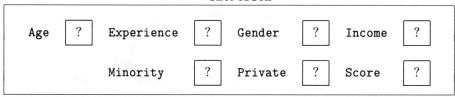

Just as you use a specific index to refer to an individual element of an array, you use a specific field name to refer to an individual field of a record. With arrays you put the index inside brackets, with records you use a period followed by the field name:

> *<record variable>* . *<field name>*

For example,

```
OnePerson.age
OnePerson.gender
OnePerson.income
```

To give a value to these fields, you would say:

```
OnePerson.age        := 20;
OnePerson.experience := 3;
OnePerson.gender     := 'F';
OnePerson.income     := 50;
```

```
OnePerson.minority   := TRUE;
OnePerson.private    := TRUE;
OnePerson.score      := 95;
```

After these statements execute, `OnePerson` would look like this:

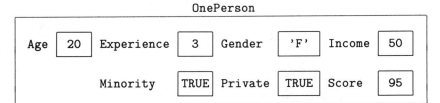

OnePerson

As with arrays, there are limitations on record objects because they are structured entities. You cannot directly compare record variables using the relational operators:

```
IF (person1 = person2) THEN
    WRITELN ('They are equal.');
```

You also cannot use READ/READLN or WRITE/WRITELN with record structures. To perform comparing, reading, or writing operations on such a type, you must build them yourself.

You can, however, copy one of these objects to another:

```
person1 := person2;
```

This command instructs the computer to copy the value of every component of **person2** into the corresponding component of **person1**. Thus this seemingly simple command might actually generate a great deal of work.

9.2.1 Records and Information Hiding

Just as the inner details of procedures are invisible outside the procedure, the inner details of a record declaration are invisible outside the record. If you define type **PersonInfo** in the main program, you do not introduce the field names of **PersonInfo** as definitions in the main program. Only the word **PersonInfo** is introduced as a definition. The other words are inside the record and are invisible.

This is another application of information hiding. The field names inside of **PersonInfo** can't possibly conflict with the field names of other record structures or with other words that might be defined in the program, so you can define several different record structures each with the same field name. This is handy when you want to use a common name such as **length** in more than one structure. This is just like the freedom you have to use the same names, such as **row** and `column`, for local variables in several different procedures, with each set of variables being independent of the others.

There is a negative aspect to this information hiding that frustrates many first-time programmers. If you use a field name outside the context of its record variable, the Pascal system will not understand you. If you write a statement such as

```
minority := TRUE;
```
not right, must be [OnePerson.minority := TRUE

the computer might report that the identifier `minority` is not declared. It is declared in the `PersonInfo` structure, but without the context of a specific record variable, the computer will be confused. If you get such error messages when you believe you have declared an identifier, it is probably because you are not properly accessing the record variable.

9.2.2   The WITH Statement

While you can appreciate the information hiding aspect of record field names, sometimes you may want to go the other way so you can say, "For this code, I want to open up a record variable so that its field names are visible." You can do this using a `WITH` statement. It has this syntax:

```
WITH <record variable> DO
     <statement>
```

The `WITH` statement makes the field names visible only for the statement controlled by the `WITH`. Because you will usually want more than one statement, you use a `BEGIN/END` block. Thus you could use a `WITH` statement to assign a series of values to fields as follows:

```
WITH OnePerson DO
BEGIN
    age := 20;
    experience := 3;
    gender := 'F';
    income := 50;
    minority := TRUE;
    private := TRUE;
    score := 95
END;
```

This is much simpler than the tedious solution of saying:

```
OnePerson.age        := 20;
OnePerson.experience := 3;
    . . .
```

You can nest WITH statements inside of WITH statements, just as you nested loops inside of loops and IF/THEN/ELSE statements inside of IF/THEN/ELSE statements. Such nesting can lead to a name conflict if both record variables have a field of the same name. Chapter 12 explains how such conflicts are resolved.

Pascal provides a shorthand way of expressing nested WITHs. The extended syntax of the WITH statement is

```
WITH <record var#1>, <record var#2>, ..., <record var#n> DO
    <statement>
```

This is defined as being equivalent to

```
WITH <record var#1> DO
    WITH <record var#2> DO
        ...
            WITH <record var#n> DO
                <statement>
```

9.3 Data Abstraction

Most programming techniques that you have examined so far can be categorized as methods of procedural abstraction. You have seen how to develop structured solutions to problems by breaking them down into procedures, subprocedures, sub-subprocedures, and so on. While you have touched on the techniques of data abstraction, these subjects have not been examined in depth.

DATA ABSTRACTION

Reasoning about the essential properties of a data type independent of a specific implementation.

You haven't needed powerful abstraction techniques before now because even though you have seen how to declare arrays and records, all the objects you have manipulated have had only a single level of structure. You are about to explore how to declare and manipulate multilevel structures.

Most of the procedural abstraction principles you have examined have corresponding data abstraction principles. Just as you can decompose a complex task into subtasks, you can also decompose a complex object into components. This decomposition makes the overall problem easier to solve because it allows you to focus on one part of the problem at a time. And just as you can develop a program in a top-down or bottom-up way, you can also develop a complex data object in a top-down or bottom-up way.

You have developed procedures and functions that are reusable tools, but you haven't yet built a type that is adaptable enough that you can reuse it. Now you will.

9.3.1 Building a Type

The process of building first involves specification and then implementation. You specify a type by describing its domain and operations. Be as specific as you can. If you are building a type for storing words, you shouldn't be satisfied with describing the domain as "all words." Such a definition is too ambiguous. Does it include such words as "isn't" and "merry-go-round" that have nonalphabetic characters? Does it include other nonalphabetic sequences of characters such as "$13.99"? Does it allow multiword terms such as "big deal"?

You generally describe the domain with some precise, but not overly complex statement such as "the domain of words contains all contiguous sequences of alphabetic characters." Such a simple definition is bound to either include values that you don't want or exclude values that you do want. For example, saying that words are composed of only alphabetic characters will exclude such words as "isn't" and "merry-go-round," but if you change your definition to allow apostrophes and dashes, then you end up with values that clearly aren't words, such as "- - -'hi'- - -." And what about empty sequences of characters, are those words or not? You need to consider all such special cases and weigh the alternatives. In the end you will probably adopt a definition that isn't perfect but which is simple enough to guarantee that you don't undertake an impossible task.

Sometimes you will want to identify a special property that all elements of the domain share. Such a property is referred to as a *data invariant* because it does not vary from domain value to domain value.

DATA INVARIANT

A property shared by all elements in the domain of a type.

For example, if you are describing dictionaries, you might want to include the invariant that they all are alphabetized. An invariant gives you both leverage and added burden. The leverage comes from the fact that any subprogram that manipulates a dictionary has the precondition that

`pre : dictionary is in alphabetical order`.

This precondition can greatly simplify many subprograms. The added burden comes from the fact that any subprogram that changes the dictionary has to guarantee the postcondition that

`post : dictionary is still in alphabetical order`.

Data invariants are most useful when you can't really imagine manipulating the structure if the invariant weren't true. For example, your conception of a dictionary might be so linked to alphabetical order that you can't imagine manipulating a dictionary that isn't alphabetized.

Once you specify the domain, you must consider what operations you want to perform on objects in the domain. The operations will vary from type to type, but here are some kinds of operations that are often included:

Kind of operation	Explanation
Creation	Initializing a variable
Inspection	Examining a variable or piece of variable
Modification	Changing the value of a variable or variables
Display	Showing the value of a variable
Comparison	Comparing two or more variables

You probably won't specify all the operations initially. You should, however, be sure to include enough that any other reasonable operation can be implemented later. This is usually accomplished by providing a core set of primitive operations that allow you to do most anything, even if in a clumsy way, and generally involves one or more creation, inspection, and modification operations. You can usually define the display and comparison operations in terms of these three. For example, if you specify a type for storing words, your core might be

Operation	Kind
Initialize a variable to an empty word	Creation
Copy the value of one variable to another	Creation
Find the nth character of a word	Inspection
Find the length of a word	Inspection
Append a character to the end of a word	Modification

This doesn't seem like much, but it is enough. To uppercase a variable called `OldWord`, for example, you can do the following. It is a roundabout way to uppercase a word, but it works.

```
initialize NewWord to an empty word.
for n := 1 to (length of OldWord) do
begin
      set NextChar to nth character of OldWord.
      uppercase NextChar.
      append NextChar to NewWord.
end
copy value of NewWord to OldWord.
```

Once you select the set of operations for the type, you are done with the specification part and are ready to start implementing it. This usually involves three steps. First, you must choose an appropriate Pascal structure for storing the type, usually a built-in structure close in its capabilities to what you intend, but which needs some enhancement. Second, you must consider the Pascal structure chosen and identify those operations which are so simple to perform that they need not be written out as separate subprograms. Finally, you should develop an appropriate set of subprograms to perform those operations which are more complex. In implementing these operations, you must remember your specification for the domain, especially any data invariants you specified.

9.3.2   Specifying a Simple List Type

To specify a type for storing a list of items, you first consider the domain of the new structure. What constitutes a list? Simply defined, a *list* is a collection of elements of the same type, with one element designated as the first, another as the second, another as the third, and so on. Here is a list of numbers:

5, 10, 1, 19, 7, 13, 204

Notice that nothing in your definition precludes repetition. Here is a list of words with repetition:

swimming, fun, computers, tedious, dancing, fun, Pascal, tedious

There are a few problems with this definition. What if the list is infinite?

1, 2, 3, 4, 5, 6, 7, 8, 9, ...

Lists such as these are fundamentally different from finite lists and are stored and manipulated in different ways. Therefore, you should restrict yourself to finite lists. Another question is whether the list can be empty. If you manipulate lists that change over time, it is likely that they will start out empty or will become empty. Thus you should allow this special case.

That takes care of specifying the domain of the type. Now consider the operations you want to perform on objects of the domain. The following operations will provide the core from which all other operations can be built:

Operation	Kind
Initialize a variable to an empty list	Creation
Copy the value of one list variable to another	Creation
Find the nth element of a list	Inspection
Find the length of a list	Inspection
Change the nth element of a list to some new value	Modification

Here are some additional operations that you will find useful:

Operation	Kind
Read part of a file into list	Creation
Write value of a list to output file	Display
Perform an operation on all list elements	Modification
Compare two lists for equality	Comparison

9.3.3 Implementing the Type

Now that you know what you want to build, you can start building. A structure that you have already examined that resembles the one you have specified here is the partially filled array discussed in Chapter 7. That structure stores a variable number of elements all of the same type and lets you easily perform several of the operations you have specified. Here are the declarations used to define one of those structures:

```
CONST LineLength = 70;
TYPE  LineList   = ARRAY [1..LineLength] OF CHAR;
VAR   line       : LineList;
      length     : INTEGER;
```

The odd thing about this structure is that it requires two variables to store the information. This is a bad idea. Your variable declarations should follow your intuitions. If you think of a list as a single entity, you should declare it that way. You shouldn't create multiple variables for storing a single object. The extra variables make the program harder to understand and complicate variable manipulation and parameter passing.

The solution is to add another level of structure that combines the length with the array in a single data object. Since the length and the array are of different types, you use a record structure to put them together:

```
CONST LineLength = 70;
TYPE  LineList   = ARRAY [1..LineLength] OF CHAR;
      LineType   = RECORD
                     chars  : LineList;
                     length : INTEGER
                   END;
VAR   line       : LineType;
```

Because of the record structure, you now have a single type called **LineType** that stores both the array and its length. This lets you declare a single variable for storing the line. Here is a picture of its structure with an example of how it might store a list of six characters:

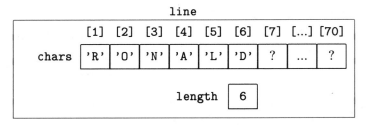

Notice that elements [7] through [70] are not initialized. This will not cause a problem as long as you use the length variable to avoid referencing nonexistent list elements.

The structure pictured above is a very specific list type that stores characters. Here is a version of the constant and type declarations that is more generic:

```
CONST MaxLength    = <maximum length of list>;
TYPE  ElementList  = ARRAY [1..MaxLength] OF <element type>;
      ListType     = RECORD
            elements : ElementList;
            length   : INTEGER
      END;
VAR   list         : ListType;
```

The two boxes above can be filled in to create any specific list type desired. But this still isn't quite what you intended. Your domain description has no maximum size for a list, whereas this array implementation does. This slight deviation from the specification obviously introduces a limitation that you didn't intend, but you can't really do better at this point. Later in the book you will examine a list structure that can grow dynamically as the program executes, growing and shrinking to just the right size. Such a structure is obviously more flexible, but even it is limited, since there is a limit to how much data any given computer can store. Thus not all the things that you plan for during the specification phase can actually be realized during the implementation phase.

With this implementation, several of the operations that you specified can be performed directly:

Operation	Pascal
Initialize a variable to an empty list	`list.length := 0;`
Copy value of one variable to another	`list2 := list1;`
Find the nth element of a list	`list.elements [n]`
Find the length of a list	`list.length`
Change the nth element of a list	`list.elements [n] := value;`

The other operations are more complex and will be developed over the course of the next few sections.

9.3.4 Reading and Writing with Lists

The simplest manipulation that you can perform on a partially filled array is to write its contents to an output line. Here is a procedure using the structure from Chapter 7:

```
PROCEDURE WriteLineList (line   : LineList;
                         length : INTEGER);
VAR index : INTEGER;
BEGIN
    FOR index := 1 TO length DO
        WRITE (line [index]);
    WRITELN
END;
```

Adapting this to your new structure is not difficult. The two parameters are collapsed to one because the record variable contains both the array and its length, and by using a WITH statement to open up the record variable, you can make the field's **length** and **chars** visible, which allows you to write the procedure in almost the same way:

```
PROCEDURE WriteLineList (line : LineType);
VAR index : INTEGER;
BEGIN
    WITH line DO
        FOR index := 1 TO length DO
            WRITE (chars [index]);
    WRITELN
END;
```

This procedure fits your new structure, but it describes a very specific writing task. You won't always be writing characters, you won't always be ending with a WRITELN statement, and sometimes, you might want to use a field width. The following description is more general, using the generic declarations for type ListType and boxes to indicate those parts of the procedure which might change from application to application:

```
PROCEDURE WriteList (list : ListType);
VAR index : INTEGER
BEGIN
    <write any text that is to appear before list>;
    WITH list DO
        FOR index := 1 TO length DO
            WRITE (elements [index]: <field width>);
    <write any text that is to appear after list>
END;
```

By filling in the boxes appropriately, you can use this procedure to write out almost any list. Now do the same for reading. In Chapter 8 you examined this procedure for reading a line of characters into an array:

```
PROCEDURE TransferLineTo (VAR line   : LineList;
                          VAR length : INTEGER);
```

```
BEGIN
    length := 0;
    WHILE NOT EOLN AND (length < LineLength) DO
    BEGIN
        length := length + 1;
        READ (line [length])
    END;
    READLN
END;
```

Changing the procedure to match your new structure, you get:

```
PROCEDURE TransferLineTo (VAR line : LineType);
BEGIN
    WITH line DO
    BEGIN
        length := 0;
        WHILE NOT EOLN AND (length < LineLength) DO
        BEGIN
            length := length + 1;
            READ (chars [length])
        END;
        READLN
    END
END;
```

Again, this describes a very specific file reading task. You won't always be reading characters, you won't always be reading to the end of the line, and you won't always want to do a READLN afterwards. So again, switching to the generic declarations for type ListType and using boxes to indicate what parts of the procedure are likely to change from application to application, you get:

```
PROCEDURE ReadList (VAR list : ListType);
BEGIN
    <perform any actions that need to be done before reading>;
    WITH list DO
    BEGIN
        length := 0;
        WHILE   <more data to read> AND (length < MaxLength) DO
        BEGIN
            length := length + 1;
            READ (elements [length])
        END
    END;
    <perform any actions that need to be done after reading>
END;
```

Here is a slight variation of the procedure that uses a sentinel loop:

```
PROCEDURE ReadList (VAR list : ListType);
VAR next : <element type>;
BEGIN
    <perform any actions that need to be done before reading>;
    READ (next);
    WITH list DO
    BEGIN
        length := 0;
        WHILE (next <> <sentinel>) AND (length < MaxLength) DO
        BEGIN
            length := length + 1;
            elements [length] := next;
            READ (next)
        END
    END;
    <perform any actions that need to be done after reading>
END;
```

9.3.5 Performing an Operation on List Elements

You will often want to perform the same operation on each list element. For example, suppose you are storing the characters of a word and want to apply the character-uppercasing operation developed in Chapter 6:

```
PROCEDURE TurnToUppercase (VAR character : CHAR);
BEGIN
    IF (character IN ['a'..'z']) THEN
        character := CHR (ORD (character) - ORD ('a') + ORD ('A'))
END;
```

This is a straightforward task. You use a FOR loop to call the procedure once for each element:

```
PROCEDURE UppercaseList (VAR line : LineType);
VAR index : INTEGER;
BEGIN
    WITH line DO
        FOR index := 1 TO length DO
            TurnToUppercase (chars [index])
END;
```

This easily converts to generic form:

```
PROCEDURE ChangeList (VAR line : LineType);
VAR index : INTEGER;
BEGIN
    WITH line DO
        FOR index := 1 TO length DO
            <operation to be performed> (elements [index])
END;
```

9.3.6 Comparing Lists

You will often want to compare lists. Suppose you have the following declarations:

```
CONST MaxNums     = 100;
TYPE  NumberList  = ARRAY [1..MaxNums] OF INTEGER;
      ListType    = RECORD
            nums   : NumberList;
            length : INTEGER
      END;
VAR   list1       : ListType;
      list2       : ListType;
```

Consider the variables `list1` and `list2`. Since they are structured variables, you cannot compare them directly using the relational operators:

```
(list1 = list2)
```

However, it is possible to compare them by building on simpler comparisons. Pascal doesn't allow direct comparisons of structured objects, but these two lists are composed of simple integers and Pascal can compare them. In other words, you need to build on comparisons such as

```
(list1.length   = list2.length)
(list1.nums [1] = list2.nums [1])
(list1.nums [2] = list2.nums [2])
```

These comparisons involve complex variable names, but the variables are of type `INTEGER`, so you can do this.

You start by writing the header of the subprogram for comparing two lists. Because the point of this operation is to answer a yes/no question ("Are they equal?"), it makes sense to make this a `BOOLEAN`-valued function:

```
FUNCTION Equal (one, two : ListType) : BOOLEAN;
```

Your first pseudocode can describe what it means for the two lists to be different:

```
        if (lengths are different) or (some elements differ) then
                report that lists are not equal.
        else
                report that lists are equal.
```

To expand this, you need to explain how to compare elements from the different lists. This obviously involves a counter:

```
        if (lengths are different) then
                report that lists are not equal.
        else
        begin
                for pos going 1 to length do
                        compare element [pos] of each list.
                report whether lists are equal.
        end
```

You can refine this further by realizing that you don't really want a FOR loop. Because you can stop comparing once you encounter a difference between the two lists, you want a WHILE loop:

```
        if (lengths are different) then
                report that lists are not equal.
        else
        begin
                pos := 1.
                while (element [pos] of each list are equal) do
                        pos := pos + 1.
                report whether lists are equal.
        end
```

The problem with this WHILE loop is that it can terminate only when it encounters a difference between the two lists. However, this might never happen. If they are truly equal, you don't expect to see a difference. In that case, you want to terminate the loop because you notice that you have compared all elements:

```
        if (lengths are different) then
                report that lists are not equal.
        else
        begin
                pos := 1.
                while (element [pos] of each list are equal) and (more to see) do
                        pos := pos + 1.
                if (elements are still equal) then
                        report that lists are equal.
                else
                        report that lists are not equal.
        end
```

This is easily translated into Pascal, but there is one special case that isn't handled properly by this pseudocode. What if both lists are empty, with a length of 0? This pseudocode will try to compare the first elements of each, which is not what you want to do. You need to add a third branch to the IF/THEN/ELSE:

```
if (lengths are different) then
        report that lists are not equal.
else
        if (lengths are 0) then
                report that lists are equal.
        else
        begin
            pos := 1.
            while (element [pos] of each list are equal) and (more to see) do
                    pos := pos + 1.
            if (elements are still equal) then
                    report that lists are equal.
            else
                    report that lists are not equal.
        end
```

This is now easily translated into Pascal:

```
FUNCTION Equal (one, two : ListType) : BOOLEAN;
VAR pos : INTEGER;
BEGIN
    IF (one.length <> two.length) THEN
        equal := FALSE
    ELSE
        IF (one.length = 0) THEN
            equal := TRUE
        ELSE
        BEGIN
            pos := 1;
            WHILE (one.nums [pos] = two.nums [pos]) AND (pos < one.length) DO
                pos := pos + 1;
            equal := (one.nums [pos] = two.nums [pos])
        END
END;
```

Notice that unlike the other subprograms developed in this chapter, the WITH statement doesn't make this procedure easier to write. That is so because you are referring to fields within two record variables of identical structure, which means that you need to specifically refer to one or the other by using the dot notation.

This function doesn't require a generic version because nothing will change from list to list except that the array **nums** might be called something else.

9.3.7 A Complete List Implementation

Now that you have examined all the subprograms necessary to implement a list structure, try creating a list that stores individual characters of a word. To simplify things, define a word as a sequence of nonblank characters. This allows these simple words:

```
this        and        that        are        words
```

as well as these more complex words:

```
isn't        merry-go-round        John's        cup-of-tea
```

Because the definition permits any sequence of nonblanks, it even allows sequences of characters that don't look like words:

```
"Arriba!"        $294.35        2+2=4        ---dashes---
```

With this simple definition, however, you will not have much trouble implementing the type. Include a procedure for uppercasing the letters of a word as the operation to be performed on all list elements. A simple program will suffice because the program is less important than the implementation of the type. The program is to read the first two words from an input line, compare them for equality, and report the result to the output file. This task is to be repeated for every line in the file. The program should also ignore the case of letters. Thus if the input file looks like this:

```
first line of file.
second line.
third third
fifth will be empty


    wow!        wow!
that's all folks!
```

the output file would look like this:

```
"FIRST" is not equal to "LINE"
"SECOND" is not equal to "LINE."
"THIRD" is equal to "THIRD"
"FIFTH" is not equal to "WILL"
"" is equal to ""
"WOW!" is equal to "WOW!"
"THAT'S" is not equal to "ALL"
```

Here is the program:

```
(* pre   : program is supplied with a file of words.            *)
(* post  : the first two words from each line (if any) are read and *)
(*        : compared for equality.  The result is reported to the   *)
```

```
(*              : output file.                                        *)
(* parameters : INPUT-in, OUTPUT-out.                                 *)

PROGRAM CompareWords (INPUT, OUTPUT);
CONST MaxWordLen = 15;           (* maximum number of characters in a word *)
TYPE  CharList   = ARRAY [1..MaxWordLen] OF CHAR;
      WordType   = RECORD
            chars  : CharList;   (* list of characters in word         *)
            length : INTEGER     (* number of characters in word       *)
      END;
VAR   word1      : WordType;     (* first word from input line         *)
      word2      : WordType;     (* second word from input line        *)

PROCEDURE ReadChar (VAR character : CHAR);
(* post       : next input character from file is returned, unless EOLN, in *)
(*             : which case a space is returned.                       *)
(* parameters : character-out.                                         *)
BEGIN
    IF NOT EOLN THEN
        READ (character)
    ELSE
        character := ' '
END;    (* ReadChar *)

PROCEDURE TurnToUppercase (VAR TheChar : CHAR);
(* post       : if TheChar is a lowercase alphabetic, it is changed to *)
(*             : corresponding uppercase char; otherwise, no change.   *)
(* parameters : TheChar-in/out.                                        *)
BEGIN
    IF TheChar IN ['a'..'z'] THEN
        TheChar := CHR (ORD (TheChar) - ORD ('a') + ORD ('A'))
END;    (* TurnToUppercase *)

PROCEDURE UppercaseWord (VAR word : WordType);
(* post       : all lowercase characters in word are turned to         *)
(*             : corresponding uppercase characters.                   *)
(* parameters : word-in/out.                                           *)
(* requires   : type WordType; procedure TurnToUppercase.              *)
VAR index      : INTEGER;   (* loop counter                            *)
BEGIN
    WITH word DO
        FOR index := 1 TO length DO
            TurnToUppercase (chars [index])
END;    (* UppercaseWord *)
```

```
PROCEDURE WriteWord (word : WordType);
(* post        : word is written to output file enclosed in "quotes." *)
(* parameters  : word-in.                                              *)
(* requires    : type WordType.                                        *)
VAR index      : INTEGER;   (* loop counter                           *)
BEGIN
    WRITE ('"');
    WITH word DO
        FOR index := 1 TO length DO
            WRITE (chars [index]);
    WRITE ('"')
END;   (* WriteWord *)


PROCEDURE ReadWord (VAR word : WordType);
(* post        : leading blanks on current input line skipped; next   *)
(*              : contiguous sequence of nonblanks is read into word;  *)
(*              : input cursor positioned after blank following word or *)
(*              : at EOLN if no blank follows word.                    *)
(* parameters  : word-out.                                             *)
(* requires    : constant MaxWordLen; type WordType; and procedure     *)
(*              : ReadChar.                                             *)
VAR next       : CHAR;   (* next character from input line            *)
BEGIN
    ReadChar (next);
    WHILE (next = ' ') AND NOT EOLN DO
        READ (next);
    WITH word DO
    BEGIN
        length := 0;
        WHILE (next <> ' ') AND (length < MaxWordLen) DO
        BEGIN
            length := length + 1;
            chars [length] := next;
            ReadChar (next)
        END
    END
END;   (* ReadWord *)
```

```
FUNCTION Equal (one, two : WordType) : BOOLEAN;
(* post        : returns TRUE if lengths are equal and if elements in *)
(*             : corresponding positions of two words are all equal;  *)
(*             : returns FALSE otherwise.                             *)
(* parameters : one-in, two-in.                                      *)
(* requires    : type WordType.                                      *)
VAR pos        : INTEGER;   (* current position of comparison scan    *)
BEGIN
    IF (one.length <> two.length) THEN
        equal := FALSE
    ELSE
        IF (one.length = 0) THEN
            equal := TRUE
        ELSE
        BEGIN
            pos := 1;
            WHILE (one.chars [pos] = two.chars [pos]) AND (pos < one.length) DO
            pos := pos + 1;
            equal := (one.chars [pos] = two.chars [pos])
        END
END;   (* Equal *)


PROCEDURE GetWords (VAR word1 : WordType;
                    VAR word2 : WordType);
(* pre         : input cursor at beginning of line.                      *)
(* post        : first two words from input line read into word1 and word2; *)
(*             : word1 and word2 turned to uppercase; input cursor at    *)
(*             : beginning of next line.                                 *)
(* parameters : word1-out, word2-out.                                   *)
(* requires    : type WordType; procedures ReadWord and UppercaseWord.   *)
BEGIN
    ReadWord (word1);
    ReadWord (word2);
    UppercaseWord (word1);
    UppercaseWord (word2);
    READLN
END;   (* GetWords *)


PROCEDURE ReportEquality (word1 : WordType;
                          word2 : WordType);
(* post        : Output line describing equality or nonequality of word1 *)
(*             : and word2 is produced.                                 *)
(* parameters : word1-in, word2-in.                                     *)
```

```
(* requires    : type WordType; and procedure WriteWord.
BEGIN
    WriteWord (word1);
    IF equal (word1, word2) THEN
        WRITE (' is equal to ')
    ELSE
        WRITE (' is not equal to ');
    WriteWord (word2);
    WRITELN
END;   (* ReportEquality *)


BEGIN   (* main program *)
    WHILE NOT EOF DO
    BEGIN
        GetWords (word1, word2);
        ReportEquality (word1, word2)
    END
END.   (* main program *)
```

There isn't much work involved in implementing the type given the generic subprograms we have worked out, but a few points are worth comment. Consider the **ReadWord** procedure. Since the domain includes all sequences of nonblank characters, the easiest way to read a word is to use a sentinel loop looking for a space. But what if there are too many characters to fit in the array? Procedure **ReadWord** merely skips the extra characters and truncates the word. You will also notice in procedure **ReadWord** that the simple READ statement has been replaced with a special procedure called **ReadChar**. The **ReadChar** procedure is more careful than the simple READ in that it will not read past end-of-line. This behavior is usually desirable.

Look at the decomposition tree for this program:

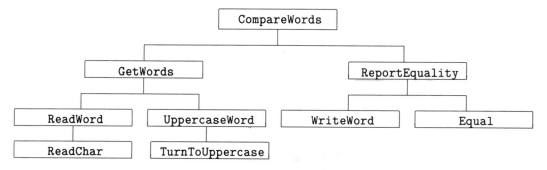

This program looks complex but is actually simple. The **TurnToUppercase** procedure comes from the software library and the **ReadChar** procedure is easy to create. The four subprograms at the next level of decomposition are also easy to write because you have generic versions of them (developed earlier in the chapter). Thus the only original code in this program is in procedures `GetWords` and `ReportEquality`. If you examine them closely, however, you will see that they too are extremely simple.

9.4 Specifying a More Complex List Type

Now that you have built one type, try another. This time build one with a data invariant. As with simple lists, define your domain as all finite sequences of elements of a single type that have a first element, second element, and so on. However, add the restriction that there be an ordering function and that each successive element in any list be greater than or equal to its predecessor. Thus your data invariant is that elements of the list appear in nondecreasing order. Nondecreasing order is slightly different than increasing order, which doesn't allow for duplicates, as nondecreasing order does. The gap between successive elements can be very small or very large. The data invariant says nothing about the magnitude of increase, it merely says that there can be no decrease, for example,

1, 1, 3, 6, 23, 104, 105, 106, 994, 999

Now that you have specified the domain, you can specify the operations. Here is a set of core operations that will allow you to build most others:

Operation	Kind
Initialize a variable to an empty list	Creation
Copy value of one variable to another	Creation
Find the nth element of a list	Inspection
Find the length of a list	Inspection
Insert a value into a list	Modification

This is the same set of core operations as before, except for the last one. In the simple list, you could change the nth element of a list. You can't do that here because changing an element in the middle of a list might cause the data invariant to be violated. The insert operation, however, will let you add to a list so that the data invariant is guaranteed.

In addition to the core operations, include these operations:

Operation	Kind
Read part of a file into list	Creation
Write value of a variable to output file	Display
Compare two lists for equality	Comparison
Search a list for a specific value	Inspection

You should exclude the operation which modifies every element of the list because such a modification might violate the data invariant, and you should include a new operation for searching a list to see if and where it stores a specific value.

9.4.1   Implementing the Complex List Type

Use the same declarations you used for the simple list:

```
CONST MaxLength    = <maximum length of list>;
TYPE  ElementList  = ARRAY [1..MaxLength] OF <element type>;
      ListType     = RECORD
          elements : ElementList;
          length   : INTEGER
      END;
VAR   list         : ListType;
```

Again, several of the operations you specified can be performed directly:

Operation	Pascal
Initialize a variable to an empty list	`list.length := 0;`
Copy value of one variable to another	`list2 := list1;`
Find the *n*th element of a list	`list.elements [n]`
Find the length of a list	`list.length`

The only core operation that cannot be performed directly is insert. Two of the other operations, writing a list and comparing two lists for equality, are the same as they were for the simple list. The Read and Search operations, however, require more thought.

9.4.2   Inserting into a Sorted List

You must carefully consider the data invariant in implementing this procedure. The invariant lets you assume that the list starts out in order, but it also requires that you keep it that way when you add the new element.

First, examine the general problem of insertion, and then tackle the problem of where to insert. Assume that you have a list that holds up to 100 integers and that currently it has 50:

List

	[1]	[2]	[3]	[4]	[..]	[48]	[49]	[50]	[51]	[..]	[100]
numbers	12	17	20	23	..	83	85	93	?	..	?

length   50

If you want to insert the value 43 between the current twenty-fifth and twenty-sixth elements, you can't say

    list [26] := 43;

since this would wipe out the current value of the twenty-sixth element. You must first make room for the new element and then store it in the twenty-sixth element:

List (before)

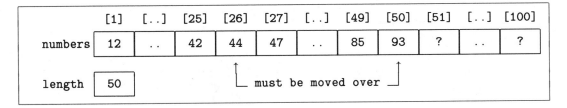

List (after)

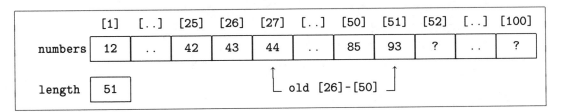

Here is a good start on the pseudocode:

shift elements [position] through [length] one to the right.
store value in elements [position].
increment length.

To improve this, you need to expand what you mean by shifting a series of elements. Changing the values of a series of array elements involves a series of assignment statements of the form:

```
elements [27] := elements [26];
elements [28] := elements [27];
      . . .
elements [50] := elements [49];
elements [51] := elements [50];
```

or, more generally:

```
elements [index + 1] := elements [index];
```

You want a loop to perform all these assignments. Thus here is a second attempt at the pseudocode

for index going position to length do
    elements [index + 1] := elements [index].
store value in elements [position].
increment length.

This is almost right, but it has one tiny bug. Let's use a piece of the array you were working with above to see what the problem is:

[26]   [27]   [28]

| 44 | 47 | 48 |

The first two iterations of the loop execute the statements:

```
elements [27] := elements [26];
elements [28] := elements [27];
```

Let's see what each does. After the first assignment statement, you get

[26]   [27]   [28]

| 44 | 44 | 48 |

After the second, you get

[26]   [27]   [28]

| 44 | 44 | 44 |

This is not shifting at all, it is copying the value 44 to all array positions [27] through [51]. You can't shift element [26] to position [27] until it is freed up. It is like sitting down in a chair where someone else is sitting. However, there is a way to make this work—by going from right to left rather than left to right. Take advantage of the fact that there is nothing stored in element [51] and start by moving element [50] to [51]. This makes element [50] a free space, so you can move element [49] into it. That makes [49] a free space, and so on. This shifting process works because you start with a free array element and free up another element every time through the loop. Here is the improved pseudocode:

> for index going (length) downto (position) do
>   elements [index + 1] := elements [index].
> store value in elements [position].
> increment length.

This is easily implemented in Pascal:

```
WITH list DO
BEGIN
    FOR index := length DOWNTO position DO
        elements [index + 1] := elements [index];
    elements [position] := value;
    length := length + 1
END
```

This is the general insertion algorithm, but how do you modify it so that the insertion takes place at the right point? Suppose your list looks like this:

2, 4, 6, 8, 10, 12, 14

Consider inserting a value such as 7. You can express this in pseudocode with a WHILE loop:

> start position at last list element.
> while (element [position] > value) do
>   position := position − 1.

This will calculate the appropriate value of `position` so that the value should be inserted after element [position]. You can translate this directly into Pascal:

```
WITH list DO
BEGIN
    position := length;
    WHILE (elements [position] > value) DO
        position := position - 1
END;
```

This code is almost right. It doesn't take into account two very special cases, however. Suppose that the value you are inserting is less than all other elements currently in the list. That means the WHILE loop will search beyond array element [1] for a value that is less than the one you are inserting. In this case, the value should be stored as the new element [1]. This means that you want position to have the value 0. The problem with that is that you will get an array index out of bounds if you make a reference to element [0]. An easy fix is to introduce a flag to avoid the array reference:

```
WITH list DO
BEGIN
    position := length;
    done := (elements [position] < value);
    WHILE NOT done DO
    BEGIN
        position := position - 1;
        IF position = 0 THEN
            done := TRUE
        ELSE
            done := (elements [position] < value)
    END
END;
```

There is another special case you need to consider. What happens if the list is empty? This means that length is 0 and will cause an array index out of bounds before the loop even executes when you try to give an initial value to done. An easy fix is to wrap up the loop in an IF/THEN that tests for a length of 0:

```
WITH list DO
BEGIN
    position := length;
    IF (length > 0) THEN
    BEGIN
        done := (elements [position] < value);
        WHILE NOT done DO
        BEGIN
            position := position - 1;
            IF position = 0 THEN
                done := TRUE
            ELSE
                done := (elements [position] < value)
        END
    END
END;
```

This will find the proper place to insert the value. Now all you have to do is combine this with the insertion algorithm. The insertion algorithm involves a loop going from right to left, and this loop goes from right to left, which means you can combine the two into one big loop. The insertion algorithm is then completed by adding the two assignment statements that store the value and increment the length. This is your insertion algorithm:

```
PROCEDURE InsertInto (VAR list  : ListType;
                          value : <element type>);
VAR position : INTEGER;
    done     : BOOLEAN;
BEGIN
    WITH list DO
    BEGIN
        position := length;
        IF (length > 0) THEN
        BEGIN
            done := (elements [position] < value);
            WHILE NOT done DO
            BEGIN
                elements [position + 1] := elements [position];
                position := position - 1;
                IF position = 0 THEN
                    done := TRUE
                ELSE
                    done := (elements [position] < value)
            END
        END;
        elements [position + 1] := value;
        length := length + 1
    END
END;
```

9.4.3 Searching for a Value

You will often want to know if a specific value is stored in a list: Does this word have any apostrophes? Did this student get a 100 on any exams? Is 0 somewhere in this list of temperatures? You want to answer the question, "Is <*a certain value*> in <*a certain list*>?" You can do this in a yes/no way, returning a BOOLEAN that indicates whether or not the value appears. However, when the value does appear in the list, you will often want to know where it appears. So instead you should develop a subprogram that returns the position of a particular value in a list. If the value does not appear, the subprogram returns a position of 0. Thus the subprogram will return both the yes/no information (nonzero/zero position) as well as the positional information, killing two tasks with one subprogram.

The simplest way to search involves scanning the list from beginning to end. Written in pseudocode, we have

```
scan the list for the value.
if found then
     return index.
else
     return 0.
```

To scan the array, you need to be able to index it. Thus you can refine the pseudocode:

```
set index to 1.
while (value not found) do
     increment index.
if found then
     return index.
else
     return 0.
```

This is almost directly translatable into Pascal, but you have forgotten one thing. What happens if the value doesn't appear? How do you exit from the WHILE loop? You need to change the loop to allow a second possibility. You continue if you haven't found the value and if there are values left in the list to examine. To account for this, you need to introduce the length:

```
set index to 1.
while (value not found) and (index < length) do
     increment index.
if found then
     return index.
else
     return 0.
```

This, now, can be easily translated into Pascal:

```
FUNCTION PositionOf (value : <element type>;
                     list  : ListType) : INTEGER;
VAR index : INTEGER;
```

```
BEGIN
    index := 1;
    WITH list DO
    BEGIN
        WHILE (elements [index] <> value) AND (index < length) DO
            index := index + 1;
        IF elements [index] = value THEN
            PositionOf := index
        ELSE
            PositionOf := 0
    END
END;
```

This simple algorithm is called *sequential search* because it examines all elements in sequence. You can do better than that, though, if you take into account the data invariant. To understand why you want a different algorithm, consider how you would solve the problem of finding a phone number in the phone book. Using the sequential-search algorithm, you start with the first name in the book and go through them one at a time until you find the one you are looking for or reach the end of the book. A person would be crazy to do that. Similarly, a programmer would be crazy to use a sequential-search algorithm on a list that he knows is sorted.

Most people deal with the phone book by turning to the middle of the book, seeing how close they are, and deciding whether they need to go backwards or forwards. They then flip to a new page either before or after the current one. Eventually, this leads them to a single page. At this point, most people switch to sequential search and scan the page from top to bottom. There is a simple extension of this idea that leads to an efficient method for searching a long list. The trick is to keep dividing the list in half, until you get down to a single element or find that you've got nothing left to search. Here are a few examples.

Consider a list with eight integers stored in it:

	[1]	[2]	[3]	[4]	[5]	[6]	[7]	[8]
list	1	3	6	12	18	93	123	146

Apply this technique to the array to see how it works. You need three different variables that keep track of the low index, the high index, and the midpoint of the two. Start by initializing `low` and `high` with the lowest and highest indexes and setting the `middle` to the midpoint:

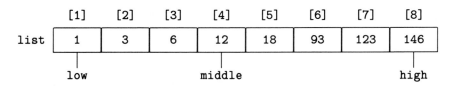

Search for the number 93. In this algorithm, you always keep your attention on the middle element. You start by looking at the fourth element. It is less than 93. Therefore, the target must be to the right of the fourth element so you can move **low** to the right of it:

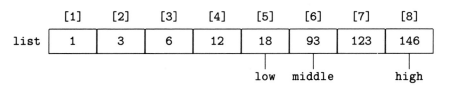

You can see that you have located the element because **middle** now points to it and **middle** is where you focus your attention. You find that the sixth element equals 93, your target value, so you return 6 as the position.

What happens when the value doesn't lie in the middle like this? Search for the number 18. Again, you start with the middle element:

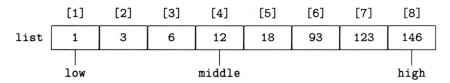

The fourth element is less than 18, so you move **low** to the right of it:

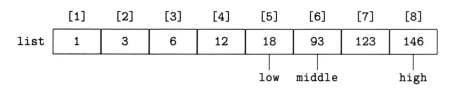

Remember, you always examine the middle element; it doesn't matter that **low** is pointing to the value you want. You now examine the sixth element. It is larger than 18. Therefore, your target must be to the left of the sixth element. This lets you reset the value of **high** to the left of the sixth element, leaving

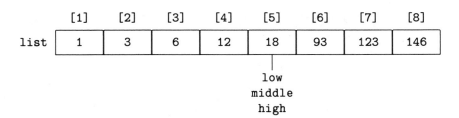

You have pinpointed the element. The fifth element stores the target value 18. Thus you return the position 5 as your answer. Situations where a value appears in the middle of a long list are less likely to occur than pileups such as the one above.

What happens when the algorithm fails to find a value? Suppose you search for the number 7. You start with the following, focusing on the middle element:

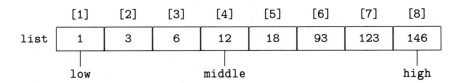

The fourth element is larger than 7, so you look to its left:

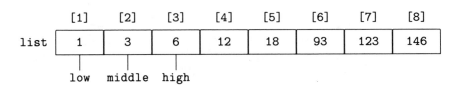

You now examine the second element. It is less than 7, so you look to its right:

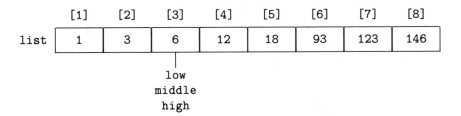

You get another pileup, but something different happens this time. The third element is less than 7, so you look to the right to find your target by moving the `low` pointer to the right:

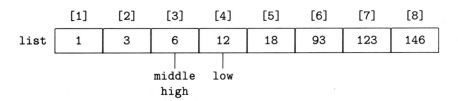

The low pointer is now larger than the high pointer. The pointers are saying, in effect, that the value must be stored at an index greater than or equal to 4 and less than or equal to 3. There are no numbers in this range. This is the signal that you aren't going to find a 7 in this list. Thus you stop searching and report a position of 0.

When the value actually appears in the array, this algorithm either finds it along the way at the middle of a long list or it creates one of those one-element pileups on top of the target. If the element doesn't appear, you also reach a pileup but end up resetting the low pointer to a value larger than the high pointer.

Here is a pseudocode description of the algorithm:

```
set low to 1.
set high to length.
set found to false.
while (not found) and (low <= high) do
begin
      calculate the midpoint of Low and High, store as Middle.
      if (element at the midpoint is target value) then
            set found to true.
      else
            if (element at midpoint is less than target value) then
                set low to (middle + 1).
            else
                set high to (middle - 1).
end
if (found) then
      return middle.
else
      return 0.
```

This is easily translated into Pascal:

```
FUNCTION PositionOf (value  : <element type>;
                     list   : ListType) : INTEGER;
VAR low     : INTEGER;
    high    : INTEGER;
    middle  : INTEGER;
    found   : BOOLEAN;
BEGIN
    WITH list DO
    BEGIN
        low := 1;
        high := length;
        found := FALSE;
        WHILE (NOT found) AND (low <= high) DO
        BEGIN
            middle := ((low + high) DIV 2);
            IF (elements [middle] = value) THEN
                found := TRUE
            ELSE
                IF elements [middle] < value THEN
                    low  := middle + 1
                ELSE
                    high := middle - 1
        END;
        IF found THEN
            PositionOf := middle
        ELSE
            PositionOf := 0
    END
END;   (* PositionOf *)
```

9.4.4 Reading into a List

Reading values into a list is not complicated, but you have to decide how to handle problems such as duplications. A simple approach would be to allow duplication, in which case your pseudocode would be

```
initialize list.
while (more to read) do
begin
    read next value.
    insert value in list.
end
```

If you want to avoid duplicates, you would have to test to see whether the next value is already in the list before you insert it. You can use the `PositionOf` function to do so:

```
initialize list.
while (more to read) do
begin
     read next value.
     if PositionOf (next value, list) = 0 then
          insert value in list.
end
```

You can easily translate this into Pascal:

```
PROCEDURE ReadList (VAR list : ListType);
VAR next :  <element type>;
BEGIN
    WITH list DO
    BEGIN
        length := 0;
        WHILE <more to read> DO
        BEGIN
            READ (next);
            IF PositionOf (next, list) = 0 THEN
                InsertInto (list, NextWord)
        END
    END
END;   (* ReadList *)
```

9.4.5 Another Complete List Implementation

Let's build a more complicated sorted list type using the results of the last few sections. A useful sorted list is a dictionary. You can build on the `WordType` that you already have. The only problem you encounter is lines such as the following:

```
IF (elements [middle] = value) THEN
```

The problem is that each element of the list is a structured variable of type `WordType`. This means you can't perform direct comparisons such as these. To fix this, use the comparison function that you wrote when you implemented `WordType`:

```
IF equal (elements [middle], value) THEN
```

Here is a complete program that compiles a dictionary of all the words appearing in an input file. As an example, when fed the program written earlier in this chapter as an input file, it produces the following output file:

"QUOTES."	,	')	');	('
('"')	('"');	('A')	('A'))	(*
(CHARACTER)	(CHARS	(IF	(INPUT,	(LENGTH
(NEXT	(NEXT)	(NEXT);	(ONE,	(ONE.CHARS
(ONE.LENGTH	(ORD	(POS	(THECHAR)	(VAR
(WORD	(WORD1	(WORD1);	(WORD1,	(WORD2);
*)	+	-	0)	0;
1	15;	1;	:	:=
<	<>	=	A	AFTER
ALL	ALPHABETIC,	AND	ANY)	ARE
ARRAY	AT	BEGIN	BEGINNING	BLANK
BLANKS	BOOLEAN;	CASE	CHANGE.	CHANGED
CHAR);	CHAR;	CHARACTER	CHARACTER-OUT.	CHARACTERS
CHARACTERS.	CHARLIST	CHARLIST;	CHARS	CHR
COMPARED	COMPAREWORDS	COMPARISON	CONST	CONSTANT
CONTIGUOUS	CORRESPONDING	COUNTER	CURRENT	CURSOR
DESCRIBING	DO	EACH	ELEMENTS	ELSE
ENCLOSED	END	END.	END;	EOF
EOLN	EOLN,	EQUAL	EQUAL;	EQUALITY
EQUALITY.	EXTRA	FALSE	FILE	FILE.
FIRST	FOLLOWING	FOLLOWS	FOR	FROM
FUNCTION	GETWORDS	IF	IGNORED	IN
INDEX	INPUT	INPUT-IN,	INTEGER	INTEGER;
INTO	IS	IT	LEADING	LENGTH
LENGTHS	LINE	LINE.	LIST	LOOP
LOWERCASE	MAIN	MAXIMUM	MAXWORDLEN	MAXWORDLEN)
MAXWORDLEN;	MORE	NEXT	NEXT;	NO
NONBLANKS	NONEQUALITY	NOT	NUMBER	OF
ON	ONE-IN,	ONE.LENGTH)	OR	ORD
OTHERWISE,	OTHERWISE.	OUTPUT	OUTPUT);	OUTPUT-OUT.
PARAMETERS	POS	POSITION	POSITIONED	POSITIONS
POST	PRE	PROCEDURE	PROCEDURES	PRODUCED.
PROGRAM	READ	READCHAR	READCHAR.	READLN
READWORD	RECORD	REPORTED	REPORTEQUALITY	REQUIRES
RESULT	RETURNED,	RETURNED.	RETURNS	SCAN
SECOND	SEQUENCE	SKIPPED;	SPACE	SUPPLIED
THAN	THE	THECHAR	THECHAR-IN/OUT.	THEN
TO	TRUE	TURNED	TURNTOUPPERCASE	TWO

TWO-IN.	TWO.CHARS	TWO.LENGTH)	TYPE	UNLESS
UPPERCASE	UPPERCASE;	UPPERCASEWORD	UPPERCASEWORD.	VAR
WHICH	WHILE	WITH	WORD	WORD-IN.
WORD-IN/OUT.	WORD-OUT.	WORD.	WORD1	WORD1-IN,
WORD1-OUT,	WORD2	WORD2)	WORD2);	WORD2-IN.
WORD2-OUT.	WORD2;	WORD;	WORDS	WORDS.
WORDTYPE	WORDTYPE)	WORDTYPE);	WORDTYPE.	WORDTYPE;
WRITE	WRITELN	WRITEWORD	WRITEWORD.	WRITTEN
['A'..'Z']	[1..MAXWORDLEN]	[INDEX])	[INDEX]);	[LENGTH]
[POS]	[POS])			

Here is the complete program:

```
(* pre       : program is supplied with a file of words.           *)
(* post      : program reports in alphabetical order all words appearing in*)
(*            : input file.                                         *)
(* parameters : INPUT-in, OUTPUT-out.                               *)

PROGRAM ManipulateDictionaries (INPUT, OUTPUT);
CONST MaxWordLength = 15;          (* maximum number of characters in a word *)
      MaxDictLength = 1000;        (* maximum number of words in a dictionary*)
      WordsPerLine  = 5;           (* number of words displayed on each line *)
TYPE  CharList     = ARRAY [1..MaxWordLength] OF CHAR;
      WordType     = RECORD
          chars     : CharList;    (* list of characters in word             *)
          length    : INTEGER      (* number of characters in word           *)
      END;
      WordList     = ARRAY [1..MaxDictLength] OF WordType;
      DictType     = RECORD
          words     : WordList;    (* list of words in dictionary            *)
          length    : INTEGER      (* number of words in dictionary          *)
      END;
VAR   dictionary   : DictType;     (* dictionary of input file words         *)

(* procedures ReadChar, TurnToUppercase, ReadWord, UppercaseWord, WriteWord,*)
(* and function Equal are the same as before.                               *)

PROCEDURE WriteSpaces (number : INTEGER);
(* post      : given number of spaces is written to output file. *)
(* parameters : number-in.                                       *)
VAR count     : INTEGER;   (* loop counter                       *)
```

```
BEGIN
    FOR count := 1 TO number DO
        WRITE (' ')
END;   (* WriteSpaces *)

FUNCTION Less (VAR one, two : WordType) : BOOLEAN;
(* post       : returns TRUE if one is alphabetically less than two; *)
(*            : returns FALSE otherwise.                             *)
(* parameters : one-in, two-in; both passed as VAR to improve speed. *)
(* requires   : type WordType.                                       *)
VAR ShortLen : INTEGER;   (* length of shorter word                  *)
    pos      : INTEGER;   (* current position of comparison scan     *)
BEGIN
    IF (one.length < two.length) THEN
        ShortLen := one.length
    ELSE
        ShortLen := two.length;
    IF (ShortLen = 0) THEN
        less := (one.length < two.length)
    ELSE
    BEGIN
        pos := 1;
        WHILE (one.chars [pos] = two.chars [pos]) AND (pos < ShortLen) DO
            pos := pos + 1;
        IF (one.chars [pos] = two.chars [pos]) THEN
            less := (one.length < two.length)
        ELSE
            less := (one.chars [pos] < two.chars [pos])
    END
END;   (* Less *)

FUNCTION PositionOf (VAR value : WordType;
                     VAR dict  : DictType) : INTEGER;
(* pre        : elements of dict are in sorted order.                *)
(* post       : if value is in dict, position is returned; otherwise 0 *)
(*            : is returned.                                         *)
(* parameters : value-in, dict-in; both passed as VAR to improve speed. *)
(* requires   : types WordType and DictType; functions Less and Equal. *)
VAR low    : INTEGER;   (* low index of search                       *)
    high   : INTEGER;   (* high index of search                      *)
    middle : INTEGER;   (* midpoint of low and high                  *)
    found  : BOOLEAN;   (* was value found?                          *)
```

```
BEGIN
    WITH dict DO
    BEGIN
        low := 1;
        high := length;
        found := FALSE;
        WHILE (NOT found) AND (low <= high) DO
        BEGIN
            middle := ((low + high) DIV 2);
            IF equal (words [middle], value) THEN
                found := TRUE
            ELSE
                IF less (words [middle], value) THEN
                    low  := middle + 1
                ELSE
                    high := middle - 1
        END;
        IF found THEN
            PositionOf := middle
        ELSE
            PositionOf := 0
    END
END;   (* PositionOf *)


PROCEDURE InsertInto (VAR dict : DictType;
                      VAR word : WordType);
(* pre        : elements of dict are in sorted order.           *)
(* post       : new word is inserted into dict in proper place. *)
(* parameters : dict-in/out; word-in (passed as VAR to improve speed). *)
(* requires   : types WordType and DictType; and function Less. *)
VAR position : INTEGER;   (* current position for scan/move     *)
    done     : BOOLEAN;   (* are you done scanning and moving?   *)
BEGIN
    WITH dict DO
    BEGIN
        position := length;
        IF (length > 0) THEN
        BEGIN
            done := less (words [position], word);
            WHILE NOT done DO
            BEGIN
                words [position + 1] := words [position];
                position := position - 1;
```

```
                    IF position = 0 THEN
                        done := TRUE
                    ELSE
                        done := less (words [position], word)
                END
            END;
            words [position + 1] := word;
            length := length + 1
        END
END;   (* InsertInto *)


PROCEDURE ReadDict (VAR dict : DictType);
(* pre        : input cursor at beginning of a file of words.           *)
(* post       : words are read into dictionary; input cursor at end-of-file.*)
(* parameters : dict-out.                                                *)
(* requires   : types WordType and DictType; procedures ReadWord,        *)
(*            : UppercaseWord, InsertInto; and function PositionOf.      *)
VAR NextWord  : WordType;    (* next word read from input file          *)
BEGIN
    WITH dict DO
    BEGIN
        length := 0;
        WHILE NOT EOF DO
        BEGIN
            ReadWord (NextWord);
            IF NextWord.length > 0 THEN
            BEGIN
                UppercaseWord (NextWord);
                IF PositionOf (NextWord, dict) = 0 THEN
                    InsertInto (dict, NextWord)
            END
            ELSE
                READLN
        END
    END
END;   (* ReadDict *)


PROCEDURE WriteDict (VAR dict : DictType);
(* post       : all words in dict are reported to output file, with *)
(*            : WordsPerLine words on each line.                     *)
(* parameters : dict-in, passed as a VAR to improve speed.          *)
(* requires   : type DictType; and procedures WriteWord.            *)
VAR index     : INTEGER;   (* loop counter                          *)
```

```
BEGIN
    WITH dict DO
        FOR index := 1 TO length DO
        BEGIN
            WriteWord (words [index]);
            IF (index MOD WordsPerLine = 0) THEN
                WRITELN
        END
END;   (* WriteDict *)


BEGIN   (* main program *)
    ReadDict (dictionary);
    WriteDict (dictionary)
END.    (* main program *)
```

9.5 Key Concepts

- The record structure allows you to store several variables of differing types. Each component of a record is called a field.

- The engineering principles that apply to creation of programs and subprograms should also be applied to creation of data types. Data abstraction requires that you consider the essential properties of a type independent of its implementation. With data abstraction, you can decompose a complex data object into smaller components that can be independently developed. Abstraction also allows you to create types general enough in purpose that they can be part of your software library to be used again in other programs.

- A data invariant is a property shared by all elements in the domain of a type. For example, in defining the domain of dictionaries you might specify the invariant that a dictionary has words appearing in alphabetical order.

- To build a type you first describe it abstractly by specifying its domain and the operations that can be performed on objects of its type. The operations that you specify will almost always include some kind of creation, inspection, and modification tasks. Your abstract data type might also specify some operations for display and comparison, although you can often build such operations in terms of the others.

9.6 Self-Check Exercises

1. Which of the following are linear structures?

Normal phone book
Purse containing address book, meeting calendar, stray notes, etc.
Card file showing the entire Library of Congress catalogue
Genealogy showing the ancestral descent of a family
Filing cabinet with folders sorted alphabetically
Standard deck of playing cards, shuffled and ready to use

2. Define a `RECORD` structure suitable for storing a twentieth-century date.

Exercises 3 and 4 make reference to the following declarations which would be used by a university wanting to keep track of a list of students, storing for each: name, age, current campus address, and permanent home address.

```
TYPE StringType  = ARRAY [1..20] OF CHAR;
     AddressType = RECORD
         street1 : StringType;
         street1 : StringType;
         city    : StringType;
         state   : StringType;
         zip     : INTEGER
     END;
     PersonType  = RECORD
         name    : StringType;
         age     : INTEGER;
         home    : AddressType;
         current : AddressType
     END;
     PersonList  = ARRAY [1..100] OF PersonType;
VAR  people      : PersonList;
```

3. How would you change the character variable which stores the third letter of the ninth person's hometown to an X? Do so once without `WITH` statements and again using `WITH` statements to simplify the statement.

4. What code will write out the sum of the local zip codes of the first two students in the array? Why won't a `WITH` statement simplify this code?

5. Define a type suitable for storing a list of temperature readings taken from a standard wall thermometer.

6. Given the following type:

```
TYPE Complex = RECORD
         x : REAL;
         y : REAL
     END;
```

Write a FUNCTION called **equal** that takes two complex numbers as arguments and returns a BOOLEAN value indicating whether or not the two numbers are exactly equal (TRUE means equal, FALSE means different).

7. For the two programs in this chapter, a *word* was defined as a sequence of nonblank characters. Suppose you had to work with a more strict definition, that a word is composed only of word characters, where a *word character* is either a letter (lowercase or uppercase), a dash, or a hyphen. What modification(s) would have to be made to program ManipulateDictionaries to cause it to use this definition of a word and to skip over all nonword characters?

8. How would you modify FUNCTION **equal** in program ManipulateDictionaries so that it ignores the case of the words it is comparing (e.g., reporting JiM equal to jIm)?

9. The program ManipulateDictionaries has two BOOLEAN FUNCTIONs for comparing words: **less** and **equal**. Combine them into a single FUNCTION that returns a value of type CHAR rather than of type BOOLEAN, returning '<' when the first word is less, '=' when the words are equal, and '>' when the first word is greater. Which of the FUNCTIONs (**less** or **equal**) is most similar to the new FUNCTION?

10. What modifications would be necessary to program ManipulateDictionaries to make it sort words by increasing length rather than sorting them alphabetically?

11. Suppose you are writing a program to process a file of names that appear one per line, as in

```
Wallingford, Phoebe
MARTIN, TAD
Chandler, Adam
Martin, Tad
```

and you want to produce an alphabetical listing of all names indicating their position in the list and with quotes around them, as in the following (notice that case is not being ignored):

Position	Name
1	"Chandler, Adam"
2	"MARTIN, TAD"
3	"Martin, Tad"
4	"Wallingford, Phoebe"

Listed below are the names of the 11 subprograms and the main program from ManipulateDictionaries. For each, indicate whether it could in this new program be used without any changes, used with one or two lines changed, used with three or more lines changed, or not used at all.

Equal	InsertInto	Less	ManipulateDictionaries
PositionOf	ReadChar	ReadDict	TurnToUppercase
UppercaseWord	WriteDict	WriteSpaces	WriteWord

12. How would you modify the dictionary program so that it keeps track of the number of occurrences of each word in the input file? This number should be

reported in parentheses after the word in the output file, as indicated below. You can assume that no word appears more than 999 times.

DO	(10)	EACH	(1)	ELEMENTS	(1)		
ELSE	(4)	ENCLOSED	(1)	END	(3)		
END.	(1)	END;	(10)	EOF	(1)		
EOLN	(3)	EOLN,	(1)	EQUAL	(9)		

9.7   Programming Problems

1. A secretary at the office where you work has to keep track of petty cash payments that range up to $75. For each transaction, he records the date and amount. He records each transaction in two places: in a log book kept in the petty cash container and in a receipt book that is used to make receipts for the individuals getting petty cash. The log book and receipt book agree for the most part, but there are always discrepancies. You are to write a program that allows the secretary to enter a series of transactions first from the log book and then from the receipt book. Your program will help the secretary identify discrepancies. The program is to print out all transactions in order first by date (i.e., early dates first, all one date's transactions grouped together) and second by amount (i.e., on each date, the amounts will appear in increasing order). It should produce a four-column output such as the following, citing any discrepancies:

Date	Log Book	Receipt Book	Discrepancy
2/23/86	15.98	15.98	
2/23/86	23.45	-----	Missing receipt
2/23/86	-----	45.23	Missing in log
2/24/86	2.29	2.29	
2/24/86	4.98	4.98	

2. An instructor of yours has asked you to write him a program to aid him in manipulating his midterm grades. He wants to be able to enter the scores from a file where each line contains a score and name, as in

```
72 Tad Martin
48 Phoebe Wallingford
97 Palmer Cortland
```

The scores are between 0 and 100. Your program is to read in these scores and compute an adjusted score. The adjusted score is based on the median score (the score that the person in the middle of the distribution got). The formula is

```
(new score) := (old score) * 75/median + 5
```

If a student gets a new score over 100, it should be set back to 100. After calculating new scores, your program is to produce a printout such as the following. The table should show scores from lowest to highest.

```
Number of Students = 103
Original Median    = 60.1
Adjusted Median    = 79.3
```

Student Name	Original Score	Adjusted Score
Phoebe Wallingford	48	65
Tad Martin	72	95
Palmer Cortland	97	100

3. A member of your family has put a great deal of time into creating a file of birthdays for your family members:

```
9/23/1959      Martin, Hillary
2/4/1958       Martin, Tad
9/23/1926      Wallingford, Langley
12/18/1927     Wallingford, Phoebe
```

You have been asked to write a program that shows these birthdays tallied for each day of the year (indicating each person who has that birthday and the year of birth for that person). The dates should appear in increasing calendar order from January 1 toward December 31. Thus, for the four lines above, you would produce this output:

```
Date          Birthdays
------------------------------------------
 2/ 4         Martin, Tad          (1958)
 9/23         Wallingford, Langley (1926)
              Martin, Hillary      (1959)
12/18         Wallingford, Phoebe  (1927)
```

4. The Morse code is an encoding of the characters into either dots and dashes or long and short sounds. Here is the encoding of the alphabet:

A	.-	G	--.	M	--	S	...	Y	-.--
B	-...	H	....	N	-.	T	-	Z	--..
C	-.-.	I	..	O	---	U	..-		
D	-..	J	.---	P	.--.	V	...-		
E	.	K	-.-	Q	--.-	W	.--		
F	..-.	L	.-..	R	.-.	X	-..-		

You are going to write a program that decodes a message given a decoding scheme such as the one above. The program will take input like this:

```
-. --- .--    .. ...    - .... .      - .. -- .
```

This input is really composed of three characters: dots, dashes, and spaces. The spaces are used to separate different characters and different words. There are two spaces between letters and six spaces between words. A carriage return also marks the end of a word. Using the code above, you can decode this as "NOW IS THE

TIME." Your program is to read an input file with a decoding scheme followed by a text to be decoded. The decoding part of the file will be a series of lines of the form:

<character> <sequences of dots and dashes>

This part of the file is terminated by a blank line. What follows is an encoded text (a series of dots, dashes, and spaces) that you are to translate. You should store each character with its code in a list sorted by code. You want it sorted by code so that when you are translating, you can use a binary search to quickly look up what character corresponds to a code you have just read from the input file.

5. Write a program that produces as output a listing of all the unique words in a file (ignoring case) with a list of the line numbers they appear on. Your program should ignore punctuation and define a word as a sequence of alphabetic characters. Your program should capitalize every word (not uppercase it, but just turn the first letter to a capital). Some words will appear so many times that you won't be able to keep track of all their line references, so you can report just the first 10 line references. Thus you might get output like this:

```
Word                Lines it appears on
-----------------------------------------------------------------
A                   1, 3, 4, 7, 12, 19, 21, 23, 24, 29, etc.
After               45, 108, 143
All                 67
Alphabetic          8, 19, 114
And                 1, 6, 10, 12, 20, 22, 24, 26, 27, 28, etc.
```

Try analyzing some of your programs by running them as input through this program. The listing that results will indicate for each identifier where that identifier is used (e.g., all places where a given variable is referred to). Such listings can be useful for very large programs.

10

PROGRAM TESTING

10.1 Introduction

When you build a program, you want to be confident that it works. This is called *program validation* and it is a major branch of current computer science research. The goal of program validation is to demonstrate that a program or program segment is valid or correct. You will find that people talk about "validating programs" much the same way they talk about "guarantying national security." Everybody has a different conception of what is involved. For some it means minor commitment; for others it means total involvement to guaranty success.

Suppose, for example, that you are going to write a program to automate the grade records for a school. Your program might use input files containing grade reports for each course to produce individual grade reports and various student listings such as an honor roll. What will it mean for your program to be correct? How will you validate it?

A first-level answer is to demonstrate that the program takes a typical set of input files and produces correct output. But correctness implies much more. What about atypical input files? What about a student who fails all of his classes or a student who is enrolled in two thousand classes or a class with no students? A true software engineer also considers these unusual cases in the process of validation.

After extensive testing of typical and atypical cases, you can declare that the program seems to work on all valid input files. However, even then you shouldn't abandon your quest for correctness. How will your program handle invalid data? Your blender at home is intended to mix things such as ice cream and crushed ice, but what happens if you drop a one pound steak into it and turn it on high speed? What if the grade program encounters a grade report for a nonexistent student or finds two different grades for a student in the same class? A well-built program has a property called *robustness*. This means it can handle not only legal inputs, but also illegal ones. A robust program always produces reasonable output, even when it is fed unreasonable input. To claim correctness for your program, you should anticipate such illegalities and decide how your program will handle them. This is called *recovering from errors* or the process of *error recovery*.

Even this view of program correctness is not sufficient to satisfy many modern-day computer scientists. Chapter 8 described a new field called *program verification* that is more formal in its approach. A disciple of program verification demands proof. You can't prove a program correct by showing lots of input files for which it works. That is like trying to prove that all humans are blond by producing a crowd composed entirely of blonds. The evidence can be shattered by a single counterexample. Similarly, even extensive program testing that finds no errors won't make a program correct if you have failed to consider a special input file that causes an error. Thus a poor test run can prove a program flawed, but a good test run can't ever prove a program correct.

Testing, therefore, can indicate the correctness of a program, but it is not a guaranty. The only guaranty lies in a rigorous analysis of the program's logic, similar to the analysis of procedure **swap** in Chapter 8. As pointed out there, however, a formal program-proving model is beyond the scope of this book. That leaves testing. To explore this subject, this chapter gives some general guidelines on developing test data and then demonstrates those principles in the testing and development of a large program.

10.2 Developing Test Data

Data values tend to fall into natural categories of legal and illegal input. For example, if you are reading test scores, you might say that anything between 0 and 100 is legal and anything else is illegal. If you are writing a program to process words using an array, you might say that words vary in length from 0 to 25, from an empty word to a word that fills the array. If you consider the set of legal values and the set of illegal values, you will find that there are certain values very close to the boundary between the two.

In the test score case, if you use a number line to examine the different scores you get:

```
-3 -2 -1  0  1  2  3  ...  98  99  100  101  102  103
          └─────────────────────────┘
                   legal scores
```

Here the values on the boundary are the scores 0 and 100. They divide the numbers into three ranges: illegal values less than 0, legal values, and illegal values greater than 100.

For the program that manipulates words, you would examine the different possible lengths:

-3 -2 -1 0 1 2 3 ... 23 24 25 26 27 28

legal lengths

Here the values on the boundary are the words of length 0 and the words of length 25. They divide this set of data values into three ranges: illegal values less than 0, legal values, and illegal values greater than 25.

There are four kinds of data that you normally test for.

- Typical values

- Degenerate values

- Boundary values

- Special values

Typical values are values in the middle of the range of legal values. *Degenerate values* are those outside the range, illegal values. If you have different ranges of illegal values, you choose values from each range. *Boundary values* are those on the boundary between typical and degenerate. A boundary typically has two adjacent values, one that is legal and one that is degenerate. Both are boundary values. *Special values* vary from problem to problem. Special values are different from the norm and should therefore be tested. For example, if you were writing a program to manipulate names, your typical cases might be:

```
Joe Ordinary
Jane Seymour
```

You will, however, want to test special cases such as

```
Doctor Peter H. Simon Willifred, III (Esq.)
```

You test typical values because you want to know how the program performs on the values you intend as input. You test degenerate values because you at least want to be aware of how your program behaves when it is given illegal input. You test the boundary values because this is often where a solution breaks down. Often the program works for most of the typical cases, but breaks down on the boundary. If you find that the program behaves properly inside the boundary, outside the boundary, and on the boundary itself, you can be fairly confident that it works.

Given that the boundary values for test scores are 0 and 100, a minimal set of test data is as follows:

Score	Reason for inclusion
-1	Boundary degenerate value
0	Boundary legal value
50	Typical value
100	Boundary legal value
101	Boundary degenerate value

You would probably want to add more values to this set of test data to increase your confidence, but this tests each major case.

To test the word program, you can form a minimal set of test data by using words with the following lengths:

Length	Reason for inclusion
-1	Boundary degenerate value
0	Boundary legal value
14	Typical value
25	Boundary legal value
26	Boundary degenerate value

10.3 Case Study: The Justify Program

To give you an idea of how to perform such testing, let's step through the development of a program, purposely going through nonworking versions of the solution to see how to test it at each development stage.

Consider the problem of reading in text and justifying it to fit within certain margins. You fit as many words as possible on a line, but do not exceed some given margin. The following file (from *An Unfinished Woman* by Lillian Hellman) and an allowed margin of 65 characters:

```
I know as little
about the nature of romantic love as I knew when I was eighteen,
but I do know about the deep pleasure of continuing interest,
the excitement of wanting to know what somebody else thinks,
will do, will not do,
the tricks played and unplayed, the short cord
that the years make into rope and, in my case, is there,
hanging loose, long after death.
```

produces this output:

```
I know as little about the nature of romantic love as I knew when
I was eighteen, but I do know about the deep pleasure of
continuing interest, the excitement of wanting to know what
somebody else thinks, will do, will not do, the tricks played and
```

unplayed, the short cord that the years make into rope and, in my case, is there, hanging loose, long after death.

It will be easier to examine this problem if, while you are testing and developing your procedures, you produce output such as the following:

```
123456789|123456789|123456789|123456789|123456789|123456789|12345
+----------------------------------------------------------------+
|I know as little about the nature of romantic love as I knew when|
|I was eighteen, but I do know about the deep pleasure of         |
|continuing interest, the excitement of wanting to know what      |
|somebody else thinks, will do, will not do, the tricks played and|
|unplayed, the short cord that the years make into rope and, in my|
|case, is there, hanging loose, long after death.                 |
+----------------------------------------------------------------+
```

This output has a border around it so that the left and right margins are clearly visible. It also has column numbers at the top that make it easier to distinguish the different columns. You should include debugging code in your program that produces output such as this while in the testing phase.

This task is easy to perform, but it has many potential errors, particularly on the border. To define the three different cases here, you need to consider text-justifying tasks that are typical, border, and degenerate. These cases are determined line-by-line, since the point of the program is to fit each line to the given margin. Suppose you have a word that when written to the current output line will leave you with N columns filled in. That word is legal on this line only if N is in the range of 1 to 65. You don't have to consider the case less than 1, however, because any word written to the output line will leave us in column 1 or higher. Thus the range of legal values for N is

$$1 \quad 2 \quad 3 \quad ... \quad 38 \quad 39 \quad 65 \quad 66 \quad 67 \quad 68$$

legal values of N

The typical cases occur when you want to add words that leave you in such columns as 10 or 25 or 50. The border case occurs when a word leaves you in column 65. This happens with the following three lines:

```
123456789|123456789|123456789|123456789|123456789|123456789|12345
+----------------------------------------------------------------+
|I know as little about the nature of romantic love as I knew when|
|somebody else thinks, will do, will not do, the tricks played and|
|unplayed, the short cord that the years make into rope and, in my|
+----------------------------------------------------------------+
```

You want to be sure that your program produces correct results for $N = 65$. You also want to make sure it rejects any solutions where $N = 66$ or more.

You want an EOF loop that reads in words and writes them back out. To perform the justification, you have to check to make sure the next word fits before you write it on a line. Thus a simple character-by-character echo will not work. You need to look one word ahead. Thus your pseudocode will be something like this:

```
while (not at end-of-file) do
begin
    read a word.
    if (the word doesn't fit on current line) then
        go to a new line.
    write the word.
end
```

Your definition of a word here is a liberal one: a sequence of nonblank characters. This includes some character sequences that don't look like words:

$234.59   "Wow!!"   Hi!

From the point of view of justifying text, however, it is easiest if you include these sequences in the domain of your WordType.

Before you can write any of the procedures, you have to create a new type for storing a word. Because a word is a list of characters, you can use the list type from Chapter 9.

```
CONST MaxWordLen = 25;
TYPE  CharList    = ARRAY [1..MaxWordLen] OF CHAR;
      WordType    = RECORD
            chars  : CharList;
            length : INTEGER
      END;
VAR   word        : WordType;
```

Because you need a procedure for reading a word and another for writing a word, let's write them separately.

10.3.1 Building and Testing WriteWord in Isolation

Many students feel that they have to type their entire program into the computer before they can test it. This is not true. You can test your program procedure by procedure, so that you find your errors gradually rather than having to face all of them at once.

You can do this in many ways. The simplest is to write main programs that don't correspond to the final program you intend to write. These "dummy" main programs can set up the test cases that you want to perform. Let's see how you can use a dummy program to test a single procedure such as the procedure

`WriteWord` developed in Section 9.3.4. Because you don't want the word to appear in quotes here, that part of the procedure has been removed.

```
PROCEDURE WriteWord (word : WordType);
VAR index : INTEGER;
BEGIN
    WITH word DO
        FOR index := 1 TO length DO
            WRITE (chars [index])
END;
```

There is only one problem with this procedure. It is not robust. What happens if the length is not in range? If it is too small, the procedure doesn't ever execute the `WRITE` statement. This is probably acceptable behavior in such a case. If it is too large, though, the procedure will execute the `WRITE` statement too many times, eventually making a reference to a nonexistent element of the array. You want to avoid this special case, so you should modify the procedure to take it into account. The standard practice in such cases is to produce some kind of error message that indicates that an overflow has occurred. For example, you can write a series of asterisks in place of a word.

To test it, you feed it words of varying lengths to see if it can write them all out properly. These lengths form an appropriate set of test data for words:

    -1   0   14   25   26

However, you might want to add a few more test cases:

    -1   0   1   7   14   25   26   35

You can construct a test program to use these data easily. All you need is one word variable. You initialize all the characters of the word to something that is easily read, such as the letters of the alphabet; then you set the length to each of these values in turn and ask the `WriteWord` procedure to do its thing on each. You will, of course, also want to report which of the lengths is being used. You also probably want to put quotes around what is written by the procedure so that you can see exactly what it outputs (and not miss the fact that it produces extra spaces, for example). All this is incorporated into the following procedure called `test` that calls up `WriteWord` and produces appropriate statistics about the call. Here is the program with `WriteWord` and its testing code:

```
PROGRAM Test1 (OUTPUT);
CONST MaxWordLen = 25;
TYPE  CharList   = ARRAY [1..MaxWordLen] OF CHAR;
      WordType   = RECORD
           chars  : CharList;
           length : INTEGER
      END;
```

```
VAR   word        : WordType;

PROCEDURE WriteWord (word : WordType);
VAR index : INTEGER;
BEGIN
    WITH word DO
        FOR index := 1 TO length DO
            IF length > MaxWordLen THEN
                WRITE ('*')
            ELSE
                WRITE (chars [index])
END;   (* WriteWord *)

PROCEDURE PerformTest (word       : WordType;
                       TestLength : INTEGER);
BEGIN
    word.length := TestLength;
    WRITE ('For length = ', TestLength:2, ', word = "');
    WriteWord (word);
    WRITELN ('"')
END;   (* PerformTest *)

PROCEDURE CreateTestWord (VAR word : WordType);
VAR letter : CHAR;
    index  : INTEGER;
BEGIN
    letter := 'A';
    WITH word DO
        FOR index := 1 TO MaxWordLen DO
        BEGIN
            chars [index] := letter;
            letter := SUCC (letter)
        END
END;   (* CreateTestWord *)

BEGIN   (* main program *)
    CreateTestWord (word);
    PerformTest (word, -1);
    PerformTest (word, 0);
    PerformTest (word, 1);
    PerformTest (word, 7);
    PerformTest (word, 14);
    PerformTest (word, 25);
    PerformTest (word, 26);
```

```
        PerformTest (word, 35);
END.    (* main program *)
```

When the program is executed, this is the output:

```
For length = -1, word = ""
For length =  0, word = ""
For length =  1, word = "A"
For length =  7, word = "ABCDEFG"
For length = 14, word = "ABCDEFGHIJKLMN"
For length = 25, word = "ABCDEFGHIJKLMNOPQRSTUVWXY"
For length = 26, word = "*************************"
For length = 35, word = "***********************************"
```

As you can see, the procedure does what you want for all cases. Notice that in the case of a word that is too long, an appropriate overflow message is written rather than the contents of the word. This tells the user that something has gone wrong.

10.3.2   Building and Testing ReadWord in Isolation

You can also adapt procedure **ReadWord** from what was written in the last chapter. Just as you did there, you can use the sentinel reading loop with a space as a sentinel. Thus you start with

```
PROCEDURE ReadList (VAR list : ListType);
VAR next :  <element type>;
BEGIN
    <perform any actions that need to be done before reading>;
    READ (next);
    WITH list DO
    BEGIN
        length := 0;
        WHILE (next <> <sentinel>) AND (length < MaxLength) DO
        BEGIN
            length := length + 1;
            elements [length] := next;
            READ (next)
        END
    END;
    <perform any actions that need to be done after reading>
END;
```

You can also use a dummy program for testing procedure **ReadWord**. This allows you to reduce the overall task to debug. You already know that **WriteWord** works, so you can use it to help you test **ReadWord**.

You need to make some design decisions about the preconditions and post-conditions of the procedure. Where will the input cursor be positioned before you start executing? What if there are spaces before or after the word? Since **ReadWord** is a low-level procedure, it would be best not to expect too much of it. Typical conditions for such a procedure are

> pre : input cursor is positioned at an alphabetic character.
> post : characters are read until the first nonalphabetic character is
> encountered; the word read in is returned via a VAR parameter.

What happens, however, if the input cursor isn't positioned at an alphabetic character? An easy answer is to allow the procedure to conceivably return an empty word:

> pre : input cursor at beginning of a word of length <= MaxWordLen.
> post : characters of word are read until a space is read; input
> cursor after space; if input cursor at space to begin
> with, space is read and word with length 0 is returned.

These are workable preconditions and postconditions. This specifies a sentinel loop, as you expected. In testing the procedure, you should be aware of two different kinds of tests. One involves using different lengths for words. You can use the same test cases used for **WriteWord**, except you can't generate a word with negative length. Another test involves testing typical line positions and special line positions. Typical words appear in the middle of lines, but a special kind of word is one that appears at the beginning of a line. Therefore, a simple input file to create is one that has two words per line (one at the beginning and one in the middle), both of the same length. You can create a different line for each different length you want to test.

Here is a sample input file:

```
a a
massive massive
merry-go-round merry-go-round
longlonglonglonglongstuff longlonglonglonglongstuff
longlonglonglonglongstuffs longlonglonglonglongstuffs
supercalifragilisticexpialidotious. supercalifragilisticexpialidotious.
```

Here is the program:

```
PROGRAM Test2 (INPUT, OUTPUT);
CONST MaxWordLen = 25;
TYPE  CharList   = ARRAY [1..MaxWordLen] OF CHAR;
      WordType   = RECORD
          chars  : CharList;
          length : INTEGER
      END;
VAR   word       : WordType;
```

```
(* procedure WriteWord should appear here. *)

PROCEDURE ReadWord (VAR word : WordType);
VAR next : CHAR;
BEGIN
    READ (next);
    WITH word DO
    BEGIN
        length := 0;
        WHILE  (next <> ' ') AND (length < MaxWordLen) DO
        BEGIN
            length := length + 1;
            chars [length] := next;
            READ (next)
        END
    END
END;   (* ReadWord *)

BEGIN   (* main program *)
    WRITELN ('Length      Text');
    WRITELN ('-------------------------------------');
    WHILE NOT EOF DO
    BEGIN
        ReadWord (word);
        WRITE (word.length:4, '        "');
        WriteWord (word);
        WRITELN ('"')
    END
END.   (* main program *)
```

Notice that the main program produces a table showing the length and text of each word read from the file. The output generated by this program follows:

```
        Length      Text
        ---------------------------------------
            0       ""
            1       "a"
            1       "a"
            7       "massive"
            7       "massive"
           14       "merry-go-round"
           14       "merry-go-round"
           25       "longlonglonglonglongstuff"
           25       "longlonglonglonglongstuff"
           25       "longlonglonglonglongstuff"
            0       ""
           25       "longlonglonglonglongstuff"
            0       ""
           25       "supercalifragilisticexpia"
            9       "idotious."
           25       "supercalifragilisticexpia"
            9       "idotious."
```

Some funny things show up here. Procedure `ReadWord` properly handles the border case of length 0, the typical cases of lengths 1, 7, and 14, and the border case of length 25, but it does something odd for the degenerate cases of length 26 and 35. Look at the result for 'supercalifragilisticexpialidotious.' The program outputs two words 'supercalifragilisticexpia' and 'idotious.' An 'l' is missing in the middle, but otherwise these two words put together form the original. The 'l' is missing because you are using a sentinel loop that looks one character ahead. When the program first processes the word, it reads 26 characters, but it doesn't store the twenty-sixth character because that would cause an array index out of bounds. The next 9 characters remain in the input file, and the next call on `ReadWord` reads them as if they were a 9-letter word.

This is probably not the way you want the procedure to behave. `ReadWord` should read a word in its entirety, even if the array isn't big enough to store all the characters. In other words, you should store a truncated version of the word. But since this value is not the correct value, you must signify the error to the user somehow. The simplest way is to create a word with length greater than 25. Then the `WriteWord` procedure will print the overflow message that you built into it.

You can do this easily. You simplify the `WHILE` loop to continue until it encounters a space. That way you will be sure each word is read in its entirety. To prevent overflowing the array and getting an array index out of bounds error, you put the array assignment inside an `IF/THEN` that tests to see that length is within range. This leads to the following procedure:

```
PROCEDURE ReadWord (VAR word : WordType);
VAR next : CHAR;
BEGIN
    READ (next);
    WITH word DO
    BEGIN
        length := 0;
        WHILE  (next <> ' ') DO
        BEGIN
            length := length + 1;
            If (length <= MaxWordLen) THEN
                chars [length] := next;
            READ (next)
        END
    END
END;   (* ReadWord *)
```

Using this version of the procedure, you obtain this output:

Length	Text
0	""
1	"a"
1	"a"
7	"massive"
7	"massive"
14	"merry-go-round"
14	"merry-go-round"
25	"longlonglonglonglongstuff"
25	"longlonglonglonglongstuff"
26	"*************************"
26	"*************************"
35	"***********************************"
35	"***********************************"

An overflow message is printed for the words of length 26 and 35. After this test, you can be fairly certain that ReadWord works properly.

10.3.3 Building the Framework of the Main Program

You left off with the following pseudocode:

```
while (not at end-of-file) do
begin
    read a word.
```

> if (the word doesn't fit on current line) then
>   go to a new line.
> write the word.
end

This loop is word-oriented. Word-oriented loops are not as common as line-oriented loops, but they can be done. You just have to be careful to deal with spaces and ends of lines properly. If you have exactly one space between words in the input file, this loop works perfectly because `ReadWord` processes both the word and the space after it. If the file looks like this:

word space word space word space word space word space word space

`ReadWord` works perfectly because the input line is processed in this order:

word space   word space   word space   word space   word space   word space
‿   ‿   ‿   ‿   ‿   ‿
ReadWord ReadWord ReadWord ReadWord ReadWord ReadWord

Six calls on the procedure process the six words and the spaces that follow. Suppose, however, that you have

word space space space word space space word space

What happens? The first call on `ReadWord` processes this:

word space space space word space space word space
‿
ReadWord

A second call on `ReadWord` processes this:

word space   space   space word space space word space
‿   ‿
ReadWord   ReadWord

The second call will return an empty word. If you continue calling the procedure you end with

word space   space   space   word space   space   word space
‿   ‿   ‿   ‿   ‿   ‿
ReadWord   ReadWord ReadWord   ReadWord   ReadWord   ReadWord

Six executions of `ReadWord` process the file. However, three of the words that are read in are empty. You will want to skip these empty words because they are generated by extra spacing between words, not by words themselves. Thus you modify the pseudocode to

```
while (not at end-of-file) do
begin
    read a word.
    if (the word is not empty) then
    begin
        if (the word doesn't fit on current line) then
            go to a new line.
        write the word.
    end
end
```

If you skip empty words, they can't cause a problem. The three words in the input file above should be processed just fine, with the extra spaces in between them being processed as empty words by **ReadWord**. Thus this pseudocode works well for files that have varying numbers of spaces between words.

What about ends-of-lines? You have already noted that they look like spaces if read as normal characters. Suppose you have this file:

word eoln word space word eoln word space word eoln word eoln

If you read the ends-of-lines as spaces, **ReadWord** does the following:

word eoln	word space	word eoln	word space	word eoln	word eoln
ReadWord	ReadWord	ReadWord	ReadWord	ReadWord	ReadWord

Six executions of **ReadWord** process this file properly. Therefore, treat ends of lines as spaces and the program should work well.

There are two tricky cases left that you should consider. You have seen files that start with words and end with spaces, but what about files that start with spaces or files that end with words? Here is a file that does both:

space word eoln word space word eoln word space word

Here is how **ReadWord** processes this file:

space	word eoln	word space	word eoln	word space	word ???
ReadWord	ReadWord	ReadWord	ReadWord	ReadWord	ReadWord

The leading space doesn't cause a problem because it is read as an empty word and skipped. However, the word at the end does. You execute **ReadWord** and try to process characters until it sees a space. If there is no space to be seen because there is nothing left in the file, you'll run into problems. This is a problem that, fortunately, you will never have to deal with. Chapter 6 mentioned that you are guarantied to have an end-of-line character right before the end-of-file character. Because you are treating the end-of-line as a space, you are guarantied to have a space right before the end-of-file character. This means that this special case will never come up.

Thus this simple pseudocode does, in fact, handle all the special cases. Now, you should refine it. Here's what you have:

```
while (not at end-of-file) do
begin
    read a word.
    if (the word is not empty) then
    begin
        if (the word doesn't fit on current line) then
            go to a new line.
        write the word.
    end
end
```

You can fill in all these pieces except the test about whether or not the word fits on the current line. It will take time to get that right, so do something simpler first: limit each output line to 10 words at most and refine the pseudocode:

```
var count : integer;
    set count to 0.
    while (not at end-of-file) do
    begin
        read a word.
        if (the word is not empty) then

            if (count = 10) then
            begin
                go to a new line.
                set count to 0.
            end
            write the word.
            increment count.
        end
    end
```

This is easily translated into Pascal:

```
BEGIN   (* main program *)
    NumWordsOnLine := 0;
    WHILE NOT EOF DO
    BEGIN
        ReadWord (word);
```

```
              IF word.length > 0 THEN
              BEGIN
                   IF (NumWordsOnLine >= 10) THEN
                   BEGIN
                       WRITELN;
                       NumWordsOnLine := 0
                   END;
                   WriteWord (word);
                   NumWordsOnLine := NumWordsOnLine + 1
              END
        END
END.    (* main program *)
```

If you execute this program on the data file you saw earlier, you get

```
Iknowaslittleaboutthenatureofromanticlove
asIknewwhenIwaseighteen,butIdo
knowaboutthedeeppleasureofcontinuinginterest,theexcitement
ofwantingtoknowwhatsomebodyelsethinks,willdo,
willnotdo,thetricksplayedandunplayed,theshort
cordthattheyearsmakeintoropeand,inmy
case,isthere,hangingloose,longafterdeath.
```

This result is good and bad: good that the spaces and ends of lines in the input file are ignored and only real words are processed, and bad that you have no spacing between words. You want to write a space between every pair of words on these output lines, so that each will look like

word, space, word, space, word, space, ..., word, space, word

This raises a classic fence-post problem. You want a word at the beginning and end of the line. Thus on an output line of 10 words you need 9 spaces to separate them. You could try to use the standard fence-post solution to this. A better solution, however, is to realize that all words are terminated with one of two possible terminators: most words are terminated with a space, but words at the ends of lines are terminated by ends-of-lines. You already have an IF/THEN that terminates the tenth word with an end-of-line:

```
IF (NumWordsOnLine >= 10) THEN
BEGIN
    WRITELN;
    NumWordsOnLine := 0
END;
```

All you have to do is add an ELSE part that terminates the other 9 words with a space:

```
ELSE
    WRITE (' ');
```

Here is the output of this version of the program:

```
 I know as little about the nature of romantic love
as I knew when I was eighteen, but I do
know about the deep pleasure of continuing interest, the excitement
of wanting to know what somebody else thinks, will do,
will not do, the tricks played and unplayed, the short
cord that the years make into rope and, in my
case, is there, hanging loose, long after death.
```

These output lines each have 10 words separated by 9 spaces and terminated by an end-of-line. The output also has a couple of bugs. There is an extra space before the first word of the first line, and although you can't tell, there is no end-of-line after the last word. The algorithm is working like this:

```
for (each word) do
begin
    write out terminator for last word.
    write out this word.
end.
```

You get an extra terminator the first time around because there is no "last word" when working on the first word. Also, you don't get the terminator for the very last word because of this order. You wouldn't have this problem if the algorithm were

```
for (each word) do
begin
    write out this word.
    write out terminator for this word.
end.
```

The terminator of every word is written out just after the word, fixing both the problems above. You can make the program work this way for the simple 10-word-per-line program, but not for the justify task. In the justify task, you don't know whether to terminate the word with a space or an end-of-line until you read the next word. Therefore, you're stuck with the first pseudocode. There is a way to fix it, though. You make a special case out of the first word and add code after the loop to terminate the last word:

```
set FirstWord to true.
for (each word) do
```

```
begin
    if FirstWord then
        set FirstWord to false.
    else
        write out terminator for last word.
    write out this word.
end.
write out terminator for last word.
```

The flag `FirstWord` keeps track of whether this is the first word of the file. If it is, the program remembers that the next word is not the first. Otherwise, it proceeds normally. After the loop, it writes out the terminator for the last word of the file. Here is a Pascal main program that implements this strategy:

```
BEGIN    (* main program *)
    NumWordsOnLine := 0;
    FirstWord := TRUE;
    WHILE NOT EOF DO
    BEGIN
        ReadWord (word);
        IF word.length > 0 THEN
        BEGIN
            IF FirstWord THEN
                FirstWord := FALSE
            ELSE
                IF (NumWordsOnLine >= 10) THEN
                BEGIN
                    WRITELN;
                    NumWordsOnLine := 0
                END
                ELSE
                    WRITE (' ');
            WriteWord (word);
            NumWordsOnLine := NumWordsOnLine + 1
        END
    END;
    WRITELN
END.    (* main program *)
```

Notice that the main loop has three cases being distinguished by the nested **IF/THEN/ELSE**: the very first word of the file, for which you do nothing; what would be the eleventh word on a line, for which you go to a new line; and the other words in the middle of lines, for which you write a space beforehand. The **WRITELN** after the loop finishes up the last line of output. Here is the output this version generates:

```
I know as little about the nature of romantic love
as I knew when I was eighteen, but I do
know about the deep pleasure of continuing interest, the excitement
of wanting to know what somebody else thinks, will do,
will not do, the tricks played and unplayed, the short
cord that the years make into rope and, in my
case, is there, hanging loose, long after death.
```

This, then, constitutes your framework for the main program. All you have to do is figure out when to go to a new line of output. This program does it after 10 words have been written to the line. The justify program will need a more sophisticated judgment based on word lengths.

10.3.4 Dealing with Current Column

Now you have to fill in the details of how words fit on lines. You do this by keeping track of the number of characters written to the output line so far (`CurrentColumn`). Using this, the maximum column (`MaxColumn`), and the length of the next word, you can tell whether or not the next word fits. First, you should modify the program so that it knows about the current column.

This involves a variable that is initialized to 0 at the beginning of every line and incremented every time a word is written out. Here is a pseudocode description of its use:

```
set CurrentColumn to 0.
for (each word) do
begin
    if (writing to a new line) then
        set CurrentColumn to 0.
    write out this word.
    add length of word to CurrentColumn.
end.
```

Thus you can modify the main program:

```
BEGIN   (* main program *)
    CurrentColumn := 0;
    NumWordsOnLine := 0;
    FirstWord := TRUE;
    WHILE NOT EOF DO
    BEGIN
        ReadWord (word);
```

```
              IF word.length > 0 THEN
              BEGIN
                  IF FirstWord THEN
                      FirstWord := FALSE
                  ELSE
                      IF (NumWordsOnLine >= 10) THEN
                      BEGIN
                          WRITELN;
                          NumWordsOnLine := 0;
                          CurrentColumn := 0
                      END
                      ELSE
                          WRITE (' ');
                  WriteWord (word);
                  NumWordsOnLine := NumWordsOnLine + 1;
                  CurrentColumn := CurrentColumn + word.length
              END
          END;
          WRITELN
      END.    (* main program *)
```

This program performs the same task as the one in the last section, but it has an additional variable `CurrentColumn` to keep track of the column. How do you check to see that it is being calculated correctly? You can do this check and build some debugging code into the program at the same time. The output will be easier to understand if there are special characters written at both the left and right margins to create a border around the output. You need the value of `CurrentColumn` to do this. At the same time, modify the program so that it doesn't always put 10 words per line. Instead, have it put 1 word on the first line, 2 on the second, and so on, until it reaches 8 words on a line. Then it starts back at 1 word on the next line and so on.

Here is what you get when we execute the new program:

```
|I                                      |
|know as                                |
|little about the                       |
|nature of romantic love                |
|as I knew when I                        |
|was eighteen, but I do know             |
|about the deep pleasure of continuing interest,|
|the excitement of wanting to know what somebody|
|else                                   |
|thinks, will                           |
|do, will not                            |
```

```
|do, the tricks played            |
|and unplayed, the short cord     |
|that the years make into rope    |
|and, in my case, is there, hanging |
|loose, long after death.         |
```

Again, there is good news and bad news. The good news is that there are a different number of words on each line and that a border appears. The bad news is that the border isn't even. However, it's not that uneven. If you look closely, you'll notice that it follows a pattern. It is off by one more for every word written to the output line. For one word the border is right, for two it is off by one, for three it is off by two, and so on.

The solution is not difficult to fathom. You keep track of the column number by starting it at 0 for a given line and then adding the length of each word that is written to the output line. However, spaces as well as words are written to the line, and you didn't account for those spaces in your calculation of the column. Not only that, your calculation is off by one more for every new word written to the output line. You might think of fixing this by changing this line:

```
CurrentColumn := CurrentColumn + word.length
```

to the following:

```
CurrentColumn := CurrentColumn + word.length + 1
```

The idea is that when you add the length of the word to the column, you will also add one extra for the space that separates it from the rest of the line. This won't work either, though, because not every word has a space written before it. Therefore, you want to leave this line alone and make a change near the line that actually writes out the separating space. You need a pair of lines:

```
BEGIN
    WRITE (' ');
    CurrentColumn := CurrentColumn + 1
END
```

This is the most straightforward way to account for every extra space written to the output line. By pairing the WRITE with an increment, you guaranty the appropriate update whenever the WRITE is performed. With these modifications, the program produces this output:

```
|I                                |
|know as                          |
|little about the                 |
|nature of romantic love          |
|as I knew when I                 |
|was eighteen, but I do know      |
|about                            |
```

```
|the deep                        |
|pleasure of continuing          |
|interest, the excitement of     |
|wanting to know what somebody   |
|else thinks, will do, will not  |
|do,                             |
|the tricks                      |
|played and unplayed,            |
|the short cord that             |
|the years make into rope        |
|and, in my case, is there,      |
|hanging                         |
|loose, long                     |
|after death.                    |
```

This output shows that the current column variable is taking on the correct values and produces the bordered output you want for debugging.

10.3.5 Final Details of Justify

Now that you have a program that reads and writes a file of words and keeps track of its current output column, you can fill in the last detail of the program. You need to tell it when to go to a new line. The expression (`MaxColumn - CurrentColumn`) describes the number of columns left on the current input line. If the next word's length is less than or equal to that, it will fit. Therefore, you can get rid of the code that deals with `NumWordsOnLine` and instead use this test:

> if (word.length > (MaxColumn − CurrentColumn)) then
>   go to new line.

This leads to the following main program. To make the output easier to read, you can also modify the program to produce lines at the beginning and end of the text to indicate column numbers.

```
BEGIN (* main program *)
   Setup (CurrentColumn, FirstWord);
   WHILE NOT EOF DO
   BEGIN
      ReadWord (word);
      IF word.length > 0 THEN
      BEGIN
         IF FirstWord THEN
            FirstWord := FALSE
```

```
        ELSE
            IF (word.length > MaxColumn - CurrentColumn) THEN
                GoToNewLine
            ELSE
            BEGIN
                WRITE (' ');
                CurrentColumn := CurrentColumn + 1
            END;
            WriteWord (word);
            CurrentColumn := CurrentColumn + word.length
        END
    END;
    WriteClosing
END.  (* main program *)
```

If you execute this program, you get this output:

```
123456789012345678901234567890123456789 0
+----------------------------------------+
|I know as little about the nature of    |
|romantic love as I knew when I was      |
|eighteen, but I do know about the deep  |
|pleasure of continuing interest, the    |
|excitement of wanting to know what      |
|somebody else thinks, will do, will not |
|do, the tricks played and unplayed, the |
|short cord that the years make into rope|
|and, in my case, is there, hanging loose,|
|long after death.                       |
+----------------------------------------+
123456789012345678901234567890123456789 0
```

Again, good news and bad news. If you look closely, you'll see that the program works for every input line whose length is 65 or less, but not for the input line of length 66. This leads to the slight bulge in the preceding text.

This seems to be a border problem. If you are going to write a word on the input line, you will write not only the word, but also a leading space. Thus you need (`length + 1`) columns, not just (`length`) columns. Thus the test

```
(word.length > MaxColumn - CurrentColumn)
```

should be

```
(word.length + 1 > MaxColumn - CurrentColumn)
```

This slight modification to the program makes it work properly.

10.3.6   Parting Words about Justify

You should now turn the program just developed into a well-structured program. To clean it up, you should do three things. First, add comments to each procedure, constant, and variable. Second, take the special code for creating the heading, the footing, and the border and put it inside IF/THEN statements that look at a global constant called Debugging. These extra output elements were produced to aid in development, but they were never intended to be part of the final output. Third, take the huge main program and break it up into smaller pieces.

Before looking at the final version, consider the following information about its structure. It has 10 procedures in it. Here is a breakdown of the various routines and the categories I would give them:

Level	Category	Procedure/function name
1	Low level	WriteCols, WriteDashes
2	File-manipulating tool	WriteChars
2	Word-manipulating tools	WriteWord, ReadWord
3	Convenience procedures	Initialize, GoToNewLine, Writespace, ProcessWord, WriteClosing
4	Top level	main program

The level indicates the relative complexity of the routine. They have been defined in this order in the file (except for WriteChars, which had to precede WriteDashes).

The simplest routines in this program are the two procedures that produce the debugging header and trailer information. Next are the tools taken from the software library. These perform low-level tasks, but they are essential to the proper functioning of the program. At level 3 are five procedures created by the breakup of the main program. These procedures are not interesting in themselves. You wouldn't imagine using them again in another program, the way you would the tools. Finally, at the highest level of abstraction is the main program. Most of the design decisions are evident in the main program. Therefore, in reading this program, pay attention to the main program and the level 2 procedures. The other parts of this solution are not that interesting.

Here is a structure diagram of the program:

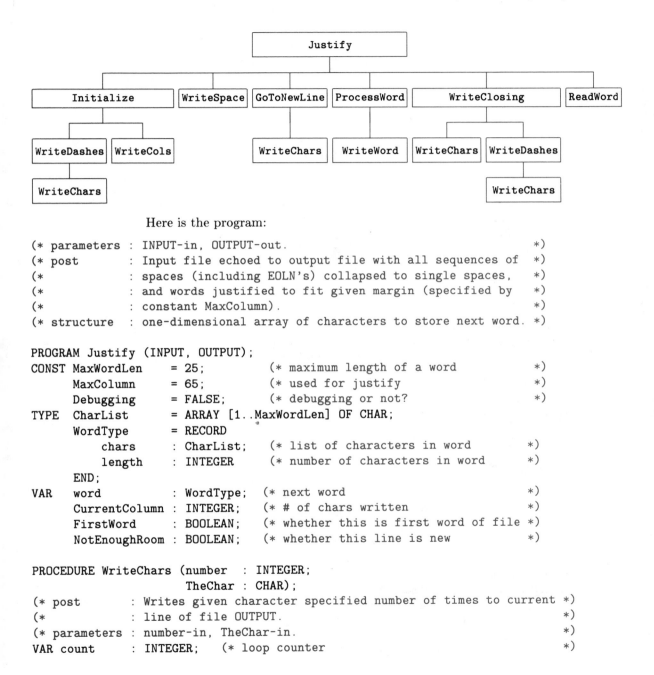

Here is the program:

```
(* parameters : INPUT-in, OUTPUT-out.                             *)
(* post       : Input file echoed to output file with all sequences of *)
(*             : spaces (including EOLN's) collapsed to single spaces,  *)
(*             : and words justified to fit given margin (specified by  *)
(*             : constant MaxColumn).                              *)
(* structure  : one-dimensional array of characters to store next word. *)

PROGRAM Justify (INPUT, OUTPUT);
CONST MaxWordLen    = 25;          (* maximum length of a word        *)
      MaxColumn     = 65;          (* used for justify                *)
      Debugging     = FALSE;       (* debugging or not?               *)
TYPE  CharList      = ARRAY [1..MaxWordLen] OF CHAR;
      WordType      = RECORD
          chars     : CharList;    (* list of characters in word      *)
          length    : INTEGER      (* number of characters in word    *)
      END;
VAR   word          : WordType;    (* next word                       *)
      CurrentColumn : INTEGER;     (* # of chars written              *)
      FirstWord     : BOOLEAN;     (* whether this is first word of file *)
      NotEnoughRoom : BOOLEAN;     (* whether this line is new         *)

PROCEDURE WriteChars (number  : INTEGER;
                      TheChar : CHAR);
(* post       : Writes given character specified number of times to current *)
(*             : line of file OUTPUT.                              *)
(* parameters : number-in, TheChar-in.                            *)
VAR count       : INTEGER;    (* loop counter                   *)
```

```
BEGIN
    FOR count := 1 TO number DO
        WRITE (TheChar)
END;   (* WriteChars *)

PROCEDURE WriteCols;
(* post      : header showing column numbers is output. *)
(* requires  : constant MaxColumn.                      *)
VAR count    : INTEGER;   (* loop counter               *)
BEGIN
    WRITE (' ');
    FOR count := 1 TO MaxColumn DO
        IF (count MOD 10 = 0) THEN
            WRITE ('|')
        ELSE
            WRITE ((count MOD 10):1);
    WRITELN
END;   (* WriteCols *)

PROCEDURE WriteDashes;
(* post      : header composed of dashes is output.           *)
(* requires  : constant MaxColumn and procedure WriteChars. *)
BEGIN
    WRITE ('+');
    WriteChars (MaxColumn, '-');
    WRITELN ('+')
END;   (* WriteDashes *)

PROCEDURE WriteWord (word : WordType);
(* post       : all data values in array are written out.        *)
(* parameters : word-in.                                          *)
(* errors     : if length > MaxWordLen, overflow message written. *)
(* requires   : constant MaxWordLen and type WordType.            *)
VAR index     : INTEGER;   (* loop counter                        *)
BEGIN
    WITH word DO
        FOR index := 1 TO length DO
            IF length > MaxWordLen THEN
                WRITE ('*')
            ELSE
                WRITE (chars [index])
END;   (* WriteWord *)
```

```
PROCEDURE ReadWord (VAR word : WordType);
(* pre         : input cursor at beginning of word of length <= MaxWordLen.  *)
(* post        : characters are read from file into array; length set        *)
(*              : appropriately; characters of word are read until a space is *)
(*              : read; input cursor after space; if input cursor at space to *)
(*              : begin with, space is read and word of length 0 is returned; *)
(*              : if word too long, length set appropriately but extra        *)
(*              : characters are ignored.                                     *)
(* parameters  : word-out.                                                   *)
(* requires    : constant MaxWordLen and type WordType.                      *)
VAR next         : CHAR;   (* next character from input line                 *)
BEGIN
    WITH word DO
    BEGIN
        READ (next);
        length := 0;
        WHILE (next <> ' ') DO
        BEGIN
            length := length + 1;
            IF (length <= MaxWordLen) THEN
                chars [length] := next;
            READ (next)
        END
    END
END;  (* ReadWord *)


PROCEDURE Initialize (VAR CurrentColumn : INTEGER;
                      VAR FirstWord      : BOOLEAN);
(* post       : program variables initialized; leading debugging code      *)
(*             : written to output if debugging in effect.                 *)
(* parameters : CurrentColumn-out, FirstWord-out.                          *)
(* requires   : constant debugging; procedures WriteCols and WriteDashes.  *)
BEGIN
    CurrentColumn := 0;
    FirstWord := TRUE;
    IF debugging THEN
    BEGIN
        WriteCols;
        WriteDashes;
        WRITE ('|')
    END
END;  (* Initialize *)
```

```
PROCEDURE GoToNewLine (VAR CurrentColumn : INTEGER);
(* post        : output cursor at new line; CurrentColumn set to 0; border *)
(*             : characters written out if debugging in effect.           *)
(* parameters : CurrentColumn-out.                                        *)
(* requires   : constants debugging and MaxColumn; procedure WriteChars.  *)
BEGIN
    IF debugging THEN
    BEGIN
        WriteChars (MaxColumn - CurrentColumn, ' ');
        WRITELN ('|');
        WRITE ('|')
    END
    ELSE
        WRITELN;
    CurrentColumn := 0
END;   (* GoToNewLine *)


PROCEDURE WriteSpace (VAR CurrentColumn : INTEGER);
(* post        : leading space written out; CurrentColumn incremented. *)
(* parameters : CurrentColumn-in/out.                                  *)
BEGIN
    WRITE (' ');
    CurrentColumn := CurrentColumn + 1
END;   (* WriteSpace *)


PROCEDURE ProcessWord (    word         : WordType;
                       VAR CurrentColumn : INTEGER);
(* post        : contents of word written out; CurrentColumn incremented *)
(*             : by word length.                                         *)
(* parameters : word-in; CurrentColumn-in/out.                           *)
(* requires   : procedure WriteWord.                                     *)
BEGIN
    WriteWord (word);
    CurrentColumn := CurrentColumn + word.length
END;   (* ProcessWord *)

PROCEDURE WriteClosing (CurrentColumn : INTEGER);
(* post        : footer lines written out if debugging in effect.  *)
(* parameters : CurrentColumn-in.                                  *)
(* requires   : constants debugging and MaxColumn; and procedures  *)
(*             : WriteChars and WriteDashes.                        *)
```

```
BEGIN
    IF debugging THEN
    BEGIN
        WriteChars (MaxColumn - CurrentColumn, ' ');
        WRITELN ('|');
        WriteDashes
    END
    ELSE
        WRITELN
END;   (* WriteClosing *)


BEGIN   (* main program *)
    Initialize (CurrentColumn, FirstWord);
    WHILE NOT EOF DO
    BEGIN
        ReadWord (word);
        IF word.length > 0 THEN
        BEGIN
            NotEnoughRoom := (word.length + 1 > MaxColumn - CurrentColumn);
            IF FirstWord THEN
                FirstWord := FALSE
            ELSE
                IF NotEnoughRoom THEN
                    GoToNewLine (CurrentColumn)
                ELSE
                    WriteSpace (CurrentColumn);
            ProcessWord (word, CurrentColumn)
        END
    END;
    WriteClosing (CurrentColumn)
END.   (* main program *)
```

One last element of the program you still need to test is whether the program constants really give you the kind of flexibility you think they do. Consider the output you would get with these settings:

```
CONST MaxWordLen    = 8;
      MaxColumn     = 50;
      Debugging     = TRUE;
```

These constants specify a restrictive word size, slightly smaller margins, and debugging turned on. You have some overflow messages with these settings, but the program executes as it should:

```
123456789|123456789|123456789|123456789|123456789|
+---------------------------------------------------+
|I know as little about the nature of romantic love|
|as I knew when I was ********* but I do know about|
|the deep pleasure of ********** ********* the      |
|********** of wanting to know what somebody else   |
|thinks, will do, will not do, the tricks played   |
|and ********* the short cord that the years make   |
|into rope and, in my case, is there, hanging       |
|loose, long after death.                           |
+---------------------------------------------------+
```

10.4 Top-Down versus Bottom-Up Construction

The development and testing of program `Justify` in the last few sections are done in a bottom-up way. You start by testing the simplest tool, `WriteWord`; then use that to test the next tool, `ReadWord`. When both tools are tested, you test the main program. Even there, you built the main program slowly: first, a program that outputs a fixed number of words per line; then, a program that outputs a variable number of words but in a definite pattern; then, a program that keeps track of the current output column to draw a border; and finally, a program that performs justification.

Thus, you start at the bottom of the program structure and work up. You begin in the detailed parts of the program and move toward the more abstract. This is called *bottom-up testing and development*, or simply *bottom-up construction*. Bottom-up construction requires the use of dummy main programs that test low-level procedures.

You can just as easily do your work in the reverse order. For example, you can write a dummy version of the `ReadWord` procedure that always does the same thing. Since `ReadWord` is a procedure with an out parameter:

one way is to create a dummy black box that always gives the same word with the same length:

```
PROCEDURE ReadWord (VAR word : WordType);
BEGIN
    WITH word DO
    BEGIN
        length := 4;
        chars [1] := 'd';
        chars [2] := 'u';
        chars [3] := 'm';
        chars [4] := 'b'
    END
END;
```

An alternative is to set every element of the array to a single character (a dash, for example) and then use the pseudo-random number generator to produce different lengths:

```
PROCEDURE ReadWord (VAR word : WordType);
VAR index : INTEGER;
BEGIN
    WITH word DO
    BEGIN
        FOR index := 1 TO MaxWordLen DO
            chars [index] := '-';
        length := RandomInt (1, MaxWord, seed)
    END
END;
```

You could also write a dummy version of the `WriteWord` procedure that always does the same thing. That procedure has one in parameter:

```
      word
        ↓
┌─────────────┐
│ WriteWord   │
└─────────────┘
```

You don't care what characters are actually written to the output line, but if you want to make sure that the output is being justified to within the specified margin, it would be nice if the procedure at least pays attention to the length of the word and does the right thing.

There is a simple solution for this:

```
PROCEDURE WriteWord (word : WordType);
BEGIN
    WRITE ('supercalifragilisticexpialidotious':word.length)
END;
```

This version of the procedure always writes the same series of letters, but it writes a different number of letters depending on `length`. In other words, the field width of the string constant will only write out the first `length` characters of this nonsense word. Therefore, this is a dummy version of `WriteWord` that produces words with the correct lengths, even though they are all the same word.

These are not the procedures you will use in the final program, but they serve as placeholders for `ReadWord` and `WriteWord` while you test the main program. Such procedures are often called *stub procedures* or simply *stubs*. This technique is sometimes called *stub programming*.

By using stubs, you would discover bugs in the main program first. You would correct the spacing between words, the way you manipulate `CurrentColumn`, and the test for whether or not a word fits. You would build the debugging procedures for writing headings before any other procedures. This technique might actually make it easier to test the boundary and degenerate cases, because you can cause the `ReadWord` procedure to spew out whatever values you want (for example, it might be useful to have it produce only one-letter words).

After you are sure that the main program works properly, you can write the real version of `WriteWord` or `ReadWord`. You would test that part of the solution until you are sure it works, and then you would fill in the other procedure.

This is called *top-down testing and development*, or *top-down construction*. You start with the main program and work downward, debugging the highest levels of abstraction first down to the more detailed pieces of code. Top-down construction requires the use of stub procedures that take the place of the not yet completed low-level routines.

The top-down construction of this program would have taken almost the same time and effort as the bottom-up construction. In this case, then, it doesn't really matter which technique you use. There will be other problems, however, where one seems more natural than the other. For example, if you are unable to clearly see how the main program is going to be broken down into pieces, bottom-up construction is almost impossible. You can't build up when you don't know where to start. However, if the procedures of the main program are difficult to simulate, then top-down construction might be more trouble than it's worth. It might be easier to build each procedure independently, testing each individually, and then fit those pieces together into the main program, debugging the highest-level code last. Finally, you might find that you prefer one technique over the other, that one seems more natural to your problem-solving skills. You should keep both techniques in mind and choose the one that is most natural for you and for the problem being solved.

10.5 Key Concepts

- To validate a program or subprogram, test it to see that it matches its specification.

- Any program or subprogram will have a set of legal values that are to be processed. It will often also have a set of illegal or degenerate values. The boundary between legal and illegal introduces boundary values. A good set of test data should include some typical legal values, some degenerate values, some boundary values (all, if possible), and any special values that require special handling.

- A useful technique for developing and testing programs is to build the program from the bottom up. Low-level procedures are written and tested before the main program. Dummy main programs are used for developing and testing each low-level procedure.

- Another useful technique for developing and testing programs is to build the program from the top down. High-level code is written and tested before the low-level details are worked out. Stub procedures and functions are used for developing and testing the high-level code.

10.6 Self-Check Exercises

1. What is the difference between program verification and program validation? Between program testing and program debugging?

2. Suppose you are building a procedure such as `InsertInto` from the last chapter that inserts a new integer into a sorted list in its proper place so that they all appear in increasing order. Design a sufficient set of tests to perform on `Insert`, indicating both the value to be inserted and the current value of the list. Assume the list holds no more than 500 numbers.

3. Suppose you are building a procedure that will read in lines of text and write them back out again centered within a certain margin. Develop a set of test data for the procedure, specifying what margin is used and what line is being centered. Assume the structure for holding the line can hold no more than 100 characters.

4. Suppose that you have a `FUNCTION` called `Median` with header below that returns the median value in a sorted list of integers (i.e., the value appearing in the middle).

   ```
   FUNCTION Median (VAR list : ListType) : INTEGER;
   ```

   Identify a series of test cases to be tried using this `FUNCTION`. Be sure to indicate what values are to be stored in the list for each test. Assume that `ListType` can store no more than 250 integers.

5. Suppose that you are going to be manipulating dates in a program. If your program is only supposed to handle dates in the twentieth century, what would be a sufficient set of dates to use as test data?

6. Consider `FUNCTION` `Less` written in the last chapter:

   ```
   FUNCTION Less (one, two : WordType) : BOOLEAN;
   ```

It compares two words to see if one is alphabetically less than another. Write a dummy main program that will allow you to test this FUNCTION. You can assume that procedures ReadWord and WriteWord are available to you.

7. Suppose that you are going to manipulate sorted lists of integers that follow the generic list declarations of Chapter 9:

```
CONST MaxNum      = 200;
TYPE  NumList     = ARRAY [1..MaxNum] OF INTEGER;
      ListType    = RECORD
          nums      : INTEGER;
          NumsNums  : INTEGER
      END;
```

You are writing a program in a top-down way and you want to test the main program. Your main program calls procedures ReadList, ModifyList, and WriteList. You are to write a stub procedure for ReadList using pseudo-random number generation to produce sorted lists of integers that can be used for testing the main program. The procedure will eventually have this header:

```
PROCEDURE ReadList (VAR list : ListType);
(* post : All integer values in input file are read into list in  *)
(*       : proper sorted order, eliminating duplicates.            *)
```

but for the time being, a seed variable is also being passed. You are to use this variable to write ReadList:

```
PROCEDURE ReadList (VAR list : ListType;
                    VAR seed : INTEGER);
```

8. Suppose that you are writing a stub for a FUNCTION that evaluates two poker hands to see whether the first hand wins:

```
FUNCTION FirstWins (VAR hand1, hand2 : HandType) : BOOLEAN;
```

Assume that you have a procedure called WriteHand that displays a poker hand. You can write a simple stub that randomly chooses one player or the other as the winner, but suppose you have reached a point in your program development where it is important that the FUNCTION return the right answer. Is there any way you can do this as a stub and delay writing the details of the FUNCTION?

9. Given the following input and a margin of 30:

```
this is some text right here on this very long line.
```

program Justify produces output such as the following:

```
this is some text right here
on this very long line.
```

Suppose you want to produce output like the following:

```
(this) (is) (some) (text)
(right) (here) (on) (this)
(very) (long) (line.)
```

In other words, you want every word to be written out inside of parentheses, but you still want to stay within the specified margin. What modifications would have to be made to the program to make it behave this way?

10. Suppose you want to improve program `Justify` so that it will hyphenate whenever possible. If a word appears in the input file that has dashes in it (such as "merry-go-round"), you can split this word into merry- / go-round or merry-go- / round. How would you modify `Justify` to perform this kind of hyphenation whenever possible?

11. Suppose that you are creating a type called `InventoryType` and that you are going to develop the following program:

```
BEGIN
    ReadInventory (inventory);
    SortInventory (inventory);
    WriteInventory (inventory)
END.
```

The program will first read an inventory listing from a file, then reorder the inventory records so that they are in sorted order, and finally write out the inventory to a new file. In what order should you develop and test these procedures? Briefly explain.

10.7 Programming Problems

1. You are going to write a program that allows you to do simple text formatting by embedding commands in a file. Lines that are not command lines are simply echoed to the output file. All commands are of the form:

```
@<char>
```

an at-sign in column 1 and then a single character. The commands you should implement are

Command	Meaning
@d	Switch to double space.
@s	Switch to single space.
@c	Center the next line using a margin of 80 columns.
@h	Make the next line a heading (i.e., turn it to all uppercase letters and write a line of dashes under it of the same length to emphasize it).
@b	Begin an itemize environment where 1) each successive line 2) is indented and 3) numbered.
@e	End an itemize environment

The program should start in double-space mode, unless the file has an **@s** command at the very beginning. You should recognize the command in either lowercase or uppercase form (that is, **@B** is the same as **@b**). Given this input:

```
@h
Programming Problems
Students have these problems with programs:
@b
procrastination
confusion
limited computer time
@e
What will we do?
```

this output should be generated:

```
PROGRAMMING PROBLEMS
--------------------
Students have these problems with programs:
    1) procrastination
    2) confusion
    3) limited computer time
What will we do?
```

2. You are to expand on the generic list procedures and functions developed in Chapter 9. You are to write a procedure with the following header (in its generic form):

```
PROCEDURE DeleteValue (VAR list  : ListType;
                       value : <element type>;
                       found : BOOLEAN);
```

```
(* pre  : list is a legal list of integers appearing in increasing order. *)
(* post : If given value appears in list, found is set to TRUE and value  *)
(*       : is deleted from the list.  All other elements remain in their  *)
(*       : proper order.  If the value does not appear, found is set to   *)
(*       : FALSE and the list is unchanged.                               *)
```

You will obviously test your procedure on a specific type of list, but it should be general enough to be used for any of the lists we have examined.

3. You are going to write a program that allows a user to explore the lines of hierarchy in an organization. The program will read a data file of person entries, one per line, where a person entry contains

    <person's name>/<person's boss>

    For example:

    ```
    Tad Martin/Adam Chandler
    Robin McCall/Greg Nelson
    Josh Dubitsky/Adam Chandler
    Charlie Brent/Tad Martin
    ```

    The program will read in the data file, displaying the name of each person to the user. Then it will ask the user what person should be displayed in more detail. Once the user has made a choice, the program should show the view of the hierarchy from that person's perspective: showing all the bosses above and all the employees below. For example, for Adam Chandler, you would get

```
Adam Chandler's bosses are    : <none>
Adam Chandler's employees are : Tad Martin, Charlie Brent, Josh Dubitsky
```

An employee can see only up and down, but not across. Thus from Tad Martin's perspective, Josh Dubitsky is neither an employee nor a boss, even though Adam Chandler is their common boss.

This program will be easiest to write if you use the generic routines in Chapter 9 to develop some procedures and functions for manipulating an alphabetical list of person entries, where a person entry contains a name and a boss.

For example, consider the problem of finding all the employees of a person (including all the employees of the employees). You can do this by using two-person lists: one to keep track of who is left to be explored (**explore**) and one to keep track of all the employees seen so far (**employees**). This pseudocode should get you started on your way to solving this problem. It is written in terms of a variable called **TargetPerson**, the person the user has asked about:

set explore and employees to empty lists.

for (all people) do

       if (boss of person = TargetPerson) then

           InsertInto (explore, person).

>   while (explore is not empty) do
>   begin
>   remove NewPerson from the explore list (probably the last entry).
>   if PositionOf (NewPerson, employees) <> 0 then
>   begin
>   InsertInto (employees, NewPerson).
>   for (all people) do
>   if (boss of person = NewPerson) then
>   InsertInto (explore, person).
>   end
>   end.

4. Suppose that an input file has a series of names, one per line:

```
Mr. Adam Chandler
Mrs. Phoebe English Tyler Wallingford
Professor Langley Wallingford
Dr. Joe Martin
```

It is often more convenient to have the names separated into first and last:

Last name	First name
Chandler	Mr. Adam
Wallingford	Mrs. Phoebe English Tyler
Wallingford	Professor Langley
Martin	Dr. Joe

In all these cases, the last name is simply the last word on the input line. You are going to write a procedure **SplitLine** with this specification:

```
PROCEDURE SplitLine (VAR first : WordType;
                     VAR last  : WordType);
(* pre  : Input cursor at beginning of a line with a name on it. *)
(* post : Last word on input line is returned as the last name,  *)
(*       : all other words are made part of the first name; input *)
(*       : cursor at beginning of next line.                      *)
```

Use the same **WordType** as you did in **Justify**. These words can have spaces in them, but you can use the same structure and the same procedures and functions that you used in **Justify**. There are many cases that this procedure will get wrong. For example, if the input line contains "Tad Martin, ESQ," the first name will be set to "Tad Martin," and the last name will be set to "ESQ." The procedure will get 90 percent of the names right, so don't worry about these mistakes.

As you complete this assignment, you should be thinking about tools that might be useful in future programs. You should start by creating a new word-manipulating procedure, one that appends one word to the end of another. Then write procedure `SplitLine` in terms of the append operation.

5. In this assignment you will examine issues of numeric precision and representation. You are going to create a type called `ExtendedReal` with more digits of accuracy than a normal variable of type `REAL`. You can accomplish this by storing it as an array of digits. With an array you can ask for thousands of digits.

One of the problems with storing `REAL` values is that they vary so widely in magnitude. Some programs require calculations very close to zero, and others require calculations whose results are incredibly large. To accommodate this variety, a `REAL` is stored in two parts: as a series of digits (mantissa) and as an exponent. Thus you will store an `ExtendedReal` as an array of digits along with an exponent. With an exponent of type `INTEGER`, you should have a wide range of `REAL` values.

Another purpose for having an exponent is that it allows you to store all the significant digits, excluding zeros at the beginning of the number. If someone tells you a value is equal to

0.0000000000000002831

this value may be expressed with 20 digits, but it has only 4 digits that are significant. With an exponent you can eliminate leading zeros:

$2.831 * 10^{-16}$

Plan on first building some tools for manipulating variables of type `ExtendedReal`; then look at a specific application. A good set to start with would be

```
PROCEDURE Init (VAR number : ExtendedReal;
                    value  : INTEGER);
(* post : Number is initialized to given integer value. *)


PROCEDURE Divide (VAR number   : ExtendedReal;
                      quotient : INTEGER);
(* post : Number is divided by given integer value. *)


PROCEDURE WriteOut (number : ExtendedReal);
(* post : Current value of number is written to output file. *)


PROCEDURE AddTo (VAR number1 : ExtendedReal;
                number2 : ExtendedReal);
(* post : The value of number2 is added to number1. *)
```

Values are transferred from `INTEGER`s into extended reals, not from `REAL`s into extended reals. It is easier to write the code for `INTEGER`s, and it leads to more precise calculations. If you want to store a number such as 0.28434 in an extended real, you can store the `INTEGER` 28,434 and then divide by 100,000.

Once you have these tools built, you can use your new type to perform a precise calculation: the approximation of *e*. E is equal to

$$1 + \frac{1}{1!} + \frac{1}{2!} + \frac{1}{3!} + \frac{1}{4!} + \cdots$$

Thus you can approximate *e* with a loop such as the following:

```
var e : ExtendedReal;
    number : ExtendedReal;
begin
    Init (number, 1);
    Init (e, 2);
    count := 2;
    while (still not close enough) do
    begin
        divide (number, count);
        AddTo (e, number);
        count := count + 1
    end
end
```

PART TWO

EXTENSIONS

11

EXTRA PASCAL DATA TOPICS

11.1 Introduction

The next two chapters discuss topics that were skipped while you were learning about design, tool building, and testing. Some are language features and some are concepts that will be useful in more advanced programs. You should study them before going on.

This chapter covers data structures. You will learn more about files and how you can manipulate them, and you will learn some important new types. First, you will learn how to create your own simple types that take on whatever set of values you specify. Then you will learn about a different kind of array, a packed array.

11.2 Enumerated Types

In Chapter 7 you saw that Pascal lets you define new types using arrays and subranges. The story doesn't end there. Pascal also lets you invent new simple types that take on whatever values you specify. For example, if you want to define a type that takes on the values of the days of the week, you can do so with a user-defined ordinal type or an enumerated type. Here's how:

```
TYPE  DayType = (Monday, Tuesday, Wednesday, Thursday, Friday,
                 Saturday, Sunday);
```

You define the type by enumerating all its possible values, by specifying its domain. Each of these values must be a legal Pascal identifier. You can't do this:

```
TYPE Illegal = (34X, #, -, +);
```

None of these values is a legal identifier. The general form of the enumerated type declaration is

(*<identifier>*, *<identifier>*, ..., *<identifier>*)

Defining an enumerated type introduces the domain of the type into the vocabulary of Pascal. Every identifier in the enumeration list becomes a constant of that type. Thus the definition of **DayType** introduces seven new constants into the program. The words **Monday**, **Tuesday**, and so on become constants of type **DayType** that you can manipulate like any other constant. Therefore, if you had a variable of type **DayType**:

```
VAR day : DayType;
```

you could give it a value by saying

```
day := Monday;
day := Tuesday;
     . . .
day := Sunday;
```

The other properties of enumerated types stem from the fact that they are ordinal types. Remember, ordinal types have an implicit ordering of the domain with a first element, a next element, and so on. The ordering of the enumerated type is derived from its definition. The enumeration list has a first element, a second element, and so on that defines the order of the type.

In the example, the first value listed in the definition is **Monday**: this means that **Monday** is considered the smallest value of type **DayType**. **Tuesday**, which is listed next, is considered the second value of type **DayType** and so on up to **Sunday**, which is considered the last value of type **DayType**.

This has several implications. First, you can compare different days for their ordering. The following statement tests whether one day occurs earlier in the week than another day:

```
IF day1 < day2 THEN
    <something>
```

You can also use the built-in ordinal functions introduced in Chapter 6—the **SUCC**, **PRED**, and **ORD** functions. **SUCC** returns the next element, the successor; **PRED** returns the previous element, the predecessor; and **ORD** returns the ordinal value.

For type **DayType**,

```
SUCC (Monday) returns Tuesday
SUCC (Tuesday) returns Wednesday
. . .
SUCC (Saturday) returns Sunday
SUCC (Sunday) causes an error
```

Similarly,

```
PRED (Monday) causes an error
PRED (Tuesday) returns Monday
. . .
PRED (Saturday) returns Friday
PRED (Sunday) returns Saturday
```

The ORD function converts from type DayType to type INTEGER. The ordinal values of an enumerated type always start at 0.

```
ORD (Monday) returns 0
ORD (Tuesday) returns 1
. . .
ORD (Sunday) returns 6
```

Remember, FOR loops can be controlled by variables of ordinal type. Thus you can say:

```
FOR day := Monday TO Sunday DO
    <something>
```

You can also make CASE statements controlled by expressions of ordinal type:

```
CASE day OF
    Monday  : <something>;
    Tuesday : <something else>;
            . . .
    Sunday  : <something else again>
END;
```

And you you can define an array indexed by DayType:

```
TYPE DayList = ARRAY [DayType] OF INTEGER;
```

About the only thing you can't do with an enumerated type that you can do with types such as CHAR is to read and write them. The standard READ/READLN and WRITE/WRITELN will not work for enumerated types. Thus enumerated types are most useful for internal manipulations, unless you are willing to build procedures for reading and writing them.

11.3 File Variables

This section delves more deeply into type TEXT. Here you will learn how to create objects of type TEXT and how to manipulate them.

The programs you have written so far have all dealt with a single source of input and a single source of output. It is possible to get by with a limited knowledge of file variables because there is a lot of magic built into the language for two objects called INPUT and OUTPUT. INPUT and OUTPUT are both predefined variables of type TEXT, which is why you have never had to declare them. You are allowed to declare your own file variables as you would declare any variables, by naming them and specifying their type:

```
VAR OutFile : TEXT;
    InFile  : TEXT;
```

This defines two new variables of type TEXT (i.e., file variables). You might find it strange to think of a file as a variable, but it shouldn't take too much imagination to realize why that is. The file variable keeps track of two pieces of information. First, it keeps track of what state it is in. Files can either be open for reading, open for writing, or not opened at all. Second, it keeps track of the pointer into the file, either the input cursor or the output cursor depending on whether it is reading or writing. Because the state of a file can change as a program executes (e.g., the input or output cursor moves), a file object changes as the program executes and is therefore a variable.

File variables have one unusual property that other variables do not have: they are usually bound to external entities. For example, the predefined variable INPUT is usually bound to the user's keyboard, so that anything typed by the user becomes input to the program. Similarly, OUTPUT is usually bound to the user's screen, so that the program can display information. It is also possible to bind file variables to other devices such as printers, disk drives, and so on or to external files stored in the secondary memory of the computer. The exact mechanism for such binding varies from Pascal system to system. But there is one general rule that you should follow: any file variable that is to be bound to an external entity should appear in the program header. Thus if you write a program and intend to use the two file variables above and the built-in variables INPUT and OUTPUT, you would use a header such as this:

```
PROGRAM FileMania (INPUT, OUTPUT, InFile, OutFile);
```

The first operations you should learn for objects of type TEXT are the procedures that open the file. While it might be obvious from the names that InFile is for reading and OutFile is for writing, Pascal cannot figure that out and will not know how to open them. You open files by using either the RESET or REWRITE command. RESET opens the file for reading, REWRITE opens it for writing. Their general syntax is

```
RESET   ( <file variable> );
REWRITE ( <file variable> );
```

as in

```
RESET   (InFile);
REWRITE (OutFile);
```

These are executable statements, so you can include them in your program wherever appropriate. You just have to be sure to open your files before you manipulate them. The usual place to perform the RESET and REWRITE is at the beginning of program execution.

Programs that use the built-in INPUT and OUTPUT are simple to write because you always READ from one place and always WRITE to one place. This is not the case when you introduce other file variables. You can now write programs that read from two or more places and write to two or more places. This means you must specify where input is to be obtained and where output is to be directed. This involves a change in many low-level functions and procedures you have learned. Here are new syntax descriptions of READ/READLN, WRITE/WRITELN, and EOLN/EOF

```
WRITE   ( <file variable>, <item>,     <item>,     . . ., <item>     )
WRITELN ( <file variable>, <item>,     <item>,     . . ., <item>     )
READ    ( <file variable>, <variable>, <variable>, . . ., <variable> )
READLN  ( <file variable>, <variable>, <variable>, . . ., <variable> )
EOLN    ( <file variable> )
EOF     ( <file variable> )
```

In each case, you specify a file variable. This is how you designate which file variable to use. Thus suppose you had the following declarations:

```
VAR in1  : TEXT;
    in2  : TEXT;
    out1 : TEXT;
    out2 : TEXT;
```

Here are READ/READLN statements and EOLN/EOF function calls that you would use to manipulate in1 versus in2 versus INPUT:

File INPUT	File in1	File in2
READ (x, y)	READ (in1, x, y)	READ (in2, x, y)
READLN (x, y)	READLN (in1, x, y)	READLN (in2, x, y)
EOLN	EOLN (in1)	EOLN (in2)
EOF	EOF (in1)	EOF (in2)

You would do similar things for the output files:

File OUTPUT	File out1	File out2
WRITE ('hi')	WRITE (out1, 'hi')	WRITE (out2, 'hi')
WRITELN ('ho')	WRITELN (out1, 'ho')	WRITELN (out2, 'ho')

You might wonder how you have managed so far. Wirth's attitude is, "It should be simple to do simple things." If you want to use just one input and one output file, he reasoned, it should be easy to do. This is why he included predefined variables called INPUT and OUTPUT. There is an automatic RESET done on file INPUT opening it for reading, and there is an automatic REWRITE done on file OUTPUT opening it for writing. In addition, if you don't include the file variable in a READ or READLN statement or an EOLN or EOF function call, Pascal will assume you mean INPUT. Thus the following are equivalent:

```
READ    (x, y);              READ    (INPUT, x, y);
READLN  (x, y);              READLN  (INPUT, x, y);
EOLN                         EOLN    (INPUT)
EOF                          EOF     (INPUT)
```

In a similar way, OUTPUT is the default file for writing, so these are equivalent:

```
WRITE    ('hi');             WRITE    (OUTPUT, 'hi');
WRITELN  ('ho');             WRITELN  (OUTPUT, 'ho');
```

11.3.1 File Window

Remember, TEXT files are similar to decks of cards. One text file property is similar to a rule common in card games. Once you take a card off the deck, you can't put it back. For files, this means that once you read something from a file, you can't put it back.

For this reason it is sometimes useful to know what the next character is before you read it. With a deck of cards you can cheat by peeking at the top card without removing it. You can do something similar in Pascal, peeking at the next character without actually reading it.

Let's look at something you can't do without this peeking capability. Suppose you want to write a procedure to skip any blanks in the input file but not to read in the nonblank that follows. Basically, you want to say

for (next group of blanks in input file) do
    read the blank.

The problem is trying to specify the test of this loop. Without the peeking capability, you can find out what character is next in the file only by actually reading it. Thus you would have to use your standard sentinel loop:

read a character.
while (character is a blank) do
     read another character.

In the deck analogy, this is like saying

take a card.
while (the card is blank) do
     take another card.

This method not only skips leading blanks, it also ends up reading the first nonblank. This method, then, is better described as obtaining a nonblank character. The Pascal code that would accomplish this is

```
PROCEDURE GetNonBlank (VAR NextChar : CHAR);
BEGIN
    READ (NextChar);
    WHILE (NextChar = ' ') DO
        READ (NextChar)
END;
```

This procedure might prove useful in some cases, but it's not what you set out to do. You set out to skip blanks on the input line, not to read an extra character.

To accomplish the skip blanks operation, you need the peeking ability. Every file has a window associated with it. The *file window* allows you to peek at the top card. In other words, the file window tells you what the input cursor is positioned at. So if input looks like this:

```
This is<eoln>Some input<eoln><eof>
          ↑
```

the character 'S' is currently in the file window. You can examine the value of the file window without moving the input cursor. In other words, you can look to see that you are positioned at 'S' before you decide whether or not to read it. The window for file INPUT is referenced by

```
INPUT^
```

You put the special up-arrow character after the file name to indicate the file window. Using this window, you can write your pseudocode properly:

while (a blank is in the file window) do
     skip the blank by reading it.

In the deck analogy, this is like saying

while (the top card is a blank) do
     discard the top card.

The big difference between this loop and the other is that when you encounter a nonblank character, you notice it by looking through the window (peeking at the top card) rather than reading the character in. In fact, this pseudocode might lead to no iterations of the loop at all. If the file window starts out with a nonblank, we do nothing.

Here is a procedure that implements this strategy:

```
PROCEDURE SkipBlanks;
VAR next : CHAR;
BEGIN
    WHILE (INPUT^ = ' ') DO
        READ (next)
END;
```

The SkipBlanks procedure is more widely applicable than GetNonBlank because it gives you the option of reading or not reading the nonblank character. Thus SkipBlanks is more versatile. In fact, GetNonBlank can be written in terms of SkipBlanks:

```
PROCEDURE GetNonBlank (VAR NextChar : CHAR);
BEGIN
    SkipBlanks;
    READ (NextChar)
END;
```

There are two subtleties of INPUT^. First, when the input cursor is positioned at the *<eoln>*, the value of INPUT^ will be a blank. Second, it is an error to inspect the value of INPUT^ when EOF is true. The combination of these two can be deadly. For example, suppose you have the following situation:

```
Stuff       <eoln>    <eoln> <eoln><eof>
     ↑
```

If you use INPUT^ to skip blanks, you will skip over all the blanks and all the *<eoln>*'s until you hit the *<eof>*. You will then reach an execution error. Also, you probably don't want your SkipBlanks procedure to be zooming past *<eoln>*'s anyway. If your data are line-oriented, for example, you don't want your program to skip over the *<eoln>* that marks the end of the current data line. The solution is to rewrite the SkipBlanks procedure with a second exit condition for the WHILE loop:

exit (if EOLN is true) or (if INPUT^ is not a blank)

By applying DeMorgan's law, you get

continue (if NOT EOLN) and (if INPUT^ is a blank)

Here is the rewritten procedure:

```
PROCEDURE SkipBlanks;
VAR next : CHAR;
BEGIN
    WHILE NOT EOLN AND (INPUT^ = ' ') DO
        READ (next)
END;    (* SkipBlanks *)
```

The `SkipBlanks` procedure is one of the most powerful tools you have seen. You should definitely add it to your software library in some form or other. It is a particularly helpful procedure for error checking of input files because you often want to move the file window to the first nonblank character so that you can tell whether or not the input looks okay.

11.3.2   File Variables as Parameters

Since files are defined as variables of a certain type, you shouldn't be surprised that they can be passed to a subprogram as a parameter. Since the various file operations all change either the status of the file or the position of the file cursor, all the file manipulations change the current value of the file variable. For this reason, you will almost always want to make file variables **VAR** parameters. Pascal makes this a bit more imperative by requiring that all file variables be passed as **VAR** parameters. This is one of those places where the added restriction makes the language a little easier to implement at the machine level.

As an example of a procedure with file parameters, let's rewrite the `Skip-Blanks` procedure so that you can use it to skip blanks in any input file:

```
PROCEDURE SkipBlanks (VAR InFile : TEXT);
VAR next : CHAR;
BEGIN
    WHILE NOT EOLN (InFile) AND (InFile^ = ' ') DO
        READ (InFile, next)
END;
```

Notice that all the file manipulations (EOLN, INPUT^, and READ) have to be fixed to refer to `InFile`. This version of the procedure is more adaptable because you can use it on any input file. For example, you can skip blanks in INPUT by saying

```
SkipBlanks (INPUT);
```

If you have input files called `in1` and `in2`, you can skip blanks in them by saying

```
SkipBlanks (in1);
SkipBlanks (in2);
```

11.4 NonTEXT Files

Before you explore Pascal's general notion of a file, you need to better understand type TEXT. Otherwise, you won't know when to use type TEXT and when to use the new file types you will examine. The elements of a file of type TEXT are all of type CHAR. However, you can use TEXT files to manipulate more than just characters. You can write out numbers and string constants and you can read in numbers.

Consider this input line:

    12+18

Chapter 6 described this line as having three elements: a number followed by a plus character followed by a number. This is not the way Pascal thinks of the line, though. The correct interpretation is that it has five characters that can be interpreted several ways. The digit characters can be interpreted either as characters or as parts of a number. Many interpretations are possible:

'1'	'2'	'+'	'1'	'8'
CHAR	CHAR	CHAR	CHAR	CHAR

12	'+'	18
INTEGER	CHAR	INTEGER

12	'+'	'1'	'8'
INTEGER	CHAR	CHAR	CHAR

This works because values of type INTEGER have an external character representation. They can be represented as sequences of characters. This external representation is readable by people, whereas the internal representation of an integer value is usually readable only by a computer. When you output integer values, you convert them from their internal machine format to their external character representation. When you tell Pascal to execute this statement:

    WRITELN ('Number = ', 349:1);

it first translates the string constant and number into characters:

```
WRITELN ('N', 'u', 'm', 'b', 'e', 'r', ' ', '=', ' ', '3', '4', '9');
```

Then it writes out the sequence of characters. Thus at the lowest level, the file is manipulated as a sequence of characters. This is why the file window, INPUT^, is a single character. Remember, by using the file window, you can look ahead one character.

The general file type declaration looks like this:

    FILE OF <component type>

For example,

```
TYPE IntegerFile = FILE OF INTEGER;
     RealFile    = FILE OF REAL;
     CharFile    = FILE OF CHAR;
     BooleanFile = FILE OF BOOLEAN;
```

These declarations define four file types, one to hold components for each of the simple primitive types. A declaration such as this defines the structure of a file. The actual data of a file are stored in a variable of appropriate type:

```
VAR  integers   : IntegerFile;
     reals      : RealFile;
     characters : CharFile;
     booleans   : BooleanFile;
```

If you store values in files such as these, they will not be stored as external character representations and will probably not be readable by humans. They will be stored in the machine's internal format.

The line-oriented operations (`READLN`, `WRITELN`, `EOLN`) are not available for general file structures, but the other operations are:

Operation	Purpose
RESET (*<file variable>*) ;	Open file for reading
REWRITE (*<file variable>*) ;	Open file for writing
READ (*<file variable>*, *<variables>*) ;	Read values from file
WRITE (*<file variable>*, *<variables>*) ;	Write values to file
EOF (*<file variable>*)	Test for end of file

Here is an example of an application where you might want to use a nonTEXT file. Suppose you are performing an experiment where you take a sequence of many temperature readings that you want to record somehow. One way to record them is to put one reading per line in a TEXT file:

```
74.5
73.8
72.9
 .  .  .
```

Another way to record them is by using a file of REAL numbers:

```
TYPE RealFile = FILE OF REAL;
VAR  reals    : RealFile;
```

How would this work? Consider a program that prompts a user for a series of numbers and stores them in a file with the preceding structure. An execution should look something like this:

```
next temperature (RETURN to quit)? 73.234
next temperature (RETURN to quit)? 74.129
```

```
next temperature (RETURN to quit)? 77.243
next temperature (RETURN to quit)? 78.334
next temperature (RETURN to quit)?
```

Here is a program that performs this task:

```
PROGRAM StoreTemperatures (INPUT, OUTPUT, temperatures);
TYPE RealFile        = FILE OF REAL;
VAR  temperatures    : RealFile;
     NextTemperature : REAL;
     quit            : BOOLEAN;
BEGIN
    REWRITE (temperatures);
    REPEAT
        WRITE (OUTPUT, 'next temperature (RETURN to quit)? ');
        quit := EOLN (INPUT);
        IF NOT quit THEN
        BEGIN
            READLN (INPUT, NextTemperature);
            WRITE (temperatures, NextTemperature)
        END
    UNTIL quit
END.
```

Notice that for every file operation this program specifies what file to use, even when it uses the built-in files INPUT and OUTPUT. This makes the program easier to read. There are three files in the program: INPUT and OUTPUT for terminal interaction and temperatures for the file of temperatures. All three are included in the program header because all three are external files.

The program starts by opening the file temperatures for writing by calling REWRITE. The program then repeatedly prompts for a temperature and checks to see if the user wants to quit. If the user types RETURN immediately, it exits the loop in the main program. Otherwise, the program reads a REAL number from the terminal and writes this value to file temperatures. In reading from the terminal, the program converts the sequence of character's typed by the user to a REAL value in internal format that is stored in the variable NextTemperature. NextTemperature is written to the file temperatures, which will cause it to be written in internal format.

To see the contents of such a file, you would execute a program such as this:

```
PROGRAM WriteTemperatures (OUTPUT, temperatures);
TYPE RealFile        = FILE OF REAL;
VAR  temperatures    : RealFile;
     NextTemperature : REAL;
```

```
BEGIN
    RESET (temperatures);
    WHILE NOT EOF (temperatures) DO
    BEGIN
        READ (temperatures, NextTemperature);
        WRITELN (OUTPUT, NextTemperature:8:3)
    END
END.
```

Here is its output given the preceding log of execution:

```
73.234
74.129
77.243
78.334
```

You must weigh the advantages against the disadvantages when you decide whether or not to store a series of data items in a file that uses internal format.

There are three primary advantages to a file such as this stored in internal format. First, the file will probably take less space because the internal representation is often more compact than the character representation. Second, the file will take less time to READ and WRITE because no conversion between internal and external format is required. Finally, converting back and forth between internal and external format can introduce a loss in accuracy in numerical data. Thus this might lead to more accurate results.

There are some disadvantages that you should remember as well. First, because a file in internal format is not readable by people, you must write a program to examine its contents. This is often undesirable. Data can only be modified by a Pascal program, which is also undesirable, because often a data file is more easily modified by a text editing system. Finally, the data are not easily transferred from one computer to another when they are stored in internal format, because different computers tend to use different internal formats.

11.4.1   More on the File Window

You have seen how to use the window for a file of type TEXT to look ahead one character. The concept applies to general files as well. Every Pascal file has a window on the next data item in the file. The window is of the same type as the components of the file. For example, the file you examined in the last section was defined by

```
TYPE RealFile      = FILE OF REAL;
VAR  temperatures  : RealFile;
```

The file window for this file is referred to by putting an up-arrow after the file name:

`temperatures^`

This gives you a window on the next value to be read from the file. It is of type **REAL**, because the components of the file are of type **REAL**. Suppose the file initially has these components and that the input cursor is positioned at the first element of the file. At this point, the file window has the value 70.3, because that is the next value to be read.

```
70.3  71.5  72.0  72.4  73.6  74.5  74.6  74.5  74.2  74.1  73.8 <eof>
 ↑
```

As an example of how to use the file window, let's write a procedure for skipping zeros in an input file such as this. It parallels the procedure for skipping blanks in a **TEXT** file:

```
PROCEDURE SkipZerosIn (VAR reals : RealFile);
VAR number : REAL;
BEGIN
    WHILE (reals^ = 0.0) DO
        READ (reals, number)
END;
```

11.4.2 GET and PUT

The **READ** and **WRITE** operations are built on more primitive operations called **GET** and **PUT**. **GET** advances the file window when the file is open for reading, **PUT** advances the file window when the file is open for writing. The following statement:

```
READ (temperatures, number);
```

is defined to be equivalent to the following statements:

```
number := temperatures^;
GET (temperatures);
```

The **READ** operation is really two steps: use the value of the file window to give a value to a variable and move forward in the file. The **GET** operation by itself has no impact on any variables other than the file variable. It merely advances to the next element in the file.

You should be asking yourself, "Is this useful? Will I ever need to use one step of the **READ** operation without using the other?" Consider executing just the **GET**, eliminating the assignment statement step. If you do this repeatedly, you will advance the file window without remembering what you have passed by. Do you want to do that or not? You probably will, sometimes. The repeated **GET** operation is an easy way of skipping over parts of the input file that don't interest you. Thus this gives you another way of skipping. Here is a rewritten version of the `SkipBlanks` procedure that performs only the `GET` part of the `READ`, eliminating the need for a dummy variable:

```
PROCEDURE SkipBlanks (VAR InFile : TEXT);
BEGIN
    WHILE NOT EOLN (InFile) AND (InFile^ = ' ') DO
        GET (InFile)
END;    (* SkipBlanks *)
```

You can also use the `GET` operation to eliminate variables if you want to. Since you have a window on the file, you don't really need an extra variable to store values from the file. For example, one of your simple echoing operations was performed by

```
PROCEDURE EchoLine;
VAR next : CHAR;
BEGIN
    WHILE NOT EOLN DO
    BEGIN
        READ (next);
        WRITE (next)
    END
END;
```

Look at the `READ` and `WRITE` at the center of this procedure. If you expand those two statements using `GET`, you find

```
next := INPUT^;
GET (INPUT);
WRITE (next);
```

There is no reason that the `GET` has to happen before the `WRITE`, so you can change the order:

```
next := INPUT^;
WRITE (next);
GET (INPUT);
```

Now you can probably see that the variable **next** is not necessary. In the first two statements above, you move the value of `INPUT^` into **next** and then write out the value of **next**. Why not use `INPUT^` in the first place? This leads to

```
PROCEDURE EchoLine;
BEGIN
    WHILE NOT EOLN DO
    BEGIN
        WRITE (INPUT^);
        GET (INPUT)
    END
END;
```

Thus the GET procedure can eliminate some variables that would normally be used to store the next value read from the file.

PUT is the corresponding action for writing to a file.

```
WRITE (integers, number);
```

is defined as being equivalent to:

```
integers^ := number;
PUT (integers);
```

The two steps for the WRITE statement are: give the file window the indicated value and move forward in the file (i.e., put this component into the file and get ready to produce another).

The assignment statement is more intimately tied to PUT than it is to GET because the standard states that it is an error to perform a PUT when the file window is uninitialized. This means that there has to be some kind of assignment to the file window before the PUT happens. When the PUT does happen, the current value is pushed into the file and the file window again becomes uninitialized. Therefore, every PUT must be preceded by an assignment to the file window.

The repeated GET without assignment is useful for skipping over unwanted input. The repeated PUT without assignment is not only not useful, it is illegal. As noted above, you have to assign a value to the file window before you PUT, so there is no parallel application there. The other application of the GET was to remove the need for extra variables. There is a similar application of PUT, but it only really helps with highly structured files.

In conclusion, you shouldn't take GET and PUT very seriously. They may save a local variable here or there, but a local variable never hurt anyone. If you start using such procedures as GET and PUT that you don't understand well and for no really good reason, you're going to start creating unnecessary bugs in your programs. READ and WRITE give you all the functionality you need, and you should stick with them unless you want to become a master of Pascal trivia and obscure bugs.

11.5 Sets

A set is used in Pascal to store a collection of values all of one type. In this respect, a set is very much like an array or a file. However, a set has two important distinguishing properties. First, it does not keep track of repeated occurrences of a value. Each value is either in or not in the set. Second, it does not keep track of the order of elements. There is no concept that one appears first, another appears second, and so on. A set is merely a collection of values. A set type is defined very much like a file type, using the following syntax:

```
SET OF <component type>
```

as in

```
TYPE IntegerSet = SET OF INTEGER;
     CharSet    = SET OF CHAR;
     BooleanSet = SET OF BOOLEAN;
```

The type listed after the word OF defines the component type of the set. This is called the *base type* of the set. Thus these declarations define three set types, one to store components for each of the simple primitive types except type REAL. A declaration such as this defines the structure of a set. The actual values of a set are stored in a variable of the appropriate type:

```
VAR  integers    : IntegerSet;
     characters  : CharSet;
     booleans    : BooleanSet;
```

The base type must be ordinal. Remember, all the simple types you have seen are ordinal except type REAL. Another restriction on sets comes from the Pascal standard. Each Pascal implementation is allowed to put a limit on what types can be base types of a set. In particular, each implementation will choose a limit on the maximum size of the domain of a type used as the base type of a set. Here are a few different types that illustrate this point (assuming type CHAR is represented in ASCII):

Type	Kind	Domain	Values in domain
INTEGER	Primitive	-MAXINT..+MAXINT	2 * MAXINT + 1
BOOLEAN	Primitive	FALSE, TRUE	2
CHAR	Primitive	CHR (0)..CHR (127)	128
1..10	Subrange	1, 2, 3, 4, ..., 10	10
-20..+20	Subrange	-20, -19, ..., 19, 20	41
'A'..'Z'	Subrange	'A', 'B', ..., 'Y', 'Z'	26
'a'..'b'	Subrange	'a', 'b'	2

As you can see, since subrange types have restricted domains, they have a smaller number of values in the domain. This means that they are more likely to be usable as a base type of a set. Thus it is more likely that you will define sets using declarations such as the following:

```
TYPE  IntegerRange = 1..50;
      CharRange    = 'A'..'Z';
      IntegerSet   = SET OF IntegerRange;
      CharSet      = SET OF CharRange;
VAR   integers     : IntegerSet;
      characters   : CharSet;
```

This defines two sets, one that stores integers between 1 and 50 and one that stores characters between 'A' and 'Z'.

11.5.1 Set Operations

Sets are also structured types that have constants associated with them. You have been using them since chapter 6 when you first studied constants such as

```
['A'..'Z']
[1, 3, 5, 7, 9, 11]
```

These sets are constant in the sense that the elements of the set do not change. The first set above always contains the 26 uppercase letters. The second set always contains the odd integers between 1 and 11. One set constant you have not yet examined is the empty set, specified as

```
[]
```

The interesting property of this constant is that it is compatible with every set type. This means that you can assign any set variable to be the empty set, no matter what its type is.

Let's now look at the set operations. Suppose you define the following set variables:

```
VAR int1 : IntegerSet;
    int2 : IntegerSet;
    int3 : IntegerSet;
```

The simplest operation you can perform on such a variable is to assign it a constant value, as in

```
int1 := [1, 3, 5];
int2 := [2, 4, 6];
int3 := [1, 2, 3];
```

You can form more complicated set expressions by using the following operators:

Operator	Meaning	Example	Value
+	Union	int1 + int3	[1, 2, 3, 5]
-	Difference	int2 - int3	[4, 6]
*	Intersection	int1 * int3	[1, 3]

The union operator returns the set of elements that appears in either the first set or the second set. The difference operator returns the set of elements that appears in the first set but not in the second. The intersection operator returns the set of elements that appears in both the first set and the second set. Each operator takes two operands. The two operands must be sets of the same type. The result is a set of the same type. Thus you can form very complex expressions such as

```
int1 + (int2 * int3) - [4, 5, 6]
```

There are also two comparison operators available:

Operator	Meaning	Example	Value
<=	Subset	int1 <= int2	FALSE
>=	Superset	[1..10] >= [1..3]	TRUE

These relational operators behave as they do for other expressions, taking two operands (sets of the same type) and returning a BOOLEAN. The subset operation returns TRUE if and only if all elements of the first set are also in the second. The superset operation is the inverse, returning TRUE if and only if all elements of the second set are also in the first.

Finally, there is one other set operator that you have used with set constants but not with set variables or expressions:

<value>   IN   *<set expression>*

The value must be in the base type of the set expression. The result is of type BOOLEAN, TRUE if and only if the value appears in the set. Thus you have formed tests such as

```
(character IN ['a'..'z'])
```

More generally, you can form complex tests such as

```
((2 * 3 - 4 * 8 + 45) IN (int1 * int2 - int3))
```

There are no other built-in set operations. You can't, for example, READ or WRITE set values in a standard TEXT file.

These new set operators follow the same rules of precedence, even though they are used to specify operations that are quite different from numerical computations. Thus the levels of precedence are as follows:

Level	Name	Operators						
1	Negation	NOT						
2	Multiplicative	*	/	DIV	MOD	AND		
3	Additive	+	−	OR				
4	Relational	=	<>	<	>	<=	>=	IN

11.6 Packed Structures

You have seen type declarations such as the following:

```
TYPE list1 = ARRAY [1..10] OF CHAR;
```

In defining a structured type (ARRAY, RECORD, FILE, or SET), you can put the keyword PACKED before the structure name, as in

```
TYPE list2 = PACKED ARRAY [1..10] OF CHAR;
```

This language feature potentially provides memory savings in a program. Saying that you want a structure PACKED commands the compiler to try fitting it in in as little space as possible, even if it will then take more time to access. Thus you can sometimes gain memory efficiency at the cost of some time efficiency. Another drawback of PACKED structures is that you cannot pass any of their individual components as VAR parameters. For example, if you define a variable of type list2:

```
VAR OneList : list2;
```

you can do all the normal manipulations on the structured object OneList. This means that you can pass OneList as either a value or a VAR parameter. However, this is not true of the components of OneList. There are 10 components of OneList:

```
OneList [1]
OneList [2]
     . . .
OneList [10]
```

Each of these is of type CHAR. You can perform most of the operations of type CHAR on these components, but you cannot pass one of these components as a VAR parameter to a procedure. For example, if you have an uppercasing procedure with the following header:

```
PROCEDURE TurnToUppercase (VAR OneChar : CHAR);
```

you cannot pass any of the components of OneList to this procedure. In other words, you can't say:

```
TurnToUppercase (OneList [1]);
TurnToUppercase (OneList [2]);
          . . .
TurnToUppercase (OneList [10]);
```

This limitation does not apply to value parameters. You can pass the individual elements of the packed structure as value parameters.

Keep in mind that the effect of packing a type varies from Pascal to Pascal. Many systems don't do anything for a packed type. Thus you might be asking for trouble by packing a structure.

Another thing to remember is that packing is effective only when individual components do not take much space to store in memory. There are only 128 characters in ASCII, so it is not difficult to encode them in a small amount of space. INTEGERs, however, have a much wider range. Therefore, it is almost never worthwhile to pack a structure of INTEGER components. The same is true of REALs. It is not, however, true of BOOLEANs, enumerated types, and subrange types. A good rule to follow if you want to pack some of your structures is to find those whose component type has a small domain. It is not worth packing a structure with a large domain.

11.6.1   String Types

Pascal has a special type called a *string* that has some useful properties. Pascal defines a string as "a packed array of CHAR whose lower index is 1 and whose higher index is greater than 1." The following are all string types:

```
TYPE string10 = PACKED ARRAY [1..10] OF CHAR;
     string20 = PACKED ARRAY [1..20] OF CHAR;
     string30 = PACKED ARRAY [1..30] OF CHAR;
     string40 = PACKED ARRAY [1..40] OF CHAR;
```

The following are not strings:

```
TYPE UnPacked = ARRAY [1..10] OF CHAR;
     BadIndex = PACKED ARRAY [100..200] OF CHAR;
```

The most interesting property of strings is that they have constants associated with them. In fact, you have been using constants of type string since Chapter 1. The following are all string constants of the type string10:

```
'Hillary   '
'Martin    '
'Long Words'
'short     '
```

In other words, any string constant with 10 characters in it is considered to be of the type

```
PACKED ARRAY [1..10] OF CHAR;
```

More generally, a string constant of length n is considered to be of type

```
PACKED ARRAY [1..n] OF CHAR;
```

String constants have to match exactly in length for them to be considered in the domain of a given string type. Therefore, if you use type string20 defined above, you must be sure to make all your constants of that type exactly 20 characters long. If you don't, you will get a compiler error.

The other interesting properties of string constants are that they can be compared like simple types and can be written out. You can compare two strings of the same type using the standard relational operators, as in

```
('Hillary    ' < 'Wilson     ')
```

or

```
('James      ' > 'Jameson    ')
```

The computer uses what is called *lexicographic order*, which means that it orders things the way people alphabetize things. For example, in comparing 'Hillary' to 'Wilson', you notice that the first letters are different. This means that the first letters determine the order: in this case, 'H' is less than 'W', so 'Hillary' is less than 'Wilson'.

With 'James' and 'Jameson', the first five characters are all the same. Therefore, you use the sixth character to determine the order. The sixth character of the first is a space, and the sixth character of the second is a lowercase 'o'. In ASCII, the space comes first; this means that 'James' is less than 'Jameson'.

Just as you can write out string constants:

```
WRITELN ('This is a string.');
WRITELN ('And so is this.');
```

you can write out string variables:

```
VAR string1 : string20;
    string2 : string30;
BEGIN
    string1 := 'Hillary Wilson       ';
    string2 := 'On the good ship lollipop      ';
    WRITELN (string1);
    WRITELN (string2);
END.
```

When you write out string variables, all components of the variable are output unless you specify otherwise. You are allowed to specify a field width which you can use to truncate the right-most characters of the string. For example, the variable **string1** above has 14 characters in it with 6 spaces as padding at the end. If you want to output just the 14 characters, you would say

```
WRITELN (string1:14);
```

11.7 Key Concepts

- Enumerated types allow you to create your own simple types that take on any values you specify. You therefore have great flexibility in building a new simple type and can add significantly to the readability of a program.

- You can define variables that correspond to files and can pass file variables as parameters to subprograms. The simple file processing you have done before was made possible by built-in properties of the predefined file variables INPUT and OUTPUT.

- A file variable can be initialized for reading with the RESET command or initialized for writing with the REWRITE command. Each file has a window associated with it. When a file is opened for reading, the file window keeps track of the next element to be read. When opened for writing, the file window keeps track of the next element to be written.

- NonTEXT files can be defined for storing files with elements of any type. Such files are usually stored in the internal format of the computer. This kind of storage can often lead to smaller files and faster access time, but it is more difficult to manipulate such a file outside of the program.

- You can define a structured type called a set, all elements of which are of the same ordinal type. The elements of a set are not ordered and the number of occurrences of each value is not stored. Thus, each value of the base type is either in or not in the set.

- PACKED structures can sometimes save storage space on the computer, but they usually lead to slower execution.

- A PACKED ARRAY OF CHAR with a low index of 1 is called a string type in Pascal and has special properties, including constants of the type, direct comparison of values, and the ability to write out values of the type.

11.8 Self-Check Exercises

1. Using type DayType from Section 11.2, write a FUNCTION NthDay with the following specification:

    ```
    FUNCTION NthDay (n : INTEGER) : DayType;
    (* post   : Returns the nth day of the week, Monday = 1, *)
    (*         : Tuesday = 2, ..., Sunday = 7.               *)
    (* errors : If n < 1 or n > 7, returns Monday.           *)
    ```

2. Again using type DayType, write procedure WriteDay with the following specification. Given this procedure, write some code that will write out the days of the week, one per line, from Monday to Sunday.

```
PROCEDURE WriteDay (day : DayType);
(* post : Value of day is written to OUTPUT as 'Monday,' *)
(*      : or 'Tuesday' or 'Wednesday,' etc.              *)
```

3. The people who maintain your computer system guaranty that `PACKED` structures save a significant amount of space in your Pascal environment. Yet you can't seem to get any savings in the declarations below, not even when you `PACK` both `DateType` and `DateList`. Why not?

```
TYPE  DateType  = PACKED RECORD
               month  : INTEGER;
               day    : INTEGER;
               year   : INTEGER
           END;
      DateList  = PACKED ARRAY [1..5000] OF DateType;
```

4. Is this a string type? If so, what are some examples of constants of this type?

```
TYPE String = PACKED ARRAY [1..1] OF CHAR;
```

5. What Pascal types does this string belong to?

```
'Isn''t it two o''clock?'
```

6. What is the output of the following program?

```
PROGRAM FileStuff (OUTPUT);
TYPE BoolFile = FILE OF BOOLEAN;
VAR  DataFile : BoolFile;
     number  : INTEGER;
     next    : BOOLEAN;

BEGIN
    REWRITE (DataFile);
    WRITE (DataFile, TRUE);
    WRITE (DataFile, FALSE);
    REWRITE (DataFile);
    FOR number := 1 TO 10 DO
        WRITE (DataFile, (number MOD 2 = 0) OR (number MOD 3 = 0));
    RESET (DataFile);
    WHILE NOT EOF (DataFile) DO
    BEGIN
        READ (DataFile, next);
        WRITELN (OUTPUT, next)
    END
END.
```

7. Using `SkipBlanks` and the file window, write a procedure with the following specification that will safely read an integer from a file. In other words, the procedure is

supposed to make sure that the input cursor isn't positioned before garbage characters such as 'XYZZY' that would generate an error if read as an integer. Keep in mind that you know it is safe to read an INTEGER if you are positioned at a digit.

```
PROCEDURE SafeIntRead (VAR InFile : TEXT;
                       VAR number : INTEGER;
                       VAR okay   : BOOLEAN);
(* pre    : InFile is open for reading and EOF is not TRUE.      *)
(* post   : Leading blanks are skipped, a sign (if present) is   *)
(*         : skipped, if it safe to read an integer at that point, *)
(*         : then the integer is read and returned in Number with *)
(*         : okay set to TRUE (making appropriate adjustments if a *)
(*         : sign was read).  If it is not safe to read an INTEGER *)
(*         : then Number is set to 0 and Okay is set to FALSE.    *)
```

8. Assuming the declaration

   ```
   TYPE IntFile = FILE OF INTEGER;
   ```

   how do you characterize the task being performed by the following PROCEDURE?

   ```
   PROCEDURE Mystery (VAR file1, file2 : IntFile);
   BEGIN
       RESET (file1);
       REWRITE (file2);
       WHILE NOT EOF (file1) DO
       BEGIN
           file2^ := ABS (file1^);
           PUT (file2);
           GET (file1)
       END
   END;
   ```

9. Given INTEGER variables X, Y, and Z, use sets to more elegantly express the following test:

   ```
   (x >= 1) AND (x <= 8) AND (y >= 1) AND (y <= 8) AND (z >= 1) AND (z <= 8)
   ```

10. Write a generic procedure EchoLine that uses file parameters to generalize the task of echoing a line of input. You should follow the specification given below. What call on EchoLine would echo a line of the standard INPUT file to the standard OUTPUT file?

```
PROCEDURE EchoLine (VAR InFile  : TEXT;
                    VAR OutFile : TEXT);
(* pre  : InFile open for reading, OutFile open for writing,      *)
(*       : NOT EOF (InFile).                                       *)
(* post : All characters on current input line of InFile echoed   *)
(*       : to OutFile; input cursor in InFile moved to beginning of *)
(*       : next input line; output cursor in OutFile moved to      *)
(*       : beginning of next output line.                          *)
```

11.   What is the output of the following program?

```
PROGRAM SetStuff (OUTPUT);
TYPE IntSet = SET OF 1..30;
VAR   set1   : IntSet;
      set2   : IntSet;
      set3   : IntSet;
      number : INTEGER;

PROCEDURE WriteSet (VAR ints : IntSet);
VAR number : INTEGER;
BEGIN
    FOR number := 1 TO 30 DO
        IF number IN ints THEN
            WRITE (number:3);
    WRITELN
END;

BEGIN
    set1 := [];
    set2 := [1..30];
    set3 := [1..30];
    FOR number := 1 TO 10 DO
    BEGIN
        set1 := set1 + [2 * number];
        set2 := set2 - [3 * number];
        set3 := set3 * ([1..(11 - number)] + set1)
    END;
    set1 := set1 - set2;
    set2 := set2 * set3;
    set3 := (set1 + set2) * set3;
    WriteSet (set1);
    WriteSet (set2);
    WriteSet (set3)
END.
```

11.9 Programming Problems

1.   Write a program that compares two input files for equality, reporting any line pairs that differ. Such a program is provided by most operating systems. It is usually used to verify that two files are identical or to pinpoint minor differences between an earlier and a later version of a file. Instructors sometimes use such programs to see whether a student has cheated by copying another student's program.

You should build in program constants to specify whether blank lines, spaces, and the case of words should be ignored. This program is supplied with two input files and produces one output file. The output file should contain notations such as

```
file 1, line 13: FUNCTION IsEqual (word1, word2 : WordType) : BOOLEAN;
file 2, line 13: FUNCTION Equal (word1, word2 : WordType) : BOOLEAN;
```

If all lines match, the output file should simply report that the files are equal.

2. This assignment is based on a party game called MadLibs. It involves reading from both a file and a terminal and writing to both a file and a terminal. The program is given an input file with a story in it. The story has various identified holes that need to be filled in. For example, the input file might look like this:

```
Dear [significant other],
     It's really late, and this place is really [adjective].  I wish I
could [verb].  Hopefully my program will [verb] soon.
                     Love and [plural noun],
                     [name]
```

Everything in brackets is to be filled in by the user. But the user isn't shown the surrounding text, only the words that appear inside brackets. The user interaction will go like this:

```
Okay, let's fill in the pieces of another MadLib. . .

significant other? Mike
adjective? zesty
verb? chew
verb? crunch
plural noun? anchovies
name? Queen Elizabeth
```

Your program is to insert the user's responses in place of what appears in brackets. This yields an output file such as this:

```
Dear Mike,
     It's really late, and this place is really zesty.  I wish I
could chew.  Hopefully my program will crunch soon.
                     Love and anchovies,
                     Queen Elizabeth
```

The output file is often amusing. The level of amusement usually depends on how silly the user is in filling in the blanks. Your program should be able to process any Madlib data file, asking the user to fill in the blanks while it produces a Madlib output file. Your program does not have to display this output file. The user can be expected to display the output file after your program finishes executing.

3. Just for a moment, put yourself in the place of a secretary who has to send out virtually the same letter to 50 different people. Suppose there are just 5 places where the various letters differ, but the secretary has to manually create the 50 different versions because his boss doesn't believe in impersonal form letters. Your task is to write some software to help the secretary out. Your program is going to take two files as input: a body file and a control file. The body file will contain the generic version of the letter. Those parts of the letter which change from version

to version will be indicated by including a name for the part inside <braces>, as in

```
                              December 11, 1986
<name>
<addr1>
<addr2>
<addr3>

Dear <nickname>,
  .   .   .
```

This file has five things to fill in, called name, addr1, addr2, addr3, and nickname. This is the file that will be processed many times, once for each different letter. The control file specifies the set of letters to create and the values to fill in for each, as in

```
name =Mr. James Smith
addr1 =3298 River Rd.
addr2 =Boulder, CO   28473
nickname =Jimmy

name =Ms. Jacqueline Reedy
  .   .   .
```

The control file should be executed as follows. Your program should read the lines of the file until it reaches a blank line. Each line will be of the form

```
name =value
```

You should read and record both the name and the value stored on each line. When you encounter a blank line, you are to generate a copy of the body file. As you go through the body file, echo anything not in braces. If you find something in braces, see if you have a recorded value for it. If not, fill it in with a blank. Otherwise, replace it with the value provided by the control file. For example, in processing the first letter, you will discover that there is no value for addr3. This is fine, just leave it blank in the output file. But filling in the other pieces, you should get

```
                              December 11, 1986
Mr. James Smith
3298 River Rd.
Boulder, CO   28473


Dear Jimmy,
  .   .   .
```

Once you have finished echoing the body file, you should return to the control file and repeat the process for the next letter. The last entry in the control file will be terminated by a blank line and then an EOF.

One area for improvement that you might consider is checking for errors and reporting them to the user. This could be done one of several ways. Your program could report errors to the terminal, so that the person running the program will be warned about a potential problem. Or your program might generate another output file, one listing errors and warnings.

4. A Keyword In Context (KWIC) index is an alphabetical listing of words (the keywords) including the context in which the keywords appear. Usually, by *context* we mean the entire line in which the word appears. Often KWIC indexes are used to list the titles of scientific articles.

Usually in a KWIC index there are certain words that are not considered keywords, including common articles and prepositions such as "a," "the," "for," "to," etc. The words that remain (shown in the example below in all capitals) are words that should be indexed:

```
STRANGER in a STRANGE LAND
GLORY ROAD
The MAN WHO SOLD the MOON
The MOON is a HARSH MISTRESS
```

Place every keyword in the same position in the center of the line. If two lines appear with the same keyword (e.g., MOON), it doesn't matter which line is printed first:

```
                    GLORY Road
        The Moon is a HARSH Mistress
Stranger in a Strange LAND
                The MAN Who Sold the Moon
   The Moon is a Harsh MISTRESS
 The Man Who Sold the MOON
                The MOON is a Harsh Mistress
            Glory ROAD
        The Man Who SOLD the Moon
    Stranger in a STRANGE Land
                STRANGER in a Strange Land
        The Man WHO Sold the Moon
```

Write a program to read a file and produce a KWIC index of the lines contained there. The file will contain a list of titles or phrases to index, with one entry per line, each no longer than 60 characters.

A second input file will supply you with the list of words that you should ignore when it comes to making the index. Several such words might appear on each line of the file, as in

```
in a
the is a for of
```

Your program should capitalize the keywords, as in the example above, but should not change the case of the other words.

5. You are going to write a program that runs a game of interactive bingo. Your program should start by explaining to the users what will happen and should ask how many players will be participating and what their names are. Suppose just two players named Sue and Bob are going to play. You should give each of them $1000 to start with. Then you will repeat the process of playing a set of bingo cards, taking bets from each player and tallying the results of a round, until the players no longer wish to continue.

Playing a set of bingo cards involves doing the following. First, your program makes the bingo cards. A bingo card looks like this:

```
+----+----+----+----+----+
| 24 |  8 | 23 |  1 |  3 |
| 27 | 20 |  4 |  9 | 25 |
|  2 | 18 | 37 | 22 | 30 |
| 17 | 32 | 39 | 28 |  6 |
| 12 | 10 | 29 | 11 | 34 |
+----+----+----+----+----+
```

It has 25 squares, each with a number. The numbers are chosen at random from some predetermined range (in this case, from 1 to 50). No two squares are allowed to have the same number. Each player gets a bingo card such as this one generated at random by the computer. Then the round begins. The computer picks at random one of the numbers in the predetermined range. Suppose it picks 12. Since 12 appears on the card above, imagine covering it up (in fact, your program will take care of this for the user). Then the computer picks a different number from the range. Maybe it chooses 40. It doesn't appear on the card above, so the card doesn't change. Then the computer picks another number, and another, and another. Eventually Sue and Bob find themselves in a situation such as this:

```
                  Sue                                          Bob
+----+----+----+----+----+              +----+----+----+----+----+
| 24 |  8 | 23 |  1 |  3 |              | -- | 11 | -- | -- |  8 |
| 27 | -- |  4 | -- | -- |              | 14 | -- | -- |  2 | -- |
|  2 | -- | 37 | -- | -- |              | 36 | -- | 31 | 23 | -- |
| -- | 32 | 39 | -- | -- |              |  4 | 27 | 10 | -- | 35 |
| -- | 10 | -- | 11 | -- |              |  3 | -- | -- | 37 | -- |
+----+----+----+----+----+              +----+----+----+----+----+
```

Many numbers have been picked and many of the squares on the cards are covered up. Eventually one of the players will get five squares in a row that are covered up. That player wins. In fact, if the next number called is 31, then Bob wins with a diagonal five-in-a-row coming from the upper-left corner to the lower-right corner. If the number is instead 3, then Sue wins with five-in-a-row covered up in her fifth column.

As soon as a player gets a five-in-a-row (called a BINGO), the cards are put away. The player who gets a bingo first wins whatever he or she bet. If more than one player gets a bingo simultaneously, all of them win whatever they bet. Those who don't have a bingo when the round is over lose whatever they bet. After tallying the results of this round, your program should ask whether the players wish to continue. If they do, you should prompt for each player's bet, generate more bingo cards, and start another round.

Your program is to play round after round with the users until they report that they don't want to continue. Your program shouldn't let a player bet more money than he or she has, but if a player goes bankrupt (down to $0), the bank should lend him or her an extra $1000. When the players report that they no longer wish to play, the program should show a summary of how much each player ended up with, taking into account any $1000 loans made from the bank.

The game is in some sense completely determined by the computer, since it generates the original cards and picks the series of numbers in each round. In fact, the computer could run the round without interacting with the users at all. But this is not polite. As your program chooses new numbers to be covered up on the bingo cards, it should pause and say something such as this:

```
                  Sue                                          Bob
    +----+----+----+----+----+              +----+----+----+----+----+
    | 24 |  8 | 23 |  1 |  3 |              | -- | 11 | 29 | -- |  8 |
    | 27 | 20 |  4 | -- | -- |              | 14 | -- | -- |  2 |  6 |
    |  2 | -- | 37 | -- | -- |              | 36 | -- | 31 | 23 | -- |
    | -- | 32 | 39 | -- |  6 |              |  4 | 27 | 10 | -- | 35 |
    | -- | 10 | 29 | 11 | -- |              |  3 | -- | -- | 37 | -- |
    +----+----+----+----+----+              +----+----+----+----+----+

Next bingo number = 20 (hit RETURN to continue). . .
```

This program poses challenging data-manipulation problems. For example, how will you write an algorithm that looks at a bingo card to see whether it has a bingo? Sets provide a nice solution. You basically translate the bingo card into its 12 five-in-a-rows (5 rows, 5 columns, 2 diagonals) and make a set out of each. Given this card:

```
    +----+----+----+----+----+
    | 24 |  8 | 23 |  1 |  3 |
    | 27 | 20 |  4 |  9 | 25 |
    |  2 | 18 | 37 | 22 | 30 |
    | 17 | 32 | 39 | 28 |  6 |
    | 12 | 10 | 29 | 11 | 34 |
    +----+----+----+----+----+
```

you would construct the following 12 sets:

```
Row 1   [24,  8, 23,  1,  3]        Col 1   [24, 27,  2, 17, 12]
Row 2   [27, 20,  4,  9, 25]        Col 2   [ 8, 20, 18, 32, 10]
Row 3   [ 2, 18, 37, 22, 30]        Col 3   [23,  4, 37, 39, 29]
Row 4   [17, 32, 39, 28,  6]        Col 4   [ 1,  9, 22, 28, 11]
Row 5   [12, 10, 29, 11, 34]        Col 5   [ 3, 25, 30,  6, 34]
Diag 1  [24, 20, 37, 28, 34]        Diag 2  [12, 32, 37,  9,  3]
```

These 12 sets keep track of the potential bingos. As your program picks new numbers to be covered up on the cards, it should keep the numbers in a set. If you do that, it is very easy to decide whether a given five-in-a-row has been finished. You merely test to see whether the set corresponding to that five-in-a-row is a subset of the set of numbers chosen by the computer. If it is, then you've found a bingo.

Don't be misled by this different view of a bingo card. Your program should use this different view for manipulating the card, but it shouldn't abandon the other view of the card as a 5 by 5 grid of numbers. The user expects to communicate using that view of the card, so your program must maintain both views. There is no reason that your program can't use one view of the bingo card for calculations and another view of the card for user interaction.

12

EXTRA PASCAL CONTROL TOPICS

12.1 Introduction

This chapter covers control structures. You will examine two: an alternative to the WHILE loop and an alternative to the IF/THEN/ELSE statement. Next, you will study the concept of scope: where various definitions are valid in a program. Scope rules are important to your understanding of how Pascal programs work. After you understand scope, you will again consider functions, looking at ways to guaranty that they return a value and exploring the dangers of functions with side effects.

12.2 CASE Statements

The IF/THEN/ELSE statement provides a two-way branch in program execution. You can use a single test to distinguish between two different statements that you might want to execute. The obvious generalization allows more than two branches since you might want to branch in one of many different directions depending on the value of a variable. For example, the following program reports an insurance company's policy about tickets:

```
(* parameters : OUTPUT-out.                                           *)
(* post       : Output file reports punishments for various numbers of *)
(*            : traffic tickets.                                       *)
```

```
PROGRAM Tickets (OUTPUT);
CONST MaxTickets = 5;          (* maximum number of tickets        *)
VAR   count      : INTEGER;    (* loop counter for number of tickets *)

PROCEDURE ReportPunishmentFor (NumberOfTickets: INTEGER);
(* parameters : NumberOfTickets-in.                                      *)
(* post       : punishment for NumberOfTickets is reported to output file. *)
BEGIN
    IF (NumberOfTickets = 0) THEN
        WRITELN ('It is a joy to have you as a customer.')
    ELSE
        IF (NumberOfTickets = 1) THEN
            WRITELN ('Everybody makes mistakes, no premium change.')
        ELSE
            IF (NumberOfTickets IN [2, 3]) THEN
                WRITELN ('You are a bad driver, premium increased 10%.')
            ELSE
                IF NumberOfTickets = 4 THEN
                    WRITELN ('You are dangerous, premium increased 50%.')
                ELSE
                    WRITELN ('You are reckless, we cancel your policy.')
END;    (* ReportPunishmentFor *)

BEGIN   (* main program *)
    FOR count := 0 TO 5 DO
    BEGIN
        WRITE ('For ', count:1, ' tickets:  ');
        ReportPunishmentFor (count)
    END
END.    (* main program *)
```

Here is its output:

```
For 0 tickets:  It is a joy to have you as a customer.
For 1 tickets:  Everybody makes mistakes, no premium change.
For 2 tickets:  You are a bad driver, premium increased 10%.
For 3 tickets:  You are a bad driver, premium increased 10%.
For 4 tickets:  You are dangerous, premium increased 50%.
For 5 tickets:  You are reckless, we cancel your policy.
```

The nested **IF/THEN/ELSE** structure provides five different branches, but it is clumsy. Pascal provides an alternative:

```
CASE NumberOfTickets OF
    0    : WRITELN ('It is a joy to have you as a customer.');
    1    : WRITELN ('Everybody makes mistakes, no premium change.');
    2, 3 : WRITELN ('You are a bad driver, premium increased 10%.');
    4    : WRITELN ('You are dangerous, premium increased 50%.');
    5    : WRITELN ('You are reckless, we cancel your policy.')
END;
```

This **CASE** statement is controlled by the variable **NumberOfTickets**. Depending on its value, you execute one of five different statements. This is a more readable format.

The general form of the **CASE** statement is

```
CASE <expression> OF
    <value list> : <statement>;
    <value list> : <statement>;
              . . .
    <value list> : <statement>
END
```

There is a single expression that controls the branching of the **CASE** statement. Each branch has a series of values associated with it. All values must be constants. You cannot use variables or complex expressions as values of a **CASE** branch. If there is more than one value, the values are separated by commas. After the values for a single branch, a single statement appears. A colon separates the values from the statement. Different branches are separated by semicolons. You use the keyword "END" to indicate the end of the list of branches. There is no corresponding **BEGIN** for this **END**. This is one of only two places in Pascal where an **END** has no **BEGIN** associated with it.

Each branch has only a single statement. You can include more than one, however, by using a **BEGIN/END** block, as you have all along. **BEGIN/END** blocks embedded in **CASE** statements are particularly ugly, however. In the insurance example, for instance, suppose you want to not only report the punishment, but also take the action. Because many of the branches involve a second step, the action to be performed, you end up with something such as this:

```
CASE NumberOfTickets OF
    0    : WRITELN ('It is a joy to have you as a customer');
    1    : WRITELN ('Everybody makes mistakes, no premium change');
    2, 3 : BEGIN
             WRITELN ('You are a bad driver, premium increased 10%');
             premium := premium * 0.10
           END;
    4    : BEGIN
             WRITELN ('You are dangerous, premium is increased 50%');
             premium := premium * 0.50
           END;
```

```
    5    : BEGIN
             WRITELN ('You are reckless, we cancel your policy');
             CancelService
           END
END;
```

This code is highly unreadable. It is also difficult to maintain, especially when there are many CASE branches. The BEGIN/END pairs also lead to frequent problems because the CASE itself has an END with no BEGIN. A better solution is to create procedures for these two-step branches:

```
CASE NumberOfTickets OF
    0    : WRITELN ('It is a joy to have you as a customer.');
    1    : WRITELN ('Everybody makes mistakes, no premium change.');
    2, 3 : DealWith2or3 (premium);
    4    : DealWith4 (premium);
    5    : DealWith5
END;
```

12.2.1 Limitations of CASE

There are some restrictions on CASE. First, the expression that controls a CASE must be of an ordinal type. You can't have CASE statements that depend on REAL-valued expressions or on structured types. However, you can have CASE statements that depend on expressions of type CHAR. A typical CASE using a character follows. It uses seven different values to distinguish four branches.

```
WRITE ('command (? for help) ---> ');
READLN (command);
CASE command OF
    'i', 'I' : insert;
    'p', 'P' : print;
    'd', 'D' : delete;
    '?'      : GiveInstructions
END;
```

Another restriction on the CASE statement is that no value can be duplicated. You can't, for example, say

```
CASE command OF
    'i', 'p', 'd' : UpperCase (command);
    'i', 'I'      : insert;
    'p', 'P'      : print;
    'd', 'D'      : delete;
    '?'           : GiveInstructions
END;
```

The problem with this CASE statement is that the lowercase letters appear in the first branch and in later branches. The purpose of the CASE statement is to execute exactly one of the branches, so you can't have a single value appearing in the list of more than one branch.

Another restriction on the CASE statement is that the controlling expression, when evaluated, must match one of the branches. The CASE statement used to report punishment for different numbers of tickets, for example, has five different branches that specify six values, 0 through 5. This CASE statement has no branch for numbers less than 0 nor for numbers greater than 5. Executing the CASE statement with a number outside this range is an error.

This error, however, is treated differently by different systems. Some systems will merely skip the CASE statement if no branch matches. Other systems generate warnings but not errors. Yet other systems generate execution errors. There are many ways around the error. Some Pascal systems extend the syntax of the CASE statement to allow you to say something such as this:

```
CASE NumberOfTickets OF
    0       : WRITELN ('It is a joy to have you as a customer.');
    1       : WRITELN ('Everybody makes mistakes, no premium change.');
    2, 3    : WRITELN ('You are a bad driver, premium increased 10%.');
    4       : WRITELN ('You are dangerous, premium increased 50%.');
    ELSE      WRITELN ('You are reckless, we cancel your policy.')
END;
```

The final branch of this CASE statement is like the ELSE branch of the IF/THEN/ELSE. It says: "If none of the previous values match, use this statement instead." This is not standard Pascal, but most Pascal systems have an extension such as this. Some use the keywords OTHERS or OTHERWISE.

If your Pascal system does not have such an extension, or if you want to stick to standard Pascal, there is a way out. You can put this CASE inside an IF/THEN/ELSE and move the extra branch outside of the CASE:

```
IF (NumberOfTickets IN [0..4]) THEN
    CASE NumberOfTickets OF
        0       : WRITELN ('It is a joy to have you as a customer.');
        1       : WRITELN ('Everybody makes mistakes, no premium change.');
        2, 3    : WRITELN ('You are a bad driver, premium increased 10%.');
        4       : WRITELN ('You are dangerous, premium increased 50%.');
    END
ELSE
    WRITELN ('You are reckless, we cancel your policy.')
```

The CASE statement has some functionality that the IF/THEN/ELSE does not. It lets you express a series of branches using a single controlling expression. The inverse question is interesting as well. Are there applications of the

IF/THEN/ELSE that cannot be done easily with a CASE? The answer is yes and no.

Consider this nested IF/THEN/ELSE:

```
IF number < 0 THEN
    WRITELN ('negative')
ELSE
    IF number = 0 THEN
        WRITELN ('zero')
    ELSE
        WRITELN ('positive')
```

This is a nested IF/THEN/ELSE construct with three branches. Can you express it using a CASE statement? To do so, you would have to come up with an expression that returns one of three different values depending on the sign of the number. You can't come up with such an expression given the tools that you now possess. This would imply, then, that IF/THEN/ELSE statements are more powerful than CASE statements.

There is a way, though. Remember that type BOOLEAN is an ordinal type. This means that you can have CASE statements controlled by BOOLEAN expressions whose branches are specified by BOOLEAN constants. In other words, you can say

```
CASE <boolean expression> OF
    TRUE  :  OneThing;
    FALSE :  AnotherThing
END;
```

This CASE statement, however, is equivalent to

```
IF <boolean expression> THEN
    OneThing
ELSE
    AnotherThing;
```

You can reduce the IF/THEN/ELSE to a CASE and nest CASE statements just as you nest IF/THEN/ELSE statements. Thus you can write the preceding example as follows. There is nothing that you can construct with the IF/THEN/ELSE that you couldn't construct with the CASE.

```
CASE (number < 0) OF
    TRUE  : WRITELN (negative');
    FALSE : CASE (number = 0) OF
                TRUE  : WRITELN ('zero');
                FALSE : WRITELN ('positive')
            END
END;
```

There is another side to the argument, though. Nested IF/THEN/ELSE statements are easier to read than nested CASE statements. You can tell this just by looking at the example above. Therefore, you should continue to use IF/THEN/-ELSE statements except where you find yourself wanting one of many branches depending on some expression.

12.3 REPEAT Loops

You have already examined one indefinite loop, the WHILE loop. Pascal has a second loop that is sometimes more convenient to use. Its general syntax is

```
REPEAT
     <statement>;
     <statement>;

          . . .

     <statement>
UNTIL <test>
```

You don't need a BEGIN/END to nest several statements in a REPEAT loop. The REPEAT and UNTIL keywords mark the beginning and end, an unusual deviation for Pascal.

Just as with the WHILE loop, the test is specified by a BOOLEAN expression. As the wording suggests, however, the test has the reverse meaning. The WHILE loop's test is a continuation condition—you continue executing while the test returns TRUE. The REPEAT loop's test is an exit condition—you repeat execution until the exit condition becomes TRUE.

Finally, as the syntax suggests, the REPEAT loop performs its test at the bottom of the loop:

```
loop
     execute controlled statements.
     perform test.
     exit if test returns TRUE.
end of loop
```

This means that the REPEAT loop will always execute its contents at least once. The first test is not performed until after the first iteration.

Let's look at a concrete example to understand the implications of this. Here is a REPEAT loop that echoes characters:

```
REPEAT
     READ (next);
     WRITE (next)
UNTIL EOLN;
```

This loop is like the following WHILE loop:

```
WHILE NOT EOLN DO
BEGIN
     READ (next);
     WRITE (next)
END;
```

Since the test in the WHILE loop has the opposite meaning of the test in the REPEAT loop, it is not surprising that the REPEAT is formulated using EOLN, whereas the WHILE is formulated using the negation of that, NOT EOLN. As noted, the REPEAT loop requires no BEGIN/END. The major difference between these loops, however, is their behavior. Because the WHILE loop performs its test at the top of the loop, it is possible it won't execute its controlled statement at all. If EOLN is TRUE immediately (i.e., if you have a blank line), the WHILE loop does nothing. The REPEAT loop, however, would charge ahead in this case and try to READ and WRITE the EOLN character. Thus the only behavioral difference occurs on an empty input line.

The WHILE loop is the better one to use in this case because you don't want to try to echo empty lines. There are many applications where the REPEAT is more natural, however. Consider a sentinel loop where you want to actually echo the sentinel. There is no easy way to do this with a WHILE loop. You can't say

```
WHILE (NextChar <> sentinel) DO
BEGIN
    READ (NextChar);
    WRITE (NextChar)
END;
```

The problem with this loop is that it requires priming. What value does NextChar have the first time the loop is executed? You could fix this by assigning NextChar a value outside the loop, but the REPEAT loop offers a more elegant solution:

```
REPEAT
    READ (NextChar);
    WRITE (NextChar)
UNTIL (NextChar = sentinel);
```

The REPEAT is the better construct because you know that you always want to READ and WRITE at least one character, the sentinel. Therefore, this is the more natural construct to use for this loop. REPEAT loops can also be applied to terminal interaction. For example, if you want to write a program to play a game with the user, you would say

```
REPEAT
    PlayGame
UNTIL UserIsBored;
```

Presumably, the user wants to play the game at least once, so the REPEAT is appropriate.

12.4   Scope of Identifiers

In Chapter 3 you learned about lifetime, a concept that refers to execution. This section introduces a concept called *scope* that involves a static view of the program, a concept that pertains to the form rather than the action of a program.

Pascal affords you many opportunities to define new words. It even sometimes allows you to define the same word twice in a single program. Each definition that you make in a program is valid for some part of the program and not valid for other parts. You call the portion where the definition is valid the *scope* of the definition.

SCOPE OF AN IDENTIFIER

That portion of a program where the identifier's definition is valid.

You can describe scopes by mapping out different parts of a program listing. You can draw a box or set of boxes that enclose parts of the program and say, "This is the scope of that word. Here is where it is valid."

The major scopes of a program listing are determined by blocks. To map out the scopes, you draw a box around each block. You do not, however, include the headers in the boxes. Consider some complete programs and the scopes within them. Start with this short program that demonstrates some important concepts:

```
PROGRAM Simple  (OUTPUT);
  VAR number :  INTEGER;

  PROCEDURE DoubleNumber;
  VAR answer :  INTEGER;
  BEGIN
      answer := 2 * number;
      WRITELN ('Doubling ', number:1, ' yields ', answer:1)
  END;


  BEGIN
      WRITELN ('This program will double an integer.');
      WRITELN ('What integer should I use?  ');
      READLN (number);
      DoubleNumber
  END.
```

There can be scopes inside of scopes. The outer box is the scope of the program block. The inner box is the scope of the procedure block. First, consider the main program's point of view. Scope rules follow the principle of information hiding. The main program is not allowed to look inside the procedure's scope. As far as the main program is concerned, then, the inner box might as well be black. If you play this game for a moment and ignore the inner box, reading from top to bottom in the outer box, you see

```
VAR number : INTEGER;

PROCEDURE DoubleNumber;

BEGIN
   . . .
END.
```

Thus the declaration part of the program block defines two words: a variable called **number** and a procedure called **DoubleNumber**. These two are the only new words defined in the execution part of the program. The program block is complete in the sense that every object used in the execution part is defined in the declaration part. The scope boxes provide another way of seeing this. Put your pencil on a word in the main program that is not a keyword. Don't put your pencil on a word such as "BEGIN" or "WRITELN," put it on a word such as "number." Try to move your pencil to where **number** is defined without crossing any lines. You can do it. You can do this with **DoubleNumber** as well. Therefore, these references are all local: they are inside of this single scope.

Now consider things from the procedure's point of view. Inside the inner box you find a declaration part with a local definition for a variable called **answer**. In the execution part you find two non-Pascal keywords being used—"answer" and "number." **Answer** is a local definition, because playing your pencil game you can trace a path from it to its definition without crossing a scope boundary. But you can't do the same with **number**. To connect **number** with its definition, you have to cross a scope boundary and go to the outer box.

As you know, this is allowed. It is okay for procedure **DoubleNumber** to look outside to the main program to find a definition, even though the main program isn't allowed to look inside **DoubleNumber**. This is one of the basic principles of scope—you are always allowed to look out and never allowed to look in.

Thus the definition of variable **number** is valid everywhere in the program. Such variables are called *global variables*. The definition of variable **answer** is valid only inside the procedure. As you have already seen, such variables are called *local variables*.

What if a global variable and a local variable have the same name? Is that a conflict? Consider this simple program:

```
PROGRAM Questionable  (OUTPUT);
   VAR number :  INTEGER;

   PROCEDURE Work;
      VAR number :  INTEGER;
      BEGIN
         number := 12;
         WRITELN (number)
      END;


   BEGIN
      number := 10;
      work
   END.
```

By your simple rule, the scope of the global variable is the entire program. The scope of the local variable is obviously just the procedure. Outside the procedure (in the main program, for example), it is clear that the global variable is the only defined variable. But what about inside the procedure? Are both variable definitions valid there?

The answer is no. Within the procedure's scope, the local definition overrides the global definition. This means that the global variable really has a "hole" in its scope. It is valid everywhere except inside the procedure.

When this program executes, it will, for a time, have two different objects with the same name. Dynamic allocation ensures that the two objects will be distinct, that they won't interfere with one another. The only potential problem is the name confusion. The scope rules, however, clear up any such confusion.

It's like having a communal refrigerator and a private refrigerator. Both can exist, both can be used, both can be independent of each other, but they can cause confusion about what is meant by the word "refrigerator." The interpretation of that word will depend on where you are. If you are in a room with a refrigerator, you will assume that the name refers to the local refrigerator. Outside that room, however, or in a room without a refrigerator, you will assume that the word refers to the communal refrigerator. This is the same way the scope rules works.

Global and local variables of the same name, then, do not conflict with each other. This does not mean that conflicts do not arise. You can't, for example, introduce two meanings for the same word in the same scope. Consider the following program:

```
PROGRAM Illegal (OUTPUT);
   VAR work :   INTEGER;

   PROCEDURE Work;
   BEGIN
       WRITELN ('working');
   END;


   BEGIN
       work;
       work := 14;
       WRITELN (work);
   END.
```

The declaration part of the program defines a variable called **work** and a procedure called **work**. Since both definitions appear in the same scope, this is illegal because the computer has no way of knowing what is meant by **work**.

Another rule of scope is that words must be defined wherever they are used. As you have seen, Pascal requires that you declare every object that you use. When you use an undefined word, you get an error message such as "Identifier not declared." The error is detected at compile time, because it is an error in the form of the program. As you are learning the rules of scope, you might encounter this error even when a word has been defined somewhere else in the program. This can happen when you inadvertently define a word in the wrong place, so that the scope of the definition is not what you planned. In such a case, you should interpret the error message as "This identifier is not defined right here, even though it might be defined for some other part of the program."

Here is a summary of the rules of scope:

RULE ONE OF SCOPE

You cannot define a word more than once within the same scope (i.e., no ambiguity).

RULE TWO OF SCOPE

The most local (innermost) definition of a word takes precedence. If a word is not defined in a scope in which it is used, the computer looks outside this scope to the containing scope for the definition. If it doesn't find it there, it looks to the containing scope of that scope, and so on.

RULE THREE OF SCOPE

Application of rule two must eventually find a definition for every word in a program (i.e., no undefined words).

One curious thing about these scopes is the definition of the program title in the program header. It is not inside the big box that encloses the whole program. By convention, you say that the title of the program is a definition in an even larger scope. It would not be a conflict, then, to define a variable or procedure called `Figures` within a program entitled `Figures`.

12.4.1   A Confusing Scope Example

To make sure you understand the scope rules, let's study a more complex example:

```
PROGRAM Mystery  (OUTPUT);
    VAR a :   INTEGER;
        b :   INTEGER;

    PROCEDURE One;
    VAR b :   INTEGER;
    BEGIN
        a := 2;
        b := 3;
        a := a + b
    END;

    PROCEDURE Two;
    VAR a :   INTEGER;
    BEGIN
        a := 2;
        b := 3;
        b := a * b
    END;

    BEGIN
        One;
        Two;
        WRITELN (a, b)
    END.
```

The main program has definitions for variables A and B and for procedures One and Two. Inside the scope for procedure One is a local definition for a variable B. This local definition takes precedence over the definition of B as a global variable. Similarly, procedure Two has a definition for a variable A that takes precedence over the definition of the global variable A.

Procedure One makes reference to variable A without a local definition for A. Therefore, the computer looks outside this scope to the containing scope and connects this reference to the global variable A. Similarly, procedure Two makes a nonlocal reference to the global variable B.

Let's simulate the program. You start with the global variables A and B:

A | ? | B | ? |

When you call procedure One, a local variable called B is allocated:

A | ? | B | ? | B (local) | ? |

Scope rules tell you that the local variable B will be manipulated by this procedure, not the global variable. Thus the first two statements have this effect:

A | 2 | B | ? | B (local) | 3 |

The third has this effect:

A | 5 | B | ? | B (local) | 3 |

When you exit the procedure, the local variable goes away:

A | 5 | B | ? |

The global variable B is still uninitialized. When you call procedure Two, you allocate another local variable called A:

A ⬛ 5   B ⬛ ?   A (local) ⬛ ?

Again, scope rules tell you that the local variable **A** will be manipulated, not the global variable. The first two statements leave you with

A ⬛ 5   B ⬛ 3   A (local) ⬛ 2

And after the third, you have

A ⬛ 5   B ⬛ 6   A (local) ⬛ 2

When you exit the procedure, the local variable **A** goes away:

A ⬛ 5   B ⬛ 6

The output generated by this program is

5   6

The nonlocal references in this program make it hard to decipher. Because it is more difficult to see what is going on, you should try to avoid such references whenever possible.

12.4.2 Parameters and Scope

Another way of defining words is by using them as parameters. The big question for parameters is whether they are inside the scope of a procedure or outside it. The answer is inside.

Here is a variation of the **Boxes** program developed in Chapter 3:

```
PROGRAM DrawBoxes2  (OUTPUT);
VAR height :   INTEGER;
    width  :   INTEGER;

PROCEDURE WriteSpaces  (number:  INTEGER);
VAR count :  INTEGER;
BEGIN
    FOR count := 1 TO number DO
        WRITE (' ')
END;


PROCEDURE DrawLine  (width:  INTEGER);
VAR col :  INTEGER;
BEGIN
    WRITE ('+');
    FOR col := 1 TO (width - 2) DO
    WRITE ('-');
    WRITELN ('+')
END;


PROCEDURE DrawBox  (height, width:  INTEGER);
VAR row :  INTEGER;
BEGIN
    DrawLine (width);
    FOR row := 1 TO (height - 2) DO
    BEGIN
    WRITE ('|');
    WriteSpaces (width - 2);
    WRITELN ('|')
    END;
    DrawLine (width)
END;


BEGIN
    height := 10;
    width := 20;
    DrawBox (height, width);
    DrawBox (width, height)
END.
```

If you play the pencil game to match up words with definitions, you will find that the main program and procedures WriteSpaces and DrawLine all use local references. Procedure DrawBox is the only one that makes a nonlocal reference. Inside DrawBox are two calls on DrawLine and one on WriteSpaces. These words are not defined locally, they are defined in the main program's scope.

Since the parameters are inside the inner scopes, it is not a conflict to have global variables with the names height and width and parameters with the names height and width. To make this clearer, consider what happens on the two different calls of DrawBox. Before the procedure gets called, you will have allocated and initialized the global variables height and width:

height `10`   width `20`

When you first call DrawBox, you will create local copies of these variables in the value parameters height and width:

height (global var) `10`   width (global var) `20`

height (local copy) `10`   width (local copy) `20`

Lining up the first procedure call with the procedure header, you see that the global variable height corresponds to the value parameter height and the global variable width corresponds to the value parameter width. This is true because of the order in which the words appear, not because the words match. In particular, when you call DrawBox a second time with the parameters in reverse order, you make your copies in reverse order:

height (global var) `10`   width (global var) `20`

height (local copy) `20`   width (local copy) `10`

Height is now a local copy of the global variable width because in the second procedure call width appears as the first actual parameter and is matched with the first formal parameter—height.

12.4.3 Functions and Scope

The names of user-defined functions have an odd status. If you have a program that defines a function called **sign**, there are two different scopes, one for the program and one for the function, as indicated by the following program:

```
PROGRAM Sample  (OUTPUT);

FUNCTION Sign  (number:  REAL) : INTEGER;
BEGIN
    sign := 0;
    IF number < 0 THEN
        sign := -1;
    IF number > 0 THEN
        sign := 1
END;

BEGIN (* main program *)
    WRITELN (sign (34.5));
    WRITELN (sign (-74.8));
    WRITELN (sign (17))
END. (* main program *)
```

The scope boxes are drawn as they would be for a procedure, but that is not quite right. The function name has a dual syntactic purpose. It is, first of all, a definition in the scope in which it appears. Thus the outer scope (the main program) refers to **sign** in order to call the function. It is also, however, a definition in the scope that it defines. Inside the function definition, the name "**sign**" is used to assign a value to the function, to specify what value to return. The better way to draw the scope boxes would be to split the name in two, indicating that it is a definition in both scopes. This leads to ugly boxes, so I don't recommend it. However, you should remember this when answering questions of scope when a function is concerned. It would be a conflict, for example, to define a local variable called "**sign**" inside of function **sign**.

12.5 More on Functions

Now that you are writing more complicated programs that manipulate complex data structures, you should have occasion to use functions more often. As previously mentioned, Pascal requires that a function always return a value, and if it fails to do so, the bug will, in most Pascal systems, be difficult to locate.

Therefore, spend a little time reconsidering functions and examining techniques for avoiding such bugs.

Consider a function that returns the sign of a number. Call it **sign** and have it return −1 for negative numbers, 0 for 0, and +1 for positive numbers. Here's a flawed definition of the function:

```
FUNCTION Sign (number: REAL) : INTEGER;
BEGIN
    IF number < 0 THEN
        sign := -1
    ELSE
        IF number > 0 THEN
            sign := 1
END;
```

This kind of nested IF/THEN/ELSE statement executes at most one of the controlled statements. The final IF/THEN has no ELSE part to it, which means that there is conceivably a case where no statement is executed. This happens when number equals zero. Neither of the tests match, so neither of the assignment statements is executed, and the function terminates without specifying a value to be returned. This is the problem you want to avoid. One easy fix is to put in the extra ELSE branch:

```
FUNCTION Sign (number: REAL) : INTEGER;
BEGIN
    IF number < 0 THEN
        sign := -1
    ELSE
        IF number > 0 THEN
            sign := 1
        ELSE
            sign := 0
END;
```

This construct always executes exactly one of the controlled statements. This means that you can be sure that the function always returns a value. This kind of nested IF/THEN/ELSE construct, then, is useful in distinguishing what value to return for a function.

It is not, however, always convenient to form such a cleanly structured nested IF/THEN/ELSE. With a more complex function definition that does not fit this form, you have a more difficult time convincing yourself that it always returns a value.

Here is a more general-purpose fix. It takes advantage of the possibility to assign a value to the function more than once:

```
BEGIN
    <function name> := <default value>;
    . . .
    IF <something> THEN
        <function name> := <other value>;
    . . .
    IF <something else> THEN
        <function name> := <yet another value>;
    . . .
END
```

By starting the function with an assignment, you can assure yourself that the function will always return some default value. The rest of the function, then, can be devoted to calculating other possible values to return. You can apply this to the **sign** function by saying 0 is the default value to return:

```
FUNCTION Sign (number: REAL) : INTEGER;
BEGIN
    sign := 0;
    IF number < 0 THEN
        sign := -1;
    IF number > 0 THEN
        sign := 1
END;
```

This definition says, "Assume it's zero unless proven otherwise. If it's negative, return −1. If it's positive, return +1." You should use this strategy for more complex function definitions.

Here is an example of where the judgment of soundness is difficult to make. Consider the following definition of **sign**:

```
FUNCTION Sign (number: REAL) : INTEGER;
BEGIN
    IF number < 0 THEN
        sign := -1
    ELSE
        IF number > 0 THEN
            sign := 1
        ELSE
            IF number = 0 THEN
                sign := 0
END;
```

This nested IF/THEN/ELSE is like the flawed function definition above. There is an unspecified ELSE part for the final IF/THEN, which means that there is a possibility that none of the controlled statements will be executed. If you think about it, though, you will realize that one of the three cases listed must be true. There is no number which is nonnegative, nonpositive, and nonzero. Therefore, this function is not flawed. It will always return a value. Realizing this, however, requires a sophisticated observation, one a compiler is unable to make. Even human beings might find it difficult to convince themselves that this function is sound. I strongly recommend, therefore, that in your function definitions you either use the nested IF/THEN/ELSE that always executes exactly one function assignment or assign a default value to the function at the beginning of its execution.

As you have seen, some functions require you to define a local variable that is manipulated during the body of the function and is then returned as the value of the function. For example, consider the manipulations on the local variable fact in the following function:

```
FUNCTION Factorial (n: INTEGER): INTEGER;
VAR fact  : INTEGER;
    count : INTEGER;
BEGIN
    fact := 1;
    FOR count := 2 TO n DO
        fact := fact * n;
    factorial := fact
END;
```

This provides a third strategy for designing functions that will be guaranteed to return a value:

```
BEGIN
    . . .
    <manipulate local variable>
    . . .
    <function name> := <local variable>
END
```

You still must be cautious to assign a value to the local variable, however, so the techniques of the last section might prove useful. For example,

```
BEGIN
    <local variable> := <default value>;
    . . .
    <manipulate local variable>
    . . .
    <function name> := <local variable>
END
```

12.5.1 Functions with Side Effects

As you have seen, even though the usual case for a function is to have all value parameters, you are not restricted by the language to use just value parameters. This can be useful, but it can also lead to dangerous and unpredictable program behavior. Let's first see where it would prove useful.

Go back to the first function you saw with a side effect:

```
FUNCTION Random (    low   : REAL;
                     high  : REAL;
                 VAR seed  : INTEGER) : REAL;
BEGIN
   seed := (29 * seed + 1) MOD 1024;
   random := (seed/1024) * (high - low) + low
END;    (* Random *)
```

This function converts the seed into a random number. The other purpose of the function, however, is to reset the value of **seed** so that you get a different random number the next time around. If you say

```
number := random (1.0, 10.0, seed);
```

this statement gives a random value to number, but also changes the value of **seed**. The change in **seed** is the side effect. It is not immediately obvious to a person glancing at this statement that **seed** might change. In fact, this statement makes it appear that only **number** is changing, that it is a function of **seed**. This is an argument against using such a function.

Imagine the frustrated person debugging a program that says

```
seed := 500;
number := random (1.0, 10.0, seed);
WRITELN (seed, number);
```

This person will be surprised to find that **seed** has changed value between the assignment statement and the WRITELN. In this simple case, it is fairly straightforward to look up the definition of the **random** function to understand what is happening. However, what if the statement is

```
number := factorial (TRUNC (miles (seed), 8 * random (1.0, 10.0, seed))));
```

Here you must look at the definitions of **factorial**, **miles**, and **random**, and you have to convince yourself that the built-in TRUNC function has nothing to do with it.

In the case of **random**, you decided that its side effect is not as important as the ease of expression that it provides, so you feel the side effect is justified.

Consider a more extreme example of a function with side effects. Suppose you want to prompt the user at the terminal to answer a yes/no question. You want a subprogram that returns a value describing whether the user types "yes" or "no." To do so, you can write a procedure:

```
PROCEDURE AskYesNo (VAR yes: BOOLEAN);
VAR response: CHAR;
BEGIN
    WRITE ('Yes or No? ');
    READLN (response);
    yes := response IN ['y', 'Y']
END;
```

This procedure reads a single character from the input line of the terminal and sets a flag accordingly. The flag is the single **VAR** parameter of the procedure. Remember, functions work well for boxes with single **VAR** parameters. Thus you might write

```
FUNCTION Yes : BOOLEAN;
VAR response: CHAR;
BEGIN
    WRITE ('Yes or No? ');
    READLN (response);
    yes := response IN ['y', 'Y']
END;
```

This is an unusual function. It has no parameters because its value is determined completely by side effects. To evaluate the function, you prompt the user for a character and return a value for the function. This is far from calculating functions.

Consider its use. Given this function definition, you might say

```
WRITELN ('Do you want instructions?  ');
IF yes THEN
    ShowInstructions;
```

Think of when various actions take place:

first execute WRITELN
then execute IF/THEN

To execute the IF/THEN, however, you need to evaluate its test:

first execute WRITELN
then evaluate function Yes.
if TRUE, then execute ShowInstructions.

The user is prompted when you evaluate function **yes**. In other words, to evaluate the test controlling the IF/THEN, you must prompt the user. This means that there is really a hidden step in all this. You don't really have

```
WRITELN
IF/THEN
```

You have

```
WRITELN
prompt and read
IF/THEN
```

This terminal interaction is obscured because it is part of function **yes**. There is another problem with such functions. Suppose you have code such as the following:

```
REPEAT
    PlayGame;
    WRITELN ('Do you want to play again? ')
UNTIL NOT yes;
```

It is difficult to distinguish the function call from a simple **BOOLEAN** variable. Somebody reading the program wouldn't know whether to turn to the variable section or the function section to find a definition. Also, a person wanting to modify this code might be tempted to do the following:

```
REPEAT
    PlayGame;
    WRITELN ('Do you want to play again? ');
    IF yes THEN
        WRITELN ('Okay, sport!  Here we go again. . .')
UNTIL NOT yes;
```

This would be an innocent enough modification if **yes** were a variable and not a function. Since it is a function, however, this added IF/THEN statement generates another call on **yes** which causes extra prompting of the user. In other words, the user will be prompted twice each time through the loop. This is obviously not what you want.

The use of functions with side effects is, at best, a questionable practice. Those who prefer the elegance of expressions tend to favor functions with side effects. Those who are more procedure-oriented and like to see all the actions clearly laid out step by step denounce such functions as "bad style." This is not an either/or decision. People usually pick some point along the continuum.

12.6 Key Concepts

■ The CASE statement is a generalization of the IF/THEN/ELSE that allows for many branches controlled by one expression of ordinal type.

■ The REPEAT loop is an alternative to the WHILE loop that performs its test at the bottom rather than the top of the loop. Using a REPEAT loop instead of a WHILE often simplifies code because it eliminates the need for priming.

■ Every identifier introduced in a Pascal program will have a scope within which the definition is valid. The program and its subprograms each introduce a local scope. You cannot define a word more than once within the same program/subprogram scope; the most local definition of a word takes precedence. And every word that is not a Pascal keyword must be defined.

■ To guarantee that a FUNCTION will return a value, you might want to assign a default value at the beginning.

■ You will generally want to avoid writing a FUNCTION that has a side effect such as changing a variable defined outside the FUNCTION.

12.7 Self-Check Exercises

1. What are the two places in a Pascal program where an END occurs without a corresponding BEGIN?

2. Translate the following WHILE loops into equivalent REPEAT loops:

```
number := 1;                    index := 0;
WHILE (number < 10) DO          WHILE (index < length) DO
BEGIN                           BEGIN
    READ (number);                  WRITELN (list [index]);
    sum := sum + number             index := index * 2
END;                            END;
```

3. How many scope conflicts does this program have?

```
PROGRAM Fun1;
CONST fun1 = 13;
VAR   fun2 : INTEGER;
```

```
              PROCEDURE Fun3;
              VAR fun1 : CHAR;
                  fun3 : INTEGER;

                      PROCEDURE fun2;
                      VAR fun1 : REAL;
                      BEGIN
                          (* point A *)
                      END;

              BEGIN
                  (* point B *)
              END;

              BEGIN
                  (* point C *)
              END.
```

4. The following program is supposed to write out a row of Pascal's triangle, but it doesn't seem to be working. For example, for row 2, the answer should be

   1   2   1

   but the program is displaying

   2   1   0

   The three values are calculated as

$$\frac{\text{fact (2)}}{\text{fact (0) * fact (2)}} \qquad \frac{\text{fact (2)}}{\text{fact (1) * fact (1)}} \qquad \frac{\text{fact (2)}}{\text{fact (2) * fact (0)}}$$

   What is the problem?

```
PROGRAM Strange (INPUT, OUTPUT);
VAR cnt : INTEGER;
    num : INTEGER;

FUNCTION Fact (n : INTEGER) : INTEGER;
VAR cnt : INTEGER;
BEGIN
    num := 1;
    FOR cnt := 1 TO n DO
        num := num * cnt;
    fact := num
END;
```

```
BEGIN
    WRITE ('What row of the table do you want? ');
    READLN (num);
    FOR cnt := 0 TO num DO
        WRITE (fact (num) DIV (fact (cnt) * fact (num - cnt)):3);
    WRITELN
END.
```

5. What is the output of the following program?

```
PROGRAM Cracked (OUTPUT);
VAR e : CHAR;

FUNCTION f : CHAR;
BEGIN
    f := 'f';
    WRITE ('z')
END;

FUNCTION G : CHAR;
BEGIN
    e := SUCC (e);
    g := e;
    WRITE (e)
END;

FUNCTION H : BOOLEAN;
BEGIN
    h := (f <> 'f') OR (g <> 'g');
    WRITE ('!')
END;

BEGIN
    e := 'd';
    WHILE h DO
        e := e
END.
```

6. What is the scope of the identifier you use to name a program?

7. Will it be easier to avoid problems with full evaluation using **REPEAT** loops rather than **WHILE** loops?

8. Under what circumstances does the following **FUNCTION** return a value?

```
FUNCTION FOO (n : INTEGER) : INTEGER;
VAR count : INTEGER;
    num   : INTEGER;
```

```
BEGIN
    IF (n < 0) THEN
    BEGIN
        num := n MOD 3;
        foo := num
    END
    ELSE
    BEGIN
        num := 0;
        FOR count := 1 TO n DO
        BEGIN
            num := num + count;
            foo := num
        END
    END
END;
```

9. What is the output of the following program?

```
PROGRAM Silly (OUTPUT);
VAR a, b, c : INTEGER;

PROCEDURE First (VAR a : INTEGER);
VAR b : INTEGER;
BEGIN
    a := a * 2;
    b := a + c;
    c := c DIV 10
END;

PROCEDURE Second (VAR a : INTEGER;
                      b : INTEGER);
BEGIN
    b := b + 1;
    a := b * c;
    c := a + c
END;

BEGIN
    a := 10;
    b := 20;
    c := 30;
    second (c, b);
    WRITELN ('A = ', a:1, ', B = ', b:1, ', C = ', c:1);
    first (b);
    WRITELN ('A = ', a:1, ', B = ', b:1, ', C = ', c:1);
    first (a);
    WRITELN ('A = ', a:1, ', B = ', b:1, ', C = ', c:1);
```

```
       second (b, a);
       WRITELN ('A = ', a:1, ', B = ', b:1, ', C = ', c:1);
       first (c);
       WRITELN ('A = ', a:1, ', B = ', b:1, ', C = ', c:1)
   END.
```

10. Write some code that gives a value to the **CHAR** variable **grade** depending on the value of an **INTEGER** variable **score**. **Grade** is to be set to **'A'** for a score of 91 to 100, **'B'** for 81 to 90, **'C'** for 71 to 80, **'D'** for 61 to 70, and **'F'** for other values.

12.8 Programming Problems

1. Write and test a procedure that compares two poker hands to see which is better. Surround the procedure with a dummy main program that prompts a user for two poker hands and reports which is better. The user can enter each card as a two-character sequence, as in

```
card ? AD
card ? 3C
card ? 4D
card ? OH
card ? JS
```

This specifies the hand: ace of diamonds, three of clubs, four of diamonds, ten of hearts, and jack of spades. The rank of the hands is as follows:

Royal flush	10, J, Q, K, A all from same suit
Straight flush	Cards are sequential, all from same suit
Four of a kind	Four cards, all same rank
Full house	Three cards, all same rank, and pair, same rank
Flush	All from same suit
Straight	Cards are sequential
Three of a kind	Three cards, all same rank
Two pair	Two pairs of cards, each same rank
One pair	Two cards, same rank

Ties are broken by looking at the high card. For example, a jack-high flush (7, 8, 9, 10, J) would beat an eight-high flush (4, 5, 6, 7, 8).

2. You are going to write a program that is generally called a tickler. The program helps to remind the user of important dates and events. The user will want a simple but powerful program. It is difficult for a programmer to guide user interaction well, so probably the best way to keep the program simple and useful is to do very little interaction with the user. This can be accomplished by having the program obtain most of its information from a **TEXT** file stored on the user's account. As long as the format of the file isn't too difficult to learn, the user should be able to quickly make use of the program.

You should design your own tickler file format. A user can then create a file of events, and your tickler can start sending out reminders. In order to work properly, your program needs to know the current date. This is usually available from your Pascal system, but not always in an obvious way. In worst case you can just ask the user to enter the date every time the program runs.

Here are some questions that your tickler might want to keep track of:

- What is the event?
- Who else is participating?
- When will it take place?
- Where will it take place?
- How long in advance does the user want to be reminded?
- How often does the user want to be reminded?
- Is it permanent (a birthday) or temporary (a one-time meeting)?

3. Write an interactive program that draws a calendar for a user. It should prompt for the year the user is interested in and should then produce output such as the following:

```
Calendar For The Year 2001
--------------------------

                             January
Monday    Tuesday  Wednesday Thursday  Friday   Saturday  Sunday
+---------------------------------------------------------------+
|    1        2         3        4        5         6        7   |
|    8        9        10       11       12        13       14   |
|   15       16        17       18       19        20       21   |
|   22       23        24       25       26        27       28   |
|   29       30        31                                        |
+---------------------------------------------------------------+


                             February
Monday    Tuesday  Wednesday Thursday  Friday   Saturday  Sunday
+---------------------------------------------------------------+
|                               1        2         3        4    |
|    5        6         7        8        9        10       11   |
|   12       13        14       15       16        17       18   |
|   19       20        21       22       23        24       25   |
|   26       27        28                                        |
+---------------------------------------------------------------+
```

Keep in mind that leap years occur every 4 years, except every even century, when they don't occur (such as 1900), except every even fourth-century, when they do occur (such as 2000). You might also find it useful to know that January 1, 1601, was a Monday. Before you start writing this program, you probably want to develop some new types for storing months, days, and years. Enumerated types are particularly well suited to the months and days of the week.

4. Write an interactive program that translates an integer into its English equivalent. For example, if given the input 193, the program should report

```
one-hundred ninety-three
```

5. You are going to write a program to process a file of grades. The input file has a series of student entries, one per line. Each entry has

<name of student>: *<units>* *<grade>* *<units>* *<grade>* ... *<units>* *<grade>*

as in

```
Tad Martin: 3 A 2 B 4 F 1 P
Hillary Wilson: 2 A 4 P 3 B 5 A
```

The first line indicates that Tad Martin has four grades reported, a 3-unit A, a 2-unit B, a 4-unit F, and a 1-unit P. The second line indicates that Hillary Wilson has a 2-unit A, a 4-unit P, a 3-unit B, and a 5-unit A. The meaning of the letter grades is

Grade	Meaning	Points
A	Excellent	4.0
B	Good	3.0
C	Satisfactory	2.0
D	Unsatisfactory	1.0
F	Failing	0.0
P	Pass	n/a

You are to read in each student's record and calculate a weighted grade point average (GPA). Each grade accumulates quality points. A 2-unit B accumulates 6 points: (2 units) * (3.0 for B). A 5-unit A accumulates 20 points: (5 units) * (4.0 for A). Pass grades are not included in the GPA calculation. The overall GPA is computed as

$$\frac{\text{Sum of quality points}}{\text{Sum of graded units (i.e., not counting P grades)}}$$

Your program should read the data file and produce as output a report for each student such as the following:

```
Info for Tad Martin:
      3 unit A
      3 unit B
      4 unit F
      1 unit P
Total Graded Units  = 10
Total Pass Units    = 1
Weighted GPA        =  2.10
```

The reports should appear in order of increasing GPA, from the poorest students to the best.

In addition, you should produce a Dean's honor roll, also sorted by GPA. This is a shorter list of students who made a GPA higher than 3.0 and should list just the student's name, total graded units, and GPA:

```
Student's                       Graded           Weighted
Name                            Units            GPA
----------------------------------------------------------
Hillary Wilson                  10               3.7
```

13

MULTILEVEL
DATA STRUCTURES

13.1 Introduction

This chapter explores the techniques you should employ in writing programs that use data structures with several levels of decomposition. Good data abstraction techniques should be applied whenever creating such a structure, just as good procedural abstraction techniques should be applied when creating a program with several levels of structure. The chapter presents two different structures, developing the implementation and presenting a complete program for each structure.

13.2 Structure of an Employee Database

Many businesses have electronic databases that store information about employees. One such database is examined here so that you can better understand how they are structured and manipulated.

A data object that stores the name, office phone number, and office number for a series of employees is usually called a *directory database* because it has information that is useful for contacting or locating people. This object has at least two obvious levels of structure: a level that stores three pieces of information for each employee and a level that stores information for many different employees. Which should be the higher level of structure? Should you keep a list of employee entries, each with three pieces of information? Or should you keep three lists of information, one for employee names, one for employee offices, and one for employee phones?

The answer is easy if you consider that the three pieces of information for a specific employee are tied together in an important way. You would lose a lot of information if you lost track of which name corresponds to which office and phone. If you store the information as three lists, keeping track of that correspondence will be cumbersome because the lists will be dependent on each other. Thus the better decomposition is the list of employee entries because it minimizes the dependence between different components. This is the same reasoning you use to choose between two decompositions of a task.

To store the name and phone number for an employee, you must store individual characters within them, and this means another level of structure. Think more specifically about each level.

To store the characters of the name and phone, you want an array. It is advantageous to pack the arrays so that they become string types that can be compared directly and written to the output file. This also allows you to examine how a string is typically manipulated.

To store the three pieces of information for an individual employee, you use a record because the three pieces of information are of different types. A name will tend to be longer than a phone number, and an office number can be expressed as a simple INTEGER.

To store the list of employee entries, you can use the generic list definitions presented in Chapter 9:

```
CONST MaxLength    = <maximum length of list>;
TYPE  ElementList  = ARRAY [1..MaxLength] OF  <element type>;
      ListType     = RECORD
          elements : ElementList;
          length   : INTEGER
      END;
VAR   list         : ListType;
```

Examine the following declarations that ultimately define the type DirectoryType. Be sure to identify each of the four levels of this structure.

```
CONST NameLength   = 20;
      PhoneLength  = 8;
      MaxPerson    = 250;
TYPE  NameType     = PACKED ARRAY [1..NameLength] OF CHAR;
      PhoneType    = PACKED ARRAY [1..PhoneLength] OF CHAR;
      PersonType   = RECORD
          name     : NameType;
          phone    : PhoneType;
          office   : INTEGER
      END;
```

```
        PersonList      = ARRAY [1..MaxPerson] OF PersonType;
        DirectoryType   = RECORD
            people      : PersonList;
            NumPeople   : INTEGER
        END;
VAR     directory       : DirectoryType;
```

Before leaving the structure issue, study the following illustrations. They should clear up any confusion you have. Notice that the declarations declare only one variable, `directory`, where all the database information is stored. Look at the first two levels of structure of this object. At the highest level, this variable is a record with two components: `people` and `NumPeople`. `NumPeople` is a simple `INTEGER` variable, but `people` is an array indexed from 1 to 250.

Directory

To see the next two levels of structure, you open up the components of the `people` array. When you do so, you find records with three components in each, two of which are arrays.

13.2.1 Manipulating the Database

To better understand how to manipulate the database, consider the problem of transferring information from a file into the database. Suppose you have this file:

```
Flintstone, Fred    555-1908    208
Bunny, Bugs    327-9843    319
Oil, Olive    238-1955    250
Gonzales, Speedy    498-1276    304
Quest, Johnny    497-1265    320
Sam, Yosemite    239-4423    100
Gator, Wally    294-1354    208
Duck, Daffy    672-3834    145
```

Each line contains the information for one employee: name, phone number, and office number. If these three pieces of information are not lined up in columns, as above, you need some rule for separating the three parts of the line. Since names are generally composed of letters and phone numbers of digits, assume that the first digit on the line marks the end of the name and the beginning of the phone number. Also assume that the phone number is always eight characters long, so that you know when the phone number ends and the office number begins.

The task of reading this file into your structure is complex enough that you will want to decompose it. The most straightforward decomposition is to parallel the data decomposition:

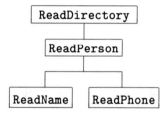

You don't need a procedure to read the office number because it is a simple **INTEGER** that can be processed with the built-in **READ** or **READLN**. You can develop these procedures in either a top-down or bottom-up way. Using top-down, **ReadDirectory** should be written first. You can again make use of the generic list operations developed in Chapter 9:

```
PROCEDURE ReadList (VAR list : ListType);
BEGIN
    <perform any actions that need to be done before reading>;
    WITH list DO
    BEGIN
        length := 0;
        WHILE <more data to read> AND (length < MaxLength) DO
        BEGIN
            length := length + 1;
            READ (elements [length])
        END
    END;
    <perform any actions that need to be done after reading>
END;
```

In this case, there is nothing special to be done before or after reading, and the test for more data is filled in with (NOT EOF). In Chapter 9 you were processing lists whose elements could be read directly. Consequently, you used the built-in READ statement. You can't do the same for the people array because its elements are structured objects. Instead, you call procedure ReadPerson. Putting this all together, you get

```
PROCEDURE ReadDirectory (VAR directory : DirectoryType);
BEGIN
    NumPeople := 0;
    WHILE NOT EOF AND (NumPeople < MaxPerson) DO
    BEGIN
        NumPeople := NumPeople + 1;
        ReadPerson (people [NumPeople])
    END
END;
```

ReadPerson is a simpler procedure to write because it always reads in exactly three things. It will be passed a single element of the people array, so it has a parameter of type PersonType. This is a record, so you again use a WITH statement to make its fields visible. Thus its outer shell looks like this:

```
PROCEDURE ReadPerson (VAR person : PersonType);
BEGIN
    WITH person DO
    BEGIN
            . . .
    END
END;
```

Inside the shell, you must specify how to read the three items. You will first read the name, then the phone number, and then the office number, because this is the order in which they appear on the input line. You should have a READLN to complete reading the line of input. Because you plan to write procedures for reading the name and phone strings and the office number is a simple integer, the preceding shell is filled in with

```
ReadName (name);
ReadPhone (phone);
READLN (office)
```

Now you have to write ReadName and ReadPhone. Of the two, ReadPhone is the easier, since you are assuming that the phone is always expressed as a string of eight characters. Since you know how many characters there are, you can use a simple FOR loop:

```
PROCEDURE ReadPhone (VAR phone : PhoneType);
VAR index : INTEGER;
BEGIN
    FOR index := 1 TO PhoneLength DO
        READ (phone [index])
END;
```

The ReadName procedure is more difficult because the names vary in length from line to line. You do know that a digit on the input line signals the end of the name, so you can use the file window (INPUT^) to see whether or not you've reached the end of the name.

You intend to manipulate the name as a string so that you can do direct comparisons and WRITE operations, but to do so you must make sure that every element of the array is initialized. If the name you are reading has only 12 characters, you must initialize the other 8 to something else. The obvious thing to do is to set them to all blanks. This is called *padding* the array. Here is one way to do this:

read characters from input line.
pad rest of array.

This is not the best way to solve the problem because it involves writing two different loops, neither of which is very simple. The better approach to the problem is to realize that you are giving a value to every element of the array, but sometimes you are getting the value from the input line and sometimes you are using a space to pad:

for (every element of array) do
    if (more to read from input line) then
        read next array element from input line.
    else
        set next array element to a space.

This loop is easy to write because it always goes from 1 to the maximum size of the array. For the name reading task, the test for the IF/THEN/ELSE should be whether or not the file window is a digit. Thus you can refine this to

```
for index going 1 to NameLength do
    if (file window is not a digit) then
            read name [index] from input line.
    else
            set name [index] to a space.
```

This is easily translated to Pascal:

```
PROCEDURE ReadName (VAR name : NameType);
VAR index : INTEGER;
BEGIN
    FOR index := 1 TO NameLength DO
        IF NOT (INPUT^ IN ['0'..'9']) THEN
            READ (name [index])
        ELSE
            name [index] := ' '
END;   (* ReadName *)
```

These four procedures make it possible to transfer the contents of the file into the database. This simple procedure call will set the whole process in motion:

```
ReadDirectory (directory)
```

13.2.2 A Complete Database Program

Now that you have seen the basic techniques used to manipulate very complex data objects, you can create a complete program that performs a useful task with your database: a program that transfers the directory information from the file to the database structure and then produces three lists sorted three different ways: by name, by phone, and by office.

The directory information is most useful when it is presented in some ordered way. For example, you may want the information in alphabetical order by employee, so that you can quickly access information for a given employee. You also might want to see the information sorted by office number, so that you could easily look up who is in what office. And occasionally, you may want to see the information sorted by phone number, so that when the phone company tells you an expensive phone call was made from a certain phone, you can find out who made it.

You have already written the procedures for reading the directory information from the file. Writing the other parts of the program is so similar to the process you went through to write the reading procedures that it is not necessary to work through the details here. Basically what is needed is a tool for sorting the directory (similar to the procedure developed in Section 17.1.1) and a tool for writing the directory (similar to the procedure developed in Section 9.3.4). As with the reading procedures, you have to develop a set of lower-level procedures that manipulate individual elements of the list. For the sorting task, you need to develop a procedure for comparing two-person entries to see whether one is less than the other. For the writing task, you need to develop a procedure for writing a single-person entry. It turns out that for these tasks you don't have to write procedures to manipulate an individual name or phone number because as string types they can be directly compared and written out.

There are two details of this program that deserve comment. First, the procedures for sorting and writing need to know what kind of directory listing you are making. There are three kinds of listings, so there are three ways of comparing and three ways of writing. To deal with this variety, an enumerated type with three values is introduced:

```
TYPE DirectoryKind = (ByName, ByPhone, ByOffice);
```

This type lets you specify what kind of directory you are making. The low-level comparison and writing procedures need to be passed this information, since the procedure behaves differently in each case. At the main program level, a **FOR** loop is used to produce the various kinds of directories.

Second, the directory variable is always passed as a **VAR** parameter, even when it is used as an in parameter, because value parameters create local copies of their parameters and this is a very large structure to copy. With a very large structure such as this, the inefficiency of copying outweighs the advantages of protection.

Here is a structure diagram of the program:

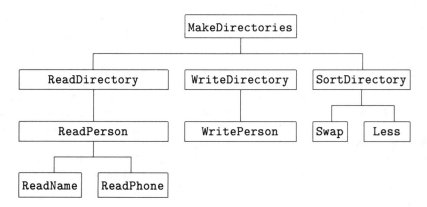

Notice that the three procedures at the first level of decomposition all manipulate directories, the four procedures at the second level manipulate person records, and the procedures at the lowest level manipulate string variables. Thus the procedural decomposition parallels the data decomposition, as intended.

When you produce a program such as this, you should order the procedures according to their level of abstraction. This way, the program listing starts with low-level details and gradually moves toward high-level abstraction. Therefore, the procedures appear in this order:

Level	Category	Procedure name
1	String manipulation	`ReadName, ReadPhone`
2	Person manipulation	`ReadPerson, WritePerson, Less, Swap`
3	Directory manipulation	`ReadDirectory, SortDirectory, WriteDirectory`

Here is the complete program:

```
(* pre        : Program is supplied with an input file of employee entries.   *)
(*             : Each entry should appear on a separate line and should be of  *)
(*             : the form:                                                     *)
(*             :     <name>  <phone number>  <office number>                   *)
(*             : The name can be any sequence of non-digit characters of       *)
(*             : length less than or equal to NameLength.  The phone number    *)
(*             : must start with a digit and should be PhoneLength characters  *)
(*             : long.  The office number should be a simple integer.          *)
(* post        : Three directory listings are produced: one sorted by name,    *)
(*             : one sorted by phone number, and one sorted by office number.  *)
(* parameters  : INPUT-in, OUTPUT-out.                                         *)
(* structure   : Names and phone numbers are stored as string variables; the   *)
(*             : office number is stored as a simple integer.  These three     *)
(*             : elements are collected in a RECORD to store one employee      *)
(*             : entry.  The database is stored as an array of these entries   *)
(*             : and a length variable telling how many entries there are.     *)
(*             : These two pieces of information are bundled in one RECORD.    *)

PROGRAM MakeDirectories (INPUT, OUTPUT);
CONST NameLength   = 20;       (* number of characters in a name          *)
      PhoneLength  = 8;        (* number of characters in a phone number  *)
      MaxPerson    = 250;      (* maximum # of people in database         *)
      width        = 3;        (* output field width for office number    *)
      filler       = ' ';      (* appears between directory columns       *)
TYPE  NameType     = PACKED ARRAY [1..NameLength] OF CHAR;
      PhoneType    = PACKED ARRAY [1..PhoneLength] OF CHAR;
      PersonType   = RECORD
         name      : NameType;
         phone     : PhoneType;
         office    : INTEGER
      END;
```

```
          PersonList      = ARRAY [1..MaxPerson] OF PersonType;
          DirectoryType   = RECORD
              people      : PersonList;
              NumPeople   : INTEGER
          END;
          DirectoryKind   = (ByName, ByPhone, ByOffice);
VAR       directory       : DirectoryType;     (* database of information *)
          KindOfDirectory : DirectoryKind;     (* loop variable          *)

PROCEDURE ReadName (VAR name : NameType);
(* pre        : Input cursor at beginning of a name; name terminated by a *)
(*             : digit.                                                    *)
(* post       : All characters up to digit read into array; rest of array *)
(*             : padded with spaces.                                      *)
(* parameters : name-out.                                                *)
(* requires   : constant NameLength and type NameType.                   *)
(* algorithm  : for each array element either read or pad.               *)
VAR index      : INTEGER;   (* loop counter                              *)
BEGIN
    FOR index := 1 TO NameLength DO
        IF NOT (INPUT^ IN ['0'..'9']) THEN
            READ (name [index])
        ELSE
            name [index] := ' '
END;   (* ReadName *)

PROCEDURE ReadPhone (VAR phone : PhoneType);
(* pre        : Input cursor at beginning of a phone with exactly *)
(*             : PhoneLength characters.                          *)
(* post       : PhoneLength characters read into array.          *)
(* parameters : phone-out.                                       *)
(* requires   : constant PhoneLength and type PhoneType.         *)
VAR index      : INTEGER;   (* loop counter                      *)
BEGIN
    FOR index := 1 TO PhoneLength DO
        READ (phone [index])
END;   (* ReadPhone *)

PROCEDURE ReadPerson (VAR person : PersonType);
(* pre        : Input cursor at beginning of input line containing a    *)
(*             : person entry.                                          *)
(* post       : Person entry read into RECORD; input cursor at next line. *)
(* parameters : person-out.                                            *)
(* requires   : type PersonType; and procedures ReadName and ReadPhone. *)
```

```
BEGIN
    WITH person DO
    BEGIN
        ReadName (name);
        ReadPhone (phone);
        READLN (office)
    END
END;   (* ReadPerson *)

PROCEDURE ReadDirectory (VAR directory : DirectoryType);
(* pre        : Input cursor at beginning of a file of people entries.   *)
(* post       : People entries read from file until EOF is encountered or *)
(*            : array is full.                                            *)
(* parameters : directory-out.                                           *)
(* requires   : constant MaxPerson; type DirectoryType; and procedure    *)
(*            : ReadPerson.                                               *)
BEGIN
    WITH directory DO
    BEGIN
        NumPeople := 0;
        WHILE NOT EOF AND (NumPeople < MaxPerson) DO
        BEGIN
            NumPeople := NumPeople + 1;
            ReadPerson (people [NumPeople])
        END
    END
END;   (* ReadDirectory *)

PROCEDURE Swap (VAR first, second: PersonType);
(* parameters : first-in/out, second-in/out.                             *)
(* post       : The values in First and Second are exchanged.            *)
(* requires   : type PersonType.                                         *)
VAR temp      : PersonType;   (* temporary storage place                 *)
BEGIN
    temp   := first;
    first  := second;
    second := temp
END;   (* Swap *)

FUNCTION Less (person1         : PersonType;
               person2         : PersonType;
               HowToCompare    : DirectoryKind) : BOOLEAN;
(* post       : Words are compared; result is true if person1 is less *)
(*            : than person2 by given criterion, false otherwise.      *)
```

```
(* parameters : person1-in, person2-in, HowToCompare-in.              *)
(* requires   : types PersonType and DirectoryKind.                   *)
BEGIN
    CASE HowToCompare OF
        ByName   : less := (person1.name   < person2.name);
        ByPhone  : less := (person1.phone  < person2.phone);
        ByOffice : less := (person1.office < person2.office)
    END
END;   (* Less *)


PROCEDURE SortDirectory (VAR directory : DirectoryType;
                             HowToSort : DirectoryKind);
(* post       : Elements of directory are sorted by given criterion.  *)
(* parameters : directory-in/out, HowToSort-in.                       *)
(* requires   : types DirectoryType and DirectoryKind, procedure Swap.*)
(* algorithm  : selection sort.                                       *)
VAR count1    : INTEGER;    (* outer loop counter                     *)
    count2    : INTEGER;    (* inner loop counter                     *)
    smallest  : INTEGER;    (* index of smallest element              *)
BEGIN
    WITH directory DO
        FOR count1 := 1 TO (NumPeople - 1) DO
        BEGIN
            smallest := count1;
            FOR count2 := (count1 + 1) TO NumPeople DO
                IF Less (people [count2], people [smallest], HowToSort) THEN
                    smallest := count2;
            Swap (people [count1], people [smallest])
        END
END;   (* SortDirectory *)


PROCEDURE WritePerson (person    : PersonType;
                       HowToWrite : DirectoryKind);
(* post       : Information for given person is written; order specified by *)
(*             : given criterion.                                      *)
(* parameters : person-in, HowToWrite-in.                              *)
(* requires   : types PersonType and DirectoryKind.                    *)
BEGIN
    WITH person DO
        CASE HowToWrite OF
            ByName   : WRITELN (name, filler, phone, filler, office:width);
            ByPhone  : WRITELN (phone, filler, name, filler, office:width);
            ByOffice : WRITELN (office:width, filler, name, filler, phone)
        END
```

```
END;   (* WritePerson *)

PROCEDURE WriteHeader (HowToWrite : DirectoryKind);
(* post       : Header for given directory is written. *)
(* parameters : HowToWrite-in                          *)
(* requires   : type DirectoryKind.                    *)
BEGIN
    CASE HowToWrite OF
        ByName   : WRITELN ('Directory listing by Name');
        ByPhone  : WRITELN ('Directory listing by Phone');
        ByOffice : WRITELN ('Directory listing by Office')
    END;
    WRITELN ('--------------------------')
END;   (* WriteHeader *)

PROCEDURE WriteDirectory (VAR directory : DirectoryType;
                              HowToWrite : DirectoryKind);
(* post       : Directory information is written to output file using *)
(*             : the format specified by HowToWrite.                  *)
(* parameters : directory-in, HowToWrite-in.                          *)
(* requires   : types DirectoryType and DirectoryKind; procedures     *)
(*             : WriteHeader and WritePerson.                         *)
VAR index     : INTEGER;   (* loop variable                           *)
BEGIN
    WITH directory DO
    BEGIN
        WriteHeader (HowToWrite);
        FOR index := 1 TO NumPeople DO
            WritePerson (people [index], HowToWrite);
        WRITELN
    END
END;   (* WriteDirectory *)

BEGIN   (* main program *)
    ReadDirectory (directory);
    FOR KindOfDirectory := ByName TO ByOffice DO
    BEGIN
        SortDirectory (directory, KindOfDirectory);
        WriteDirectory (directory, KindOfDirectory)
    END
END.   (* main program *)
```

13.3 Structure of a Picture

Now that you know how to store a database of information, let's examine how to store the characters of a picture. You have already seen how to store a row of characters in a one-dimensional array using declarations such as the following:

```
CONST MaxWidth = 80;
TYPE  LineType = ARRAY [1..MaxWidth] OF CHAR;
```

By storing an array of these `LineType` arrays, you would, in effect, be storing a list of lines, which is exactly what a two-dimensional picture is. Therefore, one way to create a two-dimensional object is to define it in terms of a one-dimensional object:

```
CONST MaxWidth    = 80;
      MaxHeight   = 100;
TYPE  LineType    = ARRAY [1..MaxWidth] OF CHAR;
      PictureType = ARRAY [1..MaxHeight] OF LineType;
```

Suppose you declare a variable with this type:

```
VAR picture : PictureType;
```

What does `picture` look like? It has 100 elements in it, which means you would expect to draw it like this:

```
          Picture

  [1]    ┌─────┐
         │  ?  │
  [2]    ├─────┤
         │  ?  │
  [3]    ├─────┤
         │  ?  │
  [4]    ├─────┤
         │  ?  │
 [...]   ├─────┤
         │ ... │
 [100]   ├─────┤
         │  ?  │
         └─────┘
```

However, each of those 100 elements is itself an array with 80 elements, which means it really looks like this:

Picture

	[1]	[2]	[3]	[4]	[5]	[6]	[7]	[8]	[...]	[80]
[1]	?	?	?	?	?	?	?	?	...	?
[2]	?	?	?	?	?	?	?	?	...	?
[3]	?	?	?	?	?	?	?	?	...	?
[4]	?	?	?	?	?	?	?	?	...	?
[...]	...	...	...	...	...	...	...	...	...	...
[100]	?	?	?	?	?	?	?	?	...	?

You can see now that this is called a *two-dimensional array* because it has both rows and columns. It is composed of 100 rows each with 80 columns. The name

    picture

is a reference to the entire two-dimensional object. The description

    picture [3]

is a reference to a one-dimensional object, a specific row of the figure (the third row). Since this refers to an array, you can also refer to

    picture [3] [5]

This is a reference to an object of type **CHAR**, the fifth character of the third row of the figure. Pascal provides a shorthand for this:

    picture [3, 5]

or, more generally,

    list [x₁, x₂, ..., xₙ]

is short for

    list [x₁] [x₂] [...] [xₙ]

In both cases, the meaning is, "Take the x_1 element of List, then take the x_2 element of that, ..., and the x_n element of that." There is a similar shorthand for multidimensional array declarations. Instead of defining **PictureType** in terms of **LineType**, you can say

```
TYPE PictureType = ARRAY [1..MaxHeight] OF
                         ARRAY [1..MaxWidth] OF CHAR;
```

In shorthand, you can write this as

```
TYPE PictureType = ARRAY [1..MaxHeight, 1..MaxWidth] OF CHAR;
```

In general, the declaration

```
ARRAY [lo₁..hi₁, lo₂..hi₂, ..., loₙ..hiₙ] OF <whatever>
```

is equivalent to

```
ARRAY [lo₁..hi₁] OF
    ARRAY [lo₂..hi₂] OF
        . . .
            ARRAY [loₙ..hiₙ] OF
            <whatever>
```

In both cases the primary index is $lo_1..hi_1$, the next is $lo_2..hi_2$, and so on. Even though Pascal lets you declare multidimensional structures this way, it is usually better to use the declaration you started with of a `LineType` and a `PictureType`. The reason is simple. If you declare both types, you can pass parameters of either type. Without the declaration of `LineType`, you can never pass an individual line as a parameter. Sometimes you will want to manipulate structures line by line, so it is best to have this declaration.

13.3.1 Manipulating a Picture

Consider using a two-dimensional array such as a piece of graph paper to draw figures in the Cartesian plane (with x and y axes). You might decide that in this case you don't really want the row and column numbers to start at 1. To make it easier to manipulate the entire plane, you might instead make the center of the array the origin of the plane with row and column numbers of 0. This is not difficult to arrange. Here is the declaration of an array that is small enough that it can be drawn on most computer terminals:

```
CONST MaxRow      = 6;
      MaxCol      = 35;
TYPE  PictureType = ARRAY [-MaxRow..+MaxRow, -MaxCol..+MaxCol] OF CHAR;
```

This array has 13 rows and 71 columns. If you want to initialize it to look like a piece of graph paper, you should have most of it be blank, but indicate the x and y axes. There are several ways to initialize the array. The easiest approach is to

blank out the whole array.
draw the x axis.

draw the y axis.
label the origin and axes.

The odd thing about this approach is that the drawing of the axes over-writes elements of the array that were blanked previously. While this may seem wasteful, it isn't. The number of elements in a single row or single column is very small compared to the total number of elements. Blanking the whole array requires a doubly nested FOR loop that iterates over all possible row and column values. The next two steps require only a single FOR loop, because in each case either the row or the column is held constant. The last step involves some simple assignments. You can, therefore, introduce FOR loops to refine this pseudocode:

```
for (each row) do
    for (each column) do
        set picture element at [row, column] to a blank.
for (each column) do
    set picture element at [0, column] to a dash.
for (each row) do
    set picture element at [row, 0] to a vertical bar.
set picture element at [0, 0] to a plus to label the origin.
set picture element at [-1, MaxCol] to a y to label the y axis.
set picture element at [MaxRow, -1] to an x to label the x axis.
```

This easily expands to Pascal:

```
PROCEDURE InitializePicture (VAR picture : PictureType);
VAR row    : INTEGER;
    column : INTEGER;
BEGIN
    FOR row := -MaxRow TO +MaxRow DO
        FOR column := -MaxCol TO +MaxCol DO
            picture [row, column] := ' ';
    FOR column := -MaxCol TO +MaxCol DO
        picture [0, column] := '-';
    FOR row := -MaxRow TO +MaxRow DO
        picture [row, 0] := '|';
    picture [0, 0] := '+';
    picture [-1, MaxCol] := 'x';
    picture [MaxRow, -1] := 'y'
END;
```

One of the problems you encounter when manipulating a structure such as this is that you can't test the new procedures that you develop if you have no way to display the values in the structure. Therefore, you should write a procedure to display this picture. Otherwise, you'll never know whether your procedure works or not.

The picture-writing procedure is similar to this procedure. It also has a double FOR loop that varies over all the possible row and column numbers:

```
for (each row) do
begin
    for (each column) do
        write the picture element at [row, column].
    go to a new line.
end
```

As you write this picture, you must be careful about the order in which you do it. It isn't enough to simply write out each row and column position, you should try to get them to line up properly. Your normal conception of the graph paper is that the rows go positive to negative, top to bottom, and columns go negative to positive, left to right. The first row you write out will be at the top of the picture, so your row loop should go positive to negative. The first column you write out will be at the left, so the column loop should go negative to positive. Thus your pseudocode can be refined to

```
for row going +MaxRow downto −MaxRow do
begin
    for column going −MaxCol to +MaxCol do
        write the picture element at [row, column].
    go to a new line.
end
```

This is easily translated into Pascal:

```
PROCEDURE WritePicture (picture : PictureType);
VAR row       : INTEGER;
    column    : INTEGER;
BEGIN
    FOR row := +MaxRow DOWNTO -MaxRow DO
    BEGIN
        FOR column := -MaxCol TO +MaxCol DO
            WRITE (picture [row, column]);
        WRITELN
    END
END;
```

Let's consider a more interesting problem, drawing a line using a specific character (`LineChar`). There are many ways to specify a line. One of the easiest is to use the slope/intercept form:

$$y = slope * x + intercept$$

This leads to the following header:

```
PROCEDURE DrawLine (VAR picture   : PictureType;
                        slope     : REAL;
                        intercept : REAL;
                        LineChar  : CHAR);
```

A simple way to draw the line is to place one `LineChar` character in the appropriate row of every column. Thus your pseudocode should start with

```
for (every column) do
begin
        using slope and intercept, find corresponding row.
        change picture [row, column] to LineChar.
end
```

This can easily be refined by introducing row and column variables and by introducing a calculation for row number using the slope and intercept:

```
var row, column : integer;
begin
        for column := −MaxCol to +MaxCol do
        begin
            row := slope * column + intercept.
            picture [row, column] := LineChar.
        end
end
```

Only two issues remain before translating to Pascal. First, the expression for calculating **row** returns a **REAL** value. You need to add a call on **ROUND** to find the nearest integer. Second, depending on the line, not all columns of the picture are supposed to have `LineChar` written to them. If the line is very steep, the row values for the leftmost and rightmost columns will be outside the range of the picture. You could fix this by calculating the beginning and ending column numbers, but it is easier to add an `IF/THEN` that assigns a value to `picture [row, column]` only if the row value is in range. Thus the pseudocode becomes

```
var row, column : integer;
begin
        for column := −MaxCol to +MaxCol do
        begin
            row := round (slope * column + intercept).
            if abs (row) <= MaxRow then
                picture [row, column] := LineChar.
        end
end
```

This easily translates to Pascal:

```
PROCEDURE DrawLine (VAR picture   : PictureType;
                        slope     : REAL;
                        intercept : REAL;
                        LineChar  : CHAR);
VAR row    : INTEGER;
    column : integer;
```

```
                    BEGIN
                        FOR column := -MaxCol TO +MaxCol DO
                        BEGIN
                            row := ROUND (column * slope + intercept);
                            IF ABS (row) <= MaxRow THEN
                                picture [row, column] := LineChar
                        END
                    END;
```

Here is a complete and documented program that uses all these procedures to draw a pair of lines:

```
(* post       : A picture with two lines drawn in a Cartesian *)
(*             : plane is output by the program.              *)
(* parameters : OUTPUT-out.                                   *)

PROGRAM GraphPaper (OUTPUT);
CONST MaxRow     = 6;              (* highest numbered row    *)
      MaxCol     = 35;             (* highest numbered column *)
TYPE  PictureType = ARRAY [-MaxRow..+MaxRow, -MaxCol..+MaxCol] OF CHAR;
VAR   picture    : PictureType;

PROCEDURE InitializePicture (VAR picture : PictureType);
(* post       : characters of picture are initialized to look like a *)
(*             : piece of graph paper.                               *)
(* parameters : picture-out.                                         *)
(* requires   : constants MaxRow and MaxCol; type PictureType.       *)
(* algorithm  : first set all elements to blanks; then draw x-axis;  *)
(*             : then draw y-axis; then fill in special characters.  *)
VAR row      : INTEGER;   (* loop counter                            *)
    column   : INTEGER;   (* loop counter                            *)
BEGIN
    FOR row := -MaxRow TO +MaxRow DO
        FOR column := -MaxCol TO +MaxCol DO
            picture [row, column] := ' ';
    FOR column := -MaxCol TO +MaxCol DO
        picture [0, column] := '-';
    FOR row := -MaxRow TO +MaxRow DO
        picture [row, 0] := '|';
    picture [      0,       0] := '+';
    picture [     -1, MaxCol] := 'x';
    picture [ MaxRow,     -1] := 'y'
END;   (* InitializePicture *)
```

```
PROCEDURE WritePicture (picture : PictureType);
(* post        : current contents of picture are sent to output. *)
(* parameters  : picture-in.                                      *)
(* requires    : constants MaxRow and MaxCol; type PictureType.   *)
VAR row        : INTEGER;    (* loop counter                      *)
    column     : INTEGER;    (* loop counter                      *)
BEGIN
    FOR row := +MaxRow DOWNTO -MaxRow DO
    BEGIN
        FOR column := -MaxCol TO +MaxCol DO
            WRITE (picture [row, column]);
        WRITELN
    END
END;  (* WritePicture *)


PROCEDURE DrawLine (VAR picture  : PictureType;
                        slope     : REAL;
                        intercept : REAL;
                        LineChar  : char);
(* post        : An approximation of a line is drawn in picture.  Line *)
(*              : is specified by its slope, intercept, and character to *)
(*              : be drawn with.                                   *)
(* parameters  : picture-out, slope-in, intercept-in, LineChar-in. *)
(* requires    : constants MaxRow and MaxCol; type PictureType.    *)
(* algorithm   : For each column, calculate corresponding row and fill *)
(*              : in LineChar if row number is in range.           *)
VAR row        : INTEGER;    (* loop counter                      *)
    column     : INTEGER;    (* loop counter                      *)
BEGIN
    FOR column := -MaxCol TO +MaxCol DO
    BEGIN
        row := ROUND (column * slope + intercept);
        IF ABS (row) <= MaxRow THEN
            picture [row, column] := LineChar
    END
END;  (* DrawLine *)


BEGIN  (* main program *)
    InitializePicture (picture);
    DrawLine (picture, 0.2, 3, '*');
    DrawLine (picture, -0.5, -4, '.');
    WritePicture (picture)
END.   (* main program *)
```

Here is the output it produces:

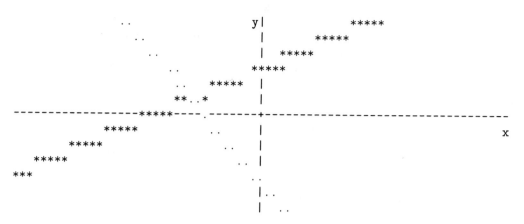

13.4 Key Concepts

- Complex data structures often have several levels associated with them. A program that uses such a structure is easier to write if you implement the different levels independently.

- A database is often stored in Pascal as an array of records, with a length variable to keep track of how many entries are in the database.

- Because an array can have elements of any type, it can have elements that are themselves arrays. Such a structure is called a multidimensional array. Pascal has special notations that make it easier to manipulate these multidimensional arrays.

- A picture is often stored in Pascal as a two-dimensional array of characters.

- When defining a multilevel structure, it is often useful to introduce **type** declarations for more than just the overall structure, including a declaration for each intermediate level. Such definitions allow you to pass parameters of an intermediate type (e.g., passing a single line of a picture to a low-level procedure).

13.5 Self-Check Exercises

1. Program **MakeDirectories** produces directories sorted by name, phone number, and office number. Suppose you want to also keep track of each person's age and produce a directory sorted by age. What modifications need to be made?

2. Suppose that you are going to write code for a database of student grades and course records. Students take classes, and classes have students in them. Which will be your top level of structure? If you make students the top level, then you will have to search through many student records to find out information about a class. If you make courses the top level, then you will have to search through many course records to find out information about a student. What do you do?

3. Consider this pair of parallel declarations for a database:

```
CONST MaxString  = 40;              CONST MaxString   = 40;
      MaxBook    = 1000;                  MaxBook     = 1000;
TYPE BookType    = RECORD           TYPE StringType   = PACKED ARRAY [1..
       title,                                            MaxString] OF CHAR;
       author,                            BookType      = RECORD
       publisher : PACKED ARRAY [1..        title    : StringType;
                   MaxString] OF CHAR;      author   : StringType;
       price     : REAL;                    publisher : StringType;
       year      : INTEGER;                 price    : REAL;
     END;                                   year     : INTEGER
VAR  books       : ARRAY [1..MaxBooks]    END;
                   OF BookType          BookList      = ARRAY [1..MaxBook]
     NumBooks    : INTEGER;                               OF BookType;
                                        BookDatabase  = RECORD
                                          books    : BookList;
                                          NumBooks : INTEGER
                                        END;
                                   VAR  database      : BookDatabase;
```

How do these declarations differ? Can you do some things with one that you can't do with the other, or is one just longer than the other?

4. Given the following declaration for storing a chessboard:

```
CONST Size    = 8;
TYPE  PieceType = (empty, pawn, bishop, knight, rook, queen, king);
      ColorType = (black, white);
      SquareType = RECORD
           piece : PieceType;
           color : ColorType
      END;
      BoardType = ARRAY [1..Size, 1..Size] OF SquareType;
VAR   board   : BoardType;
```

how do you refer to each of the following:

The first row

The second column

The bottom row

The square in the upper left-hand corner

The whole board

The lower right-hand corner's color

The four centermost squares

5. There is a family of lines that can't be drawn by procedure `DrawLine` developed in Section 13.3.1. What unusual property do they have?

6. You have seen structure diagrams used to describe the procedural decomposition of a program, but structure diagrams can be used to describe many kinds of decomposition. In particular, you can also use them to describe data decomposition. Draw a structure diagram for type `DirectoryType` developed in Section 13.2. Just as you don't include calls on low-level procedures such as `WRITELN` in your procedural decomposition diagrams, you shouldn't include low-level types such as `INTEGER` or `CHAR` in your data decomposition diagrams. Only include types defined by the program.

7. The database design of Section 13.2 declares two different types for storing strings of characters:

```
CONST NameLength  = 20;
      PhoneLength = 8;
TYPE  NameType    = PACKED ARRAY [1..NameLength] OF CHAR;
      PhoneType   = PACKED ARRAY [1..PhoneLength] OF CHAR;
```

What are the advantages and disadvantages of this versus declaring a single string type, as in

```
CONST StringLength = 20;
TYPE  StringType   = PACKED ARRAY [1..NameLength] OF CHAR;
```

8. Given the declaration

```
VAR grid : ARRAY [1..10, 1..40] OF CHAR;
```

Is the following statement legal? If so, what does it do?

```
grid [2] := grid [8];
```

9. The lines drawn in Section 13.3.1 have a slope that should make them very flat, yet they appear to be almost at a diagonal. Why is that?

13.6 Programming Problems

1. Write a program that simulates watershed for a large geographic area. The program is supplied with a two-dimensional grid of elevations. To simulate rainfall and its aftereffects, you will simulate the flow of a set of raindrops through the area. Put one drop of rain on each grid point and let it flow downhill. In other words, for each point in the grid, find the surrounding point with the lowest elevation. The water currently in the grid point flows into that new grid point, unless it is at a higher elevation. If the elevation is higher all around a point, then the water collects rather than flows out of it. Such points represent lakes. Eventually

all the water will either flow off the map or collect in these low spots. For each grid point, you need to keep track of how many raindrops it has currently and the total number of raindrops that have passed through the point. You will find that points with a great deal of rain flowing through them probably are rivers. As the simulated watershed moves over this terrain, you should periodically generate outputs indicating where the water is currently. When the water stops flowing, you should produce some summary data showing such things as grid points that collected water and grid points that had a great deal of water flow through them.

2. Write a program that manages a chessboard for two players. Imagine that two people are going to run your program instead of pulling out a real chessboard. Your program should set up the board for them and should then alternate asking for moves from the two players, updating the board, and printing out the current board often enough that the players know what is going on. Ideally, your program will check moves made by each user to verify that they are legal by standard rules of movement in chess. Once your program does check whether a given move is legal, it can be expanded to also watch out for check. The following pseudocode describes how:

check := false.
for (each piece of opponent) do
        if (moving piece to king's square is legal) then
            check := true.

If your program has reached the point where it recognizes check, you can get it to recognize checkmate by building one more procedure on top of these others. The strategy is outlined in the following pseudocode:

if (king is in check) then
begin
        mate := true.
        for (each of the player's pieces) do
            for (every square on the board) do
                if (moving piece to this square is legal) then
                begin
                        pretend to move the piece there.
                        see if king is still in check.
                        if not, mate := false and quit this loop.
                end
end

This pseudocode might look like a lot of work for the computer to perform, but it really isn't that much, because when a game reaches check, there are not very many pieces open and not many real options for moving pieces around.

3. You are to write a Pascal program that simulates the execution of a special programming language called turtle which was designed to direct a small mechanical robot that looked like a turtle. The turtle was connected to a computer which could direct it to run around on a large sheet of paper. The turtle had a felt pen attached to its tummy and it could press the pen on the paper. Directions in turtle language are specified by an integer between 0 and 7, indicating one of the following points of the compass:

5 6 7

4 X 0

3 2 1

turtle has the following commands:

PENUP	Raise pen so that no footprint is left when the turtle leaves.
PEN <*char*>	Lower pen so that <*char*> will be left after turtle moves.
GO <#>	Move <#> squares in the direction turtle is facing. If pen is down, drop the current character in each square turtle leaves, overwriting any old character. Don't drop a character in the final square since turtle is still in it. If pen is up, don't drop characters.
TURN <#>	Turn <#> clicks clockwise. Suppose turtle is facing in direction 6, then the command TURN 3 leaves turtle facing in direction 1.
ERASE	Erase entire grid. Keep same location and direction.
DRAW	Print the current page on the output file.
HOME	For the programmer's convenience, moves turtle directly to the upper-left-hand corner, facing in direction 0.
CENTER	Another convenience command moves turtle to center of page.

In the PEN command, the <*char*> argument should be interpreted to be the first nonblank character after the PEN command. <*char*> can be any nonnegative integer.

Your Pascal program should accept as input a file containing commands from the preceding language. It should read each command and simulate it. The output should be printed to the file OUTPUT. There may be more than one command on a line. At least one space must separate each command, but there might be more than one.

4. Wolf Island is populated with wolves and rabbits. Wolves eat rabbits, and rabbits eat grass. Below is a set of rules for the movement, reproduction, and feeding of the creatures. Your job is to simulate the population shift on the island based on these rules. Reproduction is asexual and merely involves splitting a creature into two offspring. Each wolf starts out with a given number of foodergs and loses one fooderg each day. If a wolf eats a rabbit, the wolf gains foodergs. If a wolf's fooderg total drops to zero, the wolf dies and is removed from the island.

The user should be prompted for the following parameters of the simulation:

Probability that a particular wolf will reproduce on any given day

Probability that a particular rabbit will reproduce on any given day

Amount of energy each wolf starts with

Amount of energy a wolf gains when it eats a rabbit

Total number of days to run the simulation

Report interval: how many days to run before reporting to the user

The wolves move first. If a rabbit is in an adjacent square (horizontally or vertically), a wolf moves into the square, eats the rabbit, and increases its foodergs. If no rabbits are around, the wolf randomly chooses one of the empty adjacent squares or its own square (each with equal probability). If it is reproduction time for a wolf, it makes its move to a new square, but another wolf appears afterwards in the old square. Each of the two split wolves receives half the foodergs of the original wolf. If the wolf is moving to its own square, the clone is stillborn and the wolf still loses half its foodergs.

Next, the rabbits move. Each rabbit moves to an empty adjacent square or stays in its own square (each possibility equally probable). Rabbits reproduce just like wolves, but they don't have to worry about foodergs—grass is plentiful.

Write a program that performs the simulation and prints out maps of the island showing where the wolves and rabbits are. Print your pictures at time unit 0 (the initial configuration), 1, 2, 3, 4, 5, and multiples of the report interval, up to the last day of the simulation or until all the rabbits are eaten or all the wolves are dead.

The input file will contain up to 20 lines each with up to 20 characters. Individual characters have the following meanings:

Char	Meaning
`' '`	Water
`'.'`	Island
`'R'`	Rabbit
`'W'`	Wolf
`missing`	Water

5. You have been asked to complete someone else's programming project. Unfortunately, that person didn't ever start writing the program; he spent his whole time playing with the data. Now you have data files that are in very good order, but you have to write all the code. Your program is going to help people explore genealogy (their ancestral roots). The place where you work has a gigantic collection of family records, and your predecessor has done a good job of getting the data all ready for you.

You have two files to work with. The information about individuals is stored in the first. Each entry in the file corresponds to a different person. The file has one line for each person. Each line has

<immediate family index> <marrge family index> <gender> <last name>/<first name>

The first two items on the line are integers that refer to the other data file. They specify which immediate family this person belongs to and which family by marriage he or she belongs to. The *immediate family* is defined as the family in which the person is a child, not a parent. Conversely, the person is a parent, not a child in the *family by marriage*.

After the two integers there will be a single character, either 'M' or 'F', to indicate gender. After that comes the last name, followed by a slash, followed by the first name. Here are some sample lines:

```
348 948 M Martin/Tad
509 742 M Chandler/Adam
123 604 F Kane/Erica
```

The first sample line indicates that a male named Tad Martin has family number 348 as his immediate family and family number 948 as his family by marriage.

The second input file contains family information. Each line contains the information for one family and contains

<parent index> <parent index> <child index> ... <child index>

In other words, the line contains nothing but integers that refer back to the person file. The first two integers refer to the parents in the family, not necessarily in any order. If there are children, an integer will appear after the parents' integers for each child in the family.

By now you are probably wondering what these integer indexes represent. This is where your predecessor comes in. She spent all her time checking and cross-checking and correcting these references so that now you have two data files that are highly interconnected. A *person index* refers to the line number in the people file where the person record can be found. Similarly, a *family index* refers to the line number in the family file where the family can be found.

To give you an idea of how these references can be used, consider the problem of finding the names of a person's in-laws from this database. Starting with the person, you would go to the marriage family, find the parent index not equal to this person's index (which is the spouse), then come back to the person entry for the spouse, then go to the immediate family of the spouse, and then use the parent indexes to come back to the person entries for the in-laws:

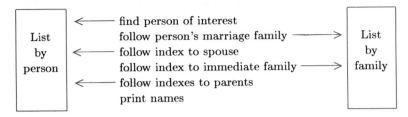

The program you are to write is an interactive one to be used by visitors investigating their own genealogy. What they want to see mostly is a large list of names of people they are related to. Thus your program has to search through the database and report as many people as possible who are related to the user.

You should approach this problem from several different angles. Write a procedure that explores parental relations. Show the father and the mother, then the grandfathers and grandmothers, and so on. Write another procedure that explores child relations. Show the children, the grandchildren, and so on. Write a third procedure to explore sibling relations. Then write a procedure to find aunts and uncles and another for nephews and nieces. If you are really ambitious, go after cousins.

There is just one other thing your program should do besides just spewing out countless relations for each user. Another common question asked at the center by visitors is, "What is the relationship between Mr. X and Ms. Y? How are they related?" Sometimes people are just trying to find out what their own relationship is to someone. You should write a procedure to search for an identifiable family path between two people.

14

WRITING LARGE
INTERACTIVE PROGRAMS

14.1 Introduction

It is possible that sometime you will write a complex interactive program. If so, you should read this chapter carefully. The first part covers general principles you should follow when constructing interactive programs. The last part is devoted to an in-depth examination of a substantial programming problem, the game of Jotto.

14.2 User Interface Principles

The user interface of a program is the way the program communicates with a user.

> **USER INTERFACE** ────────────────────────
> The way that a program communicates with a user.

Whenever you design a program, you should take into account the user interface issues. How will your program communicate with the user? What happens if the user makes a mistake? What if the user asks for help? These are questions that you should ask before you write a program. These design issues are often called the *human engineering* of the program, the techniques that make a program usable.

Here are some general principles of user interface that you should apply to your programs.

RULE ONE OF USER INTERFACE

The user should feel in control.

This might seem obvious, but it is often overlooked. People are frustrated by anything that they cannot control.

RULE TWO OF USER INTERFACE

Programs should check for user errors.

You must anticipate that users will make mistakes. Interactive programs have to be built around this assumption. A program shouldn't die just because a user types in something unexpected.

RULE THREE OF USER INTERFACE

Programs should provide interactive help to users.

Error checking is important, but it is not enough to address the fundamental problem of users getting confused and making mistakes. More often than not, error messages are meaningless. Users need the ability to learn about the system from the system. This is called *interactive help*. Interactive help is as important as error checking.

RULE FOUR OF USER INTERFACE

Programs should provide emergency exits.

A user caught in a tedious loop feels that he has lost control. This violates the first principle. You should realize that people are going to fall into traps you don't anticipate, are going to misunderstand something that is perfectly clear to you, or are going to find a stray bug that you didn't uncover in your testing. Human-engineered software should have emergency exits: there should always be a clearly labeled exit sign for users in trouble. In programming, this translates into the option to quit from any level in a program and return to a higher level or to escape the program altogether. Thus you should build loops that allow users to either perform the task or quit. A user should always be able to say, "I don't like what's going on here, let me out."

> **RULE FIVE OF USER INTERFACE**
> The user interface should be consistent.

This is a very important point, particularly for a program that will be written by more than one person. Conventions should be decided on during the design process of a program, and programmers should use those conventions consistently. For example, how will you tell the user he has made a mistake? How should a user ask for help? How detailed are the instructions going to be? And so on.

> **RULE SIX OF USER INTERFACE**
> Programs should work intuitively.

Interactive programs should, whenever possible, revolve around the intuitions of the user. For example, if you are going to write a program to play tic-tac-toe with the user, you will at some point have to ask the user to choose a square. The most intuitive way to do so is to show a picture of the two-dimensional board and have the user point to the chosen square. This solution is more intuitive than having the user specify a row and column number. It is difficult to implement on most systems, however, since pointing devices are just now becoming common attachments to computers.

> **RULE SEVEN OF USER INTERFACE**
> Programs should not force the programmer's model on the user and should not force the user's model on the programmer.

This is an extension of the previous point. There is often an intuitive user model for some action. For example, suppose that you are going to have the user manipulate a two-dimensional grid of numbers. The intuitive user model is a two-dimensional grid of numbers. But suppose that you know in advance that most of the numbers are going to be zeros. In this case, it might be more efficient to store the grid in some way that eliminates all the zeros. Here you have a conflict where the programmer would like to represent the information one way and the user likes to think of the information another way. The correct resolution is to write translation routines that allow both the programmer and the user to get what they want. The program can store the information internally in one format, but the user will see and manipulate the information in the other.

14.2.1   Error Checking on Yes/No Questions

Consider a simple interactive error-checking procedure. Suppose you ask a user a yes/no question and you expect an appropriate response. Usually, you read just the first character of the response to see whether it is a 'Y' for yes or an 'N' for no. Here is a pseudocode version of the steps involved in prompting and reading once:

> ask "yes or no?".
> read the first character of the response.
> if the character is a 'y' or a 'Y', assume the response is yes.

This can easily be translated into a procedure. Because it needs to tell you what the user's answer was, you should include a **VAR** parameter (here called **UserSaysYes**). This is a simple flag that will be set to true if the user says yes and will be set to false otherwise. Here is the simple procedure:

```
PROCEDURE AskUser (VAR UserSaysYes : BOOLEAN);
VAR response : CHAR;
BEGIN
    WRITE ('yes or no? ');
    READLN (response);
    UserSaysYes := (response IN ['y', 'Y'])
END;
```

The problem with this way of obtaining values is that the user might type something other than yes or no. For example, suppose that the user doesn't understand the question and responds

> **yes or no? help!**

This procedure would assume that the user typed no, because the response didn't start with 'y' or 'Y'. You can improve things if you make sure the user types either a yes or a no. In other words, you keep asking the question until you see a response that starts with 'Y' or a response that starts with 'N'. Obviously, you need an indefinite loop to do so. The **REPEAT** is the more natural because you know that you want the user to answer the question at least once. Here is the modified procedure:

```
PROCEDURE AskUser (VAR UserSaysYes : BOOLEAN);
VAR response : CHAR;
BEGIN
    REPEAT
        WRITE ('yes or no? ');
        READLN (response)
    UNTIL (response IN ['y', 'Y', 'n', 'N']);
    UserSaysYes := (response in ['y', 'Y'])
END;
```

The **REPEAT** loop causes this procedure to stay in the prompt/read cycle until the user has typed something that starts with either 'Y' or 'N'. Once the user does type one of these two responses, you give a value to the parameter **UserSaysYes**. With this version of the procedure, the user who asks for help won't get it. But your program also won't assume that the user said no when asking for help. The interaction will instead go something like this:

```
yes or no? help!
yes or no? ?
yes or no? maybe
yes or no? I think this is an attitude problem.
yes or no?
```

Even though a user might be frustrated that your program doesn't provide more help, he will at least know what is going on and will eventually realize that the program will only accept a yes or no answer.

This is a useful tool to have when you write interactive programs, and you should add it to your software library. You would use it by giving a series of commands such as the following (assuming that you have a **BOOLEAN** variable defined called **yes**):

```
WRITELN ('Do you want instructions?');
AskUser (yes);
IF yes THEN
    GiveInstructions;
. . .
```

14.2.2   General Solution for Error Reporting

A good piece of pseudocode to start with for interactive error checking is

```
repeat
    obtain values.
    check values.
    if (not okay) then
        report error.
until okay
```

Whenever you approach a new error-checking task, you should break it down into at least these three steps.

You will examine error checking that is complex enough that you have to inform users when they make errors. The error checking you do will involve testing several errors. Your first inclination might be to perform the appropriate tests and then execute a statement such as the following:

```
IF NOT good THEN
    WRITELN ('That was not legal.  Please try again.');
```

This is not enough. Many users won't know why a guess is illegal. Thus you should generate different error messages for each of the different errors. But what happens if the user makes more than one mistake? Do you report all of them? This is a matter of aesthetics, but I think that the answer is no. It is sufficient to report one mistake. If you report more, you are bound to cause confusion. Also, often a user realizes his mistake. Users don't want to be bothered with long explanations of the plethora of errors buried in bad responses; they want to start over again quickly.

This attitude leads to a particular way of structuring error-checking loops. Look at the set of errors you want to test for and order them, picking one error to test for first, another to test second, another to test third, and so on. Then make a nested IF/THEN/ELSE construct that tests each in succession. Because it is a nested structure, it will stop when one of the errors is encountered. Thus the error-checking loops look like this:

```
repeat
      prompt and read.
      let good = (truth value of test #1).
      if not good then
            write error message #1.
      else
      begin
            let good = (truth value of test #2).
            if not good then
                  write error message #2.
            else
            begin
                  let good = (truth value of test #3).
                  if not good then
                        write error message #3.
                  else
                  begin
                        . . .
                              let good = (truth value of test #n).
                              if not good then
                                    write error message #n.
                  end
            end
      end
until good
```

In other words, the error messages become the THEN parts of this nested construct. When an error is encountered, you write its error message and exit the nested IF/THEN/ELSE with **good** equal to FALSE. This will bring you back around the REPEAT loop to prompt, read, and test again.

Notice that the final test has an IF/THEN, but no ELSE part. This is so because if an input passes all the tests, you don't have anything else to do. In such a case, you terminate the IF/THEN/ELSE with **good** equal to TRUE, which will exit the outer loop.

This pseudocode can serve as the template for most interactive error-checking tasks you will encounter in Pascal. All you have to do is fill in the blanks by telling the procedure how to prompt and read, what tests to perform, and what error messages to produce.

Sometimes there are good reasons for putting one test before another. Some tests depend on others. For example, if you ask the user to type a positive number, you should first check that a number appears and then check that the number is positive. It doesn't work the other way around, because it doesn't make sense to test whether a number is positive if there is no number. Other times you will put one test before another because you think it is a more important issue, one that is more important for the user to know about. For example, suppose you walk into a hotel bar and a stranger comes up to you and says, "Cousin Jaime! What are you doing here? How odd that we're staying at the same hotel!" Your response would not be, "You're mistaken, I'm not staying at this hotel." You would address the more fundamental confusion and say, "You're mistaken, I'm not your cousin." Sometimes there aren't logical reasons for ordering one test before another, and you can pick randomly.

14.2.3 Improving the Solution

One of the user interface principles is to provide interactive help, but you haven't done so in this error-checking loop. One change you can make is to identify a special input used to ask for help. You can, for example, decide that if the user types a question mark as his first character, you will interpret it as a request for help rather than as data. You can modify the procedure to produce a short help message when the user types the question mark. You can also change the error messages to tell the user to type a question mark for more help.

Here is a modified pseudocode that includes the idea of interactive help:

```
repeat
    initialize good to false.
    prompt and read.
    if (first char typed) = '?' then
        provide help.
    else
    begin
        check for errors.
        if (not good) then
            tell user to type '?' for help.
    end
until good
```

Thus your nested IF/THEN/ELSE with the many different tests being performed is nested one level deeper in this procedure because it becomes the ELSE part that is executed when the user doesn't ask for help.

Another problem with your solution is that it prompts and prompts and prompts until the user types something legal. This is an example of a tedious loop without an emergency exit. You can put one in your error-checking/help-giving template to get an error-checking/help-giving/emergency-handling loop by using the same trick as before. You identify another input as the quit request. It's impossible to choose one input that would work for all possible loops you might write, but one that seems to work a lot of the time is an empty input. If you ask the user to provide a response and he hits the carriage return without typing anything, that's a pretty good sign of apathy. Sometimes a blank input is a legal input, in which case you must choose something else, but it does seem to work in many cases.

You should be careful, however, not to go too far in the other direction. Quitting a program is usually a serious thing, because a user can't go back once out. Sometimes people accidentally hit the return key and don't want to find themselves leaving the program automatically. Therefore, to be cautious, if the user types a return, you should ask whether he really wants to quit before actually exiting him from the loop.

Here is an expanded pseudocode that incorporates the error checking, the help, and the emergency exit:

```
repeat
    initialize good to false.
    prompt.
    if (end-of-line) then
        check for quit
    else
    begin
        read.
        if (first char typed) = '?' then
            provide help
        else
        begin
            let good = (truth value of test #1).
            if not good then
                write error message #1.
            else
            begin
                . . .
                let good = (truth value of test #n).
                if not good then
                    write error message #n.
            end
        end
    end
```

```
        end
    until good or (user wants to quit)
```

14.2.4   Error-Checking Example: Jotto

To practice with these concepts, try solving a fairly tough error-checking task:
a procedure for the game of Jotto. An important point about Jotto is that it
is a word-guessing game that uses five-letter words. Both the answers and the
guesses are five letters. If you write a computer program that allows a user to
play Jotto, you will need to read in guesses made by that user. The guess is only
legal if it is exactly five characters long and if each character is a letter. Thus
you must build a tool called `GetGuess` that obtains a legal guess from the user
at the terminal. Here are the declarations you will use and the procedure header
for `GetGuess`:

```
CONST WordSize = 5;
TYPE  WordType = PACKED ARRAY [1..WordSize] OF CHAR;

PROCEDURE GetGuess (VAR word : WordType);
```

You don't need to keep track of lengths in this game because all words are
guarantied to be the same length, and using a **packed array** rather than a
normal array will simplify writing and comparing words.

All you need to do is to fit this to your template. You need to prompt and
then check EOLN to see whether the user is trying to quit. If not, you read
the response into the array **word**. You have already seen enough word reading
procedures so you don't have to review that task again. Here is the procedure
you will use:

```
PROCEDURE ReadWord (VAR word   : WordType;
                    VAR length : INTEGER);
BEGIN
    length := 0;
    WHILE NOT EOLN AND (length < WordSize) DO
    BEGIN
        length := length + 1;
        READ (word [length])
    END
END;
```

The next step, checking for help, is easy to do. After the reading procedure
is executed, you say

```
IF word [1] = '?' THEN
    <give help>
ELSE
    <error check>
```

Now you must figure out how to do the error checking. EOLN should be true after the loop. If it's not, the user typed extra characters beyond the five you want. Putting in an EOLN check will take care of words that are too long. You also need to check that the user didn't type too few characters. This is easily accomplished by examining the value of length. If it is less than WordSize, you reject the input. Finally, you need to check that all the characters typed by the user were letters, not digits, punctuation marks, or other characters. This is a task you might perform often, so it is worth making it a separate function. You make it a function because you have a word going in and a yes/no piece of information coming out. This is a straightforward application of a flag. Here is a pseudocode description for it:

```
repeat
    set good to truth value of (next character is a letter).
until (not good) or (no more characters)
```

You use the REPEAT/UNTIL instead of the WHILE because you know that you want to examine at least one character. Therefore, the REPEAT is the more natural construct. If you use a WHILE, you have to initialize the flag outside the loop, a step that this loop does not require. To expand this pseudocode, you need to introduce a means of indexing the various elements of the array:

```
set index to 0.
repeat
    increment index.
    set good to truth value of (word [index] is a letter).
until (not good) or (index = word length)
```

This easily translates to Pascal:

```
FUNCTION AllLetters (word : WordType) : BOOLEAN;
VAR index : INTEGER;
    good  : BOOLEAN;
BEGIN
    index := 0;
    REPEAT
        index := index + 1;
        good := (word [index] IN ['a'..'z', 'A'..'Z'])
    UNTIL NOT good OR (index = WordSize);
    AllLetters := good
END;
```

You have three different error checks to perform:

Error	Means of checking
Too much input	NOT EOLN
Too little input	(length < WordSize)
Not all letters	NOT AllLetters (word)

For the problem that you are solving, it doesn't make sense to test the five characters of the word to see if they are letters if the user didn't type five characters. If you do, you are likely to test an uninitialized element of the array. And why bother testing the five characters if you know the user typed more than five? Therefore, you should definitely put the letter testing last. The other two are a toss-up. Let's go with the order here.

Number	Test
1	Too many characters
2	Too few characters
3	Not all letters

You now have all the pieces you need. It's just a matter of fitting them into your template. Below is a high-level set of procedures that call **ReadWord** and **AllLetters** written in this section as well as **AskUser** written earlier. It also calls a procedure **WriteHelp** that displays a help message (not reproduced here because of its length).

```
PROCEDURE CheckQuit (VAR quit : BOOLEAN);
BEGIN
    READLN;
    WRITELN ('    Do you want to quit?');
    AskUser (quit);
    IF NOT quit THEN
        WRITELN ('    Okay, you can keep guessing.  Type "?" for help.')
END;

PROCEDURE PerformChecks (VAR good   : BOOLEAN;
                             word   : WordType;
                             length : INTEGER);
BEGIN
    good := EOLN;
    IF NOT good THEN
        WRITE ('    You typed more than ', WordSize:1, ' characters.')
    ELSE
```

```
    BEGIN
        good := (length = WordSize);
        IF NOT good THEN
            WRITE ('    You typed less than ', WordSize:1, ' characters.')
        ELSE
        BEGIN
            good := AllLetters (word);
            IF NOT good THEN
                WRITE ('    You are only allowed to type letters.')
        END
    END;
    IF NOT good THEN
        WRITELN (' Please try again.  Type ? for help.')
END;


PROCEDURE GetGuess (VAR word : WordType;
                    VAR quit : BOOLEAN);
VAR length : INTEGER;
    good   : BOOLEAN;
BEGIN
    quit := false;
    REPEAT
        good := false;
        WRITE (' next guess (RETURN to quit)? ');
        IF EOLN THEN
            CheckQuit (quit)
        ELSE
        BEGIN
            ReadWord (word, length);
            IF word [1] = '?' THEN
                WriteHelp
            ELSE
                PerformChecks (good, word, length);
            READLN
        END
    UNTIL good OR quit
END;
```

Notice that the READLN is done at the bottom of the REPEAT loop in procedure GetGuess because if you perform it before you call PerformChecks, it will discard any extra characters at the end of the line and the test for too long a word won't work.

Here is an example of the kind of interaction you would see if you executed procedure GetGuess:

```
next guess (RETURN to quit)? help
  You typed less than 5 characters.  Please try again.  Type ? for help.
next guess (RETURN to quit)? who cares?
  You typed more than 5 characters.  Please try again.  Type ? for help.
next guess (RETURN to quit)? ?

Type a 5-letter response.  The rules of the
game say that a guess has to be exactly 5
letters long and composed entirely of letters
of the alphabet.

next guess (RETURN to quit)? r2d2!
  You are only allowed to type letters.  Please try again.  Type ? for help.
next guess (RETURN to quit)? whyme
```

14.3 Case Study: Jotto

Now it's time to turn your attention to the large interactive program. By developing it slowly and carefully, you can learn something about how to write such programs. An explanation of the Jotto game comes first, followed by a plan for attacking the problem.

Jotto is a guessing game that uses five-letter words. You are going to write a program that will play the game with a user. Suppose you have a file with over 3000 five-letter words in it to use as a Jotto dictionary. The computer will randomly select a word from the dictionary and will then ask the user to guess it. Suppose the computer randomly selects BOOTY.

To guess the word, the user must use five-letter words as guesses. After making a guess, the computer reports how many jots the guess gets. A jot is a letter match. Thus if the user guesses OGRES, the computer calculates

```
B O O T Y
 /
O G R E S
```

OGRES gets one jot when compared with BOOTY. The O can only match once. Every letter in each word is allowed to match at most once. Letters don't have to match in the same position. Position is irrelevant. If the user then guesses FOOLS, the computer calculates

```
B O O T Y
  | |
F O O L S
```

FOOLS gets two jots when compared with BOOTY. If the user then guesses TUBBY, the computer calculates

TUBBY gets three jots when compared with BOOTY. The double B in TUBBY can match only once against the single B in BOOTY. Each exact pair of characters that matches constitutes another jot. Because each letter can be used once at most, it is not possible to get more than five jots. It is, however, possible to get five jots without being right. Consider

Each of these words is composed of the same five letters, but they are not the same word. Thus SPEAR and PEARS each get five jots when compared with the other. You also get five jots if you compare either of these to RAPES, PARES, PARSE, or REAPS.

Most game-playing programs have more or less the same main program, usually structured like this:

> explain game to user.
> do any necessary preparation that happens only once.
> repeat
>> do any necessary preparation that happens each game.
>> play the game.
>> ask user if he wants to play again.
> until (user doesn't want to play).

You use the **REPEAT** loop because you assume a user is going to play at least one game. Given that every loop will have an emergency exit, it shouldn't be a problem if a user accidentally executes the program and decides to leave. To expand the pseudocode, you have to think about necessary preparations and whether they happen only once or in every game. Since this is a guessing game, it is a good idea to figure out what the user is supposed to guess. To do so, you need to read in the Jotto dictionary. This only has to happen once. Once you have the dictionary read in, you can randomly select a word from it to play the game. You want to select a different word for each play of the game. Thus the pseudocode expands to

> explain game to user.
> read in the dictionary.
> repeat
>> select a word at random from the dictionary.
>> play the game, making user try to guess random word.
>> ask user if he wants to play again.

until (user doesn't want to play).

You let the user play the game over and over until he gets tired of it. To play one guessing game, you will

repeat
    get user's next guess.
    if (guess is wrong) then
        tell how many jots he gets.
until (guess is right)
tell user how many guesses it took him to get this word.

14.3.1   A Development Strategy

From this program you should realize that REPEAT loops can come in handy, particularly in interactive programs. This program has three nested loops. On the outside, you have

repeat
    PlayGame.
until (user is tired)

Inside **PlayGame**, you have

repeat
    GetGuess.
until (guess is right)

Inside **GetGuess**, you have

repeat
    prompt for, read, and check a guess.
until (guess is legal)

Fortunately, you already built and tested this inner loop when you wrote procedure **GetGuess**. One good strategy for attacking the problem is from the inside out. Thus you might have three development stages:

Stage	What program will do
1	Gets a guess, performing error checking
2	Plays the game, keeping track of number of user guesses
3	Plays multiple games

This isn't a bad development plan, but it can be improved. There are two aspects of this program that are challenging. The first is reading in the dictionary and randomly selecting words from it. The second is reporting the jots for a given guess. Both of these are necessary to play the game correctly, so the structure above implies that they are part of stage 2. If so, you will be spending a long time on that stage and might not ever make it to stage 3. Stage 2 is such a quantum leap higher than stage 1 that you might become discouraged.

The best way to incorporate these two other tasks into the plan is to make them stages themselves. It doesn't matter where they appear, but a logical progression is as follows:

Stage	What program will do
1	Gets a guess, performing error checking
2	Plays the game, keeping track of number of user guesses, always with the same word and not reporting jots
3	Reads the dictionary and randomly selects a word for the PlayGame procedure
4	Reports jots for guesses
5	Plays multiple games

You've already completed stage 1, so let's get started on the other four.

14.3.2   Stage 2 Jotto

To finish this stage, you need to develop the main parts of the `PlayGame` procedure. Remember, its pseudocode is

```
repeat
     get user's next guess.
     if (guess is wrong) then
          tell how many jots he gets.
until (guess is right)
tell user how many guesses it took him to get this word.
```

Stage 1 provided you with the procedure for getting a guess, so that much is finished. You don't have to worry about reporting jots yet, but you do have to devise some way of testing whether the guess is right or not. This decision requires knowledge of the answer, so you have to assume that the procedure is passed the correct answer as a parameter. The answer and guess are both of type `WordType`. They are string types, so they can be compared directly.

Now you can attack the pseudocode of `PlayGame` a little. You know that you'll need a variable to store the user's guess and that it will be of type `WordType`. You also know that it will get its value by calling `GetGuess`. You don't have to calculate jots yet, so you can just put in a dummy `WRITELN` statement. The jots will be worked out in stage 4. Therefore, you can expand the pseudocode to

```
    var guess : WordType;
    begin
        repeat
            GetGuess (guess);
            if (guess <> RightAnswer) then
                write "You're wrong, and I'd normally tell you jots."
        until (guess = RightAnswer).
        tell user how many guesses it took him to get this word.
    end
```

The only thing you have left to do is to figure out the number of guesses. This is a simple counting operation:

```
    var guess : WordType;
        NumGuesses : integer;
    begin
        NumGuesses := 0;
        repeat
            GetGuess (guess);
            NumGuesses := NumGuesses + 1.
            if (guess <> RightAnswer) then
                write "You're wrong, and I'd normally tell you jots."
        until (guess = RightAnswer).
        report the value of NumGuesses.
    end
```

This procedure plays the game properly, but it has a major defect in its user interface. It has a REPEAT loop that requires the user to guess over and over and over until the answer is right. Given that there are over 3000 possible words, this could prove tedious. You need to build another emergency exit. This is easy to build, because you have an exit in the low-level GetGuess loop. In fact, GetGuess was modified to have a second parameter to pass on exactly this information, a BOOLEAN variable telling whether or not the user quit. This makes the modifications to the pseudocode simple. You introduce a local BOOLEAN to keep track of whether or not the user quits, the variable gets its value from the innermost loop in GetGuess, and you create an exit in this loop by modifying the UNTIL part of the REPEAT loop so that it will exit not only if the user gets the right answer, but also if he quits.

It is only sporting to give the right answer to the user who decides to quit. Otherwise, he may not believe there is such a word. Thus you can add this to the end of your pseudocode:

```
    if quit then
        report correct answer.
```

This is easily translated:

```
PROCEDURE PlayGame (RightAnswer: WordType);
VAR guess     : WordType;
```

```
    NumTries  : INTEGER;
    quit      : BOOLEAN;
BEGIN
    NumTries := 0;
    REPEAT
        GetGuess (guess, quit);
        IF NOT quit THEN
        BEGIN
            NumTries := NumTries + 1;
            IF (guess <> RightAnswer) THEN
                WRITELN ('  wrong.  Normally I would report the jots.')
        END
    UNTIL (guess = RightAnswer) OR quit;
    WRITELN ('  You made ', NumTries:1, ' guesses.');
    IF quit THEN
        WRITELN ('Correct answer = ', RightAnswer)
END;
```

To test this procedure, you would write a dummy main program such as the following:

```
BEGIN
    WRITE ('What should the answer be this time? ');
    GetGuess (answer);
    PlayGame (answer)
END.
```

This lets you test the behavior of the PlayGame procedure on a known word. You should perform tests such as this before starting with unknown words. It ensures that PlayGame loops when incorrect words are guessed and terminates when the correct word is guessed. If it doesn't behave this way, you must debug PlayGame before proceeding to stage 3.

14.3.3 Stage 3 Jotto

How do you deal with the dictionary? Assume you have a text file of Jotto words:

```
ABYSS
ABUSE
ABOVE
ABOUT
ABORT
```

What kind of errors can there be in the dictionary file? All kinds. What will happen if you read in a string such as "R2D2!"? The user is required to guess only alphabetic characters because of all the error checking and will never be able to get the right answer. If you see errors such as this, it is best to ignore the word and not put it in the dictionary.

Case makes a difference in type CHAR; 'ABYSS' will not equal 'abyss'. This is not what you want to happen. Therefore, you must figure a way to deal with such discrepancies. The simple solution is to turn everything to one case. For example, you can turn each word to uppercase letters as it is read in. You need to remember this, but you should think more about the dictionary before you figure out how to uppercase all the words in it.

Because you want to be able to randomly pull any word out of the dictionary, the file is too limited. You need to transfer the information from the file into an array. You already have a WordType defined as

```
CONST WordSize = 5;
TYPE  WordType = PACKED ARRAY [1..WordSize] OF CHAR;
```

We can define a type for dictionaries using the generic list declarations from Chapter 9:

```
CONST MaxWord       = 3100;
TYPE  WordList      = ARRAY [1..MaxWord] of WordType;
      DictionaryType = RECORD
          words       : WordList;
          length      : INTEGER
      END;
```

You also need to define a file variable used to read values from the dictionary file:

```
VAR DictionaryFile : TEXT;
```

The easiest way to read words from the dictionary is to alter your existing word reading procedure to take a file parameter. This way it can be used to read from either the terminal or the dictionary file. You then can do error checking in the procedure for reading the dictionary to ignore any words that aren't composed of all letters or that aren't of length 5. With the modified version of the procedure, you can say the following to read from the terminal:

```
ReadWord (INPUT, word, length);
```

and you can say the following to read from the dictionary file:

```
ReadWord (DictionaryFile, word, length);
```

One of the virtues of this solution is that all Jotto words are read through the single ReadWord procedure. This offers us a nice fix to the problem of case. Since all the words are read in this procedure, you can turn everything to uppercase inside that procedure. First, you resurrect a tool for turning a character to uppercase:

```
PROCEDURE TurnToUppercase (VAR character : CHAR);
BEGIN
    IF (character IN ['a'..'z']) THEN
        character := CHR (ORD (character) - ORD ('a') + ORD ('A'))
END;
```

Remember from Chapter 11, however, that we can't call this procedure on the individual characters of a PACKED ARRAY. Thus you must modify ReadWord slightly:

```
PROCEDURE ReadWord (VAR InFile : TEXT;
                    VAR word   : WordType;
                    VAR length : INTEGER);
VAR next : CHAR;
BEGIN
    length := 0;
    WHILE NOT EOLN (InFile) AND (length < WordSize) DO
    BEGIN
        length := length + 1;
        READ (InFile, next);
        TurnToUppercase (next);
        word [length] := next
    END
END;
```

Given this procedure for reading a single word, the procedure for reading the dictionary is easy. We start with the generic list reading procedure from Chapter 9:

```
PROCEDURE ReadList (VAR list : ListType);
BEGIN
    <perform any actions that need to be done before reading>;
    WITH list DO
    BEGIN
        length := 0;
        WHILE <more data to read> AND (length < MaxWord) DO
        BEGIN
            length := length + 1;
            READ (elements [length])
        END
    END;
    <perform any actions that need to be done after reading>
END;
```

The test in this case is NOT EOF. Before reading, you need to open the file for reading, and nothing special has to happen after reading. The only minor modifications you have to make to this procedure are to add a check on the legality of the word, removing it if necessary, and to add a command to go to a new input line:

```
PROCEDURE ReadDictionary (VAR dictionary : DictionaryType);
BEGIN
    RESET (DictionaryFile);
    WITH dictionary DO
    BEGIN
        length := 0;
        WHILE NOT EOF (DictionaryFile) AND (length < MaxLength) DO
        BEGIN
            length := length + 1;
            ReadWord (DictionaryFile, words [length], WordLength);
            IF NOT AllLetters (words [length]) OR (length <> WordSize) THEN
                length := length - 1;
            READLN (DictionaryFile)
        END
    END
END;
```

Next, you have to figure out how to randomly select a word from the dictionary. If you pull your pseudorandom number generation tools out of your software library, you'll almost be done. You can copy procedure GetSeed and function RandomInt into the program and declare a **seed** variable at the same time. Then you can get some random integers. You want to select a random word out of the dictionary. This means that you want to select a random array index between 1 and the total number of words. You don't want to choose something higher than the number of words, because then you would be examining an uninitialized word. Thus you will ask the RandomInt function for a random integer between 1 and NumberOfWords:

```
RandomInt (seed, 1, NumberOfWords);
```

Therefore, you can use it to select a random word by saying

```
answer := dictionary [RandomInt (seed, 1, NumberOfWords)];
```

The function call inside the brackets will generate a random index into the dictionary array. The selected element will be assigned to the variable **answer**, presumably of type WordType. To make use of this statement, you modify the main program:

```
BEGIN
    GetSeed (seed);
    ReadDictionary (dictionary);
    answer := dictionary [RandomInt (seed, 1, NumberOfWords)];
```

```
        WRITELN ('Answer = ', answer);
        PlayGame (answer)
  END.
```

In this program, the `PlayGame` procedure will be given a random word from the dictionary. To keep track of what is going on, though, it writes out the value of the word before executing `PlayGame`. You won't leave this code in the final version of the program, because it wouldn't be a very interesting guessing game if the computer told you the answer before you began guessing. But for purposes of debugging and development, you need this kind of information.

14.3.4 Stage 4 Jotto

How do you report jots to the user? In terms of lines of code contributed to the final solution, this stage contributes the least: a single 16-line procedure. However, it is tricky enough that it deserves to be separated from the rest.

The calculation of jots is not difficult to perform. The tough part is figuring out how to express the process that you have stored in your head as a Pascal procedure. So how do you calculate jots? If letters had to match in location, then the calculation would be easy. You could simply compare the first elements, the second, and so on until the fifth. But you need to consider many more possibilities than this.

To faciliate discussion of the problem, write the header for the procedure:

```
PROCEDURE ReportJotsFor (word1, word2 : WordType);
```

You could be passed words such as the following:

	[1]	[2]	[3]	[4]	[5]
word1	'B'	'O'	'O'	'T'	'Y'

	[1]	[2]	[3]	[4]	[5]
word2	'T'	'U'	'B'	'B'	'Y'

There are a lot of wrong ways of approaching this problem and only one really good simple way that works. Consider one of the wrong ways. As noted earlier, you can't just compare elements in the same position. In this case, for example, the B in position [1] of `word1` can match the B in either element [3] or [4] of `word2`. In other words, you can potentially match element [1] of `word1` with any of the elements of `word2`. To calculate the contribution of element [1], then, you might say

```
if (word1 [1] matches any letter in word2) then
    jots := jots + 1.
```

You can do the same for element [2] of word1:

if (word1 [2] matches any letter in word2) then
    jots := jots + 1.

In fact, you can turn this into a general strategy:

jots := 0;
for index going 1 to 5 do
    if (word1 [index] matches any letter in word2) then
        jots := jots + 1.

Here's what happens when you follow this strategy:

jots starts at 0.
word1 [1] matches word2 [3],   so jots now = 1.
word1 [2] doesn't match,   so jots still = 1.
word1 [3] doesn't match,   so jots still = 1.
word1 [4] matches word2 [1],   so jots now= 2.
word1 [5] matches word2 [5],   so jots now = 3.

This is the right answer. And if you try to use this algorithm on other word pairs, you will find that it works most of the time. But it has one big bug. Think of what would happen if the two words above were switched in order. Order is supposed to be unimportant, so you should get the same answer. You start with

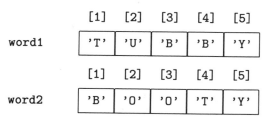

jots starts at 0.
word1 [1] matches word2 [4],   so jots now = 1.
word1 [2] doesn't match,   so jots still = 1.
word1 [3] matches word2 [1],   so jots now= 2.
word1 [4] matches word2 [1],   so jots now= 3.
word1 [5] matches word2 [5],   so jots now = 4.

Here, the algorithm gives the wrong answer of 4 jots. The problem is that both the B's in TUBBY are matched with the single B in BOOTY, which is not supposed to happen. Letters can only match once, so the B in BOOTY can only contribute 1 jot, not 2.

There are many tricks you might employ to fix this problem, but there's only one that makes sense. Imagine how you would solve this problem with a piece of paper and a pencil. You would probably cross out any character that has already been matched. In the preceding algorithm, you start with

You first examine element [1] of word1. It matches element [4] of word2, so you have 1 jot and do the following:

You cross out the T's, so they can no longer be matched. Then you compare element [2] of word1 with the elements of word2. It doesn't match, so nothing happens. Then you compare element [3] of word1 with word2. It matches element [1] of word2, so you increase the number of jots to 2 and do the following:

On the next iteration of the loop, you compare element [4] of word1 with the elements of word2. The B stored in element [4] of word1 matches what was stored in element [1] of word2, but since you crossed out element [1] of word2, it doesn't matter: there's no match. You still have 2 jots. You end by comparing element [5] of word1 with the elements of word2 and find that it matches element [5] of word2. Thus you increase the number of jots to 3 and once more cross out the Y's, leaving

This is the strategy you want to follow to count up the jots. Since you want to wipe out some of the characters stored in these two words, you should make sure that any manipulations made by your procedure are on local copies and not on the original arrays.

Your basic pseudocode, then, is

```
for index going 1 to 5 do
    if (word1 [index] matches any letter of word2) then
    begin
        jots := jots + 1.
        wipe out the value of word1 [index].
        wipe out the value in word2 that it matched.
    end
```

The difference between this pseudocode and the earlier version is the presence of the two commands to wipe out the values that match. To expand this pseudocode, you start by clarifying what you mean by (word1 [index] matches any letter of word2). You would test for such a relationship by examining all the elements of word2, all indexes between 1 and 5. Thus you want a nested loop that varies over the indexes of word2:

```
for index1 going 1 to 5 do
    for index2 going 1 to 5 do
        if word1 [index1] = word2 [index2] then
        begin
            jots := jots + 1.
            wipe out the value of word1 [index1].
            wipe out the value of word2 [index2].
        end
```

This is almost your Pascal procedure. You just need to specify how to wipe out the values. Even here there is room for minor bugs. Since the arrays store all letters, you can change the characters to some nonalphabetic value. The nonalphabetic value won't match any of the letters of the word, so that will, in effect, wipe out the value. The bad solution is

```
for index1 going 1 to 5 do
    for index2 going 1 to 5 do
        if word1 [index1] = word2 [index2] then
        begin
            jots := jots + 1.
            word1 [index1] := '!'.
            word2 [index2] := '!'.
        end
```

Here, you wipe out the values by setting them to exclamation marks. The bug is that there are exclamation marks in both words. Thus eventually you may get a match on the exclamation marks. This does actually happen if you use FOR loops. You can eliminate the bug by changing the FOR loops to WHILE loops that stop once a match is found. A simpler solution, however, is to store different characters in each array so there can be no match:

```
for index1 going 1 to 5 do
    for index2 going 1 to 5 do
        if word1 [index1] = word2 [index2] then
```

```
begin
    jots := jots + 1.
    word1 [index1] := '!'.
    word2 [index2] := '*'.
end
```

In this case, since you store one punctuation mark in one word and another in the other, they can never mistakenly match. This is easily turned into a procedure. By making **word1** and **word2** value parameters, the procedure will have its own local copies to manipulate. It won't matter to the outside world if this procedure resets some of the letters of those words to exclamation marks and asterisks: changing a value parameter never affects the outside world.

```
PROCEDURE ReportJotsFor (word1, word2 : WordType);
VAR index1    : INTEGER;
    index2    : INTEGER;
    jots      : INTEGER;
BEGIN
    jots := 0;
    FOR index1 := 1 TO WordSize DO
        FOR index2 := 1 TO WordSize DO
            IF word1 [index1] = word2 [index2] THEN
            BEGIN
                jots := jots + 1;
                word1 [index1] := '!';
                word2 [index2] := '*'
            END;
    WRITELN ('You got ', jots:1, ' jots')
END;
```

The last step is to insert a call on this procedure inside **PlayGame** where your pseudocode includes it.

14.3.5 Stage 5 Jotto

Now you're ready for the big time: filling in the details of the main program. Your goal here is to make the program play multiple times. Reaching that goal is easy, but the program still has several loose ends that you need to tie up.

Here is the pseudocode for the main program:

explain program to user.
read in the dictionary.
repeat
    select a word at random from the dictionary for the user to guess.
    play the Jotto guessing game.
    ask user if he wants to play again.
until (user doesn't want to play).

You only have three pieces to fill in here that aren't in place: explaining the program, asking the user if he wants to play again, and looping until he says no. The explanation is easy to accomplish by defining an Introduction procedure that gives the rules of the game.

When you wrote procedure DoQuit developed in stage 1, you copied the AskUser procedure to the program to verify whether the user really wants to quit. You can use the same procedure to find out whether the user wants to play again:

```
WRITELN ('Do you want to play again?');
AskUser (yes);
```

You can then examine the value of the variable **yes** to see what the response is. You can set up the loop easily by having it go until **yes** becomes **FALSE** (i.e., when the user says he doesn't want to play again).

You can get triple mileage out of the **AskUser** procedure by also asking users if they want instructions. That way people who run the program more than once and who don't need instructions will have the option of skipping them.

14.3.6 Discussion of Jotto

The Jotto program has grown incredibly since you started. It has a total of 13 procedures and 2 functions. The order in which you declare them should not be haphazard. You should try to group them into logical categories and logical levels as follows:

Level	Category	Procedure name
1	Low-level	Instructions, WriteHelp
2	CHAR tool	TurnToUppercase
2	Pseudorandom number tools	GetSeed, RandomInt
2	User-interface tool	AskUser
2	Word manipulating tools	AllLetters, ReadWord
3	Convenience procedures	PerformChecks, CheckQuit, SetUp
4	Midlevel	GetGuess, ReportJotsFor
5	High level	ReadDictionary, PlayGame
6	Top level	Main program

Before going further, consider an analogy that will help you understand these six levels. Suppose that you are going to spy on Julia Child in her kitchen to find out the secrets she doesn't share on TV. As you watch her prepare a meal, you will see many different things, each with a different level of importance. At level 1 are skills like using a measuring spoon or cracking an egg that are so trivial they aren't worth paying attention to. At level 2, however, you start noticing techniques that she uses, little tricks of the trade. How does she cream the butter and the sugar so well? What is she doing with that wooden spoon?

How does she create those lovely swirls on the cake? These are low-level details, but they are important because they are the learned habits of an expert cook and they will find application over and over again in other cooking tasks. At level 3, you start noticing the larger things that she has gathered together for the meal: a bottle of wine, a head of lettuce, a bag of tomatoes, two steaks wrapped in butcher paper, and so on. There are many of these little packages that are all going to be part of the meal. The packages by themselves do not teach you anything; the important thing is how she prepares a meal using them. So you move on to level 4. Here you find her making a sauce which, even though it is not the meal, is crucial. You pay close attention to exactly how she does it. At level 5 is a stack of hand-written recipes from her kitchen counter. These are the high-level secrets that tell the big story. At level 6 is the dinner menu. The menu is pretty much known from having examined the other levels, so the phrases "filet mignon" and "black forest cake" are not helpful. They are too high level and reveal no secrets.

The point of this analogy is that there is no simple rule about what is interesting in a solution and what is not. The higher level isn't always the more interesting level; or the lower level, the least important. A complex solution such as this tends not to be terribly interesting at either the highest or lowest level. Levels 1 and 6 in this program did not involve any design decisions, they were predictable. The more interesting levels start at 2 and 5. At level 2 you see tools that will prove useful for later programs, and you start to understand what makes a successful low-level procedure. Level 2 procedures are the tricks of the trade, the bits of technique that make a good solution possible. At level 5 you see the central procedures of the program, the central nervous system of the whole program. Most of the design decisions are in these two procedures. Level 4 is also of interest to you right now, since you haven't written many procedures at this level. With practice, though, level 4 will also become boring because there are simple techniques for producing such procedures.

The level 3 procedures are very different from the level 2 procedures, and you should notice the difference. They serve different purposes in the program. Consider as an example `GetGuess`. It grew to almost two pages of code. It was totally unmanageable in that form, so you created two spinoff procedures that did nothing but take a large chunk of code away (`CheckQuit` and `PerformChecks`). These procedures have helped structure the solution and have helped to partition the complexity of the `GetGuess` task into smaller subtasks. However, the procedures you generate as a result will probably never be used in another program. Procedures such as these are too special purpose, too strongly tied to the procedure they come from. The code might be detailed and abundant, but it is straightforward and boring. They are like Julia Child's packages of food which, while certainly substantial, have no secrets to reveal.

`ReportJotsFor` is something of an anomaly because it is vital to the workings of the program and has a high risk of being bug-ridden, but it doesn't have the kind of central place you would expect of a level 4 procedure (i.e., calling other procedures and functions or being called from the main program). I almost categorized it as a level 2 word manipulating tool, but I think that since getting this procedure just right is so tricky and so important, it deserves the higher classification.

The key to writing a large program such as this is the ability to perform well at levels 4, 5, and 2. If you can perform well at levels 4 and 5, then you know how to construct a large program. If you perform well at level 2, you know how to make it work. You can definitely perform well at level 1 and probably at level 6 as well. It doesn't require great insight into a problem to see its first-level decomposition. The more difficult parts are the level 4 and 5 decompositions and the level 2 details. You don't have to worry about level 3 at all, because these procedures naturally appear when a level 4 or 5 procedure or the main program becomes too long or is executing statements that seem too low level.

To help you in your study of this program, here's a structure diagram of it. You might find it worth noting that the relative position of the procedures and functions in this diagram has very little to do with their level as listed in the table above.

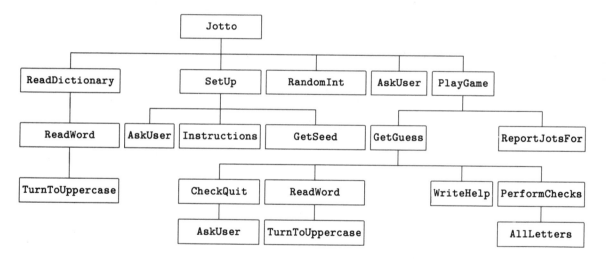

14.4 The Complete Jotto Program

Here, finally, is the Jotto program:

```
(* pre       : Program is supplied a jotto dictionary file of no more than *)
(*            : MaxWordwith lines, with one legal jotto word per line.       *)
(* post      : User plays the guessing game of jotto with the computer      *)
(*            : until he gets bored and says he wants to quit.               *)
(* parameters : DictionaryFile-in, INPUT-in, OUTPUT-out.                     *)
```

```
PROGRAM Jotto (DictionaryFile, INPUT, OUTPUT);
CONST WordSize      = 5;                                 (* letters/word     *)
      MaxWord       = 3100;                              (* max dict length  *)
TYPE  WordType      = PACKED ARRAY [1..WordSize] OF CHAR;(* stores a word    *)
      WordList      = ARRAY [1..MaxWord] OF WordType;    (* stores dict      *)
      DictionaryType = RECORD
           words      : WordList;
           length     : integer
      END;
VAR   DictionaryFile : TEXT;                             (* dictionary file  *)
      dictionary     : DictionaryType;                   (* holds dictionary *)
      answer         : WordType;                         (* secret word      *)
      seed           : INTEGER;                          (* for random       *)
      yes            : BOOLEAN;                           (* user said yes?   *)

PROCEDURE Instructions;
(* post : Jotto instructions are displayed for the user. *)
BEGIN
    WRITELN;
    WRITELN ('This is the game of Jotto.  I will think of a five-letter');
    WRITELN ('word, and you will try to guess it.  I will give you hints');
    WRITELN ('along the way.  For each word, I will tell you the number of');
    WRITELN ('"jots" it gets.  A "jot" is a letter match.  A letter can only');
    WRITELN ('match once, though.  So the word BOOTY would have one jot when');
    WRITELN ('compared with OGRES, two jots when compared with FOOLS or');
    WRITELN ('COLOR.  Notice that you can get five jots and still not get');
    WRITELN ('the word.  If the word is PEARS, you will get five jots for');
    WRITELN ('SPEAR, RAPES, PARES, PARSE, or REAPS.')
END;    (* Instructions *)


PROCEDURE WriteHelp;
(* post     : Help message about legal versus illegal jotto words is *)
(*          : displayed for user.                                    *)
(* requires : constant WordSize.                                     *)
BEGIN
    WRITELN;
    WRITELN ('    Type a ', WordSize:1, '-letter response.  The rules of the');
    WRITELN ('    game say that a guess has to be exactly ', WordSize:1);
    WRITELN ('    letters long and composed entirely of letters');
    WRITELN ('    of the alphabet.');
    WRITELN
END;    (* WriteHelp *)
```

```
PROCEDURE TurnToUppercase (VAR character : CHAR);
(* post       : character is turned to uppercase, if a lowercase letter. *)
(* parameters : character-in/out.                                        *)
BEGIN
    IF character IN ['a'..'z'] THEN
        character := CHR (ORD (character) - ORD ('a') + ORD ('A'))
END;   (* TurnToUppercase *)

PROCEDURE GetSeed (VAR seed: INTEGER);
(* post       : User is prompted for initial value of seed. *)
(* parameters : seed-out.                                    *)
BEGIN
    WRITELN ('I need an integer to seed the random number generator.');
    WRITE ('Give me a seed ---> ');
    READLN (seed);
    WRITELN
END;   (* GetSeed *)

FUNCTION RandomInt (VAR seed : INTEGER;
                        low  : INTEGER;
                        high : INTEGER) : INTEGER;
(* pre        : 1 <= seed <= 1024; low <= high.                          *)
(* post       : A pseudorandom value is returned with low <= value <= high; *)
(*            : seed is modified to a new value in [1..1024].            *)
(* parameters : low-in, high-in, seed-in/out.                            *)
BEGIN
    seed := (29 * seed + 1) MOD 1024;
    RandomInt := TRUNC ((seed/1024) * (high - low + 1)) + low
END;   (* RandomInt *)

PROCEDURE AskUser (VAR UserSaysYes : BOOLEAN);
(* pre        : User has been asked a yes or no question.       *)
(* post       : User is forced to type either Y or N; if user types Y, *)
(*            : UserSaysYes is set to TRUE, otherwise FALSE.    *)
(* parameters : UserSaysYes-out.                                *)
(* algorithm  : Loop until user types legal response.           *)
VAR response : CHAR;   (* user response                         *)
BEGIN
    REPEAT
        WRITE ('    yes or no? ');
        READLN (response)
    UNTIL (response in ['y', 'Y', 'n', 'N']);
    UserSaysYes := (response in ['y', 'Y'])
END;   (* AskUser *)
```

```
FUNCTION AllLetters (word : WordType) : BOOLEAN;
(* post      : Returns TRUE if all elements of word are alphabetic, *)
(*            : otherwise returns FALSE.                             *)
(* parameters : word-in.                                            *)
(* requires   : constant WordSize.                                  *)
VAR index    : INTEGER;   (* used to index over word               *)
    good     : BOOLEAN;   (* whether only letters have been seen    *)
BEGIN
    index := 0;
    REPEAT
        index := index + 1;
        good := (word [index] IN ['a'..'z', 'A'..'Z'])
    UNTIL NOT good OR (index = WordSize);
    AllLetters := good
END;   (* AllLetters *)


PROCEDURE ReadWord (VAR InFile : TEXT;
                    VAR word   : WordType;
                    VAR length : INTEGER);
(* pre       : Input cursor is at beginning of a word.                  *)
(* post      : WordSize characters are read, or all characters to EOLN are *)
(*            : read, whichever happens first; length set appropriately;   *)
(*            : input cursor positioned after last character that is read;  *)
(*            : all characters converted to uppercase.                  *)
(* parameters : InFile-in/out, word-out, length-out.                    *)
(* requires   : constant WordSize; type WordType; procedure TurnToUppercase. *)
VAR next    : CHAR;   (* next character from input line               *)
BEGIN
    length := 0;
    WHILE NOT EOLN (InFile) AND (length < WordSize) DO
    BEGIN
        length := length + 1;
        READ (InFile, next);
        TurnToUppercase (next);
        word [length] := next
    END
END;   (* ReadWord *)


PROCEDURE PerformChecks (VAR good   : BOOLEAN;
                         word   : WordType;
                         length : INTEGER);
(* pre       : If there are extra characters at end of line for last *)
(*            : READ, input cursor is still positioned at it.        *)
```

```
(* post        : The three checks on legality are performed on word.   *)
(*             : i.e., check for: too many characters, too few          *)
(*             : nonalphabetic characters with error messages directed  *)
(*             : to the user as appropriate; good set to FALSE if an    *)
(*             : error is seen, TRUE otherwise.                         *)
(* requires    : constant WordSize, type WordType, function AllLetters. *)
(* parameters  : word-in, length-in, good-in/out.                      *)
(* algorithm   : Nested IF/THEN/ELSE to distinguish three errors.  The  *)
(*             : order in which they will be reported is: too much, too *)
(*             : little, and finally nonalphabetics.                   *)
BEGIN
    good := EOLN;
    IF NOT good THEN
        WRITE ('    You typed more than ', WordSize:1, ' characters.')
    ELSE
    BEGIN
        good := (length = WordSize);
        IF NOT good THEN
            WRITE ('    You typed less than ', WordSize:1, ' characters.')
        ELSE
        BEGIN
            good := AllLetters (word);
            IF NOT good THEN
                WRITE ('    You are only allowed to type letters.')
        END;
    END;
    IF NOT good THEN
        WRITELN (' Please try again.  Type ? for help.')
END;   (* PerformChecks *)


PROCEDURE CheckQuit (VAR quit : BOOLEAN);
(* pre         : User typed a carriage return when prompted for a guess. *)
(* post        : User is asked to clarify that he wants to quit.  If he   *)
(*             : doesn't, then he is told how to get help (just in case). *)
(* parameters  : quit-out.                                              *)
(* requires    : procedure AskUser.                                     *)
BEGIN
    READLN;
    WRITELN ('    Do you want to quit?');
    AskUser (quit);
    IF NOT quit THEN
        WRITELN ('    Okay, you can keep guessing.  Type "?" for help.')
END;   (* CheckQuit *)
```

```
PROCEDURE SetUp (VAR seed : INTEGER);
(* post        : User is given instructions if he wants; seed for random *)
(*             : sequence is initialized.                                 *)
(* parameters : seed-out.                                                 *)
(* requires    : type WordList; procedures AskUser, Instructions, and     *)
(*             : GetSeed.                                                  *)
VAR yes        : BOOLEAN;    (* whether or not user says yes              *)
BEGIN
    WRITELN ('Do you want instructions?');
    AskUser (yes);
    IF yes THEN
        instructions;
    WRITELN;
    GetSeed (seed)
END;    (* SetUp *)

PROCEDURE GetGuess (VAR word : WordType;
                    VAR quit : BOOLEAN);
(* post        : A legal Jotto word is read from the user at the terminal or *)
(*             : the user indicates that he wants to quit.  Thus either Quit *)
(*             : will be FALSE and Word will have a value, or vice-versa.    *)
(* parameters : word-out, quit-out.                                         *)
(* requires    : type WordType; procedures CheckQuit, ReadWord, WriteHelp,   *)
(*             : PerformChecks.                                              *)
(* algorithm   : Loop until legal value is typed by user.  Provide error     *)
(*             : messages as appropriate, provide help if user types '?'.    *)
VAR length     : INTEGER;    (* length of word read from the terminal       *)
    good       : BOOLEAN;    (* whether or not the input is legal           *)
BEGIN
    quit := FALSE;
    REPEAT
        good := FALSE;
        WRITE ('  next guess (RETURN to quit)? ');
        IF EOLN THEN
            CheckQuit (quit)
        ELSE
        BEGIN
            ReadWord (INPUT, word, length);
            IF word [1] = '?' THEN
                WriteHelp
            ELSE
                PerformChecks (good, word, length);
            READLN
        END
```

```
        UNTIL good OR quit
END;    (* GetGuess *)


PROCEDURE ReportJotsFor (word1, word2 : WordType);
(* post       : Words are compared; number of jots is calculated; result *)
(*             : displayed for the user.                                  *)
(* parameters : word1-in, word2-in.                                       *)
(* algorithm  : Every element of the first word is compared with every    *)
(*             : element of the second word.  Whenever a match is         *)
(*             : encountered, the matching characters are wiped out so     *)
(*             : they won't match again.                                  *)
VAR index1   : INTEGER;   (* used to scan indices of first word          *)
    index2   : INTEGER;   (* used to scan indices of second word         *)
    jots     : INTEGER;   (* total number of character matches           *)
BEGIN
    jots := 0;
    FOR index1 := 1 TO WordSize DO
        FOR index2 := 1 TO WordSize DO
            IF word1 [index1] = word2 [index2] THEN
            BEGIN
                jots := jots + 1;
                word1 [index1] := '!';
                word2 [index2] := '*'
            END;
    WRITELN (' ', jots:1, ' jots')
END;    (* ReportJotsFor *)


PROCEDURE ReadDictionary (VAR dictionary: DictionaryType);
(* pre        : DictionaryFile is bound to a file of not more than MaxWord *)
(*             : jotto words, one per line.                                *)
(* post       : All words from file read into dictionary; length set      *)
(*             : appropriately; DictionaryFile window at EOF; if illegal   *)
(*             : words are seen, they are not inserted in dictionary.      *)
(* parameters : dictionary-out.                                           *)
(* requires   : type DictionaryType; variable DictionaryFile; and procedure *)
(*             : ReadWord.                                                 *)
(* algorithm  : EOF loop.                                                 *)
VAR WordLength : INTEGER;   (* length of next word read from dictionary   *)
BEGIN
    RESET (DictionaryFile);
    WITH dictionary DO
    BEGIN
        length := 0;
        WHILE NOT EOF (DictionaryFile) AND (length < MaxWord) DO
```

```
        BEGIN
            length := length + 1;
            ReadWord (DictionaryFile, words [length], WordLength);
            (* If illegal word, then take out of dictionary. *)
                length := length - 1;
            READLN (DictionaryFile)
        END
    END
END;   (* ReadDictionary *)


PROCEDURE PlayGame (RightAnswer: WordType);
(* pre        : RightAnswer selected from jotto dictionary.          *)
(* post       : User is prompted for guesses until word is guessed; user *)
(*             : is informed at the end how many guesses it took.    *)
(* parameters : RightAnswer-in.                                      *)
(* requires   : type WordType; procedures GetGuess and ReportJotsFor. *)
VAR guess     : WordType;    (* user's current guess               *)
    NumTries  : INTEGER;     (* number of user guesses             *)
    quit      : BOOLEAN;     (* if user decides to quit on this word *)
BEGIN
    WRITELN;
    NumTries := 0;
    REPEAT
        GetGuess (guess, quit);
        IF NOT quit THEN
        BEGIN
            NumTries := NumTries + 1;
            IF (guess <> RightAnswer) THEN
                ReportJotsFor (guess, RightAnswer)
        END
    UNTIL (guess = RightAnswer) OR quit;
    IF quit THEN
        WRITELN ('Correct answer = ', RightAnswer)
    ELSE
        WRITELN ('  You got it!');
    WRITELN ('  You made ', NumTries:1, ' guesses.');
    WRITELN
END;   (* PlayGame *)


BEGIN   (* main program *)
    SetUp (seed);
    ReadDictionary (dictionary);
```

```
    REPEAT
        WRITELN;
        WRITELN ('I''m thinking of a word . . .');
        WITH dictionary DO
            answer := words [RandomInt (seed, 1, length)];
        PlayGame (answer);
        WRITELN ('Do you want to play again? ');
        AskUser (yes)
    UNTIL NOT yes;
    WRITELN ('Okay, bye for now.')
END.    (* main program *)
```

Here is a log of execution:

```
Do you want instructions?
    yes or no? y

This is the game of Jotto.  I will think of a five-letter
word, and you are supposed to guess it.  I will give you hints
along the way.  For each word, I will tell you the number of
"jots" it gets.  A "jot" is a letter match.  A letter can only
match once, though.  So the word BOOTY would have one jot when
compared with OGRES, two jots when compared with FOOLS or
COLOR.  Notice that you can get five jots and still not get
the word.  If the word is PEARS, you will get five jots for
SPEAR or RAPES or PARES or REAPS.

I need an integer to seed the random number generator.
Give me a seed ---> 23

I'm thinking of a word . . .

next guess (RETURN to quit)? fools
0 jots
next guess (RETURN to quit)? spare
2 jots
next guess (RETURN to quit)? pours
1 jots
next guess (RETURN to quit)? price
1 jots
next guess (RETURN to quit)? north
2 jots
next guess (RETURN to quit)? rings
3 jots
```

```
next guess (RETURN to quit)? green
3 jots
next guess (RETURN to quit)? grays
4 jots
next guess (RETURN to quit)? rangy
You got it!
You made 9 guesses.

Do you want to play again?
    yes or no? y

I'm thinking of a word . . .

next guess (RETURN to quit)? about
2 jots
next guess (RETURN to quit)? sheer
0 jots
next guess (RETURN to quit)? gloom
1 jots
next guess (RETURN to quit)? steam
1 jots
next guess (RETURN to quit)? slips
2 jots
next guess (RETURN to quit)? erupt
2 jots
next guess (RETURN to quit)? clock
1 jots
next guess (RETURN to quit)? slant
3 jots
next guess (RETURN to quit)? sting
3 jots
next guess (RETURN to quit)? sling
3 jots
next guess (RETURN to quit)? until
You got it!
You made 11 guesses.

Do you want to play again?
    yes or no? n
Okay, bye for now.
```

14.5 Key Concepts

- The user interface of a program is the way in which it interacts with a user. Carefully design the user interface of an interactive program.

- In a well-designed program the user feels in control, implying that emergency exits are available to the user.

- A well-designed program will check for user errors and will provide interactive help.

- A well-designed program behaves in the way the user expects it to: capitalizes on any intuitions the user might have; the user interface is consistent; and the programmer's model is not forced on the user. These characteristics can be achieved without forcing the user's model on the programmer because you can write procedures that translate from one model to the other.

14.6 Self-Check Exercises

1. Suppose that you are writing a program that plays a board game with a user and that you need to find out from the user which square of the board he would like to move to next. The user is supposed to supply you with two numbers that specify the row and column numbers of the square. If you would like to build error-checking code that distinguishes the following user errors, what would be a logical hierarchy for the tests?

   - Square is illegal.
   - Square is occupied.
   - First value entered is not a number.
   - Second value entered is not a number.

2. Suppose that you are going to write an interactive program that manipulates playing cards. In particular, you want to write a procedure **Discard** that shows a user what cards he currently holds in his hand and asks him to pick a card to discard. The user will specify the card as two characters: one to indicate the rank (1 = one, 2 = two, ..., 9 = nine, 0 = ten, J = jack, Q = queen, K = king, A = ace) and one to indicate the suit (S = spades, H = hearts, C = clubs, D = diamonds). Suppose that you want to test the user errors listed below. What would be a logical hierarchy for the tests?

   - The card specified by the user is not in his hand.
   - Suit character is illegal.
   - The user typed more than two characters.
   - Rank character is illegal.

3. You are going to write a procedure **ChooseCard** that would be used by procedure **Discard** mentioned in Exercise 2. The procedure should follow the general error-checking template, prompting for user input repeatedly until it passes all four tests outlined in Exercise 2. You should be able to formulate **BOOLEAN** expressions for three of the four tests, but the test for whether or not a card is in the user's hand depends on the implementation of a hand. You can assume that your procedure is passed the hand, as indicated in the following header:

```
PROCEDURE ChooseCard (VAR hand : HandType;
                      VAR rank : CHAR;
                      VAR suit : CHAR);
```

You can test whether the rank and suit characters correspond to a card in the hand by calling a **BOOLEAN FUNCTION** called InHand:

```
InHand (rank, suit, hand)
```

4. Function **AllLetters** seems like a fairly powerful tool that you might want to use again. In another context, though, you might not be searching for the same thing. You are going to make use of the set types defined in Chapter 11 to make **AllLetters** even more flexible. Assuming you have this definition:

```
TYPE CharSet = SET OF CHAR;
```

rewrite **AllLetters** so that it becomes something called **AllInSet** with the header below, a function with a second parameter specifying what set to check against. What call would be the equivalent of the current **AllLetters**? How would you check a word to see that it is all in uppercase?

```
FUNCTION AllInSet (word : WordType;
                   chars : CharSet) : BOOLEAN;
```

5. What will happen in program **Jotto** if all words in the dictionary are illegal? How can you address this potential problem?

6. What changes would have to be made to program **Jotto** to make it play the same word-guessing game for four-letter words?

7. In program **Jotto** the user is told how many character matches he has, but he isn't told whether they are in the right position or not. Suppose you want to change the game so that it doesn't report merely jots, but rather it reports two different things called "fermis" and "picas." A fermi is a character match in the right position and a pica is a character match in the wrong position. If you have the opportunity to report either a fermi or a pica (as with the O in BOOTY and NOSES), you should report the fermi. What changes would have to be made to the program to accommodate this new scheme?

8. One of the standard rules of **Jotto** not enforced by this program is that all guesses are supposed to be real words, not just stray combinations of letters such as XYZZY. Can you think of a way that the program could at least partially check the user's input to see if it is a legal word?

9. Suppose you want to expand program Jotto so that it not only makes up words for the user to guess, but also makes guesses at a word that the user has thought

up. Programming a good guessing strategy is challenging, but a simple approach would be to

set current guess list to jotto dictionary.

repeat

    make a guess from the current guess list.

    eliminate words from current guess list.

until (you get it right) or (current guess list is empty)

It turns out that you have a powerful tool available to you for eliminating words from the current guess list once you've made a guess and found out how many jots it gets, and it needs only slight alterations. Can you think of what tool could help with this task?

10. You are going to write the main program for a simple interactive game program. To simplify things, you can make use of procedures `GetSeed` and `AskUser` and function `RandomInt`. Your program is going to play a guessing game against the user. On each round of the game, your program will choose a new random answer between 1 and 100. Then either the user or the program will get a chance to guess at the answer. In order to win, you don't have to guess the exact answer, you only have to guess a number that ends in the same digit (i.e., a number that has the same value in MOD 10 as the answer). You can also make use of the following procedures to obtain the user and computer guesses:

```
PROCEDURE UserGuess (VAR guess : INTEGER);
BEGIN
    WRITE ('What is your guess? ');
    READLN (guess);
END;

PROCEDURE ComputerGuess (VAR guess : INTEGER;
                         VAR seed  : INTEGER);
BEGIN
    guess := RandomInt (seed, 1, 100);
    WRITELN ('I guess ', guess:1);
END;
```

Your program must give the user the option of whether or not to go first, and it must report the winner at the end. A sample session with this game might look like this:

```
Do you want to go first?
    yes or no? y
What is your guess? 44
Answer = 100
I guess 82
Answer = 72
I win!
```

14.7 Programming Problems

1. Write an interactive program that allows two players to play tic-tac-toe. It should ask the names of the players and should allow them to have a series of games. For each game, it should

    - Ask which player should go first.

    - Ask the player for his move specified as two integers, row and column, each between 1 and 3. Loop until a legal move is specified.

    - Put either an "X" or "O" in the square specified by the user, whichever is appropriate.

    - Show the current board.

    - If the most recent player hasn't just won, switch to the other player and go to 2.

    - Report which player has won.

    - Find out whether the players want to have another game.

    Your program should allow the players to halt a game if they want to. You might also consider having your program recognize a situation where neither player can win (a cat's game).

2. You are going to write a program to play an interactive word-guessing game called hangman. You will need access to a dictionary of words, but it doesn't have to be an incredibly large dictionary. Your program plays the part of the hangman. The user is allowed to make a series of guesses as to which characters appear in the word. Every time the user makes a wrong guess, your program moves a little closer to having a complete picture of a hanged man. If the picture is complete before the user gets the word, the user loses.

    The way the game works is that your program first chooses a word at random from the dictionary. Then it shows the user how many letters the word has. The usual way to indicate this is by a series of blanks. For example, if the word is "biking," you should show the user this:

    ___ ___ ___ ___ ___ ___

    Then you allow the user to start guessing characters. If the user guesses a character in the word, then you don't add to your hangman picture, but you do display to the user where the character appears in the word (even if it appears more than once). Thus if the user guesses "i," the program should display

    ___ i ___ i ___ ___

    It is also courteous to display all the character the user has guessed, but you might decide to make the user keep track of this personally. There is no set number of body parts to use in hangman, so you can decide for yourself how hard you want the game to be. Obviously, the more body parts you draw, the longer the user gets to guess. Here is a sample of the stages you might go through with a hangman figure with 10 body parts (head, torso, 2 legs, 2 arms, 2 feet, and 2 hands):

```
+--+     +--+     +--+     +--+     +--+     +--+     +--+     +--+     +--+     +--+
|  |     |  |     |  |     |  |     |  |     |  |     |  |     |  |     |  |     |  |
|  0  |  0  |  0  |  0  |  0  |  0  |  0  |  0  |  0  |  0
|        |  |     |  |     |  |     | /|    | /|\   | /|\   |_/|\   |_/|\   |_/|\_
|        |        |  \    | / \    | / \    | / \   | / \_  | / \_  |_/ \_  |_/ \_
|        |        |        |        |        |        |        |        |        |
+-----   +-----   +-----   +-----   +-----   +-----   +-----   +-----   +-----   +----
```

3. You are going to write a program to play blackjack·with up to 10 users. The program will act as dealer and will keep track of everything needed to play the game, including the dealing of the cards and whether a player has busted.

In blackjack, every player, including the dealer, is dealt two cards. The dealer must show the value of one of his cards. The object is to get as close to 21 as possible without going over by summing the cards in your hand. Face cards have a value of 10, and aces may have a value of either 1 or 11 depending on which is more advantageous. After the first two cards are dealt to each player, the dealer gives each player the option of hitting or staying. A "hit" means that the player would like another card. The card is dealt face up. A "stay" signifies that the player is satisfied with his hand and the dealer should go to the next player. A player may hit as many times as he wants as long as the sum of all the cards in the hand does not exceed 21. Once all the players have either stayed or busted, then the dealer must play his hand. The dealer is required to hit if his cards total to less than 17. Once the dealer's total is 17 or greater, the dealer must stay. After this has been completed, the remaining hands are compared to the dealer's. If the dealer's total is greater than a given player's, then the dealer wins the bet. If, however, a player's total is greater than the dealer's, then the player gets back twice the amount of the bet. If the player and the dealer have the same score, then the player pushes and his bet is simply returned to him. If the player busts (goes over 21), he automatically loses. If the dealer busts, all players that are still in the game automatically win. After bets have been taken or returned, the dealer shuffles the cards and deals out a new hand.

Your program should be the dealer and should monitor what happens throughout the game. It should do the following things initially:

■ Find out how many people are playing the game, and optionally explain the rules to those who have never played before. It should find out how much money they are each bringing to the game.

■ Initialize the deck.

■ Find out the betting limit for all the rounds of play.

For every round it should do the following:

■ Take bets for this round. If a player bets zero or is out of money, he will not be dealt any cards. If a player tries to bet more than he has, he should be told that the bet was too large and be given a chance to give a new bet.

■ Reshuffle the deck of cards. For each person betting (and the dealer), deal out two cards.

- For each player, ask whether this player would like to hit or stay. If the player decides to stay, go to the next player. If the player decides to hit, give him a card and determine whether or not that card will make him bust. If so, take the bet away. Otherwise, go back and ask again whether this player would like to hit or stay.

- Once each player has finished, play out the dealer's hand.

- Once the dealer's total is determined, go back to the players still remaining in this round and determine who won. Update each player's money pool according to whether they won or lost.

- Ask about playing another round. If so, go back to the beginning. You are going to write a program.

4. Following the idea suggested in Exercise 9, you are going to write an expanded version of program Jotto that not only allows a user to guess a word selected by the computer, but also allows the computer to guess a word selected by the user. For each round of guessing, you should do the following:

- Choose a word for the user to guess.

- Let the user decide who goes first.

- Alternate guessing, allowing the user to guess the computer's word and allowing the computer to guess the user's word.

- If the player guesses correctly, then end the round and ask the user what his word was. Check the word against the jots reported by the user and complain if he has given any inaccurate information. If the computer guesses correctly, then ask the user whether he wants to end the round or keep guessing. If the user wants to guess more, let him.

- Record the winner of the round.

- Ask the user if he wants to play again. If yes, go back to the beginning.

When the user says he is no longer interested in playing anymore, your program should end by reporting how many rounds were won by the user and how many were won by the computer.

The pseudocode strategy outlined in Exercise 9 actually plays quite a good game. You shouldn't need anything more powerful than that, unless you are going to take on Jotto champions. One minor point about that strategy, though, is that you don't always want to choose from your guess list. For example, if your guess list is reduced to words that all get 4 or 5 jots when compared with the correct answer, then you aren't making much progress by guessing them one at a time. Often a word that will get 0 jots when compared with the word gives you more information. Thus you probably want to choose your guesses from the guess list only when it is either very large or very small. When its size is in the medium range, guess from the whole dictionary. Don't limit your program.

5. Write a program that simulates an automatic teller. The program should start by reading a data file of customer records, one per line, where each record stores:

<customer number> <secret code> <status of accounts>

The status of accounts is a list of account identifiers and balances. The identifiers are

C   Checking
M   Money market
P   (Plastic) credit card
S   Savings

Thus some customer records might look like this:

```
1345   13843 C 349.24 S 623.45 P -238.44
93843  78342 C 459.19 M 13274.19
```

The first line indicates that customer number 1345 has secret code 13843 and has $349.24 in checking, $623.45 in regular savings, and a debit of $238.44 for a credit card. The second line indicates that customer number 93843 has secret code 78342 and has $459.19 in checking and $13,274.19 in a money market savings account.

The first line of the input file should contain a special customer number and code that identify a bank manager. This customer number will be used to shut down the automatic teller at the end of the day.

After reading the data file, the program should follow these steps:

- Determine which customer is next. This requires prompting for a customer number and secret code and checking to see that the customer number is legal and that the secret code matches.

- If the customer number is the special bank manager number, then skip to the last step.

- Prompt for a command and carry it out. The user's input should be checked to be sure a legal command is specified. The commands should include deposit, withdraw, transfer, and account balance inquiry. Users should be able to access any of their accounts with any of these commands, except obviously silly commands such as transferring money from one account to the same account.

- Ask the customer if he wants to perform another transaction. If yes, go back to the preceding step. If no, go back to the beginning.

- Write out the new account balances to an output file in the same format as the input file.

15

INTRODUCTION
TO RECURSION

15.1 Introduction

All human languages allow self-reference, i.e., statements that refer to themselves. Self-reference arises from the fact that sentences can be about sentences:

The sentence below has eight words.
The sentence above starts with "The."

Self-referencing sentences make statements about themselves:

This sentence was written on May 14, 1985.

This statement tells something about itself. While it is natural to construct such self-references, not all of them are as simple. Linguists and philosophers have long recognized the problem of self-reference. Consider a person who claims:

I am telling you a lie.

This self-referencing statement is very confusing. If it is true, you can conclude that the person is lying, which would indicate that the statement is false. If it is false, the person is telling you a lie, which would indicate that the statement is true. The statement being true implies that it is false, which implies it is true, which implies it is false, which implies it is true, and so on. There is no resolution. This is a famous problem known as the *liar's paradox*.

Allowing self-reference in a language opens a Pandora's box of good and bad. The good part is that you can express certain things straightforwardly that might otherwise be difficult to express. The bad part is that you create the possibility of incomprehensible statements such as the liar's paradox. Pascal allows self-reference, and it too opens a Pandora's box of good and bad.

15.2 Recursion

Pascal is a language for expressing algorithms, not ideas or beliefs, so where does self-reference come in? It arises in three places: self-referencing procedures, self-referencing functions, and self-referencing types. Because a procedure can call another procedure, you can have procedures that call themselves. Similarly, since a function can call another function, you can have functions that call themselves. Finally, since types can be defined by other types, you can have types that are defined in terms of themselves.

The word "recursive" describes self-referencing structures such as these: recursive procedures, recursive functions, recursive types. The technique of writing recursive code is called *recursion*.

RECURSION (RECURSIVE) ────────────────────

A problem-solving technique where a structure is defined in a self-referential way (i.e., in terms of itself).

The terminology stems from the recurring structure name in the structure definition, as in a procedure whose name recurs in the definition of its execution part.

A certain class of problems is more easily and more elegantly solved by recursive algorithms. This is the good part of Pandora's box. You will also see, though, that recursion is a dangerous tool. You have to be careful not to create a recursive definition such as the liar's paradox. In addition, recursion can introduce extreme inefficiency if you use it inappropriately. Finally, recursive code requires special debugging techniques. This is the bad part of Pandora's box.

In preceding chapters you have used loops to perform actions more than once. This technique is called *iteration*. You will find that you can use recursion instead of iteration. In fact, from the point of view of programming, recursion and iteration are equally powerful techniques. Some people prefer recursion, some prefer iteration, and many people fall somewhere in between. Designers of programming languages tend to build their biases into their languages. The language LISP, for example, is built around the power of recursion. Conversely, languages such as FORTRAN, COBOL, and BASIC rely solely on iteration. Pascal is somewhere in the middle: it allows recursive definitions, but it is not designed around recursion.

The question of when to use recursion and when to use iteration often generates fierce arguments among computer scientists. This book will stay neutral—showing you places where recursion is obviously superior and places where it is obviously inferior. It is up to you to decide the gray areas.

15.2.1 From Iteration to Recursion

Let's examine an iterative procedure that you have written and see how you could rewrite it as a recursive procedure. It turns out that the recursive solution you end up with is highly inefficient. However, it makes a good introduction to the concept because you have already seen its iterative solution.

Suppose you have a procedure for generating a line of stars:

```
PROCEDURE WriteStars (number: INTEGER);
VAR count : INTEGER;
BEGIN
    FOR count := 1 TO number DO
        WRITE ('*');
    WRITELN
END;
```

This procedure uses a FOR loop to create an output line with a specified number of stars. How can you turn it into a recursive procedure?

All recursive definitions have the same basic form. They define simple cases and recursive cases. The simple cases, also called *base cases*, have the property that they can be solved immediately. The recursive cases have the property that they reduce a task to a simpler one from the same domain. As you will see, a recursive definition doesn't make sense unless it has both these parts.

With WriteStars, the trick is to exploit the fact that the procedure can perform an entire family of star-writing tasks. It can make a line of 0 stars, 1 star, 2 stars, and so on. The recursive case has to reduce a complex star-writing task to a simpler star-writing task. The solution is simple: write out a single star. This reduces the problem to another star-writing task, but one that is simpler. The simplest star-writing task is when you are asked to create a line with 0 stars and all you have to do is a WRITELN.

Thus you can formulate a recursive definition by saying

```
if (number <= 0) then
    writeln.
else
begin
    write one star.
    call WriteStars with (number - 1).
end
```

Notice that this procedure has no loop. It manages to repeat the writing action by creating many procedure calls instead of using a loop. Like this definition, most recursive definitions are expressed as nested IF/THEN/ELSE constructs that distinguish the various simple and recursive cases.

Understanding such a definition requires a leap of faith. The odd part of this procedure is in the recursive case where you call WriteStars. It is odd because in the process of executing WriteStars you call WriteStars. Suppose you call WriteStars from the main program. WriteStars gets the work done by calling WriteStars. This doesn't seem right. In a business, this would be like having an employee get his work done by putting it in an envelope and mailing it to himself. On the surface, it doesn't seem to work, because the employee would just keep mailing the work and would never get it done. However, if you consider that each time procedure WriteStars executes, it does a little bit of the work, then you will realize that it does work. This is like having the employee do a bit of the work and then mail the rest to himself. When he gets the rest, he does a bit more and mails it to himself again, and so on. Since the employee does a bit of work every time, he eventually will finish.

Here is a Pascal version of the procedure:

```
PROCEDURE WriteStars (number: INTEGER);
BEGIN
    IF (number <= 0) THEN
        WRITELN
    ELSE
    BEGIN
        WRITE ('*');
        WriteStars (number - 1)
    END
END;
```

If you call the procedure and ask it to produce a line of four stars, it will lead to this execution:

```
call WriteStars (4);
    WRITE ('*');
    call WriteStars (3);
        WRITE ('*');
        call WriteStars (2);
            WRITE ('*');
            call WriteStars (1);
                WRITE ('*');
                call WriteStars (0);
                    WRITELN;
                    return.
                return.
            return.
        return.
    return.
```

The way you perform the four-star writing task is to reduce it to a three-star writing task by writing out one star and then performing the remaining three-star writing task by calling the procedure again. This writes a star and calls the procedure to perform the remaining two-star writing task, and so on. When the procedure is asked to perform the zero-star writing task, it realizes that all that needs to be done is a simple WRITELN, which it does and then returns. Thus the first four procedure calls each result in the writing of one star and the fifth results in the execution of a WRITELN. The result is that four stars are written out with a WRITELN at the end.

As you have probably deduced, the recursive step gets off the hook of doing most of the work by calling the procedure again. Thus the recursive case tells how to reduce the complexity a little bit. You can't solve a task by constantly spawning new tasks, though, so this process has to end somewhere. This is where the simple case comes in: it stops the whole process.

Another way to think about this is to consider the problem of going down a ladder. In theory, you really only need to know two things to climb down a ladder. You need to know how to get from one step to the one below it, and you need to know how to get off the ladder. If you can get down one step and if you can step off, then you can climb down any ladder no matter how high it is. The rule for getting down from step to step is like the recursive case that simplifies a task to another from the same domain. The rule for stepping off the ladder is like the simple case that stops the whole process.

Now that you have seen a recursive version of a procedure that is really better written iteratively, consider a recursive procedure that is not very easy to write iteratively.

15.2.2   Reversing Lines of Text

At the end of Chapter 7 you wrote a program that uses an array to reverse the lines of text of an input file. As you might guess, there is a simple recursive solution to this problem. It doesn't require an array or any other special data structure. It manipulates the input line one character at a time. Obviously, "line reversing" is not specific enough to pin down this domain of tasks, so use preconditions and postconditions to formalize what exactly the tasks are:

```
PROCEDURE ReverseLine;
(* pre  : Input cursor at beginning of a (possibly empty) series    *)
(*          of characters.                                          *)
(* post : Characters from input line are echoed to output line in   *)
(*          reverse order; output cursor at end of that line; input  *)
(*          cursor at EOLN.                                          *)
```

To devise a recursive definition for this procedure, you must figure out how to handle the simple case and how to handle the recursive case. The simple case is the line of zero characters, the empty line. This occurs when you are positioned at EOLN before the procedure executes. In this case, you have no characters to echo. Thus the postcondition is satisfied automatically. You don't have to do anything in the simple case.

What about the recursive case? You must think about how you can reduce a complex line-reversing task to a simpler line-reversing task. "Simpler" means a shorter line. The easiest way to do this is to read a single character from the input line, which will make it shorter. If the line starts out with five characters:

```
hello
↑
```

you first read the 'h', which leaves you with

```
hello
 ↑
```

Then you recursively call the procedure to reverse the rest.

The problem being solved by the recursive call is the following line-reversing task:

```
ello
↑
```

This task involves reversing four characters, which is a simpler task than reversing the five-character line above. If you believe that the procedure works properly (leap of faith), you conclude from the postconditions that it leaves the input cursor at the end of the current line and produces this output:

```
olle
```

This is the reverse of the four-character line. You can complete the five-character line by writing the 'h' at the end of it:

`olleh`

Thus your recursive step is simply:

```
read a character.
ReverseLine.
write the character.
```

First, you reduce the complexity by reading in a character and making the line shorter. Then you recursively call the procedure to solve this simpler line-reversing task. Last, you write out the character read from the beginning of the line. You can use an IF/THEN/ELSE construct to distinguish the simple and recursive cases. Your first pseudocode description, then, might be

```
if (at end-of-line) then
     do nothing.
else
begin
     read a character.
     ReverseLine.
     write the character.
end
```

There are a couple of modifications you might want to make. First, you don't need a "do nothing" branch in your IF/THEN/ELSE. This two-way branch can be turned into a simple IF/THEN. You can also improve the code by introducing the idea of a local character variable:

```
var next : char;
begin
     if (not at end-of-line) then
     begin
          read (next);
          ReverseLine;
          write (next)
     end
end
```

As you can see, this is virtually Pascal. Here is the entire procedure embedded in a simple Pascal program that prompts for a line of input and then uses **ReverseLine** to echo it in reverse order:

```
PROGRAM ReverseLines (INPUT, OUTPUT);

PROCEDURE ReverseLine;
VAR next : CHAR;
BEGIN
    IF NOT EOLN THEN
    BEGIN
        READ (next);
        ReverseLine;
        WRITE (next)
    END
END;    (* ReverseLine *)

BEGIN
    WRITE ('Give me a line to reverse ---> ');
    ReverseLine;
    WRITELN
END.
```

Here is a log of five executions showing how the program behaves with an empty line, a one-character line, a two-character line, a three-character line, and a very long line:

```
Give me a line to reverse --->

Give me a line to reverse ---> h
h

Give me a line to reverse ---> hi
ıh

Give me a line to reverse ---> hi!
!ih

Give me a line to reverse ---> Gee, isn't this fun!
!nuf siht t'nsi ,eeG
```

This recursive version of ReverseLine has several properties worth noting. First, it uses all simple character variables, which is appealing. Data structures shouldn't be introduced where they are not needed. Second, it is a very short program. This is a general property of recursive definitions which are very dense. You should examine a third property of this program having to do with the local variable **next**, but first examine some of Pascal's details that make recursion work.

15.2.3 Dynamic Scope

To explain the behavior of a recursive procedure, a new picture is needed: a dynamic scope representation of a program's execution. When this book first talked about scope, it examined lexical scope, the surface structure of a program. *Dynamic scope* does not describe the surface structure, the order of definition, it describes runtime behavior, the order of execution. Procedure and function calls are the important events for dynamic scope. In Chapter 3 you examined the activation of program and procedure blocks. You will again be examining activations, because every activation creates a new dynamic scope.

In a dynamic scope, you include information about what happens as execution proceeds. You list the series of statements that are executed in the order that they are executed. You start by building a large dynamic scope for the main program and list the statements of the main program in their order of execution. When one of these statements is a procedure or function call, in addition to listing the procedure or function call, you also attach a new dynamic scope box nested in the larger scope to represent that block's activation. Inside such a box, you trace the execution of the procedure or function. Similarly, if that procedure or function calls other procedures or functions, you create more dynamic scopes that are more deeply nested. Reading such a scope listing from top to bottom gives a detailed accounting of what goes on inside the computer as a program executes.

To understand this, look at a simple program. Here is a simplified version of the figures program examined in Chapter 1 with lexical scope boxes indicated:

```
PROGRAM DrawFigures (OUTPUT);

  PROCEDURE DrawCone;
  BEGIN
      WRITELN ('  /\');
      WRITELN (' /  \');
      WRITELN ('/    \')
  END;

  PROCEDURE DrawV;
  BEGIN
      WRITELN (' \    /');
      WRITELN ('  \  /');
      WRITELN ('   \/')
  END;

  PROCEDURE DrawDiamond;
  BEGIN
      DrawCone;
      DrawV;
      WRITELN
  END;

  PROCEDURE DrawX;
  BEGIN
      DrawV;
      DrawCone;
      WRITELN
  END;

  BEGIN
      DrawDiamond;
      DrawX
  END.
```

The lexical scopes show that the four procedures are all defined in the outermost scope of the main program. This is the description of the surface structure. Remember, the order of procedure definition is independent of the order of procedure execution.

To understand the execution, you would draw a dynamic scope representation of the program. Before drawing the full program representation, look at some of the different perspectives within it.

In general, each procedure and function executes independently of the others and doesn't know or care about what is happening either inside the inner scopes it activates or outside in the outer scope that contains it. In other words, information hiding applies to dynamic scopes as well as lexical scopes. From the main program's point of view, things look like this:

execute program `DrawFigures`

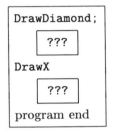

In other words, as far as the main program is concerned, the execution of this program involves two steps, `DrawDiamond` and `DrawX`. After these two steps, the program terminates. The inner details of these procedure activations are invisible to the main program. However, if you open up the `DrawDiamond` box you see:

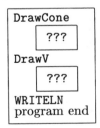

Here you see the other two program procedures but not their inner details. You must go one level deeper, for example, into `DrawCone`:

```
WRITELN ('   /\');
WRITELN ('  /  \');
WRITELN (' /    \')
procedure end
```

Here you finally encounter an innermost dynamic scope. *Innermost scopes* are those which don't activate other procedures or functions. To understand recursion, you must habitually look at things from a single procedure's point of view. The main point is that a procedure or function doesn't know what is happening inside the dynamic scopes it activates, nor does it know what is happening in the dynamic scope that activates it. It can't look in, and it can't look out. This is actually a desirable property provided that procedures can't interfere with each other.

Here is the complete dynamic scope representation:

execute program `DrawFigures`

```
DrawDiamond;
    DrawCone;
        WRITELN ('   /\');
        WRITELN ('  /  \');
        WRITELN (' /    \')
        procedure end

    DrawV;
        WRITELN (' \    /');
        WRITELN ('  \  /');
        WRITELN ('   \/')
        procedure end

    WRITELN
    procedure end

DrawX
    DrawV;
        WRITELN (' \    /');
        WRITELN ('  \  /');
        WRITELN ('   \/')
        procedure end

    DrawCone;
        WRITELN ('   /\');
        WRITELN ('  /  \');
        WRITELN (' /    \')
        procedure end

    WRITELN
    procedure end

program end
```

15.2.4 How Recursion Works

Now you can more fully understand the low-level details of how the recursive **ReverseLine** procedure works. You will see that the analogy of the employee who mails his work to himself is not accurate. A more accurate analogy is an employee who creates a completely independent clone of himself, who he hands the work on to. This clone might in turn create another clone who might create another, and so on. The key point is that each new recursive call creates a completely independent procedure activation as if it were cloning itself.

You have seen that procedures are basically independent of each other and that if they declare their own local objects, those objects are protected from outside interference. Recursive procedures add a new wrinkle to the question of independence. Recursive procedures lead to multiple activations of the same procedure at the same time. At one point, the recursive **WriteStars** procedure had five versions in existence. The problem is that these different activations are, in one sense, all different, but are, in another sense, all the same. Are they independent or not? The answer is yes.

Lexical scope rules guaranty the independence of different procedures, but they don't tell anything about recursive procedures. This is why dynamic scope rules are important. Dymanic scoping explains the independence of different activations of a single procedure. For example, the **ReverseLine** procedure has a local variable called **next**. A new local variable will be allocated for each activation of the procedure. This means that each different version of the procedure has its own character variable to manipulate. As you will see, this property of independence is what makes recursion work.

To explore this, examine a dynamic scope representation of **ReverseLine**'s execution on the three-character line **'hi!'**. Look at each scope independently. Here is the main program's perspective:

execute program **ReverseLines**

```
WRITE ('Give me a line to reverse -->');
ReverseLine;

    ┌─────┐
    │ ??? │
    └─────┘

WRITELN
program end
```

The action of the main program is easy to understand from this perspective. It prompts, reverses, and completes the output line. If you open up the **ReverseLine** box, you see

```
allocate variable Next
EOLN is FALSE, so execute THEN
READ (next); (next now = 'h')
ReverseLine;
    ┌─────┐
    │ ??? │
    └─────┘
WRITE (next); (next still = 'h')
procedure end, deallocate variable next
```

This activation of ReverseLine has its own variable called next to manipulate. The variable is allocated just before execution and is deallocated just after. You use it to read the first character, the 'h'. This leaves the length-2 line 'i!'. You tuck away the 'h' in the local variable next while you recursively call the procedure to reverse the length-2 line. If it works properly, then the line is reversed to

!i

After the recursive call, you untuck the 'h' and write it at the end of this line:

!ih

It is important to remember that even though this activation of ReverseLine creates an inner activation of ReverseLine, the inner activation is independent and does not interfere with this execution. In fact, that inner activation creates two more inner activations which do not matter to this outermost activation of the procedure. All that the outermost activation cares about is that the length-2 line is reversed properly.

Thus, as long as this inner ReverseLine does its job on the length-2 line, you're set. If you open up this inner ReverseLine, you see

```
allocate variable Next
EOLN is FALSE, so execute THEN
READ (next); (next now = 'i')
ReverseLine;
    ┌─────┐
    │ ??? │
    └─────┘
WRITE (next); (next still = 'i')
procedure end, deallocate variable Next
```

This inner activation allocates its own local variable **next**. Any manipulations it performs on its variable will not affect the other activations of **ReverseLine**. Again, this procedure doesn't care about the details of the inner **ReverseLine** scope as long as it successfully reverses the length-1 line that remains after the 'i' is read in.

If you open up this **ReverseLine**, you see

```
allocate variable Next
EOLN is FALSE, so execute THEN
READ (next);  (next now = '!')
ReverseLine;
    ┌─────┐
    │ ??? │
    └─────┘
WRITE (next);  (next still = '!')
procedure end, deallocate variable Next
```

This inner activation also gets its own local variable, so that it is independent of the other activations. It reads in the last character from the line and recursively calls **ReverseLine** to reverse the empty line.

Finally, if you open that scope box, you find an innermost activation:

```
allocate variable Next
EOLN is  TRUE, so skip  IF/THEN
procedure end, deallocate variable Next
```

Even this activation has its own variable **next**, even though it is never used. The computer notices that **EOLN** is **TRUE**, so this procedure does nothing. This then starts you coming out of the nested activations. You come back to the length-1 activation and write out the '!'. Then you come back to the length-2 activation and write out the 'i'. Then you come back to the length-3 activation and write out the 'h'. Finally, you come back to the main program and execute the **WRITELN** that terminates the line and ends the program's execution.

Putting all this together, here is a complete dynamic representation of this execution:

execute program `ReverseLines`

> ```
> WRITE ( 'Give me a line to reverse -->');
> ReverseLine;
> ```
> > allocate variable `Next`
> > `EOLN` is `FALSE`, so execute `THEN`
> > `READ (next);` (next now = 'h')
> > `ReverseLine;`
> > > allocate variable `Next`
> > > `EOLN` is `FALSE`, so execute `THEN`
> > > `READ (next);` (next now = 'i')
> > > `ReverseLine;`
> > > > allocate variable `Next`
> > > > `EOLN` is `FALSE`, so execute `THEN`
> > > > `READ (next);` (next now = '!')
> > > > `ReverseLine;`
> > > > > allocate variable `Next`
> > > > > `EOLN` is `TRUE`, so skip `IF/THEN`
> > > > > procedure end, deallocate variable `Next`
> > > >
> > > > `WRITE (next);` (next still = '!')
> > > > procedure end, deallocate variable `Next`
> > >
> > > `WRITE (next);` (next still = 'i')
> > > procedure end, deallocate variable `Next`
> >
> > `WRITE (next);` (next still = 'h')
> > procedure end, deallocate variable `Next`
>
> ```
> WRITELN
> ```
> program end

A positive point about this program is that it uses exactly as much space as it requires. To reverse a line of 100 characters, for example, the program produces 101 nested `ReverseLine` scopes, each with its own `next` variable. Thus the program will only allocate a few variables for a short reversing task and will allocate as much as it needs for a long reversing task. It isn't wasteful, nor does it suffer from an arbitrary maximum length, both of which are problems in the array solution.

15.2.5   Local Variables in Recursive Procedures

To help you understand the function of the local variable in procedure **Reverse-Line**, consider what would happen if the program instead had a global variable:

```
PROGRAM ReverseLines (INPUT, OUTPUT);
VAR next : CHAR;

PROCEDURE ReverseLine;
BEGIN
    IF NOT EOLN THEN
    BEGIN
        READ (next);
        ReverseLine;
        WRITE (next)
    END
END;   (* ReverseLine *)

BEGIN
    WRITE ('Give me a line to reverse ---> ');
    ReverseLine;
    WRITELN
END.
```

The difference between this version of the program and the earlier one is that all the activations of **ReverseLine** in this program share the same variable **next**. This is disastrous. Here is a trace of execution for the length-3 line **'hi!'**:

execute program `ReverseLines`

```
allocate variable Next
WRITE ( 'Give me a line to reverse -->');
ReverseLine;

    EOLN is FALSE, so execute THEN
    READ (next);  (next now = 'h')
    ReverseLine;

        EOLN is FALSE, so execute THEN
        READ (next);  (next now = 'i')
        ReverseLine;

            EOLN is FALSE, so execute THEN
            READ (next);  (next now = '!')
            ReverseLine;

                EOLN is TRUE, so skip IF/THEN
                procedure end

            WRITE (next);  (next still = '!')
            procedure end

        WRITE (next);  (next still = '!')
        procedure end

    WRITE (next);  (next still = '!')
    procedure end

WRITELN
program end, deallocate variable Next
```

In this program, there is only one allocation and deallocation of Next, since it is global. Because there is only one variable Next, each change wipes out the previous value. Thus the final value of Next will be whatever it was last changed to. In general, this will be the final character of the line, in this case the ' ! '. Thus you shouldn't be surprised that this is how it behaves:

```
Give me a line to reverse --->


Give me a line to reverse ---> h
h

Give me a line to reverse ---> hi
ii
```

```
Give me a line to reverse ---> hi!
!!!


Give me a line to reverse ---> Gee, isn't this fun!
!!!!!!!!!!!!!!!!!!!!!
```

The local variables of a recursive procedure provide a kind of memory of their own. In this case, you reverse an $(n + 1)$-character line by setting aside the first character in a local variable, then recursively calling the procedure to reverse the smaller n-character line, and finally writing out the character that was set aside. The local variable lets you remember the first character while the recursive call grinds away at the rest of the line. When you write your own recursive definitions, you must be careful to use local variables to make each activation of a recursive procedure or function independent of the other activations.

15.3 A More Complex Recursive Procedure

The `WriteStars` and `ReverseLine` recursive definitions are both of the same form. In each you reduce an $(n + 1)$-size problem to an n-size problem. This is an intuitive and straightforward way to reduce, and it works on many occasions, but not always. Often there is a different kind of recursive simplification that is not so intuitive and not so straightforward. This section examines one such problem.

The problem involves evaluating expressions, so first, a few words about that.

15.3.1 Prefix, InFix, and Postfix Notations

Consider the plus operator which is used to form expressions such as this:

```
2 + 3
```

This describes the plus of two values, in this case 2 and 3. If you think about it a minute, you will realize that plus is really a function. It takes two numbers as input and returns another number, the sum of the operands. You could create your own plus function that does the same work as the plus sign:

```
FUNCTION Plus (x, y: INTEGER): INTEGER;
BEGIN
    plus := x + y
END;
```

Think about how the plus function differs from the plus sign. They can both be used to add numbers together, but you use slightly different syntax for each, as indicated below:

```
sum := x + y;              sum := plus (x, y);
a   := b + c + d;          a   := plus (b, plus (c, d));
foo := a * (b + c);        foo := a * plus (b, c);
```

You put the plus sign between the two operands, whereas you put the plus function name before the two operands. Yet both seem like the natural thing to do. The only difference is that the function has a name, whereas the plus sign is a punctuation mark. There seems to be cultural bias for putting words at the beginning and punctuation in the middle.

There is a third possibility, however. The operator could go in front, such as with the plus function, or the operator could go in the middle, such as with the plus sign, or the operator could go at the end:

```
2 3 +
```

Each of these conventions has a name. These terms are the first of a series of related terms that you will see elsewhere in this book. You use the following prefixes to describe the three possibilities:

Prefix	Name of notation	Where operator appears
Pre	Prefix notation	Before operands
In	Infix notation	In between operands
Post	Postfix notation	After operands

Prefix notation is used mostly for named functions. *Infix* notation is most familiar because it is used for virtually all arithmetic: $+ - */ \hat{}$. *Postfix* notation, also called *Reverse Polish Notation* (RPN), is used extensively for internal computer representations of expressions. It was widespread among early calculator users because it was cheaper to make an RPN calculator than one that worked the way people do.

Prefix and postfix notations do not require parentheses. There are no ambiguous cases. The only notation that requires parentheses is the one used most by humans, the infix notation.

Now, to the problem.

15.3.2   Writing a Prefix Evaluator

You want to write a procedure that will evaluate a prefix expression read from an input line. To simplify the problem, use only the operators $+$, $-$, $*$, and $/$ and limit yourself to unsigned integers. This means that whenever you see a $+$ or $-$, you can assume that it is an operator with two operands that follow rather than a sign in front of an integer. Use the DIV operator for division. Here is a good starting specification for the procedure you are to build:

```
PROCEDURE Evaluate (VAR result : INTEGER);
(* pre        : Input cursor at beginning of a legal prefix    *)
(*             : expression composed of unsigned integers and the *)
(*             : operators +, -, *, and /.                      *)
(* post       : Input cursor at first character after expression; *)
(*             : Result set to value of prefix expression.  Note: *)
(*             : DIV operator used for integer division.        *)
(* parameters : Result-out.                                     *)
```

Before you can come up with a recursive solution, you have to examine the family of prefix evaluation tasks. Some expressions, such as the one on the left below, are more complex than others:

- / * 7 6 5 / + 4 3 + 2 1   + 2 2

The simple case is a prefix expression with no operators; in other words, a simple integer:

1

Evaluating this prefix expression is easy; you read in the integer and return it as the value of the expression. The next simplest solution has exactly one operator. Since it has only one operator, its two operands must be numbers:

+ 2 3

To be more specific, this is really

+	2	3
operator	operand #1	operand #2

The next level of complexity involves two operators:

* 4 + 5 6

This expression is easier to understand when the operands have been identified:

*	4	+ 5 6
operator	operand #1	operand #2

To evaluate the overall expression, you first have to evaluate operand #1, which is obviously 4, and operand #2, which isn't so easy:

+ 5 6

Once this operand has been evaluated, you can multiply by 4. Here is the same idea expressed in infix notation:

4 * (5 + 6)

The parentheses tell you that you have to add before you multiply. The complex prefix expressions all fit a basic pattern. They are all of the form

<operator> <operand #1> <operand #2>

The important thing to realize about the pattern is that each operand is a prefix expression. Therefore, you really know that a complex prefix expression is composed of

<operator> <prefix expression> <prefix expression>

Each subexpression must be simpler than the overall expression, because the overall expression starts with an operator that is not part of either subexpression. Therefore, the overall expression has at least one more operator than either subexpression does.

The observation that a prefix expression is composed of two simpler prefix expressions is what you need to design the recursive case. You evaluate a complex prefix expression by breaking it into two simpler subexpressions that you recursively evaluate. Once you determine the values of the subexpressions, you can determine the value of the overall expression by applying the given operator to the two values obtained from the recursive calls. Here is a pseudocode description of the recursive case:

    read the leading operator.
    evaluate the first operand.
    evaluate the second operand.
    apply the leading operator to the operands and return that as result.

To further refine this pseudocode, consider what kinds of variables you need. Think about what variables a single activation would need to make it independent of the other activations. Consider the recursive case above. You need a place to set aside the operator while recursively calling `Evaluate` for the first operand. Similarly, you need a place to set aside the first operand while recursively calling `Evaluate` for the second operand. Finally, you need a place to store the second operand when the second recursive call is completed. Thus you need three local variables: `operator`, `operand1`, and `operand2`.

You can come up with a pretty good pseudocode approximation by putting together the simple case, the recursive case, and the three local variable declarations:

    var operator : char;
        operand1 : integer;
        operand2 : integer;
    begin
        if (positioned at a number) then
            read (result).
        else
        begin
            read (operator).

```
                    evaluate (operand1).
                    evaluate (operand2).
                    apply Operator to Operand1 and Operand2, return that as Result.
              end
          end
```

As usual, the THEN part defines the simple case and the ELSE part defines the recursive case. You have only two things to fill in for this pseudocode.

First, you have to figure out how to test to see if you are "positioned at a number." The easy way to do so is to pull procedure SkipBlanks out of your software library and put it just before the IF/THEN/ELSE. This way you know that you will be positioned either at the first digit of a number or at an operator character. INPUT^ will let you perform the actual test.

The second thing you have to fill in is how to apply the given operator to the operands. Because there are four possibilities for each of the four operators, this is the perfect chance to use a CASE statement controlled by the operator variable.

Here is a complete program that implements the pseudocode with these two refinements. The program prompts the user for a prefix expression and calculates the result:

```
(* pre         : The user must know what a legal prefix expression is.     *)
(*              : No error checking is done.                               *)
(* post        : user is prompted for an expression in prefix notation; the *)
(*              : value of the expression is reported.                     *)
(* parameters  : INPUT-in, OUTPUT-out; terminal I/O.                      *)

PROGRAM PrefixEvaluator (INPUT, OUTPUT);
VAR answer : INTEGER;   (* value of user's prefix expression *)

PROCEDURE SkipBlanks;
(* post  : Any blanks on current input line skipped, input *)
(*       : cursor at first nonblank or at EOLN.            *)
VAR next : CHAR;   (* dummy variable used to skip blank     *)
BEGIN
    WHILE NOT EOLN AND (INPUT^ = ' ') DO
        READ (next)
END;   (* SkipBlanks *)

PROCEDURE Evaluate (VAR result : INTEGER);
(* pre         : Input cursor at beginning of a legal prefix expression   *)
(*              : composed of unsigned integers and the operators +, -, *, *)
(*              : and /.                                                   *)
(* post        : Input cursor at first character after expression; Result set *)
(*              : to value of prefix expression.  Note:  DIV operator used for *)
```

```
(*             : integer division.                                *)
(* parameters : Result-out.                                       *)
(* algorithm  : recursion:                                        *)
(*             :  simple case    = unsigned-number;               *)
(*             :  recursive case = <oper> <prefix sub-expr> <prefix sub-expr> *)
VAR operator  : CHAR;        (* operator character                *)
    operand1  : INTEGER;     (* first operand                     *)
    operand2  : INTEGER;     (* second operand                    *)
BEGIN
    SkipBlanks;
    IF INPUT^ IN ['0'..'9'] THEN
        READ (result)
    ELSE
    BEGIN
        READ (operator);
        evaluate (operand1);
        evaluate (operand2);
        CASE operator OF
            '+':  result := operand1 + operand2;
            '-':  result := operand1 - operand2;
            '*':  result := operand1 * operand2;
            '/':  result := operand1 DIV operand2
        END
    END
END;   (* Evaluate *)


BEGIN   (* main program *)
    WRITELN ('This program evaluates prefix expressions composed of');
    WRITELN ('integer constants and the operators + * - and /.');
    WRITE ('Give me a prefix expression ---> ');
    evaluate (answer);
    WRITELN ('Answer = ', answer:1)
END.   (* main program *)
```

Here is a log of three executions that evaluate prefix expressions of increasing complexity:

```
This program evaluates prefix expressions composed of
integer constants and the operators + * - and /.
Give me a prefix expression ---> 1
Answer = 1

This program evaluates prefix expressions composed of
integer constants and the operators + * - and /.
Give me a prefix expression ---> +  2  3
```

```
Answer = 5

This program evaluates prefix expressions composed of
integer constants and the operators + * - and /.
Give me a prefix expression ---> *  4  +  5  6
Answer = 44
```

15.3.3 Understanding the Prefix Evaluator

Examine the dynamic scopes of program `PrefixEvaluator` from the outside in to better understand how it works. Because procedure `SkipBlanks` is not of much interest, it isn't expanded into dynamic scope boxes here. The third execution was the most interesting, so it is traced here. From the main program's point of view you have:

execute program `PrefixEvaluator`

```
allocate variable Answer
WRITELN ('This program evaluates prefix expressions composed of');
WRITELN ('integer constants and the operators + * - and /');
WRITE ('Give me a prefix expression --> ');
evaluate (answer);

   ┌───────┐
   │  ???  │
   └───────┘

Answer now = 44;
WRITELN ('Answer = ', answer:1)
program end
```

This picture helps you understand the intent of the main program—prompt, evaluate, and report the result. The main program has only one variable, **answer**, used to store the result of the evaluation. The variables that are actually used for the evaluation are all inside the dynamic scope for procedure **evaluate**. Open it up to see what you have:

```
allocate variables Operator, Operand1, Operand2
SkipBlanks;
INPUT^ = '*',  so execute ELSE
READ (operator); (sets operator to '*')
evaluate (operand1);

    ???

operand1 now = 4
evaluate (operand2);

    ???

operand2 now = 11
result := operand1 * operand2; (sets result to 44)
procedure end, variables deallocated
```

The big difference between this recursive procedure and the others you have examined is that you have two nested procedure activations. The procedure has its own local variables to keep track of the part of the calculation it is performing. Remember, the overall expression is

$$
\underbrace{*}_{\text{operator}} \quad \underbrace{4}_{\text{operand \#1}} \quad \underbrace{+\ 5\ 6}_{\text{operand \#2}}
$$

At this level you only know about multiplying the two operands 4 and 11. These two numbers come from the recursive calls, but this outer procedure doesn't know how the values are calculated. It picks off the leading operator to reduce the complexity of the problem and relies on the recursion (leap of faith) to do the rest. If you open the first recursive activation to see how the first operand is evaluated, you see

```
allocate variables Operator, Operand1, Operand2
SkipBlanks;
INPUT^ = '4', so execute THEN
READ (result) (sets result to 4)
procedure end, variables deallocated
```

This is the simple case where you are positioned at an integer. The local variables are not used, but they do no harm by being allocated one moment and deallocated the next. This brings you back to the outer procedure's activation with a value of 4 coming back to its local operand1 variable. If you open up the second recursive call, you find

```
allocate variables Operator, Operand1, Operand2
SkipBlanks;
INPUT^ = '+',  so execute ELSE
READ (operator); (sets operator to '+')
evaluate (operand1);
    [ ??? ]

operand1 now = 5
evaluate (operand2);
    [ ??? ]

operand2 now = 6
result : operand1 + operand2; (sets result to 11)
procedure end, variables deallocated
```

This inner activation is calculating the value of the subexpression

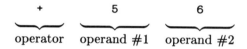

$$\underbrace{+}_{\text{operator}} \quad \underbrace{5}_{\text{operand \#1}} \quad \underbrace{6}_{\text{operand \#2}}$$

This inner activation has its own local variables that keep track of its **operator**, **operand1**, and **operand2**. This avoids possible interference with other activations (here it avoids a problem with the outer activation). It has two more inner activations that both lead to the simple case, so they look just like the activation examined above.

Putting all these together, here is a complete dynamic scope representation of the third excution:

execute program **PrefixEvaluator**

> allocate variable **Answer**
> WRITELN ('This program evaluates prefix expressions composed of');
> WRITELN ('integer constants and the operators + * - and /');
> WRITE ('Give me a prefix expression --> ');
> evaluate (answer);
>
>> allocate variables **Operator, Operand1, Operand2**
>> SkipBlanks;
>> INPUT^ = '*', so execute ELSE
>> READ (operator); (sets **operator** to '*')
>> evaluate (operand1);
>>
>>> allocate variables **Operator, Operand1, Operand2**
>>> SkipBlanks;
>>> INPUT^ = '4', so execute THEN
>>> READ (result); (sets **result** to 4)
>>> procedure end, variables deallocated
>>
>> operand1 now = 4
>> evaluate (operand2);
>>
>>> allocate variables **Operator, Operand1, Operand2**
>>> SkipBlanks;
>>> INPUT^ = '+', so execute ELSE
>>> READ (operator); (sets **operator** to '+')
>>> evaluate (operand1);
>>>
>>>> allocate variables **Operator, Operand1, Operand2**
>>>> SkipBlanks;
>>>> INPUT^ = '5', so execute THEN
>>>> READ (result); (sets **result** to 5)
>>>> procedure end, variables deallocated
>>>
>>> operand1 now = 5
>>> evaluate (operand2);
>>>
>>>> allocate variables **Operator, Operand1, Operand2**
>>>> SkipBlanks;
>>>> INPUT^ = '6', so execute THEN
>>>> READ (result); (sets **result** to 6)
>>>> procedure end, variables deallocated
>>>
>>> operand1 now = 6
>>> **result** := operand1 + operand2; (sets **result** to 11)
>>> procedure end, variables deallocated
>>
>> operand1 now = 11
>> **result** := operand1 * operand2; (sets **result** to 44)
>> procedure end, variables deallocated
>
> **Answer** now = 44;
> WRITELN ('Answer = ', answer:1)
> program end

The reduction performed by the recursive case need not be simple. In the other examples, you saw reductions such as 10, 9, 8, 7, and so on always reducing the complexity by one level. Things are not so simple and predictable here. If you start with an expression with 10 operators, you pick off the leading operator and then recursively call to evaluate the two subexpressions. Picking off the leading operator leaves 9 operators, but since you have two recursive calls, you don't know how the 9 are distributed. You might have one subexpression with 9 operators and the other with none, or one with 8 and the other with 1, or one with 7 and the other with 2, and so on. The reduction here is into two smaller pieces of unpredictable complexity. The unpredictability doesn't matter, though, as long as both pieces are smaller than the original. Reduction can follow unusual patterns as long as it always reduces the complexity.

15.3.4 Three More Recursive Prefix Evaluators

An interesting thing about the program written in the last section is that minor modifications to it can produce interesting results. For example, it prompts for a prefix expression and writes just an answer. Suppose you want to echo the expression as you read. So if the user types

```
Give me a prefix expression ---> *  4  +  5  6
```

you should answer

```
The answer for * 4 + 5 6 = 44
```

This is a trivial modification to the procedure. All you have to do is echo everything you read except the spaces. Every time you read an operator or number, you immediately echo. To space things out somewhat, you can put a space before each operator and number. Here is the modified body of procedure **Evaluate** with two new **WRITE** statements that echo the expression:

```
BEGIN
    SkipBlanks;
    IF INPUT^ IN ['0'..'9'] THEN
    BEGIN
        READ (result);
        WRITE (' ', result)
    END
    ELSE
    BEGIN
        READ (operator);
        WRITE (' ', operator);
        evaluate (operand1);
        evaluate (operand2);
        CASE operator OF
```

```
'+':  result := operand1 + operand2;
'-':  result := operand1 - operand2;
'*':  result := operand1 * operand2;
'/':  result := operand1 DIV operand2
      END
   END
END;   (* Evaluate *)
```

You would also have to change the main program:

```
WRITE ('Give me a prefix expression ---> ');
WRITE ('Answer for');
evaluate (answer);
WRITELN (' = ', answer:1)
```

You need to have the **'Answer for'** WRITE statement before the recursive call, because echoing the expression takes place during the execution of **evaluate**. These simple modifications to the program cause it to echo the prefix expressions as they are being evaluated.

But what if you don't like prefix notation and want to see it echoed in postfix notation? This also is not a difficult modification. The key lines are the following:

```
READ (operator);
WRITE (' ', operator);
evaluate (operand1);
evaluate (operand2);
```

Remember that procedure **evaluate** echoes as it executes. Therefore, the order above says to echo the operator first and then echo the two operands. If you want to echo the operator after the two operands, you change it to

```
READ (operator);
evaluate (operand1);
evaluate (operand2);
WRITE (' ', operator);
```

Moving the WRITE statement down causes the procedure to echo in postfix. Thus if the user types

Give me a prefix expression ---> * 4 + 5 6

the program will respond with

Answer for 4 5 6 + * = 44

You have written a program that translates from prefix notation to postfix notation, a handy fringe benefit that few would have anticipated. If you want to, you can try to do the infix notation by putting the WRITE statement between the two operand evaluations:

```
READ (operator);
evaluate (operand1);
WRITE (' ', operator);
evaluate (operand2);
```

This produces the following output for the input above:

```
Answer for 4 * 5 + 6 = 44
```

This is not what you want. Because infix notation is ambiguous, you have to modify the procedure to have it parenthesize when necessary. Believe it or not, even this is not a major modification (see Exercise 9 in Section 15.6).

15.4 Some Efficiency Considerations

The power of recursion is great, but naturally there is a price to pay. It is very easy to misuse recursion and to create highly inefficient solutions to problems. Recursion is like a credit card. The freedom causes many people to spend and spend without thinking about the consequences. Only later do they discover that they are deeply in debt.

You should remember that every activation of a procedure, whether recursive or not, takes up a certain amount of space in the computer's memory. This means that, in general, recursive solutions require more computer memory than nonrecursive solutions.

Recursive solutions can also lead to gross time inefficiency. The simplest example of a disaster in time efficiency is the recursive Fibonacci definition. It looks harmless enough, but deep down it has tentacles. The Fibonacci sequence is a series of integers in which each term is the sum of the two previous terms. It starts with the numbers 1, 1, so the sequence is

```
1, 1, 2, 3, 5, 8, 13, 21, 34, 55, 89, . . .
```

You can easily express this series mathematically. You can specify the first two elements of the sequence by saying

```
fib (1) = 1
fib (2) = 1
```

To obtain the rest of the sequence, you have to indicate that every term is the sum of the two previous terms:

```
for n > 2,  fib (n) = fib (n - 1) + fib (n - 2)
```

For the other problems examined, you had to figure out how to come up with a recursive definition by finding the simple cases and the recursive case. For Fibonacci, you have it already done for you. The two simple cases are fib (1) and fib (2). The recursive case is given by the definition above that expresses fib (n) in terms of the two previous Fibonacci numbers. Thus recursion seems like a perfect fit. Here is a recursive function that calculates the Fibonacci numbers:

```
FUNCTION Fib (number : INTEGER): INTEGER;
BEGIN
    IF number <= 2 THEN
        fib := 1
    ELSE
        fib := fib (number - 1) + fib (number - 2)
END;   (* Fib *)
```

This definition is very elegant, but extremely inefficient. The biggest problem is that the same Fibonacci values are calculated many times. Some values are calculated an incredible number of times. For example, here is a trace of what happens when you calculate fib (6):

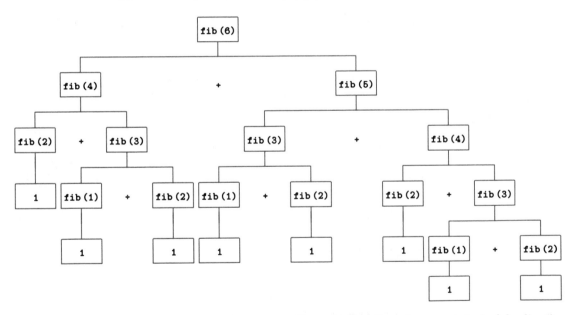

You can see in this structure diagram that there is a great deal of duplication. The following table shows how many times each of the Fibonacci numbers has to be calculated in order to find the value of fib (6):

Fibonacci number	Times calculated
1	3
2	5
3	3
4	2
5	1
6	1

It is ludicrous to calculate a value again, and again, and again. And it doesn't get any better; it gets worse. In calculating fib (20), for example, you calculate fib (1) 2584 times.

Let this be a warning. Recursive definitions might look harmless, but in fact, they may be lethal. A definition such as this that recursively calculates the same value over and over takes a considerable amount of computer time.

15.5 Key Concepts

- Pascal allows subprograms to call themselves, which leads to recursive definitions. Recursion as a technique is as powerful as iteration, but some tasks are more elegantly solved recursively.

- Every recursive definition includes one or more simple cases and one or more recursive cases. A simple case is one that can be solved immediately. A recursive case involves performing some piece of the overall task that reduces the problem to a simpler one in the same domain. Thus, after performing the simplification, a recursive call will complete the overall task.

- To better understand the execution of a program, consider its dynamic scope representation, which indicates the order in which subprograms are invoked.

- Recursion is possible in Pascal because each activation of a procedure is independent of any other activations of a procedure. For example, each activation will have its own local variables.

- Arithmetic expressions can be written in prefix notation, with the operator appearing before the operands; in infix notation, with the operator appearing between the operands; or in postfix notation, with the operator appearing after the operands.

- Recursive definitions can potentially lead to subprograms that are time or memory inefficient or both.

15.6 Self-Check Exercises

1. Rewrite the following iterative procedure so that it uses recursion:

```
PROCEDURE ReadData (VAR sum : INTEGER);
VAR next : INTEGER;
BEGIN
    sum := 0;
    WHILE NOT EOLN DO
    BEGIN
        READ (next);
        sum := sum + next
    END
END;
```

2. Rewrite the following iterative function so that it uses recursion:

```
FUNCTION Factorial (n : INTEGER) : INTEGER;
VAR product : INTEGER;
    count   : INTEGER;
BEGIN
    product := 1;
    FOR count := 2 TO n DO
        product := product * count;
    factorial := product
END;
```

3. Consider an integer function called **F** with two **INTEGER** arguments:

```
FUNCTION F (m, n : INTEGER) : INTEGER;
```

The following table provides a recursive definition for the function. Write the function from the definition (note that **SQR** refers to the built-in squaring function in Pascal).

Kind of case	Case	Result
Simple	n = 0	Answer = 1
Recursive	n MOD 2 = 0	Answer = SQR (f (m, n DIV 2))
Recursive	n MOD 2 = 1	Answer = m * f (m, n - 1)

4. Consider the following recursive function. What is the value of **Mystery (10, 25)**? What about **Mystery (180, 36)**?

```
FUNCTION Mystery (x, y);
BEGIN
    IF y = 0 THEN
        mystery := x
    ELSE
        mystery := mystery (y, x MOD y)
END;
```

5. Write a recursive procedure that writes out an integer value in binary. When you express a value in binary, you think of it as a sum of powers of 2:

$$46 = 101110 = 1 * 2^5 + 0 * 2^4 + 1 * 2^3 + 1 * 2^2 + 1 * 2^1 + 0 * 2^0$$

$$= 32 + 8 + 4 + 2 = 46$$

There is a simple recursive way to write the binary digits of an integer. It comes from the observation that you know what digit the number ends in. If the number is even, it ends in 0; if it is odd, it ends in 1.

Look at the following table. It shows digits obtained by dividing 46 by 2 over and over until the value gets down to 1. Reading down the digits column, you see 011101, which is the reverse of the binary representation of 46: 101110. Thus you can easily determine one digit of the binary representation, the last one, and the other digits are determined by (number DIV 2).

Number	Kind	Digit
46	Even	0
23	Odd	1
11	Odd	1
5	Odd	1
2	Even	0
1	Odd	1

Try to generalize your procedure so that it can write in other bases.

6. Write a procedure with the header below that counts in binary. For example, if asked to count for 5 digits, the procedure should display all 32 values between 00000 and 11111 in succession. (*Hint*: You might want to define a recursive procedure inside of CountBinary.)

PROCEDURE CountBinary (NumDigits : integer);

7. Suppose that you have some marbles that you want to lay down in a one-line combination on the ground. If you have two green marbles and three blue marbles, how many different combinations can you make? The answer is 10, as shown below:

```
green green blue  blue  blue        blue  green blue  green blue
green blue  green blue  blue        blue  green blue  blue  green
green blue  blue  green blue        blue  blue  blue  green green
green blue  blue  blue  green       blue  blue  green blue  green
blue  green green blue  blue        blue  blue  green green blue
```

You are to write a recursive function that calculates the number of combinations for any number of green and blue marbles:

FUNCTION Combos (green, blue : INTEGER) : INTEGER;

8. Consider the following procedure:

```
PROCEDURE Strange (VAR x : INTEGER;
                       y : INTEGER;
                   VAR z : INTEGER);
BEGIN
    IF z = 0 THEN
    BEGIN
        z := z + 1;
        strange (x, y, z);
        z := -z
    END
    ELSE
    BEGIN
        IF x > y THEN
            x := x DIV 10
        ELSE
            IF x < y THEN
                y := y DIV 10
            ELSE
                z := -x;
        IF z > 0 THEN
            strange (y, x, z)
    END
END;
```

Assuming integer variables A, B, and C have been defined, what values will the variables have after the following call on procedure **Strange**?

```
a := 1092;
b := 105;
c := 0;
strange (a, b, c);
```

9. Modify procedure **Eval** so that it evaluates a prefix expression as it echoes it in proper infix notation with parentheses in appropriate places.

10. Trace the function and procedure calls generated by the call below, indicating the order that the various calls take place in and what parameters are being passed.

```
SumOdds (sum, 6)
```

How many calls on **NthOdd** does this calculation generate? How many calls on **SumOdds**?

```
FUNCTION NthOdd (n : INTEGER) : INTEGER;
BEGIN
    IF n = 1 THEN
        NthOdd := 1
    ELSE
        NthOdd := 2 + NthOdd (n - 1)
END;
```

```
          PROCEDURE SumOdds (VAR sum : INTEGER;
                                 n   : INTEGER);
          BEGIN
             IF n = 0 THEN
                sum := 0
             ELSE
             BEGIN
                SumOdds (sum, n - 1);
                sum := sum + NthOdd (n)
             END
          END;
```

11. What is the output of the program below? How would you characterize the task performed by procedure **Unknown**?

```
          PROGRAM ResultHidden (OUTPUT);
          CONST MaxString = 20;
          TYPE  StringType = PACKED ARRAY [1..MaxString] OF CHAR;
          VAR   string    : StringType;
                length    : INTEGER;

          PROCEDURE Unknown (string : StringType;
                             length : INTEGER;
                             n      : integer);
          VAR index : INTEGER;
              temp  : CHAR;
          BEGIN
             IF n = length THEN
                WRITELN (string:length)
             ELSE
                FOR index := n TO length DO
                BEGIN
                   temp := string [n];
                   string [n] := string [index];
                   string [index] := temp;
                   unknown (string, length, n + 1)
                END
          END;

          BEGIN
             string := 'ABCD                ';
             length := 4;
             unknown (string, length, 1)
          END.
```

15.7 Programming Problems

1. Write a recursive program to solve the "jealous wives" problem. It seems that N couples must cross a river using a boat which cannot hold more than two people. None of the women will allow her husband to be on the same side of the river or in the boat with any other woman (or women) unless she also is present. Assuming that both husbands and wives can row, how do the N couples get across under the stated conditions?

    Run your program for $N = 1, 2, 3,$ and 4. Your output should include the initial problem, the moves you make, and a "picture" of the current state of the puzzle after each move. Your final output should produce only the moves and picture for those states which are on the "solution path."

2. A famous puzzle called the "towers of Hanoi" can be handily solved using recursion. The puzzle involves manipulating disks and three different towers where the disks can be placed. You are given a certain number of disks (four in the example below) on one of the three towers. The disks have decreasing diameters, with the largest disk on the bottom:

    The object of the puzzle is to get all the disks from one tower to another, say, from A to B. The third tower is provided as temporary storage space as you move disks around. You are only allowed to move one disk at a time, and you are not allowed to place a disk on top of a smaller one (i.e., one with smaller diameter).

    Examine the rather simple solutions for 1, 2, and 3 disks, and see if you can't discern a pattern. Then write a program that will solve the "towers of Hanoi" puzzle for any number of disks.

3. There are many problems in computer science that are best represented using an abstract structure called a *graph*, such as the one below. A graph is composed of individual nodes (indicated by letters below) and edges connecting the nodes:

    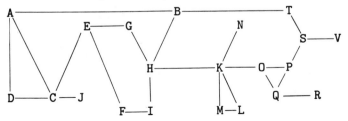

    You are to create three new types: `NodeType`, `GraphType`, and `PathType`. A variable of type `NodeType` stores the name of a node (simple characters will do) and a list of nodes adjacent to it (i.e., nodes that are connected by an edge to the node), as indicated in the following example:

name	neighbors
A	C, D, T

name	neigbors
B	A, H, T

name	neighbors
C	A, D, E, J

A variable of type **GraphType** should simply store a list of nodes. The generic list declarations from Chapter 9 should be fine for this. Finally, a **PathType** should be a simple list of Node Names. For example, the graph above has many paths between nodes A and T. Two of these paths are described by the node sequences (A, B, T) and (A, D, C, E, G, H, B, T).

Once you have declared these three types, you are to write a procedure that searches for all paths between two nodes. This operation can be expressed elegantly in a recursive procedure.

4. Another famous puzzle involves placing eight queens on a standard chessboard in such a way that no two threaten each other. Write a recursive program that explores all possible placements of eight queens on the board, reporting all configurations where no two queens are in jeopardy.

5. Suppose you have a two-dimensional picture represented as described in Chapter 13. You define a region of the picture to be a set of connected blank squares. Two squares are connected if there is a path from one to the other each of whose steps involves moving either one row or one column (but not both) to another blank square. Consider the grid below.

	[1]	[2]	[3]	[4]	[5]	[6]	[7]	[8]	[9]	[10]
[1]	*					*		*		
[2]	*	*	*	*		*			*	*
[3]				*		*	*			
[4]		*		*			*	*	*	
[5]						*				*

Element [3, 1] is connected to [5, 5], because you can move from one to the other with a series of horizontal and vertical moves to empty squares. The same is not true of elements [1, 7] and [1, 5]. There is a wall between them (mostly in column 6). The picture above has four regions in it. You will see them more clearly if they are filled in. Let's fill the region surrounding square [2, 2] with the character 1, fill the region around [1, 7] with 2, the region surrounding [1, 9] with 3, and the region around [5, 7] with 4. This yields the following:

	[1]	[2]	[3]	[4]	[5]	[6]	[7]	[8]	[9]	[10]
[1]	*	1	1	1	1	*	2	*	3	3
[2]	*	*	*	*	1	*	2	2	*	*
[3]	1	1	1	*	1	*	*	2	2	2
[4]	1	*	1	*	1	1	*	*	*	2
[5]	1	1	1	1	1	*	4	4	4	*

Diagonal moves are not allowed. Element [2, 8] is in a different region from element [1, 9], even though there is a diagonal move connecting them.

Your task is to write code to perform this region-filling task. Your program should read an initial picture from a file and should then allow a user to specify various regions to be filled in. As you saw above, a good way to specify these region-filling tasks is by specifying a square in the region and the character to use for filling.

6. You are going to write a program that plays a game of strategy against a user. The first player has a guaranteed win, so the game is in some sense uninteresting, but the winning strategy is not immediately obvious, and it leads to an interesting application of recursion. Both players take turns knocking down a series of numbered pins until all the pins have been knocked down. The player to take the last pin wins. The game starts with all pins up, as in

```
0  1  2  3  4  5  6  7  8  9
_____

!  !  !  !  !  !  !  !  !  !
```

Each player is allowed to knock down one, two, or three adjacent pins. Suppose the first player knocks down pins 3 and 4:

```
0  1  2  3  4  5  6  7  8  9
_____

!  !  !        !  !  !  !  !
```

The pins retain their original position relative to one another. Therefore, the second player would not be allowed to knock down pins 2 and 5, because they are not adjacent, even though they have no pins between them.

The recursive strategy involves searching for a winning move by examining all possible moves, and all possible countermoves, and all possible countercountermoves, and so on. The pseudocode for the recursive procedure looks like this:

```
procedure FindWin (var move : MoveType);
begin
        search for trivial win (i.e., knocking down the last pin)
        if (no win found) then
                search for a nontrivial win.
end.
```

Searching for a trivial win involves checking to see if a legal move would knock down the last pins. The other search procedure is more complex. To understand its logic, you should realize that every configuration of pins is either a guaranteed win for the player, or a guaranteed loss, assuming the other player is playing a perfect game. Thus every configuration of the board can be classified as either a winning configuration or a losing configuration. For example:

0	1	2	3	4	5	6	7	8	9	Kind	Move
!										Winning	0
!	!									Winning	0-1
!	!	!								Winning	0-2
!		!								Losing	none
!		!	!							Winning	2
!	!			!	!					Losing	none

To search for a complicated winning move, you consider all your possible moves:

```
for (each possible move you can make)
      consider move.
```

For each move, you want to decide whether it puts you in a good playing position. How do you find that out? If you are in a good playing position, then you have found a move that puts you into a winning configuration. This would mean that your opponent has no countermove to make. You can find out that your opponent has no countermove because you have a procedure that finds winning moves: it's the procedure you are writing. This is where the recursion comes in. Thus the pseudocode is

```
var countermove : MoveType; (* used to store opponent's countermove *)
begin
        for (each possible move you can make) do
        begin
                pretend you make the move (change the current configuration).
                FindMove (CounterMove);
```

```
            if (CounterMove is empty) then
            begin
                this move is a guaranteed win.
                exit from loop.
            end.
            unpretend you make the move (put configuration back to normal)
        end
    end
```

16

RECURSIVE
DATA STRUCTURES

16.1 Introduction

You have examined many data structures that seem severely limited in what they can do at runtime. You can't, for example, increase the size of an array dynamically. You would have to start the program over and recompile with a larger array size. But Pascal has dynamic memory allocation. Every time a procedure is activated, its local variables are allocated. Every time a procedure terminates, its local variables are deallocated. If the system does dynamic allocation of local variables, there is no reason that it can't do dynamic allocation of other kinds of variables. For example, it should allow you to create a data structure that can dynamically grow and shrink as memory demands change during the execution of a program.

Pascal does allow you to design such data structures. They are dynamic in the sense that you start with an empty structure and give commands to allocate memory to your structure as you need it. If you need lots of memory, you allocate lots; if you need a little, you allocate a little. Thus these structures have a flexibility that arrays do not. Before you can deal with such a structure, though, you need to learn some of the basics of dynamic memory management.

16.2 Creating and Destroying Dynamic Variables

Dynamic variables are not allocated before a program executes. Instead, you allocate space for them during execution. However, dynamic variables do not appear magically. You need some way to reference them. You do this with pointer variables. Pascal pointer types, also called *pointers*, evoke strong feelings from most who have studied them. Sentiments range from distress and anger to wonder and exhaltation.

The value of a pointer variable is a reference to another variable. For example, a company that keeps employee files and that employs both a husband and a wife has no reason to copy information from one folder into the other. It makes more sense to store a reference to the other folder (e.g., a folder number) in each. Pointer variables work similarly, storing a reference to data rather than the data themselves.

Pointer types are defined by an up-arrow (^) in front of a type name:

```
TYPE PtrInt  = ^INTEGER;
     PtrReal = ^REAL;
     PtrChar = ^CHAR;
     PtrBool = ^BOOLEAN;
```

You should pronounce an abbreviation such as `PtrInt` as "pointer to integer." Given these type declarations, you can define some pointer variables:

```
VAR  int1 , int2  : PtrInt;
     real1, real2 : PtrReal;
     char1, char2 : PtrChar;
     bool1, bool2 : PtrBool;
```

These eight variables do not store integers, reals, characters, or booleans. They store references to integers, reals, characters, and booleans. You can use these variables to reference dynamic variables, but dynamic variables are not allocated before program execution. Therefore, these eight pointers initially point to nothing. To make them point to a dynamic variable, you need to call the built-in procedure `NEW`, which has the following syntax:

```
NEW ( <pointer-variable> )
```

When you call `NEW`, a dynamic variable is allocated with the pointer variable pointing to it. For example, consider the two pointer variables `int1` and `int2`. They are initially undefined:

int1   `?`

int2   `?`

Suppose you start your program with

```
NEW (int1);
NEW (int2);
```

These two calls on NEW create two dynamic variables, which will be of type INTEGER because you declared the pointers as variables that point to integers. Thus two integer variables are dynamically created, each uninitialized with a pointer variable pointing to it:

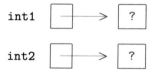

In the preceding diagram, there are four variables. The two on the right are integer variables, created dynamically by the calls on NEW. They are unnamed variables because of their dynamic creation. The two variables on the left are named variables. The top one is named int1, and the bottom one is named int2. These variables store references (or pointers) to integer variables, but they are not integers themselves—they merely point to integers.

How do you refer to the two dynamic variables if they are unnamed? You go through the pointer variables. This process is called *dereferencing*. You dereference a pointer variable by putting an up-arrow after its name:

Pointer Variable	Dereferenced Variable
int1	int1
int2	int2

Thus you might say:

```
int1^ := 12;
int2^ := 15;
```

Since you use the up-arrow to dereference each of these pointers, you are referring to the dynamic variables they point to and not to the pointers themselves. Thus it makes sense to assign integer values. These two statements give you

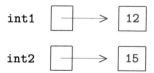

What happens if you say

```
int1^ := int2^ * 2;
```

You again use the up-arrow to dereference, so these are references to the dynamic variables and not references to the pointer variables. This statement says to double the second integer and store the result in the first integer:

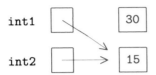

You can manipulate these integer variables as you manipulate any other integer variables. You just have to remember that they are referred to in a funny way by dereferencing other variables.

If you decide that you no longer need a dynamic variable, you can free up its space by giving the built-in command DISPOSE. It has the same syntax as NEW:

```
DISPOSE ( <pointer variable> )
```

For example,

```
DISPOSE (int1);
```

deallocates the dynamic variable that int1 points to. This means its space is now available for other dynamic variables, and int1 again becomes uninitialized.

16.2.1   Some Pointer Variable Considerations

There are some things you can't do and some things you don't want to do with pointer variables. Consider these statements:

```
int1 := 19;
int1^ := int2;
```

Both of these are illegal statements. In the first statement, you try to set the pointer variable to 19. You can't set the pointer to an integer value because it is a pointer, not an integer. If you dereference the pointer, you can assign a value of 19, because then you will be referring to the integer that int1 points to. The second assignment statement has a similar problem. On the left you dereference the first pointer variable, which means you are referring to the integer variable it points to. On the right you refer to the second pointer variable. You are mixing apples and oranges. On the left you dereference, so you have an integer; on the right you don't dereference, so you have a pointer. You can't assign a pointer to an integer: this statement is illegal.

Here is another statement to consider:

```
int1 := int2;
```

Here, you are referring to the pointer variables on both sides of this assignment statement. Because you are referring to the pointers and not the dynamic variables they point to, the pointer variables change, not the integers. This statement says to make **int1** point to the same thing **int2** points to:

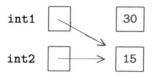

Int1 and **int2** point to the same dynamic variable. There's nothing theoretically wrong with this, and while you may want many references to a single variable and create data structures where there are many different pointers all to the same variable, this probably isn't what you want here.

What about that second dynamic integer with the 30 stored in it? No pointer variable references it now, so what happens to it? Can you change **int1** to point back to it? Unfortunately, an assignment statement such as the one above is not reversible, and all references to the integer variable are lost. It is somewhere in the computer's memory. If you allocate this variable and then throw it away, the computer will oblige you. You can use the **NEW** statement to create a third dynamic integer variable and make **int1** point to it, but you can't do anything about that lost variable. This is a mistake you should try to avoid.

If you think of the references as strings attached to helium balloons, with the dynamic variables as the helium balloons and the two pointer variables as two children each with a balloon, you can draw the variables this way:

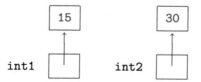

When you execute the statement

```
int1 := int2;
```

it is like the first child grabbing the friend's balloon and letting go of his or her own. Once the balloon is released, it floats off into the cosmos. Therefore, when you manipulate pointer variables, you should be cautious about throwing away dynamic variables by resetting pointers.

Earlier you saw not only the declaration of `int1` and `int2` as variables of type `PtrInt`, but also the declaration of `real1` and `real2` as variables of `PtrReal`, where

```
TYPE PtrReal = ^REAL;
```

What happens if you try the following?

```
real1^ := 13.5;
```

This causes an execution error because the pointer `real1` was never initialized. Remember, dynamic variables are not allocated until runtime and even then only when you use the procedure `NEW` to allocate the variable. Thus you first have to say something like

```
NEW (real1);
NEW (real2);
```

This allocates the dynamic variables and sets up references for the pointer variables:

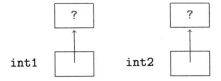

Then you could say

```
real1^ := 17.64
real2^ := SQRT (real1^);
```

This gives you:

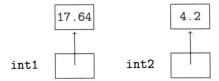

16.2.2 How to Point to Nothing

There is a special pointer value, `NIL`, that you will use often. `NIL` corresponds to an empty pointer, and you should think of it as "pointing to nothing." You can set any pointer variable to this value to make it point to nothingness:

```
real1 := NIL;
bool1 := NIL;
bool2 := NIL;
```

You usually represent the NIL value by putting a slash through the box for the variable:

real1 ◨   bool1 ◨   bool2 ◨

Why would you want to set something to NIL? Without such an action, your pointers remain uninitialized. There is a big difference between an uninitialized pointer and a pointer that has been initialized to NIL. It is illegal to inspect the value of an uninitialized variable. Therefore, any reference to an uninitialized pointer variable might cause an execution error. It is legal, however, to inspect the value of a variable that has been initialized to NIL. NIL lets you distinguish between variables that are not initialized and variables that are initialized to point to nothing.

16.2.3 Pointer Variables and Value Parameters

There is one last point about pointer variables that is confusing but critically important. With a pointer variable, your old ideas about parameter passing aren't adequate anymore. For example, suppose you want to pass one of these integer pointers to a procedure and want to guaranty that the procedure doesn't alter anything. By using a value parameter, you can guaranty that the pointer variable isn't changed:

```
PROCEDURE Bad (int : PtrInt);
BEGIN
    int := NIL
END;
```

This procedure has no effect because the pointer variable is a value parameter. But suppose the procedure does this:

```
PROCEDURE Bad (int : PtrInt);
BEGIN
    int^ := 0
END;
```

This procedure isn't changing the pointer, it dereferences the pointer and changes the dynamic variable. This is legal Pascal, and it does set the value of the dynamic variable to 0. The value parameter is useless as a protection mechanism because this is a pointer variable. All the procedure needs is a reference to the dynamic variable. Once it has that reference, it can change it.

As you write pointer applications, you must think about parameter passing and about how any changes actually occur.

16.3 A Recursive Type: Lists

The first recursive structure you will study is called a *linked list*. A linked list is a linear structure, like an array or a file, in that it stores a series of values all of the same type, but it is a dynamic object. If there are no data to store, the linked list will be empty. If there are a great deal of data to store, you will allocate many dynamic variables and create a very large linked list. There are other properties of linked lists that will interest you once you start exploring them.

The individual components of a linked list are usually called the *elements* of the list. You refer to a linked list by pointing to its first element, unless the list is empty, in which case you point to NIL. Thus you are inventing a new pointer type that references a list element.

Since this is a recursive type, you can give a recursive definition. The simplest list is empty, no data items, and you use a NIL pointer to reference it. Thus if you have a variable called `list` that points to a linked list, it would look like this when empty:

List ⧅

This list doesn't point to any dynamic variables. More complicated lists have a first element (a dynamic variable) that contains a data field and a pointer to another list:

Dynamic Variable

List ──▶ | *<data>* | *<pointer to list>* |

Suppose that you are storing characters in the data fields of the list. The dynamic variable above stores a single character and a pointer to another list. What can you use as values for the pointer? Anything you have seen so far. For example, you can store NIL to represent an empty list:

List ──▶ | Z | ⧅ |

`List` now points to a single element (value Z) that points to nothing. Thus `list` has just one element. Once you have this list, you can use the recursive definition again to introduce another dynamic variable, making the new variable point to this list:

List ──▶ | X | ──▶ | Z | ⧅ |

Now you have `list` pointing to a dynamic variable (value X) that points to a dynamic variable (value Z) that points to nothing. Thus this list stores two values.

You can continue using the recursive definition to get more and more complicated lists, as indicated below. Each line of the table represents a list constructed by applying the recursive definition and using the list on the previous line as the list for the new dynamic variable to point to.

List	Representation
()	List ⬜
(Z)	List ☐ → | Z |
(X, Z)	List ☐ → | X | → | Z |
(S, X, Z)	List ☐ → | S | → | X | → | Z |

Thus the recursive definition tells you how to take a list of length n and add a new first element to it to make it a list of length $(n + 1)$.

Try to write some declarations for this type. You run into a funny problem. The variable `list` is a pointer to an element. If each element is of type `ListType`, then `list` should be of this type:

```
TYPE PtrList = ^ListType;
```

To define `ListType`, you need a record with a data field and a pointer to another list:

```
TYPE ListType = RECORD
          data : CHAR;
          next : PtrList
      END;
```

`PtrList` is defined in terms of `ListType`, and `ListType` is defined in terms of `PtrList`. Which should be declared first? Pascal's rule that every word must be defined before it is used prevents you from putting either one first. Wirth anticipated this problem, so he invented a loophole. He said that the definition of a pointer type may precede the definition of the type it points to. Here the pointer to a list can be defined before the list type it points to. Thus you can define both types by saying the following, but it would not be okay if you switched the order of the declarations:

```
TYPE PtrList =  ListType;
     ListType = RECORD
          data : CHAR;
          next : PtrList
     END;
```

16.3.1   Getting Started with Linked Lists

Now that you have defined the structure for a linked list, let's see how to manipulate one. You need a variable to point to the list:

```
VAR list : PtrList;
```

With a pointer variable, you can call `NEW` and create some elements. You start out with `list` uninitialized:

list ?

You can initialize it by calling `NEW`:

```
NEW (list);
```

This creates a dynamic variable of the appropriate type and makes `list` point to it. Since `list` is of type `PtrList`, it points to something of type `ListType`, so the variable created is of type `ListType`:

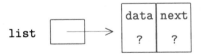

The dynamic variable starts out uninitialized. Consider some of the names involved here:

Name	What It Refers to	Type
list	Pointer to list	PtrList
list^	Dereferenced pointer, refers to dynamic record	ListType
list^.data	Data field of dynamic record	CHAR
list^.next	Pointer field in dynamic record	PtrList

You can give a value to the **data** field within the record by saying

```
list^.data := '!';
```

If you want to create a second element, you can say

```
NEW (list^.next);
```

Now you have these variables to reference:

Name	What It Refers to	Type
list	Pointer to list	PtrList
list^	Dereferenced pointer, first dynamic record	ListType
list^.data	Data field of first record	CHAR
list^.next	Pointer field of first record	PtrList
list^.next^	Dereferenced pointer, second dynamic record	ListType
list^.next^.data	Data field of second record	CHAR
list^.next^.next	Pointer field of second record	PtrList

You can see that between the up-arrows, the periods, and the multiple occurrences of words such as 'next', this can be quite confusing. Try it another way. Examine in detail what this program does:

```
PROGRAM SimpleListStuff;
TYPE PtrList  = ^ListType;
     ListType = RECORD
          data : CHAR;
          next : PtrList
       END;
VAR  list     : PtrList;

BEGIN   (* main program *)
    NEW (list);
    list^.data := 'f';
    NEW (list^.next);
    list^.next^.data := 'u';
    NEW (list^.next^.next);
    list^.next^.next^.data := 'n';
    list^.next^.next^.next := NIL
END.    (* main program *)
```

Start with

```
list   [ ? ]
```

The first statement is a call on NEW, which creates a dynamic variable:

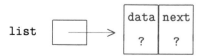

The fields of this dynamic variable are uninitialized. You refer to them as `list^.data` and `list^.next`. The next two statements of the program initialize these variables, setting the first to `'f'` and calling `NEW` to cause the second to point to a new dynamic variable:

You now have two elements in the list. The first is initialized, but the second is not. You can refer to the fields of this uninitialized record as `list^.next^.data` and `list^.next^.next`. The next two statements initialize these two fields:

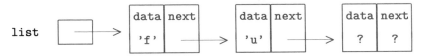

You refer to the fields of the third list element as `list^.next^.next^.data` and `list^.next^.next^.next`. The last two statements of the program initialize these fields:

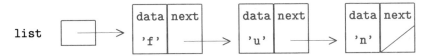

That's the end of the program, so you exit and all these dynamic variables are destroyed. So how do you know the program works? How do you know you didn't miss a bug somewhere? The problem is that these dynamic variables are like quicksilver. They're fascinating to look at but hard to get a hold of. If this were an array or a file or almost any other structure, you would know how to examine its contents.

As you have already learned, every time you create a new data structure, you have to build a library of routines for manipulating it. Your first encounters with it will probably be frustrating.

One thing you can do is to almost immediately write a procedure to display the contents of the new data structure. You can't produce any useful manipulations of an object if you can't see what's in it. As always, whenever you approach a new data structure, your first consideration should be displaying it.

16.3.2   Displaying a Linked List

Let's write a procedure to display the contents of a linked list. You can make it a simple procedure that writes the sequence of characters to an output line. You should have the procedure put quotes around the output so you can see where it begins and ends. The pseudocode for this operation is straightforward:

```
while (still elements to be processed) do
begin
        write value of next list element.
        go to next element.
end
```

There are only three things to fill in for this pseudocode. First, you need to know how to test for the end of the list. That's easy. The empty list is designated by the value NIL. This means that you can check that

```
(list <> NIL)
```

The next piece to fill in is writing the value of the next list element. To do so, you need to dereference the pointer variable to get to the record and then refer to the data field within the record to get to the character. Thus you would say

```
WRITE (list^.data);
```

The only piece left is how to go to the next element in the list. The pointer to the next element of the list is in **List^.next**. The way you move to the next element is to make this the new value of **list**:

```
list := list^.next;
```

This statement is one that appears in many list operations. It is used in most of the same places where you have used this statement with array indexes:

```
index := index + 1;
```

Putting all this together along with the quotation marks, you get

```
PROCEDURE WriteList (list : PtrList);
BEGIN
    WRITE ('"');
    WHILE (list <> NIL) DO
    BEGIN
        WRITE (list^.data);
        list := list^.next
    END;
    WRITELN ('"')
END;    (* WriteList *)
```

You should pay close attention to the various elements of this procedure because you will be using these same elements when you manipulate lists.

There is one nonproblem with this loop that should be mentioned. Remember, you are trying to be careful not to lose any of the dynamic objects that you create. Look at the way you use the parameter **list** in this procedure. It starts out pointing to the beginning of the list and ends up pointing to NIL. This means that the pointer to the list is lost after execution of the loop. It is not a problem in this case, though, because `list` is passed as a value parameter. This means that these manipulations are only on a local copy of the list pointer and will not have any disastrous effects.

If for some reason you couldn't use `list`, you would introduce a local variable to manipulate the list. This technique of declaring a local variable to access the list is another that you will find yourself using often:

```
PROCEDURE WriteList (list : PtrList);
VAR temp : PtrList;
BEGIN
    WRITE ('"');
    temp := list;
    WHILE (temp <> NIL) DO
    BEGIN
        WRITE (temp^.data);
        temp := temp^.next
    END;
    WRITELN ('"')
END;    (* WriteList *)
```

16.3.3 Simple List Insertion

Now that you have a tool for examining the contents of a linked list, let's concentrate on tools for adding information to a list. Consider the problem of adding a new element to a list. Suppose you have a list already pointed to by variable `list`:

The easy way to add an element to a list is to insert it at the front:

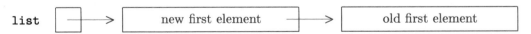

Here is a reasonable specification of such a procedure:

```
PROCEDURE InsertAtFrontOf (VAR list    : PtrList;
                                TheChar : CHAR);
(* pre  : Linked list pointed to by list has been properly    *)
(*       : initialized.                                        *)
(* post : A new element is added to the front of the list with *)
(*       : the value TheChar.                                  *)
```

In this procedure, `list` is a **VAR** parameter, as it needs to be. This is so because the new element is being inserted at the front of the list, so `list` is actually going to change in value.

Since you want to insert a new element, you have to start with a call on **NEW** to obtain a new record of type `ListType`. You might say

```
NEW (list);
```

but this isn't a good idea. `List` holds your reference to the current list. If you lose the value of `list`, you lose the list. And that's exactly what would happen as a result of this statement, because **NEW** wipes out any old value a pointer variable might have had.

The easy fix is to define a local variable for this manipulation. Therefore, you start your procedure with

```
VAR NewElement : PtrList;
BEGIN
    NEW (NewElement);
```

This creates a dynamic variable to hold the new element. You can store the character in this element by saying

```
NewElement^.data := TheChar;
```

Now you link up the new data structure. Linking is the tricky part. After you perform the statements above, you are in this situation:

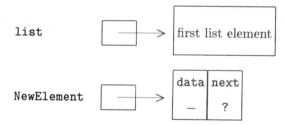

You want to rearrange this so that `list` points to this new element and so that the new element points to the current first element. There are two assignment statements involved. First, you make the new element point to the current first element by saying

```
NewElement^.next := list;
```

This gives you

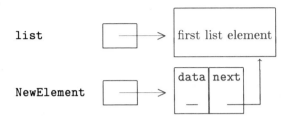

You now have two different variables pointing to the old first element of the list. This frees up `list`, so you can say

```
list := NewElement;
```

This leaves you with

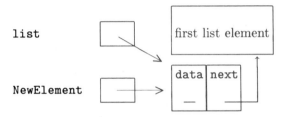

You now have `list` pointing to the new element as well as `NewElement`. The variable `NewElement` is now superfluous, since `list` has been given its value, so you can gracefully exit the procedure.

Here is a complete program with this procedure in it as well as some code to test it:

```
PROGRAM PlayWithLists1 (OUTPUT);
TYPE PtrList  = ^ListType;
     ListType = RECORD
          data  : CHAR;
          next  : PtrList
     END;
VAR  list       : PtrList;
     next       : CHAR;

PROCEDURE InsertAtFrontOf (VAR list    : PtrList;
                           TheChar : CHAR);
VAR NewElement : PtrList;
BEGIN
    NEW (NewElement);
    WITH NewElement^ DO
```

```
        BEGIN
            data := TheChar;
            next := list
        END;
        list := NewElement
    END;   (* InsertAtFrontOf *)

    PROCEDURE WriteList (list : PtrList);
    BEGIN
        WRITE ('"');
        WHILE (list <> NIL) DO
        BEGIN
            WRITE (list^.data);
            list := list^.next
        END;
        WRITELN ('"')
    END;   (* WriteList *)

    BEGIN   (* main program *)
        list := NIL;
        FOR next := 'z' DOWNTO 'a' DO
            InsertAtFrontOf (list, next);
        WriteList (list);
        FOR next := '9' DOWNTO '0' DO
            InsertAtFrontOf (list, next);
        WriteList (list);
        FOR next := 'Z' DOWNTO 'A' DO
            InsertAtFrontOf (list, next);
        WriteList (list);
        InsertAtFrontOf (list, ' ');
        InsertAtFrontOf (list, '!');
        InsertAtFrontOf (list, 'n');
        InsertAtFrontOf (list, 'u');
        InsertAtFrontOf (list, 'f');
        WriteList (list)
    END.
```

Here is its output:

```
"abcdefghijklmnopqrstuvwxyz"
"0123456789abcdefghijklmnopqrstuvwxyz"
"ABCDEFGHIJKLMNOPQRSTUVWXYZ0123456789abcdefghijklmnopqrstuvwxyz"
"fun! ABCDEFGHIJKLMNOPQRSTUVWXYZ0123456789abcdefghijklmnopqrstuvwxyz"
```

16.3.4   A Recursive List Procedure

Now consider a more complicated linked list application that is easily implemented recursively. Instead of inserting at the beginning of the list, consider an operation similar to the sorted insertion developed for arrays in Chapter 9. Here is a reasonable specification for such a procedure:

```
PROCEDURE InsertIntoSorted (VAR list    : PtrList;
                                number  : INTEGER);
(* pre  : Linked list pointed to by list has been properly    *)
(*       : initialized; elements of list appear in increasing order. *)
(* post : A new element with value number is added in its proper    *)
(*       : place, retaining sorted order.                       *)
```

To write the recursive solution, you need to think of what the simple cases are and what the recursive cases are. Given that you always point to the front of a list, the simple case is when you want to insert the new element at the front. The recursive case is when you need to insert it after the first element, in which case you want to insert it into the list pointed to by the first element. Since this list is shorter, you are reducing the complexity of the problem to be solved. Therefore, the following strategy should work:

> if (value should be inserted at front of list) then
>   insert value at front of current list.
> else
>   InsertIntoSorted (list pointed to by first element, value).

Again, you see the familiar IF/THEN/ELSE used to distinguish the simple case from the recursive case. You can improve this pseudocode by realizing that you can use the procedure written in the last section to insert at the front of a list:

> if (value should be inserted at front of list) then
>   InsertAtFrontOf (list, value)
> else
>   InsertIntoSorted (list pointed to by first element, value).

Thus you insert at the front of the current list or you recursively insert into the shorter list pointed to by the current element. Now all you have to figure out is when to use the simple case and when to use the recursive case. The simplest list is the empty list, so it represents your simplest case. But there is at least one other simple case. Assuming the list is nonempty, when would the value belong at the front of the list? Applying the reasoning worked out in Chapter 9, you should insert number if it is less than or equal to the first value stored in the list. Therefore, you can change your pseudocode to

> if (list is empty) or (number <= (data stored in first element))then
>   InsertAtFrontOf (list, value)
> else
>   InsertIntoSorted (list pointed to by first element, value).

There is a problem with this pseudocode. Full evaluation rears its ugly head. Suppose the list is empty. This means that list is NIL. What happens when the IF/THEN/ELSE above is evaluated? You end up trying to look at the data stored in the first element when there is no first element. This will lead to an execution error because you can't dereference NIL. This is another problem that you will probably come across often in writing code to manipulate pointer structures, so keep it in mind. In this case, there is a simple fix. You can create a three-way IF/THEN/ELSE so that you examine the first element of the list only if you know that it is not empty. Thus your pseudocode becomes

```
if (list is empty) then
    InsertAtFrontOf (list, number)
else
    if (number <= (data stored in first element)) then
        InsertAtFrontOf (list, value)
    else
        InsertIntoSorted (list pointed to by first element, value).
```

This is easily translated into Pascal. Here is an interactive program that tests this procedure by prompting the user for numbers and calling procedure InsertIntoSorted. Notice the slight modifications to the WriteList procedure that deal with the fact that you now have a list of numbers. In particular, the quotation marks are removed and a field width is added. Here is the program:

```pascal
PROGRAM PlayWithLists2 (INPUT, OUTPUT);
TYPE PtrList  = ^ListType;
     ListType = RECORD
           data  : INTEGER;
           next  : PtrList
     END;
VAR  list     : PtrList;
     next     : INTEGER;


PROCEDURE InsertAtFrontOf (VAR list   : PtrList;
                               number : INTEGER);
VAR NewElement : PtrList;
BEGIN
    NEW (NewElement);
    WITH NewElement^ DO
    BEGIN
        data := number;
        next := list
    END;
    list := NewElement
END;    (* InsertAtFrontOf *)
```

```
        PROCEDURE InsertIntoSorted (VAR list   : PtrList;
                                     number : INTEGER);
        BEGIN
            IF (list = NIL) THEN
                InsertAtFrontOf (list, number)
            ELSE
                IF (number <= list^.data) THEN
                    InsertAtFrontOf (list, number)
                ELSE
                    InsertIntoSorted (list^.next, number)
        END;

        PROCEDURE WriteList (list : PtrList);
        BEGIN
            WHILE (list <> NIL) DO
            BEGIN
                WRITE (list^.data:3);
                list := list^.next
            END;
            WRITELN
        END;    (* WriteList *)

        BEGIN    (* main program *)
            list := NIL;
            REPEAT
                WRITE ('Next number (0 to quit) ---> ');
                REPEAT
                    READ (next);
                    InsertIntoSorted (list, next)
                UNTIL EOLN OR (next = 0);
                READLN;
                WriteList (list)
            UNTIL (next = 0)
        END.    (* main program *)
```

Here is a log of its execution:

```
Next number (0 to quit) ---> 5
  5
Next number (0 to quit) ---> 19
  5 19
Next number (0 to quit) ---> 12
  5 12 19
Next number (0 to quit) ---> 2
```

```
   2   5 12 19
Next number (0 to quit) ---> 23
   2   5 12 19 23
Next number (0 to quit) ---> 17
   2   5 12 17 19 23
Next number (0 to quit) ---> 17
   2   5 12 17 17 19 23
Next number (0 to quit) ---> 14
   2   5 12 14 17 17 19 23
Next number (0 to quit) ---> 26
   2   5 12 14 17 17 19 23 26
Next number (0 to quit) ---> 25
   2   5 12 14 17 17 19 23 25 26
Next number (0 to quit) ---> 0
   0   2   5 12 14 17 17 19 23 25 26
```

16.3.5 Solving the Same Problem Iteratively

The problems you have solved up until now have had nice solutions, but you are about to see one that doesn't. It brings to the surface the kind of problems you can run into when manipulating a pointer structure. You are going to rewrite the procedure for inserting into a sorted list, but this time you are going to do it iteratively.

You start with the same procedure header:

```
PROCEDURE InsertIntoSorted (VAR list    : PtrList;
                                number : INTEGER);
```

List is a VAR parameter here because it might change if the element is to be inserted at the beginning of the list. If not, you must have some way to go down the list of items to find where to insert the number. You can't use list because it would destroy the pointer to the list. Therefore, you must introduce a temporary variable for manipulating the list:

```
VAR current : PtrList;
```

The manipulations on this variable require some lengthy explanations. First, think about what is going to happen when you find the right spot for the new number. If you insert 7 in the following list, for example, you expect that eventually you get to this situation:

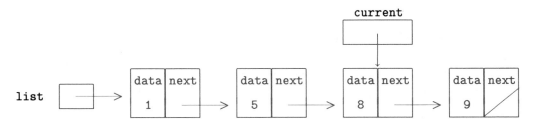

When you see the 8, you know that the value 7 belongs before this element. The problem is that you have no way of inserting a new element before this one. You can't change the list by saying

```
InsertAtFrontOf (current, number);
```

When you call the procedure to insert at the front of a list, passing it **current** as the **VAR** parameter, **current** gets changed so that it points to the new element, but the list doesn't change. **Current** refers to a local variable independent of the list, so changing **current** doesn't change the list. You end up with

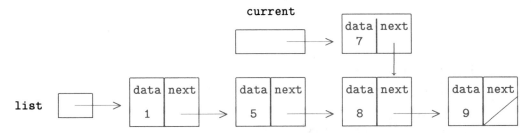

What you need to do instead is to keep track of not only the current element you are looking at, but also the previous element you were at:

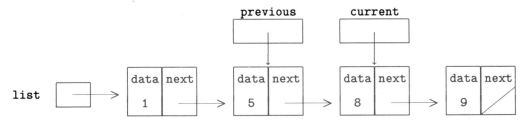

With this extra pointer, you can make the call

```
InsertAtFrontOf (previous^.next, number);
```

Previous and **current** are local variables independent of the list, but the field **previous^.next** refers to a link of the list: the Next field of the list element whose value is 5. Thus changing **previous^.next** will change the list. This leads to the result you want:

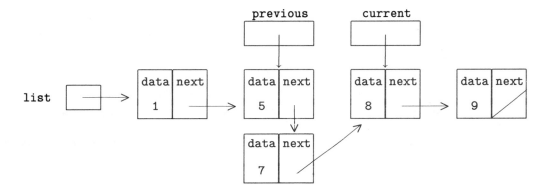

You start by initializing **current**. You don't have to initialize **previous**, since it obtains its value from **current** as you scan the list.

```
current := list;
```

You will know that the variables are positioned correctly when one of two things happen: you find a value greater than the number or you reach the end of the list. You can express these two tests as

```
(number <= current^.value) OR  (current = NIL)
```

You are going to have trouble with this expression. It's the problem of full evaluation again. If **current** is NIL, then it will cause an error to evaluate **current^.value**. However, you need to write a loop that is controlled by both these tests. The best way is to use a flag and to use an IF/THEN/ELSE to separate these two tests. You must go through the loop at least once because you must check to see if you are done, so a REPEAT loop is a better construct than a WHILE. Your basic pseudocode is

```
repeat
    give a value to "done" flag.
    if not done then
        go to next list element.
until done
```

To give a value to the flag, you perform the two preceding tests being careful to perform the NIL test before the other so you won't have the same problem:

```
IF (current = NIL) THEN
    done := TRUE
ELSE
    done := (current^.data >= number);
```

When you break out of the loop, you will know to insert the element before the current element. But what if `current` is the first element of the list? In this case, `previous` would still be uninitialized, because you wouldn't have scanned along the list at all. In such a case, you have to be careful not to insert into `previous^.next`, since it is an illegal variable reference. In this case, you have to insert into `list` directly. Thus this procedure ends with

```
if (current = list) then
    InsertAtFrontOf (list, number)
else
    InsertAtFrontOf (previous^.next, number)
```

You can now put all these pieces together into a complete procedure:

```
PROCEDURE InsertIntoSorted (VAR LinePointer : PtrList;
                                number      : INTEGER);
VAR previous : PtrList;
    current  : PtrList;
    done     : BOOLEAN;
BEGIN
    current := list;
    REPEAT
        IF current = NIL THEN
            done := TRUE
        ELSE
            done := (number <= current^.data);
        IF NOT done THEN
        BEGIN
            previous := current;
            current := current^.next
        END
    UNTIL done;

    IF current = list THEN
        InsertFront (list, number)
    ELSE
        InsertFront (previous^.next, number)
END; (* InsertSorted *)
```

This version is considerably less elegant than the recursive one.

16.4 Tree Structures

Another common recursive data structure is called a *tree*. A tree structure is a collection of nodes. Each node contains information. Here is a tree structure with seven nodes in it, each containing the name of a state:

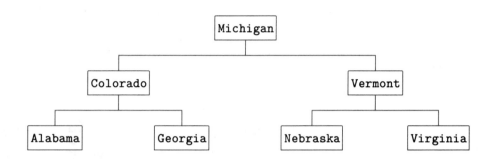

One node is designated as the root node. All other parts of the tree emanate from the root. In the preceding tree, `Michigan` is the root. Each node can have one or more nodes below it. A node with other nodes below it is called a *branch* of the tree. The nodes below it are called the *children* of the node, and the node itself is called the *parent* of the children. Thus the `Michigan` node has two children: `Colorado` and `Vermont`. They each have two children. Each node can have only one parent. Thus two different nodes can't point to the same child. A node that has no children is called a *leaf*. The preceding tree has four leaves: `Alabama`, `Georgia`, `Nebraska`, and `Virginia`. Finally, the *depth* of the tree refers to the maximum distance between the root and the leaves of the tree. All the leaves of this tree are two levels away, so this tree has a depth of 2.

Computer scientists often view the world the wrong way around, so you will understand this terminology better if you look at this picture upside down:

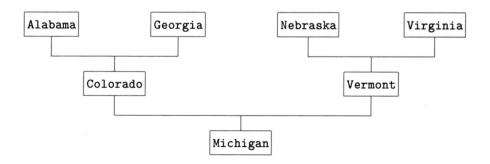

It is easier to see why Michigan is labeled the root, why Colorado and Vermont are called branches, and why Alabama, Georgia, Nebraska, and Virginia are called leaves. The restriction that each node can have only one parent implies that the branches of the tree are independent. Consider what would happen, for example, if the Georgia node had both Colorado and Vermont as a parent: you would have a leaf that appears in both branches of the tree.

An important property of trees is the fact that each branch of the root is itself a tree. These are called *subtrees*. For example, if you take away the root node, you get these two structures:

Each of these is a tree, so you call them subtrees. On the left you have a subtree of depth 1 whose root is Colorado. On the right you have a subtree of depth 1 whose root is Vermont. If you took apart the tree even further, you would find that each of these two subtrees is composed of two more subtrees of depth 0 (i.e., just single nodes).

The general concept of a tree puts no limit on the number of children that a node might have. Computer scientists, however, most often make use of a special kind of tree: the binary tree. A *binary tree* is one in which each node has at most two children.

Since each branch of the root defines a subtree, this is a recursive data structure. You can recursively describe a tree by describing the simple case and the recursive case. Just as you store a pointer to the first element of a linked list, you store a pointer to the root of a tree. Consider trees that store characters as data. The simple case is the empty tree, nothing at all, represented by the value NIL:

Tree

The recursive case involves a pointer to a dynamic record that contains a single-character data field and two pointers to the left and right subtrees:

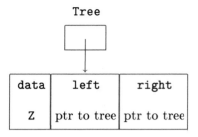

What values can you store in the fields called **left** and **right**? Any pointer to a tree you have examined so far. For example, they can both point to empty trees:

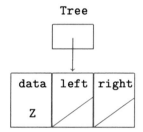

With this new tree structure, you can use the recursive definition again to define yet another tree that points to two subtrees, each like the tree above:

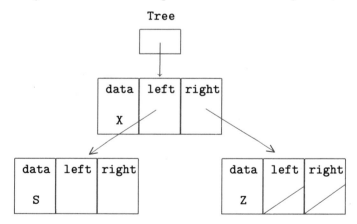

The fact that trees have this recursive definition can be exploited, since it leads to simple recursive procedures for manipulating them.

16.4.1 A Binary Tree Implementation

You implement binary trees using links and dynamic variables much the same way you construct linked lists. You use dynamic variables for the nodes of the tree and pointers to keep track of the links among nodes. Following your recursive definition, you can represent a tree by keeping track of what the root points to. For example, here is a short program that creates the tree structure discussed in the last section:

```
PROGRAM TreeSample1;
CONST MaxString   = 20;
TYPE   string     = PACKED ARRAY [1..MaxString] OF CHAR;
       PtrTree    = ^tree;
       tree       = RECORD
           contents : string;
           left     : PtrTree;
           right    : PtrTree
       END;
VAR    root        : PtrTree;

PROCEDURE NewNodeAt (VAR node  : PtrTree;
                         stuff : string);
BEGIN
    NEW (node);
    WITH node^ DO
    BEGIN
        contents := stuff;
        left := NIL;
        right := NIL
    END
END;    (* NewNodeAt *)

BEGIN
    NewNodeAt (root, 'Michigan            ');
    NewNodeAt (root^.left,  'Colorado        ');
    NewNodeAt (root^.right, 'Vermont         ');
    NewNodeAt (root^.left^.left,  'Alabama       ');
    NewNodeAt (root^.left^.right, 'Georgia       ');
    NewNodeAt (root^.right^.left,  'Nebraska      ');
    NewNodeAt (root^.right^.right, 'Virginia     ')
END.
```

Look at the type declarations where the structure is defined. Each node of the tree is defined as having a string as its contents and two pointers to the left and right subtrees. The program introduces a procedure to create a new node. That procedure gives a value to the `contents` field and sets the two subtrees to NIL. Thus procedure `NewNodeAt` creates a leaf node.

The main program starts by creating a leaf node at the root with the word 'Michigan' in its contents. Then it builds a left and right node. Finally, it creates the four leaves of the tree.

A program such as this isn't terribly interesting, because it produces no output. So let's see how you would examine the contents of a tree. You must decide in what order to write the nodes. There are three simple schemes that follow the recursive definition of the tree. You expect to write the left subtree before the right because of your Western bias that things go left to right, but where do you write the contents of the node itself? You can either write it before, in the middle, or after.

Before	In Middle	After
Write node	Write left subtree	Write left subtree
Write left subtree	Write node	Write right subtree
Write right subtree	Write right subtree	Write node

Each of these schemes has a name. They make use of the prefixes introduced when the different notations for expressions were discussed:

Prefix	Name of Scheme	Where Node is Written
Pre	Preorder traversal	Before subtrees
In	Inorder traversal	In the middle of subtrees
Post	Postorder traversal	After subtrees

The word "traversal" is used because you are traversing the various nodes of the tree. These definitions lead to a simple recursive procedure for writing the contents of the tree. For example, here is an inorder traversal of the tree:

```
PROCEDURE WriteTreeAt (root : PtrTree);
BEGIN
    IF (root <> NIL) THEN
    BEGIN
        WriteTreeAt (root^.left);
        WRITELN (root^.contents);
        WriteTreeAt (root^.right)
    END
END;    (* WriteTreeAt *)
```

You test for the simple case of an empty tree. If it is an empty tree, you have nothing to do. Otherwise, you recursively write the contents of the left and right subtrees and write the contents of the current node in between. To get a preorder traversal, you move the WRITELN before the recursive call on the left subtree. To get a postorder traversal, you move the WRITELN after the recursive call on the right subtree.

Here is the output produced by the preceding program when you add the inorder traversal procedure and call it after building the tree:

```
Alabama
Colorado
Georgia
Michigan
Nebraska
Vermont
Virginia
```

16.4.2 A Binary Search Tree

Let's explore one application of a binary tree: sorting. A simple technique for sorting is to use the tree structure to keep track of the order of a series of elements. Suppose you are going to get a series of values in random order. You can put the first node at the root and then for each remaining element put it to the left if it is less than the root and to the right if it is greater. If you recursively follow this strategy for each subtree, your tree will have the information of the ordering. For example, consider the tree that you have been studying:

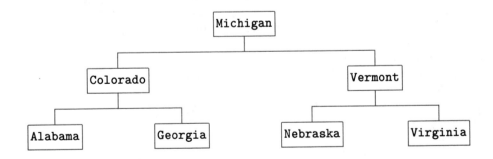

This tree has the property just described. Every node in the left subtree is less than Michigan, and every node in the right subtree is greater than it. Further, the node to the left of Colorado is less than it, and the node to the right of Colorado is greater than it. And finally, the node to the left of Vermont is less than it, and the node to the right of Vermont is greater than it. Thus the relative position of the nodes in this tree encodes the alphabetical order of the words.

You can produce an alphabetized list by writing out the tree using an inorder traversal. This way you will always write out the left subtree, then the root itself, and then the right subtree, which matches the order.

Here is a complete program that follows this strategy. It prompts the user at the terminal for a series of words and uses a recursive procedure to insert the words into the tree using this strategy.

```
(* post       : User is prompted for a series of words; words are echoed *)
(*             : in alphabetical order.                                   *)
(* parameters : INPUT-in, OUTPUT-out.                                     *)
(* data       : binary search tree stores sequence of words.             *)

PROGRAM Alphabetize (INPUT, OUTPUT);
CONST MaxString    = 20;          (* maximum size of a word   *)
TYPE  string       = PACKED ARRAY [1..MaxString] OF CHAR;   (* one word *)
      PtrTree      = ^tree;       (* pointer to a tree        *)

      tree         = RECORD       (* one node of a tree       *)
          contents : string;      (* data stored at this node *)
          left     : PtrTree;     (* pointer to left subtree  *)
          right    : PtrTree      (* pointer to right subtree *)
        END;
VAR   root         : PtrTree;     (* pointer to root of tree  *)


PROCEDURE ReadWord (VAR word : string);
(* pre        : Input line has a word of no more than MaxString characters.  *)
(* post       : Up to MaxString characters are read from input line; word is *)
(*             : padded with spaces; input cursor at beginning of next line.  *)
(* parameters : word-out.                                                    *)
(* requires   : constant MaxString.                                          *)
VAR count      : INTEGER;   (* loop counter                                  *)
BEGIN
    FOR count := 1 TO MaxString DO
        IF NOT EOLN THEN
            READ (word [count])
        ELSE
            word [count] := ' ';
    READLN
END;    (* ReadWord *)


PROCEDURE NewNodeAt (VAR node : PtrTree;
                         word : string);
(* post       : Node is initialized using given word; subtrees are empty. *)
```

```
(* parameters : node-out, word-in.                                          *)
(* requires   : types string, tree, and PtrTree.                            *)
BEGIN
    NEW (node);
    node^.contents := word;
    node^.left := NIL;
    node^.right := NIL
END;   (* NewNodeAt *)


PROCEDURE InsertAt (VAR node : PtrTree;
                        word : string);
(* post       : Word is inserted at appropriate point in tree. *)
(* parameters : node-in/out, word-in.                          *)
(* requires   : types string, tree, and PtrTree.               *)
BEGIN
    IF (node = NIL) THEN
        NewNodeAt (node, word)
    ELSE
        IF word < node^.contents THEN
                InsertAt (node^.left, word)
        ELSE
            IF word > node^.contents THEN
                InsertAt (node^.right, word)
END;   (* InsertAt *)


PROCEDURE WriteTreeAt (root : PtrTree);
(* post       : Contents of tree are written using inorder traversal. *)
(* parameters : root-in.                                              *)
(* requires   : types Tree and PtrTree.                               *)
BEGIN
    IF (root <> NIL) THEN
    BEGIN
        WriteTreeAt (root^.left);
        WRITELN (root^.contents);
        WriteTreeAt (root^.right)
    END
END;   (* WriteTreeAt *)


PROCEDURE BuildTreeAt (VAR root : PtrTree);
(* post       : User is prompted for a series of words; words are inserted *)
(*            : into tree to record their order.                           *)
(* parameters : root-out.                                                  *)
(* requires   : types Tree and PtrTree.                                    *)
```

```
VAR quit : BOOLEAN;
    word : string;
BEGIN
    REPEAT
        WRITE ('next word (RETURN to quit)? ');
        quit := EOLN;
        IF NOT quit THEN
        BEGIN
            ReadWord (word);
            InsertAt (root, word)
        END
    UNTIl quit
END;   (* BuildTreeAt *)

BEGIN   (* main program *)
    BuildTreeAt (root);
    WRITELN;
    WRITELN ('Contents of tree:');
    WRITELN ('------------------');
    WriteTreeAt (root)
END.    (* main program *)
```

Here is a log of its execution:

```
next word (RETURN to quit)? four
next word (RETURN to quit)? score
next word (RETURN to quit)? and
next word (RETURN to quit)? seven
next word (RETURN to quit)? years
next word (RETURN to quit)? ago
next word (RETURN to quit)? our
next word (RETURN to quit)? forefathers
next word (RETURN to quit)? brought
next word (RETURN to quit)? forth
next word (RETURN to quit)? upon
next word (RETURN to quit)? this
next word (RETURN to quit)? continent
next word (RETURN to quit)? a
next word (RETURN to quit)? new
next word (RETURN to quit)? nation
next word (RETURN to quit)?
```

```
Contents of tree:
-----------------
a
ago
and
brought
continent
forefathers
forth
four
nation
new
our
score
seven
this
upon
years
```

Given this execution, here is the tree it constructs:

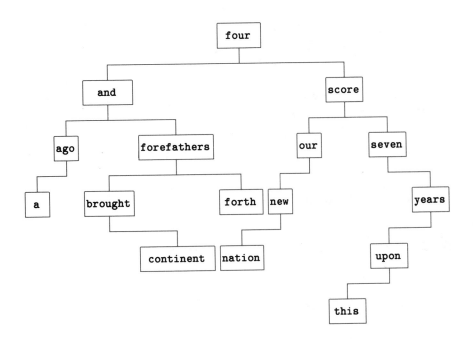

This kind of tree is called a *binary search tree* because it makes it easy to quickly search the tree for a specific value. Second, both the inserting and writing procedures were written recursively. It is fairly straightforward to rewrite the inserting procedure iteratively, but not the writing procedure. This is so because the inserting procedure follows a specific path from root to leaf, whereas the writing procedure must follow all paths from root to leaf. In other words, the inserting procedure descends the tree along a single path, whereas the writing procedure spans the tree by descending all possible paths.

16.5 Key Concepts

- Pointer types in Pascal allow creation and destruction of dynamic variables. Procedure NEW is used to create a dynamic variable and procedure DISPOSE to destroy it. The dereferencing operator (^) is used to refer to the dynamic variable pointed to by a pointer variable.

- You are not allowed to dereference a pointer variable unless it has been initialized by a call on NEW or by assignment to another pointer value.

- The special pointer value NIL is used to refer to nothingness or an empty pointer.

- You can accidentally lose all references to a dynamic variable by resetting the pointer variable that refers to it. This loss, wasteful of the computer's memory, should be avoided.

- A linked list of data values can be created out of records, each with a data field and a next field that points to the next record in the list. The empty list is represented by the value NIL. Thus in a nonempty list the last element will always have a next field with the value NIL.

- A binary tree of data values can be created out of records, each with a data field and two pointer fields to store the left and right subtrees. The empty tree is represented by the value NIL.

- Because lists and trees are recursive structures, it is often easier to write recursive subprograms to manipulate them.

16.6 Self-Check Exercises

1. What is the output of the following program?

```
PROGRAM Strange (OUTPUT);
TYPE PtrReal = ^REAL;
VAR  first   : PtrReal;
     second  : PtrReal;
```

```
    third    : PtrReal;
BEGIN
    NEW (first);
    second := first;
    first^ := 3.5;
    NEW (third);
    third^ := second^ * 2;
    WRITELN (first^:5:1, second^:5:1, third^:5:1);
    first := third;
    WRITELN (first^:5:1, second^:5:1, third^:5:1);
    second^ := second^ * first^;
    WRITELN (first^:5:1, second^:5:1, third^:5:1)
END;
```

2. What is the output of the following program?

```
PROGRAM Stranger (OUTPUT);
TYPE PtrChar = ^CHAR;

VAR  first   : PtrChar;
     second  : PtrChar;
BEGIN
    NEW (first);
    first^ := 'A';
    second := first;
    WRITELN ('second = "', second, '"');
    DISPOSE (first);
    WRITELN ('second = "', second, '"')
END;
```

3. If you are going to change the order of data values stored in a linked list, you could either swap a series of data values and leave the pointer structure intact, or you could change the underlying pointer structure and avoid swapping data values. Which is the easier method to write programs for? Which is the more efficient method?

Exercises 4 and 5 refer to the following declarations for a linked list of integers:

```
TYPE PtrList  = ^ListType;
     ListType = RECORD
          data : INTEGER;
          next : PtrList
     END;
```

4. Write an iterative function with the following header that finds the sum of the elements of a linked list:

```
FUNCTION SumOf (list : ListType) : INTEGER;
```

```
(* post : Returns the sum of the values stored in the list. *)
```

5. Write a recursive procedure with the following header that eliminates any elements of the list that have the data value 0. The order of elements should otherwise be unchanged. All elements deleted from the list should be properly freed by appropriate calls on DISPOSE.

```
PROCEDURE EliminateZeros (VAR list : ListType);
(* post : any elements with value 0 are eliminated from list. *)
```

Exercises 6 to 8 refer to the following tree:

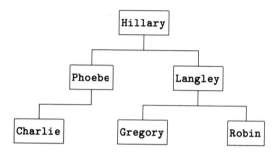

6. What names are stored in leaf nodes of this tree?
7. List the contents of this tree using a preorder traversal.
8. List the contents of this tree using a postorder traversal.
9. Given the following declarations for a tree:

```
TYPE PtrTree    = ^tree;
     tree       = RECORD
          data  : INTEGER;
          left  : PtrTree;
          right : PtrTree
     END;
```

write a recursive function with the following header that returns the total number of leaves in a tree:

```
FUNCTION NumLeaves (tree : PtrTree) : INTEGER;
(* post : Returns the total number of leaves in the tree. *)
```

16.7 Programming Problems

1. Suppose you are supplied with two input files, each with a series of integers. There might be several integers on each line of each input file. You are to write a program to read in the integers in each file and to write an output file showing the integers that appear in both input files. The integers should be written in increasing order and should be listed without duplicates.

2. Using type `WordType` implemented in Chapter 9, modify program `PlayWithLists2` from Section 16.3.4 so that it prompts the user for a series of words and reports the resulting list of words in alphabetical order.

3. You are going to write a program that would be used by a computer dating company. The customers of the company are a race of creatures called Draks. The degree to which one Drak is attracted to another is calculated as an integer between 0 and 99. Assume that attraction scores have been calculated for each possible pair of Drak customers. The computer dating company only wants to make dates for Draks that seem compatible with each other. A score of 80 to 99 seems like strong attraction, so the company considers a couple compatible if the attraction score is between 80 and 99 in both directions. A file listing compatible couples is created. Incompatible couples are not listed.

    The first line of the input file has two numbers on it. The first describes the total number of Draks. The second describes the maximum number of dates being arranged for each Drak (explained below). A list of compatible pairs appears on the subsequent lines. A compatible pair is specified by four integers: first Drak number, second Drak number, how attractive the second Drak seems to the first, and how attractive the first seems to the second. For example, the input file might be

    ```
    4 2
    1 3 82 84
    1 2 99 90
    2 4 85 95
    4 1 88 83
    ```

    The first line of this input indicates that there are four Draks and that you are trying to arrange no more than two dates for each. The other lines describe the compatibilities.

The problem that the computer dating company faces is that some Draks are quite popular and others are not. In a population of 1000 Draks, for example, you might find one who is compatible with 750 of the 1000 and another who isn't compatible with any. The computer dating company would ideally like to arrange a fixed number of dates for each client. This number is included in the first line of the input file, as described above. The sample input file specifies that at most two dates are to be arranged for each Drak. It might not be possible to arrange two for each, so some Draks might end up with only one date or perhaps none at all.

Your task is to design an algorithm that eliminates possible dates until every Drak has at most the specified number of dates. You are to design the algorithm, but there should be some justification behind the algorithm. For example, you might reason that popular Draks should have dates with the Draks they most like. Given the sample input and following this reasoning, we would notice that Drak 1 has three dates, and we would eliminate his least desirable date, the date with Drak 3. Another line of reasoning, however, would be to say that every Drak should have about the same number of dates as any other Drak. By this reasoning, we would notice that eliminating the date between Draks 1 and 3 would leave Drak 3 with no dates. Thus we would instead delete the date either with Drak 2 or Drak 4 so that Drak 3 has at least one date.

Once you have applied your algorithm to prune the set of dates, you should produce an output file which shows all the dates you have arranged. It should have one line of ouptut for each Drak and should list the dates that have been arranged. Each date should be specified by the Drak number of the date and the attraction score this Drak has for the other. The last two lines of your output should report the sum of the attraction scores and the total number of dates arranged. These are two measures of how good the solution is. The company will be making its customers happier if these numbers are large.

4. You are going to write a program that plays a guessing game with the user at the terminal. The program will repeat the following operations until the user reports that he or she is bored:

- Ask the user to think of an animal.
- Ask yes/no questions about what the user's animal is.
- Guess the user's animal.
- If not correct, then ask the user what his or her animal is; ask for a yes/no question that will distinguish the animal from the animal guessed; remember this new animal.

The data structure used by the program is a binary tree. Each branch node of the tree contains a yes/no question, with one branch representing animals for which the answer to the question is yes and the other branch representing animals for which the answer to the question is no. Each leaf node of the tree represents an animal. For example,

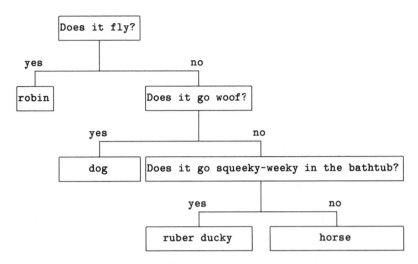

The program arrives at its guess by descending the tree. If it is at a branch node, it asks the question stored there and descends either left or right depending on the answer. When it reaches a leaf node, it guesses the animal stored in that leaf. If the guess is not right, the program prompts for the new animal and a yes/no question to distinguish it from the animal it guessed. The program then creates a new branch node with the given question and with the two animals as children. In this way the program learns about the new animal.

The program should use a data file to read in the initial value of the tree and to write out the final value of the tree. Thus the data file for the program will grow larger with each execution. The tree should be written and read using a preorder traversal, where each line of the file represents the contents of one node. Each line should start with either 'Q:' or 'A:' to indicate whether it is a question node or animal node. For example, the preceding tree would be stored as

```
Q: Does it fly?
A: robin
Q: Does it go woof?
A: dog
Q: Does it go squeeky-weeky in the bathtub?
A: rubber ducky
A: horse
```

5. Consider the problem of managing a tennis tournament. You must divide the group of players into pairs. Then each pair plays, which constitutes the first round of competition. Half the players win and half the players lose. The half that win go on to the second round. You again divide the group into pairs, and the second round is played. Again, half win and half lose. This process continues until a single winner is found. Some rounds will have an odd number of players, so sometimes you will have to give a player a "bye," which means the player sits out the round

and automatically moves into the next round. You should try not to give a single player more than one bye.

Managing this information is a fairly complicated problem for those who have to handle large tournaments, so perhaps a computer program can help. You are going to write an interactive program that helps a tournament manager. Your program will only have to perform four different commands, but it should be written in such a way that more commands could be added easily.

Your program will read in the players' names from a file. The order of the names in this file will determine the initial pairing (in general, the first two will be paired, then the next two, and so on). The file will simply contain a series of lines with one name per line.

After the data have been read in, the program should determine the initial pairings and report them to the user. The pairings will be determined by the file, except that if the file has an odd number of players, the program should randomly pick a player to take the first bye. Then the program should allow the user to give whatever sequence of commands he or she wants to. The program has to be able to show the current set of pairings, show the cumulative set of results, record the results of the current round, and give help (i.e., explain the various commands).

The problem of giving each player no more than one bye is a fairly complicated one, so you will be allowed to solve a slightly easier task. No player is to have two byes in a row (i.e., no player should sit out two rounds in a row).

Your program will probably have a fairly complicated data structure. When the tournament is over, you will want a binary tree with the winner at the top. A simple tree structure would be easy to use for this program if you knew in advance who is at the root of the tree, then knew who the children of the root are, and so on. Unfortunately, this information is not found out until the end of the tournament. Thus you start out with the names of five people, but you don't know what will appear above them in the tree. The best structure to use is a hybrid of an array and tree. You will store an array of pointers to trees. Start by storing each player in the tournament in a leaf node with an array element pointing to it. When you record the results of round 1, you can consolidate these array elements into a smaller number of trees. Repeat this process until you finally end up with just one array element, a pointer to the complete tree that describes the tournament.

17

ADVANCED COMPUTER SCIENCE TOPICS

17.1 Introduction

This chapter briefly explores some of the most significant advanced topics that have not been covered previously in this book. These topics normally are major themes in a second course in computer science. First, the chapter examines the techniques for putting lists into sorted order. Second, the chapter considers a further application of logic to programming: assertions about loops. Finally, the chapter considers more restrictive implementations of a type, implementations that completely hide the underlying structure.

17.2 Sorting

In Chapter 9 you examined a linear type that stores a series of values in increasing order. The inserting procedure that you developed maintained the list in sorted order, so that you only had to consider inserting a single value into a previously sorted list. More often you will want to take a list that is not in sorted order and put it into sorted order. There are many algorithms for doing this. You will study two different sorting algorithms here. For each, you should assume that the following declarations have been made:

```
CONST MaxLength  = 100;
TYPE  NumberList = ARRAY [1..MaxLength] OF INTEGER;
```

```
ListType    = RECORD
    nums    : NumberList;
    length  : INTEGER
END;
```

17.2.1 Selection Sort

Selection sort is a well-known algorithm for putting a list into sorted order. Each time through a loop, the smallest value is selected and put in the right place. While there are literally hundreds of such algorithms, this is one of the most intuitive. Given this list

[1]	[2]	[3]	[4]	[5]	[6]
12	123	1	18	93	146

how do you put this array into order from smallest to largest? One step would be to scan the array and find the smallest number. In this list, the smallest is **nums** [3], which equals 1. You would be closer to your goal if you were to swap **nums** [1] and **nums** [3]:

[1]	[2]	[3]	[4]	[5]	[6]
1	123	12	18	93	146

Nums [1] now has the value it should, and you only have to order the elements [2] through [6]. You can repeat this algorithm, scanning the remaining five elements for the smallest (**nums** [3], which equals 12) and swapping it with **nums** [2]:

[1]	[2]	[3]	[4]	[5]	[6]
1	12	123	18	93	146

Now **nums** [1] and **nums** [2] have the correct values. You can continue for **nums** [3], scanning the remaining four elements for the smallest (**nums** [4], which equals 18) and swapping it with **nums** [3]:

[1]	[2]	[3]	[4]	[5]	[6]
1	12	18	123	93	146

This gives you the correct values for nums [1], nums [2], and nums [3]. You can continue this process until all elements have the proper values. Here is an attempt at a pseudocode description of the algorithm:

scan elements [1] through [6] for the smallest value.
swap element [1] with the element found in the scan.
scan elements [2] through [6] for the smallest value.
swap element [2] with the element found in the scan.
scan elements [3] through [6] for the smallest value.
swap element [3] with the element found in the scan.
scan elements [4] through [6] for the smallest value.
swap element [4] with the element found in the scan.
scan elements [5] through [6] for the smallest value.
swap element [5] with the element found in the scan.

The algorithm involves a scan followed by a swap. You repeat the scan/swap five times. You don't need to perform a sixth scan/swap because the sixth element will automatically have the correct value if the first five have the correct values. This pseudocode is clumsy because it doesn't take into account the obvious looping that is going on. Here is a better approximation:

for n going from 1 to 5 do
begin
        scan elements [n] through [6] for the smallest value.
        swap element [n] with the element found in the scan.
end

You can perform the scan with the following:

set smallest to (lowest array index of interest).
for (all other index values of interest) do
begin
        if (value at [index]) < (value at [smallest]) then
                set smallest to index.
end

You can incorporate this into your larger pseudocode:

for n going from 1 to 5 do
begin
        set smallest to n.
        for index going (n + 1) to 6 do
                if element [index] < element [smallest] then
                        set smallest to index.
        swap element [n] with element [smallest].
end

This pseudocode is almost directly translatable into Pascal except for the swap process. For this, you should use the following procedure, verified in Chapter 8:

```
PROCEDURE Swap (VAR first, second: INTEGER);
VAR temp : INTEGER;
BEGIN
    temp   := first;
    first  := second;
    second := temp
END;   (* Swap *)
```

Now you can write the procedure properly:

```
PROCEDURE SelectionSort (VAR list   : ListType);
VAR count1   : INTEGER;
    count2   : INTEGER;
    smallest : INTEGER;
BEGIN
    WITH list DO
    BEGIN
        FOR count1 := 1 TO (length - 1) DO
        BEGIN
            smallest := count1;
            FOR count2 := (count1 + 1) TO length DO
                IF nums [count2] < nums [smallest] THEN
                    smallest := count2;
            Swap (nums [count1], nums [smallest])
        END
    END
END;   (* SelectionSort *)
```

17.2.2 Merge Sort

The reasoning applied in the merge sort algorithm is similar to the reasoning applied in writing recursive procedures. Not surprisingly, the merge sort is most easily written recursively. The algorithm derives from the observation that if you have two sorted sublists, you can easily merge them into a single sorted list. For example, if you have

```
1 3 6 7   2 4 5 8
-------   -------
sublist   sublist
```

you merge the sublists together by keeping a pointer into each of them. Here is a pseudocode description of the merging algorithm:

set left pointer to smallest element of left sublist.
set right pointer to smallest element of right sublist.

```
for (number of elements in entire list) do
    if (left pointer points to smaller value than right pointer) then
    begin
        include value pointed to by left pointer in new list.
        move left pointer to next value in left sublist.
    end
    else
    begin
        include value pointed to by right pointer in new list.
        move right pointer to next value in right sublist.
    end
```

Here is a trace of the eight steps involved in merging the two sublists into a new sorted list:

Unsorted List								Next Include	New List
1 left	3	6	7	2 right	4	5	8	1 from left	1
1	3 left	6	7	2 right	4	5	8	2 from right	1 2
1	3 left	6	7	2	4 right	5	8	3 from left	1 2 3
1	3	6 left	7	2	4 right	5	8	4 from right	1 2 3 4
1	3	6 left	7	2	4	5 right	8	5 from right	1 2 3 4 5
1	3	6 left	7	2	4	5	8 right	6 from left	1 2 3 4 5 6
1	3	6	7 left	2	4	5	8 right	7 from left	1 2 3 4 5 6 7
1	3	6	7	2	4	5	8 right	8 from right	1 2 3 4 5 6 7 8

After the seventh step, you have included all the elements in the left list, so the left pointer no longer points to anything. This complicates the pseudocode somewhat, because you have to deal with the special case that one of the pointers might not point to anything. The simple test in the pseudocode needs to be expanded:

```
if (left points to nothing) then
    take from right.
else
    if (right points to nothing) then
        take from left.
else
    compare values pointed to by left and right to decide.
```

This is a complex enough test that you should make a separate function for it. Assume that each pointer has the value 0 when there is nothing left to be taken from its sublist. Using this function, you can expand the pseudocode for merging. How do you specify the two sublists that are to be merged? If you assume that the left list ends at the midpoint and that the right list starts at midpoint plus 1, you can specify the two sublists using two indexes: the leftmost position of the left sublist and the rightmost position of the right sublist. The midpoint can be calculated from those two. Thus your procedure looks like the following. Function `TakeFromLeft` has been included along with a procedure called `Use`, which simplifies the code. Both are nested so that they can examine the values of variables local to procedure `Merge`.

```
PROCEDURE Merge (VAR nums  : NumberList;
                     start : INTEGER;
                     stop  : INTEGER);
VAR LeftPos  : INTEGER;
    RightPos : INTEGER;
    midpoint : INTEGER;
    index    : INTEGER;
    TempNums : NumsType;

    FUNCTION TakeFromLeft : BOOLEAN;
    BEGIN
        IF (LeftPos = 0) THEN
            TakeFromLeft := FALSE
        ELSE
            IF (RightPos = 0) THEN
                TakeFromLeft := TRUE
            ELSE
                TakeFromLeft := (nums [LeftPos] < nums [RightPos])
    END;    (* TakeFromLeft *)
```

```
    PROCEDURE Use (VAR WhichPos : INTEGER;
                       limit    : INTEGER);
    BEGIN
        TempNums [index] := nums [WhichPos];
        WhichPos := WhichPos + 1;
        IF (WhichPos > limit) THEN
            WhichPos := 0
    END;

BEGIN   (* Merge *)
    midpoint := (start + stop) DIV 2;
    LeftPos := start;
    RightPos := midpoint + 1;
    FOR index := start TO stop DO
        IF TakeFromLeft THEN
            use (LeftPos, midpoint)
        ELSE
            use (RightPos, stop);
    FOR index := start TO stop DO
        nums [index] := TempNums [index]
END;    (* Merge *)
```

The left and right position pointers are set to 0 when all elements from the sublist are included in the master list. Also, note the variable TempNums, used to store the new list. At the end of the procedure, the new sequence stored in TempNums is copied back to nums. You need such temporary storage because storing the new sequence in variable nums can potentially erase one of your sublists.

The interesting thing about this sorting algorithm is that the only hard part is the merging. The rest is solved by the funny kind of reasoning you apply when writing recursive procedures. You are writing a procedure to sort a sequence of numbers. How do you do it? If you want to use merge, you could

> sort the first half.
> sort the second half.
> merge the two halves.

You have the procedure to merge, so you just need to figure out how to sort the two halves. But you are writing a procedure that does exactly that, a procedure that sorts a sequence of values. Thus you can recursively call the sorting procedure to sort each half.

This specifies the recursive case. What about simple cases? What are the simplest lists to sort? The answer is that a list with either no elements or just one element doesn't need to be sorted at all. It takes at least two elements before you can get something in the wrong order, so the simple cases are lists of length less than 2.

Here is a procedure that implements this strategy:

```
PROCEDURE RecursiveSort (VAR nums  : NumberList;
                             start : INTEGER;
                             stop  : INTEGER);
VAR midpoint : INTEGER;
BEGIN
    IF (start < stop) THEN
    BEGIN
        midpoint := (start + stop) DIV 2;
        RecursiveSort (nums, start, midpoint);
        RecursiveSort (nums, midpoint + 1, stop);
        merge (nums, start, stop)
    END
END;   (* RecursiveSort *)
```

This procedure, like procedure **merge**, has two parameters that specify the start and stop indexes of the list. The list has two or more elements if and only if **start** is less than **stop**. Thus the test in the IF/THEN guaranties that you perform the recursive case only for lists of length 2 or more. Here is a dynamic scope trace of what happens when you call this procedure on a list of five elements:

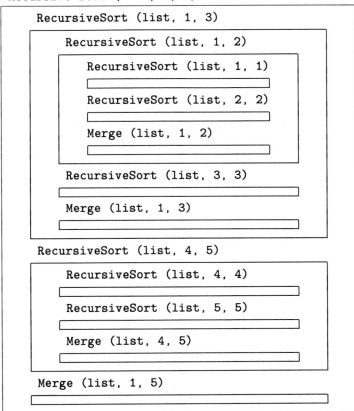

To create a procedure with the same parameter passing as procedure **InsertionSort**, you would create a procedure such as the following:

```
PROCEDURE MergeSort (VAR list : ListType);
BEGIN
    WITH list DO
        RecursiveSort (nums, 1, length)
END;   (* MergeSort *)
```

17.3 Loop Invariants

This section explores the logic of loops in more detail. Just as you use preconditions and postconditions to describe subprograms, you use invariant assertions to describe loops.

> **LOOP INVARIANT**
> An assertion that is true just before each iteration of a loop.

For example, here is an outline of a WHILE loop showing where the invariant is:

```
WHILE <test> DO
BEGIN
    (* invariant assertion is true here *)
    <body of loop>
END
```

You should think of an invariant as a relationship that is maintained while the loop performs its various iterations. It does not vary, which is why it is called an invariant. An invariant is to a programmer what a course is to a navigator. The navigator calculates the course he needs to travel and then makes sure the craft stays on that course while it moves forward. If the navigator stays on course, he will reach the destination. Similarly, the programmer figures out what relationship must be maintained among variables as the computer performs more and more iterations of the loop. If he maintains that relationship, the loop will accomplish its task.

An invariant is like both a precondition and a postcondition for the code in the body of the loop. It is a precondition in the sense that you can assume the invariant is true before the body is executed. It is a postcondition in the sense that the body of the loop has to restore the invariant so that on the next iteration it will again hold.

A loop invariant can help you in many ways. First, it precisely describes the workings of a loop. Second, it simplifies the process of verification. And third, it often helps you to write code that implements the loop. This is easiest to understand by studying an example.

Suppose you want to calculate the sum of the first n integers. You might write this code:

```
sum := 0;
number := 0;
WHILE (number < n) DO
BEGIN
    (* invariant assertion should be true here *)
    number := number + 1;
    sum := sum + number
END;
```

To fill in the invariant, consider how the loop works. What partial sum do you have before each iteration? For the first four iterations, you have

Iteration	Partial Sum
First	1
Second	$1 + 2$
Third	$1 + 2 + 3$
Fourth	$1 + 2 + 3 + 4$

You can express this relationship in terms of the variable `number`:

```
Sum = 1 + 2 + 3 + ... + number
```

This is the loop invariant, the relationship that is maintained while the loop executes. You can verify it in two steps. First, you verify it for the first iteration. The initialization before the loop guaranties that on the first iteration you have

```
Sum = number = 1
```

Thus the invariant holds on the first iteration. Now you verify that the assertion holds for subsequent iterations. On a subsequent iteration, you start out knowing that

```
Sum = 1 + 2 + 3 + ... + number
```

The first statement of the loop increments `number`. Expressing the invariant in terms of this new value of number yields

```
Sum = 1 + 2 + 3 + ... + (number - 1)
```

Thus the invariant is not satisfied at this point in execution. However, the second statement of the loop adds the new value of `number` to `sum`, which restores the invariant. Thus the invariant holds for every iteration of the loop.

If you analyze this loop further, you notice that the variable `number` takes on all the values between 1 and n consecutively. On the final iteration, you have number $=$ n. This means that after you restore the invariant on the last iteration, you get

```
Sum = 1 + 2 + 3 + ... + n
```

This is your goal. Thus verifying the loop invariant verifies that this code works.

17.3.1 Program Synthesis with Invariants

In the last section you saw how, given a loop, you can find a loop invariant that describes it in more detail and that helps to verify its correctness. This section considers the opposite situation, where you are given an invariant and are asked to construct a loop that maintains it. By doing so, you can use the invariant to write the code of the loop.

Suppose you are using a version of Pascal that doesn't have the built-in SQRT function for calculating the square root of a number. You could write your own function that approximates the square root. Here is a sample specification:

```
FUNCTION SQRT (number : REAL) : REAL;
(* pre  : number is nonnegative.                    *)
(* post : returns an approximation to the nonnegative *)
(*        : square root of the given number.          *)
```

To write this function, you must figure out how to approximate a square root. Let's explore a specific method that is easily derived from an invariant. The invariant is derived from the simple observation that while it is difficult to pinpoint the exact square root, it is fairly easy to guess something larger than it and something smaller than it. Thus you introduce two variables:

```
VAR guess1 : REAL;
    guess2 : REAL;
```

What relationship can you maintain that would express the idea that these are two approximations to the square root of number? One simple answer is

```
(guess1 * guess2 = number)
```

In other words, you make sure that the two guesses always have the same product, the number you are finding the root of. You will be done if you can maintain this relationship and eventually obtain

```
guess1 = guess2
```

In this case, each variable would store the square root. Given the fact that computers do not store numbers with an infinite degree of precision, it might not be possible to obtain this goal. Therefore, you will instead specify a threshold where you will stop iterating. For example, you might try to obtain

```
ABS (guess1 - guess2) <= 0.0001
```

This says that you will calculate the square root to within an accuracy of 0.0001. You write the code using this very general outline:

```
<initialization>
WHILE <test> DO
BEGIN
    (* invariant assertion should be true here *)
    <get closer to terminating the loop>
    <restore invariant>
END
```

You fill in this outline with the specific invariant you are using and with a test that will terminate when **guess1** and **guess2** are within the threshold:

```
<initialization>
WHILE ABS (guess1 - guess2) > 0.0001 DO
BEGIN
    (* invariant : guess1 * guess2 = number *)
    <get closer to terminating the loop>
    <restore invariant>
END
```

The most difficult part of the loop left to fill in is how to get closer. How do you improve on the guesses that you have made? You do so by decreasing the distance between the root and one of your guesses. You know from the invariant that one guess will be low and the other high:

```
<low guess>    <square root>    <high guess>
```
distance #1   distance #2

If you maintain the invariant, all you have to do is reduce one of these distances. If you reduce the first, the second will automatically be reduced, and vice versa. For example, if you find a new low guess that is closer, the invariant ensures that your new high guess will be closer as well because the product of the guesses is constant. You can accomplish the reduction by using the midpoint of the two guesses. You don't know whether the midpoint is higher or lower than the root, but it doesn't matter. Either it is lower than the root, which reduces distance 1, or it is higher than the root, which reduces distance 2. Either way you get closer. Thus you can fill in the getting closer part of your loop with

```
midpoint := (guess1 + guess2)/2;
guess1 := midpoint;
```

If this is your way of getting closer, how do you restore the invariant? You know that after these statements execute, you have

```
guess1 = midpoint
```

You want to guaranty the relationship

```
(guess1 * guess2 = number)
```

This is simple algebra. You merely set **guess2** to a value that satisfies these two equations:

```
guess2 := number/midpoint;
```

Now you have filled in the test and body of the loop. All that remains is the initialization. What guesses should you start with? You can begin with any guesses whatsoever, as long as they satisfy the invariant so that it will be true before the first iteration. A simple pair of guesses is

```
guess1 := 1;
guess2 := number;
```

This completes the function. Thus you get

```
FUNCTION SQRT (number : REAL) : REAL;
VAR guess1 : REAL;
    guess2 : REAL
BEGIN
    guess1 := 1;
    guess2 := number;
    WHILE ABS (guess1 - guess2) > 0.0001 DO
    BEGIN
        (* invariant : guess1 * guess2 = number *)
        midpoint := (guess1 + guess2)/2;
        guess1 := midpoint;
        guess2 := number/midpoint
    END;
    SQRT := guess1
END;
```

A very important property of the loop you have created is that you have a proof of its correctness. You constructed the loop from the invariant, so you know it is correct. This is what computer scientists call *program synthesis* or *program generation*, the generation of code from a logical statement of what the code is to accomplish. It is a small example of how code can be created by reasoning about program assertions. This is an important area of computer science research.

17.4 Building Data Types Revisited

In Chapter 9 you examined the building of a linear data type, starting with the abstract specification and leading to an implementation. The techniques studied, however, sometimes lead to situations you want to avoid. This is easiest to explain by example.

Suppose you want to create a type for storing a linear list of integers, not in sorted order. The type will be called `ListType` and should include at least the following operations:

Operation	Specification
InitList	Procedure to initialize a list variable, setting it to an empty list
EmptyList	Procedure to remove all the elements of a list so that it is once again empty
NthElement	Function to return the NthElement of a list variable
Length	Function to return the length of a list variable
ChangeNthElement	Procedure to change the NthElement of a list variable to some new value
NewElement	Procedure to create a new uninitialized element at the end of the list (i.e., at position (length + 1))

Suppose you are going to define `ListType` as follows:

```
CONST MaxList = 500;
TYPE  Numlist  = ARRAY [1..MaxList] OF INTEGER;
      ListType = RECORD
          nums   : Numlist;
          length : INTEGER
      END;
```

All six of the operations are easily performed on elements with this structure:

Operation	Implementation
InitList	list.length := 0;
EmptyList	list.length := 0;
NthElement	list.nums [n]
Length	list.nums [length]
ChangeNthElement	list.nums [n] := NewValue;
NewElement	list.length := list.length + 1;

In Chapter 9 you decided not to write procedures or functions for these simple operations because they can be so easily specified. However, consider what happens when you write high-level code that uses the operations in this way:

```
PROCEDURE ReadList (VAR list : ListType);
BEGIN
    list.length := 0;
    WHILE NOT EOLN DO
    BEGIN
        list.length := list.length + 1;
        READ (list.nums [list.length])
    END
END;
```

```
PROCEDURE WriteList (list : ListType);
VAR index : INTEGER;
BEGIN
    FOR index := 1 TO list.length DO
        WRITELN (list.nums [index])
END;

PROCEDURE MergeLists (VAR result : ListType;
                          list1  : ListType;
                          list2  : ListType);
VAR index : INTEGER;
BEGIN
    result.length := 0;
    FOR index := 1 TO list1.length DO
    BEGIN
        result.length := result.length + 1;
        result.nums [result.length] := list1.nums [index]
    END;
    FOR index := 1 TO list2.length DO
    BEGIN
        result.length := result.length + 1;
        result.nums [index + list1.length] := list2.nums [index]
    END
END;
```

The problem with these high-level procedures is that they are tied to the underlying implementation of ListType. Each of them makes direct reference to an array called nums and an integer called length:

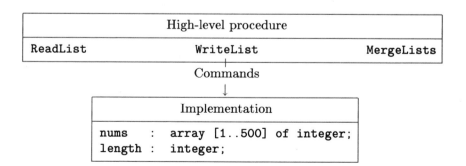

The high-level procedures are executing commands that refer to the implementation. These procedures are committing a kind of information peeking: looking inside the variables of type `ListType` and manipulating the innards directly. If the innards change, the procedures won't work anymore. There is a way to insulate high-level procedures from such changes by creating what is called an *opaque type*.

17.4.1   An Opaque Implementation

In an opaque implementation, you use procedures and functions to obscure the underlying implementation. To do so, you create procedures and functions for each of the list operations, even though they are so simple to perform that they don't seem like they should be written as procedures and functions. Thus you would create six procedures and functions:

```
PROCEDURE InitList (VAR list : ListType);
BEGIN
    list.length := 0
END;


PROCEDURE EmptyList (VAR list : ListType);
BEGIN
    list.length := 0
END;


FUNCTION NthElement (list  : ListType;
                     index : INTEGER) : INTEGER;
BEGIN
    NthElement := list.nums [index]
END;


FUNCTION Length (list : ListType) : INTEGER;
BEGIN
    length := list.length
END;


PROCEDURE ChangeNthElement (VAR list     : ListType;
                                index    : INTEGER;
                                NewValue : INTEGER);
BEGIN
    list.nums [index] := NewValue
END;
```

```
              PROCEDURE NewElement (VAR list : ListType);
              BEGIN
                  list.length := list.length + 1
              END;
```

Then you would rewrite the three high-level procedures in terms of these procedures and functions:

```
PROCEDURE ReadList (VAR list : ListType);
VAR number : INTEGER;
BEGIN
    InitList (list);
    WHILE NOT EOLN DO
    BEGIN
        NewElement (list);
        READ (number);
        ChangeNthElement (list, length (list), number)
    END
END;

PROCEDURE WriteList (list : ListType);
VAR index : INTEGER;
BEGIN
    FOR index := 1 TO length (list) DO
        WRITELN (NthElement (list, index))
END;

PROCEDURE MergeLists (VAR result : ListType;
                          list1  : ListType;
                          list2  : ListType);
VAR index : INTEGER;
BEGIN
    InitList (result);
    FOR index := 1 TO length (list1) DO
    BEGIN
        NewElement (result);
        ChangeNthElement (result, index, NthElement (list1, index))
    END;
    FOR index := 1 TO length (list2) DO
    BEGIN
        NewElement (result);
        ChangeNthElement (result, index + length (list1),
                          NthElement (list2, index))
    END
END;
```

Now these procedures are independent of the underlying structure. They make no reference to the array **nums** or to the integer **length**:

High-level procedures		
ReadList	WriteList	MergeLists

Commands
↓

Procedures and functions implementing basic operations		
InitList	NthElement	ChangeNthElement
EmptyList	Length	NewElement

Commands
↓

Implementation
nums   :   array [1..500] of integer;
length :   integer;

The high-level procedures manipulate list variables only through the set of middle-level procedures and functions. The middle level, in turn, manipulates list variables by making direct references to the implementation. Since the middle level is the only level that makes such references, it serves as a screen that hides the implementation from the high-level code.

17.4.2   Changing the Implementation

If you want to pull out the array implementation and use another, you merely rewrite the middle level of procedures and functions. The high-level code remains unchanged. For example, consider the following set of declarations for a dynamic linked list implementation:

```
TYPE PtrList     = ^ListElement;
     ListElement = RECORD
          number  : INTEGER;
          next    : PtrList
     END;
     ListType    = PtrList;
```

Here is a different set of six operations implemented for this structure:

```
PROCEDURE InitList (VAR list : ListType);
BEGIN
    list := NIL
END;


PROCEDURE EmptyList (VAR list : ListType);
VAR temp : PtrList;
BEGIN
    WHILE (list <> NIL) DO
    BEGIN
        temp := list;
        list := list^.next;
        DISPOSE (temp)
    END
END;


FUNCTION NthElement (list  : ListType;
                     index : INTEGER) : INTEGER;
VAR temp : PtrList;
BEGIN
    temp := list;
    WHILE (index > 1) DO
    BEGIN
        temp := temp^.next;
        index := index - 1
    END;
    NthElement := temp^.number
END;


FUNCTION Length (list : ListType) : INTEGER;
VAR temp  : ListType;
    count : INTEGER;
BEGIN
    count := 0;
    temp := list;
```

```
            WHILE (temp <> NIL) DO
            BEGIN
                count := count + 1;
                temp := temp^.next
            END;
            length := count
    END;

    PROCEDURE ChangeNthElement (VAR list     : ListType;
                                    index    : INTEGER;
                                    NewValue : INTEGER);
    VAR temp : PtrList;
    BEGIN
        temp := list;
        WHILE (index > 1) DO
        BEGIN
            temp := temp^.next;
            index := index - 1
        END;
        temp^.number := NewValue
    END;

    PROCEDURE NewElement (VAR list : ListType);
    VAR temp : PtrList;
    BEGIN
        IF (list = NIL) THEN
            NEW (list)
        ELSE
        BEGIN
            temp := list;
            WHILE (temp^.next <> NIL) DO
                temp := temp^.next;
            NEW (temp^.next)
        END
    END;
```

17.4.3 Opaque Types and Efficiency

An opaque type can certainly improve the modifiability of a program, but what does it cost? One answer is computer time. When a programmer knows the underlying implementation and can manipulate all the individual parts of a variable, he can write the most efficient code possible for that implementation.

When the implementation is obscured, however, often the resulting code is quite inefficient. There are a few things that can be done to improve the situation. For example, consider this high-level procedure:

```
PROCEDURE WriteList (list : ListType);
VAR index : INTEGER;
BEGIN
    FOR index := 1 TO length (list) DO
        WRITELN (NthElement (list, index))
END;
```

Suppose you are manipulating a list of 500 elements using the array implementation. Function `length` is called once and immediately returns a value. The `WRITELN` statement is executed 500 times, once for each list element. And the call on `NthElement` is performed 500 times, causing 500 individual accesses of array elements.

Now suppose you are manipulating a list of 500 elements using the linked list implementation. Function `length` is again called only once, but this time it must scan 500 list elements to determine the length. The `WRITELN` is again executed 500 times, once for each element. And you call `NthElement` 500 different times. When index is 1, `NthElement` only needs to examine one element of the list to return its result. But when the index is 2, `NthElement` needs to examine two elements. When index is 3, `NthElement` examines three elements, and so on until index is 500 and `NthElement` examines 500 elements before returning its result. This totals 125,250 different times you must examine an element of the list, which is certainly going to slow you down.

Given a situation such as this, you can usually fix the implementation so that it performs better by adding some extra fields to the list. You currently have

```
TYPE PtrList     = ^ListElement;
     ListElement = RECORD
         number  : INTEGER;
         next    : PtrList
     END;
     ListType    = PtrList;
```

You can add more to the list variable by creating a record:

```
ListType     = RECORD
    elements : PtrList;
    (* other stuff *)
END;
```

One simple fix you can make is to realize that if a certain list element is examined, it is likely that the next examination of the list will either be at the same place or somewhere very near. So you can keep track of the last list element referenced:

```
ListType      = RECORD
    elements : PtrList;
    LastPtr  : PtrList;
    LastN    : INTEGER
END;
```

This requires a slight modification in your initializing procedure. You can initialize LastN to 0 to indicate that you don't have a last pointer:

```
PROCEDURE InitList (VAR list : ListType);
BEGIN
    WITH list DO
    BEGIN
        elements := NIL;
        LastN := 0;
        LastPtr := NIL
    END
END;
```

In this implementation, you can only go forward in the linked list. This means that the LastPtr is only useful if you examine an element at the same spot or at a later spot in the list. In other words, if you call NthElement with an N that is greater than or equal to LastN, you can get some savings out of LastPtr. Otherwise you can't. Here is a rewritten NthElement procedure that takes advantage of LastPtr whenever possible:

```
FUNCTION NthElement (list  : ListType;
                     index : INTEGER) : INTEGER;
VAR temp          : PtrList;
    OriginalIndex : INTEGER;
BEGIN
    OriginalIndex := index;
    WITH list DO
    BEGIN
        IF (index >= LastN) AND (LastN > 0) THEN
        BEGIN
            temp := LastPtr;
            index := index - LastN + 1
        END
        ELSE
            temp := elements;
        WHILE (index > 1) DO
        BEGIN
            temp := temp^.next;
            index := index - 1
        END;
```

```
                    NthElement := temp^.number;
                    LastPtr := temp;
                    LastN := OriginalIndex
              END
      END;
```

You would have to change the other procedures and functions similarly to take advantage of `LastPtr`. With this fix, the linked list implementation does as well as the array implementation because the `FOR` loop examines element (n + 1) right after examining element n. This means that the preceding procedure only has to move a pointer over one element each time, which results in 500 list manipulations rather than the 125,250 you saw earlier.

Similar savings can be gained by actually storing the length in the list rather than calculating it each time. This would naturally mean that procedures such as `InitList`, `EmptyList`, and `NewElement` would have to modify the value of the variable appropriately, but it also means that function Length can simply return a value rather than having to scan down the entire list.

Another area of savings comes from storing a pointer to the last element in the list, if there is one. This way `NewElement` won't have to scan through the list to create a new element at the end.

No matter how many minor modifications are made to the type, however, it is difficult to avoid all possible sources of inefficiency. For example, you still have to perform 125,250 list manipulations if the `FOR` loop is made to go backward rather than forward, because in a singly linked list you can't go back to the previous element without starting at the beginning of the list and working forward. You can get around this as well if you want to store pointers in both directions in your list, but the real point here is that the implementor of the opaque type will never be able to anticipate all possible problems.

17.4.4   Verification with Opaque Types

Opaque types afford a new opportunity for verifying assertions about your programs. Since you know that variables of an opaque type are directly manipulated by only a small set of procedures and functions, you can concentrate on them to try to verify properties of the type.

For example, suppose that each variable of a certain opaque type is a record with a field called `score`. Also suppose that in examining the set of procedures and functions that directly manipulates the fields of the record, you find only two statements that change the value of `score`. In the initializing procedure, you find that this statement is always executed:

```
    score := 0;
```

And in an updating procedure, you find that `score` might be changed by

```
IF (score < 100) THEN
    score := score + 1;
```

If there are no other places where `score` is changed, you can prove that for any initialized variable of the opaque type, the following is true:

```
0 <= score <= 100
```

You know that this is true because `score` starts out at 0; it is possibly incremented, but only if it is strictly less than 100; and it is never changed anywhere else. This might be a useful property to prove about your program. The assertion is not so much about the program as it is about variables of a certain type. You call such assertions *data invariants*. Often it is easier to implement a type if you decide on the data invariants in advance. For example, it might be easier to write code to manipulate a list of names if you can assume that they are always in sorted order.

17.4.5 Error Recovery with Opaque Types

What happens when an error occurs in one of the procedures and functions that hide the implementation from the high-level code? You must be careful not to have these procedures and functions also hide errors, because the high-level code needs to know about them.

For example, in the array implementation of `ListType` you might call `NewElement` at a time when the array is full. What happens then? The usual thing is to have the procedure return an error flag as a parameter, which would change the procedure header to

```
PROCEDURE NewElement (VAR list  : ListType;
                      VAR error : BOOLEAN);
```

The problem with this change is that you need to call `NewElement` often, because you are using it to hide the implementation. If each of these intermediate procedures and functions requires an error flag in its parameter list, it becomes prohibitively difficult to use the opaque implementation.

Again, there is a nice solution. The real problem is that you haven't properly abstracted the list type. You conceived of a variable that stores only a series of integers. You should have conceived of a variable that also stores certain state information about the list. For example, each list can keep track of whether or not it is overfull. If you call `NewElement` when the list is completely full, then `NewElement` can record the fact that the list is now overfull. Naturally, the high-level code should be able to also see whether the list is overfull, so you will create a new operation for it.

To see how this is done, here is a revised set of declarations for the array implementation of `ListType` with an overfull flag:

```
CONST Maxlist      = 500;
TYPE  Numlist      = ARRAY [1..MaxList] OF INTEGER;
      ListType     = RECORD
          nums     : Numlist;
          length   : INTEGER;
          overfull : BOOLEAN
      END;
```

You would change three of the basic operations:

```
PROCEDURE InitList (VAR list : ListType);
BEGIN
    list.length := 0;
    list.overfull := FALSE
END;

PROCEDURE EmptyList (VAR list : ListType);
BEGIN
    list.length := 0;
    list.overfull := FALSE
END;

PROCEDURE NewElement (VAR list : ListType);
BEGIN
    overfull := (list.length = MaxList);
    IF NOT overfull THEN
        list.length := list.length + 1
END;
```

You would also add a seventh operation to allow the high-level code to examine this value:

```
FUNCTION Overfull (list : ListType) : BOOLEAN;
BEGIN
    overfull := list.overfull
END;
```

You could modify your abstraction of a list even further to include other error flags as well. For example, you probably want to set a flag whenever the intermediate procedures are asked to do something with the Nth element where N is not in the range of 1 to length.

Thus, by changing your abstraction of a type, you can often increase its usefulness without greatly increasing the complexity of the rest of the program (e.g., the parameter passing). This allows you to handle error checking for opaque types straightforwardly.

17.5 Key Concepts

- It is often useful to sort the elements of a list into some order. The selection sort is one way to do so, but you will want to use an algorithm like the merge sort for larger lists because it is more time efficient.

- A loop invariant precisely describes the workings of a loop. It defines what can be assumed to be true before each iteration of the loop and what is to be true after each iteration. Loop invariants are useful for verifying the correctness of a loop and for synthesizing the loop.

- It will be easier to modify the underlying implementation of a type if you implement it in an opaque way, creating a set of procedures and functions that hide all references to the underlying structure. Though it is often more difficult and less efficient to use a type in an opaque way, the technique simplifies any changes that you might want to make in the underlying data structure.

17.6 Self-Check Exercises

1. What modifications would have to be made to procedure `InsertionSort` to cause it to sort a list of **REAL** values rather than a list of **INTEGER** values?

2. How many calls on procedure `MergeSort` are generated by a call to sort a list of length **n**?

3. What modifications would have to be made to procedure `MergeSort` and the procedures it calls to cause it to sort in descending rather than ascending order?

4. You are going to synthesize a version of function `factorial` from an invariant. Remember, n factorial (written $n!$) is defined as

$$n! = \begin{cases} 1, & n = 0 \\ 1 * 2 * 3 * \ldots * n, & \text{otherwise} \end{cases}$$

You should use the invariant below (when `index` = n, `fact` has the desired value):

```
fact = (index - 1)!
```

Complete the following outline:

```
FUNCTION Factorial (n : INTEGER) : INTEGER;
(* pre : n >= 0. *)
VAR index : integer;
    fact  : INTEGER;
```

```
BEGIN
    <initialization>
    WHILE (index < n) DO
    BEGIN
        index := index + 1;
        <restore invariant>
    END;
    factorial := fact
END;
```

5. The invariant below can be used to synthesize a loop that performs exponentiation
    (when **TempPower** = 0, **Result** has the desired value):

    $$\text{TempPower} >= 0,\ \text{result} * \text{TempBase}^{\text{TempPower}} = \text{base}^{\text{power}}$$

    Use the invariant to complete the function outlined below.

```
FUNCTION Exponent (base, power : integer) : integer;
(* pre : power >= 0. *)
VAR result, TempBase, TempPower : INTEGER;
BEGIN
    <initialization>
    WHILE (TempPower > 0) DO
        IF (TempPower MOD 2) = 0 THEN
        BEGIN
            TempPower := TempPower DIV 2;
            <restore invariant>
        END
        ELSE
        BEGIN
            TempPower := TempPower - 1;
            <restore invariant>
        END
END;
```

6. What is the loop invariant of the outer loop of procedure **SelectionSort**?

7. Write some high-level code that implements the following operation on variables
    of type **ListType** using the opaque specification of Section 17.4.1:

```
FUNCTION SumOf (VAR list : ListType) : INTEGER;
(* post : returns the sum of the elements stored in the list. *)
```

8. Write some high-level code that implements the following operation on variables
    of type **ListType** using the opaque specification of Section 17.4.1:

```
FUNCTION Equal (VAR list1, list2 : ListType) : BOOLEAN;
(* post : returns TRUE if elements of list1 match exactly in value *)
(*      : and position the elements of list2.                      *)
```

9. Using the operations defined for type **string** in Programming Problem 5, imple-
    ment the following procedure in an opaque way:

```
PROCEDURE Append (VAR FromStr, ToStr : string);
(* post   : ToStr is appended to FromStr. *)
```

10. Using the operations defined for type `ListType` in Programming Problem 3, implement the following procedure in an opaque way:

```
PROCEDURE EmptyAndCheck (VAR list          : ListType;
                         VAR SameInReverse : BOOLEAN);
(* post : If the sequence of numbers originally in the list is the  *)
(*      : same both forwards and backwards (e.g., 1 7 9 7  1), then  *)
(*      : SameInReverse is set to TRUE, otherwise SameInReverse is   *)
(*      : set to FALSE.  List returns an empty list.                 *)
```

17.7 Programming Problems

1. Write a program that reads a series of input lines and sorts them in lexicographic order, ignoring the case of words. The program should use the merge sort algorithm so that it quickly sorts even a large file.

2. An *anagram* of a word is a rearrangement of the letters. Anagrams are puzzles that people try to solve. For example, the anagrams of "computer" include "reptomuc," "tecrumop," and "murpceto." You can write a program that solves anagrams given an input file that stores a large dictionary. Assume that you have a file available to you which lists many words, one per line. Your program should first read in the dictionary and sort it. It shouldn't sort it in alphabetical order, though. Instead, it should sort according to each word's canonical form. The *canonical* form of a word is defined to be a word with the same letters as the original but appearing in sorted order. Thus the canonical form of "COMPUTER" is "CEMOPRTU," and the canonical form of "PROGRAM" is "AGMOPRR." Thus, in sorting the dictionary, the word "PROGRAM" would be placed before the word "COMPUTER," because the canonical form of "PROGRAM" is alphabetically less than the canonical form of "COMPUTER." In turning a word to canonical form, an insertion sort is probably appropriate. To sort something as large as the dictionary, however, you will probably want to use merge sort.

After reading and sorting the dictionary, your program should prompt the user for an anagram to solve. It should then report all words that match. To find words that match, use the canonical form of the word given by the user and find all words in the dictionary with the same canonical form. Suppose that the user gives you the anagram "SIDK." This word has the canonical form "DIKS." The other words that also have this canonical form are "DISK," "SKID," and "KIDS." These are the possible solutions to the anagram.

3. Suppose that you want to store a sequence of integers in a structure where you can manipulate both the front and back of the list:

$<integer>$ $<integer>$ $<integer>$ ... $<integer>$ $<integer>$ $<integer>$
     ↑   ↑
   front   back

You are going to implement a type called `ListType` and some procedures and functions that allow variables of type `ListType` to be manipulated in an opaque way. All the operations are required to execute in time independent of the length of the list. You are to implement the following operations:

```
PROCEDURE InitList (VAR list : ListType);
(* post : List is initialized to an empty list.  This procedure *)
(*       : should be called exactly once for each list variable, *)
(*       : before the variable is manipulated in any other way.  *)
```

```
FUNCTION Empty (VAR list : ListType) : BOOLEAN;
(* post : Returns TRUE if and only if list is empty. *)
```

```
FUNCTION Length (VAR list : ListType) : INTEGER;
(* post : Returns the number of elements in the list. *)
```

```
FUNCTION Front (VAR list : ListType) : INTEGER;
(* pre  : List has at least one element.                   *)
(* post : The value stored at the front of the list is returned.  *)
```

```
PROCEDURE DeleteFront (VAR list : ListType);
(* pre  : List has at least one element.                   *)
(* post : The value at the front of the list is deleted.   *)
```

```
PROCEDURE InsertFront (VAR list  : ListType;
                           value : INTEGER);
(* post : Given value is inserted as a new element at the front of *)
(*       : the list.                                               *)
```

```
FUNCTION Back (VAR list : ListType) : INTEGER;
(* pre  : List has at least one element.                   *)
(* post : The value stored at the back of the list is returned.  *)
```

```
PROCEDURE DeleteBack (VAR list : ListType);
(* pre  : List has at least one element.                   *)
(* post : The value at the back of the list is deleted.    *)
```

```
PROCEDURE InsertBack (VAR list  : ListType;
                          value : INTEGER);
(* post : Given value is inserted as a new element at the back of *)
(*       : the list.                                             *)
```

4. You are to implement a new type called `TableType` in an opaque way. Each variable of type `TableType` will store a sequence of table entries. A table entry consists of a word and an integer value. The words will be described by values of type `WordType`, specified as follows:

```
CONST MaxWord = 25;
TYPE  WordType = PACKED ARRAY [1..MaxWord] OF CHAR;
```

You are to implement the following operations:

```
PROCEDURE InitTable (VAR table : TableType);
(* post : Table is initialized to an empty table.  This procedure *)
(*      : should be called exactly once for each table variable,  *)
(*      : before the variable is manipulated in any other way.    *)

FUNCTION EntriesIn (table : TableType) : INTEGER;
(* post : Returns the number of entries stored in the table. *)

PROCEDURE AddValue (VAR table : TableType;
                        word  : WordType;
                        value : INTEGER);
(* post : Word is turned to uppercase.  If it doesn't appear in the *)
(*      : table, then it is added with the specified value.  If it  *)
(*      : already appears in the table, then the specified value    *)
(*      : becomes its new table value.                              *)

PROCEDURE DeleteValue (VAR table : TableType;
                           word  : WordType);
(* post : Word is turned to uppercase.  If it appears in the table, *)
(*      : it is deleted from the table.                             *)

FUNCTION ValueOf (word  : WordType;
                  table : TableType) : INTEGER;
(* post : Returns table value for given word.  If word is not in the *)
(*      : table, the value 0 is returned.                            *)
```

5. You are to implement a new type called **string** in an opaque way. Each string will store a sequence of values of type **CHAR**. The operations on type **string** that you must implement are specified as follows:

```
PROCEDURE InitString (VAR str : string);
(* post : Str is initialized to an empty string.  This procedure *)
(*      : should be called exactly once for each string variable, *)
(*      : before the variable is manipulated in any other way.    *)

FUNCTION NthChar (VAR str : string;
                      n   : INTEGER) : CHAR;
(* pre    : 1 <= n <= length (str).                      *)
(* post   : Returns character at position n in str.      *)
(* errors : If n is out of range, returns a space.       *)

PROCEDURE DeleteChar (VAR str : string;
                          pos : INTEGER);
(* pre    : 1 <= pos <= length (str).                        *)
(* post   : Character at position pos is deleted from str.   *)
(* errors : If pos is out of range, str is unchanged.        *)
```

```
PROCEDURE InsertChar (VAR str : string;
                           pos : INTEGER;
                           ch  : CHAR);
(* pre     : 1 <= pos <= length (str) + 1.                    *)
(* post    : Ch is inserted into str so that it has position pos. *)
(* errors  : If pos is out of range, str is unchanged.        *)


FUNCTION Length (VAR str : string) : INTEGER;
(* post : Returns length of str.   *)


PROCEDURE EmptyString (VAR str : string);
(* post : Str is reset to an empty string. *)


PROCEDURE WriteString (VAR str     : string;
                       VAR OutFile : TEXT);
(* pre  : OutFile is open for writing.            *)
(* post : Contents of str are written to OutFile. *)


PROCEDURE ReadString (VAR str    : string;
                      VAR InFile : TEXT);
(* pre  : InFile is open for reading.                         *)
(* post : Str is initialized; characters are read from InFile and *)
(*        stored in str until EOLN is reached.                *)


FUNCTION Comparison (VAR str1, str2 : string) : CHAR;
(* post : Strings are compared for lexicographic order; returns   *)
(*        either '<', '=', or '>' depending upon whether result is *)
(*        less, equal, or greater, respectively.              *)


PROCEDURE PositionOf (VAR TargetStr : string;
                      VAR SearchStr : string) : INTEGER;
(* post : SearchStr is searched for an occurrence of the characters *)
(*        in TargetStr.  If found, the position of the first      *)
(*        character of the first occurrence of TargetStr is        *)
(*        returned; otherwise, 0 is returned.                  *)


PROCEDURE Copy (VAR FromStr : string;
                VAR ToStr   : string);
(* post : ToStr is initialized and contents of FromStr are copied to *)
(*        ToStr.  FromStr is unchanged.                       *)
```

APPENDIX A

Mathematical Details

A.1 Definition of DIV and MOD

Suppose that you have INTEGER variables A and B. This section helps you to better understand the value of (A DIV B) and (A MOD B).

For positive arguments, DIV and MOD return the quotient and remainder of INTEGER division. An INTEGER division problem can be thought of as

$$\frac{\text{dividend}}{\text{divisor}} \quad \text{yields} \longrightarrow \quad \text{quotient and remainder}$$

You expect the result that:

$$\text{divisor} * \text{quotient} + \text{remainder} = \text{dividend}$$

Consider for a moment the multiples of the divisor. The quotient defines a particular multiple of the divisor with the property that:

$$\text{divisor} * \text{quotient} \leq \text{dividend}$$
$$\text{divisor} * (\text{quotient} + 1) > \text{dividend}$$

In other words, the quotient defines the largest multiple of the divisor less than or equal to the dividend. Expressing this another way:

$$\text{divisor} * \text{quotient} \leq \text{dividend}$$
$$\text{divisor} * \text{quotient} > \text{dividend} - \text{divisor}$$

611

which leads to:

dividend − divisor < divisor ∗ quotient ≤ dividend

This in fact uniquely characterizes the quotient. If you allow the possibility that the divisor and/or dividend might be negative, you should be more explicit and say:

|dividend| − |divisor| < |divisor ∗ quotient| ≤ |dividend|

Thus, the magnitude of (A DIV B) is defined by the inequality:

|a| − |b| ≤ |b ∗ (a DIV b)| ≤ |a|

The sign of (A DIV B) is defined to be positive if A and B have the same sign, and negative otherwise. If B is 0, then (A DIV B) is undefined.

Starting again with the equation:

divisor ∗ quotient + remainder = dividend,

if you switch the remainder to the other side, you get:

divisor ∗ quotient = dividend − remainder

In other words, (dividend − remainder) is a multiple of divisor. What kind of multiple? Find out by solving for it again using the equation above:

remainder = dividend − divisor ∗ quotient

The remainder is supposed to represent what is left over, and the quotient is supposed to be sufficiently large that what's left over is less in magnitude than the divisor. Thus, you know that:

0 ≤ remainder < divisor for divisor ≥ 0
divisor < remainder ≤ 0 for divisor < 0

These two properties uniquely determine the remainder. The definition of MOD is slightly different. To calculate (A MOD B), first check B. If B is not positive, then (A MOD B) is undefined. Otherwise, it is defined as follows:

a − (a MOD b) is a multiple of b such that 0 ≤ (a MOD b) < b.

This is not the usual definition of the remainder, and in fact will not work properly with the definition above of DIV. MOD always returns a nonnegative value whereas the remainder should be negative when the divisor is negative. In other words, if A is negative, it is not the case that:

(a DIV b) ∗ b + (a MOD b) = a

In order to make this true, we would have to define (A MOD B) for negative values of A as follows:

a − (a MOD b) is a multiple of b such that b < (a MOD b) ≤ 0.

Thus, the MOD operator in Pascal doesn't really give the remainder, because its result is always nonnegative. It returns something that mathematicians call the modulus. You could define the remainder function in terms of this function as:

```
FUNCTION Rem (a, b : INTEGER) : INTEGER;
BEGIN
    IF a >= 0 THEN
        rem := a MOD b
    ELSE
        rem := -(-a) MOD b
END;
```

A.1.1   Application of DIV and MOD

This section contains a few examples of the application of DIV and MOD. Suppose you have an integer variable called **number** that you want to get the final digit of:

if **number** = 289, final digit = 9 because **number** = 280 + 9
if **number** = 347, final digit = 7 because **number** = 340 + 7

The final digit is the remainder when you divide by 10, thus the following expression will yield the final digit:

number MOD 10

The ten's digit can be gotten by the following expression:

(number DIV 10) MOD 10

The parentheses here are not necessary, but make the expression more clear. Consider two examples:

(289 DIV 10) MOD 10 = (28) MOD 10 = 8
(347 DIV 10) MOD 10 = (34) MOD 10 = 4

Another expression that yields the ten's digit is:

(number MOD 100) DIV 10

as in

(289 MOD 100) DIV 10 = (89) DIV 10 = 8
(347 MOD 100) DIV 10 = (47) DIV 10 = 4

How would you test to see if a number is even? Even numbers have no remainder when divided by 2, so you would test that

number MOD 2 = 0

How do you test if it is odd? Odd numbers are one more than an even number, so they have a remainder of 1 when divided by 2. Thus, you test whether

`number MOD 2 = 1`

How would you see if a number ends in 0? By the same reasoning, if it ends in 0, then it must be divisable by 10:

`number MOD 10 = 0`

A.2 More on Built-in FUNCTIONs

Pascal has no exponentiation operator, but it does provide `EXP` and `LN` (exponentiation and log for base *e*). You can do arbitrary exponentiation for positive exponents by noticing that

$$x = e^{\ln (x)}$$

With this, you can derive

$$x^y = (e^{\ln(x)})^y = e^{(\ln(x) * y)}$$

Thus, you can calculate X to the Y power by

`result := EXP (LN (x) * y);`

Similarly, if you want to calculate a logarithm in a base other than e, you can convert using the formula:

$$\log_b(x) = \frac{\ln (x)}{\ln (b)}$$

Thus, to calculate the logarithm to the base B of X, you would say:

`result := ln (x)/ln (b);`

Pascal offers only a limited number of trigonometric functions, because you can derive the others from the three provided functions: ARCTAN, SIN, and COS. For example, to calculate the tangent of X you would say:

`result := sin (x)/cos (x);`

If you want to calculate something like the arccosine, you have to consider what you can calculate if you know the cosine. Suppose you have a variable called `TheCos` that stores the cosine. You can't say

`theta := ARCCOS (TheCos);`

But you can calculate **theta** using **ARCTAN**. Consider this right triangle:

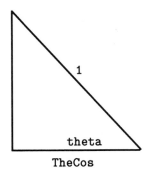

theta

TheCos

The third side of this triangle has length $\sqrt{1 - \text{TheCos}^2}$. Thus, you know that the tangent of **theta** is given by:

$$\tan(\textbf{theta}) = \frac{\text{TheCos}}{\sqrt{1 - \text{TheCos}^2}}$$

Thus, you can calculate **theta** as:

```
theta := ARCTAN (TheCos/SQRT (1 - SQR (TheCos)))
```

A.3 More on Pseudorandom Number Generation

Pseudorandom numbers are generated by creating a sequence of numbers that is irregular and that doesn't repeat itself too quickly. You do this by setting a variable **seed** to some initial value and then applying the following statement repeatedly to obtain new values for **seed**:

```
seed := (a * seed + b) MOD c;
```

Different values of A, B and C will yield different sequences. For example, you might use:

```
seed := (5 * seed + 1) MOD 8;
```

If you start **seed** at 3, you obtain this sequence:

3, 0, 1, 6, 7, 4, 5, 2,
3, 0, 1, 6, ...

Thus, you obtain all the values between 0 and 7 in a more or less random order in a sequence that repeats itself after 8 steps. If you were to use this statement instead:

```
seed := (13 * seed + 1) MOD 16;
```

and you again start **seed** at 3, you obtain

3, 8, 9, 6, 15, 4, 5, 2, 11, 0, 1, 14, 7, 12, 13, 10,
3, 8, 9, ...

This sequence generates the numbers between 0 and 15 in a fairly random order and repeats after 16 steps.

The mathematics behind pseudorandom number generation is beyond the scope of this book, but here are some hints for choosing good values of A, B and C that will give you good results most of the time. One danger of pseudorandom sequences is that you might generate an INTEGER that is too large for your computer to handle. Therefore, some of these constants are related to MAXINT:

A: You should select a value of A between $(0.01 * C)$ and $(0.99 * C)$. A should not have a regular pattern of digits and you should make sure that (A MOD 8) = 5.

B: Doesn't matter much. Good choices are 1 or A.

C: Choose a large power of 2, around $\sqrt{\text{MAXINT}}$. In choosing A and B, however, you should make sure that A * (C - 1) + B <= MAXINT.

Your pseudorandom number will behave better if you use the significant digits rather than the low-order digits. In other words, you get better behavior when you use the digits on the left-hand side (the digits that correspond to millions and billions) rather than the digits on the right-hand side (the digits that correspond to ones and tens). Here are some good choices for pseudorandom number generation for different values of MAXINT and the number of steps after which they repeat.

MAXINT	Statement	Repeats After
32767	seed := (29 * seed + 1) MOD 1024;	1024
8388607	seed := (29 * seed + 1) MOD 2048;	2048
2147483647	seed := (31421 * seed + 1) MOD 65536;	65536

APPENDIX B

The Software Library

This appendix collects together many of the more useful procedures and functions developed throughout the textbook.

B.1 Character Manipulations

```
PROCEDURE WriteSpaces (number : INTEGER);
(* post       : Writes specified number of spaces to current line of *)
(*             : file OUTPUT.                                          *)
(* parameters : number-in.                                            *)
VAR count : INTEGER;
BEGIN
    FOR count := 1 TO number DO
        WRITE (' ')
END;   (* WriteSpaces *)

PROCEDURE WriteChars (number  : INTEGER;
                      TheChar : CHAR);
(* post       : Writes given character specified number of times to current *)
(*             : line of file OUTPUT.                                        *)
(* parameters : number-in, TheChar-in.                                       *)
VAR count    : INTEGER;   (* loop counter                                    *)
```

```
BEGIN
    FOR count := 1 TO number DO
        WRITE (TheChar)
END;   (* WriteChars *)

PROCEDURE TurnToUppercase (VAR character : CHAR);
(* post       : character is turned to uppercase, if a lowercase letter. *)
(* parameters : character-in/out.                                        *)
BEGIN
    IF character IN ['a'..'z'] THEN
        character := CHR (ORD (character) - ORD ('a') + ORD ('A'))
END;   (* TurnToUppercase *)
```

B.2 Pseudorandom Number Generation

```
PROCEDURE GetSeed (VAR seed: INTEGER);
(* post       : user is prompted for initial value of seed. *)
(* parameters : seed-out.                                    *)
BEGIN
    WRITELN ('I need an integer to seed the random number generator.');
    WRITE ('Give me a seed ---> ');
    READLN (seed)
END;   (* GetSeed *)

FUNCTION Random (VAR seed: INTEGER) : REAL;
(* pre        : 1 <= seed <= 1024.                                    *)
(* post       : a pseudorandom value is returned with 0 <= Random < 1; *)
(*            : seed is modified to a new value in [1..1024].          *)
(* parameters : seed-in/out.                                          *)
BEGIN
    seed := (29 * seed + 1) MOD 1024;
    random := seed/1024
END;   (* Random *)

FUNCTION RandomInt (VAR seed : INTEGER;
                        low  : INTEGER;
                        high : INTEGER) : INTEGER;
(* pre        : 1 <= seed <= 1024; low <= high.                           *)
(* post       : A pseudorandom value is returned with low <= value <= high; *)
(*            : seed is modified to a new value in [1..1024].             *)
(* parameters : low-in, high-in, seed-in/out.                            *)
```

```
BEGIN
    seed := (29 * seed + 1) MOD 1024;
    RandomInt := TRUNC ((seed/1024) * (high - low + 1)) + low
END;   (* RandomInt *)
```

B.3 List Manipulations

All of the manipulations assume declarations like the following:

```
CONST MaxLength     = <maximum length of list>;
TYPE  ElementList   = ARRAY [1..MaxLength] OF <element type>;
      ListType      = RECORD
           elements : ElementList;
           length   : INTEGER
      END;
VAR   list          : ListType;

PROCEDURE WriteList (list : ListType);
VAR count : INTEGER
BEGIN
    <write any text that is to appear before list>;
    WITH list DO
        FOR count := 1 TO length DO
            WRITE (elements [count]: <field width>;
    <write any text that is to appear after list>
END;

PROCEDURE ReadList (VAR list : ListType);
BEGIN
    <perform any actions that need to be done before reading>;
    WITH list DO
    BEGIN
        length := 0;
        WHILE  <more data to read> AND (length < MaxLength) DO
        BEGIN
            length := length + 1;
            READ (elements [length])
        END
    END;
    <perform any actions that need to be done after reading>
END;
```

```
PROCEDURE ReadList (VAR list : ListType);
VAR next : <element type>;
BEGIN
    <perform any actions that need to be done before reading>;
    READ (next);
    WITH list DO
    BEGIN
        length := 0;
        WHILE (next <> <sentinel>) AND (length < MaxLength) DO
        BEGIN
            length := length + 1;
            elements [length] := next;
            READ (next)
        END
    END;
    <perform any actions that need to be done after reading>
END;


PROCEDURE ChangeList (VAR list : ListType);
VAR index : INTEGER;
BEGIN
    WITH list DO
        FOR index := 1 TO length DO
            <operation to be performed> (elements [index])
END;


FUNCTION Equal (one, two : ListType) : BOOLEAN;
VAR pos : INTEGER;
BEGIN
    IF (one.length <> two.length) THEN
        equal := FALSE
    ELSE
        IF (one.length = 0) THEN
            equal := TRUE
        ELSE
        BEGIN
            pos := 1;
            WHILE (one.elements [pos] = two.elements [pos]) AND
                  (pos < one.length) DO
                pos := pos + 1;
            equal := (one.elements [pos] = two.elements [pos])
        END
END;
```

```
FUNCTION PositionOf (value : <element type>;
                     list  : ListType) : INTEGER;
VAR index : INTEGER;
BEGIN
    index := 1;
    WITH list DO
    BEGIN
        WHILE (elements [index] <> value) AND (index < length) DO
            index := index + 1;
        IF elements [index] = value THEN
            PositionOf := index
        ELSE
            PositionOf := 0
    END
END;
```

B.3.1 Special Manipulations for Sorted Lists

```
PROCEDURE InsertInto (VAR list  : ListType;
                      value : <element type>);
VAR position : INTEGER;
    done     : BOOLEAN;
BEGIN
    WITH list DO
    BEGIN
        position := length;
        IF (length > 0) THEN
        BEGIN
            done := (elements [position] < value);
            WHILE NOT done DO
            BEGIN
                elements [position + 1] := elements [position];
                position := position - 1;
                IF position = 0 THEN
                    done := TRUE
                ELSE
                    done := (elements [position] < value)
            END
        END;
        elements [position + 1] := value;
        length := length + 1
    END
END;
```

```
FUNCTION PositionOf (value  : <element type>;
                     list   : ListType) : INTEGER;
VAR low    : INTEGER;
    high   : INTEGER;
    middle : INTEGER;
    found  : BOOLEAN;
BEGIN
    WITH list DO
    BEGIN
        low := 1;
        high := length;
        found := FALSE;
        WHILE (NOT found) AND (low <= high) DO
        BEGIN
            middle := ((low + high) DIV 2);
            IF (elements [middle] = value) THEN
                found := TRUE
            ELSE
                IF elements [middle] < value THEN
                    low   := middle + 1
                ELSE
                    high := middle - 1
        END;
        IF found THEN
            PositionOf := middle
        ELSE
            PositionOf := 0
    END
END;   (* PositionOf *)
```

B.3.2 Sorting Lists

```
PROCEDURE Swap (VAR first, second: INTEGER);
VAR temp : INTEGER;
BEGIN
    temp   := first;
    first  := second;
    second := temp
END;   (* Swap *)

PROCEDURE SelectionSort (VAR list   : ListType);
VAR count1   : INTEGER;
```

```
    count2   : INTEGER;
    smallest : INTEGER;
BEGIN
    WITH list DO
    BEGIN
        FOR count1 := 1 TO (length - 1) DO
        BEGIN
            smallest := count1;
            FOR count2 := (count1 + 1) TO length DO
                IF nums [count2] < nums [smallest] THEN
                    smallest := count2;
            Swap (nums [count1], nums [smallest])
        END
    END
END;   (* SelectionSort *)

PROCEDURE Merge (VAR nums  : NumberList;
                     start : INTEGER;
                     stop  : INTEGER);
VAR LeftPos   : INTEGER;
    RightPos  : INTEGER;
    midpoint  : INTEGER;
    index     : INTEGER;
    TempNums  : NumsType;

        FUNCTION TakeFromLeft : BOOLEAN;
        BEGIN
            IF (LeftPos = 0) THEN
                TakeFromLeft := FALSE
            ELSE
                IF (RightPos = 0) THEN
                    TakeFromLeft := TRUE
                ELSE
                    TakeFromLeft := (nums [LeftPos] < nums [RightPos])
        END;   (* TakeFromLeft *)

        PROCEDURE Use (VAR WhichPos : INTEGER;
                           limit    : INTEGER);
        BEGIN
            TempNums [index] := nums [WhichPos];
            WhichPos := WhichPos + 1;
            IF (WhichPos > limit) THEN
                WhichPos := 0
        END;
```

```
BEGIN    (* Merge *)
    midpoint := (start + stop) DIV 2;
    LeftPos := start;
    RightPos := midpoint + 1;
    FOR index := start TO stop DO
        IF TakeFromLeft THEN
            use (LeftPos, midpoint)
        ELSE
            use (RightPos, stop);
    FOR index := start TO stop DO
        nums [index] := TempNums [index]
END;    (* Merge *)

PROCEDURE RecursiveSort (VAR nums  : NumberList;
                             start : INTEGER;
                             stop  : INTEGER);
VAR midpoint : INTEGER;
BEGIN
    IF (start < stop) THEN
    BEGIN
        midpoint := (start + stop) DIV 2;
        RecursiveSort (nums, start, midpoint);
        RecursiveSort (nums, midpoint + 1, stop);
        merge (nums, start, stop)
    END
END;    (* RecursiveSort *)

PROCEDURE MergeSort (VAR list : ListType);
BEGIN
    WITH list DO
        RecursiveSort (nums, 1, length)
END;    (* MergeSort *)
```

B.4 Miscellaneous

```
PROCEDURE AskUser (VAR UserSaysYes : BOOLEAN);
(* pre        : User has been asked a yes or no question.         *)
(* post       : User is forced to type either Y or N; if user types Y, *)
(*            : UserSaysYes is set to TRUE, otherwise FALSE.       *)
(* parameters : UserSaysYes-out.                                  *)
(* algorithm  : Loop until user types legal response.             *)
VAR response  : CHAR;   (* user response                          *)
```

```
BEGIN
    REPEAT
        WRITE ('    yes or no? ');
        READLN (response)
    UNTIL (response in ['y', 'Y', 'n', 'N']);
    UserSaysYes := (response in ['y', 'Y'])
END;   (* AskUser *)


FUNCTION AllLetters (word : WordType) : BOOLEAN;
(* post       : Returns TRUE if all elements of word are alphabetic, *)
(*             : otherwise returns FALSE.                            *)
(* parameters : word-in.                                            *)
(* requires   : constant WordSize.                                  *)
VAR index    : INTEGER;   (* used to index over word                *)
    good     : BOOLEAN;   (* whether only letters have been seen    *)
BEGIN
    index := 0;
    REPEAT
        index := index + 1;
        good := (word [index] IN ['a'..'z', 'A'..'Z'])
    UNTIL NOT good OR (index = WordSize);
    AllLetters := good
END;   (* AllLetters *)


PROCEDURE SkipBlanks;
(* post  : any blanks on current line of file INPUT are skipped, input *)
(*        : cursor at first nonblank or at EOLN.                       *)
VAR next : CHAR;   (* dummy variable used to skip blank               *)
BEGIN
    WHILE NOT EOLN AND (INPUT^ = ' ') DO
        READ (next)
END;   (* SkipBlanks *)


PROCEDURE SkipBlanks (VAR InFile : TEXT);
(* post       : any blanks on current line of file InFile are skipped, *)
(*             : input cursor at first nonblank or at EOLN.            *)
(* parameters : InFile-in/out.                                        *)
VAR next     : CHAR;   (* dummy variable used to skip blank           *)
BEGIN
    WHILE NOT EOLN (InFile) AND (InFile^ = ' ') DO
        READ (InFile, next)
END;
```

APPENDIX C

Pascal
Syntax Summary

C.1 Reserved Keywords

AND	END	MOD	REPEAT
ARRAY	FILE	NIL	SET
BEGIN	FOR	NOT	THEN
CASE	FORWARD	OF	TO
CONST	FUNCTION	OR	TYPE
DIV	GOTO	PACKED	UNTIL
DO	IF	PROCEDURE	VAR
DOWNTO	IN	PROGRAM	WHILE
ELSE	LABEL	RECORD	WITH

C.2 Summary of Precedence

Level	Name	Operators						
1	Negation	NOT						
2	Multiplicative	*	/	DIV	MOD	AND		
3	Additive	+	–	OR				
4	Relational	=	<>	<	>	<=	>=	IN

C.3 Built-in Functions

Function	Meaning	Argument Type	Result Type
ABS	Absolute value	REAL/INTEGER	Same as argument
ARCTAN	Arctangent	REAL/INTEGER	REAL
CHR	Character	INTEGER	CHAR
COS	Cosine	REAL/INTEGER	REAL
EOF	End of file	File type	BOOLEAN
EOLN	End of line	TEXT	BOOLEAN
EXP	Power of e	REAL/INTEGER	REAL
LN	Natural logarithm	REAL/INTEGER	REAL
ODD	Is number odd?	INTEGER	BOOLEAN
ORD	Ordinal value	Ordinal type	INTEGER
PRED	Predecessor	Ordinal type	Same as argument
ROUND	Rounding	REAL	INTEGER
SIN	Sine	REAL/INTEGER	REAL
SQR	Square	REAL/INTEGER	Same as argument
SQRT	Square root	REAL/INTEGER	REAL
SUCC	Successor	Ordinal Type	Same as argument
TRUNC	Truncation	REAL	INTEGER

C.4 Page References to Important Pascal Constructs

Elements of a Program

Declarations, Blocks, Activations, and Scope

Pascal Statements and Control

Built-in Procedures: 19, 45, 173, 360, 370, 376, 543
User-Defined Procedures: 82
Assignment Statement: 41–43
Nesting and Levels of Control: 52–54
Sequential Control: Compound Statement: 53–54
Selection: IF/THEN/ELSE and CASE: 114, 389
Definite Looping: FOR: 47
Indefinite Looping: WHILE and REPEAT: 181, 395
The WITH Statement: 271–272
Calling User-Defined Functions: 122
Recursion: 496–514

Pascal Data and Expressions

Expressions and Evaluation: 33–36
Built-in FUNCTIONs: 111–113
User-Defined FUNCTIONs: 122–124
Simple Types: 37, 104, 172, 234
Structured Types: 186
ARRAY Types: 206–224
RECORD Types: 268–272
FILE Types: 186–189
SET Types: 374–375
Pointer Types: 539–544
Strings and Other PACKED Structures: 376–378

Input and Output (I/O)

Formatted Output: 43–47
General File Types: 362–372
Type TEXT: 186, 360–365, 366
Using Standard INPUT and OUTPUT: 360
Internal versus External Files: 179–181, 186–195

C.5 Pascal Syntax

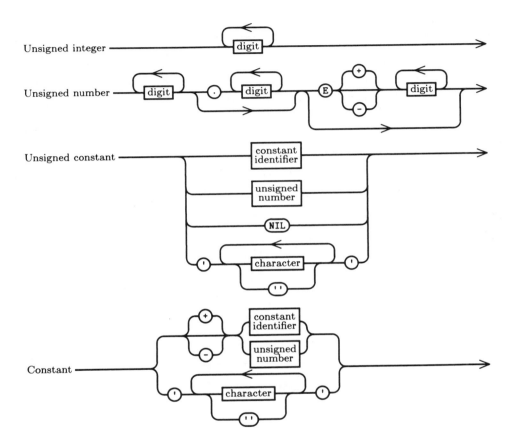

These diagrams of Pascal syntax are reprinted with permission from the *Pascal User Manual and Report, Second Edition* (Kathleen Jensen and Niklaus Wirth, Springer Verlag, New York, 1974). They were typeset by Jim Boyce on a format by Michael Plass.

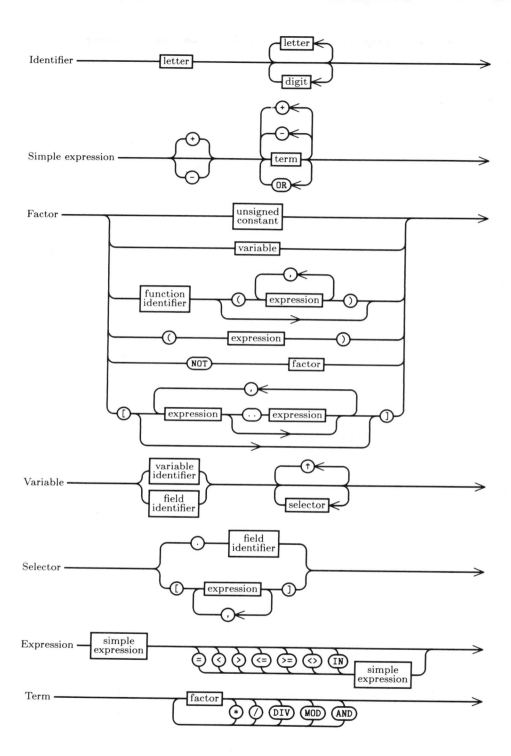

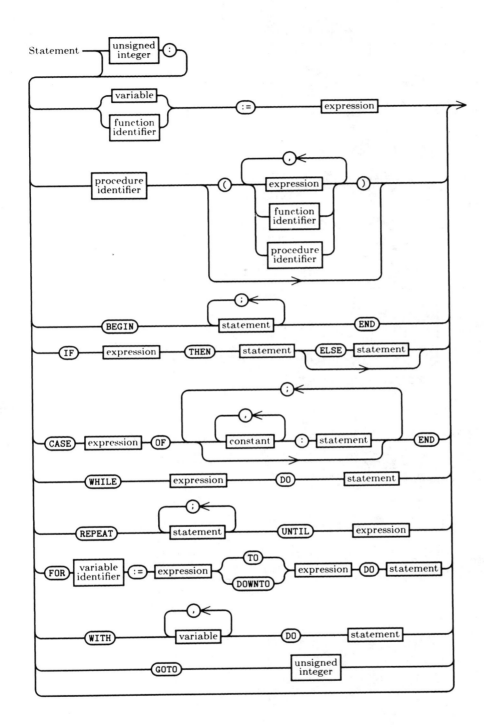

631

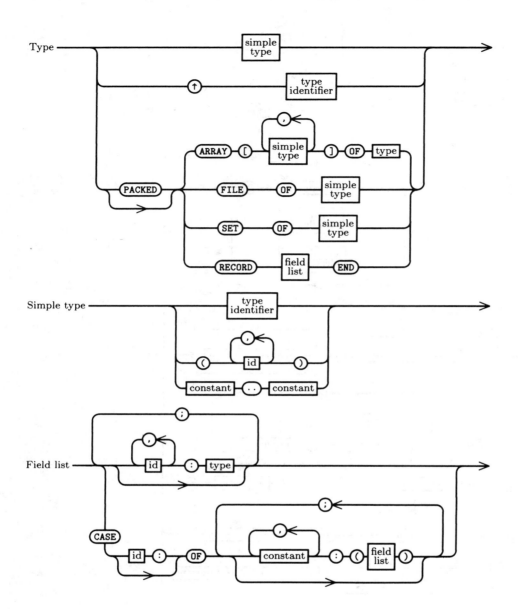

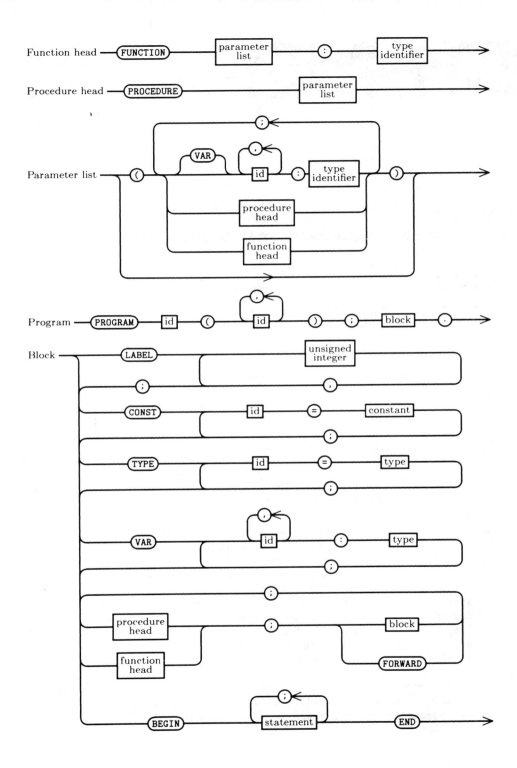

633

APPENDIX D

Answers to Selected Exercises

D.1 Chapter 1 Answers

1. You would generally need very little main memory, since you would only work on a piece of the novel at a time, but would need a great deal of secondary memory in order to store the entire novel.

3. writeln   Can be an identifier because it is a keyword, but not reserved but because this would override the definition of the built-in WRITELN statement, it shouldn't be used as an identifier.

    first-name   Can't be an identifier because of the dash.
    AnnualSalary   Can be an identifier.
    label   Can't be an identifier because it is a reserved keyword.
    22Skidoo   Can't be an identifier because it doesn't start with a letter.
    loop   Can be an identifier.
    sum_of_terms   Can't be an identifier because of the underscores.
    Warp8Scotty   Can be an identifier.

5. No, the procedures could not be defined in another order, as the structure diagram below indicates. **Third** depends on both **First** and **Second**, so it must be defined last. **Second** depends on **First**, so it must be defined after **First**.

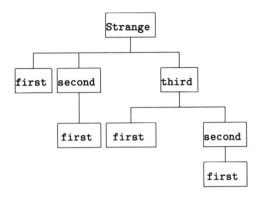

7.  ```
    PROGRAM GiveAdvice (OUTPUT);
    BEGIN
        WRITELN ('Programs can be easy or difficult');
        WRITELN ('to read, depending upon their format.');
        WRITELN;
        WRITELN ('Everyone, including yourself, will be');
        WRITELN ('happier if you choose to format your');
        WRITELN ('programs.')
    END.
    ```

D.2 Chapter 2 Answers

1. 1., because no decimal point is allowed; 2.5, because it is not an integer; 2,349, because no comma is allowed; 2.0, because no decimal point is allowed; all others are legal.

3.  ```
    VAR num1 : INTEGER;
        num2 : INTEGER;

    VAR num2 : INTEGER;
        num1 : INTEGER;

    VAR num1, num2 : INTEGER;

    VAR num2, num1 : INTEGER;
    ```

5. Afterwards, `first` = 19 and `second` = 8. The statements interchange the values of `first` and `second`.

7.  ```
    WRITELN ('Twasbrillig and the ');
    WRITELN ('slithy toves did gyre and');
    WRITELN (' gimble');
    WRITELN;
    WRITELN ('in the wabe.');
    ```
    ```

9.

```
1           FOR row := 1 TO 3 DO
(           BEGIN
2               FOR digit := 0 TO 9 DO
3                   FOR column := 1 TO 3 DO
4                       WRITE (digit:1);
2               WRITELN
)           END;
```

To create the other output, change the limits of the three loops:

```
1           FOR row := 1 TO 5 DO
(           BEGIN
2               FOR digit := 9 DOWNTO 0 DO
3                   FOR column := 1 TO 5 DO
4                       WRITE (digit:1);
2               WRITELN
)           END;
```

11. The loop will iterate four times even though the value of **number** changes as the loop executes, because the starting and ending values for the loop (in this case, 1 and 4) are evaluated before the loop is executed and are not recalculated. Thus the output is:

```
4
2
1
0
```

D.3 Chapter 3 Answers

1. Duplication occurs when two or more blocks have been activated each with an object of the same name. For example, a main program might have a variable called **count** and might call a procedure with a variable called **count**. In such a case, two objects called **count** are active while the procedure executes.

3. A value parameter is outside the black box in the sense that any value can be passed into the procedure as an actual parameter. It is inside the black box in the sense that the formal parameter name can be used locally to define the procedure.

5. When should a WRITELN be executed to go to a new line?   coding

How do you calculate the next prime?   design or coding

Are the numbers produced by the program really prime?   testing

Should the field width for the table be a global constant or parameter?   design

What will be the principle procedures of the program?   design

7. **FieldWidth** is allocated once, when the program block is activated. **Row** is allocated twice, once for each table produced. **Column** is allocated 15 times, 5 times for the first table and 10 times for the second. **Count** is allocated 17 times, once more than **Column** for each table.

9. The new version of the procedure has two nested loops rather than a single loop. The innermost loop writes the characters '-----+' to the output line, using the appropriate number of dashes to match the field width. The outermost loop repeats this process for each column. Notice that this introduces a fence-post problem (plus signs at both the left and right of the line), which is solved by writing the first plus before the loop. Here is the procedure:

```
PROCEDURE WriteSolidLine (NumColumns : INTEGER);
VAR column : INTEGER;
    count  : INTEGER;
BEGIN
    WRITE ('+');
    FOR column := 1 TO NumColumns DO
    BEGIN
        FOR count := 1 TO (FieldWidth + 1) DO
            WRITE ('-');
        WRITE ('+')
    END;
    WRITELN
END;   (* WriteSolidLine *)
```

D.4 Chapter 4 Answers

1.

```
PROGRAM InteractiveTimesTable (INPUT, OUTPUT);
VAR rows : INTEGER;   (* number of rows user wants in times table    *)
    cols : INTEGER;   (* number of columns user wants in times table *)

(* include WriteTimesTable here along with the procedures it calls *)
(* and its global constant FieldWidth.                             *)

BEGIN   (* main program *)
    WRITELN ('This program will produce a multiplication table for');
    WRITELN ('you.  I will ask you how large you want the table to');
    WRITELN ('be and then I''ll make it for you.  Here goes. . .');
    WRITE ('How many rows do you want in the table? ');
    READLN (rows);
    WRITE ('How many columns do you want in the table? ');
    READLN (cols);
    WRITELN;
    WRITELN ('Okay, here''s your table. . .');
    WriteTimesTable (rows, cols)
END.    (* main program *)
```

3.

Expression	Value
2.5 MOD 1.2	Illegal, MOD is not allowed for **REAL** operands
2.0 * 3.2 + 6.4	= 6.4 + 6.4 = 12.8
2.5 - 3.5 * 2.0/0.7	2.5 − 7.0/0.7 = 2.5 − 10.0 = −7.5
(3.5 * 2) MOD 5	Illegal, (3.5 * 2) is a **REAL**, MOD not allowed
-2.0 * 3.1	= −6.2
10.0 DIV 3	Illegal, 10.0 is **REAL**, so can't use **DIV**
12 + 15/3	= 12 + 5.0 = 17.0
8 MOD 3 + 4.5	= 2 + 4.5 = 6.5
17 MOD 6 * 2/5	5 * 2/5 = 10/5 = 2.0
-3.1 * -2.0	Illegal, multiplication has higher precedence than either minus, so we try to multiply, but can only find the operand 3.1. Can be made legal by saying −3.1 * (−2.0)

5. Unless something very unusual is happening (e.g., output being generated by other parts of the program), the only way the skewing can occur is if one or more numbers don't fit in the given format specification. Remember that when this happens the computer automatically expands the field so that it has enough space to write the number. The best strategy for fixing the problem is to increase the size of the format, say, from :8:3 to :10:3.

7. To convert from **dollars** and **cents** to **money**, you say:

```
money := dollars + cents/100;
```

To convert from **money** to **dollars** and **cents**, you say:

```
dollars := TRUNC (money);
cents := TRUNC (money * 100) MOD 100;
```

You might think the WRITELN for displaying **dollars** and **cents** is this simple:

```
WRITELN ('$', dollars:1, '.', cents:2);
```

It isn't. Remember that **cents** has to be displayed as a two-digit decimal, not a two-digit **INTEGER**. The difference occurs when **cents** is a single digit such as 5, when you would want to display it as 05. Thus the correct statement is

```
WRITELN ('$', dollars:1, '.', (cents DIV 10):1, (cents MOD 10):1);
```

9.
```
FUNCTION Min3 (first, second, third : INTEGER) : INTEGER;
BEGIN
    min3 := min (first, min (second, third))
END;
```

```
FUNCTION Min3 (first, second, third : INTEGER) : INTEGER;
BEGIN
    IF first < second THEN
        IF first < third THEN
            min3 := first
        ELSE
            min3 := third
    ELSE
        IF second < third THEN
            min3 := second
        ELSE
            min3 := third
END;
```

D.5 Chapter 5 Answers

1.
```
PROCEDURE GetAngle (VAR angle : REAL);
VAR degrees, minutes, seconds : INTEGER;
BEGIN
    WRITE (' (degrees, minutes, seconds) ---> ');
    READLN (degrees, minutes, seconds);
    angle := degrees + minutes/60 + seconds/3600
END;
```

3. With the **VAR** parameter, you can only call the procedure with variables:

```
WriteSpaces (width);
```

you can't call it with arbitrary expressions:

```
WriteSpaces (2 * width);
WriteSpaces (20);
```

5. DoCalculation (int1, int2, real1, int3);
    -legal: all types match and all actual parameters are variables
DoCalculation (int1, int2, 32.9, 27);
    -legal: all types match and all **VAR** actual parameters are variables and
        all value actual parameters are constants.
DoCalculation (int1, int2, 35/4, 2 * 3);
    -legal: all types match and all **VAR** actual parameters are variables and
        all value actual parameters are expressions.
DoCalculation (10, 20, 30.5, 40);
    -illegal: you can't pass 10 and 20 to **VAR** parameters
DoCalculation (int1, int1, real1, int3);
    -legal: even though 'int1' is passed twice
DoCalculation (int1, int2, 10, 20);
    -legal: even though 10 is passed to a **REAL** value parameter (it is converted)
DoCalculation (int2, int1, 10.5, 20.5);
    -illegal: 20.5 can't be passed to an **INTEGER** value parameter.

7. If you want to have a single subprogram, you would use a procedure rather than a function, since the function returns a single value and this conversion requires returning two values.

9. Here is the structure diagram:

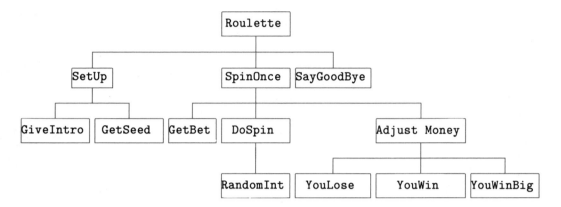

D.6 Chapter 6 Answers

1. The output is:

```
wy!y
y!!y
```

3. The correct expression is:

```
CHR (ORD (TheChar) - 4)
```

5. All.

7. The WHILE loop controls only the WRITELN statement. The assignment statement that follows has the same indentation, but there is no BEGIN/END to indicate that it is controlled by the WHILE. Thus this code will produce infinitely many output lines, each with the number 1.

9. For the first file:

```
First = '1', Second = ':', Third = '2', Fourth = '3'
```

For the second file:

```
First = '1', Second = ' ' (from the EOLN), Third = '3', Fourth = '4'
```

D.7 Chapter 7 Answers

1.

0..5	Legal
-10..+10	Legal
low..high	Legal
10..10	Legal, even though domain has only one value
-high..-low	Legal, even though named constants are negated
'0'..9	Illegal, low value is **CHAR** but high value is **INTEGER**
1..2+2	Illegal, because 2+2 is not a constant
'a'..'za'	Legal
high..low	Illegal, because low bound is greater than high bound
low..50	Legal, even though one is a named constant and one not

3.

`ARRAY [INTEGER] OF CHAR;`	Theoretically, legal, although space limitations will probably make it illegal; has (2 * MaxInt + 1) elements
`ARRAY [1..20] OF RangeType;`	Legal; has 20 elements
`ARRAY [-100..100] OF CHAR;`	Legal; even though low index is not 1, has 201 elements
`ARRAY [0..10] OF alphabet;`	Legal; has 11 elements
`ARRAY [alphabet] OF alphabet;`	Legal; has 26 elements
`ARRAY ['A'..20] OF alphabet;`	Illegal; because subrange is not legal

5. The variables match in structure, but not in type. Variable **first** is of type **ListType**. Variables **second** and **third** are of different anonymous types (different because they appear in different variable lists, even though the structure is the same). They could be made of the same type by saying:

```
VAR first  : ListType;
    second : ListType;
    third  : ListType;
```

7.
```
FUNCTION Sum (list   : ListType;
              length : INTEGER) : INTEGER;
(* returns the sum of the elements in List. *)
VAR index  : INTEGER;
    TheSum : INTEGER;
BEGIN
    TheSum := 0;
    FOR index := 1 TO length DO
        TheSum := TheSum + list [index];
    sum := TheSum
END;
```

9. The procedure is easier to write if we first write

```
PROCEDURE Swap (VAR first, second : INTEGER);
```

```
VAR temp : INTEGER;
BEGIN
    temp := first;
    first := second;
    second := temp
END;
```

The procedure is then written as

```
PROCEDURE Reverse (VAR list    : ListType;
                        length : INTEGER);
VAR index : INTEGER;
BEGIN
    FOR index := 1 TO (length DIV 2) DO
        swap (list [index], list [length - index + 1])
END;
```

D.8 Chapter 8 Answers

1.

Statement	Assertion?	Proposition?
x < y.	yes	no
Write a program that adds together two numbers.	no	no
The moon is made of green cheese.	yes	yes
z = 2 + 2.	yes	no
What is your name?	no	no
All FOR loops can be rewritten as WHILE loops.	yes	yes

3.

Expression	Operator	Operands	Results
(x > y) OR (x > 0) AND (y > 0)	>	x, y	FALSE
(FALSE) OR (x > 0) AND (y > 0)	>	x, 0	TRUE
(FALSE) OR (TRUE) AND (y > 0)	>	y, 0	TRUE
(FALSE) OR (TRUE) AND (TRUE)	AND	TRUE, TRUE	TRUE
(FALSE) OR (TRUE)	OR	FALSE, TRUE	TRUE
TRUE			
NOT (x + 2 = y) OR (x < y)	+	x, 2	12
NOT (12 = y) OR (x < y)	=	12, y	TRUE
NOT (TRUE) OR (x < y)	<	x, y	TRUE
NOT (TRUE) OR (TRUE)	NOT	TRUE	FALSE
FALSE OR (TRUE)	OR	FALSE, TRUE	TRUE
TRUE			

5. `test := (x < 0) OR NOT (y > z)`

7.
```
position := 0;
done := FALSE;
WHILE NOT done DO
BEGIN
    position := position + 1;
    IF (position > length) THEN
        done := TRUE
    ELSE
        done := (list [position] > 10)
END;
```

9.
```
FUNCTION SQRT (number : REAL) : REAL;
(* pre  : number >= 0. *)
(* post : returns an approximation to the square root of Number.*)
```

D.9 Chapter 9 Answers

1. normal phone book
> -linear, sorted by name, with a first name, second name, and so on.

purse containing address book, meeting calendar, stray notes, etc.
> -nonlinear, there is no first element, more like record than array

card file showing the entire Library of Congress catalogue
> -linear, sorted by book number, with a first book, second, etc.

genealogy showing the ancestral descent of a family
> -non-linear, because of the branching nature of families, there
> isn't a simple order with one person first, another second, etc.

filing cabinet with folders sorted alphabetically
> -linear, with a first folder in the cabinet, second folder, etc.

standard deck of playing cards, shuffled and ready to use
> -linear, with a top card, next card, next card, and so on

3. Without WITH statements, you get

```
people [9].home.city [3] := 'X';
```

Using a WITH a statement, you get:

```
WITH people [9], home DO
    city [3] := 'X';
```

5. Temperatures are **REAL** values, so you fill in the generic declarations of Section 9.3.3 to get

```
              CONST MaxTemp      = 250;
              TYPE  TempList      = ARRAY [1..MaxTemp] OF REAL;
                    ReadingsType = RECORD
                        temps    : TempList;
                        NumTemps : INTEGER
                    END;
```

7. You can start by defining a function to test whether a character is a word character:

```
FUNCTION WordChar (character : CHAR) : BOOLEAN;
BEGIN
    WordChar := character IN ['a'..'z', 'A'..'Z', '-', '''']
END;
```

Using this function, you can rewrite **ReadWord** so that it skips leading nonword characters, and reads only word characters into the word. The procedure is written as a sentinel loop testing whether **next** is a space. The procedure also has a loop at the end that scans to the end of a word if the loop terminates because the array is full. The procedure can be made to use this new definition of a word by the following replacements:

Current ReadWord	New ReadWord
(next = ' ')	NOT WordChar (next)
(next <> ' ')	WordChar (next)

9. Function **Equal** is a very simple procedure that doesn't have to do any work if the lengths of the words are unequal. Function **Less**, on the other hand, has to deal with the possibility that comparison will have to be made of words of unequal length. The same is true of function **Compare**, so function **Less** is the most similar to the new function and a good starting point. Here is the completed function:

```
FUNCTION Compare (one, two : WordType) : CHAR;
VAR ShortLen : INTEGER;
    pos      : INTEGER;
BEGIN
    IF (one.length < two.length) THEN
        ShortLen := one.length
    ELSE
        ShortLen := two.length;
    IF (ShortLen <> 0) THEN
    BEGIN
        pos := 1;
        WHILE (one.chars [pos] = two.chars [pos]) AND (pos < ShortLen) DO
            pos := pos + 1
    END;
    IF (one.chars [pos] < two.chars [pos]) THEN
        compare := '<'
    ELSE
```

```
     IF (one.chars [pos] > two.chars [pos]) THEN
         compare := '>'
     ELSE
         IF one.length < two.length THEN
             compare := '<'
         ELSE
             IF one.length > two.length THEN
                 compare := '>'
             ELSE
                 compare := '='
END;
```

11.

Subprogram/Program	In New Program
Equal	Used with no changes
InsertInto	Used with no changes
Less	Used with no changes
ManipulateDictionaries	Used with no changes
PositionOf	Used with no changes
ReadChar	Not used
ReadDict	Used with more than three lines of change, because now the file reading is line-by-line instead of word-by-word and it no longer uppercases
TurnToUppercase	Not used
UppercaseWord	Not used
WriteDict	Used with more than three lines of change, because table must be made
WriteSpaces	Unused, because no longer writing out in even columns, now writing out "quoted words"
WriteWord	Used with more than three lines of change (no call on **WriteSpaces**) and writes out "quotations"

D.10 Chapter 10 Answers

1. Program validation encompasses all endeavors to validate the correctness of a program. Program verification is a specific way of validating a program, one that involves a rigorous analysis of the program to prove it correct. Program testing is the process of trying to identify discrepancies between the program's specification and its behavior. Testing can be done independently of debugging, the process of trying to correct flaws in program logic so that its behavior more closely resembles its specification.

3. The border cases occur for empty lines and lines whose length equals the margin. Special cases worth testing are odd/even differences between length and the margin. The degenerate case of a long line is also tested.

Input Line	Margin	Reason
	20	Border, empty line
1	20	Border, single character
Exactly--20 chars!!!	20	Border, length = margin
Exactly--20 chars!!!	19	Degenerate, length > margin
Exactly--20 chars!!!	25	Special, length even/margin odd
Exactly--20 chars!!!	30	Special, length even/margin even
Exactly 17 chars!	19	Special, length odd/margin odd
Exactly 17 chars!	20	Special, length odd/margin even

5. You need to check month, day, and year values that are outside their maximum ranges. For months with 30 days, you should check that the 31st of that month is considered illegal. To make sure the last day in every month is a legal date, you should include each. Many special and typical 2/29's have to be checked (including 2/29/1900, since 1900 was not a leap year).

Date	Reason	Date	Reason
0/ 1/1986	Degenerate, month small	1/ 1/1900	Border, century start
13/ 1/1986	Degenerate, month large	12/31/1999	Border, century end
1/ 0/1986	Degenerate, day small	1/31/1986	Border, end of Jan
1/32/1986	Degenerate, day large	2/28/1986	Border, end of Feb
1/ 1/-1	Degenerate, year small	3/31/1986	Border, end of March
1/ 1/3000	Degenerate, year large	4/30/1986	Border, end of April
4/31/1986	Degenerate, illegal April	5/31/1986	Border, end of May
6/31/1986	Degenerate, illegal June	6/30/1986	Border, end of June
9/31/1986	Degenerate, illegal Sept	7/31/1986	Border, end of July
11/31/1986	Degenerate, illegal Nov	8/31/1986	Border, end of Aug
12/31/1899	Degenerate, before century	9/30/1986	Border, end of Sept
1/ 1/2000	Degenerate, after century	10/31/1986	Border, end of Oct
2/29/1901	Typical, year MOD 4 = 1	11/30/1986	Border, end of Nov
2/29/1902	Typical, year MOD 4 = 2	12/31/1986	Border, end of Dec
2/29/1903	Typical, year MOD 4 = 3	2/29/1900	Special, no leap year
2/29/1904	Typical, year MOD 4 = 0 (leap)		
3/15/1950	Typical		
7/23/1908	Typical		
10/ 7/1990	Typical		

7. In writing a stub for **ReadList** you have to be careful to satisfy the postconditions when the procedure is done executing. Thus you have to be careful to write a procedure that generates sorted lists of integers and you have to make sure that the length variable is within range. In order to ensure the range of the length variable and to guarantee a variety of different lengths, you can execute the statement:

```
NumNums := RandomInt (seed, 0, MaxNum);
```

This gives the length variable its widest possible variation within the range of legal list lengths. The procedure below generates sorted lists by picking a value for **nums [1]** and then using pseudorandom number generation to pick a positive increment for the next element, and another positive increment for the next, and so on. Two constants specify the average starting value (**AveStart**) and the average increment between values (**AveInc**). The procedure needs function **RandomInt** from the software library but is otherwise self-contained.

```
PROCEDURE ReadList (VAR list : ListType;
                    VAR seed : INTEGER);
CONST AveStart  = 100;
      AveInc    = 20;
VAR   index     : INTEGER;
      increment : INTEGER;
BEGIN
    WITH list DO
    BEGIN
        NumNums := RandomInt (seed, 1, MaxNum);
        increment := RandomInt (seed, -10 * AveInc, +10 * AveInc);
        nums [1] := AveStart + increment;
        FOR index := 2 TO NumNums DO
        BEGIN
            increment := RandomInt (seed, 1, 2 * AveInc);
            nums [index] := nums [index - 1] + increment
        END
    END
END;
```

9. Three changes need to be made. One particular procedure processes the writing of a word:

```
PROCEDURE ProcessWord (    word          : WordType;
                       VAR CurrentColumn : INTEGER);
BEGIN
    WriteWord (word);
    CurrentColumn := CurrentColumn + word.length
END;   (* ProcessWord *)
```

First, you can change this procedure to write out a left parenthesis before the word and a right parenthesis after the word. This takes care of writing out the parentheses. But you have to account for them in the various calculations involving the current column and the margin. Thus, second, increment **CurrentColumn** by two more since you have written out two extra characters. Thus the procedure becomes

```
PROCEDURE ProcessWord (    word          : WordType;
                       VAR CurrentColumn : INTEGER);
BEGIN
    WRITE ('(');
    WriteWord (word);
    WRITE (')');
    CurrentColumn := CurrentColumn + word.length + 2
END;   (* ProcessWord *)
```

The third and final part of the program that must be fixed is the test for whether or not the next word will fit on the current line:

```
NotEnoughRoom := (word.length + 1 > MaxColumn - CurrentColumn);
```

Since the word will require two more characters than before, this test needs to be changed to:

```
NotEnoughRoom := (word.length + 3 > MaxColumn - CurrentColumn);
```

11. Since you are creating a new structure, you will not be able to examine its contents easily. This will make testing and debugging difficult. Thus you should develop and test **WriteInventory** first. If you develop **SortInventory** next, you will have no way of storing appropriate test cases in the inventory variable, which will make testing difficult. You should develop **ReadInventory** next. You can use **WriteInventory** to test whether or not it is working. Once **ReadInventory** is working, you can store various test cases in files and use **ReadInventory** to load the inventory variable with your test cases. Thus **ReadInventory** is helpful for the testing and debugging of **SortInventory**. The testing can be summarized as follows.

Procedure to Test	Testing Accomplished Using
WriteInventory	Simple assignment statements
ReadInventory	Multiple test files to be read, checking that WriteInventory echoes what was in each file after a call on ReadInventory
SortInventory	Test cases read from files by ReadInventory, results written by WriteInventory

D.11 Chapter 11 Answers

1.
```
FUNCTION NthDay (n : INTEGER) : DayType;
VAR index : INTEGER;
    day    : DayType;
BEGIN
    day := Monday;
    IF n <= 7 THEN
        FOR index := 2 TO n DO
            day := SUCC (day);
    NthDay := day
END;
```

3. The reason is that the fields of **DateType** aren't specific enough. By saying they are **INTEGER**s, you are asking the computer to set aside enough space to store any value in the domain of type **INTEGER**. But in fact very few values in the domain of **INTEGER** can be used as month or day numbers. And if you limit yourself to twentieth-century dates, you can limit the year range as well. Thus the solution is to introduce some subrange types and to take `PACKED` away from `DateList`, since it won't help at that high of a level.

```
TYPE  DateType    = PACKED RECORD
                month : 1..12;
                day   : 1..31;
                year  : 0..99
            END;
        DateList  = ARRAY [1..5000] OF DateType;
```

5. The string constant has two apostrophe images, which each represent single apostrophes. Thus the constant has 21 characters in it and is of type:

```
PACKED ARRAY [1..21] OF CHAR;
```

7.
```
PROCEDURE SafeIntRead (VAR InFile : TEXT;
                       VAR number : INTEGER;
                       VAR okay   : BOOLEAN);

VAR sign: CHAR;
BEGIN
    SkipBlanks (InFile);
    IF (InFile^ IN ['+', '-']) THEN
        READ (InFile, sign)
    ELSE
        sign := '+';
    okay := (InFile^ IN ['0'..'9']);
    IF okay THEN
    BEGIN
        READ (InFile, num);
        IF sign = '-' THEN
            num := -num
    END
    ELSE
        num := 0
END;    (* SafeIntRead *)
```

9. `[x, y, z] <= [1..8]`

11. The output is:

```
6 12 18
1  2  4  8
1  2  4  6  8
```

1. After the last field of a record and after the last branch of a **CASE**.

3. There are no scope conflicts in the program. It is perfectly legal. Here is a chart showing the definition of each of the words 'Fun1', 'Fun2', and 'Fun3' at the points A, B, and C. Notice that the only nonlocal reference in this program happens at point A where Fun2 and Fun3 are defined in the containing scope (the outer procedure).

Point	Fun1	Fun2	Fun3
A	REAL	PROCEDURE	INTEGER
B	CHAR	PROCEDURE	INTEGER
C	13	INTEGER	PROCEDURE

5. This program is difficult to decipher because of the functions with side effects. Consider what happens the first time function **h** is evaluated. Evaluating **h** involves evaluating functions **f** and **g**. All three of these functions write out characters at the end of the **function**, and function **g** changes the value of the global variable **e**:

    evaluate h

    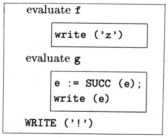

    After three evaluations of **h** the global variable **e** takes on the value 'g' and the program stops executing because function **h** returns **FALSE** instead of **TRUE** when it sees function **f** returning 'f' and function **g** returning 'g'. Thus, the output is:

    `ze!zf!zg!`

7. No. There are a few rare instances where a full evaluation problem goes away because the loop iterates once before the test is performed (e.g., it might avoid a reference to a 0th element of an array), but generally you have the same problems with full evaluation in **REPEAT** loops as you do in **WHILE** loops.

9. Here is the output generated:

    ```
    A = 10, B = 20,  C = 1260
    A = 10, B = 40,  C = 126
    A = 20, B = 40,  C = 12
    A = 20, B = 252, C = 264
    A = 20, B = 252, C = 52
    ```

D.13 Chapter 13 Answers

1. Two changes would have to be made in the declarations. **PersonType** would have to have an age field added to it, and **DirectoryKind** would have to be expanded to include a fourth value, **ByAge**. It is easiest if you insert the fourth value in the middle of the others, because many later parts of the program refer to **ByName** and **ByOffice**, the lowest and highest values in the type. **ReadPerson** would also have to be changed so that it reads in a value for the age field. Finally, the two **CASE** statements controlled by **DirectoryKind** would have to have new branches added to them (these are inside function **Less** and procedure **WritePerson**).

3. The declarations on the left are missing some of the declarations from the right. Consider the consequences of each separately.

   The left declarations have an unnamed string type. This means that you can't write any procedures with strings as parameters. This can cause a multitude of problems. You won't always be able to decompose a problem into procedures the way you want because you can't pass the necessary parameters, you can't make use of code in the software library that manipulates similar structures, and you can't use **VAR** parameters to simplify the names of your strings; you will always have to refer to them by first referring to a book record.

   The left declarations also have an unnamed **BookList** type. This probably doen't make much difference, because you never want to pass a variable of type **Book-List**; you will instead pass the whole **BookDatabase** record so that you have the length variable as well. Thus the extra declaration of **BookList** in the right-hand declarations is not there for practical reasons; it is there for stylistic ones.

   Finally, the declarations on the left bundle the book list with its length variable into a single **BookDatabase** record. The advantage of this declaration is that it simplifies parameter passing. You only have one variable to pass, not two. This will be even more important if the set of variables assoicated with the database starts to grow. With the **BookDatabase** record, new fields can be added without any increased difficulty with parameter passing. The one disadvantage of this bundling, however, is that it means you have to use **WITH** statements throughout your program.

5. Vertical lines have an infinite slope, so they can't be described by the slope/intercept form of a line. Thus, **DrawLine** can't draw any vertical lines.

7. This is certainly an issue that could be decided either way with good reason. First, consider the advantages of a single **StringType**. With a single type there will be less duplicating of procedures. In fact, perhaps you can double your effort on a single, more powerful string procedure that can handle both names and phones. This also simplifies the program, since there are fewer types for you to keep track of. These are good reasons for combining into a single string type.

   Now consider the disadvantages. First, names and phones are conceptually different kinds of data, so you shouldn't expect to store them both in the same structure. By forcing two different kinds of data into the same structure, you might end up with so many conflicts that your single structure isn't useful for either. Another consideration is space. If these strings are to be stored in the same type, each string will have to be of the maximum possible length. With a separate `PhoneType`, it is possible to store 8 characters for a phone rather than 20. This might not sound like much, but for very large databases it can be significant. This shorter length also makes it easier to write out the phone number, since it has no extra characters at the end of the string. Finally, `PACKED` arrays were chosen so that most low-level operations would be peformed with built-in procedures, so there isn't much room for shared procedures. The only procedures actually built for the name and phone strings are reading procedures, and the reading is so very different that it would be difficult to combine them. Thus there are also good reasons for keeping the types separate.

9. The characters used by most terminals and printers are much taller than they are wide. Thus even though the lines are quite flat, they appear to be diagonal because the horizontal scaling is so much tighter than the vertical scaling. To get around this, people who compose images from standard characters introduce a scaling factor into their code.

D.14 Chapter 14 Answers

1. You can't carry out the two tests on the square specified by the user if you don't even have any numbers specifying a square. Thus the two tests on whether or not the user entered numbers should happen first. Of the two tests, it makes sense to test the first number first, because if the first value is wrong, why charge ahead and look at the second? Of the two tests on the square, the test for illegal square should happen before the test on whether or not the square is occupied. Otherwise, you are likely to make a reference to an illegal square (checking to see if it is occupied), which will probably lead to an array index out of bounds or a similar fatal error. Thus the proper order for these tests is

   - first value entered is not a number
   - second value entered is not a number
   - square is illegal
   - square is occupied

3.

```
PROCEDURE ChooseCard (VAR hand : HandType;
                      VAR rank : CHAR;
                      VAR suit : CHAR);
VAR good : BOOLEAN;
BEGIN
    REPEAT
        WRITE ('What card do you want to discard (rank and suit)? ');
        READ (rank, suit);
        good := EOLN;
        READLN;
```

```
    IF NOT good THEN
        WRITELN ('You typed more than 2 characters.')
    ELSE
        BEGIN
            good := rank IN ['0'..'9','J','Q','K','A','j','q','k','a'];
            IF NOT good THEN
                WRITELN ('Illegal rank character: "', rank, '"')
            ELSE
            BEGIN
                good := suit IN ['S','H','C','D','s','h','c','d'];
                IF NOT good THEN
                    WRITELN ('Illegal suit character: "', suit, '"')
                ELSE
                BEGIN
                    good := InHand (rank, suit, hand);
                    IF NOT good THEN
                        WRITELN ('That card is not in your hand.')
                END
            END
        END;
        IF NOT good THEN
            WRITELN ('Try again.')
    UNTIL good
END;
```

5. If all the words are illegal, then `dictionary.length` will be 0 and the call on `RandomInt` in the main program to find a random word will generate

```
RandomInt (seed, 1, 0)
```

`RandomInt` returns 1 in this case, which means the main program will start a game using `dictionary.words [1]`. This won't work very well, since the word is illegal. In order to address this problem, you can modify the main program. Currently it looks like this:

```
SetUp (seed);
ReadDictionary (dictionary);
REPEAT
        . . .
UNTIL NOT yes;
WRITELN ('Okay, bye for now.')
```

You can change this to:

```
SetUp (seed);
ReadDictionary (dictionary);
IF dictionary.length = 0 THEN
    WRITELN ('Aborting Jotto, all words in file are illegal.')
ELSE
```

```
BEGIN
    REPEAT
            .  .  .
    UNTIL NOT yes;
    WRITELN ('Okay, bye for now.')
END
```

7. There are several ways that this change could be made. You might suspect that you can calculate the `fermis` and `picas` simultaneously, but it turns out that all the `fermis` have to be calculated first. Thus a first change would be to introduce a new INTEGER variable called `fermis` in `ReportJotsFor` and add the following code to the beginning of the procedure:

```
fermis := 0;
FOR index1 := 1 TO WordSize DO
    IF word1 [index1] = word2 [index1] THEN
    BEGIN
        fermis := fermis + 1;
        word1 [index1] := '!';
        word2 [index1] := '*'
    END;
```

The nice thing about adding this code is that it turns the current Jotto calculation that follows into a pica calculation, because `picas` are simply all the nonfermi jots. Since the new code takes care of all the `fermis`, we can use the existing code written in terms of jots to find `picas`. We also need to change the WRITELN at the end of the procedure:

```
WRITELN (fermis:1, ' fermis and ', jots:1, ' picas.');
```

Finally, we should change the instructions to the program to explain this new feedback given to the user.

9. The tool is `ReportJotsFor`. The slight alteration that needs to be made is that it needs to be turned into a function `JotsFor` that returns the jots rather than a procedure that reports jots to the user at the terminal. Here's how the elimination works. Suppose you have 3000 words on your current guess list and you guess the word `'ABORT'`. The user tells you how many jots you get. Suppose you get 1. You know that the correct word gets 1 jot when compared with `'ABORT'`. Therefore, you can look through all 3000 words on your current guess list and eliminate any words that don't get 1 jot when compared with `'ABORT'`. Thus you will call function `JotsFor` 3000 times on this round of elimination. This will probably reduce the size of your guess list to 400 or 500, and you'll make another guess on the next round and call `JotsFor` on each of those words to try to eliminate more.

D.15 Chapter 15 Answers

1. ```
   PROCEDURE ReadData (VAR sum : INTEGER);
   VAR next : INTEGER;
   ```
   ```

```
BEGIN
    IF EOLN THEN
        sum := O
    ELSE
    BEGIN
        READ (next);
        ReadData (sum);
        sum := sum + next
    END
END;
```

3. This recursive function performs exponentiation, carrying m to the n power.

```
FUNCTION F (m, n : INTEGER) : INTEGER;
BEGIN
    IF n = O THEN
        f := 1
    ELSE
        IF n MOD 2 = O THEN
            f := SQR (f (m, n DIV 2))
        ELSE
            f := m * f (m, n - 1)
END;
```

5. Here is the binary version:

```
PROCEDURE WriteNumber (number : INTEGER);
BEGIN
    IF number < 2 THEN
        WRITE (number:1)
    ELSE
    BEGIN
        WriteNumber (number DIV 2);
        WRITE ((number MOD 2):1)
    END
END;
```

It can be generalized for other bases:

```
PROCEDURE WriteNumber (number : INTEGER);
CONST base = 3;
BEGIN
    IF number < base THEN
        WRITE (number:1)
    ELSE
    BEGIN
        WriteNumber (number DIV base);
        WRITE ((number MOD base):1)
    END
END;
```

7. One simple case derives from the fact that you don't have any combinations if you don't have a legal number of marbles. Thus a negative number of marbles leads to no combinations. Another simple case comes from having no marbles, where there is only one way to lay them out. The recursive case comes from the observation that you really have two choices for which marble to lay down first, either you lay down a green and are left with the possible combinations of (**green** - 1) greens and (**blue**) blues, or you lay down a blue and are left with the possible combinations of (**green**) greens and (**blue** - 1) blues. Unfortunately, this version of the function is very inefficient.

```
FUNCTION Combos (green, blue : INTEGER) : INTEGER;
BEGIN
    IF (green < 0) OR (blue < 0) THEN
        combos := 0
    ELSE
        IF (green = 0) AND (blue = 0) THEN
            combos := 1
        ELSE
            combos := combos (green - 1, blue) + combos (green, blue - 1)
END;
```

9. Parentheses are needed in infix notation with an additive operand of a multiplicative operator. In other words, if you are working on either of the following operators, you have to be careful.

```
operand1 * operand2            operand1/operand2
```

The only problem comes up when one of the operands of an expression such as this is additive (i.e., is performing addition or subtraction). In order to parenthesize correctly, you need to pass an extra parameter to the procedure that specifies whether or not the parent expression (i.e., the one generating the call) is a multiplicative operator. Thus you will want to use a procedure header more like this:

```
PROCEDURE Eval (VAR result    : INTEGER;
                    MultParent : BOOLEAN);
```

You shouldn't, in general, change the parameter lists of a procedure just to suit your solution to a problem. Therefore, let's leave Eval with the current single parameter and create a nested procedure with the extra parameter.

```
PROCEDURE Eval (VAR result: INTEGER);

        PROCEDURE Inner (VAR result    : INTEGER;
                            MultParent : BOOLEAN);
        VAR operator: CHAR;
            operand1, operand2: INTEGER;
        BEGIN
            SkipBlanks;
            IF INPUT^ IN ['0'..'9'] THEN
```

```
                      BEGIN
                          READ (result);
                          WRITE (result:1)
                      END
                      ELSE
                      BEGIN
                          READ (operator);
                          IF operator in ['+', '-'] THEN
                          BEGIN
                              IF MultParent THEN
                                  WRITE ('(');
                              inner (operand1, FALSE);
                              WRITE (' ', operator, ' ');
                              inner (operand2, FALSE);
                              IF MultParent THEN
                                  WRITE (')')
                          END
                          ELSE
                          BEGIN
                              inner (operand1, TRUE);
                              WRITE (' ', operator, ' ');
                              inner (operand2, TRUE)
                          END;
                          CASE operator OF
                              '+':  result := operand1 + operand2;
                              '-':  result := operand1 - operand2;
                              '*':  result := operand1 * operand2;
                              '/':  result := operand1 div operand2
                          END
                      END
                  END;   (* Inner *)

      BEGIN   (* Eval *)
          inner (result, FALSE)
      END;   (* Eval *)
```

11. The output of the program is a series of 24 lines like the following (these are the first six):

```
WHAT
WHTA
WAHT
WATH
WTHA
WTAH
```

Procedure Unknown generates all the different combinations of the four letters stored in the string and writes out each. For words, a reordering like this is known as an *anagram*. Procedure Unknown generates all the anagrams of a word, no matter what length it is. Mathematicians call these reorderings permutations. Procedure Unknown can be used on any list structure stored in an array to generate these different permutations.

D.16 Chapter 16 Answers

1. The output is:

```
3.5   3.5   7.0
7.0   3.5   7.0
7.0  24.5   7.0
```

3. Swapping data values is generally easier to write code for, since it involves only calls on a simple swapping procedure and not any pointer manipulations. Changing the pointer structure is more efficient, however, if the data values are large. Think of a linked list as a series of boulders connected by strings. Moving the strings is more efficient than moving the boulders.

5.
```
PROCEDURE EliminateZeros (VAR list : PtrList);
VAR temp : PtrList;
BEGIN
    IF list <> NIL THEN
    BEGIN
        IF list^.data = 0 THEN
        BEGIN
            temp := list^.next;
            DISPOSE (list);
            list := temp
        END;
        IF list <> NIL THEN
            EliminateZeros (list^.next)
    END
END;
```

7. A preorder traversal yields: Hillary, Phoebe, Charlie, Langley, Gregory, Robin.

9.

```
FUNCTION NumLeaves (tree : PtrTree) : INTEGER;
BEGIN
    IF tree = NIL THEN
        NumLeaves := 0
    ELSE
        IF (tree^.left = NIL) AND (tree^.right = NIL) THEN
            NumLeaves := 1
        ELSE
            NumLeaves := NumLeaves (tree^.left) + NumLeaves (tree^.right)
END;
```

D.17 Chapter 17 Answers

1. To sort a list of REALs rather than INTEGERs, you would change the declaration of NumberList to:

    ```
    TYPE  NumberList  = ARRAY [1..MaxLength] OF REAL;
    ```

    and change the declaration of procedure Swap to start with:

    ```
    PROCEDURE Swap (VAR first, second: REAL);
    VAR temp : REAL;
    ```

3. To make the procedure sort in descending order, this line from function TakeFrom-Left (nested inside of procedure Merge)

    ```
    TakeFromLeft := (nums [LeftPos] < nums [RightPos])
    ```

    would have to be changed to

    ```
    TakeFromLeft := (nums [LeftPos] > nums [RightPos])
    ```

5.  ```
    FUNCTION Exponent (base, power : integer) : integer;
    (* pre : power >= 0. *)
    VAR result, TempBase, TempPower : INTEGER;
    BEGIN
        result := 1;
        TempBase := base;
        TempPower := power;
        WHILE (TempPower > 0) DO
            IF (TempPower MOD 2) = 0 THEN
            BEGIN
                TempPower := TempPower DIV 2;
                TempBase := TempBase * TempBase
            END
            ELSE
            BEGIN
                TempPower := TempPower - 1;
                result := result * TempBase
            END
    END;
    ```

7.

```
FUNCTION SumOf (VAR list : ListType) : INTEGER;
(* post : Returns the sum of the elements stored in the list. *)
VAR index : INTEGER;
    sum   : INTEGER;
```
```

```
        BEGIN
            sum := 0;
            FOR index := 1 TO length (list) DO
                sum := sum + NthElement (list, index);
            SumOf := sum
        END;
```

9.

```
PROCEDURE Append (VAR FromStr, ToStr : string);
VAR index : INTEGER;
BEGIN
    FOR index := 1 TO length (FromStr) DO
        InsertChar (ToStr, length (ToStr) + 1, NthChar (FromStr, index))
END;
```

INDEX

661